MULTICULTURAL COOKBOOK OF LIFE-CYCLE CELEBRATIONS

BY

LOIS SINAIKO WEBB

The rare Arabian Oryx is believed to have inspired the myth of the unicorn. This desert antelope became virtually extinct in the early 1960s. At that time several groups of international conservationists arranged to have 9 animals sent to the Phoenix Zoo to be the nucleus of a captive breeding herd. Today the Oryx population is over 1,000, and over 500 have been returned to the Middle East.

4041 North Central at Indian School Road

Phoenix, Arizona 85012-3397

www.oryxpress.com

Children should always have adult supervision when working in the kitchen. Please see "Getting Started" on page xxi for more information

Published simultaneously in Canada

Printed and Bound in the United States of America

∞ The paper used in this publication meets the minimum requirements of American National Standard for Information Science—Permanence of Paper for Printed Library Materials, ANSI Z39.48, 1984.

Library of Congress Cataloging-in-Publication Data

Webb, Lois Sinaiko.

Multicultural cookbook of life-cycle celebrations / by Lois Sinaiko Webb.
p. cm.
Includes bibliographical references and index.
ISBN 1-57356-290-4
1. Cookery, International. I. Title.
TX725.A1 W43 2000
641.59—dc21 00-032658

This book is dedicated to my wonderful friends:
Casey Myers and Francesco Camera

Special thanks to:
Mary Kegg
Kateri Angel (named after Tekakwitha, the first American Indian woman to become a Catholic saint)
Jean Ouimet, French Canadian
Ning Yu
Gretchen Facey
Ganesh N. Rajamani
Shirley Donahoo
Asghar Khan
Jan and John Blyth
Josie Wilson
Neala Gunderson
Olga Mire
Jean Seltzer
Harvey Belsky
Hedwig Somdah

Illustrations by Tim Hosler

CONTENTS

PREFACE

In all cultures, sharing food is a primary way of sustaining human relationships. In fact, the English word "companion" is derived from Latin and French words that mean "sharing bread together." Each society's culture is passed on to children through eating with the family, a setting in which individuals learn sharing, kinship and family values, and the traditions of the group.

Ever since finishing two cookbooks, one featuring recipes from most of the world's countries and one about national holidays around the world, I have had a nagging desire to write a cookbook about people and their family celebrations.

The first book, *Multicultural Cookbook for Students*, co-authored with Carol Albyn, gives an overview for each country: the geography, climate, terrain, and principal crops grown. Each overview is accompanied by an array of recipes, which feature the typical foods eaten by the majority of the people in that country.

The second book, *Holidays of the World Cookbook*, covers a country's most important celebration or its national holiday. The recipes included are for the dishes eaten in celebration of the special day.

Multicultural Cookbook of Life-Cycle Celebrations covers the life-cycle celebrations that take a person from the crib to the grave and the food eaten at these markings of life passages. As one goes into the homes and lives of people around the world, doors of understanding open, barriers come down, and new light is shed on how other cultures share their most precious family moments.

Life-cycle events are often celebrated with food. A festive feast communicates many things: a family's wealth and success, status within the society, family ties, and religious devotion. A celebration feast usually means enjoying great quantities of more expensive foods. In most cultures, a meal becomes a feast only when special breads are baked, traditional dishes are prepared, and meat is on the table.

This book takes you into the homes and kitchens of people in more than 145 countries. The countries are arranged geographically by region. Within each region, the countries are listed in the order a person in a car might tour them. Each country has a short introduction describing the country's geographic location, relevant history, and ethnic and religious breakdowns. This information is followed by examples of local life-cycle celebrations, often unique to that country or a region of that country. (Rather than describing the same life-cycle events over and over for countries with similar ethnic and religious groups, we have included an essay at the beginning of the book outlining the important life-cycle events for the world's major religions. The reader is frequently referred to the appropriate section of this essay in these introductions.)

Following the introductions are an average of three or more easy-to-follow recipes (over 500 recipes total), made with readily available ingredients. The recipes are for dishes specifically prepared to commemorate a celebration or be included in the celebration feast.

The recipes were gathered over a career of more than 30 years in the food business. They have been tried and tested by dozens of people in different parts of the world. Many old recipes were time consuming and the use of fat was excessive. Whenever possible the recipes in this book have been updated and streamlined to fit today's healthier diet and busy lifestyle.

To expand the senses and make the taste buds more adventuresome, I have included recipes for a few of the more unusual, yet easily available, foods, such as salt cod, herring, and caviar. To please the eye, there are recipes for decorative breads and Japanese Sushi as well as lovely birthday and wedding cakes and cookies. Recipes that include edible gold and silver leaf (*vark*), used in India and other regions to decorate food for special occasions, have been added. For texture, I have included recipes for unusual vegetables, such as yucca (cassava), chayote and prickly pear (cactus pear), and grain dishes. (All products are easily available at most large supermarkets, health food stores, or designated ethnic markets.) A trip to an ethnic market can be delicious, informative, and fun. If an unusual food is in a recipe, detailed information about it appears in the glossary, starting on page xxiv. These unusual foods and cooking terms are set in boldface type the first time they appear in a recipe, indicating their inclusion in the glossary.

All recipes in the book include the following:

- *Yield*, stating the number of people a recipe will serve or how many pieces it will make.
- *Ingredients*, listing how much of each food item you need to make the recipe.
- *Equipment*, listing cooking equipment, such as pans, bowls, and spoons.
- *Instructions*, telling you exactly how to make the recipe.
- *Serving suggestions*, explaining how to plate and serve the finished product, and if necessary, how it is eaten.

GETTING STARTED

Safety Tips

To make cooking an enjoyable experience it's a good idea to 1) cook safely; 2) think before you act, using common sense; and 3) make sure that you, your cooking tools, and your kitchen are clean. All experienced cooks know the importance of these few simple rules.

Don't Cook Alone. Have an Adult Help. Even apprentice chefs in restaurants never cook alone; an experienced cook is always present to teach food preparation and explain cooking equipment.

Keep Food at Proper Temperature at All Times. Cold food must be kept cold and hot food must be kept hot. Never cover food while it is cooling to room temperature, because it takes longer to cool down and there is a chance of bacteria forming. Cover to refrigerate or freeze. It is very important not to use spoiled food. If you think something may have spoiled, ask an adult if it should be discarded.

Prevent Fire Accidents. The kitchen's most dangerous equipment are stove-top burners, where most home accidents occur. Always keep a fire extinguisher (designed for stove fires) within easy reach and in working condition. To prevent stove-top accidents, follow a few simple rules:

Never turn your back on or walk away from a skillet or pan of hot cooking oil. Always have the necessary utensils and ingredients ready to go before heating the oil.

If the oil should begin to smoke or seems too hot, quickly turn off the heat. *Do not* move the pan, and *do not* throw water in the pan. Allow it to cool down and begin again.

Never leave food that is cooking unattended, unless you are making a soup or stew with plenty of liquid and cooking on low heat. Even a soup or stew must be checked from time to time while it cooks to make sure it's not drying out, sticking, or burning. If the phone rings or there are other distractions while cooking, turn off the heat, and, using a potholder, slide the pan to a cold burner. If the pot is too heavy, ask an adult to do it. Double-check the burner to make sure you turned it *off*. (A common mistake is to turn it up, thinking you have turned it to *off*.) When you return to the kitchen, if it hasn't been more than a few minutes, continue cooking where you left off.

When you finish cooking, before leaving the kitchen, make sure the oven and stove-top burners are *off*.

Keep dry, heatproof oven mitts or pot holders handy. All metal spoons and handles get hot. Use wooden mixing spoons or plastic-handled metal spoons instead. Do not use all-plastic spoons or other cooking tools for mixing hot food, because they will melt. Never transfer very hot food to plastic containers or plastic bags; some are not made to hold hot food and might melt.

When lifting the lid off a pan of hot food always direct the open lid away from you so that the steam does not come toward your face.

Accidents do happen, however, and it is a good idea to have a first aid kit with burn and cut medication on hand.

Adjust the Cooking Time. Please note that the recommended cooking time given for each recipe is approximate. This time can vary, based on thickness of the pan, thickness of the ingredients, and differing heat controls on stoves.

Keep Knives Sharp. Dull knives can be dangerous, even more so than sharp knives. A dull knife can slip off food, causing accidents. Always cut food on a cutting board, and always have an adult standing by to help. Always carry a knife by the handle with the blade pointing toward the floor; never pass a knife to another person blade first, and do not put utility knives in a dishwasher or in a sink full of soapy water. It is not only dangerous, but it is also not good for the knives. Wash knives by hand, and keep them in a safe place away from small children.

Use Caution When Working with Hot Peppers. Cover hands with gloves or plastic baggies to prevent burning. Do not touch your eyes or face as you are working; if you do, splash with cold running water.

Be Extremely Careful When Working Around Hot Grease. Always have an adult help you when cooking with hot grease or oil. When you finish using the deep fryer or other pans with grease, immediately turn off the heat or unplug the pan. Double-check to make sure the burners are *off*, not turned to high, which is a very serious and common mistake many people make. *Do not move the pan of hot grease until it is cool.* Keep a kitchen fire extinguisher in working order and handy at all times. Accidents do happen, so be prepared.

Cleanliness in the Kitchen

1. Tie your hair back or wear something on your head, such as a bandanna.

2. Roll up your sleeves and wear an apron or some protection to keep your clothes clean.

3. Do not touch any food or cooking equipment unless you have first washed and dried your hands. Wash your hands frequently while handling food to prevent cross-contamination. Raw chicken and raw eggs are two foods that can easily become infected by bacteria called salmonella. Raw chicken must be kept at a cold temperature (below 45° F.) at all times. It is best to thaw frozen chicken in the refrigerator (this can take a day or so, depending on the size) or more quickly under cold, running water. When preparing the chicken, keep the work area and all utensils sanitized (*sanitize* means to kill disease-causing bacteria by cleaning). Also, immediately after the chicken has been prepared and before any other food preparation, sanitize the work surface, utensils, and equipment again to prevent cross-contamination. Eggs keep well at 36° F. When buying eggs, look for the freshness date on the container, and check each egg to be sure there are no cracks.

4. Wash all fresh fruits and vegetables before cutting.

5. Have all the utensils and equipment clean, ready, and in good working order before beginning to cook.

6. Wipe up spills and drips at once. Good cooks clean up after themselves and always leave the kitchen spotless.

Equipment and Methods You Need to Know About

Almost every recipe you will use from this book will require the following basic equipment:

- A set of **measuring cups**. You will probably need nested cups in different sizes for measuring dry items such as flour, and you will probably need a liquid measuring cup with lines drawn on the sides to tell you how much liquid you have.
- A set of **measuring spoons** for measuring small amounts of liquid and dry items.
- A **work surface**, such as a counter top or table top, where you can put all of your equipment as you prepare your food.
- A set of **sharp knives** for cutting and dicing ingredients.

Each recipe will tell you what other equipment you will need—such as bowls, pans, or spoons—to make the food described.

GLOSSARY OF FOOD TERMS

allspice: A spice made from the dried and ground berries of the Jamaica pepper tree. Allspice tastes like a combination of cloves, nutmeg, and cinnamon, hence its name.

almond paste: A pliable mixture of ground almonds, raw egg whites, sugar, and liquid. To avoid using raw egg whites, commercial almond paste is recommended for non-cooking recipes, available at supermarkets in 6- to 8-ounce packages. Keep the paste well wrapped and refrigerated after opening. If almond paste becomes hard, it can be softened by heating for 2 to 3 seconds in a microwave oven or by placing it in a warm oven (225°–250°) for a few minutes, until almond paste is soft to the touch.

appetizers (also French: hors d'oeuvre, literally means "outside the works"): Small, light, decoratively presented finger food items eaten before the main meal, usually to appease hunger.

areca nuts: *See* **betel nuts**

arrowroot: A tasteless and colorless thickening agent.

atta (chapati flour): Very finely ground wheat flour, cream or pale yellow in color. Atta is ideal to use in unleavened flatbread recipes. Sifting out the coarse particles of bran in whole wheat flour, using a fine-hole sifter, will produce flour with a texture similar to atta. Atta is available at all Indian and Middle East food stores and some health food stores.

bamboo steamer basket: *See* **steamer pan**

basmati rice: Long-grained and nonglutinous rice (each grain cooks separately from the other).

baste: To moisten with liquid at intervals while cooking.

beetroot: The English name for **beets**.

beets: A firm, round, dark red root vegetable with leafy green tops that are also edible and nutritious. Buy beets that are firm with smooth skin. Small to medium size beets are the most tender. Beets will keep refrigerated for up to two weeks.

betel nuts: Hard round nuts, called *supari* by East Indians, that are really the astringent seeds of the betel palm (also called the areca palm). Since ancient times, they have been chewed for their stimulating effect. After having been chewed a while, the nuts soften and give off a peculiar taste. Chewing the betel nuts makes your lips, mouth, and teeth bright orange. Habitual chewing of the betel nut will stain the teeth black. The betel nut is used in many Hindu life-cycle rituals. *Paan*, the betel leaf, is spread with either white lime paste (*choona*) or red paste made from the bark of a tree (*katechu* or *kattha*). The paste is sprinkled with mixture of crushed betel nuts and spices and herbs, such as cardamom and aniseed. The leaf is folded into a small triangular wad and fastened with a whole clove. The *paan* is chewed as a digestive and mouth freshener. The betel leaf varies in taste from sweet to slightly bitter.

In Papua New Guinea (PNG) chewing the betel nut, or in Pidgin *buai*, is so common people greet each other by asking, "Do You Chew?" (meaning "do you chew betel nut?") People chew it as a little pick-me-up, a bit like a mid-morning cup of tea or coffee. The children of PNG, as young as 5 years old, take up chewing the betel with all the condiments, and they start by gnawing on the husks of the nut discarded by others. The nut is combined with mustard stick (*daka*) and crushed-coral lime (*cumbung*). The "chew" is foul tasting, and the lime used in the procedure is highly caustic and can cause terrible mouth sores.

black-eyed peas: A white pea with a black eye or dot, brought to the southern United States from Africa in the seventeenth century with the slave trade.

blanch (nuts): A process done to nuts to make it easier to peel off the skin. To blanch nuts, cover them with boiling water and let them stand for 5 minutes. Drain, and when cool enough to handle, skins will easily peel off.

blanch (vegetables): A process done to vegetables to make it easier to peel off the skin, to set color, to slightly soften the vegetables, and to remove the raw flavor. To blanch vegetables, fill a saucepan with 4 cups water for every cup of vegetables to be blanched. Bring water to a boil over high heat and add vegetables. Bring water back to a boil for 1 to 3 minutes, depending upon size of vegetables. Remove at once from heat, drain vegetables in a **colander**, and rinse them under cold running water to stop the cooking action.

blend: To mix two or more ingredients together completely into one.

blender: An appliance with whirling blades that quickly crushes and blends food.

bok choy: Meaning literally "white cabbage" in Chinese, a vegetable with thick white stems and long, narrow leaves.

boned (also **bone**): To remove bones from fowl, fish, or meat.

bread crumbs (also breadcrumbs): Dry bread crumbs and fresh (soft) bread crumbs used in various ways in different recipes. For best results, use what is called for in a recipe. Fresh white bread crumbs are made by trimming off the crust of white bread, cutting it into **cubes,** and processing it in a food processor or blender, 1 to 2 slices at a time, to desired size of crumb. Dried crumbs can be made by trimming off crust and drying bread on baking sheet in an oven heated to 250° F until crisp and lightly toasted; either crush with rolling pin or in food processor. Dry plain or seasoned bread crumbs are available at all supermarkets.

bread doneness: A test to indicate whether a loaf of bread is done; to do this test, remove bread from the oven and from the pan and tap the bottom of loaf with handle of dinner knife. If loaf sounds hollow, it is done. If it has a dull, thump sound, it is not done. Return loaf to pan, set in oven, and continue baking for at least another 10 to 15 minutes.

breadfruit: A starchy fruit with a tough, bumpy, or prickly skin. Fresh, the fruit is as big as a cannonball. It is eaten green or ripe and sometimes stands in for white potatoes. Breadfruit weighs from 2 to 5 pounds with cream-colored flesh, bland flavor, and texture that is often compared to grainy bread. They are cooked like squash or potatoes and can be used in both sweet and savory dishes. As it ripens it becomes sweeter. It is available fresh, canned, or frozen at some supermarkets and all Latin American food stores.

broccoli rabe (also **raab**, rabe, rapini [Italian], or rape): A vegetable related to both the cabbage and turnip family. It has a pungent, bitter flavor that has not been popular in the United States. It is very popular in Italy where people fry or steam it and use it in soups and salads. It is available in some supermarkets and all Asian and other ethnic food stores.

bulb baster: A kitchen tool that is used for moistening meat or fowl while it is baking. A bulb baster has a plastic or metal shaft with a heavy rubber bulb at one end. To operate, place the shaft opening in the pan drippings and squeeze the rubber bulb. By releasing the bulb, the air comes back into the bulb, drawing the liquid from the pan up into the shaft. Squeeze the bulb again to **baste** the food.

bulgur (also bulghar or burghul): *See* **wheat berries**

bundt pan: A fluted pan with a center tube.

butterfly: To split a food (such as meat, fish, or shrimp) through the middle, leaving it intact at one end. The two halves are opened, like the cover of a book or like butterfly wings. This procedure is generally done with a piece of meat or fish that is going to be stuffed. Shrimp are butterflied to make them look larger and more attractive.

cake boards: Square, rectangular, or round (called **cake circles**) pieces of cardboard that are placed under baked cakes to keep them rigid. Before setting a cake on the cardboard, cover the side it will sit on with foil. To cover a circle board with foil cut it about 2 inches larger than the circle. Wrap the excess foil over the edges and press it down in pleats on the backside of the circle. Cake boards come in different sizes and are packed 6 or 12 of one size to a box. They are available at kitchenware and craft supply stores.

cake circles: *See* **cake boards**

candied fruit (also glacé fruit): A fruit, used in cakes, breads, and other sweets, that has been boiled or dipped in sugar syrup and sometimes dipped in granulated sugar. Chopped mixed candied fruit (called fruit cake mix) and chopped pineapple, cherries, and citron come in 8-ounce (1 cup) and 16-ounce (2 cup) containers at most supermarkets. After opening, store candied fruit in an airtight container and refrigerate.

candy thermometer: *See* **thermometers; sugar syrup**

carambola (also **star fruit**): Pale yellow green fruit, with five pointed ridges around the center core. When sliced crosswise, each slice is shaped like a star. Available at most supermarkets.

cassava (also manioc and yucca): A tropical root vegetable with hard white flesh covered by dark brown, hairy bark-like skin. It has to be peeled and cooked before eating. It is a staple food in African, Caribbean, and Latin American kitchens. Tapioca is made from cassava. Cassava is cooked whole, sliced, pounded into pulp, or ground into a coarse flour. Only sweet cassava is available in the United States; the bitter variety is poisonous until it is cooked. Cakes and breads are made from cassava meal, which is made from grated, sun-dried cassava. Cassava is available fresh and in meal and flour form in Asian and Latin American food stores and some supermarkets.

cauliflowerets: The white top part of cauliflower, broken or cut off from the stems.

chafing dish: A heatproof dish or pan heated from below with a flame, hot coals, or electricity, for warming or cooking food; the name comes from the French word *chauffer*, to heat.

chard (also Swiss chard): A green leafy vegetable with reddish stalks. Buy tender greens and crisp stalks. It will keep up to three days if refrigerated.

chayote (also mirliton): A tropical round or pear-shaped squash, 3- to 8-inches long, with a thin green skin. It has white, bland-tasting flesh around one soft seed. It is prepared like summer squash or can be stuffed and baked like acorn squash. They are available in the winter at most supermarkets. Buy chayote that are unblemished and firm.

chicken doneness: To check whether chicken is fully cooked, pierce thickest part of fowl with a knife. If juices that trickle out are clear, not pinkish, the chicken is done.

cilantro: *See* **coriander**

cinnamon sugar: To make cinnamon sugar, mix 3 tablespoons sugar with 1 teaspoon ground cinnamon.

citron: A fruit of the citrus family, resembling a large, lumpy lemon, cultivated for its thick rind, which is candied or pressed; its oil is used in making liqueurs, perfume, and medicine.

coarsely chopped: Cut into ¼ to ½-inch pieces. *See also* **finely chopped**.

coconut, fresh grated: To prepare grated coconut, choose a coconut without any cracks and one that produces the sound of swishing liquid when shaken. Have an adult pierce the eyes of the coconut with a ice pick or metal skewer, drain the liquid, and save it for another use. After draining, break the coconut with a hammer and remove the flesh from the shell, levering it out carefully with the point of a strong knife. Peel off the brown membrane and cut the coconut meat into small pieces. In a food processor fitted with the shredding disk, shred the pieces a few at a time. Or grate the coconut meat on the fine side of a grater. One large coconut yields about 4 cups of grated coconut.

cod, salt: *See* **salt cod**

collard greens (also called collard): A type of cabbage with leaves that do not form a head. Buy fresh, crisp green leaves, avoiding leaves with a yellowish or wilted appearance. Available at all supermarkets.

colander: A perforated bowl-shaped container used to drain liquid from solids.

core: The center of a fruit such as an apple, pear, or pineapple that has seeds or the tough fibrous part of vegetables such as on the bottom of cabbage or celery.

coriander: An herb related to the parsley family. When fresh, it is also called Chinese parsley or by its Spanish name cilantro. Buy fresh coriander with bright green leaves. Keep refrigerated with stems in glass of water. Dried coriander seeds are available whole or ground and the dried leaves are available crushed or ground. The seeds and leaves have different flavors so when adding to a recipe be sure to use the proper kind.

corn flour: Finely ground to the consistency of flour from yellow or white cornmeal. Corn flour is used for breading and combined with other flours in baked goods. It is often confused with cornstarch, which is always white and is used as a thickening agent and sometimes for baking. Corn flour, cornstarch or cornmeal are not interchangeable in recipes. (Corn flour is available at health food stores.)

cornmeal: Made from dried corn kernels that are ground in three textures, fine, medium and coarse. Depending upon the corn used, cornmeal can be white, yellow, or blue. The color does not affect the taste.

couscous: A pasta that looks and acts like a grain. The tiny granules are made of semolina, the same hard durum wheat used for noodles. *Couscous* is the Arabic word for semolina. The term "couscous" refers to both the granules and the famous dish called couscous. All North African countries have couscous recipes; the Moroccans sprinkle in saffron, Algerians add tomatoes, and Tunisians drizzle on *harissa*, a fiery red pepper sauce. Authentic North African couscous takes about an hour to prepare and requires three steamings. Precooked couscous, found in supermarkets, takes about 5 minutes to make. To cook, follow directions on package. The larger, pearl-size couscous from Israel is available at some supermarkets and Jewish and Middle East food stores.

crawfish: *See* **crayfish**

crayfish (also called crawfish): Tiny lobster-like crustaceans that are usually found in freshwater. Live crayfish are seasonal and available only at certain times of the year. Packaged, frozen, cooked crayfish meat is available at most supermarkets all year long. It takes five pounds of live crayfish to pick out one pound of edible meat.

crème fraîche: A specialty of France; this thickened cream has a slight tangy flavor and a smooth velvety texture. It is easy to make: Combine 1 cup heavy cream and 2 tablespoons buttermilk in a glass container. Cover and let stand at room temperature (about 70° F) for 8 to 24 hours, or until very thick. Stir before covering and refrigerate up to 10 days. *Crème fraîche* can be cooked in sauces and soups without curdling.

croquettes: A mixture of meat and/or vegetables formed into small cylinders, ovals, or rounds and fried until crisp and brown.

croûtes: French for a crust, shell, or piece of bread or dough used in various savory dishes. *En croûte* means encased in pastry.

crudités: Raw vegetables, such as carrot, celery, and zucchini, cut into finger-size pieces and cauliflower and broccoli broken into small **florets** to accompany a dipping sauce as an **appetizer**.

cubed: To cut something into small (about ½-inch size) pieces of uniform size; compare to **diced**.

cuisine: A French term pertaining to a specific style of cooking or the food of a particular region or country.

dasheen: *See* **taro root**

deep fryer: A special container with a built-in thermostat used for quickly frying food. Fill deep fryer with oil according to manufacturer's directions. Heat to 375° F on deep-fryer thermometer or place the handle of a wooden spoon in the oil; if small bubbles appear around the surface, the oil is ready for frying. A **wok**, deep skillet, or saucepan with a cooking thermometer can be made into a deep fryer. A wok is ideal for deep frying. Its sloping sides enable one to decrease the amount of oil normally used for deep frying. To fry with a wok: Use only vegetable oil and fry in small batches. Some woks come with a semi-circular wire rack that may be placed above the oil for draining food after it is fried. Drain again on paper towels. To remove food from the wok, use either a slotted metal spoon or spatula or metal tongs.

devein: *See* **peeled and deveined**

diced: Food cut into very small (about ¼-inch) pieces of uniform size; compare to **cubed**.

doneness: *See* **chicken doneness; bread doneness**

double boiler: Two pans that fit together with one resting partway inside the other; it usually comes with a cover that fits either pan. Food cooks in the top pan from the heat of the boiling water in the bottom pan. A double boiler can be made by placing a metal mixing bowl over a slightly smaller pan. The boiling water should not touch the bottom of the upper bowl.

drizzle: To lightly pour a liquid or sauce in fine lines over a surface. This is done when only a little liquid or sauce is needed, usually as a decorative touch. An easy way to drizzle is to put liquid or sauce into a squirt bottle with a small hole in the nozzle.

dry-roast: *See* **roasted nuts**

Dutch oven: A cast iron pot with a tight-fitting, domed lid that is used for slow-cooking soups, stews, and cobblers.

egg wash: Combine 1 egg yolk with 2 tablespoons water or milk in cup, and using a fork, gently beat to mix.

egg whites: *See* **eggs, separated**

egg yolks: *See* **eggs, separated**

eggs, separated: To separate egg yolks from egg whites. *How to crack and separate eggs:*

1. Wash your hands. Have three bowls ready: one for the yolks (the yellow part), one for the whites, and one to crack the eggs over.

2. Hold the egg in one hand; crack it with one light, sharp blow against the rim of the bowl, or crack lightly with the dull side of a table knife. Try to make an even, crosswise break in the shell.

3. Hold the cracked egg over an empty bowl; take it in both hands, with the cracks on the upper side, and pull the crack open with your thumbs, breaking it apart into halves. As you do this, some of the egg white will drip into the bowl underneath it. Hold the yolk-filled half shell upright so it cups the yolk. Empty any remaining egg white in the other half shell into the bowl.

4. Hold the yolk-filled half over the bowl, and carefully, so the yolk doesn't break, pass it back and forth from one half shell to the other. As you do this, more egg white drips into bowl. When the yolk is free of egg white, put it into a separate bowl and continue cracking remaining eggs the same way.

If an egg is spoiled, it can be easily discarded when cracked into a separate bowl. Make sure no yolk gets in the bowl with the white because the slightest fat from the yolk will keep the whites from whipping.

elastic: A term used for dough. When dough is elastic, it springs back when you pull on it.

fenugreek: A plant with pungent, bitter-sweet edible seeds. The seeds come whole or ground and are used in African and Middle Eastern cooking. Fenugreek is often combined with other spices to make Indian curries.

fillet (also **filet,** the French spelling): A cut of meat or fish that has been trimmed of all bones and sometimes the skin. When ordering fillets from the fishmonger, always specify you want them skinless. Some fish fillets, such as tuna and catfish, are always boneless and skinless because the skin is tough and inedible.

filo: *See* **phyllo**

finely chopped: To cut into very tiny pieces. It is the same as to **mince.** (*See also* **coarsely chopped.**)

Finnan haddie: Smoked haddock, originally from the Scottish town of Findon, hence the name. Finnan haddie is available whole or in **fillets** at some supermarkets.

florets: Tender, edible tops of cauliflower and broccoli.

fold in: To combine a froth light substance, such as beaten egg whites or cream, with a heavier one and not lose air and reduce volume or lightness. To fold in, stir in a continuous, gentle circular motion from the bottom of the container to the top. Continue to fold in until the ingredients are incorporated.

fresh white bread crumbs: *See* **bread crumbs**

froth: To make foamy by adding air to the mixture; this is done by vigorously beating or whipping.

garnish: To put something on or around food, either to make it more colorful, such as adding a sprig of parsley; to make it more flavorful, such as adding syrup, icing; or to decorate it, such as with confectioners' sugar.

glacé cherries (also called candied cherries): *See* **candied fruit**

glaze: To give a shiny appearance to both savory and sweet preparations. For savory foods, coat with a light sauce; for sweets, coat with sprinkled sugar or spread thin icing.

gold leaf: *See* **silver leaf**

grater: A metal kitchen utensil with different surfaces used for grating, shredding, and slicing. Graters are found in flat, cylindrical, or box shapes, and some have a handle across the top for a firm grip. The surface used for grating is perforated with rough-edged round holes that stick out, forming a rasp-like surface. Graters usually have two grating surfaces, one for finely grating things such as spices, and a larger rasp-like surface for coarsely grating things such as cheese and for making bread crumbs. The shredder surface is perforated with ¼-inch round holes that have a raised cutting edge along the bottom side of each hole. The slicing surface has several parallel slits with a raised cutting edge along the bottom side of each slit.

grill: Cooking over heat on a perforated rack. The grill can be gas, electric, charcoal, wood, or combination. The food takes on a distinct grilled flavor, especially over a wood fire.

ground: The process of grinding different substances, ranging from coarse, used for ingredients such as meat, to fine powder, used for spices. Nuts can be ground in an electric blender, food processor, nut or coffee grinder, or **mortar and pestle.** Grind nuts, a few at a time, adding a little of the sugar called for in the recipe. Adding sugar to each batch prevents lumping up, which is caused by the oil in the nuts. The standard food processor can take 1 cup nuts and 2 teaspoons sugar; use the on-off pulse method to grind; 6 to 8 pulses should be sufficient.

guava: The fruit of a tropical shrub. It is available fresh, but it is best to buy it canned for a more consistent taste and texture.

half-sheet baking pan: A professional baking pan 18 x 13 x 1 inches. This is the maximum size pan that will fit in most home ovens.

heavy-based: A saucepan with a thick bottom such as cast iron or enameled cast iron. Food cooks more evenly in this type of pan and is less likely to burn.

herring: A saltwater fish found in the cold waters of the North Atlantic and Pacific Oceans. Over a hundred varieties of herring have been found. It is eaten fresh, pickled, smoked, and salted and is very popular in Scandinavian and Eastern European countries.

hominy: Dried white or yellow corn kernels from which the hull and germ have been removed. Hominy is sold canned, ready-to-eat, or dried (which must be soaked in water before using). Hominy grits, or simply grits, come in three grinds—fine, medium, and coarse. They are generally available at supermarkets.

hors d'oeuvre: *See* **appetizers**

icing spatula: *See* **pastry spatula**

jalapeño: Easily available hot green peppers that can be bought fresh or pickled and canned at supermarkets. When working with peppers, it is best to wear plastic or rubber gloves to protect your hands. The heat of peppers is in the seeds, and so it is best to remove and discard the seeds and membrane before using.

julienne: Cutting food, especially vegetables, such as carrots, into matchstick-sized shapes.

kiwi: A fruit known in China (as *yang tao* or Chinese gooseberry) since ancient times; it was introduced to New Zealand in 1906. When buying kiwi, select firm fruit. Kiwi that are soft can be mushy or mealy and lack flavor. To ripen kiwi, just leave in a bowl for a few days; do not refrigerate. To speed up ripening, place kiwi in a paper bag with a banana.

knead: To push down into the dough with the heels of hands. To knead, push down, turn the dough slightly, and repeat. Continue to turn and fold dough until it is smooth and **elastic**. As you knead, you will see the dough change from a flaky consistency to a more solid consistency that holds together. As you continue kneading, you will feel and see the dough become more and more elastic; it springs back each time you pick up the heel of your hand.

kosher salt: An additive-free, coarse-grained salt. It is used primarily in Jewish cooking.

lemon grass: A lemon-flavored, thick-stemmed grass that is widely used in southeast Asia, especially in Thai cooking. It is often combined with flavors of coconut, chili, and ginger. Many varieties are available; some of them are called sorrel, derived from the German word for "sour." Sorrel is also popular in French cooking. Lemon grass has long greenish-gray leaves with a white bulb-like base. (It looks something like a large green onion.) It has a sour-lemon flavor and fragrance. It is available fresh or dried in many supermarkets and in Asian food stores. Lemon grass is also called citronella. Dried lemon grass needs to be soaked in warm water to soften for about 15 to 20 minutes before using. The whole lemon grass is added to some recipes for flavoring only, and it is removed and discarded before the food is served. In other recipes, only the tender whitish-green end (about 4 to 6-inches) is used. It is finely chopped and edible.

lentils: Probably the earliest cultivated legume, dating back as early as 8000 B.C. Lentils, which have a pleasant earthy flavor, come in many varieties. The most common are the brown or green lentils. Red lentils are a salmon-color that turn yellow when cooked. Lentils don't require soaking, cook in about 20 minutes, and can easily turn mushy if left to cook too long.

liqueur: The French name for sweet alcoholic beverages usually served at the end of a meal.

lukewarm: A cooking term used to refer to heating or cooling food to a specific temperature, usually between 110°–115° F on food thermometer. Water that feels pleasantly warm to the touch is the right temperature.

manioc: *See* **cassava**

marinade: A seasoned liquid used to coat foods in order to absorb flavor or to tenderize.

marinate: To soak food, especially meat, in a sauce (**marinade**) made up of seasonings and liquids.

marzipan: A sweet mixture of almond paste, sugar, and usually egg whites. It is pliable, like modeling clay, and is often tinted with food coloring and made into different shapes to decorate cakes and other sweets. It is available in cans or plastic-wrapped logs at most supermarkets.

meat mallet: A tool used to flatten meat to a uniform thinness and to break down the meat fibers, tenderizing the meat and permitting even cooking. Also known as meat pounders, they come in different shapes and are made of wood or metal. Pound meat firmly with the meat mallet; use a lighter pressure on breast of chicken. Place the meat between two sheets of plastic wrap to prevent it from sticking to the mallet or work surface. Pound outward as well as downward to spread the meat out evenly.

melon baller: A kitchen tool with small, bowl-shaped scoops of different sizes at each end of a handle. It is used for cutting out round balls from melons.

millet: A grain native to Africa and Asia; it is a high-protein staple usually made into porridge. In the United States, it is used mostly for animal fodder.

mince: To chop very fine.

mortar and pestle: A bowl (mortar) and a grinding tool (pestle), usually used to grind spices. Both are made of a hard substance. The mortar holds the ingredients, and the pestle is held in the hand and is used to mash or grind them. You can make a mortar and pestle by simply using a metal bowl or a hard surface for the mortar and a clean, smooth rock, small enough to hold in your hand, or the head of a hammer or wooden mallet for the pestle.

mung beans: A small, dried bean popular in Indian subcontinent and Asian countries. The bean has a green skin that must be removed before cooking. Cover the beans completely in water to soak for 4 hours. After soaking, rub the beans briskly between your palms, which will loosen the skins. Pour off soaking water and discard skins. The skinless yellow bean that remains is what is used for cooking. Dried skinless yellow beans are available in Asian food stores and need no presoaking. When cooked, they have a slightly sweet flavor and velvety texture. Cook according to directions on the package or the recipe. Bean sprouts grow from mung beans.

mustard greens: Dark green leaves of the mustard plant. They have a strong mustard flavor and are available fresh, canned, or frozen at supermarkets. Buy only fresh, crisp, young leaves. Do not buy yellowish, wilted looking greens; they are old and will have an unpleasant fibrous texture.

oven-ready: Meat, fowl, or fish that is ready to cook with no preparatory work. Have the butcher or fishmonger prepare the item you are buying so it is ready for cooking according to your recipe, be it for the stovetop, oven, or grill. Fish must always be gilled, gutted, and scaled to be considered oven-ready.

paan: *See* **betel nuts**

papaya (also known as "tree melon" or *paw-paw*): A tropical fruit. They usually weigh about 1 to 2 pounds. The skin of this creamy, orange-colored fruit is a vibrant green that ripens to yellow. When selecting papaya, gently press on the fruit; if it yields to the pressure, it is ripe for eating. Cut a papaya in half lengthwise and scoop out the small, shiny (and inedible) black seeds.

parboil: To partially cook food by boiling in water for a short time to remove the raw flavor. It also speeds up the preparation of dense foods when they are combined with other ingredients that require minimum cooking.

pastry bag: A cone-shape of paper, plastic, or cloth with an opening at both ends. A metal or plastic tip is fitted onto the tip end, and the bag is filled through the large top opening with a soft, smooth mixture, such as icing, whipped cream, or other foods. When the top opening is securely closed and the bag is squeezed, the mixture is forced through the tip. The tips come in different sizes and designs. Pastry bags and tips are available in hobby and craft stores, kitchenware sections of department stores, and supermarkets.

pastry blender: A kitchen tool made of several parallel rows of stiff metal wires, bent in a U-shape. They are attached to either side of a 4- or 5-inch wide handle. As you press the wires down into the flour mixture, in a chopping motion, the fat is cut into the flour, making tiny pea-size pieces.

pastry brush: Used for applying glazes to foods. It can be a 1-inch paint brush, but it should be soft and of good quality so the bristles do not come out.

pastry spatula (also called an icing spatula): A straight, narrow blade used for applying smooth coatings of frosting to the tops and sides of cakes, and for slicing and filling layer cakes. The best are made of flexible stainless steel. They come in different lengths, but the 9-inch length blade is average.

peeled and deveined (shrimp): To peel shrimp, remove the hard shell that covers the edible flesh. This is done by holding the shrimp between the thumb and index finger of one hand and carefully pulling the tiny legs under the shrimp apart with the fingers of the other hand. The shell should easily peel off. To devein shrimp, remove the visible black (sometimes white) vein running down the back of peeled shrimp. Using a paring knife, cut the thin membrane while rinsing the shrimp under cold running water; use the point of the knife to remove the vein.

phyllo (also **filo**): Pastry sheets used in Greek, Eastern European, and Middle Eastern cooking. Available in one-pound boxes, each containing 22 paper-thin sheets, 14- x 18-inches in size (available in the freezer section of supermarkets). The pastries are paper thin and dry out quickly. Once the package is opened, keep the sheets you are not working with covered with a damp towel.

pigeon peas: A tiny grayish-yellow legume native to Africa. They are also called Congo peas and no-eyed peas. They are popular in southern states where they grow in long fuzzy pods. They are available dried, fresh, frozen, and canned in many supermarkets and most Latin American and Indian food stores.

pinch: The amount of a dry ingredient, such as salt or pepper, that can be held between the tip of the forefinger and thumb, about 1/12 teaspoon.

pine nuts: A seed of the pine tree that comes from the pine cone. They are available at supermarkets but are less expensive in Asian or Italian food stores.

piri-piri: A spicy Portuguese sauce made of chopped chili peppers, olive oil, bay leaves, and lemon rind.

pith: The spongy tissue between the skin and flesh of citrus fruits such as oranges, lemons, and grapefruit.

poach: To cook food gently in liquid held below the boiling point.

poi: *See* **taro root**

pomegranate: A golden red fruit, about the size of an apple. It grows on trees native to the Middle East. The fruit is full of tiny edible seeds imbedded in pith. The fruit dates back to ancient times and has been used in many religious rites.

proof: To dissolve and activate yeast in **lukewarm** liquid (sometimes with small amount of sugar); set yeast and water in warm place for 5 to 10 minutes until it is bubbly and expands.

puff pastry sheets (French: *pâte feuilletée*): Available frozen in most supermarkets; a 17¼ ounce box contains 2 sheets puff pastry, each 9 ½ inches square. Thaw, unwrap, and unfold pastry sheets according to directions on package. Puff pastry has to bake in a very hot, preheated oven to "puff up." Bake according to directions in each recipe. Puff pastry is made by folding and rolling dough and butter to produce many very thin butter-rich layers. During baking, the steam from the melted butter pushes the layers up to made the delicate flaky pastry.

punch down: To do this procedure, use a closed fist to punch down on the dough. This process releases the carbon dioxide air bubbles in the dough. After punching down the dough, remove it from the bowl and turn it upside down on a lightly floured work surface.

purée: A French word that means to mash, blend, process, or strain food until it reaches a smooth, lump-free consistency. Purée in a blender or food processor; adding a little liquid will help.

reduce: To boil rapidly until the amount of liquid is reduced due to evaporation. This is done to concentrate flavor in broth, to burn off alcohol in wine, and to thicken the sauce's consistency.

render: To melt fat over low heat to release the oil from animal tissue.

roasted nuts: To roast nuts, preheat oven to 375° F. Place nuts on a greased baking sheet and bake for 5 to 10 minutes, or until lightly browned. To dry-roast, put nuts or seeds in a dry pan with no liquid or oil. Shake the pan and stir with a wooden spoon until they lightly tan. Remove from heat at once so the nuts or seeds do not burn.

rose water: A sweet, clear, liquid flavoring distilled from rose petals; the petals are often imported from Bulgaria. It is available in Middle Eastern food stores, specialty food stores, and pharmacies.

roux: *See* **white sauce**

salt cod: A Mediterranean staple, especially in Portugal, where it is said there are more than 365 different ways to cook it. In the United States, salt cod was of vital importance to the New England colonies, both for eating and exporting, but gradually fell into disfavor. This was partly due to the misconception that salt cod dishes are salty. In fact, the salt is used to preserve the fish, not flavor it. Salt cod is made by curing fresh cod in brine or rock salt and then drying it either in the sun or air (the traditional way) or in temperature-controlled drying rooms. When properly reconstituted, salt cod is no more salty than fresh fish. It is all in the soaking: Change the water every 4 hours during the soaking process and refrigerate the soaking cod during the last half of the soaking; it becomes perishable after losing its salt. On average, salt cod fillets should be soaked for at least 12 hour and sometimes up to 36 hours. After soaking in the brine solution, salt cod must be soaked in cold water to soften it and remove its salt. The soaking time depends on how heavily the cod has been salted. Canadian salt cod, the type most commonly available in the United States, is often less heavily salted than other varieties and so needs less soaking. When the fish becomes soft and pliable, start tasting it. Salt cod with skin should be soaked for 48 hours; peel the skin off after soaking. Unlike some preserved foods, salt cod is very different from the fresh version. Salting and drying not only preserves the cod but also silkens the texture and enhances flavor, turning a bland fish into a distinctive product. Salt cod is sold by the pound in many ethnic markets. In food service terminology, "salt cod" refers to boneless fillet, while *bacala* means split, dried salt cod sold with the bone-in and skin-on. Other fish of the cod family are salted and dried and may also be called salt cod; the species name, such as pollock or haddock, should be on the package.

samovar: A large, metal urn-like container used for heating water, usually for tea.

sausage casing: Casing used to hold a sausage mixture together in a tube-shape. Natural casings are usually intestines of hogs and sheep. They are sold commercially cleaned. Soak in warm water for 2 to 3 hours, until casing is soft and pliable before using. Artificial casings need no preparation, but they are inedible and must be removed before eating the filling. Fill casing according to each recipe.

sauté: To fry in a small amout of oil. This term comes from a French word that means "to jump." The oil must be hot before adding the ingredients. Stir constantly while cooking the "jumping" ingredients; otherwise they absorb too much oil.

scald milk: To heat milk to just below the boiling point, when small bubbles form around the edge of the pan. Formerly, milk was always scalded to kill bacteria. Now, with pasteurized milk, air-dried milk solids, and canned milk, scalding is usually done to save time in dissolving sugar and melting fat.

Scotch bonnet: A tiny pumpkin-looking capsicum, native to Jamaica; it is one of the hottest peppers known. Since they can be difficult to find, **jalapeño** peppers or ground red pepper can be used instead.

sear: To cook the surface of food, especially meat, quickly over high heat to brown the exterior. Searing does not "seal in" juices, as commonly thought, but it does improve the flavor and appearance.

section (citrus fruit): To peel the fruit and remove all the **pith**. To section, hold the fruit over a bowl to catch all the juices. Using a serrated paring knife or grapefruit knife, carefully cut down on both sides of the fruit's membrane to release each v-shaped section of edible fruit. Repeat until all edible fruit is removed from the membrane. Squeeze the membrane in your hand to release any remaining juice into the bowl. Discard membrane.

seed: To remove and discard seeds before cutting or chopping, usually for a fruit or vegetable. To seed tomatoes, cut in half and gently squeeze tomatoes over a small bowl. Discard juice or cover and refrigerate it and the seeds for another use. This is the quickest and easiest way to remove seeds from a tomato.

segment: *See* **section (citrus fruit)**

self-rising flour: A type of flour containing leavening agents and salt for convenience.

semolina: Hard wheat flour (durum) excellent for making pasta and some breads.

serrated knife: A knife that has saw-like notches along the cutting edge, such as on a bread knife.

sesame seeds: Used for flavoring in Middle Eastern and Asian cooking. Toast sesame seeds in skillet by cooking over medium heat, tossing frequently, until lightly browned, about 5 minutes. Spread out on a plate to cool. The best places to buy sesame seeds are health food and Middle Eastern food stores.

shallots: A variety of the onion family whose bulbs form small clusters. It has a mild flavor. Peel off the thin brown skin before cooking. Buy shallots that are firm, not wrinkling or sprouting, and store in a cool dry place.

short grain: The type of rice favored for most Japanese cooking. It is more absorbent than the more familiar long-grain rice. If the rice you buy seems to have a gummy residue on the surface of the grains, put it in a strainer, wash under cold running water, and drain well. To continue, follow cooking directions on package or in recipe.

sift: To shake a dry, powdered substance (such as flour, baking powder, etc.) through a strainer/sifter to make it smooth and lump-free. (See **sifter**.)

sifter: A container, such as a flour sifter, with a strainer bottom used for sifting. (See **sift**.)

silver leaf (also ***vark*** or ***varak***)**:** Tissue-thin edible silver that is decoratively applied to sweet and savory dishes as a show of status and wealth by people in India and the subcontinent. To decorate, gently lay silver leaf on the food and it self-adheres. Sometimes just a dab, no bigger than a pea, is added to small candies. Three pieces of 2 to 3-inch squares cost about $1.00 at Indian and Middle East food stores. Gold leaf is similar but more expensive than silver leaf.

simmer: To slowly cook food just below the boiling point.

simple syrup: *See* **sugar syrup**

skimmer: A long handled tool that has a round, slightly cupped, mesh screen or metal disk with small holes for removing food items from hot liquid.

slivered: Finely sliced

slurry: A paste made by stirring together water and flour or cornstarch. It is used to thicken hot soups, stews, gravy, or sauces. After adding slurry, continue to cook for several minutes for flour to lose its raw taste.

snow peas: A legume that is totally edible, including the thin crunchy pod. The French call it *mange-tout*, which means "eat it all." Buy snow peas with crisp, brightly colored pods. If they seem limp, they are probably old. Snow peas can be eaten raw or cooked. Trim off tips at both ends of the pod just before adding to salad or cooking. Rinse under cold running water and drain well. Sometimes called Chinese snow peas, they are available fresh or frozen at most supermarkets and most Asian food stores.

sorghum: a grain similar to **millet**. It is eaten as porridge in Asian countries and in Africa is used for porridge and made into flour, beer, and molasses. In the United States it is mostly used for forage.

star fruit: *See* **carambola**

steamed pudding mold: Heat-proof containers that are wider at the top with either plain or fluted sides, with attached cover. The mold is filled with pudding mixture, and the top is clamped shut. The pudding cooks in a pot of simmering water large enough to hold the mold. Some have a center tube enabling food to cook quicker. The molds come in different sizes. If you don't have a steamed pudding mold you can make one using either a round-bottomed stainless mixing bowl or a 2- or 3-pound coffee can. Cans aren't tapered like the molds, but they work quite well. After filling the can with pudding mixture, cover the top with sheet of greased aluminum foil, placed greased side down, over the opening. Press the foil tightly against sides of can and tie with string. It is important to prevent moisture from entering the container.

steamer pan: A two-part pan with a tight-fitting cover. The upper pan is perforated and sits above boiling water in the lower pan. Food placed in the upper pan cooks by the steam from the boiling water. A steamer pan can be made by placing a metal **colander** into a larger saucepan with cover. The pan must be large enough so that the boiling water does not touch the upper container. The steamer basket (upper container) can be propped up with something heat-proof, such as a wad of foil or small metal bowl placed in the water. A bamboo steamer basket placed in a **wok** makes an excellent steamer pan. Bamboo steamer baskets come in assorted sizes, are inexpensive, and are available in kitchenware stores and Asian food stores.

steep: To soak dry ingredients in liquid (usually hot) until the flavor is incorporated (infused) into the liquid.

sugar syrup: Also known as sweet syrup. Sugar syrup has different stages and temperatures for different types of candies and desserts. To make it, heat 1 cup sugar and 1 cup water in small saucepan over high heat until sugar dissolves, about 1 minute. Add a small pinch of cream of tartar, stir, and boil rapidly until it reachs the desired stage. Use a candy thermometer or follow these tests to determine the stage:

Stage: Temperature	*Test*
Thread stage: 230°–234° F	• A little syrup forms long flexible threads when spoon is lifted from mixture.
Soft ball stage 234°–236° F	• Syrup forms a soft ball when dropped in cup of cold water.
Firm ball stage 242°–248° F	• Syrup forms a firm ball that can be easily flattened with your finger when dropped in cup of cold water.
Hard ball stage 250°–265° F	• Syrup forms a firm, pliable ball when dropped in cup of cold water.
Crack stage 270°–290° F	• Syrup forms a brittle ball • or teardrop shape when dropped in cup of cold water.
Hard crack stage 300°–310° F	• Syrup forms brittle threads when dropped in cup of cold water.
Caramelized stage* 310°–312° F	• Syrup becomes pale golden color.

* ADULT SUPERVISION REQUIRED. To caramelize sugar, follow the directions for sugar syrup, but cook over low rolling boil until syrup is pale golden color, 15 to 20 min-

utes. Carefully remove pan of syrup from heat and set it in a larger pan of simmering water. This will keep the caramelized sugar syrup liquid. If it gets too firm, remove the pan from the water and place it over direct medium heat to soften. Do not reboil or it will crystallize.

Simple syrup is a relatively thin solution of sugar syrup. It is used for glazing pastries, poaching and preserving fruit, and adding to frostings. Sugar syrup is the basis for most candies and caramelizing used on desserts. To make simple syrup, dissolve 1 cup sugar in ¾ cup water over medium heat. Bring to boil and cook for 3 to 4 minutes, or until it reaches 220° F on candy thermometer. Cool syrup and refrigerate in jar with tight fitting lid. Use as needed.

tamarind: Refers to the seed pod of the tamarind tree, about 5 inches long. When dried, its sweet-sour flavor is used to season food, much like adding lemon juice. Dried tamarind pods are available at all Asian food stores and some supermarkets. Tamarind paste, made from tamarind seeds, is more convenient and available in jars in all Asian food stores.

taro root: A plant of the arum family cultivated throughout Polynesia and the tropics for its edible, starchy roots. When the taro root is cooked and **puréed**, it looks very much like dehydrated mashed potatoes. In its natural state, its color varies from steel blue to pink to purple. The leaves of the plant, called callaloo, are eaten as a green vegetable. Like the taro root, the leaves must be cooked for at least an hour to remove a peculiarly irritating taste. A variety of taro grown in the southern United States is called **dasheen**.

temper: To raise the temperature of a cold liquid gradually by slowly stirring in a hot liquid.

thermometers: Refers to meat, cooking or candy, and deep-fryer thermometers. Meat thermometers register inside temperature of meat. Cooking or candy thermometer register heat to 400° F and are used for extremely hot ingredients. The best meat thermometer is called "instant," which gives a reading in just seconds. Deep-fryer thermometers are built in to the fryer equipment.

toasted nuts: *Toast in oven:* Spread nuts or seeds out on baking sheet and put in preheated 325° F oven until lightly golden, 12 to 15 minutes. *Toast in skillet:* Heat medium skillet over high heat until a drop of water flicked across its surface evaporates instantly. Add the nuts or seeds and shaking the pan gently, cook for 2 to 3 minutes, until the seeds are lightly toasted. *See also* **sesame seeds**.

tomatoes, peeled: To peel tomatoes, drop each in boiling water for 1 to 2 minutes. Remove with a slotted spoon and hold under cold water to stop the cooking action. If the skin has not already cracked open, poke the tomato with a small knife, and the skin easily peels off. (This is also called **blanching**.)

trim or trimmed: To trim off the inedible parts on food products, such as the stems and root ends and blemish spots on fruits and vegetables, gristle and silver skin on meat, or rind on cheeses.

truss: To tightly bind together. When applied to poultry, it is done to keep stuffing inside the bird while it cooks. Trussing can be done by sewing up the opening or inserting several metal truss pins or skewers into skin on either side of the opening and lacing it closed with string (like lacing a boot).

turnips: A root vegetable with white flesh and skin. Buy small, firm, young turnips; as they age, they get a tough, almost woody texture. Wash and **trim** just before using. They can be cooked like potatoes. Turnip greens, the leafy greens that grow above ground, are best when young. They are available at all supermarkets.

vark or **varak:** *See* **silver leaf**

wasabi: A horseradish-like root grown in Japan and sold as a paste or powder at Asian markets. The powder is soaked in a little cold water for 10 minutes before using. It is served as a condiment for dipping.

water bath: A container with food placed in a larger shallow pan of water that is heated either on the stove or in the oven. The food cooks with less intense heat. Food is also kept warm. The French call it *bain marie*.

watercress: A member of the mustard family that grows in shallow streams. The crisp, deep green leaves are used as an herb, salad green, and garnish. Its flavor is peppery and slightly pungent.

wheat berries: Whole wheat grains that have not been cooked or processed in any way. If they are in good condition, they will sprout and can even be used as seed. Wheat berries can be cooked a long time to make porridge, and they can be cooked with less liquid for a shorter time to use much as you might use rice. With a blender, you can grind wheat berries into a coarse meal. Cracked wheat is wheat berry that has been **coarsely chopped** by steel blades. It cooks faster than whole berries but not as quickly as bulgur. Bulgur (also bulghar or burghul) refers to wheat berries that have been steamed, toasted, and cracked and then either finely or coarsely ground. Bulgur can be made by boiling the wheat berries about half an hour, until barely tender, draining them thoroughly, and toasting them in flat pan in a 250° F. (warm oven) for 1 to 1½ hours, or until completely dry. In the blender, pulverize the toasted berries to either coarse or fine grind. You can buy wheat berries, cracked wheat, and bulgur in bulk or boxed in health food stores and many supermarkets.

white sauce: A sauce made by stirring a liquid, such as milk or water, into a paste made of fat (usually butter) and flour; this paste is called **roux**. For thin sauce, use 1 tablespoon each of fat and flour for each cup of liquid; for a medium sauce, use 2 tablespoons each of fat and flour for each cup of liquid; for a thick sauce, use 3 tablespoons of each for each cup of liquid.

wok: A Chinese round-bottomed metal cooking pan with sloping sides and a large cooking surface suitable for stir-frying and steaming. A special ring trivet is used to adapt the wok to Western stoves.

yeast: A natural substance that helps breads and cakes rise. In home baking, two types of yeast are used—compressed cake yeast or active dry granulated yeast. Both are living organisms and must be activated in warm liquid. One package of dry yeast may be used in place of 1 cake of yeast. To use, dissolve contents of package of dry yeast in ¼ cup **lukewarm** water. Sugar is added to yeast to quicken the action of the yeast. (Never add salt, it retards the yeast action.) When buying dry yeast make sure it is active by checking the expiration date on package. One package of dry yeast (¼-ounce) contains 2 teaspoons yeast.

zest: The outer peel of citrus fruits, removed by grating or scraping off. It is important to only remove the colored outer peel, not the white pith beneath which is bitter.

INTRODUCTION

What Is a Life-Cycle Event?

A life–cycle event, also known as a "rite of passage," is a person's progression from one stage of life to another. An individual's key life-cycle events—birth, puberty (coming of age), marriage, and death—are important occasions in most societies and cultures worldwide. Other personal milestones—celebrating birthdays and name days, graduating from school, getting a first job, paying off a mortgage, becoming a grandparent—are also occasions for marking a person's advancement in life. The events indentified as important vary from place to place, from time to time, and from one culture to another. Among most cultures, however, a new stage in life usually calls for a celebration, perhaps a ritual, and almost always food.

Sometimes life-cycle events are marked by an official rite of passage that formally removes individuals from an earlier status or role and officially places them in a new role that includes different rights and responsibilities. In other situations, life milestones are marked or celebrated without such an official rite, but with recognition and celebration of other kinds. Some of these practices are defined by religious leaders or teachings. Some are the customs of the ethnic group or national community. Often, the life-cycle celebrations are surrounded with familiar customs and traditions, anticipated by all involved.

Many of these customs are rooted in religious traditions, but some of the beliefs can be traced back to more ancient customs. Today in most countries these beliefs, often called good luck and bad luck, are still very strong. For example, throwing rice at newlyweds to send them on their way at the end of a wedding is supposed to "shower luck" on their life together. Tying shoes on their getaway car is another act for "good luck." The groom seeing the bride before the wedding is sometimes considered "bad luck." Consulting the stars for an auspicious date, rubbing oil on an infant during baptism to ward off the devil, and eating longevity noodles are all rituals that have been passed from generation to generation.

Life-cycle rituals vary from culture to culture and nation to nation. Some customs are more understandable to outsiders than others. One of the goals of this book is to show the many ways that different cultures mark the milestones in individuals' lives.

In reading these descriptions, keep in mind that rituals vary, even within the same group, and this book limits its descriptions to the most obvious and easy to understand rituals. In addition, the rituals described in these pages tend to reflect an idealized version of the tradition, one that might not be followed in every household. For example, even though it is pretty safe to say that a cake is part of most weddings, not every wedding includes a special cake.

Throughout the world, life-cycle celebrations reveal the very heart of the family and the culture. Continuing the ancestral life-cycle customs and rituals give continuity and a sense of belonging and substance to each new generation.

RELIGIOUS LIFE-CYCLE RITUALS AND CUSTOMS

To better understand life-cycle celebrations, it is important to know something about the role religion plays in these events. Throughout the world, religion and culture are entwined, and for many people religion determines which life-cycle events are celebrated, and when and how they are celebrated. Even people who don't consider themselves religious often turn to their religious heritage when reaching these rites of passage. Keep in mind, though, that religious rituals are just one facet of the life-cycle celebrations; the other facets that determine how life-cycle events are celebrated include the family and social structure, the lifestyle, and the habitat of the celebrants.

Although there are countless variations among the world's religions, this introduction will describe the most important life-cycle rituals of eight of the major religions of the world—Indigenous Religions, Judaism, Christianity, Islam, Hinduism, Buddhism, Shintoism, and Confucianism. This book cannot, of course, undertake the daunting task of explaining or comparing religions. Nor can it go beyond a very simplified presentation of how life-cycle events are celebrated. Over time, with religions crossing borders, mountains, and oceans, life-cycle rituals and celebrations frequently have changed. Local people often have altered, added to, or fused together religious and secular customs and rituals. Many of these local customs are described in the introductions to each country section of this book.

Indigenous Religions

Indegenous or traditional religions are the umbrella terms under which I have classified the religious traditions of tribes and other small groupings of people. These traditions represent some of humankinds' most ancient interpretations of the world around them. Although these indigenous religions are grouped together in this book, and also by anthropologists, the variations among religions in this category are immense. To give some idea of this diversity, consider that such groups include, but are not limited to, Africans, Maoris of New Zealand, Aborigines of Australia, and Native Americans of the Western Hemisphere. Although indigenous religions are found throughout the world, most of the descriptions that follow apply to the indigenous life-cycle events of Africa, because these religions have more followers in Africa than other parts of the world.

Even though indigenous religions differ throughout the world, and even within Africa, some general beliefs are fairly widespread. Some followers of indigenous religion believe that all things in nature have a soul and that the spirits inhabit trees, water, animals, and all other things in nature, a belief system sometimes known as animist. Other groups believe the ancestral spirits (founders of the family, lineage, or clan) affect everyday life. Many followers of indigenous religions who have been exposed to other religions will combine these beliefs with their traditional practices, incorporating rituals from both indigenous and introduced religions in life-cycle celebrations.

Traditional African Life-Cycle Rituals

Life-cycle events in an African society that follows indigenous practices usually begin with an offering to the ancestral spirits. The offerings can be baskets of food left on the family shrine or a beverage, water or something stronger, taken out and poured over the ancestral burial ground. Popular ritual foods are honey, pumpkins, and yams.

Birth

Shortly after birth, it is important to name the newborn; usually an ancestral or "spirit" name is chosen. The name is chosen according to which dead ancestor has "returned" in the child. (See Death below.) The name is more than a label; being given the name of an ancestor is to inherit something of his or her basic nature, qualities, and status.

Coming of Age (Initiation)

Among most ethnic groups, when the male reaches puberty, an initiation ceremony takes place, usually at the beginning of the dry season in May. The first stage of this ceremony is separation from all females, especially from mothers. Among most groups, circumcision is performed during this separation. The boys spend several months at camps, away from the village, where they undergo trials and are instructed in traditional beliefs and practices. Their return to the village as men is a joyful occasion, and great communal feasts are part of the celebration.

The initiation of girls is often performed on an individual basis, usually just before the first menstrual period. The initiation prepares young women for marriage and usually no celebration is held, or at most a party is given for the immediate family.

Marriage

Throughout rural Africa, the betrothal and marriage rituals are tied to the age-old concern of collective survival. The rituals, steeped in tradition, might differ slightly from tribe to tribe, but regardless of specific traditions, marriage is a union between families and communities rather than two people. Marrying within the kin group is discouraged; however, the preferred marriage is with someone belonging to the same ethnic group. In the traditional indigenous cultures, polygamy (one husband and many wives) has been the accepted family structure, in part because of the high death rate of women during childbirth.

Once a mate has been selected, the long, drawn-out courting process can take up to a year to complete in traditional cultures. The giving of premarital gifts and providing of services to each other's families help to cement the marriage agreement. Gifts from the groom's family to the family of the bride, given to validate the marriage contract, include such things as cattle, kente cloth, bags of money, beer, and food. In some communities, the men farm for their prospective in-laws as part of the nuptial contract.

In these traditional cultures, to have children is the most important responsibility of life. To be childless is to have failed the community, including the ancestors. A person without children cannot be an "ancestor" and does not participate in the continuity of communal life.

Until recent years, a girl had no say in her future. As Africa modernizes, women are speaking out, and in some communities they have the right to accept or reject the husband selected by their family. Some can actually choose their own husbands but not without first consulting the ancestral spirits for approval.

Death

In most traditional religions, ancestors are revered by the living. Not everyone who dies becomes an ancestor, however, only those who have children, who die without shame, and who are correctly buried.

Upon the death of a family member, a period of mourning forges links between the living and the dead. Those in mourning perform a number of rituals to ensure that the spirit of the dead person moves easily into the world of his or her ancestors. Families practice different rituals to retain the connection between this world and the next so that they do not lose contact with ancestors. For example, ancestral worshipers make offerings of food and drink at the grave, and some ethnic groups keep a private shrine or a "spirit house" within the family compound. When a favor is requested of the ancestor spirit a sacrifice may be made, usually a small animal such as a chicken or goat.

The most important link between ancestors and the living is the rebirth of the dead through the birth of a child. In this way, the relationship between ancestors and descendants is continuous and never ending.

In many traditional African societies, kings and chiefs are considered sacred, and they have elaborate funerals. To please their followers, it is important for ruling figures to be impressive in death, and so they are buried in full regalia. Not too many years ago, the wives and servants of the rulers were killed and buried along with the important men to help them in their afterlife.

Judaism and Jewish Life-Cycle Rituals

Judaism is the world's oldest monotheistic religion (belief in just one God), surviving for over four thousand years. It has also given rise to the Christian and Islamic traditions. Although followers of Judaism can be found all over the world, its roots are in the Middle East, particularly the region around the country of Israel, which was founded in 1948 as a Jewish state.

Judaism has split into three branches—Orthodox, Conservative, and Reform—with numerous other small variations. Although all branches observe the same life-cycle events, each interprets the rituals differently. Orthodox Jews are the most pious and generally follow rituals and customs to their full extent. Most Conservatives accept some of the rituals and customs, while most Reform Jews follow them in moderation, if at all.

One important difference between the different Jewish groups is that Orthodox Jews follow strict kosher dietary laws. The word "kosher" means "fit" or "clean." The kosher rules apply to what can be eaten, how it is processed, and how it is prepared and served. Many Conservative Jews "keep kosher," while most Reform Jews don't observe the kosher laws.

In the State of Israel, the kosher dietary laws are the law of the land and are followed by most people. For Kosher Jews, eating shellfish, pork, and certain other animals is forbidden, and the animals they do eat must be slaughtered a certain way. Dairy products must not be eaten at the same meal with meat and poultry. Wine and the traditional bread, *challah* (recipe page 105), are ritual foods included in all life-cycle celebrations.

Birth

On the eighth day after a boy is born, friends and family gather for a ceremony, observed for millennia, called a *Brit Milah*, the ceremony of circumcision (commonly referred to as a *Bris*).

The *mohel*, a person trained to perform the circumcision, does so for male infants of all Orthodox and some Conservative and Reform parents. Followed by appropriate blessings and prayers, the *mohel* completes the procedure with the skill of a fine surgeon. The baby is then comforted in the arms of its mother while the family and a few close friends invited for the ceremony adjourn to another room for a light repast. Many Conservative and Reform Jews prefer to have a doctor perform the circumcision at the hospital before the newborn is taken home. The first Friday evening after the birth of a boy the family holds a *Shalem Zachor*, a festive occasion to welcome him into the family. Sweet pastries and *nahit* (chick peas or garbanzo beans) are traditionally served.

A ceremony fairly new to Judaism celebrates the birth of a girl. *Simhat habat* is Hebrew for "rejoicing over the daughter." When a girl is born, the family's rabbi (Jewish religious leader) announces her name to the congregation during Friday night synagogue services. To celebrate the occasion, some parents and grandparents provide sweets and beverages in the reception area for the congregation following the service or a party may be held at the parents' home.

Many Jewish children are given two names—a secular name and a Hebrew name. Some are named after people in the Bible. The Hebrew name is used throughout life: at the *Bar* and *Bat Mitzvah*, at the wedding, and on the gravestone.

The Orthodox Jews have many rituals and customs not practiced by the Conservative or Reform branches of Judaism. For instance, only Orthodox Jews delay a little boy's haircut until he is 3 years old, the age at which Orthodox boys traditionally begin to study the Torah (the first five books of the Bible).

Coming of Age

Jewish parents believe nothing is more important for their children than education in both secular and Hebrew schools. After a boy completes his Jewish learning, at age 13, a coming-of-age ceremony, called a *Bar Mitzvah*, is held. For a girl, at age 12, a *Bat Mitzvah* is held. This ceremony is an important event in the lives of Jewish boys and girls because it means they are no longer looked upon as children and they are now received into the religious community. Bar and Bat Mitzvah ceremonies are a relatively recent development. Neither a ceremony nor a feast is called for in the Jewish religious law, but decades ago, Eastern European Jews began the practice of marking the day with a ceremony at the synagogue, followed by a simple party.

Although customs vary, the Bar and Bat Mitzvah services take place during the weekly Sabbath service in the synagogue or temple. The young adults read in Hebrew from the Torah, and they are called upon to give a speech, usually thanking their parents and Hebrew teachers. At the close of the service, attended by family, relatives, friends, classmates, and regular members of the congregation, it is customary for the boy or girl's parents to invite the attendees into the social hall of the temple or synagogue for a *kiddush*, the traditional Sabbath prayer over bread and wine. After the service, everyone is invited to the parent's home, a social hall, or restaurant for a celebration marked with plenty of food and the giving of gifts.

Another coming-of-age ceremony for Reform Jews is the confirmation ceremony that is celebrated after the completion of Hebrew high school. This practice arose out a belief by Reform Jews that 13 was too young an age for the coming-of-age ceremony. Today most Reform Jews celebrate both the Bar Mitzvah and the confirmation.

Marriage

In Judaism, marriage is considered to be a holy covenant (agreement) between the bride and groom. Among the Orthodox and some Conservative and Reform Jews, a marriage document (*ketubah*) is signed by the bride and groom in which they promise to take care of each other and to make a Jewish home. This document describes the rights and obligations of the bride and groom.

A bride will often wear a face veil for the wedding, especially if she is Orthodox. If the veil is worn, a veiling ritual takes place just before the ceremony when the groom veils the bride after he verifies that she is actually the woman he plans on marrying. This symbolic ritual is a reminder of the lesson learned in the Old Testament by Jacob, who was tricked into marrying Leah instead of Rachel, his true love. Leah pretended to be Rachel and covered her face with her veil so Jacob would not know the truth until the marriage was sanctioned.

A Jewish wedding can be held at any location, as long as an ordained rabbi officiates. By custom, all immediate relatives are part of the wedding party. The groom, and then the bride, are escorted down the aisle by their parents. Siblings can be attendants and grandparents may have a place in the procession.

The wedding ceremony is performed under a *huppah* (wedding canopy), which represents the couple's future home. The *huppah* is often a large embroidered cloth, or it can be a blanket of fresh flowers and greenery; sometimes it is a prayer shawl (*tallit*) belonging to a relative. The *huppah* is held up by four poles, and it is considered an honor to be one of the four people selected to hold a pole upright during the ceremony. Symbolically, the pole bearers are showing loyalty to the marrying couple. Under the *huppah*, a table is set with two glasses and a bottle of ritual wine used for the *kiddush* prayer.

Depending on the couple's cultural background, personal preference, and local custom, the language of the service will vary, possibly combining Hebrew and English. After the introduction by the rabbi, wedding vows are exchanged; the groom then places a plain gold band (without engraving or breaks) on the bride's right index finger for Orthodox and some Conservative ceremonies. If it is a Reform ceremony, it is usually placed on her left ring finger.

The rabbi then reads aloud the *ketubah* (the traditional marriage contract). At some point during the service, the bride and groom will each sip a glass of ritual wine while a traditional prayer, a *kiddush*, is recited. Near the end of the ceremony, the traditional seven blessings will be recited or sung. The Orthodox ritual is a little different. The bride may circle the groom seven times, representing the seven wedding blessings, before taking her place at his right side.

The *sheva brachot* (seven blessings) symbolize the seven days of creation and the completion of the marriage ceremony. The first blessing is upon the wine, the fruit of the vine. The second thanks God for his creation, and the third specifically praises God for his creation of human life. The fourth blessing acknowledges the separation of human life into man and woman. The fifth wishes for Jerusalem to be rebuilt and restored to its beautiful existence. The sixth declares hope that the new couple will be as happy as Adam and Eve were in the Garden of Eden. The seventh blessing thanks God for creating delight, mirth, gratification, pleasure, love, serenity, and brotherhood.

The ceremony ends with the tradition of crushing the wine glass used in the ceremony beneath the groom's heel. The glass is often wrapped in a napkin or handkerchief before the groom stamps on it. The breaking of the glass represents many things: it symbolizes the destruction of the Temple of Jerusalem and acts as a reminder that in life and in marriage there are times of sorrow and joy. The shattered glass also reminds guests and participants of how fragile life is. After the groom breaks the glass, guests clap and cheer him and call out "*Mazeltov*!" (congratulations or good luck). Immediately following the ceremony, some Jewish couples perform a traditional ritual known as *yichud* (union). The couple goes into a private room where they briefly eat some food together, usually chicken broth.

Housewarming

Chanukat habayit is the celebration for the family in their new home. It is a housewarming or a "dedication of the home." A *mezuzah*, a case containing small scrolls in Hebrew with two extracts from Deuteronomy (in the Old Testament), is fixed to the top right-hand side of the front door and each door inside the house. Prayers are said and bread and salt are brought into the house, as a symbol of good luck, before the festivities begin.

Death

After a death in a Jewish family, the funeral service is arranged as soon as possible, preferably within 24 hours of death. Funerals are kept very simple, even among wealthy families. No prayers for the dead are offered, but *kaddish*, a prayer of praise to God, is recited in their memory. When a parent dies, it is the responsibility of the children to say *kaddish* on their behalf. At Orthodox and some Conservative funerals mourning family members make a small tear in their clothes (such as on a tie or scarf) as a mark of grief.

After the funeral, mourners are invited to the departed person's family home to partake in food and drink prepared by friends or family members other than mourners. This meal is known as *seudat havra-ah* (meal of consolation). Customs vary among the different communities and Jewish groups, but the food for *seudat havra-ah* always includes hard-boiled eggs as a symbol of life and a food whose roundness suggests the continuance and eternity of life, such as lentils or bagels. In Judaism, bread is the staff of life and is served at all meals. At a time of mourning, it is especially appropriate to eat bread as the symbol of life. The *seudat havra-ah* is a *mitzvah* (blessing), not a social event, and as such mourners can drink a moderate amount of wine. Meat is symbolically the food of celebration and joy, therefore it is never served for *seudat havra-ah*.

Before entering the house, all the mourners must wash their hands. A pail of water and towels are placed just outside the front entrance of the house for this ritual. Following the funeral, a week of private mourning, called *shivah* (the seven days), is observed. During *shivah*, the grieving Orthodox Jews sit on low stools or on the floor. It is also the custom to cover mirrors and pictures hanging on the walls with cloth sheets.

On the anniversary of a parent's death, the children light a memorial candle (and recite the *kaddish*). Toward the end of every Friday night synagogue or temple service, the rabbi asks those mourning a loved one to join him in reciting the *kaddish*.

breads and wheat grain products have a religious significance in most Christian church ceremonies.

Christianity and Christian Life-Cycle Rituals

Christianity is a universal religion with more followers than any of the other world religions. Christianity is a monotheistic religion (the belief in just one God) that grew out of Judaism. The Old Testament of the Christian Bible is the same as the Jewish Torah, but Christians believe that Jesus Christ is the messiah prophesized in the Old Testament. The story of Jesus' life makes up the New Testament.

Over the centuries, cultural differences and variations in the way people worship have led to the formation of thousands of different branches, denominations, and sects within Christianity. The principal divisions in Christianity are the Protestant, the Catholic, and the Orthodox Churches. Despite these divisions, Christians share some common beliefs: Jesus Christ is the savior, Sunday is the official day of worship, and the Bible is the holy book of Christianity.

Almost all Christian churches celebrate life-cycle events with the designated rituals—baptisms, confirmation, marriage, and funeral services. The rituals and pageantry vary from the simple or few in some Protestant churches, to the symbolic pageantry in most Catholic churches and some Anglican churches, to the grand opulence in the Orthodox churches. Besides these differences in religious sects, the geographic location and the traditions and customs of local people cause rituals to vary from one country to another. Although these differences exist, the foods associated with Christian rituals are fairly universal. Red wine or grape juice and

Protestant and Catholic Life-Cycle Rituals

Birth

Baptism is the most widely accepted way of becoming a member of the Christian faith. The word "baptism" is derived from the Greek word "*baptizein*," meaning "to dip or immerse." Christian churches have infant baptisms and adult baptisms. When infants are baptized, they are either dipped into a baptism tub, called a font, or water is sprinkled on the infant's head by the minister (Protestant clergy) or priest (Catholic clergy). When an adult converts to Christianity, the baptism ceremony can be held in a church or in a river or lake. Various Christian groups observe the rituals in different ways. Among some groups, when a baby is born, parents select godparents to oversee the child's spiritual progress in case they are unable to do so. Godparents are expected to take part in the baptismal ceremony. For some groups, naming the child, christening, is part of the ceremony.

Coming of Age

Christian churches that practice infant baptism almost always have coming-of-age rituals, known as confirmation. Although confirmations can take place at any time, they are usually held at the onset of puberty, at about age 12. At these ceremonies, a young person is "confirmed" to take a more active role in the church. To be confirmed, one has to attend classes to learn more about the Christian faith.

Catholic confirmation services are a little more extensive and include many symbolic rituals. In most denominations, the ceremony is performed by a high-ranking member of the church. An emotional ritual performed by the clergy is "laying hands" on the head of the person being confirmed. This ancient ritual symbolizes the passing on of the Christian faith from one generation to the next.

Betrothal and Marriage

Christian marriage traditions vary from church to church and even from family to family. Prior to marriage the couple usually announces their intentions to marry, known as the betrothal. The length of betrothal periods are different for each marriage, with no set time period. Some Christian groups have orientation classes at the church to prepare the couple for marriage.

A Christian wedding may be an elaborate, formal church ceremony with many attendants or a very simple affair with just the bride and groom before the minister. Most Protestants hold their wedding ceremonies anywhere they like; it need not take place in the church. The wedding celebrations differ according to the customs of the country, ethnic group, city, village, and even the family.

Roman Catholic marriages must take place in the church to be officially recognized. The ceremony can be either without Mass, and only 20-minutes long, or be a more elaborate ceremony with a Mass, lasting for an hour.

It is customary for the Roman Catholic priest throughout the Mass to give instructions, which often vary from parish to parish. During the wedding ceremony, vows and rings are exchanged. Just before Communion (see next paragraph) is served, the priest gives a sign of peace, and at that time the guests turn to their neighbors, shake their hands, and say, "Peace be with you" or some other friendly greeting. Close friends and relatives often hug.

In the Roman Catholic Church, Communion is reserved for baptized Catholics. The Communion is the commemoration of Christ's Last Supper. It is the ceremony in which bread and wine are consecrated and taken as the body and blood of Christ. (Anglican and Orthodox churches also have Communion ceremonies.) To take Communion, members of the congregation walk down the center aisle to take the bread (usually a wafer) and wine and then return to their seats. After Communion, the signing of the register takes place, and the priest introduces the newly married couple to the guests. At this time the guests will often applaud, depending on local custom.

Both Catholic and Protestant wedding ceremonies are usually followed by a wedding feast. It can be a simple meal for just the wedding party or an elaborate one for thousands of guests. The feast can be a wedding breakfast, luncheon, afternoon repast, supper, or extravagant wedding reception at any time of day or evening with feasting, drinking, dancing, singing, and merrymaking.

Death

Christian customs for mourning the dead vary from country to country and from parish to parish. When a Christian dies, the body is embalmed and then washed and dressed in clean clothing in preparation for burial. Depending upon local customs and the financial situation and wishes of the family, Christian funerals can take place either at home, funeral home, church, or public hall.

The evening before a Protestant funeral, it is customary for family and friends to view the body either in the home or funeral home. Catholics generally have a Wake (prayer service), followed by the serving of food and drink. In fact, food and drink play an important role in the mourning process. As soon as friends and neighbors hear about a death it is customary for them to bring platters, bowls, and baskets of prepared food and beverages to the home of the deceased to be shared by mourners.

On the day of the burial, Protestants generally have a service at the funeral home or church. Catholics may or may not bring the casket to the church for the Mass. After the burial at the cemetery, the mourners go to the church hall or the home of the deceased to share in the food provided for the occasion.

It is customary for Catholics to have a memorial Mass said in memory of a loved one 30 days after the death and again after one year.

Eastern or Orthodox Church Life-Cycle Rituals

The Eastern or Orthodox churches are territorial or national. This arrangement is unlike the close-knit unity of the Roman Catholic Church, whose clergy are under the authority of the Pope, regardless of their location. The Orthodox churches of Greece, Russia, Armenia, Bulgaria, Serbia, and other countries are autonomous and have always been closely identified with their own country. The life-cycle rituals of Orthodox churches are more elaborate than the other Christian churches.

Birth

Parents are allowed to bring their newborns to church for the first time 40 days after its birth. At that time, the priest offers special prayers and blessings for the infant.

The baptism, usually held after the infant is three or four months old, is the first important event in a child's life. Baptism is the triple immersion of the baby by the priest in a baptismal tub filled with warm water. For the baptism, the baby's clothes are removed and discarded. After the triple dipping, the child is dried off by the godparents. The priest then performs the Chrismation, anointing the child with oil (chrism). This symbolic act is performed to keep the devil from grasping the child. Another symbolic act is for the priest to snip off a lock of the child's hair, representing the child's first donation to the church.

After the immersion, the godparents dress the baby in their gift of new clothes, all white, a symbol of purity. They also give the infant a gold cross. The child is given a Christian name, usually chosen from one of the many saints and martyrs of the church.

Name Day: Catholic and Orthodox Christian

In some Catholic and Orthodox Christian communities, instead of celebrating a birthday, the children celebrate the "name day" of the saint or martyr they were named after. The "name day" is not the birth date of the child or the saint, but rather the designated date on which the church elevated a holy or godly person or martyr to sainthood. Each country or region of the world, ethnic group, or church has its own collection of saints and martyrs.

Marriage

The traditional Orthodox wedding takes place in the church, and it is usually a very long ceremony with many symbolic rituals. Each country, ethnic group, or church adds its own unique traditions to some of the following basic rituals.

During the wedding the bride and groom wear crowns or wreaths to signify their elevation to king and queen of the home they will share. The couple jointly sip red wine from a cup to signify their togetherness, and double rings are blessed and exchanged as a visual ritual of unity. The reception feast follows at the church hall, club or hotel ballroom, restaurant, or family home.

Death

Orthodox Christian funerals are marked by long, involved rituals and ceremonies that vary by the ethnic group, the church, the community, and to some degree, the family's wishes.

The burial service is more intense and dramatic than the Roman Catholic church service, taking it to a higher level of pageantry. Among some groups, it is customary, for the family mourners to cut a lock of hair to be buried with the dead; this act symbolizes that not even death will sever the strong family ties.

Islam and Islamic Life-Cycle Rituals

Islam is the second largest universal religion, with followers in all parts of the world. Islam is a monotheistic religion with its roots in Judaism and Christianity. Muslims believe in the biblical prophets Adam, Noah, Abraham, Ishmael, Isaac, Jacob, Moses, and Jesus, but they believe that Muhammad is the last prophet sent by God and that his message is the final one. Although Muslims believe Jesus was a prophet, they don't believe he was the son of God or that he was crucified.

Islam cannot be separated from daily life and government, and so provides a framework for both secular and spiritual life. Prayer, fasting, pilgrimage, and dietary requirements are some of the long-held customs of the Muslim faith.

Muslims must pray five times a day, every day of their lives. At dawn each morning in Muslim communities, a *muezzin* (prayer announcer) enters the mosque (house of worship), climbs to the top of the minaret (tower), and usually with the help of loudspeakers and a public address system, calls the faithful to the first of the day's prayers. They are called, if not actually to enter a mosque, at least to take the time to pray wherever they are. In most Islamic countries, it is a common sight to see Muslims praying by the side of the road or in the street.

On Fridays, the Muslims gather before noon at the mosque, and the prayer (*Jum'ah*) is led by an *imam* (religious leader). In the mosque, the prayer area for the men is completely separate from the section designated for the women and children. The mosque also serves as a community center where children and adults are schooled in the Koran (the Islamic holy book).

Birth

In Muslim countries, the birth of a child is a joyous occasion. The birth of a boy is cause for a greater celebration than for the birth of a girl. When a boy grows up and marries, his wife and children become part of and strengthen his parents' extended family. Girls, however, leave their families and become part of their husband's clan when they marry.

To welcome a newborn baby into the world, an *imam* whispers the call to prayer into its ear. Another auspicious and joyous ceremony is when the baby is named. Guests are invited to a celebration feast. Roasted lamb is the traditional food served at this ceremony and most other Muslim celebrations.

Coming of Age

The major event of a boy's life is his circumcision, which normally takes place sometime between the ages of 7 and 12. It is a religious requirement for male Muslims. This ritual requires no celebration except perhaps a family dinner.

When a girl reaches puberty, she changes from the dress of a schoolgirl to the garments worn by women. From this time forward, she dons the veil (*hijab*, also called *khimar*) in public. The veiling signifies that she is now a woman and is ready for marriage. Each Muslim country has its own identifiable veiling and rules of dress for women. It is often possible to tell not only a woman's country but also what region she is from and her status in life by the veil she wears. Varying in style, some veils cover just the hair and neck and others leave only the eyes visible. Among the most devout Muslims, the veil completely covers not only a woman's head and face but it drapes down over her clothes to her ankles.

Marriage

Marriage rituals in most Muslim countries are basically similar, but some are very rigid, following Islamic law to the letter; others are a little more lenient. Most Muslim marriages are arranged by the parents, and because marriage is an agreement between families, a financial contract is drawn up to define the terms. The bride takes no part in the negotiations, nor does she see her husband until after they are married. The groom has to pay *mahr*, the bride's price, by giving the bride gold jewelry or other goods that are worth an agreed amount of money. In some countries, the bride's family, not the bride, receives the money from the groom. If a groom is wealthy, he gives both money to the family and jewelry to the bride.

The religious part of a marriage is very private and is performed separately from the more public celebration. According to strict Islamic law, at no time are men and women allowed to be together in the same room for any part of the wedding celebration, or for any other occasion for that matter. The religious part of the marriage ceremony is quite simple and is conducted by someone learned in *Shari'ah* (Islamic Law), usually the *imam*. In Islam, the *imam* is separated from the bride-to-be by a screen or closed door; he asks the bride if she will accept the prospective husband. If she agrees, the *imam* then goes to the groom and asks him, in the presence of four witnesses (they cannot be family members), if he will take the woman for his wife. His acceptance in front of witnesses makes the marriage valid, and then the *imam* officially records the contract.

According to Islamic law, polygamy (a husband with more than one wife) is allowed. A man can have no more than four wives at a time, and even then, only if he can afford to treat them all equally; otherwise he must take fewer wives.

Hajj

The *Hajj*, the pilgrimage to the Muslim holy city of Mecca, is the most important rite of passage in a Muslim man's life. Muslim men are obliged to make the pilgrimage at least once in a lifetime. The *Hajj* must be performed during a specific month.

The *Kaaba* is the sanctuary in Mecca to which all Muslims turn in prayer. The Black Stone is a sacred object set in the eastern wall of the *Kaaba*. During the *Hajj*, the faithful try to kiss or touch the stone. The Koran associates Abraham and Ishmael with the building of the *Kaaba*.

Death

When a Muslim dies, the funeral is very simple, and the body must be buried within 24 hours. The placement of the grave is important because the body must face Mecca.

The body is washed and wrapped in a white cotton shroud. Muslims are not buried in coffins; a plank is placed at the bottom of the grave, and the body is laid on top of it. The face is covered with a cloth before the body is lowered into the ground. Men carry the body on a stretcher, or, in the case of a young child, the father carries the body in his arms. Male relatives sprinkle the grave with earth before it is completely covered. The final prayers are said for the deceased at the cemetery. Muslim graves have no elaborate headstones. Only a small stone or marker is placed at the head and foot of the grave. Muslim women do not accompany the body to the burial ground because it is not considered appropriate for them, as bearers of life, to visit a place of death.

It is the custom for friends and relatives to bring food for the immediate family for three days after the burial, and in turn, the guests are offered coffee (but no food). Honey or dishes made with honey are often eaten after funerals. Muslims believe eating honey is soothing to the soul and eases the mental anguish associated with death. A widower has no required mourning period, but a widow must go into seclusion for several months after the death of her husband.

Hinduism and Hindu Life-Cycle Rituals

The origins of the Hindu religion are obscure, but elements of Hindu beliefs can be traced back at least several thousand years. It is a complicated religion with many different interpretations by the numerous sects. Each group has intricate and minutely detailed rituals, customs, and ceremonies that are deeply rooted in every stage of life.

Traditional Hindus attempt to achieve four objectives through life. The first objective is *dharma* (duty); followed by *artha* (material prosperity), *kama* (enjoyment), and finally, *moksha* (salvation). To achieve these four objectives, Hindus divide life into four segments: *bramacharya* (celibacy—student life, learning); *grihastha* (family life—enjoying life years); *vanaprastha* (retirement—delegating responsibilities to younger generations); and finally, *sanyas* (renunciation—giving up all responsibilities to prepare for death and the journey to the spirit world).

The most basic Hindu ceremonies, those pertaining to the life cycle, take place in the home. The four major life-cycle events are prenatal and birth, childhood, marriage, and death. Most Hindus keep a home shrine for daily prayer, which can be a shelf, a corner of a room, or in some homes a small room or closet. For the life-cycle ceremonies, family and friends gather around a family member who performs the ritual. When necessary, a priest is called in to take over the more complicated services.

The shrine contains pictures and/or statues of the gods and goddess, saints, and ancestors. Other ritual necessities are a container of water for sprinkling and purifying the area, a bell to summon the good spirits, an incense burner to wave in front of the gods, and a tray with flowers and food. The food offerings include fruit, freshly cooked rice, butter or *ghee*, and sugar. After a prayer is said over the food, family members eat it.

Food is an important element of Hinduism. The kitchen in a Hindu home is treated as part cooking room, part dining room, and part chapel. Since leather is considered unclean by Hindus, one may not cook or dine wearing shoes. Beef is banned, because cattle are revered as sacred.

The Hindu food laws and restrictions do not simply prohibit certain foods in the same way Muslims and Jewish people are forbidden from eating pork. Hindu food restrictions and rituals are very complex; caste, ethics, aesthetics, and faith as well as nutrition, hygiene, and diet are all interwoven into the Hindu doctrines involving food. The specific rituals and customs extend to not only what food is eaten and why it is cooked a certain way but also how and where it is served and eaten.

One unique feature interwoven in Indian society and Hinduism is the caste system that divides the Indian population into four main castes (*varnas*). The castes were established by Aryan priests after India was invaded by the Aryans around 1500 B.C. The caste divisions were originally based on racial or ethnic differences, with the Aryans occupying the higher castes. The highest caste are the *Brahmans* (priests and scholars); next are the *Kshatriyas* (nobles and warriors); below them are the *Vaishyas* (merchants and skilled artisans); and finally, there are *Shudras* (common laborers). Beyond the actual castes are the *Harijans* (outcastes), who were given the dirty and degrading jobs. The outcastes were called "untouchables" because merely to touch an outcaste, or even to be touched by an outcaste's shadow, was considered a form of ritual pollution for members of the higher *varnas*. Although officially banned by the Indian constitution since 1949, some people are still considered *Harijan*.

Within the four Indian castes are thousands of subcastes (*jati*), usually confined to local areas or regions. A *jati* is usually connected to a particular occupation, such as trash collectors, rag pickers, snake charmers, farmers, and street sweepers.

Although the Indian caste system is stronger in rural areas it still is a vital part of the Hindu religion and Indian culture. Indians' caste and subcaste positions affect the jobs available to them as well as their diet and religious practices, including how life-cycle events are celebrated.

Prenatal Period, Birth, and Early Childhood

Before birth three rites are performed during the mother's pregnancy to help the child arrive safely into the world. On the 10th or 12th day after birth, the naming ceremony is performed by a Hindu priest. The name is selected according to the baby's horoscope, and friends and relatives are invited to celebrate the event. Another ceremony, *annaprasana*, is held at six months when the infant is given its first solid food. The baby's first step and first birthday may also be observed with a religious ceremony and a party. Between the ages of one and five, girls experience a ceremonial ear-piercing; this event too is reason to rejoice and have a party.

The *mundan*, first haircut, is a very auspicious event for baby boys between one and three years of age. The father is supposed to shave the head, but usually he just cuts a few hairs while reciting the appropriate Hindu verses; the task is finished by a barber. The first hair is offered as a sacrifice to the gods. The hair cutting event usually calls for a large celebration with plenty of food.

Coming of Age

The main adolescence ritual is *upanayana*, popularly known as the "thread ceremony." Only boys between the ages of 8 and 12 in the upper three castes of the Hindu social system go through this ceremony. There are complex variations to this ritual for different Hindu sects. One of the basic principles behind this ceremony is to elevate the boy into manhood. Before the ritual he eats his last meal with his mother, and after the completion of *upanayana* he is expected to eat with the adult male family members. The "thread," or *upavita*, refers to a three-strand rope normally worn over the left shoulder and hanging under the right arm. It is a visible symbol confirming the boy's passing over into manhood.

Some of the ritual foods used in this ceremony are *ghee* (recipe page 285), coconut, corn, wheat, and rice.

Marriage

Most Hindus consider it a social obligation to be married within the religion, and marriages are arranged between members of the same caste (social group). The first thing parents have to do, with the consent of their offspring, is to find a suitable mate. Then an auspicious date and time for the marriage ceremony are chosen based on astrological charts. Nowadays more and more parents, especially in urban areas, believe the dowry or good looks are more important than the agreement of stars. This has become possible because boys and girls are not married as children as they once were.

Hindu wedding ceremonies vary greatly, depending on geographical location, sect, family customs, and personal taste. Even within the same community differences can be seen in the clothes, ornaments, rituals, food, and length of the wedding celebrations, which in some cases can last several days. Rice and *ghee* are important ritual foods.

The marriage (*vivaha*) is considered to be a gift-giving ritual by the father. He gives his daughter (*kanya*) as a gift (*dan*) to the boy's family. The biggest donation a father can make in his lifetime is *kanya dan* (the gift of his daughter).

A great many marriages take place in wedding halls, which are available on a rental basis. A priest officiates the wedding, which is held in front of a pit for the sacrificial marriage fire (*vivahahoma*). The fire is fueled by sprinkling it with *ghee*. Among most Hindus, it is the custom for the couple to circle the fire seven times, chanting vows and throwing in offerings such as rice.

During the ceremony the bride and groom each wears a garland of flowers around the neck which they exchange with each other as a token of acceptance. The father of the bride offers her hand in marriage first of all to the gods, then to the groom. The groom then assures his father-in-law that he will take care of his bride.

At some point during the ceremony, the bride may stand on a stone, representing firmness and stability, to signify loyalty and faithfulness in the marriage. The rituals and customs extend to the wedding feast, making it an important part of the total marriage ceremony.

Retirement

The 60th birthday is a milestone in a person's life and is a very auspicious date. Making it to 80 years old is as good as reaching 100; it is called *sathabishekam* which means 100. Both dates are reasons for a celebration feast with family and friends.

Death

Hindus view death as part of the never-ending cycle of birth and rebirth. According to Hindu tradition, bodies are cremated after death. Very elaborate ceremonies may continue for several weeks after the cremation, which must take place as soon as possible after death. After someone dies, the body is immediately washed and dressed in fresh clothes. Men and widows generally are covered with white shrouds, although the customs and the color of the shroud cloth can vary greatly, even within the same Hindu group. Among some Hindus, a woman is decorated as for her wedding, and her shroud is orange.

Unlike other Hindu life-cycle celebrations, friends and family do not bring food to the families in mourning. Death memorial rituals can last for several days or up to a year after the death of a loved one, depending on the beliefs of the person performing them.

Buddhism and Buddhist Life-Cycle Rituals

Buddhism originated in India in the sixth century B.C. as an offshoot of Hinduism and soon spread to other countries. Buddha, the Enlightened One, was a Hindu prince whose philosophy grew into a separate religion. Buddha considered himself not a holy man but rather a teacher who simply wanted to inform and enlighten people about life and afterlife. Buddhism was accepted by people from all walks of life and all over the world. Many different interpretations of Buddhism have developed over the years in different countries.

Life-cycle events, such as births, coming of age, and marriages, are not considered to be spiritually significant by Buddhists, although monks may bless a new baby, a marriage, or a new house. In some countries, for example Thailand, temporary ordination and a short period in the monastery may serve as a boy's entry into adulthood.

Buddhists do consider burial ceremonies important occasions. Funerals reconfirm the Buddhist teachings that nothing is permanent and that rebirth follows death. The funeral takes place in a temple or funeral hall, where priests, accompanied by the sounds of bells, gongs, and hollow wooden blocks, recite prayers over the body placed on a bier or in a coffin. Mourners then burn incense before the corpse. Twenty-four hours or more later, the body is taken to be cremated or buried.

Most Buddhists build a family altar in their home and place an ancestral tablet and other sacred articles on it. The tablet is a small lacquered, gilded board containing a picture and the name of the deceased. Incense is burned on the altar, and family members pray before it.

Families traditionally mourn their dead for 49 days and then observe the first, third, seventh, and thirteenth anniversaries by asking a priest to give a prayer service for the dead.

Shintoism and Shinto Life-Cycle Rituals

Shintoism is a Japanese religion. Its origins are unclear, but some scholars believe it is the name given to combined religious practices, some dating back to prehistoric Japan. Others believe Shintoism is simply a way of life that grew out of a natural love for everything and everyone.

Japan has thousands of Shinto shrines, sacred places where spirits (*kami*) dwell. (In the Shinto religion, the source of all creation and the unexplainable essences of the universe are called *kami*.) Different shrines are visited for specific divine powers (*shintoku*). Students visit certain shrines to seek help with their studies, and sick people come to other shrines for the healing powers. Some shrines give protection from accidents, while other shrines are popular with couples seeking to bless their marriages.

Mostly life-cycle celebrations and community festivals take place at the shrines. The Japanese often combine religions, and it is not unusual for the same person to have had a Shinto wedding and a Buddhist funeral.

Birth and Early Years

It is common, though not universal, for a baby to be brought to the Shinto shrine by its mother or grandmother so that prayers may be said for its good health. *Hatsu miyamairi* (first shrine visit) takes place on the 32nd day after birth for a boy and the 33rd day for a girl. At this ceremony, the baby is introduced to the spirits (*kami*) and becomes a member of the shrine.

The *shichi-go-san* (seven-five-three) festival is held throughout Japan on the nearest Sunday to November 15. Parents with three- and seven–year-old boys and five–year-old girls dress them in traditional kimonos and bring them to the shrine for a ceremony. At the shrine, parents give thanks for their children's good health and growth so far and pray for their future.

Coming of Age (*Seijin-no-hi*)

Seijin-no-hi is on the second Sunday in January. The once a year coming-of-age ceremony is held for all who turn 20 throughout the year. On this day, Japanese youth are granted full rights as citizens. Families spend huge amounts of money on traditional clothing and photos for a ceremony that lasts less than an hour. Most women attend this ceremony in a colorful *furisode*, a long sleeved kimono worn by single women.

Marriage

The *shinzen kekkon-sai* is a marriage ceremony before the *kami* (spirit). The majority of wedding ceremonies in Japan include Shinto rituals while others are Western-style, Christian events, popular since World War II. Shinto weddings became popular in the early 1900s after the very first royal wedding was performed by Shinto priests. Some Shinto shrines have a special hall to accommodate wedding parties. If the ceremony is not held at the shrine, the priests often officiate at public wedding halls or hotel ballrooms.

Death

Buddhist monks are looked upon as ritual specialists, and they are often called upon to chant the sutras that will benefit the deceased and to conduct all funeral rites and memorial services; the funeral services for the two religions are very similar. To help the deceased on its journeys to the beyond, mourners make offerings of paper "spirit money," along with wine, incense, and food, such as fish, fowl, and vegetables. Instead of burning incense as the Buddhists do, the Shinto mourners offer strips of white paper and twigs of the sacred *sakaki* tree.

Selecting a proper location for the grave is very important, and a *Feng shui sien sheng* (a specialist in grave placement matters) is consulted for the best site. The heirs must maintain the grave, and they are expected to make occasional offerings.

Within one hundred days of the burial, a memorial service is held in the home of the oldest male heir. The Shinto priest offers prayers and reads an account of the life of the deceased.

The Shinto ancestral tablet, containing a picture and the name of the deceased, is made of plain wood. It is dedicated by the priest and placed on the home altar along with Joss-sticks (special incense), which are lit and placed on the tablet. Newlyweds traditionally bow before the altar as a sign of respect.

According to Shinto beliefs, overseeing the proper funeral for a family member and making regular offerings to the ancestors are critical if the living descendants expect to have a successful and a good life.

Confucianism and Confucian Rites of Passage

Confucianism can be confusing to Western readers because it is more of a philosophy and way of life than a religion. Confucian teachings have influenced the beliefs and values of traditional societies in China, Korea, Japan, Vietnam, and Taiwan for centuries. Confucius (551-472 B.C.) was a teacher who taught social and ethical reforms, not religion. Respectful relationships between all people—parents and children, one another, and elders—are fundamental to Confucians.

In the old Imperial China, Confucian officials regulated the traditional rites of passage and all aspects of public behavior. Under Communism, the great majority of Chinese people still hold fast to values that were first introduced by Confucius and his followers, even though religion is officially discouraged.

Throughout Asian countries, Confucian rituals are hard to identify because they are generally fused with other religions.

Death

Today, the most important rite of passage for Confucians is death. Confucians have great respect for their ancestors; when someone dies, the funeral is a memorable occasion. Colorful decorations and elaborate rituals are carefully attended to with the help of a religious leader. Family mourners chant prayers and offer sacrifices of food, especially rice. They symbolically burn paper money, and in some cases paper cars, planes, and images of servants, all necessary items that they believe will help the spirit of the dead make a more enjoyable journey into the world of its ancestors.

MULTICULTURAL COOKBOOK OF LIFE-CYCLE CELEBRATIONS

AFRICA

Introduction

Africa is the world's second-largest continent, with perhaps the most diverse population in the world. There are well over a thousand ethnic groups, and just about as many different languages. The majority of Africans are farmers and pastoralists in rural communities where the foods, religion, daily life, and celebrations of life passages have changed little for centuries.

Christianity is the most prevalent religion in Africa, followed by Islam. About 15 percent of the population, mostly farmers and herders, practice indigenous religions. African Christians follow the life-cycle rituals prescribed by the Church, and African Muslims follow those of the Koran. It is also very common for Africans to fuse traditional local religious practices with Christianity or Islam.

In Africa, events to celebrate individuals' life milestones vary according to the family, its social status, and its wealth; the region where the people live; their communication skills; and their religious beliefs. However, throughout Africa, individuals' life-milestone celebrations are usually community affairs, and recognition of each person's progress through the key events of the life cycle is important to everyone in the family, clan, and village. Similarly, awareness of another person's status in terms of life-cycle events is of interest and significance.

In most African communities, the clothing a woman wears indicates whether she is single, married, or widowed. In southern Africa among the Ndebele women, for instance, a bride's mother-in-law makes her a *jocolo.* This is a colorfully beaded five-paneled goatskin apron that married women wear on ceremonial occasions. In parts of western Africa, a married woman wears a large and elaborate head scarf that she folds and wraps in a manner that signals her social group and status.

African men and women often wear jewelry and other ornaments that communicate their stage in life. For instance, among the Masai people in Tanzania, only married women wear brass earrings. By the presence of certain colors of beads on her headband, a Rendile woman indicates that she is barren. A Samburu woman will wear a double strand of beads looped between her ears for each son who has passed into warriorhood. Male elders of the Turkana and Pokot tribes wear leaf-shaped aluminum pendants suspended from their nostrils to announce a daughter's engagement.

Some groups in Africa communicate their status by decorating their heads and bodies with paints and dyes. Henna dye is used in parts of northern and western Africa to paint intricate patterns on the hands, feet, and face. Although the dye is sometimes used by men and children, it is more commonly applied by women of marriageable age to show they are looking for a husband—or, in some societies, that they are about to be married. Body painting, piercing, tattooing, and scarification are other ways Africans traditionally indicate milestones they have reached in life.

In Africa, music is an important component of rituals, celebrations, and healing ceremonies. The rhythms have specific meanings, which are responded to by swaying, dancing, and sometimes singing. Different musical patterns signal distinct purposes, such as songs of warriors or hunting songs that can be performed only by men. Other music is limited to women and might be played only during childbirth or for girls' initiation rites.

Channeling between the spirit world and the world of humans is another important part of life-cycle events and celebrations in some western and central Africa communities. Channeling is done through masked dances (also known as masquerades). The identity of the person wearing the mask is hidden from the audience, and "the mask" (as the dancer is known) takes on the identity of the character represented. Combined with dance steps, gestures, songs, and sounds, the "mask" becomes a powerful and energetic force connecting the spirit world with the world of humans. Masquerades are usually performed by men—members of secret societies who begin their training as children. The services of the "masks" are especially effective for funerals.

Life is harsh in many parts of Africa, so an opportunity to celebrate the achievement of a life milestone is a joyous occasion that usually includes feasting, dancing, singing, and the wearing of elaborate garments, ornate headdresses, and colorful jewelry.

TANZANIA

Tanzania (the former nations of Tanganyika and Zanzibar) is a remarkable country. It contains Kilimanjaro, the highest mountain in Africa, and the continent's biggest lakes touch its borders to the north, west, and south. Along Tanzania's eastern border is the Indian Ocean; Uganda and Kenya are to the north; Burundi, Rwanda, and Congo are to the west; and Mozambique, Zambia, and Malawi are to the south. On its island of Zanzibar in the Indian Ocean, some of the world's finest spices and coffee are grown.

The population of Tanzania includes more than 120 ethnic groups. Centuries ago, Muslims came to Tanzania as spice traders from the East, and Christian traders came from Europe, primarily Portugal. Today, the Tanzanian population is almost equally split between Muslims, Christians, and those following indigenous religions.

At least 80 percent of Tanzanians are rural. They live on the food they grow, often with no more than simple hoes to work their gardens. As in other African countries, the extended family traditionally feeds and cares for its members.

Muslims in Tanzania observe life's passages in accordance with Islam (see Islam and Islamic Life-Cycle Rituals, pp. xlix), but practices and traditions are less conservative than in the Middle East. For instance, in Tanzania, women are allowed to receive an education and to work outside the home. Islamic modesty laws, too, are relatively moderate. Tanzanian Muslim women wear dress-length, loose black garments *(buibui)* and black head scarves that tie under the chin. Tanzanian Muslim men pray five times a day and look forward to making the hajj (pilgrimage) to Mecca. It is the most important rite of passage in a Muslim man's life.

Wedding traditions are important to Tanzanian Muslims. Parents arrange marriages, and the prospective groom's family pays a bride-price, which is refunded if all goes well. Men may have as many as four wives. A bride-price usually is paid only for the first wife.

After consummating a marriage, a *walima* (wedding reception) is given by the husband for friends and family to celebrate the auspicious occasion. Tanzanian Muslim men and women celebrate together at weddings and other festivities instead of partying in separate locations, as is done in many other Islamic countries.

If the family can afford it, roast lamb (recipe page 141) or goat are prepared for the wedding feast, along with many other dishes and assorted flat breads, such as *khobaz arabee* (recipe page 115) and *mkate wa ufute* (recipe follows), as well as large bowls of fruits and nuts.

This Zanzibar recipe, which resembles pancakes, is used as flat bread. It is eaten throughout Tanzania.

Mkate wa Ufute

Yeast Pancake Bread

Yield: makes 8 to 10

1 package dry **yeast**
1 teaspoon sugar
¾ cup **lukewarm** water
1 cup all-purpose flour
¾ cup milk
3 tablespoons **sesame seeds, roasted**
6 to 8 tablespoons vegetable oil, more as needed

Equipment: Small bowl, mixing spoon, flour **sifter**, large mixing bowl, large skillet, ladle or cup, wide metal spatula, baking sheet, oven mitts, napkin-lined bread basket

1. Put yeast and sugar into small bowl and add lukewarm water. Stir once and do not disturb until frothy, 5 to 10 minutes.

2. **Sift** flour into large mixing bowl and make a well (hole) in the center. Pour yeast mixture into the well and stir to mix well. Stir in milk to make a thick batter.

Preheat oven to warm 200° F.

3. Heat 2 tablespoons oil in large skillet over medium-high heat. Using a ladle or cup, pour in enough batter to make one large round 5- or 6-inch pancake. Use the back of a spoon or the ladle to spread out the batter. Cook to brown, about 2 minutes, and using wide metal spatula, flip over to brown second side, about 1 to 2 minutes. Sprinkle with roasted sesame seeds and transfer to baking sheet. Keep in warm oven while making remaining pancakes.

To serve as bread, put in napkin-lined bread basket to keep warm. Break into chunks to scoop up stew such as ndizi na nyama *(recipe follows).*

Many side dishes, such as this stew, are prepared for Muslim wedding feasts in Tanzania. *Ndizi na nyama* has an unusual combination of flavors.

Ndizi na Nyama

Stewed Tomatoes with Bananas

Yield: serves 6 to 8

- 2 tablespoons butter or margarine
- 1 onion, **finely chopped**
- 2 tomatoes, **trimmed** and finely chopped, or 2 cups canned stewed tomatoes
- 8 bananas, peeled and cut crosswise into ½-inch pieces
- 1 cup coconut milk, homemade (recipe page 346), or canned (available at most supermarkets and all Latin American food stores)
- ½ teaspoon salt
- ½ teaspoon **ground** turmeric
- 1 teaspoon sugar, more or less to taste

Equipment: Medium saucepan with cover, mixing spoon

Melt butter or margarine in medium saucepan over medium-high heat. Add onions, stir, and **sauté** until soft, 3 to 5 minutes. Add stewed tomatoes, bananas, coconut milk, salt, turmeric, and 1 teaspoon sugar, more or less to taste. Stir well and bring to boil. Reduce heat to **simmer**, cover, and cook 15 minutes.

Serve warm or at room temperature, as a side dish with meat.

If roast lamb is too expensive for the wedding feast, other meat or fowl, sometimes both, are prepared for the celebration. Nutria (aquatic rodents) and *bata* (duck) are two favorites. This duck dish, using Zanzibar cloves, is popular throughout the East African coast. The recipe calls for dried whole red chili peppers; they are very hot, so use cautiously.

Bata Iliyokaushwa

Zanzibar Duck

Yield: serves 6

- 5 to 6 pound duck, fresh or frozen (thawed)
- 2 cups chicken broth, homemade (recipe page 106), or canned
- 2 teaspoons **ground** cloves
- dried whole red chili peppers, to taste
- 2 tablespoons cornstarch
- ½ cup water
- ½ cup frozen orange juice concentrate, thawed
- juice of 1 lime

1 green or red bell pepper, **trimmed**, **seeded**, and **finely chopped**
salt and pepper to taste
2 oranges, cut into wedges, for **garnish**
6 to 8 cups cooked rice, keep warm, for serving

Equipment: Paper towels, work surface, sharp knife, large **heavy-based** skillet, metal tongs, 12- x 9- x 2-inch baking pan, aluminum foil, serving platter

1. Rinse the duck under cold running water and wipe inside and out with paper towels. Place duck on work surface and using a sharp knife, cut the duck into serving-size pieces. Cut off any chunks of fat and set aside. Prick the duck skin in several places with the point of the knife.

2. Finely chop about 2 tablespoons duck fat and put in large skillet. Heat over medium-low heat to **render**. Increase heat to medium-high and add duck pieces. Fry on both sides, until golden brown , 10 to 15 minutes on each side. Fry in batches and, using metal tongs, transfer duck pieces to baking pan.

Preheat oven to 350° F.

3. Pour off and discard any fat left in the skillet. Pour chicken broth into skillet. Add ground cloves and dried red chili peppers to taste. Stir and bring to boil over medium-high heat.

4. In cup, combine cornstarch and water. Stir until smooth and add to chicken broth mixture. Add orange juice, lime juice, bell pepper, and salt and pepper to taste. Stir until thickened, 3 to 5 minutes, and pour over duck in baking pan. Cover with foil.

5. Bake in oven for 1 hour. To test for doneness, pierce the thigh of the duck with the point of a knife. The juice should trickle out a clear yellow. If juice is slightly pink, cook the duck for another 15 to 20 minutes.

To serve, place the duck on a serving platter and pour the sauce over it. Garnish with orange wedges and serve with rice.

KENYA

Kenya borders the Indian Ocean in East Africa. The equator runs through the middle of the country, which borders Somalia to the east, Ethiopia to the north, Tanzania to south, and Sudan to the northwest. Kenya is home to more than 70 ethnic groups, although the differences between many of them have faded as Western cultural values filter into their lives.

The standard of living in major Kenyan cities ranks high compared with that of neighboring countries. Most city workers maintain connections with their extended families living in rural areas, and they leave the city periodically to help work on their families' farms. Even among urbanites who appear to have drifted away from ancestral traditions, tribal identity remains singularly important. When two Kenyans meet in the city, they almost always identify their tribes as they introduce themselves.

Most of Kenya's population is Christian: 40 percent are Protestants and 30 percent are Roman Catholics. Most celebrate life passages by combining Christian rituals (see Protestant and Catholic Life-Cycle Rituals, page xlvi) with the traditional customs of their tribes and local religions. A small percentage of Kenyans are Muslims, most of whom live along the coast. (See Islam and Islamic Life-Cycle Rituals, page xlix) Many others practice indigenous religions. (See Traditional African Life-Cycle Rituals, page xli.)

The pastoral Masai, the best known of Kenya's tribal people, have managed to stay outside the mainstream of Kenya's development. They live a nomadic lifestyle, traveling throughout the year—mostly in the southern part of the country—to maintain their cattle herds. Among the Masai, as for most ethnic groups in Kenya, circumcision remains as the main rite for boys passing into adulthood. The Masai have a ceremony in which boys of about 14 years of age become warriors *(morans)*. After circumcision, custom requires the group of boys to go out on their own, away from their people, and build a village *(manyatta)*, where for eight years they must fend for themselves.

The Akamba people live in the eastern part of Kenya. Among the Akamba, youths of the same age, beginning at about 12, are grouped into an "age-set" *(rika)*. They will stay together as a group and pass through the various stages of life until they die. As they become older, they gain seniority rights—especially young men, but also, although to a lesser extent, young women. Young Akamba parents are known as "junior elders" and are responsible for the maintenance and upkeep of the village. Later in life, they go through a ceremony to become "medium elders," and still later, "full elders," with the responsibility for death ceremonies and administering the law. The last stage of a person's life is that of "senior elder," with responsibility for the holy places.

The Swahili people, most of whom are Muslims, live along Kenya's coast. Today, Muslims in Kenya do not adhere to strict forms of Islam; instead, they are strongly committed to the education of women, who are also encouraged to participate in all levels of business.

The Turkana live in a remote, arid region in northwestern Kenya. Due to their isolation, the Turkana are probably the ethnic group in Kenya that is least influenced by the modern world. Like the Masai, the Turkana are cattle herders, but unlike the Masai, they have discontinued the practice of circumcision rituals for young boys. Turkana women wear a variety of beaded and metal adornments that identify stages in their lives. When a young Turkana girl is ready for marriage, she announces that fact by covering her body with a mixture of ochre (red or yellow pigment) and fat. When men are ready to find a mate, they cover part of their hair with mud, which is then painted blue and decorated with ostrich and other feathers. A set of rules and rituals bring the available individuals together.

For the marriage ceremonies of the Samburu people of Kenya, a couple shows their commitment to one another by crossing sticks. The sticks—given to the bride by the groom—are also used to brand his cattle, signifying that his wife and cattle are now his possessions.

Rendile women of the northern desert of Kenya wear their hair in a coxcomb made from mud, animal fat, and ochre to show that they have given birth to their first son. This hair style is worn until the boy is circumcised or until a close male relative dies, at which time the woman shaves her head. Wide arm bracelets are also worn by Rendile women to indicate their marriage status; to announce when a firstborn son has been circumcised, they add a wide band of bracelets above the elbow on their upper arms.

All ethnic and religious groups in Kenya have one thing in common: celebrations are communal, and great quantities of food must be prepared for feasts. *Irio* is a nourishing dish that can feed hundreds of people from large cauldrons. Everyone brings a calabash (gourd container) or plastic bowl from home to be filled with this tasty dish.

Irio

Corn and Bean Mash

Yield: serves 6

1 large baking potato, chopped

2½ cups chicken broth or water

3 cups canned corn kernels

1 cup red kidney beans
16 ounces frozen chopped spinach, thawed
salt and pepper to taste

Equipment: Medium saucepan with cover, mixing spoon, medium bowl, fork or potato masher

1. Put potato in medium saucepan and cover with broth or water. Bring to boil over high heat, cover, and cook for 10 minutes. Add corn, kidney beans, and spinach. Stir and continue to cook, covered, for 10 minutes, to heat through. Remove from heat. Drain off most of the liquid into medium bowl and set aside.

2. Add margarine and salt and pepper to taste. Using a fork or potato masher, mash mixture, adding more of the drained liquid, if necessary, to make mixture the consistency of mashed potatoes.

Serve warm and everyone in the family eats from the same pan.

The Luo people live in western Kenya on the shores of Lake Victoria. Unlike most African tribes, the Luo do not circumcise adolescent boys during a coming-of-age ritual. Instead, several teeth are extracted from the boy's lower jaw. Although this has become a less-common practice, many middle-aged and older Luo men are missing a few lower teeth from this ritual in their youth.

A dish that feeds a lot of people with little cost is *mtori*. Pots of *mtori* are commonly served along with *irio* (recipe precedes) at communal feasts in Kenya.

Mtori

Plantain and Beef Soup

Yield: serves 4 to 6

2 to 3 pounds beef short ribs, cut into 3-inch lengths
8 cups water
2 teaspoons salt
3 ripe plantains (about 1½ pounds), peeled and cut into chunks
3 boiling potatoes (about 1 pound), peeled and quartered
2 onions, peeled and **coarsely chopped**
1 tablespoon butter or margarine

Equipment: Large saucepan with cover or **Dutch oven**, mixing spoon, fork, slotted spoon or tongs, cutting board, sharp knife, ladle, electric **blender**, medium bowl, individual soup bowls

1. In large saucepan or Dutch oven, put short ribs, water, and salt. Bring to boil over high heat, and using mixing spoon, skim off and discard the foam that comes to the surface. Reduce heat to **simmer**, cover, and cook for 1½ hours. Add plantains, potatoes, and onions. Stir and continue to cook for 25 to 30 minutes, or until meat and potatoes are tender when poked with a fork.

2. With slotted spoon or tongs, transfer meat to cutting board. Using sharp knife, remove bones, and cut away and discard fat and gristle. Cut meat into bite-size pieces.

3. Ladle potatoes, plantains, and liquid into electric blender. **Purée** in batches and pour into medium bowl. Return purée to large saucepan and stir in pieces of meat and butter or margarine. Cook over medium heat to heat through, 5 to 7 minutes. Add salt to taste.

Serve warm in individual soup bowls. Although called a soup, this is actually a thick stew, and in Kenya it is served as a main course.

SOMALIA

Located on the shores of the Indian Ocean, on what is known as the Horn of Africa in the northeastern part of the continent, Somalia is bordered by Djibouti on the northwest, by Ethiopia on the west, and by Kenya on the southwest. It is the only African country where everyone speaks the same language and nearly everyone is of the same ethnicity: Somali.

There are two distinct groups of Somalis: nomads whose lives revolve around the seasonal movements of their herds, and urbanites who live in the coastal towns and are involved in international trade.

For over a thousand years, Somalis have been Muslims, and life-cycle events are celebrated in accordance with Islam. (See, Islam and Islamic Life-Cycle Rituals, page xlix.) Somali Muslims also incorporate indigenous Somali customs with Islamic beliefs. For instance, ritual dances are done to placate evil forces, diseases, crop failures, marauding wild animals, and foreign invaders, while recreational dances celebrate happy events, including the coming of the rains, the harvest, marriages, and births.

Meat is a luxury in Somalia, and when it is prepared for a meal, it means that something is being celebrated. The most elaborate celebration feasts are prepared for men who have returned from the hajj (pilgrimage to Mecca). For a Muslim man, this is considered the most important rite of passage in his lifetime, and he is given a hero's welcome when he returns home. The feasting and partying may continue nonstop for several days. *Kabab barreh,* whole roast lamb (recipe page 141) or roast goat, or often both, is typically prepared for the homecoming celebration. A large assortment of other dishes are also prepared for the feast, *huris hilib* among them. This recipe uses veal, but it is equally good when made with chicken breasts or other kinds of lean, boneless meat.

Huris Hilib

Veal with Tomatoes

Yield: serves 6

1 green pepper, **trimmed**, **seeded**, and **coarsely chopped**
3 potatoes, peeled and quartered
water, as needed
2 tablespoons vegetable oil
1 onion, **finely chopped**
1 clove garlic, finely chopped
1 pound boneless lean veal or beef, cut into ½-inch cubes
salt and pepper to taste
1 tomato, **peeled** and sliced, or 1 cup canned stewed tomatoes
1/4 cup **bread crumbs**
2 tablespoons butter or margarine

Equipment: Medium saucepan with cover, mixing spoon, food processor or potato masher, rubber spatula, large skillet, greased 8-inch baking pan, oven mitts

1. Put green pepper and potatoes in medium saucepan and add just enough water to cover. Bring to boil over high heat. Reduce heat to **simmer**, cover, and cook until very tender, 20 to 25 minutes. Remove from heat and allow to cool enough to handle.

2. Transfer potato mixture, including pan juices, to food processor and **purée** until smooth and lump free, about 1 minute or mash with a potato masher.

Note: While processing, turn machine off once or twice and scrape down sides of container with rubber spatula.

Preheat oven to 350° F.

3. Heat oil in large skillet over medium-high heat. Add onions, garlic, and meat. Stir and **sauté** until meat is lightly browned, 12 to 15 minutes. Stir puréed potato mixture into the meat mixture, and add salt and pepper to taste. Gently stir to mix. Transfer to greased 8-inch baking pan

and arrange tomato slices over the top or cover with stewed tomatoes. Sprinkle with bread crumbs, salt and pepper to taste, and dot butter or margarine on top.

4. Bake in oven for 30 to 35 minutes, until top is lightly browned and mixture is bubbly.

To serve, place pan of huris hilib *on the table and serve with side dish of cooked rice or millet.*

To celebrate happy events—the birth of a son, a boy's circumcision, a man's return from Mecca, or a daughter's wedding—whole roasted lamb would be the first choice for the feast. Most Somalis can't afford such extravagance, so they might settle for a dish like this.

Skudahkharis

Lamb and Rice

Yield: serves 4

4 tablespoons vegetable oil
1 pound lean lamb, cut into bite-size pieces
1 onion, thinly sliced
1 clove garlic, **finely chopped**
2 tomatoes, chopped
1 teaspoon **ground** cumin
1 teaspoon ground cinnamon
½ teaspoon ground cloves
½ teaspoon ground cardamom
salt and pepper to taste
3 ounces (about ½ cup) canned tomato paste
2 cup raw white rice
4 cups boiling water

Equipment: Large **heavy-based** saucepan with cover or **Dutch oven**, mixing spoon, large serving platter

1. Heat oil in large heavy-based saucepan or Dutch oven over medium-high heat. Add meat, stir, and brown on all sides, 18 to 20 minutes. Add onions and garlic, stir, and **sauté** until onion is soft, 3 to 5 minutes. Stir in tomatoes, cumin, cinnamon, cloves, cardamom, salt and pepper to taste, and tomato paste. Stir to mix well, reduce heat to medium-low, and cook for 5 to 7 minutes for flavors to develop.

2. Slowly stir in rice and boiling water, and bring to boil over high heat. Reduce heat to **simmer**, cover, and cook for 18 to 20 minutes, until rice is done. Remove from heat and keep covered for 15 minutes before serving.

To serve, pile mixture on large serving platter and place it on a cloth spread out on the floor or on a low table. Everyone uses only the fingers of their right hand to help themselves with each mouthful. According to Islamic tradition, the left hand must never touch food; it is used only for personal grooming.

Somalis have close ties with Middle Eastern Muslims. Many Middle Eastern foods—especially flat breads like Jordan's *khobaz arabee* (recipe page 115)—are part of the Somali diet. Bread is used to scoop food from a bowl and pop it into the mouth.

Fatir is one of the traditional Arabic flat breads of Bedouin nomads that has crossed the Gulf of Aden to Somalia from neighboring Yemen and Saudi Arabia. The Somali nomads adopted this quick and easy-to-prepare bread as their own many years ago. The breads are baked on a *sajj*, a convex metal dome placed over an open fire. A good substitute for a *sajj* is a wok placed upside-down over a stove burner. Fatir can be cooked equally well on a flat griddle or **heavy-based** skillet.

Fatir

Barley Bread

Yield: 8 to 10 pieces

2 cups barley flour (available at all health food stores)

2 cups bread flour, more as needed
2 teaspoons salt
1½ to 2 cups **lukewarm water**
vegetable oil cooking spray

Equipment: Large **heavy-based** skillet, mixing spoon, medium mixing bowl, lightly floured work surface, kitchen towel, lightly floured rolling pin, large flat griddle or large cast iron skillet, metal tongs, wide metal spatula

1. Put barley flour into a large heavy-based skillet and heat over medium heat, stirring constantly until flour turns golden brown and gives off a pleasant roasted aroma, 5 to 7 minutes. Transfer to medium mixing bowl and cool for about 5 minutes.

2. Add 2 cups bread flour and salt to roasted barley flour, and stir to mix. Make well (hole) in center, and pour in 1½ cups warm water. Stir to moisten flour. Add remaining ½ cup warm water, a little at a time, to make dough. Using your hands, form dough into a ball. Transfer to lightly floured work surface and if dough is sticky, add bread flour, a little at a time, and **knead** for 5 to 7 minutes, until smooth. Cover with towel and let rest for about 30 minutes.

3. Divide dough into 8 equal pieces. Flatten each piece, one at a time, on lightly floured work surface. Sprinkle lightly with flour and flatten with the palm of your hand. Place side by side on work surface and cover with towel.

4. Continue with one piece of dough at a time. Using lightly floured rolling pin, flatten to about 10 inches in diameter. The bread should be very thin and will easily tear, handle with care. Prepare dough pieces one at a time: Do not roll out to 10 inches until ready to cook.

5. Prepare to cook: ADULT SUPERVISION REQUIRED. Lightly coat surface of large flat griddle or large cast iron skillet with cooking spray, and heat to medium-high. When drop of water sprinkled on hot oiled surface dances and evaporates, place one bread on surface. Using back of wide metal spatula, press down on bread to get maximum heat from hot surface. Cook for 1½ to 2 minutes, or until bottom side of bread is golden brown. Using both metal tongs and spatula, carefully turn over and cook second side until firm and golden brown, 1 to 1½ minutes. Using metal tongs and spatula, remove from heat. Wrap in towel to keep warm while rolling out and cooking each remaining bread, one at a time. Spray with cooking spray each time before placing dough on cooking surface.

Serve breads while still warm for best flavor. Tear bread into bite-size chunks and use to scoop up huris hilib *(recipe page 8) or* skudahkharis *(recipe precedes) from the serving platter. Eat with only the fingers of your right hand. According to Muslim tradition, the left hand must never touch food; it is used only for personal grooming.*

ETHIOPIA & ERITREA

Ethiopia and Eritrea are located in northeastern Africa; Ethiopia is completely landlocked, bordered by Sudan on the west, by Somalia and Djibouti on the east, by Kenya on the south, and by Eritrea on the northwest. Eritrea is located on the Red Sea coast and is bordered by Ethiopia and Djibouti on the south, and Sudan on the east and north

Ethiopia has historic links to the Islamic cultures of the Middle East and to the ancient civilizations of the Mediterranean. Unlike other African countries (except Liberia), Ethiopia was never a European colony. Eritrea was a province of Ethiopia until it declared independence in 1993, but the two countries are still closely connected, and the people are the same culturally.

Most Ethiopians and Eritreans adhere to one of the two main religions: Islam (See Islam and Islamic Life-Cycle Rituals, page xlix) and Christianity in the form of the Ethiopian Orthodox Christian Church. Others follow indigenous religions.

The Ethiopian Orthodox Church has close ties to the Coptic Church of Egypt, the head of which is the Patriarch of Cairo; thus, this Church differs in some ways from the Roman Catholic and Eastern Orthodox traditions. For Ethiopian Orthodox Christians, fasting, feasting, and worship are inseparable from daily life. Church services, accompanied by cymbals, the tolling of bells, and the chanting of rituals, often last throughout the night. All religious observances and life-milestone rituals are full of pageantry, with processions of beautifully robed clergy, some carrying *lalibela* (large filigree crucifixes) and others swinging pots of burning incense. Many priests carry ceremonial parasols of different colors and designs denoting their status in the Church; the parasol itself is symbolic of a link between heaven and earth.

Baptism at about three months of age is the first important event in an Ethiopian Christian's life. Usually, a great many infant baptisms take place on the same day. Infants are traditionally dressed in christening gowns worn by older siblings and cousins, often handed down from earlier generations. During the baptism ceremony, when the priest calls for those who will work together to raise the child in the way of the faithful, it is customary for a large number of family members and friends to come forward, signaling their commitment.

As part of the baptism ceremony, the priests, followed by the godparents carrying their godchildren, as well as family and friends, form a procession that circles the chapel and altar several times. Godparents give the baptized child a Coptic cross, blessed by the priest, for protection from the devil. The cross is suspended from a blue cotton cord called a *mateh*. Many Ethiopian Orthodox Christians wear these crosses around their necks throughout their lives.

After the baptism ceremony, there is always a party. A whole roasted bull, mutton, or lamb (recipe page 141) is the ideal centerpiece of a celebration feast, otherwise *tsebhi dereho* (recipe page 13) or other Ethiopian *wat* (stew) is prepared for the meal. Ethiopian Orthodox Christians slaughter animals in the tradition of the Old Testament, by slitting the animal's throat.

First communion is the next important milestone for Christian boys and girls, and it, too, is full of pageantry and processions. Afterward, there is a celebration at home or in a rented hall. Grandmothers and aunts often spend days preparing the feast for this happy occasion.

Along with the Church-based rites, Ethiopian and Eritrean Christian weddings involve many regional traditions. An astrologer is usually consulted to set an auspicious wedding day and to counsel the couple concerning their compatibility. At one time, it was customary during the wedding ceremony to place an armed guard by the bridal couple, to protect them from demons. Today, weddings for the masses are normally common-law unions, accompanied by feasting late into the night. Weddings of the urban elite are celebrated by long and elaborate church ceremonies and processions. Wedding receptions include music, professional performers, dancing, and feasting, usually at a celebration hall or hotel ballroom.

Ethiopian Orthodox funerals are complex ceremonies that involve elaborate rites and long processions. The traditional period of mourning by the bereaved family is 40 days. The government has tried to discourage long periods of mourning, insisting that three days is sufficient time to grieve, but traditional practices continue in many places.

Eating in Ethiopia involves many special rituals, from the washing of hands that precedes a formal dinner to the sipping from tiny cups of coffee served at the end of a meal. A traditional setting for a meal is around a gaily-colored basket-weave table called a *masob*. Before eating, soap, water, and a towel are brought to each diner to wash both hands. Only the right hand is used for eating; the left is considered unclean, even though it has been washed. Cutlery is not used in Ethiopia.

Ethiopians grow grapes for wine, which is the favorite beverage for celebrations. Other popular Ethiopian drinks are *talla* (a beer made from millet) and *tej* (an alcoholic drink made from fermented honey, similar to mead). Wine, *talla*, and *tej* flow freely at most celebrations.

Ethiopian Orthodox Christians have 160 fasting days a year, and additional days are designated for partial fasting, during which meat, eggs, milk, and other animal products are not eaten. Thus, Ethiopians have developed a variety of vegetarian dishes. *Yegomen kitfo* is not considered pure vegetarian because it includes dairy products. Spinach or other greens may be substituted for collard greens. ✺ ✺ ✺

Yegomen Kitfo

Collards with Spiced Cottage Cheese

Yield: serves 6 to 8

½ cup melted butter or margarine
2 cloves garlic, **finely chopped**
½ teaspoon **ground** cardamom
½ teaspoon ground cinnamon
½ teaspoon ground turmeric
½ teaspoon ground ginger
¼ teaspoon ground nutmeg
1½ cups (12 ounces) cottage cheese, small or large curd
salt and pepper to taste
ground red pepper to taste
2 bunches (about 20 ounces) collards or spinach, washed, drained, and **coarsely chopped**

Equipment: Medium bowl, mixing spoon, large saucepan with cover, metal tongs, medium serving bowl

1. Put melted butter or margarine into medium bowl. Add garlic, ground cardamom, cinnamon, turmeric, ginger, and nutmeg. Stir well to mix. Add cottage cheese and stir to mix well. Add salt and pepper to taste and ground red pepper to taste.

2. Put chopped collards or spinach into large saucepan and add ½ cup water. Bring to boil over medium-high heat. Reduce heat to **simmer**, cover, and cook for 15 to 20 minutes. Using metal tongs, transfer greens to medium serving bowl.

To serve, spoon cottage cheese mixture over greens or serve in separate bowl. Eat by mixing some greens and a little cottage cheese mixture together in your right hand and popping it into your mouth. Serve as a side dish with tsebhi dereho *(recipe follows) and cooked rice.*

Although many Muslim marriages in Ethiopia and Eritrea are arranged by parents (often between first cousins), educated urbanites sometimes select their own marriage partners. By tradition, every bride is expected to know how to cut a chicken into 12 pieces to make *tsebhi dereho*. The easiest way to cut a chicken into 12 pieces is to have it done by a butcher.

Tsebhi Dereho

Chicken in Red Pepper Paste

Yield: serves 6

¼ cup *berberé* (recipe follows)
2½ to 3 pound chicken, cut into 12 pieces by butcher
juice of 2 lemons
salt to taste
½ cup butter or margarine
2 onions, **finely chopped**
2 tablespoons tomato paste
4 tomatoes, **peeled** and chopped, or 16 ounces canned stewed tomatoes
2 cups water
2 teaspoons finely chopped fresh ginger, or 1 teaspoon **ground** ginger
6 whole hard-cooked eggs, peeled, for serving

Equipment: Paper towels, large bowl, large **heavy-based** ovenproof skillet with cover or **Dutch oven**, mixing spoon, oven mitts, paring knife, large serving bowl

1. Prepare *berberé*. Keep covered and refrigerated until ready to use.

2. Rinse chicken pieces under cold running water and pat dry with paper towels. Place in large bowl and sprinkle all sides with lemon juice and salt to taste.

Preheat oven to 350° F.

3. Melt butter or margarine in large heavy-based ovenproof skillet or Dutch oven over medium-high heat. Add onions and **sauté** until soft, 3 to 5 minutes. Stir in ¼ cup prepared *berberé* and mix well. Add tomato paste, chopped fresh tomatoes or stewed tomatoes, water, and ginger, and stir well. Add chicken pieces and push down to cover with tomato mixture.

4. Bake in oven, covered, for 1 to 1½ hours until chicken is done. Test **chicken doneness.**

5. Using paring knife, make 4 or 5 small slits in 6 peeled, whole hard-cooked eggs.

To serve, transfer chicken pieces to large serving bowl. Arrange hard-cooked eggs around the chicken and spoon tomato sauce over the top. Eat with h'mbasha *(recipe page 14) for sopping up sauce.*

This is the basic recipe for hot pepper paste. There are many other variations.

Berberé

Ethiopian Red Pepper Paste

Yield: 1½ to 2 cups

1 teaspoon **ground** ginger
½ teaspoon ground black pepper
½ teaspoon ground **coriander** seeds
½ teaspoon ground cardamom
¼ teaspoon ground nutmeg
¼ teaspoon ground cloves
¼ teaspoon ground cinnamon
¼ teaspoon ground **allspice**
1 onion, **finely chopped**
1 cup water, divided
8 tablespoons paprika
4 tablespoons chili powder
salt to taste
1 tablespoon vegetable oil

Equipment: Electric **blender**, rubber spatula, small saucepan, mixing spoon, 1 pint plastic or glass jar with cover

1. Put ground ginger, black pepper, coriander seeds, cardamom, nutmeg, cloves, cinnamon, allspice, finely chopped onion in blender. Add ¼ cup water and **blend** into smooth paste. Add little more water if paste is too thick. Turn off blender, once or twice and use rubber spatula to scrape down sides of bowl.

2. Put paprika and chili powder in small saucepan. Add blended mixture and remaining water and salt to taste, and stir until smooth. Cook over medium heat 5 to 7 minutes for flavor to develop. Do not boil. Remove from heat and cool

to room temperature. Spoon paste into 1 pint plastic or glass jar. Carefully pour oil over surface of paste and cover tightly.

Continue, tsebhi dereho *(recipe precedes: Step 1. Prepare* berberé*) or use in other recipes calling for* berberé *or hot pepper sauce. Refrigerate for up to 5 months.*

Ethiopians eat bread with every meal, and this is one of the most popular types.

H'Mbasha

Spiced Bread

Yield: 4 small loaves

- 1¼ cups **lukewarm** water
- 1 package dry active **yeast**
- 1 teaspoon **ground fenugreek**
- ½ teaspoon ground **coriander** seeds
- ½ teaspoon ground cardamom
- 1 teaspoon salt
- 1 egg
- 2 cups all-purpose flour
- 2 cups whole wheat flour
- 4 tablespoons warm melted butter or margarine

Equipment: Large mixing bowl, mixing spoon, lightly floured work surface, kitchen towel, fork or knife, large **heavy-based** skillet with cover or griddle with cover (this could be a piece of foil or lid from large saucepan), metal tongs, **pastry brush**, napkin-lined bread basket

1. Pour warm water into large mixing bowl and add yeast. Stir and let set for 5 to 10 minutes, until frothy. Add ground fenugreek, coriander, cardamom, salt, and egg, and stir well. Add all-purpose and whole wheat flour, a little at a time, and use your hands to mix together. Transfer to lightly floured work surface and **knead** until smooth, 7 to 10 minutes. Clean and lightly grease large mixing bowl. Place dough into bowl and turn to grease all sides. Cover with towel and keep in warm place to rise to double in bulk, 1 to 1½ hours.

2. Transfer dough to lightly floured work surface, **punch down** and divide into 4 pieces. Using your hands, lightly flatten each piece into a round flat loaf, about ¼-inch thick. Using fork or knife, mark the top of each loaf with cross-hatch design. Cover loaves with towel.

3. Preheat heavy-based skillet or griddle until drop of water sprinkled on surface sizzles away on contact. Place one or two loaves in dry skillet or griddle and cover. Reduce heat to medium and cook for 7 minutes. Turn over and continue cooking second side for another 7 minutes uncovered. Using metal tongs, remove from pan or griddle and place on work surface. Using pastry brush, brush loaves with warm butter or margarine, place in napkin-lined bread basket and cover. Continue to cook remaining loaves the same way.

Serve either warm or at room temperature. Hold the bread in your right hand, use your teeth to break off bite-size pieces. Never use your left hand. According to Muslim tradition, the left hand must never touch food; it is used only for personal grooming. The bread is used as a scoop to carry food from the bowl to your mouth.

UGANDA

Uganda, in eastern Africa, is bordered on the north by Sudan, on the east by Kenya, on the west by Congo, and on the south by Tanzania and Rwanda. The country includes Lake Victoria, the second-largest freshwater lake in the world and the source of the great White Nile River. Few African countries are as well endowed as Uganda with water and fertile land, which makes subsistence comparatively easy for the large Ugandan population. Formerly a British colony, it became an independent nation in 1962.

Most Ugandans are Christians, almost equally divided between Protestants and Roman Catholics. (See Protestant and Catholic Life-Cycle Rituals, page xlvi.) The rest of the population is either Muslim (see Islam and Islamic Life-Cycle Rituals, page xlix) or followers of indigenous religions. (See Traditional African Life-Cycle Rituals, page xli.) The Ugandan constitution guarantees religious freedom.

The Nile forms a natural dividing line that separates Uganda's south—home to the Bantu people, the country's largest ethnic group—from the north, where the Nilotes live. Nilotes are a group of related peoples who live near the source of the Nile. One of these groups, the Karamojong people, are notable for having tenaciously maintained their long-standing traditions; for instance, only recently have they begun wearing clothes. The Karamojong men tend their longhorn cattle, often singing and talking to them. Women are responsible for raising grain and other foods to supplement the basic diet of milk and blood from the cattle. Cattle are slaughtered only for feasts on special occasions.

Cattle represent wealth and prestige. Among the Karamojong—and all Ugandan herding groups—giving cattle to the bride's father in the bride-price negotiation is one of the most important parts of the marriage. It binds two families together, and all the relatives in both families are expected to help make the marriage work. Only after a marriage has been validated according to traditional beliefs will the couple arrange a church wedding. For Christian weddings, there is a church ceremony and a reception afterward.

Christian Ugandan men are permitted to have only one wife. Most adhere to this rule, although some marry only their first wife in church and then take another wife, or perhaps several others, in accordance with traditional African practice.

Death is marked by elaborate funeral rites. When someone in a community dies, everyone is expected to attend the funeral. A person who ignores a death is thought to harbor ill feelings toward the bereaved family and toward the community in general. A wake can last several days and involves singing, ritual dances, prayers, and feasting. Guests contribute to the expense of the food and drink. Mourners express their sorrow by emotional crying, shouting, and wailing. The dead are buried on land that belonged to them, not in cemeteries. The corpse is place in the ground, usually in a coffin, beside the main dwelling of the living compound.

Matoke, which means green cooking bananas, is also the name for this dish. Green plantains are one of the most important foods in Uganda, and this dish would almost certainly be on the menu for a feast at a wedding, a funeral, or other life-cycle event.

Matoke

Mashed Green Plantains

Yield: serves 4

1 cup peanut butter
2 cups cold water
2 tablespoons peanut oil
1 onion, **finely chopped**
salt to taste
ground red pepper to taste
4 green plantains (available at all Latin American food stores and some supermarkets)
½ cup boiling water, more if necessary

Equipment: **Blender**, rubber spatula, small bowl, paring knife, **steamer pan**, metal spatula, medium mixing bowl, potato masher or fork, wooden mixing spoon

1. Prepare sauce: Put peanut butter, water, peanut oil, and onion in blender. **Blend** until smooth, about 1 minute. Turn off blender once or twice and use rubber spatula to scrape down sides of container. Transfer peanut butter mixture to small bowl, and add salt to taste and ground red pepper to taste.

2. Prepare plantains: Using paring knife, slice down the length of plantain skin on two sides, cut off both ends, and peel skin off. Cut plantains in half lengthwise.

3. Steam plantains: Pour water into bottom pan of steamer and set top pan or rack in place. Lay plantain pieces in top pan or rack. Bring water to boil over high heat. Reduce heat to **simmer**, cover, and steam until soft but not mushy, 15 to 20 minutes. Using metal spatula, transfer to medium mixing bowl.

Note: Check water level carefully during steaming to be sure there is at least 1 inch of water at all times in bottom pan. Add more hot water, if necessary.

4. Using potato masher or fork, mash plantains until smooth. Add ½ cup boiling water and beat until consistency of very thick mashed potatoes. Add more boiling water, a little at a time, if necessary to achieve correct consistency. Add salt to taste.

5. **Drizzle** peanut sauce over mashed plantains.

Serve while still warm as a nutritious starch side dish with chickennat *(recipe follows).*

A little chicken or meat combined with other ingredients can go a long way to feed a hungry crowd at a wedding or funeral.

Chickennat

Chicken in Peanut Sauce

Yield: serves 4 to 6

2½ to 3 pounds chicken, cut into serving-size pieces
salt and pepper to taste
½ cup butter or margarine
2 cups water
2 onions, **finely chopped**
1 cup peanut butter
2 **egg yolks**
1 tablespoon parsley, **coarsely chopped** for **garnish**

Equipment: Paper towels, large **heavy-based** skillet with cover or **Dutch oven**, mixing spoon, metal tongs, plate, small bowl, whisk, large serving bowl

1. Rinse chicken under cold running water and pat dry with paper towels. Sprinkle with salt and pepper to taste.

2. Melt butter or margarine in large heavy-based skillet or Dutch oven over medium-high heat. Add chicken pieces and water, and sprinkle in finely chopped onions. Bring to boil. Reduce heat to **simmer**, cover, and cook for 45 minutes to 1 hour, or until chicken is tender. Test **chicken doneness**. Using metal tongs, remove chicken pieces and place on plate.

3. Put peanut butter in small bowl. Remove about ¾ cup chicken broth from pan and stir into peanut butter until well mixed. Stir egg yolks into peanut butter mixture. Whisking constantly, slowly add peanut mixture to remaining chicken broth. Return chicken pieces to skillet or Dutch oven, cover, and simmer to heat through, 7 to 12 minutes.

To serve, transfer to large serving bowl and sprinkle with parsley. Serve with rice, putu *(recipe page 29), or* matoke *(recipe precedes).*

MOZAMBIQUE

Mozambique is a long, narrow country on the southern coast of East Africa. It is bordered by the Indian Ocean on the east; by Tanzania on the north; by Malawi, Zambia, and Zimbabwe on the west; and by South Africa and Swaziland on the south.

A Portuguese colony until it gained independence in 1975, sharp cultural contrasts remain between the coastal cities, which were strongly influenced by Portuguese traders, and the interior of the country, where people follow ancient traditions and customs. Most Mozambicans are engaged in subsistence farming.

There are 10 major ethnic groups in Mozambique. The largest group is the Makua, living mostly in the north. Two-thirds of the population of Mozambique follow indigenous religions, about one-tenth are Muslims, and the rest are Christians, mostly Roman Catholics. Muslims and Christians generally blend local traditions with their religious celebrations. (See Islam and Islamic Life-Cycle Rituals, page xlix, and Protestant and Catholic Life-Cycle Rituals, page xlvi.)

Traditional rituals are observed by most Mozambicans for life passages. At the time of a marriage, nothing is more important to the families of the bride and groom than negotiating *lobola*, bride-price. The traditional payment is in the form of hoes—farming tools. Among the 10 to 15 hoes that are given as *lobola*, there is a special marriage hoe, called a *beja*, which is not made to be used. It is carefully kept and passed along to the next generation, to be used again in the payment of a bride-price.

Mozambique has an extensive coastline, and more than 50 rivers run through the country. Thus, it is only natural that fish and shellfish are important to the Mozambican diet. *Camarão de coco* is a wonderful way to fix shrimp for the *lobolo* meal or for a wedding feast.

CAMARAO DE COCO

COCONUT SHRIMP

Yield: serves 6

2 to 2½ pounds shrimp (48 to 54 shrimp), **peeled and deveined**
¼ cup butter or margarine, more if necessary
1 onion, **finely chopped**
4 cloves garlic, finely chopped
2 tablespoons fresh parsley, finely chopped, or 3 teaspoons dried parsley flakes
½ teaspoon **ground** red pepper, more or less to taste
2 teaspoons ground cumin
3 peeled tomatoes, chopped or 12-ounce canned stewed tomatoes
salt and pepper to taste
2 cups coconut milk, homemade (recipe page 346), or canned

Equipment: **Colander**, large **heavy-based** skillet, slotted spoon, medium bowl, mixing spoon

1. Put peeled and deveined shrimp in colander and rinse under cold running water. Drain well.

2. Melt ¼ cup butter or margarine in large heavy-based skillet over medium-high heat. Add shrimp and tossing constantly, **sauté** until opaque pinkish-white, 3 to 5 minutes. Remove shrimp with slotted spoon and place in medium bowl. Add onion and garlic to same skillet, and add more butter or margarine, if necessary. Stir and sauté until onions are soft, 3 to 5 minutes. Add parsley, ½ teaspoon ground red pepper, more or less to taste, cumin, tomatoes, and salt and pepper to taste. Stir well, reduce heat to medium, and continue cooking for flavor to develop, 3 to 5 minutes. Stir in coconut milk and

blend well. Return shrimp to skillet, toss to mix, and cook 3 to 5 minutes to heat through.

Serve at once over rice.

For a wedding or funeral feast, cauldrons of *sopa de peixe*—a specialty of coastal Mozambicans—might be prepared. This soup can be made with any available fish, seafood, and vegetable combination. In Mozambique, soups are eaten together with all the other dishes served at a meal.

Sopa de Peixe

Fish and Vegetable Soup

Yield: serves 6

2 tablespoons vegetable oil
3 onions, chopped
2 cloves garlic, **finely chopped**
½ teaspoon **ground** red pepper, more or less to taste
2 white potatoes, peeled and chopped
2 sweet potatoes, peeled and chopped
2 cups finely chopped cabbage
3 peeled tomatoes, chopped or 12-ounce canned stewed tomatoes
6 cups water
1 pound skinless fish fillets, fresh or frozen (thawed), cut into chunks
1 pound small size shrimp, **peeled and deveined**
salt and pepper to taste

Equipment: Large saucepan with cover or **Dutch oven**, mixing spoon

Heat oil in large saucepan or Dutch oven over medium-high heat. Add onions and garlic. Stir and **sauté** until onions are soft, 3 to 5 minutes. Stir in ground red pepper to taste, add white potatoes, sweet potatoes, cabbage, chopped or stewed tomatoes, and water. Bring to boil and stir. Reduce heat to **simmer**, cover, and cook for 30 to 40 minutes, until vegetables are almost mushy but still tender. Add fish and shrimp and toss gently to mix. Cover and cook for 7 to 12 minutes until fish is opaque white and shrimp are opaque and pinkish-white. Add salt and pepper to taste.

To serve fish soup, as they do in Mozambique, pour each serving into bowl made from a gourd or use a plastic bowl. Pour soup over rice or steamed millet *(recipe follows).*

Millet or cornmeal porridge is served at every meal in Mozambique, much as potatoes or bread are served with meals in Western countries. A feast would be incomplete if one or the other were not on the menu. Millet is one of the most important grains in Africa.. Buy millet at a health food store, and be sure to get hulled millet, not birdseed.

Steamed Millet

Yield: serves 6

3½ cups water
1 teaspoon salt
2 cups millet
½ cup boiling water
3 tablespoons butter or margarine

Equipment: Medium **heavy-based** saucepan with cover, mixing spoon

Pour water into medium heavy-based saucepan, and add salt and millet. Bring to boil over medium-high heat. Stir, reduce heat to **simmer**, cover, and cook for 20 minutes. After 20 minutes, stir to fluff millet, and taste it. (When fully cooked, millet has a texture similar to cooked white rice.) If it seems too dry, yet still has a little crunch, add ¼ cup boiling water, cover, and continue cooking 10 minutes more. Remove from heat and stir in butter or margarine. Keep covered until ready to serve.

Serve millet as a side dish with fish, meat, or vegetables.

MADAGASCAR

Madagascar is an island in the Indian Ocean off the southeastern coast of Africa. Most of the island's flora and fauna, and the sea creatures in the surrounding waters, are found nowhere else in the world. Even the people of Madagascar have distinctive customs and lifeways that differ from those of other Africans. In many ways, Madagascar isn't African in anything but the geographical sense, although the country does participate in African political affairs.

The Malagasy people are descended primarily from Indonesian seafarers, black Africans, and Arabs. According to legend, Indonesians first arrived on the island a couple of thousand years ago, and after they took up residence, they acquired wives and slaves from the neighboring coast of Africa. Arabs came as traders and stayed.

Although one language is spoken in Madagascar, there are 18 recognized ethnic groups, each with its own customs, traditions, and territory. For centuries, rivalry has existed between them. Most groups are subsistence farmers, though some are herders who raise humpbacked *zebu* (cattle). About 40 percent of the Malagasy are Christian, divided almost equally between Protestants and Roman Catholics.

The Christian Malagasy have incorporated some of the customs and ideologies of Islam into their practices. Belief in *vintana* (fate or destiny), thought to have roots in Islamic cosmology (study of the universe), is incorporated into every facet of their lives. The date and time of a birth, circumcision, marriage, or burial are either good or bad, according to an individual's *vintana*. All auspicious occasions are planned around a person's *vintana*; for instance, the name of a newborn is chosen only after consulting an astrologer for a reading on the child's *vintana*.

Boys are circumcised at a very young age, and this is an occasion that is always accompanied by a huge feast with drinking and singing.

Among Malagasy pastoralist groups, *zebu* (cattle) are an extremely important item of prestige and wealth. Formerly, no young male passed to manhood until he had rustled someone's cattle and bragged about it. (This is now forbidden, however.) Still, even today, no self-respecting man can marry without his bride's price in cows. Even more important is for a man to possess cattle for slaughter at his funeral—it would bring disgrace to his family if he were to die without this property. The more bulls killed for a funeral, the greater a man's glory, proclaimed forever by horned skulls displayed on the stone walls of his tomb, along with elaborately carved drawings of his cattle. The greatest sacrifice is cattle, and only at funerals do these herders kill and eat their *zebu*. At lesser occasions, chickens, rice, honey, rum, sugar cane, or sweets are given in sacrificial ceremonies.

In Madagascar, meat is eaten only on special occasions. *Varenga* (recipe follows) is always eaten with mountains of *vary* (rice)—a way to make small quantities of meat go a long way. Served along with the main dish and *vary* are *brêdes* (recipe page 20) and a small bowl of *rano vola* (also called *ranon 'apango*), which is a rice broth made by simply adding boiling water to the residue left in the pot used to cook rice. Plenty of *mofo* (bread) is needed to sop up the juices. ❂ ❂ ❂

Varenga

Shredded Beef

Yield: serves 4 to 6

2 pounds lean boneless chuck steak, cut in 2-inch chunks
water, as needed
1 teaspoon salt
2 cloves garlic, **finely chopped,** or 1 teaspoon garlic granules
1 onion, finely chopped
4 to 6 cups cooked white rice, keep warm, for serving

Equipment: Medium saucepan with cover or **Dutch oven**, mixing spoon, fork, plate, serving platter

Place beef in medium saucepan or Dutch oven and add water to cover by at least 1 inch. Add salt, garlic, and onion. Bring to a boil over high heat and stir. Reduce heat to **simmer**, cover, and cook for about 2 hours, or until meat is so tender you can easily shred it with your fingers. During cooking, add more hot water if necessary to keep the meat well covered. To test doneness: Using a fork, remove a piece of meat from the pan, put on a plate and let cool enough to handle. Using your fingers, the meat should easily shred apart.

To serve, mound cooked rice on a serving platter and spoon meat and pan juices on top. Serve with a basket of mofo.

The greens used for *brêdes* can be anything you can get from the garden or market; such as spinach, **chard** (also Swiss chard), **mustard greens**, **turnip** greens, **collard greens**, or **broccoli rabe** (also raab), or combination. Spinach is used in this recipe.

Brêdes

Boiled Greens

Yield: serves 3 to 4

1 pound fresh spinach or other greens
2 cups water
salt and pepper to taste

Equipment: **Colander**, medium saucepan with cover, mixing spoon

1. Wash spinach carefully under cold running water to rinse out sand. Drain well in a colander.

2. Pour water into medium saucepan and bring to boil over high heat. Add spinach and salt and pepper to taste. Reduce heat to **simmer**, cover, and cook until tender, 15 to 20 minutes.

Serve as a side dish or pour over vary *(rice).*

In Madagascar, a feast celebrating a life passage would be incomplete without *voankazo* (tropical fruit). The most popular are *voasary* (oranges) and *akondro* (bananas). *Banane flambée* (flaming bananas) is Madagascar's unofficial national dessert.

This is an easy and dramatic way of ending a special meal. The recipe calls for rum, which has a high alcohol content. The alcohol burns away in 3 or 4 seconds.

Banane Flambée

Flaming Bananas

CAUTION: ADULT SUPERVISION REQUIRED

Yield: serves 4

4 bananas
1/4 cup light rum
4 tablespoons butter or margarine
1/2 cup dark brown sugar
1/2 teaspoon **ground allspice**

Equipment: Fork, paring knife, aluminum foil, baking sheet, oven mitts, small saucepan, medium **heavy-based** skillet with cover, mixing spoon, kitchen matches or long-handled outdoor grill lighter, individual dessert dishes

Preheat oven to 400° F.

1. With a fork, pierce through the banana peel in 3 or 4 places. Using a paring knife, make lengthwise slits in the peel along both the inside and outside curves stopping about 1 inch from the bottom end of the banana. Lay the bananas that are fully encased in the peel, on the foil-covered baking sheet, so the slits are on the sides.

2. Bake in the oven for 10 to 15 minutes, or until the skins darken and the bananas feel tender when pressed gently with your finger. Remove from the oven and gently lift off and discard the top peel. Leave the underside peel intact.

3. About 5 minutes before serving, warm the rum in a small saucepan over low heat.

4. Prepare to cook: Melt the butter or margarine in a medium heavy-based skillet over medium heat. Stir in brown sugar and allspice. Gently lay the bananas, one at a time, flesh side down into the skillet. Lift off and discard the remaining peel. Spoon the butter or margarine mixture over the bananas and reduce heat to low.

5. Ignite flame: Use caution and stand away from the skillet when igniting the flame. Pour the warm rum over the bananas and using a kitchen match or long-handled outdoor grill lighter, carefully ignite the alcoholic vapors directly above the bananas. The flaming stops in just a few seconds. Cover the bananas until ready to serve.

To serve, spoon bananas with pan juices into individual dessert dishes. Eat at once while warm.

SWAZILAND

The smallest country in the Southern Hemisphere, the kingdom of Swaziland is surrounded on three sides by South Africa, and its fourth side borders Mozambique.

Although nearly half the population of Swaziland belongs to the Zion Apostolic Church, many Swazi people include traditional indigenous practices with their Christian rituals and celebrations. (See Protestant and Catholic Life-Cycle Rituals, page xlvi, and Traditional African Life-Cycle Rituals, page xli.) African Christian churches in Swaziland—and elsewhere in Africa—have been trying to stop polygamy and to discourage *loboa*, the bride-price practice. However, most African ethnic groups feel pride in their heritage and allegiance to the ways of their ancestors. Indeed, the payment of *loboa* validates the union of two people, legalizes marriage, and legitimates the children.

In traditional Swazi culture, a newborn remains nameless until he or she is three months old. The naming day is a big celebration, with everyone invited to view the ritual and take part in singing, dancing, and feasting. At three years of age, a baby is weaned and left in the care of siblings and grandparents while its mother works in the fields. At about age six, Swazi boys and girls are given a small cut in each ear lobe as their first test of bravery. From that time forward, they are expected to control their emotions in public.

Unlike many other traditional African societies, there are no special Swazi puberty ceremonies for boys. However, the Swazi royal family uses this period of passage from boyhood to manhood to encourage national unity. The Swazi nation is maintained by a system of age-related royal regiments *(libutfo)*, which boys must join when they reach puberty. Boys from different clans have the same age-mates through each advancement. The strong bonds that develop between the boys help decrease problems that might someday arise between clans, while promoting national pride and loyalty to the king.

When girls reach puberty, they take part in *umhlanga* in late August or early September—the exact date is selected by the royal astrologers. *Umhlanga* is a week-long celebration for marriageable young women, who come from all over the kingdom to help repair the *indlunkulu* (great house) of the queen mother. After arriving, the girls spend a day resting, then set off in search of reeds, sometimes not returning for several days. *Umhlanga* is essentially a fertility celebration that gets its name from the large reeds gathered by the girls. On the sixth and seventh days, a reed dance is performed by the young women before the king, the queen mother, and important guests and onlookers. This dance is a showcase of potential wives for the king, who is encouraged to make a selection from the performing group. Afterward, there is always an elaborate feast for the dancers and spectators.

All wedding ceremonies include a grand feast and, depending upon the budget, cattle, goats, or sheep (recipe page 141) are roasted for the event. Along with the roasted meat, great quantities of food, such as *kurma* (recipe page 23), *borrie rys* (recipe page 27) and *putu* (recipe page 29) are prepared for revelers.

Respect for both ancestors and the aged plays a large part in the complex structure of Swazi traditional society. Funerals are grand celebrations, and people come from miles around for the festivities. Cattle are usually slaughtered for the feast, which can go on for a week or more, depending upon the importance of the deceased. When the headman of a village dies, he is buried at the entrance of the *sibaya*, a circular enclosure made of stacked reed stalks that is the center of community life. The *sibaya* is where the village's council of elders meets and where the best grain is stored.

At every meal, the Swazi people set aside a little food and pour a little home-brewed beer or sour milk onto the ground as an offering to the spirits of their ancestors

Curry dishes are commonplace in Swaziland, and several different kinds are often prepared for weddings and funeral feasts. The spices used in curries are always hand-ground for each dish. Grinding may be done with a mortar and pestle, or by placing the spices on a hard surface and pounding them with a round rock. Every cook has her own blend of spices that varies with different types of food. The following is a mild curry recipe that can be made hotter by adding more dried red peppers, to taste. For this recipe, use whole spices. Home-ground spices are not as finely pulverized as commercial blends, but they are fresher, therefore better.

Homemade Curry Powder

1 whole dried red pepper, more if necessary
6 cardamom pods
1 stick cinnamon, broken into small pieces
24 whole **coriander** seeds
4 whole cloves
10 cumin seeds
4 whole fennel seeds
10 **fenugreek** seeds
5 whole white or black peppercorns
1 teaspoon **ground** turmeric

Equipment: **Mortar and pestle** or electric **blender** or nut grinder

Put cardamom pods, broken cinnamon stick, coriander, cloves, cumin, fennel, fenugreek, peppercorns, turmeric, and 1 whole red pepper in the mortar. Using the pestle, pound as smooth as possible; or put in blender or nut grinder and **blend** or grind until smooth. If you want a more spicy curry powder, grind in more red peppers, one at a time, if necessary.

For best flavor, use curry powder within three or four months of making it. Store spice mixture in tightly covered jar in cool, dark place.

Curried chicken is a popular way to prepare fowl, and this is just one of a dozen or more variations. Curry dishes are generally included in life-cycle celebration feasts.

Kurma

Curried Chicken

Yield: serves 4 to 6

2½ to 3 pounds chicken, cut into serving-size pieces
1 cup yogurt
2 tomatoes, chopped
curry powder, homemade (recipe precedes), or commercial
1 tablespoon grated fresh ginger, or 1 teaspoon **ground** ginger
1 clove garlic, **finely chopped**
2 tablespoons vegetable oil
2 onions, finely sliced
1 cup water

Equipment: Paper towels, large mixing bowl, mixing spoon, small bowl, plastic food wrap, large skillet with cover or **Dutch oven**, serving bowl

1. Wash chicken pieces and pat dry with paper towels. Put clean chicken pieces in large mixing bowl.

2. Put yogurt, tomato, curry powder, ginger, and garlic in small bowl, and stir to mix well. Pour yogurt mixture over chicken and turn the pieces until they are well coated. Cover with plastic wrap and refrigerate for 3 to 4 hours to **marinate**.

3. Heat oil in large saucepan or Dutch oven over medium-high heat. Add onion and **sauté** until soft, 3 to 5 minutes. Stir in water and mix well. Add chicken pieces with **marinade**, and bring to boil. Reduce heat to **simmer**, cover, and cook for 45 minutes to 1 hour, or until chicken is tender. Test for **chicken doneness**.

To serve, transfer to serving bowl and serve with brêdes *(recipe page 20),* putu *(recipe page 29), and/or cooked rice.*

SOUTH AFRICA

South Africa is on the southern tip of Africa and has coastlines on both the Atlantic and Indian Oceans. It shares borders with Namibia, Zimbabwe, Botswana, Mozambique, and Swaziland. It also contains the kingdom of Lesotho within its borders.

The people of South Africa are of diverse cultures and origins. Under the many years of apartheid (government-enforced racial segregation), South Africans were classified into four major groups: whites (Afrikaners of Dutch ancestry, along with people of English and French ancestry); Blacks (regardless of ethnic group); coloureds (descendants of indigenous Africans who intermarried with the earliest European and Malay settlers); and Asians (descendants of Indians and Pakistanis brought to South Africa as indentured laborers). Apartheid was outlawed in 1994, and at the turn of the twentieth century, South African society is in a period of flux.

Most South Africans are Christians. The largest denomination in the country is the Dutch Reformed Church, called the DRC or the *Nederduitse Gereformeerde Kerk,* which serves mainly Afrikaners. There are also more than 4,000 African indigenous churches that broke off from various missionary churches. These churches, run by and for blacks, are organized as the African Independent Churches (AIC). The AIC churches incorporate traditional local religious practices with Christian celebrations, especially for life-milestone events such as baptisms, weddings, and funerals.

Indigenous African religions are adhered to by about 40 percent of South Africans, mostly in rural areas. Many of those who adhere to traditional religions also have some contact with Christianity, and they often incorporate aspects of it into their indigenous religions.

Having marriages arranged by the families involved is an accepted practice throughout Africa. (See Traditional African Life-Cycle Rituals, page xli.) In South Africa, when a Zulu girl is ready for marriage (which can be as young as 9 or 10 years of age), relatives of her suitor must pay *lobola* to her parents. A few years ago, it was the custom to pay the bride-price in cattle; now they pay cash.

The boy's father, mother, older sister or brother, and an uncle or two accompany him to meet his future in-laws. In anticipation of their arrival, the bride's family cleans, polishes, paints, and repairs until everything in the house and yard are clean and orderly. It is important for the bride-to-be to let her future in-laws know she helped with the work so they know she is worth all they have come to pay as *lobola.*

When the day arrives on which the two families are to meet, the dining table is covered with a freshly washed and ironed tablecloth and set with tableware brought out for important occasions. A sumptuous meal, easily the best meal of the year, is prepared. It usually consists of roast chicken, *borrie rys* (recipe page 27), pumpkin or squash casserole, green vegetables, **beetroot**, custard and jelly, assorted breads, cakes and pies such as *melk tert* (recipe page 27), soft drinks, and beer. Everyone is dressed in their best attire, but only the bride's father and an uncle or male neighbor, acting as witnesses, sit at one end of the table opposite the prospective in-laws. The bride-to-be, her mother, sisters, and female relatives do not eat with the guests—they are busy serving food and clearing away dirty dishes.

The future bride is forbidden to be present during *lobola* negotiations. One of the relatives is the go-between and takes over the meeting. A price is offered for the girl, which her father can accept or refuse. Discussion of the price may go back and forth until agreement is reached. When a deal has been struck, a verbal agreement is made in front of the witnesses, and the marriage is official. In the eyes of the community and the parents, the marriage is legitimate. *Lobola* is usually made in installments, and it is the custom for the *makoti* (bride) to live with her husband, at his parents' house, without shame or violating any taboos, until all the payments have been made. The couple then moves to their own hut. Zulu men can take as many wives as they wish as long as they can afford *lobola* for each one.

Lobola or not, wives have no rights in the eyes of the South African government without going before a magistrate and obtaining a marriage license. The Christian churches of South Africa are also opposed to *lobola*, polygamy, and child brides. However, these are long-standing and revered traditions of the region.

When an event involves feeding a large group, such as to pay *lobola*, to celebrate a christening dinner, or in connection with a funeral—or, when the wedding budget is lean—a *bredie* (a thick, flavorful, meat and vegetable stew) might be prepared for the feast. The inexpensive cuts of meat used in the *bredie* go a long way to feed a crowd of people. Both the stew and the name are of Malay origin—Malay laborers were brought to Cape Town in the eighteenth century by the Dutch during their many voyages to the East while trying to establish control of the Spice Trade. Malay cooking is called Cape Malay cuisine, and it is now popular throughout South Africa.

Bredies are almost always made with the fattier cuts of lamb or mutton, which gives the dish a rich flavor. A bredie is named for the main vegetable it is cooked with—tomatoes, green beans, cauliflower, or pumpkin. A famous bredie is *waterblommetjie*, made with a special water flower that grows wild in Cape Town ponds.

Imbotyi Eluhlaza Bredie

Green Bean and Lamb Stew

Yield: serves 4

- 2 tablespoons vegetable oil
- 1½ pounds boneless lamb shoulder, cut into bite-size chunks
- 1 cup onions, chopped
- 2 cloves garlic, **finely chopped**
- 3 teaspoons finely chopped fresh ginger root, or 1 teaspoon **ground** ginger
- 2 cups water
- 2 potatoes, peeled and cut into bite-size pieces
- 1 pound fresh string beans, **trimmed**, washed, and cut crosswise into 1-inch lengths, or frozen cut green beans (thawed)
- ground red pepper, to taste
- ½ teaspoon ground thyme
- salt and pepper to taste

Equipment: Large **heavy-based** skillet or **Dutch oven**, slotted spoon, plate, mixing spoon, serving platter

1. Heat oil in large heavy-based skillet or Dutch oven over medium-high heat. Add lamb and brown all sides, 7 to 12 minutes. Using slotted spoon, transfer to plate. Drain off and discard all but about 2 tablespoons fat. Add onions, garlic, and ginger root. Stirring constantly, cook over medium-high heat for 3 to 5 minutes, until onions are soft. Return lamb to skillet with any liquid that has accumulated. Add water, bring to boil, and stir well. Reduce heat to **simmer**, cover, and cook 1 to 1½ hours, or until meat is tender.

2. Add potatoes, cover, and cook 10 minutes.

3. Add green beans, ground red pepper to taste, thyme, and salt and pepper to taste. Stir, cover, and cook for 20 minutes, or until meat and vegetables are tender.

To serve, mound on serving platter. Bredies *are traditionally served with hot boiled rice or* borrie rys *(recipe page 27).*

Pinangkerrie (made with **tamarind** and the green leaves from an orange tree) and *denningvleis* (recipe follows) are two very popular curry dishes often served at wedding feasts. They can easily be made in large quantities and heaped on platters. Guests help themselves from the platter, either using the fingers of the right hand, a fork, or a spoon. The left hand must never touch food; it is used only for personal grooming.

Denningvleis

Dried Fruit and Meat Curry

Yield: serves 6 to 8

1 cup dried apples
½ cup pitted prunes
½ cup seedless raisins
2 cups warm water
4 tablespoons vegetable oil, divided
1½ pounds boneless lean beef chuck, cut into 1-inch cubes
1 teaspoon salt
2 onions, **finely chopped**
2 tablespoons curry powder (preferably Madras type) (available at all Asian food stores and some supermarkets)
3 tablespoons dark brown sugar, more or less to taste
2 tablespoons red wine vinegar
1 tablespoon strained fresh lemon juice
hot water, if necessary
½ cup salted peanuts, **coarsely chopped**, for **garnish**
2 bananas, for garnish

Equipment: Medium mixing bowl, mixing spoon, large **heavy-based** saucepan with cover or **Dutch oven**, plate, slotted spoon, fork, large serving platter

1. Put dried apples, prunes, and raisins in medium mixing bowl. Add water and let soak for 1 hour, stirring occasionally.

2. Heat 2 tablespoons oil in large heavy-based saucepan or Dutch oven over medium-high heat. Add cubes of meat and sprinkle with salt. Stirring constantly, brown on all sides, 7 to 12 minutes. Using slotted spoon, transfer browned meat to plate.

3. Heat remaining 2 tablespoons oil in large saucepan or Dutch oven over medium-high heat. Add chopped onions and **sauté** until soft, 3 to 5 minutes. Reduce heat to low, stir in curry powder, and return browned meat, including juices, to onion mixture. Add apples, prunes, and raisins (including their soaking water), 3 tablespoons brown sugar, more or less to taste, vinegar, and lemon juice. Stir to mix well. Increase heat to high, bring to boil, and stir. Reduce heat to low, cover, and cook for 1 to 1½ hours, or until meat is fully cooked and easily pierced with a fork. During cooking, if mixture seems too dry, stir in just enough hot water, if necessary, to keep mixture from sticking.

To serve, mound curry on large serving platter. For garnish, sprinkle curry mixture with coarsely chopped peanuts and arrange peeled and sliced bananas over the top. Denningvleis *is traditionally served with* borrie rys *(recipe follows).*

Among South African Whites, most funerals follow Western-style Christian traditions. Usually a notice is placed in the local paper stating the date, time, and place of the funeral. Many people are cremated, in which case a service is held in the chapel at the crematorium. If there is a burial, there will be a service at a church, followed by a procession behind the hearse to the cemetery. Tea, drinks, or even a light meal may be served after the funeral at the home of the deceased's family.

Tribal African funerals follow very special rituals, with ancestors usually playing a major role. The funeral and mourning period can take days or even weeks to complete. Blacks living in South African cities often take leave from work to return to rural homeland areas to bury their relatives. Funerals are most often conducted according to indigenous traditions and tribal customs. Even among sophisticated Christian urbanites, an eldest son will carry out the ritual of sacrificing a bull at his father's funeral, in keeping with traditional practices.

Borrie is the Afrikaans word for turmeric or yellow. *Borrie rys* is customarily served with curry dishes, such as *denningvleis* (preceding recipe), or a stew, such as green bean and lamb bredie (recipe page 25). Historically this is known as "funeral rice" because it is often served at funeral feasts.

Borrie Rys

Turmeric Rice (also Funeral Rice)

Yield: serves 4

2 cups water
1 tablespoon butter or margarine
1 cup long-grain rice
½ teaspoon turmeric
½ teaspoon salt
¼ teaspoon cinnamon
¼ cup seedless raisins

Equipment: Medium saucepan with cover, mixing spoon, fork, serving bowl

In medium saucepan, heat water and butter or margarine over high heat until water boils. Stir in rice, turmeric, salt, and cinnamon. Reduce heat to **simmer**, cover, and cook for 15 to 20 minutes, until rice is tender. Remove from heat, add raisins, and fluff with fork. Cover and let rest 10 minutes before serving for flavor to develop.

To serve, transfer to serving bowl to accompany denningvleis *(recipe page 26) or* green bean and lamb bredie *(recipe page 25).*

All kinds of pies, both savory and sweet, are favored by South Africans. This *melk tart* is a classic recipe that all South Africans seem to love. It is included in the wedding banquet menus of several fine South African hotels.

Melk Tert

Milk Pie

Yield: serves 8

4½ tablespoons cornstarch
¾ cup sugar
¼ teaspoon salt
3½ cups milk
1 egg, beaten
½ teaspoon almond extract
½ teaspoon vanilla extract
1 (9-inch) frozen single-crust pie shell (baked according to directions on package)
cinnamon sugar, for **garnish**

Equipment: Small bowl, medium **heavy-based** saucepan, whisk, cake knife

1. In small bowl, combine cornstarch, sugar, and salt.

2. Pour milk into medium heavy-based saucepan, and whisk in egg and cornstarch mixture. Whisking constantly, cook over medium heat until thickened, 7 to 12 minutes. Do not boil. Reduce heat to low if necessary, to prevent burning. Whisk in almond and vanilla extracts. Cool to lukewarm and pour mixture into baked pie shell. Refrigerate until set, 3 to 4 hours. Before serving, sprinkle top with cinnamon sugar mixture.

To serve, cut in wedges and serve as dessert.

Cookies are often made into different shapes using a cookie cutter. For a christening party, the cookies might be cut into the shape of a teddy bear, a carriage, or a cradle. For weddings, heart shapes are popular.

Caramongscraps

Cardamom and Coconut Cookies

Yield: about 3 dozen

1½ cups all-purpose flour
½ teaspoon **ground** cardamom
1½ teaspoons baking powder
5 tablespoons butter or margarine, at room temperature
½ cup sugar

1 **egg yolk**
2 tablespoons milk
½ cup finely grated coconut
½ teaspoon grated **lemon peel**
1 cup chopped mixed candied fruit (available at all supermarkets)

Equipment: Flour **sifter**, medium mixing bowl, large mixing bowl, electric mixer or mixing spoon, lightly floured work surface, lightly floured rolling pin, 2-inch cookie cutter or water glass, 2 or 3 nonstick cookie sheets, oven mitts, metal spatula, wire cake rack, plate

1. **Sift** the flour, ground cardamom, and baking powder into medium mixing bowl.

2. Put butter or margarine in large mixing bowl, and using electric mixer or mixing spoon, beat until creamy, about 1 minute. Beat in sugar, a little at a time, until light and fluffy, 2 to 3 minutes. Beating constantly, add egg yolk, milk, and flour mixture, ½ cup at a time, beating well after each addition. Using mixing spoon, stir in the coconut and lemon peel.

Preheat oven to 350° F.

3. On lightly floured work surface, using lightly floured rolling pin, roll out dough to about 1/8 inch thick. Using cookie cutter or rim of glass, cut dough into desired shapes and place about ½ inch apart on cookie sheet. Press about ½ teaspoon candied fruit in center of each cookie. Bake in batches, if necessary.

4. Bake in oven for 10 to 12 minutes, or until the cookies are golden brown at the edges. Remove from oven and let cookies rest 10 minutes before using metal spatula to transfer to wire cake rack to cool.

To serve arrange cookies on plate. They keep well in tightly covered jar for 2 to 3 weeks.

LESOTHO

The tiny kingdom of Lesotho is totally surrounded by South Africa. With mainly natural borders, Lesotho is situated in rugged mountain terrain. The people call their country the "Kingdom in the Sky," since it claims to have the highest low-elevation point of any country in the world. The people are referred to as MoSotho (singular) and BaSotho (plural).

Cattle and horses are symbols of wealth in Lesotho. Goats are kept for slaughter, and angora goats and merino sheep provide most rural people with cash income from the mohair and wool. Flocks are tended by shepherd boys in their early teens, who are sent into the hills for a few years before returning to their villages as men to be given land of their own.

Most people in Lesotho are nominally Christian, primarily Roman Catholics. All life-milestone celebrations involve a combination of Christianity and indigenous beliefs. (See Protestant and Catholic Life-Cycle Rituals, page xlvi, and Traditional African Life-Cycle Rituals, page xli)

Newborns are baptized a few weeks after birth. Godmothers are selected for girls and godfathers for boys. After a church service, there is a family celebration and gifts are brought for the newborn.

Lesotho Christians take great pride in their children's accomplishments, especially their first communion. The parents of children who make their first communion together share the expenses for the day-long communal feast and celebration.

At death, the BaSotho are traditionally buried in a sitting position, facing the rising sun, "ready to leap up when called." All burials are followed by a communal feast, which includes one or two cows slaughtered for the occasion.

A stiff porridge, eaten throughout Africa, is called *putu* in Lesotho. It is known as *nsima* in Zambia and Malawi, *ugali* in Kenya and Tanzania, *oshifima* in Namibia, and *mealie-meal* in South Africa. It is the same as Italy's *polenta* and Romania's *mamaliga*, but in Africa this porridge is eaten at every meal. It also can be made with milk instead of water.

PUTU

STIFF CORNMEAL PORRIDGE

Yield: serves 4 to 6

1 cup white **cornmeal**
1 cup milk
1 cup water
1 teaspoon salt

Equipment: Small bowl, mixing spoon, medium saucepan, greased serving platter

1. Put cornmeal into small bowl and slowly stir in milk to make smooth paste.

2. Pour water into medium saucepan, add salt, and bring to boil over high heat. Stirring constantly, slowly add cornmeal paste and continue stirring for 2 or 4 minutes, until thickened. Reduce heat to low and stir frequently. Cook until mixture thickens, becomes stiff, and pulls away from sides of pan, 10 to 15 minutes. Remove from heat. Transfer to greased serving platter. Using greased or damp hands, shape into a smooth round loaf. *Putu* becomes firm, like a loaf of bread, when it cools.

To eat, tear off a small chunk and use it to scoop up stew and other foods or sauces.

During the wedding reception *dihotse* are set out in bowls for guests to munch on while they sit around, listen to speeches, and visit with friends. The seeds should be eaten one at a time to savor the flavor, not in handfuls.

DITHOTSE

ROASTED MELON SEEDS

Yield: serves 2 to 4

2 cups pumpkin or squash seeds
3 teaspoons salt

Equipment: **Colander**, large **heavy-based** skillet, metal spatula, small serving bowl

1. Put seeds in colander and wash under running water, rubbing them well to remove any pulp. Sprinkle wet seeds with salt and toss to mix well.

2. Heat dry heavy-based skillet over medium heat, and add salted seeds. Cook for 5 to 7 minutes, tossing constantly with metal spatula. Seeds are ready when they have cracked open.

To serve, put seeds in a small serving bowl and set out as a snack. The edible part of the seed is inside the shell.

ZIMBABWE

Zimbabwe is a landlocked country in south-central Africa surrounded by Botswana on the west, Mozambique on the east, South Africa on the south, and Zambia on the north. It was known as Rhodesia from 1895 to 1980. Today, more than 50 percent of the population are Christians, with the largest number belonging to the Roman Catholic Church. Most Zimbabweans combine local religions with Christianity. (See Protestant and Catholic Life-Cycle Rituals, page xlvi, and Traditional African Life-Cycle Rituals, page xli.)

In Zimbabwe, indigenous religious beliefs about the spirits of ancestors are widely held.

Ancestors, including recently deceased relatives, may speak to the living through human hosts. When these human hosts (or spirit mediums) enter a trance, they are thought to speak the words of the ancestor's spirit. The most important ancestors are great chiefs and storied warriors from centuries ago, and the mediums who are their living hosts hold a place of high status in society and are powerful and influential. The ancestor spirits are given attention and respect so that they will watch over and guard their descendants.

Weddings in Zimbabwe center around the bride-price. The Christian churches have discouraged bride-price, but it is an ancient tradition that continues among all but the most sophisticated and educated urbanites. Two payments are involved. In years past, the *rutsambo* (the first payment) was simply a hoe (a garden tool)—but now it is usually a large cash payment, along with whatever else the future father-in-law requests. This might be anything from new clothes for his family to livestock. Once *rutsambo* is paid, the couple can live together as husband and wife. The second payment, *roora*, is usually delivered in installments; it may be cash or cattle. The husband is in no hurry to hand over the final payments until he is fully satisfied that his wife will fulfill all of her obligations.

When Zimbabwe's president Robert Mugabe married in the early 1990s, the Roman Catholic Pope gave his blessing, well-wishers gave livestock, and dancers dressed in animal skins entertained the 6,000 guests. Wedding rings were exchanged, and the normally austere president sported red and white orchids on the lapel of his dark business suit. Among the wedding gifts were chickens, turkeys, and cattle. The Shona people gave pottery articles as part of the new bride's belongings.

The wedding feast included dozens of whole roasted steers (Zimbabwe is one of the world's great beef producers); game meat, such as crocodile, *kudu* (large antelope), and impala; cauldrons of rice; bean stews; vegetable stews made with tomatoes; *courgettes* (zucchini); corn on the cob; mixed greens; and a large quantity of tropical fruits, such as papayas, mangos, and bananas. Most people drank beer or an nonalcoholic drink called *shandy*, made with ginger beer, a few drops of angostura bitters, and soda water. Some preferred *rock shandy* made with lemonade, soda water, and angostura bitters—both are served over ice.

A wedding feast in Zimbabwe traditionally includes *sadza*—corn porridge—the same as *putu* (recipe page 29). When eaten with a sauce of vegetables or beans, it is called *sadza ne muriwo*. ۞ ۞ ۞

Sadza ne Muriwo

Vegetable Sauce with Cornmeal Porridge

Yield: serves 4

putu (recipe page 29)
2 tablespoons vegetable oil
1 onion, **finely chopped**
3 tomatoes, finely chopped or 16 ounces canned stewed tomatoes
salt and pepper to taste
4 cups (about 1 pound) shredded cabbage

Equipment: Medium saucepan with cover, mixing spoon, serving bowl

1. Prepare *putu* and keep warm.

2. Heat oil in medium saucepan over medium-high heat. Add onion, stir, and **sauté** until soft, 3 to 5 minutes. Add finely chopped or stewed tomatoes, and salt and pepper to taste, and shredded cabbage. Toss to mix and bring to boil.

Reduce heat to **simmer**, cover, and cook for 12 to 15 minutes, or until cabbage is tender.

Serve as a side dish with putu *in a separate serving bowl. To eat, take a handful of* putu *in your right hand, form it in a ball and use it to scoop up a little vegetable mixture to put into your mouth. The left hand must never touch food; it is used only for personal grooming.*

Sadza is often made with peanuts, such as *sauce arachide* (recipe page 67) or for special occasions, such as weddings and funerals, it is combined with *nyama* (meat).

Sadza ne Nyama

Cornmeal Porridge with Meat Stew

Yield: serves 4 to 6

putu (recipe page 29)
1 pound beef, cut into bite-size pieces
1 teaspoon **ground** cumin
1 teaspoon ground **cilantro**
ground red pepper to taste
2 tablespoons vegetable oil
2 onions, **finely chopped**
2 cloves garlic, finely chopped
2 cups water
1 cup coconut milk, homemade (recipe page 346) or canned
2 potatoes, peeled and chopped

Equipment: Large saucepan with cover or **Dutch oven**, mixing spoon, slotted spoon, plate

1. Prepare *putu.*

2. Sprinkle meat with cumin, cilantro, and ground red pepper to taste.

3. Heat oil in large saucepan or Dutch oven over medium-high heat. Add meat, stir, and **sauté** until browned on all sides, 5 to 7 minutes. Using slotted spoon, transfer meat to plate. Add onions and garlic to saucepan, stir, and sauté until onions are soft, 3 to 5 minutes. Return meat and juices on plate to pan. Add water, stir, and bring to boil. Reduce heat to **simmer**, cover, and cook for 30 to 40 minutes, or until meat is tender.

4. Stir in coconut milk, add potatoes, and carefully toss to stir. Cover and simmer for 25 to 30 minutes, until potatoes are tender.

Serve in a bowl, have putu *in separate container. Cooked rice is often served along with this dish.*

For Zimbabwean wedding and funeral feasts—to make sure there is plenty for everyone—dozens of side dishes, sauces, and stews are prepared to eat along with the roasted meat. One of the most popular stews is *dovi*.

Dovi

Beef Stew in Peanut Butter Sauce

Yield: serves 4 to 6

2 tablespoons vegetable oil
2 onions, **finely chopped**
2 cloves garlic, finely chopped
2 green bell peppers, **trimmed**, **seeded**, and chopped
2 pounds lean beef, **cubed**
4 tomatoes, chopped, or 16 ounces canned chopped tomatoes
2 cups water
½ cup smooth peanut butter
salt and pepper to taste
ground red pepper to taste
1 package (10 ounces) spinach or other greens, fresh or frozen (cooked according to directions on package), keep warm, for serving

Equipment: Large saucepan with cover or **Dutch oven**, mixing spoon, serving bowl

1. Heat oil in large saucepan or Dutch oven over medium-high heat. Add onions and garlic,

stir, and **sauté** until onions are soft, 3 to 5 minutes. Add green pepper, cubed beef, fresh or canned tomatoes, and water. Bring to boil and stir. Reduce heat to **simmer**, cover, and cook until beef is tender, 35 to 45 minutes.

2. Thin peanut butter with about ½ cup hot liquid from pan until mixture has consistency of pancake batter. Stir in half the peanut butter mixture to meat mixture. Add salt and pepper to taste and ground red pepper to taste. Continue to cook, uncovered until sauce thickens, 20 to 25 minutes.

3. Transfer cooked spinach or greens to serving bowl, and pour remaining half of peanut butter mixture over them.

Serve dovi *in one bowl and spinach or greens in another. The greens and meat stew are eaten together. Using the fingers of your right hand, take a little meat mixture and then greens at the same time, pop into your mouth. The left hand must never touch food; it is used only for personal grooming.*

BOTSWANA

Botswana, a landlocked country in southern Africa, is one of the world's most sparsely populated nations. About 90 percent of the Batswana people, as they are called, live along the country's eastern border, which it shares with South Africa and Zimbabwe. It shares the western border with Namibia.

Farming and herding have been the traditional means of subsistence, but today that is changing. Since Botswana's independence in 1966, the population shift to urban areas has been overwhelming. Due to the country's high unemployment, many men have turned to South Africa for work in mines and on farms.

About 60 percent of the Botswana are Christians. However, indigenous religions and traditional beliefs remain important to all Batswana, even those who have become Christians. Traditional rituals are commonly combined with Christian rituals. (See Protestant and Catholic Life-Cycle Rituals, page xlvi, and Traditional African Life-Cycle Rituals, page xli.)

Weddings among the *San* (Bushmen) of Botswana's Kalahari involve a considerable amount of ritual. Prior to the wedding day, the bride fasts in silence, and for four days she remains in a branch enclosure that is set up outside the village. At the end of the period of seclusion, the village women shave the heads of the bride and groom, who are then bathed and prepared for scarification. In this ceremony, they are cut simultaneously and their blood is intermingled as a symbol of their union. When the pattern of cuts has been completed on their bodies, a mixture of ashes and medicinal roots is rubbed into the cuts to ensure the formation of raised scars. Scarification is a way of announcing that the couple has gone through a purification ritual.

Wedding and funeral feasts in Botswana almost always include tripe, the stomach lining of an animal (usually a cow). The honeycomb tripe from the second stomach of a cow is the most tender and flavorful. When properly prepared, it is considered a delicacy in many parts of the world.

MOGODU

TRIPE IN TOMATO SAUCE

Note: This recipe takes 2 days.

Yield: served 6

2 pounds oven-ready honey comb tripe (available at some supermarkets and most butchers; honey comb tripe has been

partially cooked by the meat packing company.)
- water, as needed
- 1½ teaspoons salt, or more as needed
- 1½ cups milk
- 1 onion, finely sliced
- 3 tomatoes, **peeled** and **finely chopped** or 16 ounces canned whole tomatoes, chopped
- 1 bay leaf
- 3 tablespoons vegetable oil
- 3 tablespoons all-purpose flour

Equipment: Knife, medium bowl with cover, medium saucepan with cover, tongs, work surface, medium **heavy-based** saucepan with cover or **Dutch oven**, mixing spoon, medium serving bowl

1. Preparing oven-ready honey comb tripe before cooking: Using knife, trim and discard any gristle, and wash tripe thoroughly under cold running water. Place in medium bowl and cover generously with cold water. Cover and refrigerate to soak overnight. Discard water and transfer tripe to a medium saucepan. Add fresh cold water to cover and 1 teaspoon salt. Bring to boil, quickly reduce heat to **simmer**, and cook for 15 minutes. Drain and discard water. (The tripe must always be cooked very gently or it will become tough and rubbery.)

2. Wash and dry medium saucepan or use new medium saucepan. Pour milk into clean medium saucepan and add 2 cups fresh cold water, ½ teaspoon salt, and prepared tripe. Heat over medium-high heat until small bubbles appear around edge of pan. Reduce heat to simmer, cover, and cook for 1 hour.

3. Remove tripe with tongs, drain excess over pan, and place on work surface. Cut tripe into strips about ½ inch wide and 3 to 4 inches long. Set aside milk mixture.

4. Heat oil in second medium heavy-based saucepan or Dutch oven over medium-high heat. Add onions, stir, and **sauté** until soft 3 to 5 minutes. Reduce heat to simmer, and add tomatoes and bay leaf.

5. Combine flour and ½ cup milk mixture to make **slurry**. Stir slurry into onion mixture. Stirring constantly, add remaining milk mixture left in first saucepan. Add tripe and stir to coat. Cover and cook for 1 hour, or until tripe is very tender. Remove and discard bay leaf. Add salt and pepper to taste.

To serve, transfer to serving bowl and serve with rice, boiled potatoes, or noodles.

In Botswana's urban areas, a favorite way of celebrating a birth, a first communion, or a birthday is by having a *braii* (barbecue). A large amount of meat, usually goat, is spit-roasted for the occasion. For wealthier families, beef is the meat of choice. Stuffing yourself is a tribute to the host; it shows that you are aware he can afford the luxury of meat.

Beverages are usually drunk after the meal, not with it. In the cities and among men in the villages, beer and palm wine are favorite party drinks. In the villages, older men and women drink mild alcoholic home brews, either *bojalwa*, made from sorghum, or *kadi*, made from fermented roots and sugar.

Mealie-meal is the same as Lesotho's *putu* (recipe page 29)—a staple that is served at almost every meal. At tea time it is served thinned, while at other times it is thickened and served with sauce and/or *mopani*. *Mopani* are caterpillars that are cooked in hot ash for 15 minutes, boiled in salt water, or sun-dried. Dried *mopani* are either deep-fried, roasted, eaten raw, or ground up.

Samosas made their way from India to Botswana by way of South Africa. They are a favorite finger food that is prepared for every celebration feast.

Samosas Nama ya kgomo

Ground Meat Fritters

CAUTION: HOT OIL USED

Yield: about 15 pieces

2 tablespoons vegetable oil, divided
½ pound lean **ground** pork
1 medium onion, **finely chopped**
2 cloves garlic, finely chopped
1 medium potato, **parboiled**, peeled, and finely **diced**
½ teaspoon ground red pepper, more or less to taste
¼ cup finely chopped fresh **coriander** leaves
salt and pepper to taste
15 frozen square egg roll wrappers, thawed (available in all Asian food stores and in the freezer section of most supermarkets)
vegetable oil for deep frying

Equipment: Small skillet, mixing spoon, medium mixing bowl, work surface, knife, damp kitchen towel, large plate, **deep fryer**, deep-fryer **thermometer** or wooden spoon, baking sheet, paper towels, wooden spoon, slotted metal spoon or metal tongs

1. Heat 1 tablespoon oil in small skillet over medium-high heat. Crumble in ground pork, stir, and **sauté** until browned, 3 to 5 minutes. Transfer pork to medium mixing bowl. Add remaining 1 tablespoon oil to small skillet and heat over medium-high heat. Add onion and garlic, stir, and sauté until onion is soft, 3 to 5 minutes. Add garlic mixture to pork in medium mixing bowl. Add diced potato, ½ teaspoon ground red pepper, more or less to taste, coriander leaves, and salt and pepper to taste. Toss to mix well.

2. Using knife, cut thawed egg roll wrappers in half to make 3- x 6-inch strips. Work with one strip at a time, keeping the others covered with damp towel to prevent drying out.

3. Fill pastries: Place a cup with water near work surface. Place 1 egg roll wrapper strip on work surface. Spoon 1 tablespoon meat mixture centered at one end of strip, about 2 inches up from bottom edge. Fold a corner of the bottom edge diagonally over the filling to meet the other side, forming a triangle. Moisten finger in cup of water and dab along the 2 open edges to dampen. Press down on the edges to seal in filling. Repeat making egg roll wrappers into triangular packages. Place each package on large plate.

Repeat assembling pastries.

4. Prepare deep fryer: ADULT SUPERVISION REQUIRED. Place several layers of paper towels on baking sheet. Heat oil to 375° F on fryer thermometer or oil is hot enough when small bubbles appear around wooden spoon handle when dipped in oil. Deep fry in small batches, 3 or 4 at a time, until golden brown, 2 to 3 minutes. Remove with slotted metal spoon or metal tongs and drain on paper towels.

To serve, place pastries on platter and eat while still warm for best flavor. Hot pepper sauce or ground red pepper is often sprinkled on the fritters. Have guests help themselves using only the fingers of the right hand. The left hand is used for personal grooming; it must never touch food.

NAMIBIA

Namibia, located along the Atlantic coast of southern Africa, is bordered by Angola and Zambia on the north, Botswana on the east, and South Africa on the south. It gained independence in 1990. Namibia means "place of no people," but the country is hardly that. The population includes 10 ethnic groups (4 of which predominate), along with a large group of coloureds (people of mixed ancestry) and Afrikaners (whites with ties to South Africa). Many urban Namibians have adopted Western ways, but in rural areas, traditional life ways are still practiced.

Most Namibians profess Christianity, with the majority affiliated with the German Lutheran sect of Protestantism. (See Protestant and Catholic Life-Cycle Rituals, page xlvi.) However, Church views on certain issues, especially on marriage, have been untenable for many Namibians. According to traditional beliefs, a man has the right to refuse to take as his wife any woman who is unable to get pregnant, although Christian churches consider premarital sex inappropriate. In actuality, many nominal Christians in Namibia have a church wedding only after the birth of the first child.

At puberty, women of the Himba ethnic group shave the front and top of their heads, leaving the hair in back long, which they braid with strands of plant fibers. After marriage, they take locks of hair from their brothers and their new husband and braid it in with their own. Their plaited hair is also plastered with a mixture of butter, ash, and ochre.

Every life-cycle celebration calls for a feast. Among the pastoral Herero and Himba ethnic groups, cattle—a form of wealth—are slaughtered only on very special occasions. Along with beef roasted on a spit, *oshifima*, which is the same as *putu* (recipe page 29), would be served with this dish of fresh black-eyed peas. ۞ ۞ ۞

Oshingali

Black-eyed Peas

Yield: serves 4

4 cups **black-eyed peas**, fresh or frozen (thawed)
1 teaspoon salt
ground red pepper, to taste

Equipment: Large bowl, **colander**, large saucepan with cover, mixing spoon

1. Prepare fresh black-eyed peas: Put fresh peas in large bowl and cover generously with cold water. Soak for about 5 minutes to soften. Using both hands, rub and gently squeeze the peas as they continue to soak. The skins will loosen and float to the top. Skim off and discard skins as they float to the top. Drain peas in colander and rinse under cold running water.

2. Put prepared fresh or frozen peas in large saucepan, and add just enough water to cover peas. Bring to boil over medium-high heat. Reduce heat to **simmer**, cover, and cook until tender. When tender, sprinkle in salt and ground red pepper to taste.

Serve, along with the cooking water, over oshifima *or another porridge such as* tuo zaafi *(recipe page 64).*

Groundnuts (peanuts) are plentiful in Namibia. For this recipe the peanuts can be either boiled or **roasted**. If using roasted peanuts, simply sprinkle them over the cooked spinach or other greens before serving. This recipe is made with boiled peanuts.

Um'bido

Greens and Peanuts

Yield: serves 6

water, as needed
1 cup shelled, skinless peanuts
2 packages (10 ounces each) spinach or other greens, fresh or frozen (thawed)
2 tablespoons butter or margarine
salt and pepper to taste

Equipment: Medium saucepan with cover, mixing spoon, **colander**, serving bowl

1. Fill medium saucepan halfway with water and bring to boil over high heat. Add shelled, skinless peanuts, and bring back to boil. Reduce heat to **simmer**, cover, and cook for 20 to 25

minutes, until soft. Add spinach or other greens and stir. Cover and cook 5 to 7 minutes, or until tender. Place colander in sink and drain spinach mixture.

2. Transfer to serving bowl, toss with butter or margarine, and sprinkle with salt and pepper to taste.

Serve with stiff porridge and oshingali *(recipe precedes).*

Peanuts are an important food in Namibia. *Kuli-kuli* is often served with stews, sauces, and soups, or crumbled over boiled yams, cassava, and mashed plantains.

Kuli-Kuli (also Kulikuli)

Peanut Patties

CAUTION: HOT OIL USED

Yield: about 12 patties

2 pounds shelled, **roasted** peanuts
¼ cup peanut oil, more or less as needed
1 onion, **finely chopped**
ground red pepper, to taste
peanut oil, for **deep-frying**

Equipment: **Blender**, rubber spatula, medium bowl, medium skillet, slotted metal spoon, wax paper, work surface, **deep fryer**, paper towels, baking sheet, deep-fryer **thermometer** or wooden spoon, napkin-lined bread basket

1. Put nuts in blender and **blend**, switching blender on and off, until nuts are broken into small pieces. While blender is running, slowly **drizzle** just enough of the ¼ cup oil through feed tube until mixture is a smooth paste, adding more if needed. Transfer to medium bowl.

2. Heat 1 tablespoon oil in medium skillet over medium-high heat. Add onion and **sauté** until soft, 3 to 5 minutes. Stir in ground red pepper to taste and salt to taste. Add to ground peanuts in medium bowl. Gather into a ball and mixture should hold together.

3. Divide dough into 12 equal balls and flatten each into a patty. Place on wax-paper-covered work surface.

4. Prepare deep fryer: ADULT SUPERVISION REQUIRED. Place several layers of paper towels on baking sheet. Heat oil to 375° F on fryer thermometer or oil is hot enough when small bubbles appear around a wooden spoon handle when it is dipped in the oil. Deep fry in small batches, 3 or 4 at a time, until golden brown and crisp on both sides, 2 to 3 minutes. Remove with slotted metal spoon and drain on paper towels.

Serve the patties in a napkin-lined bread basket and eat as you would biscuits. Kuli-kuli *keeps well in an airtight container for up to one week.*

ANGOLA

Angola is on the southwest coast of Africa, bordered by the Democratic Republic of the Congo and the Republic of Congo to the north, Zambia to the east, and Namibia to south. In the late 1400s, Portuguese colonists—slave traders and farmers—began settling in Angola. These Portuguese colonists imported chili peppers, maize, tobacco, tomatoes, pineapples, sweet potatoes, manioc, and bananas to Angola from Latin America. They also planted orange, lemon, and lime trees, and they introduced the domestic pig into Africa. Angola broke from Portugal and gained its independence in 1975.

The largest ethnic group in Angola is the Mbundu people, about half of whom are Christians, mostly Roman Catholics. Most Angolan Christians combine Church teachings with traditional religious practices when celebrating important life-cycle events. (See

Protestant and Catholic Life-Cycle Rituals, page xlvi, and Traditional African Life-Cycle Rituals, page xli.)

Baptism ceremonies take place within a few weeks after birth. The ceremony is followed by a celebration with singing, dancing, and a huge feast. Guests are expected to bring gifts for both the mother and the father, usually a small amount of money. Typically, a pig is slaughtered and roasted (recipe page 348) for the occasion.

As in many other parts of Africa, when boys reach puberty, they go through secret rituals to mark their transition to manhood. They are taken away to a camp for a month of seclusion where they are circumcised, educated in the social and moral values of the community, and put through rigorous tests of endurance. During this rite of passage, the leaders wear elaborate costumes representing the spirits of deceased chiefs and heroes. After the month-long process, the boys return to the village as "new men." Upon their return, there is a great celebration with a communal feast—ideally, meat roasted on a spit.

In Angola, a wedding ceremony can be very simple or quite lavish, depending on the family's wealth. If the family is poor, the ceremony is likely to be at home with just the couple, their families, and a religious leader. More expensive weddings might involve the entire community and take place in a rented celebration hall with music, dancing, and great quantities of food. Among Angola's Bantu people, cattle and sheep are currency, and meat is eaten only at wedding and funeral feasts.

The Angolans learned how to prepare and cook **salt cod** from the Portuguese. Today, Angolans love it as much as the Portuguese do. It is often on the menu at a celebration feast. Salt cod must be soaked overnight to soften it and to remove salt before cooking.

❂ ❂ ❂

Bacalhau Gomes Sa

Salt Cod with Boiled Potatoes

Note: This recipe takes 2 days.

Yield: serves 4 to 6

1 to 2 pounds dried **salt cod** (available at all Latin American food stores and some supermarkets)
water, as needed
3 bay leaves
6 medium potatoes, washed
¼ cup olive oil
2 onions, chopped
2 cloves garlic, **finely chopped**
1 green pepper, **trimmed**, seeded, and chopped
¼ teaspoon oregano
½ cup fresh parsley, finely chopped
12 black olives, for **garnish**
3 hard-cooked eggs, shelled and sliced, for garnish

Equipment: Medium bowl, work surface, medium saucepan, slotted spoon, plate, **colander**, knife, vegetable peeler, large **heavy-based** skillet, mixing spoon, serving platter

1. Put salt cod in medium bowl and cover with plenty of cold water. Set on work surface to soak overnight. The next day transfer fish to medium saucepan, and discard soaking water. Cover fish generously with fresh cold water, add bay leaves, and bring to boil over medium-high heat. Reduce heat to **simmer** and cook 20 minutes. Using slotted spoon, remove fish and transfer to plate. Discard cooking liquid and clean medium saucepan.

2. Put potatoes in clean medium saucepan and cover generously with fresh water. Bring to boil over high heat. Reduce heat to simmer, cover, and cook until tender, not mushy, 15 to 20 minutes. Drain potatoes in colander. When cool enough to handle, peel and chop into bite-size pieces.

3. Heat oil in large heavy-based skillet. Add onions, garlic, and green pepper. Stir and sauté until onions and pepper are soft, 3 to 5 minutes. Reduce heat to medium, add potatoes, oregano, and parsley. Toss to mix well. Break fish into bite-size chunks and carefully **fold in** to onion mixture. Heat through, 3 to 5 minutes.

To serve, transfer to serving platter and garnish with olives and egg slices.

Traditionally, *caldeirada* is made with goat. Lamb, which is more easily available, is recommended for this recipe.

Caldeirada de Cabrito

Lamb and Potato Casserole

Yield: serves 4 to 6

4 slices bacon, **coarsely chopped**
2 pounds lean boneless lamb shoulder, cut into 2-inch chunks
salt to taste
2 tablespoons vegetable oil
2 onions, **finely chopped**
2 cloves garlic, finely chopped
1 green bell pepper, seeded, **trimmed**, and **coarsely chopped**
2 cups canned tomatoes, chopped and drained
3 tablespoons finely chopped fresh parsley, or 2 teaspoons dried parsley flakes
½ teaspoon **ground** red pepper, more or less to taste
½ teaspoon ground cloves
2 tablespoons finely chopped fresh **coriander**, or 2 teaspoons dried crushed cilantro leaves
4 potatoes, washed, peeled, and cut crosswise into ¼-inch slices
2 bay leaves
1½ cups water

Equipment: Large **heavy-based** skillet, slotted spoon, paper towels, plate, ladle, heatproof casserole with cover or **Dutch oven**

1. Fry bacon in large heavy-based skillet over medium-high heat until lightly browned but not crisp. Using slotted spoon, transfer bacon to drain on paper towels.

2. Sprinkle lamb on all sides with salt to taste. Add oil to bacon fat remaining in skillet and heat over medium-high heat. Add lamb, 8 to 10 pieces at a time, and turning frequently, brown on all sides, 7 to 12 minutes. Transfer cooked pieces of lamb to plate. Continue to fry in batches until all lamb pieces are browned.

3. Add onions, garlic, and bell pepper to skillet. Stirring constantly, **sauté** until onions and pepper are soft, 3 to 5 minutes. If necessary, lower heat to prevent burning. Add chopped canned tomatoes, stir, and cook for 5 to 7 minutes for flavors to develop. Remove from heat. Stir in parsley, ½ teaspoon ground red pepper, more or less to taste, ground cloves, coriander or dried cilantro leaves, and drained bacon pieces. Add salt to taste and stir well.

4. Ladle about 1 cup tomato mixture into heatproof casserole or Dutch oven and spread to coat bottom. Spread half of the sliced potatoes on top. Add half of the lamb and cover with another cup of tomato mixture. Spread remaining potatoes evenly in the casserole. Add remaining lamb pieces and any liquid that accumulated from them. Ladle remaining tomato mixture over the top. Tuck bay leaves down into casserole or Dutch oven and pour water around sides of mixture.

5. Set casserole or Dutch oven over medium-high heat and bring to boil. Reduce heat to **simmer**, cover, and cook 1 to 1½ hours, until meat is tender. Before serving, remove and discard bay leaves.

Serve directly from cooking container and have plenty of broa *(recipe follows) for sopping up the sauce.*

The Portuguese colonists brought their breads to Angola, where bread is now part of the national cuisine. *Broa* is one of Portugal's favorite breads.

Broa

Portuguese Corn Bread

Yield: 1 loaf

1½ cups **cornmeal**, divided
1½ teaspoons salt
1 cup boiling water
1 tablespoon vegetable oil
1 package active dry **yeast**
1 teaspoon sugar
¼ cup **lukewarm** water
2 cups sifted all-purpose flour, more or less as needed

Equipment: **Blender** or food processor, rubber spatula, large mixing bowl, mixing spoon, plastic food wrap, lightly floured work surface, kitchen towel, lightly greased baking sheet, oven mitts, wire cake rack

1. Pulverize cornmeal in blender or food processor, ½ cup at a time, until fine and powdery. The bread can be made without this step but the bread texture will not be as smooth.

2. Put 1 cup powdered cornmeal and salt into large mixing bowl. Stirring constantly, slowly pour in boiling water. Stir until smooth. Stir in oil and let cool to lukewarm.

3. Stir to dissolve yeast and sugar into lukewarm water, leave for 5 to 10 minutes, until **froth** forms.

4. When cornmeal mixture is lukewarm, stir in yeast mixture. Beat in remaining cornmeal and 1 cup all-purpose flour to make soft dough. If mixture is sticky, add ¼ cup flour at a time, until smooth and no longer sticky. Cover with plastic wrap and set in warm place to rise to double in bulk, 30 to 40 minutes.

5. Transfer dough to lightly floured work surface, **punch down** and **knead** in ¾ to 1 cup flour, enough to make firm dough. Knead for 3 to 5 minutes until dough is smooth and **elastic**. Shape dough into a round ball, place on lightly greased baking sheet and flatten to about 7 inches across. Cover with towel and let rise in warm place to double in bulk, 30 to 40 minutes.

Preheat oven to 350° F.

6. Bake in oven for 45 to 50 minutes, until golden brown and done. Test the **bread doneness**. Transfer to wire cake rack to cool.

Serve bread fresh from the oven for best flavor. Cut into slices or break into chunks and use to sop up gravies and juices.

The Portuguese influence in Angola is evident in many dishes, including this dessert pudding. Desserts are something most Africans know nothing about. African languages have no word for dessert, so this dessert is called pudding. This would be served as a refreshing ending at a first communion dinner or wedding feast.

Cocada Amarela

Yellow Coconut Pudding

Yield: serves 8

2 cups sugar
6 cups water
4 whole cloves
4 cups unsweetened finely grated coconut, homemade (recipe page 346), or canned (available at all Latin American food stores and most supermarkets)
12 eggs
ground cinnamon, for **garnish**

Equipment: Medium saucepan, mixing spoon, candy **thermometer** or cup cold water, slotted spoon, medium mixing bowl, whisk, individual dessert dishes

1. Put sugar, water, and cloves into medium saucepan. Stirring constantly, bring to boil over medium-high heat. Continue to boil briskly without stirring until syrup reaches 230° F on candy thermometer, or when a few drops spooned into a cup of cold water immediately forms coarse threads, 15 to 20 minutes. Reduce heat to low and with slotted spoon, remove and discard cloves. Add coconut, 1 cup at a time, stirring well after each addition. Continue to cook, stirring frequently, for 8 to 10 minutes, or until coconut becomes translucent. Remove pan from heat.

2. In medium mixing bowl, beat egg yolks with whisk until slightly thickened, about 1 minute.

3. **Temper** eggs: Stirring constantly, pour 1 cup hot coconut mixture into eggs and beat well. Slowly pour tempered egg mixture into coconut syrup, stirring constantly, until well mixed. Stirring frequently, cook over medium heat until mixture thickens enough to pull away from sides of pan, 7 to 12 minutes.

4. Spoon mixture into individual dessert dishes.

Serve at room temperature or refrigerate for about 2 hours. Before serving, sprinkle lightly with cinnamon.

DEMOCRATIC REPUBLIC OF THE CONGO

In 1997, Zaire—once known as the Belgian Congo—was renamed the Democratic Republic of the Congo. The nation is surrounded by Congo Republic, the Central African Republic, the Sudan, Uganda, Rwanda, Burundi, Tanzania, Zambia, Angola, and the Atlantic Ocean.

Ruled by Belgium for many years, as the former name implies, the Democratic Republic of the Congo won its independence in 1960. Since its independence, the country has been dominated by dictators, particularly Joseph-Desiré Mobutu. It was Mobutu who renamed the country Zaire, and the new name was chosen after Mobutu was overthrown.

Seventy-five percent of the nation's people are Christians, mostly Roman Catholics. All life-cycle celebrations are a combination of Christian and traditional rituals. (See Protestant and Catholic Life-Cycle Rituals, page xlvi, and Traditional African Life-Cycle Rituals, page xli.)

Urban women in the Democratic Republic of the Congo enjoy freedoms that women of marriageable age living in rural villages would not be permitted to have. Traditionally, parents choose a young woman's husband, arrange the marriage with his parents, and accept the dowry.

Fish are caught in the many rivers and lakes that run through the country. This dish would be prepared in large quantities to serve guests at a wedding or mourners at a funeral feast.

Mbisi ye Kalou na Loso

Fish and Kale

Yield: serves 6

- 3 tablespoons vegetable oil
- 1 onion, **finely chopped**
- 1 bell pepper, stemmed, **seeded**, and chopped
- 1 (10-ounce) box frozen kale, thawed
- 1 cup water
- 1½ pounds fresh skinless firm fish **fillets**, cut into finger-size pieces (cod, red snapper, catfish, trout, or halibut)
- salt and pepper to taste
- **ground** red pepper to taste

Equipment: Medium saucepan with cover or **Dutch oven**, mixing spoon, fork

1. Heat oil in medium saucepan or Dutch oven over medium-high heat. Add onion and green pepper. Stir and **sauté** until onion is soft, 3 to 5 minutes.

2. Add kale and water, and bring to boil. Lay fish pieces over the top and sprinkle with salt and pepper to taste and ground red pepper to taste. Reduce heat to **simmer**, cover, and cook for 15 to 20 minutes, or until fish flakes easily when pierced with a fork.

Serve as main course with sliced yams or sweet potatoes.

ZAMBIA

In south-central Africa, the landlocked nation of Zambia is surrounded by Angola, Zaire, Tanzania, Malawi, Mozambique, Zimbabwe, Botswana, and Namibia. A British colony that was federated as Northern Rhodesia at one time, Zambia became an independent country in 1964.

Zambia has more than 70 ethnic groups—but no single group is predominant. More than half the population is Christian, the majority of whom are Roman Catholics.

The population of Zambia is divided almost equally between subsistence farmers and those who have left rural life to live in the modern cities. When Zambians move away from the farms that were passed down to them from previous generations, they give up their right to the land. They also give up kinship with the ethnic group of which they have been part. To take the place that kinship groups occupy in rural life, regional self-help societies have sprung up in cities to give people a place to turn in times of need.

Due to the high infant mortality rate, babies in Zambia are baptized soon after birth. Other than attending church for the ceremony, there is not much festivity. However, when children reach the age of 9 or 10 and have their first communion, there is always a large communal celebration. Children by this time are on the road to a healthy life, and a celebration is in order.

When boys and girls reach puberty, they go through coming-of-age ceremonies. For boys, secret initiation ceremonies take them to a remote area to be circumcised and then to hunt and learn about the rituals and customs of their people. An important part of the girls' ceremony is instructions on being a wife and mother.

Before marriage, *lobola*—bride-price—is paid by a groom to the bride's father. Traditionally, *lobola* was paid in cattle, and for those with no cattle, payment was made in the form of services performed by the groom. The payment is a form of insurance, meant to protect the bride from being badly treated by her husband. It can be returned to the husband's family if the wife finds cause to leave him, although that is rare.

Zambians do not ordinarily eat meat. Cattle are a form of wealth, and they are slaughtered only on important occasions such as weddings and funerals. Maize (corn) was introduced to Africa from South America about 200 years ago, and it has been an important food ever since. *Nshima*, a Zambia specialty, is usually served with sauce made from spinach or other greens. This is a favorite dish to add to the feast menu for a first communion, wedding, or funeral. Cornmeal porridge without the sauce of greens is called *bidia* in the Democratic Republic of the Congo, *nshima* in Zambia, and *putu* (recipe page 29) in Lesotho. ۞ ۞ ۞

Nshima

Cornmeal Porridge with Sauce of Greens

Yield: serves 4 to 6

4 tablespoons vegetable oil, divided
1 onion, sliced
2 tomatoes, **finely chopped**
2 pounds fresh spinach or fresh **broccoli rabe**, rinsed, **trimmed**, and drained well
salt and pepper to taste
4 cups water
1 cup coarsely **ground** yellow **cornmeal**

Equipment: Large saucepan with cover, wooden mixing spoon, medium saucepan, small serving bowl, serving platter

1. Prepare sauce: Heat 2 tablespoons oil in large saucepan over medium-high heat. Add onion, stir, and **sauté** for 3 to 5 minutes until soft. Add remaining 2 tablespoons oil, tomatoes, spinach or broccoli rabe, and salt and pepper to taste. Reduce heat to **simmer**, cover, and cook until wilted and tender—3 to 6 minutes for broccoli rabe and 7 to 12 minutes for spinach. Keep warm until ready to serve.

2. Prepare porridge: Pour water into medium saucepan and bring to boil over high heat. Stirring constantly, slowly add cornmeal. Reduce heat to low, stir frequently and cook for 15 minutes, or until mixture pulls away from sides of pan. Remove from heat, sprinkle in salt and pepper to taste, and stir.

To serve, put sauce in small serving bowl and put porridge on a serving platter. As the porridge cools it gets firm. To eat nshima, *pull off a small chunk of porridge and use it to scoop up the sauce.*

Throughout the world, corn and beans are two crops commonly grown together. The beans return to the soil the nutrients taken out by the corn. Before harvesting, the corn is usually left on the stalk to dry. The hard kernels of either white or yellow corn are removed from the cob, pounded, and soaked for a couple of days in slaked lime or lye to break up the grain; the hull and germ are removed. What is left is sun dried and sold as **hominy**. When hominy is broken into fairly large pieces or is very coarsely ground, it's called samp or pearl hominy. When finely ground, it's called hominy grits or simply grits, a cereal beloved in the southern United States. Samp is not easily available, and a good substitute for this recipe is canned hominy. *Samp ye dinawa* would be one of the many side dishes served with meat at a wedding feast or other life-cycle celebration.

Samp ye Dinawa

Corn and Bean Mash

Yield: serves 4 to 6

2 tablespoons vegetable oil
1 onion, **finely chopped**
1 tomato, chopped
1 (14 ounces) canned **hominy**, drained (available at all supermarkets)
2 (14 ounces each) canned red beans
salt and pepper to taste
½ teaspoon **ground** red pepper, more or less to taste

Equipment: Large skillet with cover, mixing spoon

Heat oil in large skillet over medium-high heat. Add onion, stir, and **sauté** until soft, 3 to 5 minutes. Add chopped tomatoes, stir, and cook until soft, 2 to 3 minutes. Add drained hominy, red beans with juice, salt and pepper to taste, and ½ teaspoon ground red pepper, more or less to taste. Stir, reduce heat to **simmer**, cover, and cook for 12 to 15 minutes, to heat through and to blend flavors.

Serve as a side dish with meat.

Lemon grass grows throughout this region of Africa. Lemon grass tea is a popular refreshing drink for those who prefer something other than beer at celebration feasts.

Zanibta or Malava

Lemon Grass Tea

Yield: serves 2

3 leaves of fresh **lemon grass**
2 cups boiling water
sugar, to taste

Equipment: teapot, spoon, strainer, cup

Put tea leaves in teapot and pour in boiling water. Leave to infuse for 3 minutes. If you wish to add sugar to taste, add it now. Stir and strain tea into cup.

Serve tea while hot, adding more sugar if necessary.

RWANDA AND BURUNDI

Rwanda and Burundi are small and very similar nations in central Africa that border one another. The two landlocked nations are surrounded by the Democratic Republic of the Congo, Uganda, and Tanzania.

In both, nearly every family lives in a self-contained compound, and the few urban areas are grouped around government centers. Both countries have three ethnic groups: the Hutu, the Tutsi, and the Twa (tropical forest foragers, sometimes called Pygmies). The Hutu make up the largest part of the population, while only about 15 percent of the people are Tutsi, and less than 1 percent are Twa. European missionaries arrived in the region around 1890, and today most people are Roman Catholics. In practice, almost all combine indigenous religions with Catholic rituals. (See Protestant and Catholic Life-Cycle Rituals, page xlvi; and Traditional African Life-Cycle Rituals, page xli.)

When the Tutsi settled in the Rwanda and Burundi area several centuries ago, the Hutu were living there as well-established farmers. The Tutsi were herders, to whom cattle-owning meant wealth, prestige, and power. The Tutsi took control of the region, reducing the Hutu to serfdom through a contract known as *ubuhake*, an agreement whereby the Hutu would serve the Tutsi in exchange for protection and for the use, but not the ownership, of cattle.

Over time, there have been many intermarriages between the Tutsi and the Hutu, and the distinction between them has become one of class rather than of ethnicity. If you are wealthy, it is thought, you must be a Tutsi—even if you were born a Hutu. If, as a Tutsi, you became poor, you are looked down upon and called a Hutu.

Ever since the Tutsi's arrival, they have used their cattle as a form of wealth. For instance, before a wedding, the groom's family traditionally gives a cow to the bride's family. During the *gusaba*—the bride-price ceremony—the bride's family refers to her as *mutumwinka* ("you are exchanged for a cow"). The cow symbolizes the union between the two families.

Because of the importance of cattle, people associate *amata* (milk) with happiness, and because wealthy Tutsi and Hutu drank *ubuki* (an alcoholic beverage made from fermented honey), *ubuki* is associated with success and good fortune. Before long, the combination of milk and honey became sacred. All Rwandans greet friends at the New Year with "*Uzagire umwaka w'amata n'ubuki*" ("Have a year of milk and honey").

An important tradition at weddings is sharing a beverage, *ubuki* mixed with milk, from a washtub-sized bowl. After the bride and groom take the first sips, three or four people at a time take turns sipping the beverage through three-foot-long reed straws. The proportion of milk to *ubuki* varies, according to taste.

Kubandwa are puberty rites to initiate young boys, about 12 years old, into adulthood. The young Hutu and Tutsi male initiates are circumcised then go through rigorous endurance exercises. On their return to their families, there is always a large communal feast with whole roasted bull, mutton, or lamb (recipe page 141). After the puberty rites, men become *intore* (warriors) before they marry and settle down.

The following recipe, *Ibiharage*, is one of the many side dishes served for the communal feast.

IBIHARAGE

FRIED BEANS

Yield: serves 4 to 6

2 tablespoons vegetable oil
3 onions, **finely chopped**
2 cloves garlic, finely chopped
4 cups cooked white beans, canned or homemade (follow directions on package)
salt and pepper to taste
ground red pepper to taste

Equipment: Large skillet, mixing spoon

Heat oil in large skillet over medium-high heat. Add onions and garlic. Stir and **sauté** until onions are soft, 3 to 5 minutes. Add beans, salt and pepper to taste, and ground red pepper to taste, stir, reduce heat to **simmer** and cook for 7 to 12 minutes to heat through and for flavor to develop.

Serve as a side dish with meat.

Cassava (also manioc) is a **tuber** that is a nutritious starch, like potatoes. It is used to thicken soups and stews. As African slaves traveled, cassava has traveled too—for instance, it is used by cooks in the West Indies and Brazil, where it is known as *farinhe de mandioca*.

MUHOGO TAMU

BEEF AND CASSAVA STEW

Caution: Use care handling peppers. Wrap your hands in plastic wrap or slip them into plastic sandwich bags. If you accidentally touch your eyes while handling peppers, rinse them out at once under cold running water.

Yield: serves 6

water, as needed
salt and pepper, as needed
1 pound **cassava**, peeled and cut into ½-inch cubes
¼ cup vegetable oil
1 onion, **finely chopped**
1 teaspoon **ground** turmeric
1½ pounds lean beef, cut into ½-inch cubes
2 tomatoes, cut each into 6 wedges
1 cup coconut milk, homemade (recipe page 346), or canned (available at all Latin American food stores and some supermarkets)
1 fresh green chili pepper, **seeded** and finely chopped, or ¼ teaspoon ground red pepper
3 tablespoons finely chopped fresh cilantro, or 1 tablespoon dried **coriander**

Equipment: Medium saucepan with cover, fork, **colander**, large skillet with cover, mixing spoon, small bowl, serving bowl

1. Fill medium saucepan two-thirds full with water and add ½ teaspoon salt. Bring to boil over

high heat and add cassava cubes. Bring water back to boil. Reduce heat to **simmer**, cover, and cook until fork tender but not mushy, 10 to 15 minutes. Drain in colander placed in the sink.

2. Heat oil in large skillet over medium-high heat. Add onion, stir, and **sauté** until soft, 3 to 5 minutes. Stir in turmeric, add beef, and toss to brown all sides, 7 to 12 minutes. Add tomatoes and 1 cup water, and stir to mix well. Bring to boil, and stir. Reduce heat to simmer, cover, and cook until beef is tender, 45 minutes to 1 hour.

3. In small bowl, combine coconut milk, finely chopped chili pepper or ground red pepper, and cilantro or coriander. Stir to mix well. Pour spicy coconut milk over beef in skillet. Add drained cassava and toss to mix. Simmer for 10 to 15 minutes to heat through and for flavor to develop.

To serve, transfer to serving bowl and set on a cloth spread on the floor. After washing their hands, guests sit around the bowl and each person eats from the section of bowl in front of them, using only the fingers of the right hand. The left hand must never touch food; it is used only for personal grooming.

All celebrations call for great quantities of food. Fried beans, as in this recipe, are a favorite snack food. Platters of *kosari* are set out for guests, especially children, to munch on at weddings and other life-cycle celebrations. Omit the meat and one of the eggs to make vegetarian *kosari*.

Kosari

Bean Balls with Meat

CAUTION: HOT OIL USED

Yield: serves 4

1½ cups dried **black-eyed peas**
½ cup warm water
2 eggs
½ teaspoon chili powder
salt and pepper to taste
2 onions, grated
1 pound lean, **ground** beef
2 cups vegetable oil, for frying

Equipment: **Blender**, rubber spatula, medium mixing bowl, mixing spoon, paper towels, baking sheet, large **heavy-based** skillet, wooden spoon or cooking **thermometer**, slotted spoon

1. In blender, grind dried peas, turning machine off and on, for about 1 minute to break up. With blender running, add warm water, a little at a time, through feed tube to make a smooth paste, the consistency of a thick milk shake. Turn off machine once or twice and scrape down sides of container using rubber spatula. Transfer to medium mixing bowl.

2. Add eggs, chili powder, grated onions, and salt and pepper to taste. Crumble in beef and using your hands, mix well.

3. Prepare to skillet-fry: ADULT SUPERVISION REQUIRED. Place several layers of paper towels on baking sheet. Heat oil in large heavy-based skillet over medium-high heat. Oil is hot enough when small bubbles appear around a wooden spoon handle when it is dipped in the oil or when cooking thermometer registers 375° F.

4. Carefully drop tablespoonfuls of bean mixture, a few at a time, in oil and fry until browned on all sides, 2 to 3 minutes. Remove with slotted spoon and drain on paper towels. Continue to fry in batches.

Serve warm or at room temperature. Use kosari *to scoop up stews or sauces or alone as a finger food snack.*

CENTRAL AFRICAN REPUBLIC

The Central African Republic lies deep in the interior of Africa, just above the equator. The landlocked nation is surrounded by Cameroon, Chad, the Sudan, the Democratic Republic of the Congo, and the Republic of Congo. The area was ravished by slave traders from the sixteenth to the nineteenth centuries. Ruled by France, the Central African Republic proclaimed its independence in 1960.

Country-wide, about one quarter of the people are Roman Catholics, and there is also a small Muslim population in the north. The remainder of the population practices indigenous religions. (See Protestant and Catholic Life-Cycle Rituals, page xlvi; Islam and Islamic Life-Cycle Rituals, page xlix; and Traditional African Life-Cycle Rituals, page xli.)

One of the 80 ethnic groups in the Central African Republic is the tropical forest foragers (Pygmies), who live in the rain forest in the southwestern section of the country. They are descendants of some of the earliest inhabitants of the region. The lifeway of these hunter-gathers is distinct from that of the village-based farmers who live throughout rest of the country. As elsewhere in Africa, music accompanies the Pygmies' life-cycle celebrations, but it is also a prominent part of all their daily tasks—cooking, hunting, gathering berries, and bartering. Among the tropical forest foragers, everyone is a musician—men and women, young and old alike. Everyone participates in singing, clapping, stamping, or playing musical instruments.

The majority of people in the Central African Republic are farmers who live in clusters of villages. At puberty, young boys in their age group spend months in secret camps, making the transition from boyhood to adulthood under the supervision of elders. After graduation, it is taboo for the boys to eat with their mothers—from that time forward, they must eat with the men.

Marriage aims to strengthen existing families rather than to establish new ones. Parents arrange marriages for their children, and once the bride-price is paid, the marriage is confirmed.

Life-cycle celebrations in the Central African Republic give people a change from the routine of daily life. Along with music, life-cycle celebrations include feasts. If either meat, fish, or chicken is available, it must be included in the meal. Beer made from millet is the beverage most men drink on a daily basis, but palm wine is prepared for special celebrations and is used for the libations.

Vegetables are an important part of the African diet, and they are included in every feast. Spinach is a common substitute for the "bitter leaf" that is traditional in African cooking. *Gombo épinard* (recipe below) also can be made with kale, turnip greens, or any combination of greens.

Gombo Épinard

Spinach Stew

Yield: serves 4 to 6

- 2 tablespoons vegetable oil
- 2 onions, **finely chopped**
- 2 tomatoes, thinly sliced
- 1 green pepper, finely chopped
- 2 (10 or 12 ounces each) boxes frozen chopped spinach, thawed
- salt and pepper to taste

½ cup smooth or chunky peanut butter
¼ cup water

Equipment: Large skillet with cover, mixing spoon

1. Heat oil in large skillet over medium-high heat. Add onions, stir, and **sauté** until soft, 3 to 5 minutes. Add tomatoes and green pepper, stir, and cook 3 to 5 minutes until green pepper is soft.

2. Squeeze spinach to remove as much liquid as possible and crumble into tomato mixture. Add salt and pepper to taste, and stir well. Reduce heat to **simmer**, cover, and cook for 5 to 7 minutes.

3. Stir peanut butter with water to make a smooth paste. Stir peanut butter paste into tomato mixture. Reduce heat to medium and cook, uncovered, for 10 to 12 minutes for flavor to develop. Stir frequently to prevent sticking.

Serve as a side dish with broasheht *(recipe page 56) and* dundu oniyeri *(recipe page 57).*

Ground *egussi* (also *eggussi*) seeds, a thickening agent used in this soup, are from the egussi melon, native to Africa. Egussi seeds are available in African food stores and multi-ethnic food markets. Pumpkin seeds can be substituted if *egussi* is unavailable. In West Africa, *egussi potage* is made with whatever meat is available, or it can be made with fish or fowl.

Egussi Potage (also Eggussi Potage)

Thick Meat Soup

Caution: Use care handling peppers. Wrap your hands in plastic wrap or slip them into plastic sandwich bags. If you accidentally touch your eyes while handling peppers, rinse them out at once under cold running water.

Yield: serves 4

1 cup egussi seeds or pumpkin seeds (see above)
water, as needed
½ cup dried **crayfish** or dried shrimp
1 pound lean boneless beef or lamb, **cubed**
salt to taste
2 tablespoons vegetable oil or palm oil (available at ethnic food stores)
2 onions, **finely chopped**
3 fresh chili peppers, **trimmed**, **seeded**, and finely chopped, or 1 teaspoon **ground** red pepper, more or less to taste
3 tomatoes, chopped
1 bunch (about 10 ounces) fresh spinach, washed and **coarsely chopped**

Equipment: **Blender**, rubber spatula, medium saucepan with cover, large skillet with cover, mixing spoon

1. Put egussi or pumpkin seeds in blender and pulse for 1 or 2 seconds to **coarsely grind** seeds. With blender running, add water, through the feed tube a little at a time, to make a smooth mixture, the consistency of a milk shake. Turn off machine once or twice and use rubber spatula to scrape down sides of container. Add dried crayfish or dried shrimp and **blend** until smooth, about 10 seconds. Set aside.

2. Put beef or lamb cubes in medium saucepan, and add salt to taste. Add enough water to cover beef or lamb, and bring to boil over medium-high heat. Reduce heat to **simmer**, cover, and cook until tender, 45 minutes to 1 hour.

3. Heat oil in large skillet over medium-high heat. Add onions and **sauté** until soft, 3 to 5 minutes. Add chopped chili peppers or 1 teaspoon ground red pepper, more or less to taste. Stir and sauté 1 minute to release flavor. Reduce heat to medium, add tomatoes and ground seed mixture. Stirring frequently, cook 5 to 7 minutes until tomatoes are soft.

4. Add tomato mixture and spinach to meat. Stir, cover, and cook until spinach is tender and flavor has developed, 12 to 15 minutes. Add salt to taste.

To serve, the consistency should be thick enough to eat with your fingers when scooped up with stiff porridge putu *(recipe page 29). It is also good alone or over rice.*

CAMEROON

Cameroon, located on the west coast of Africa, is bordered by Nigeria, Chad, the Central African Republic, the Republic of Congo, Equatorial Guinea, and Gabon. The area was free of colonial rule until the 1880s, when Germany gained control. After World War I, control was split between Britain and France. The legacy of this split is reflected in the fact that it is the only African nation where the French and English languages both have official status. Cameroon became an independent nation in 1960.

Indigenous religious beliefs (see Traditional African Life-Cycle Rituals, page xli) influence the Muslims (see Islam and Islamic Life-Cycle Rituals, page xlix) who live in the north and the Christians (see Protestant and Catholic Life-Cycle Rituals, page xlvi)—mostly Roman Catholics—who live in the south. Many in Cameroon have never converted from local religions.

Among urban Christians, childbirth usually takes place in a hospital or clinic. A few weeks after the baby is born, friends and relatives are invited to a party called "*born hause.*" Guests bring gifts for the newborn, and the family provides food and drink during the day-long celebration.

Children are baptized when they are about 5 or 6 weeks old. Baby girls have godmothers and boys have godfathers, not godparents. Some parents have a second baptism for their child at the time of first communion, at about 8 years of age. For first communion, girls wear white dresses with short veils and boys wear white shirts and long black pants. Families share the work and expense for the communal feast and party, which generally takes place in a rented "celebration hall" after the church ceremony.

For traditional Africans, marriage is still a union of families, but young Christian urbanites in Cameroon typically choose their own marriage partners. When a boy finds the girl he wants to marry, he must ask the oldest member of the girl's family for permission. The elder can be a grandparent, an aunt, or an uncle (female elders wield as much power as male elders). The elder accepts or rejects the suitor and asks a bride-price. The bride-price (also called the "dues") varies from group to group. A pig and goat, perhaps a cow, and a sum of money are typical components of the required dues. The boy's family then arranges to come with their son to meet with the elder of the girl's family; this is called "knock door." At this visit, the boy's family brings the requested bride-price items, and, if expectations are satisfied, the marriage is approved.

Christian men are allowed one wife, and Muslims can have up to four. Those adhering to local beliefs and practices may have as many wives as they can afford.

Weddings can take place at any hour of the day, but the reception never begins before six in the evening. Wedding reception rituals are carefully orchestrated by a master of ceremonies (also called the announcer). He welcomes the guests and is in charge of all activities during the evening. During the reception, he sits with the bride and groom, the chairlady and chairman, and the best man at the "high table." The chairlady is a friend of the bride and makes a glowing speech about her. The chairman does the same for the groom. While the speech-making takes place, platters of appetizers, popcorn, and *roasted melon seeds* (recipe page 29) are brought to guests. The speech-making usually takes three hours, after which a wedding cake (*English fruitcake*, recipe page 202) is cut by the bride and groom and wedding gifts are opened before everyone partakes in a buffet dinner. Toward the end of the evening, after much partying, a large pot of *pepper soup* (recipe page 70) is set out for guests, along with plenty of *French bread* (recipe page 51); it settles their stomachs and sobers them up.

When a Christian dies in Cameroon, it is common for several hundred people—most of whom may be total strangers to the family—to come from miles around for the funeral. The body is placed in a coffin at the mortuary, and after a requiem Mass at the church, it is interred in a cemetery. It is customary for family members and other mourners to throw a handful of dirt on top the casket after it is lowered into the ground. During the funeral, women friends prepare a funeral feast. Great quantities of food, including pigs, goats, and even a cow or two, are prepared for the crowd of mourners, who stay all week long.

Widows wear black for one year, and at the end of the mourning period, there is another huge feast. Again, throngs of people show up to share in the memorial feast, which usually is announced over the radio. Again, livestock is slaughtered for the occasion. To prepare for the designated end of the mourning period, it is the custom for all family members to have garments sewn from the same fabric. This is done to show solidarity and to distinguish the family from other mourners.

Egussi is a dish prepared for feasts held for special occasions. *Egussi* are seeds from a vegetable similar to squash or pumpkin. In Cameroon, the fish mixture is put in plantain leaves to cook. A good substitute for plantain leaves is quart-size heavy-duty plastic freezer bags wrapped in aluminum foil.

Egussi (also Eggussi)

Steamed Fish Dumplings

Yield: serves 10 to 15 people

water, as needed

2 pieces (about 1 pound) dried smoked fish (available at all African food stores and most multi-ethnic supermarkets)

1 to 1½ pounds fresh catfish **fillets**

3 cups egussi seeds (available at all African food stores and most multi-ethnic supermarkets)

½ cup dried **crayfish** (available at all African food stores and most multi-ethnic supermarkets)

ground red pepper or **piri-piri**, to taste (available at all African food stores and most multi-ethnic supermarkets)

salt to taste

½ cup vegetable oil

Equipment: Medium saucepan, slotted spoon, **colander**, knife, small bowl, work surface, electric **blender**, rubber spatula, large mixing bowl, 1 cup-size ladle or measuring cup, 6 or 7 quart-size plastic heavy-duty freezer bags, aluminum foil, **steamer pan**, metal tongs

1. Fill medium saucepan two-thirds full with water and add dry smoked fish. Bring to boil over high heat and cook for 15 minutes. Add fresh catfish fillets and cook for 10 minutes more. Set colander in sink, drain both types of fish into colander, and cool enough to handle. Remove catfish from colander and place on work surface.

2. Cut catfish fillets into ½-inch cubes and put in small bowl. After cooking, the dried smoked fish becomes soft and pliable. Using your

hands, carefully remove and discard skin and bones from smoked fish. Add the edible smoked fish pieces to the catfish cubes, making a total of 2 to 3 cups combined fish.

3. Pour egussi seeds out on work surface and carefully pick through them to remove and discard any broken shell or other debris.

4. Put 1½ cups egussi seeds in blender, add ½ cup water, and **blend** until smooth. Add just enough water, a little at a time, until mixture resembles a smooth, thick milk shake, 3 to 5 minutes. Transfer to large mixing bowl.

5. Put remaining 1½ cups seeds in blender, and add dried crayfish and ½ cup water. Blend as before, adding just enough water, a little at a time, until mixture resembles a smooth, thick milk shake, 3 to 5 minutes. Add to first batch already in large mixing bowl, and stir with rubber spatula. Stir in dried, smoked fish and catfish, ground red pepper or piripiri to taste (½ teaspoon for mild), salt to taste, and oil. Stir to mix well.

6. Fill each heavy-duty plastic bag with 1 cup of fish mixture. Press mixture to bottom of bag, press out air as you roll it up and seal top. (Each bag should be cylinder shaped, about 7 inches long.) Wrap each bag in foil to make watertight.

7. Fill steamer pan with at least 4 cups water and bring to boil over high heat. Stack foil packages in the steamer so they are above the boiling water. Cover tightly and cook for 1½ to 2 hours. Maintain water level, adding hot water to steamer pan as needed (about every 10 to 15 minutes). After 1½ hours open a package to check for doneness. When fish mixture is firm and holds together, it is done. If not done, continue steaming for about 30 minutes more.

To serve, remove foil and cut open plastic bag. For best flavor, serve at room temperature. Cut each fish dumpling crosswise into ½-inch thick slices. Serve with boiled plantains (recipe follows).

Doh Doh

Boiled Plantains

Yield: serves 10 to 15

6 to 8 ripe plantains
salt to taste

Equipment: Knife, large saucepan with cover, slotted spoon, fork, serving dish

1. Using sharp knife, cut tips off both ends of plantain, make a lengthwise cut in the skin, and peel off.

2. Cut plantain crosswise into 4 or 5 chunks. Put in large saucepan, cover with water, and bring to boil over medium-high heat. Cover and boil 15 to 20 minutes until tender when poked with fork. Remove with slotted spoon and put on serving dish. Sprinkle with salt to taste.

Serve at room temperature to eat with eggussi.

GABON

Situated on the western coast of Africa, Gabon is covered almost entirely by a dense tropical rain forest. It is bordered by Equatorial Guinea, Cameroon, and the Republic of Congo. The original inhabitants of Gabon were the Babinga, or Pygmies, who were in the area at least 7000 years ago. Although it was first explored by the Porticoes, it eventually fell under French control. It became an independent country in 1960.

Nearly all Gabonese are Bantu, whom Christian missionaries began converting during the nineteenth century. Today, most Gabonese are either Roman Catholics or Protestants. They follow the Christian life-milestone events prescribed by their churches (see Protestant and Catholic Life-Cycle Rituals, page xlvi), but there is considerable influence from indigenous religions. (See Traditional African Life-Cycle Rituals, page xli.)

The majority of people live in small villages near the ocean or on the shores of the many rivers that run through the country. Fish is one of their most important foods, and *egussi* (recipe page 49) and *boulettes de poisson* (recipe page 77) are favorite ways of preparing fish for feasts.

More French people now live in Gabon (and Cameroon) than during colonial times. The French have influenced not only the language but the food, especially the bread. French bread is eaten at every meal in Gabon and Cameroon.

Instead of calling bread *pain* as the French do, people in Cameroon and Gabon call French bread *gâteau*, which in French actually means pastry or cakes.

Gâteau

French Bread

Yield: 2 loaves

- 4 cups all-purpose flour
- 2 teaspoons salt
- 1½ tablespoons sugar, divided
- 1¼ cups **lukewarm** water, divided
- 1 package active dry **yeast**
- ½ cup milk, **scalded** and cooled to lukewarm
- 1½ teaspoons solid shortening

Equipment: Flour **sifter**, large mixing bowl, small bowl, mixing spoon, damp kitchen towel, lightly floured work surface, knife, 9- x 12- x 2-inch baking pan, wax paper, scissors, pencil, ruler, greased baking sheet, dry kitchen towel, oven mitts, wire cake rack

1. **Sift** flour with salt and ½ tablespoon sugar into large mixing bowl.

2. In small bowl, sprinkle yeast over ¼ cup lukewarm water until dissolved and bubbly, 5 to 10 minutes. Add lukewarm milk, remaining 1 cup lukewarm water, shortening, and remaining 1 tablespoon sugar. Stir to dissolve.

3. Make a well (hole) in center of flour mixture and pour in yeast mixture. Stir thoroughly to mix but do not **knead**. The dough will be soft. Cover with damp towel and set in warm place to rise to double in bulk, 1½ to 2 hours.

4. **Punch down** dough and lightly knead in bowl. Transfer to lightly floured work surface and cut in half with knife. Cover with damp towel.

5. Fill baking pan halfway with water and place in bottom of oven. (Steam from the pan of water ensures a crisp crust.)

Preheat oven to 400° F.

6. Cut wax paper 10 x15 inches. Using pencil and ruler, mark a 9- x12-inch rectangular pattern on dull side of wax paper. Place wax paper, shiny-side up on work surface, and sprinkle lightly with flour. Place one piece of dough in center of pattern and pat it out to size of pattern. Roll up dough, jelly roll-style, into a tight, 12-inch long cylinder. It helps to pull up on the edge of wax paper to make the first few turns firm. Remove wax paper, lightly flour work surface, and continue to roll the cylinder back and forth, while pressing down, making it about 15 inches long. Using your hands, taper ends slightly. Repeat, making second loaf with remaining dough.

7.Place loaves side by side on greased baking sheet, leaving at least 2-inches between. Using scissors, cut 3 or 4 diagonal slits about ¼ -inch deep across the tops. Cover with dry towel, set in warm place to rise to almost double in bulk, 20 to 30 minutes.

8. Bake in oven 15 minutes at 400° F, reduce heat to 350° F and bake 30 minutes longer or until loaves are crisp and brown. Cool on wire cake rack.

Serve bread soon after it cools for best flavor and texture. To eat, break bread into chunks.

For special occasions, such as first communion celebrations, chicken would be one of several dishes prepared for the feast. In Gabon, palm nuts are used in this recipe, but other nuts work equally well.

Poulet au Gnemboue

Chicken Gabon-style

Yield: serves 4 to 6

1 cup ground nuts (peanuts, palm nuts, almonds, or macadamia nuts, or combination)
1½ cups water, more as needed
2½ to 3 pounds frying chicken, cut into serving-size pieces
½ teaspoon **ground** red pepper
salt and pepper to taste
2 tablespoons vegetable oil
2 onions, **finely chopped**
2 cloves garlic, finely chopped

Equipment: Electric **blender**, rubber spatula, paper towels, wax paper, work surface, large saucepan with cover or **Dutch oven**, mixing spoon

1. Put nuts and 1½ cups water in blender and **blend** until smooth.

2. Rinse chicken pieces under cold running water and pat dry with paper towels. Place chicken pieces on wax-paper-covered work surface and sprinkle all sides with ground red pepper and salt and pepper to taste.

3. Heat oil in large saucepan or Dutch oven over medium-high heat. Add onions and garlic, stir, and **sauté** until soft, 3 to 5 minutes. Add blended nut mixture, stir, and cook for 3 minutes. Add chicken pieces to the nut mixture. Reduce heat to medium, cover, and cook until chicken is tender, 1½ hours. Check often and stir, adding water if needed to prevent sticking. The nut mixture should be the consistency of thick gravy.

Serve with side dish of boiled plantains *(recipe page 50) and* French bread *(recipe page 51) for sopping up nutty gravy.*

SUDAN

The largest nation on the African continent, Sudan has 500 miles of coastline along the Red Sea. It shares its other borders with Ethiopia and Eritrea to the east; Kenya, Uganda, and Congo to the south; Chad and the Central African Republic to the west; and Egypt and Libya to the north.

Sudan has two distinct cultures (Arab and black African) and over 500 ethnic groups. There are great differences between the Dinka people who travel with their herds; subsistence farmers like the Zandes who work with ancient tools and farming methods; and the very westernized Sudanese urbanites who enjoy high-tech living.

Most people living in the northern two-thirds of the country belong to the large Muslim community, which comprises 70 percent of Sudan's total population. These Sudanese live in walled compounds, and most men wear *jellabiahs* (Arabic dress) and turbans. Women are covered with loose-fitting garments called *tobes*. In the southern part of the country, however, most Sudanese are Christians. These people live in clusters of beehive-shaped huts, and although many men wear *jellabiahs*, which are comfortable in the hot climate, they don't wear turbans. Women wear Western-style dresses.

The Muslims and Christians in Sudan have customized the standard rituals of their faith to include local traditions and beliefs. (See Islam and Islamic Life-Cycle Rituals, page xlix; Protestant and Catholic Life-Cycle Rituals, page xlvi; and Traditional African Life-Cycle Rituals, page xli.)

The Dinka people have lived in the Sudan region since about the tenth century. Most are Muslims. They are semi-nomadic people who raise herds of cattle, which give them respect and status. With cattle, a man can purchase a bride, pay taxes, and buy staples. The cattle provides meat and milk for his family, and the smoke from burning cow dung keeps mosquitoes away.

The Dinkas are devoted to their cows, which they believe are a link with the spiritual world. When a Dinka boy reaches puberty, he is given a young calf. This becomes his "namesake ox," after which he himself is named. For the next few years, he identifies closely with the young bull, imitating and emulating it as the two mature together. Scarification signifies a boy's initiation into adulthood. This is done by making deep cuts across a boy's forehead to resemble horns. It is an ordeal that must be endured without any show of pain.

Among the Dinka, the family of a prospective husband is expected to pay the bride-price in the form of cattle. The number of cattle exchanged for the bride is negotiated between the future in-laws. A beautiful bride can cost a future husband many head of cattle, adding considerable wealth to her family. Thus, when Dinka girls reach marrying age, they are fattened up by their families to make them more desirable. To add to their allure, marriageable girls wear beaded bodices made of dozens of rows of tiny beads strung horizontally across the chest and back. The beads are applied in patterns that indicate the family's prosperity, and cowrie shells are attached to promote fertility.

All life-cycle celebrations in Sudan include a communal feast. This recipe for *bani-bamia* combines two African favorites, lamb and okra. (Okra in Africa is known as lady fingers.) ۞ ۞ ۞

Bani-Bamia

Lamb and Okra Stew

Yield: serves 4

2 tablespoons vegetable oil
2 onions, thinly sliced
2 cloves garlic, **finely chopped**
1½ pounds lean boneless lamb or other lean meat, cut into 2-inch chunks
1 cup canned tomato paste
3 cups water
salt and pepper to taste
10-ounce package frozen whole okra, thawed
6 cups cooked rice, kept warm, for serving

Equipment: Large saucepan with cover or **Dutch oven**, mixing spoon, small bowl, large serving platter

1. Heat oil in large saucepan or Dutch oven over medium-high heat. Add onions and garlic, stir, and **sauté** until soft, 3 to 5 minutes. Add lamb and brown on all sides, 7 to 12 minutes.

2. In small bowl, combine tomato paste with water. Add tomato mixture to lamb mixture in large saucepan. Add salt and pepper to taste and bring to boil. Reduce heat to **simmer**, cover, and cook until meat is tender, 45 to 50 minutes. Add okra and cook, covered until okra is tender, 8 to 10 minutes.

To serve, spoon lamb mixture over cooked rice in large serving platter.

The foods of Sudan are a combination of Middle Eastern and African cooking. This easy salad recipe is served as a side dish with roast lamb (*méchoui*, recipe page 75) for weddings and other special occasions.

Shorbat Robe

Yogurt and Cucumber Salad

Yield: serves 6

2 cucumbers, peeled and chopped

1 cup plain yogurt
salt and pepper to taste
2 cloves fresh garlic, **finely chopped**, or 1 teaspoon garlic granules
2 hard-cooked eggs, chopped, for **garnish**
2 tomatoes, chopped, for garnish
1 onion, sliced, for garnish

Equipment: Medium bowl with cover, mixing spoon, serving bowl

Put cucumber in medium bowl, **fold in** yogurt, salt and pepper to taste, and garlic, and **blend** well. Cover and refrigerate until ready to serve. At serving time, transfer to serving bowl, sprinkle with hard cooked eggs, tomatoes, and onion slices.

To serve, place bowl of shorbat robe *on the table and have guests help themselves. To eat, tear off a piece of* khobaz arabee *(recipe page 115) and use to scoop up some onion, egg, and tomato with each bit of salad. Eat with* ful sudani *(recipe follows).*

This is a favorite Arab dish that is popular in all Middle Eastern and North African countries. A bowl of *ful sudani* is on the table for all celebrations. Often bowls of the cooked beans are set out as a snack at parties.

Ful Sudani

Sudan-style Beans

Yield: serves 4
½ pound or 2 cups dried butter beans, soaked overnight and drained
2 tablespoons olive oil
1 tablespoon lemon juice
salt and pepper to taste
½ teaspoon **ground** cumin

Equipment: Medium saucepan with cover, mixing spoon, **colander**, medium mixing bowl, potato masher or fork

1. Put drained beans in medium saucepan and cover with fresh water. Bring to boil over high heat. Reduce heat to **simmer**, cover, and cook until tender but not mushy, 1 to 1½ hours.

2. Place colander in sink and drain beans. Transfer beans to medium mixing bowl. Add oil, lemon juice, and salt and pepper to taste, and stir. Mash slightly with potato masher or fork.

Serve at room temperature for best flavor. Eat the beans with the fingers of your right hand. According to Muslim tradition, the left hand must never touch food; it is used only for personal grooming.

CHAD

Chad, a landlocked country situated in north-central Africa, is bordered by Libya on the north, Sudan on the east, the Central African Republic and Cameroon on the south, and Nigeria and Niger on the east. It is a rural country that encompasses three different climatic zones. Nomadic pastoralists roam the northern Sahara desert region with their camels, goats, and sheep. The central region is home to semi-nomadic horsemen who herd cattle and sheep and still hunt with spears. The southern Sarh region, home to the Sara people, has the largest number of people, the most cities, and the best farming.

Chad, at the crossroads of African and Arab cultures, has over 200 ethnic groups. Those living in the upper two-thirds of the country are mostly Muslims. Elsewhere, the people of Chad primarily follow indigenous religious practices, except for urbanites who were converted to Christianity during the French colonial period, which ended in 1960 when independence was won.

Muslims in Chad marry within their clan, usually to first cousins; as specified in the

Koran, men are limited to four wives. Men who instead follow traditional local practice sometimes have several dozen wives, guaranteeing a large number of children to support the father in his old age.

In Chad, when a girl is ready for marriage, she is initiated by female elders. These women tell her what to expect and help prepare her for the realities of married life. The girl learns secret codes and languages to help her communicate with other married women, should the need arise. A girl goes directly into marriage after a suitor shows interest in her, once he and his bride-price are accepted by the girl's father or a family elder.

When a girl's family agrees to marry her to a man from a different clan and the negotiations of the bride-price have been completed, a week-long ceremony takes place in the settlement of the girl's family. Paying the bride-price actually cements the marriage; it is the same as a marriage certificate. What follows is a dancing, singing, and feasting celebration.

The bride misses the festivities, however, as she must stay in seclusion until she says goodbye to her family and friends and departs with her husband to his settlement. On the bride's arrival to her new home, her in-laws give her gifts, such as small animals. If her husband has other wives, they are there to welcome her into the family.

Every life-milestone celebration in Chad includes a feast. Among Muslims and other Chadians, whole roasted lamb (recipe page 141) is the centerpiece of the celebration. There are always dozens of vegetable dishes to go along with the meat. ۞ ۞ ۞

Courgette avec Groundnuts

Zucchini with Peanuts

Yield: serves 4 to 6

- 2 tablespoons vegetable oil
- 1 onion, **finely chopped**
- 2 cloves garlic, finely chopped
- 3 to 4 zucchini (about 1½ to 2 pounds), sliced crosswise and **blanched**
- 1 tablespoon lemon juice
- salt and pepper to taste
- 1 ½ cups **roasted** peanuts, **coarsely chopped**

Equipment: Large skillet with cover, mixing spoon, fork

Heat oil in large skillet over medium-high heat. Add onion and garlic, stir, and **sauté** until onion is soft, 3 to 5 minutes. Add zucchini and toss to mix. Reduce heat to medium, add lemon juice and salt and pepper to taste. Toss, cover, and cook until zucchini is tender, 7 to 12 minutes. Either mash zucchini mixture with a fork or serve chunky. Sprinkle with peanuts before serving.

Serve with tuo zaafi *(recipe page 64) or plain boiled rice.*

Some of the cooked vegetable dishes are as simple as this recipe.

Maize avec Épinards

Corn with Spinach

Yield: serves 4

- 2 pounds fresh spinach, washed and **coarsely chopped**
- 1 cup water
- 2 tablespoons vegetable oil
- 10-ounce package frozen corn kernels, thawed
- 2 onions, **finely chopped**

ground red pepper to taste
salt and pepper to taste

Equipment: Large saucepan with cover, **colander**, large skillet with cover, mixing spoon

1. Put coarsely chopped spinach in large saucepan, add water, and bring to boil. Reduce heat to **simmer**, cover, and cook 5 to 7 minutes, until tender. Drain in colander.

2. Heat oil in large skillet over medium-high heat. Add onions, stir, and sauté until soft, 3 to 5 minutes. Add corn, stir, and cook for 3 minutes. Reduce heat to medium. Squeeze spinach over the sink to extract all the water. Crumble dried spinach into skillet, and toss to mix. Add salt and pepper to taste and ground red pepper to taste. Cover and cook for 7 to 12 minutes to heat through.

Serve vegetables either hot or at room temperature.

If roasted lamb, *méchoui* (recipe page 75), is too expensive, cheaper cuts of meat would be made into *broashehts*. Roasting meat on skewers has always been a favorite among Africans. This recipe is popular not only in Chad but throughout most of Africa.

Broasheht

Brochettes (Grilled Meat on Skewer)

Note: This recipe takes 2 days.

CAUTION: GRILL OR BROILER USED

Yield: serves 4

1 teaspoon **ground** paprika
1 teaspoon ground cinnamon
2 cloves garlic, **finely chopped**
salt and pepper to taste
ground red pepper to taste
2 tablespoons vinegar
2 pounds lean lamb, mutton, or beef, cut into 1½ to 2-inch cubes
2 onions, quartered, and each quarter separated into 3 or 4 pieces
½ cup finely chopped **roasted** peanuts, for serving
4 cups rice (cooked according to directions on package), kept warm for serving

Equipment: Small bowl, mixing spoon, rubber spatula, large resealable plastic bag, 8 metal or wooden 8- or 10-inch skewers (if using wooden skewers, soak in water for at least 30 minutes before using so they don't burn), charcoal **grill** or broiler pan, metal tongs, oven mitts, serving platter

1. Put paprika, cinnamon, garlic, salt and pepper to taste, and ground red pepper to taste in small bowl, and stir in vinegar to make into paste. Using spatula, spread paste over inside of resealable plastic bag. Add meat, press out most of the air, and seal bag. Press on all sides of bag to massage paste into meat until evenly coated. Refrigerate for at least 6 hours or overnight.

Prepare to grill or broil: ADULT SUPERVISION REQUIRED. Have an adult help prepare charcoal grill or preheat broiler.

2. Thread 4 meat cubes on a skewer, separating each chunk of meat with a piece of onion and ending with cube of meat on each end. Carefully squeeze meat and onion tightly together.

3. Place skewers side by side on prepared grill or broiler pan. Using metal tongs, turn to brown all sides, and cook to desired doneness, 15 to 20 minutes. Transfer to serving platter and sprinkle finely chopped nuts over meat before serving.

Serve skewered meat with cooked rice. Allow 2 skewers per person.

NIGER

A landlocked country in Saharan Africa, Niger is surrounded by Mali, Algeria, Libya, Chad, Benin, Burkina Faso, and Nigeria. It shares not only its name, but a fair proportion of its people, with neighboring Nigeria. Niger's largest ethnic group, the Hausa people, have kinfolk living across the border in the northern two-thirds of Nigeria.

In both countries, the people are predominantly Muslims, although there also are small communities of Christians. All groups fuse local religious beliefs with Islam or Christianity, and rituals and customs vary greatly from group to group. (See Islam and Islamic Life-Cycle Rituals, page xlix, and Protestant and Catholic Life-Cycle Rituals, pp. xlvi.)

Although Niger is primarily a country of small villages, with the majority of people working as subsistence farmers, the nomadic Wodaabé people are herders who constantly travel with their cattle—a sign of wealth and prestige—over Niger's sub-Saharan steppe.

Most Wodaabé parents arrange the betrothal of their children, usually to a first cousin, when the child is born or is very young. Years later, after marrying, a Wodaabé man may have up to three more wives, but they must all be from outside his clan. If a marriage has not been arranged by the parents, a boy can abduct the girl he wants for his wife. By slaughtering a sheep, followed by a short celebration, the two are considered wed.

The Wodaabé are very concerned with physical appearance, and having beautiful children is of utmost importance to married couples. During courtship, to win the attention of the eligible girls, single men sometimes participate in a "beauty contest." The main event is a performance for which the men blacken their lips to make their teeth seem whiter. The men dance and perform for hours, displaying their looks and charisma to entice the young girls standing on the sidelines.

Some girls ultimately make a choice, and if a marriage proposal results, the man takes a calabash full of milk to her parents. If they accept, he then brings them the bride-price: three cattle that are slaughtered for the feast that follows.

Cattle are usually slaughtered and roasted for celebration feasts, which also include cauldrons of millet porridge, the same as *tuo zaafi* (recipe page 64). Yams, too, are always served on holidays and at life-cycle celebrations. They are a mainstay of the African diet; a symbol of survival that is given ceremonial status. White African yams (also called *coco-yams* or *water-yams*) can be found in some Asian food stores. Sweet potatoes can be substituted.

Dundu Oniyeri

Fried Yam Slices

CAUTION: HOT OIL USED

Yield: serves 6

4 cups water, more as needed
1½ teaspoons salt, divided
2 pounds white yams (see above) or sweet potatoes, peeled and sliced ½ inch thick
2 eggs
1 cup all-purpose flour
½ teaspoon **ground** cinnamon
½ teaspoon ground black pepper
½ teaspoon ground paprika
1 cup vegetable oil, for frying

Equipment: Large saucepan with cover, **colander**, paper towels, baking sheet, small shallow bowl, fork, pie pan, wax paper, work surface, large **heavy-based** skillet, wooden spoon, slotted metal spatula

1. Pour 4 cups water in large saucepan. Add ½ teaspoon salt and yams or sweet potatoes. Bring to boil over high heat. Reduce heat to **simmer**,

cover, and cook until tender but still firm, 20 to 35 minutes. Drain in colander.

2. Prepare to skillet-fry: Place several layers of paper towels on baking sheet. Put eggs in small shallow bowl and using fork, beat in 1/4 cup water, and set next to stove. Put flour in pie pan and stir in cinnamon, black pepper, remaining salt, and paprika. Set flour mixture next to beaten egg mixture next to stove. Dip a yam slice in flour mixture, then in egg mixture, and into flour again. Shake off excess each time. Place on wax-paper-covered work surface. Continue to coat all the pieces.

3. Fry yams: ADULT SUPERVISION REQUIRED. Heat oil in large heavy-based skillet over medium-high heat. Oil is hot enough when small bubbles appear around a wooden spoon handle when it is dipped in the oil. Fry yams, in batches, until golden brown on both sides, 3 to 5 minutes. Using slotted metal spatula, transfer to paper towel-covered baking sheet to drain.

Serve warm fried yams as a side dish with bondo gombo *(recipe follows).*

Lamb is a favorite meat of Muslims in Africa. In Africa, *gombo* means okra, which is used in this lamb gumbo.

Bondo Gombo

Lamb Gumbo with Whole Wheat Dumplings

Yield: serves 6

- 4 tablespoons vegetable oil
- 2 pounds lean stewing lamb, cut into 1-inch cubes
- 1 onion, **finely chopped**
- 3 tablespoons all-purpose flour
- 1 cup tomato paste
- 6 cups water
- 10-ounce package frozen sliced okra, thawed
- salt and pepper to taste
- *whole wheat dumplings*, for serving (recipe follows)

Equipment: Large saucepan with cover or **Dutch oven**, mixing spoon

1. Heat oil in large saucepan or Dutch oven over medium-high heat. Add meat and brown on all sides, 7 to 12 minutes. Add onions and stir. Reduce heat to medium and cook until soft, 3 to 5 minutes. Sprinkle in flour and stir until smooth. Add tomato paste and water and stir. Cover and **simmer** over medium heat until meat is tender, 1 to 1½ hours. Carefully **fold in** okra and simmer until soft, 10 to 15 minutes. Add salt and pepper to taste.

2. Prepare *whole wheat dumplings.*

Serve the bondo gombo *from the cooking pot. Arrange dumplings on top of gumbo or serve separately. Either way, the dumplings are used to sop up the meat sauce.*

Whole Wheat Dumplings

Yield: serves 6 to 8

- 1 cup **whole wheat flour**
- 1 cup water, more as needed
- 1 ½ teaspoons salt, divided

Equipment: **Double boiler** with cover, mixing spoon, medium saucepan, slotted spoon

1. Put flour in top pan of a double boiler. Stir in 1 cup water and ½ teaspoon salt to make a smooth paste. Fill bottom pan of double boiler halfway with water and bring to boil over high heat. Reduce heat to **simmer**. Set flour mixture over simmering water, cover, and cook 30 minutes. Remove from heat.

2. Fill medium saucepan two-thirds full with water and bring to boil over high heat. Add 1 teaspoon salt and reduce heat to rolling boil. Drop dumplings, one tablespoonful at a time into water. Do not crowd pan. Cook 5 to 7 minutes. When dumplings float to the top, cook 5 minutes longer. Remove with slotted spoon and keep warm. Continue to cook in batches.

Continue, bondo gombo *(recipe precedes: Step 2. Prepare dumplings).*

NIGERIA

Nigeria is on the west coast of Africa, and shares its other borders with Benin, Niger, Cameroon, and Chad. It is divided into three very distinct regions—northern, southwestern, and southeastern—separated naturally by a Y-shaped division through the center of the country formed by the Niger River and its tributary, the Benue. The three regions differ in languages, religions, traditions, and alliances. The northern two-thirds of the country, known as the Holy North, is where the Muslim Hausa and Fulani peoples live. The southwest is home to the Yoruba people, about half of whom are Christian and half Muslim. The southeast is inhabited by the Ibos, who are mostly Roman Catholics.

Throughout Nigeria, puberty initiation rites and ceremonies are conducted for both boys and girls. Today, the initiation rites of most ethnic groups are painless, unlike *sharo,* a practice of the Fulani people of the north. *Sharo* has been illegal for many years, but it is still practiced in remote regions of the country. It involves two boys, usually best friends. Each, in turn, must flog the other three times with a large stick. The boy being hit cannot show that he is feeling any pain, or he will be disgraced before the girls in the village and will not be able to marry.

There are several forms of marriage in Nigeria. In the south, Christian urbanites have monogamous marriages, while traditional Nigerian marriages are polygamous. In the Holy North, Muslim men marry up to four wives. In polygamous marriages, the first wife is usually the leader among the wives. Frequently, she is the only one for whom a full dowry has been paid.

During traditional courtship, the suitor's family visits the girl's family, bringing quantities of *mmanya,* a type of wine—this is called "the carrying of the wine." Libations are poured, and ancestors are called upon to bless the union.

In parts of Nigeria (as well as in neighboring Togo) a bride-to-be resides in a fattening room for 14 days prior to her wedding. Female family elders put her through an intensive feeding and beautifying regime, hoping she will be more pleasing to her husband.

In Nigeria, as well as in Togo and Benin, everyone in the clan or village takes part in the wedding feast. Meat is the main food, served with great quantities of pounded yams, fritters, grilled plantains, soups, porridges, and stews. After the wedding feast, a bride goes to her husband's home, thus confirming her marriage to the family. The Ibo community in eastern Nigeria then refer to her as *nwuye any,* which means "our wife."

Black-eyed peas (*ewa*) and bananas (*dodo*) are a favorite dish in Nigeria. The following recipe would be one of the many side dishes served at a wedding feast.

Ewa and Dodo

Black-eyed Peas with Fried Bananas

CAUTION: HOT OIL USED

Yield: serves 6

1 cup plus 1 tablespoon vegetable oil, divided
1 onion, **finely chopped**
6 cups cooked **black-eyed peas** with liquid, homemade (follow directions on package) or canned

1 large tomato, finely chopped
3 tablespoons canned tomato paste
7 ounces canned water packed tuna or salmon
ground red pepper, to taste
3 bananas, peeled and cut crosswise into ¼-inch slices
salt to taste

Equipment: Medium saucepan with cover, mixing spoon, paper towels, baking sheet, large skillet, metal slotted spoon, serving bowl

1. Heat 1 tablespoon oil in medium saucepan over medium-high heat. Add onions, stir, and **sauté** until soft, 2 to 3 minutes. Add peas with liquid, chopped tomato, and tomato paste. Stir, reduce heat to **simmer**, and cook for 10 minutes. Using mixing spoon, **fold in** tuna or salmon, and salt and ground red pepper, to taste. Simmer for 10 minutes without stirring. Cover and keep on medium-low heat.

2. Prepare to skillet-fry: ADULT SUPERVISION REQUIRED Place several layers of paper towels on baking sheet. Heat remaining 1 cup oil in large skillet over medium-high heat. Add bananas and fry on both sides until golden brown, 3 to 5 minutes. Remove with metal slotted spoon and drain on paper-towel-covered baking sheet. Sprinkle with salt to taste.

To serve, sprinkle dodo *(fried bananas) over* ewa *(black-eyed peas) in a serving bowl.*

Chinchin is simply fried dough sprinkled with sugar. It is popular under different names in almost every country in the world. Platters of *chinchin* are prepared for many life-cycle celebrations. They are a favorite sweet snack, especially among children.

Chinchin

Fried Pastries

CAUTION: HOT OIL USED

Yield: about 2 dozen
2 cups all-purpose flour
1 teaspoon baking powder
1 teaspoon **ground** nutmeg
½ teaspoon salt
1 tablespoon vegetable shortening, at room temperature
¾ cup hot water, more or less as needed
vegetable oil, for deep frying
confectioners' sugar, for **garnish**

Equipment: Large mixing bowl, mixing spoon, kitchen towel, lightly floured work surface, lightly floured rolling pin, knife, **deep fryer**, paper towels, baking sheet, wooden spoon, slotted metal spoon or metal tongs, serving platter

1. In large mixing bowl, mix flour, baking powder, nutmeg, and salt. Using clean hands, **blend** in shortening until mixture resembles fine crumbs. Add just enough hot water, a little at a time, to make a soft dough that holds together, leaving sides of bowl clean. Divide dough into 2 balls, and cover with towel to prevent drying out.

2. On lightly floured work surface, using lightly floured rolling pin, roll one ball into a rectangle, about ¼ inch thick. Sprinkle with flour if dough seems sticky. Using a knife, cut dough into 1- x 6-inch strips . Cover with towel and repeat with second ball.

3. Prepare deep fryer: ADULT SUPERVISION REQUIRED. Place several layers of paper towels on baking sheet. Heat oil to 375° F on fryer thermometer or oil is hot enough when small bubbles appear around a wooden spoon handle when it is dipped in the oil. Deep fry in small batches, 3 or 4 at a time, until golden brown, 2 to 3 minutes. Remove with slotted metal spoon or metal tongs and drain on paper towel-covered baking sheet.

To serve, stack pastries on serving platter and sprinkle with confectioners' sugar, for garnish.

In Eastern Nigeria, a man of importance is given two funerals. After his death, such a man is buried promptly and secretly. Although it is common knowledge that the man has died, people keep silent about it until the family is ready for the public announcement of a second funeral. Because of the expense of providing food and drink for everyone who attends, months—perhaps even years—may pass before the bereaved family can afford the festivities. The deceased man's estate is not distributed among his heirs until after the second funeral.

Grubombo is a basic recipe throughout much of Africa. A hearty one-dish meal can be made by adding shrimp, cubed fish **fillets**, chunks of meat, chicken, sausage, or any combination of those ingredients to the okra mixture (*gombo* means okra). The Créoles of southern Louisiana learned how to make gumbo from the slaves who brought *grubombo* with them from Africa. Serve *grubombo* as a vegetarian dish over rice or as a side dish. It is best to use fresh okra (not canned) for this recipe.

Grubombo

Stewed Okra and Tomatoes

Yield: serves 6 to 8

- 2 tablespoons vegetable oil
- 2 onions, **finely chopped**
- 1 pound fresh whole okra (small pods), **trimmed**
- 28 ounces canned whole tomatoes, chopped
- 1 **jalapeño** (hot green chili pepper), trimmed, **seeded**, and finely chopped
- salt and pepper to taste

Equipment: Medium **heavy-based** saucepan with cover or **Dutch oven**, mixing spoon

1. Heat oil in medium heavy-based saucepan or Dutch oven over medium-high heat. Add onions, stir, and **sauté** until soft, 3 to 5 minutes. Add okra, tomatoes, and jalapeño, and bring to boil. Stir, reduce heat to **simmer**, cover, and cook until okra is tender, 10 to 15 minutes. Stir in salt and pepper to taste. Simmer, uncovered, for 5 to 10 minutes to thicken.

Serve as a side dish or as a sauce over rice, meat, or chicken.

Gnamacoudji

Pineapple Ginger Drink

Yield: about 8 cups

- 6 cups hot boiled water
- 1 cup grated or **finely chopped** fresh ginger root, or 4 tablespoons **ground** ginger
- 5 blades fresh **lemon grass**, or 5 tablespoons dried, soaked for 30 minutes and drained
- ½ cup fresh mint leaves, or 2 tablespoons dried mint leaves
- 16 ounces canned frozen pineapple juice concentrate
- 2 cups confectioners' sugar, more or less as needed
- 2½ teaspoons vanilla extract
- ice cubes, as needed for serving

Equipment: Medium saucepan with cover, mixing spoon, strainer, large pitcher, coffee filter, beverage glasses

1. Heat water in medium saucepan over high heat. Bring to boil for 3 minutes and remove from heat. Add ginger, lemon grass, and mint to hot water. Stir, cover, and allow to **steep** for 1 hour.

2. Put strainer lined with a coffee filter over large pitcher, pour the ginger mixture through to filter into the pitcher. Discard residue left in filter. Add pineapple juice, 2 cups confection-

ers' sugar, more or less to taste, and vanilla extract to ginger mixture, and stir well. Taste and add a little more sugar, if necessary to sweeten.

Serve in beverage glasses over ice for a refreshing drink.

GHANA

Ghana (once known as Gold Coast) is situated just above the equator in West Africa, bordering the Atlantic Ocean, Togo, Burkina Faso, and Côte d' Ivoire (Ivory Coast). Ghana is home to more than 50 small ethnic groups. More than half of Ghana's people are Christians, and about 12 percent are Muslims. The rest—mostly rural folk—practice indigenous religions. (See Protestant and Catholic Life-Cycle Rituals, page xlvi; Islam and Islamic Life-Cycle Rituals, page xlix; and Traditional African Life-Cycle Rituals, page xli.)

The clothing Ghanaians wear tells a great deal. For important events—naming ceremonies, weddings, and funerals—men wear *kente* cloth, a beautifully patterned hand-woven textile. *Kente* cloth is made into a garment about the size of a bed sheet that is worn draped over the left shoulder, with the right shoulder left bare, toga-style. The designs and colors of the *kente* cloth differ for each specific occasion, and the intricate patterns are rich in symbolism. For example, *kente* cloth woven with threads of red, a Ghanaian color of mourning, is worn by men of the Akan people when they dance the funeral rituals.

In Ghana, the traditional belief is that when a person dies, they are actually going on a journey; that life continues after death. Ghanaians often spend everything they have on funerals, and one of the hardest struggles in life is to make enough money for the eventual funeral. Part of the cost is for highly individual coffins, which are created by woodcarvers to reflect objects of special importance to the customer. There is such a demand for these creative coffins that when a person dies before theirs is ready, the body may have to be kept in a mortuary for several months. Families bury their dead with the comforts and adornments of life; for instance, hand-woven cloth, jewelry, and money are placed in the coffin.

Ghanaians love festivals. Funerals draw large crowds: often hundreds of people come for a celebration that is more jubilant than sad. During a Christian funeral ceremony, there will be a blending of Christian and traditional practices, such as when the officiating clergyman pours a libation over the coffin to ask blessings from the deceased.

Aprapransa is a delicacy of the Akwapim people, but it is eaten by all Ghanaians. When it is prepared for special occasions, smoked **herring** is added to the dish. The recipe calls for palm butter, a pulp made from palm nuts. Canned palm butter is available in some Latin American and other specialty food stores, but peanut butter is an acceptable substitute. ۞ ۞ ۞

Aprapransa

Palm Nut Stew

Yield: serves 4

1 tablespoon vegetable oil or red palm oil (available in Latin American food stores)
1 onion, **finely chopped**
1 cup cooked **black-eyed peas**, dried (cook according to directions on package), or canned
2 to 4 tablespoons palm butter (see above) or peanut butter

4 tomatoes, finely chopped and divided
water, as needed
3 tablespoons masa flour (available at all Latin American food stores and all supermarkets)
1 tablespoon lemon juice
salt and pepper to taste

Equipment: Large skillet, mixing spoon, serving bowl

1. Heat oil in large skillet over medium-high heat. Add onion, stir, and **sauté** until soft, 3 to 5 minutes. Add cooked black-eyed peas, palm butter or peanut butter, half the chopped tomatoes, and 2 cups water. Stir and bring to a boil. Reduce heat to **simmer** and cook for 5 minutes, for flavor to develop.

2. Stir in masa flour, lemon juice, and salt and pepper to taste. Reduce heat to simmer. Cook uncovered, for 10 to 15 minutes, or until thickened. Stir occasionally to prevent sticking.

To serve, transfer to serving bowl and sprinkle the top with remaining chopped tomatoes.

Ghanaians slaughter and roast cattle to feed the throngs of people who come to a funeral and stay for the feast. There are always cauldrons of cooked rice, *tuo zaafi* (recipe page 64), boiled yams, and stews such as this recipe.

Fante Mbire Flowee

Beef and Mushroom Stew

Yield: serves 6
2 pounds lean round steak
salt and pepper to taste
4 tablespoons all-purpose flour
2 tablespoons vegetable oil
2 onions, **finely chopped**
1 pound mushrooms, wiped with damp paper towel and sliced
2 cups canned stewed tomatoes
2 cups water
6 cups cooked rice (cooked according to directions on package), kept warm for serving

Equipment: Work surface, plastic wrap, **meat mallet**, knife, **Dutch oven** or large skillet with cover, spoon

1. Prepare steak: Place steak on work surface and sprinkle with salt and pepper and 2 tablespoons flour. Cover with plastic wrap and pound with meat mallet to tenderize meat by breaking down fibrous tissue. Turn the steak over, with plastic wrap on the bottom. Sprinkle the second side with remaining 2 tablespoons flour. Cover with plastic wrap and pound with meat mallet. Unwrap steak and cut into 2-inch chunks.

2. Heat 2 tablespoons oil in Dutch oven or large skillet over high heat. Add steak, stir, and **sear** on all sides, 5 to 7 minutes. Add onions and mushrooms, stir, and cook until onions are soft, 3 to 5 minutes. Add stewed tomatoes and water, and bring to boil. Stir, reduce heat to **simmer**, and cover. Stirring occasionally, cook for 1 hour, or until meat is tender. If mixture seems thin, cook uncovered for 12 to 15 minutes or until mixture thickens.

To serve, pour meat mixture over cooked rice in large bowl. Place the bowl in center of a cloth placed on the floor. Everyone eats from the bowl, using only the fingers of their right hand. The left hand must never touch food; it is used only for personal grooming.

This dish below would be prepared for a baptism celebration, first communion, or wedding feast. It is eaten with *tuo zaafi* (recipe page 64).

Hkatenkwan

Ginger Chicken and Okra

Yield: serves 4 to 6

2½ to 3 pound chicken, cut into serving-size pieces
1 tablespoon peeled and **finely chopped** fresh ginger, or 1 teaspoon **ground** ginger
1 onion, finely chopped
8 cups water
2 tablespoons tomato paste
2 tomatoes, **cored** and chopped
1 cup chunky peanut butter
½ teaspoon ground red pepper, more or less to taste
1 cup eggplant, peeled and **cubed**
1 pound whole okra, fresh or frozen, **trimmed**
salt and pepper to taste

Equipment: Large saucepan with cover or **Dutch oven**, slotted spoon, trivet

1. Put chicken pieces, ginger, onion, and water in large saucepan or Dutch oven. Bring to a boil over high heat. Reduce heat to **simmer**, cover, and cook until chicken is tender, 1 hour. Using slotted spoon, remove chicken pieces and keep warm.

2. Add tomato paste, tomatoes, peanut butter, ground red pepper, more or less to taste, eggplant, okra, and salt and pepper to taste. Bring to boil over medium-high heat, stir, and cook 5 minutes. Reduce heat to simmer, cover, and cook 10 minutes. Return chicken pieces and lay on top of vegetables. Cover and simmer for 15 minutes or until chicken is heated through.

To serve set the saucepan or Dutch oven on trivet in the middle of the table and have guests help themselves.

Porridge is a simple way to cook grains such as cornmeal, sorghum, or millet. Porridge is to Africans what bread is to Europeans and rice is to Asians. *Tuo zaafi*, made with millet, is such a staple. Muslims would serve it with *mechoui* (recipe page 75) and Christians would serve it with suckling pig (recipe page 348) at the wedding feast or other life-cycle celebrations.

Tuo Zaafi

Millet Porridge

Yield: serves 4

1 cup **millet** (available at all health food stores), soaked overnight
6 cups canned beef broth
2 tablespoons vegetable oil
1 onion, **finely chopped**
1 potato, peeled and chopped
2 carrots, **trimmed** and sliced crosswise
1 cup finely chopped cabbage
½ cup milk
salt and pepper to taste
2 tomatoes, quartered, for **garnish**

Equipment: Strainer, medium saucepan with cover, mixing spoon, medium skillet

1. Drain soaked millet in strainer placed over sink, and discard soaking water. Put millet in medium saucepan, add beef broth, and bring to boil over medium-high heat. Reduce heat to **simmer**, cover, and cook for 45 minutes, or until tender.

2. Heat oil in medium skillet over medium-high heat. Add onions, stir, and **sauté** until soft, 3 to 5 minutes. Add potatoes, carrots, and cabbage and stir. Reduce heat to simmer, cover, and cook until vegetables are soft, 12 to 15 minutes.

3. Add potato mixture to cooked millet, and stir to mix well. Add milk, stir, and cook uncovered over medium-low heat to thicken to desired consistency, 7 to 12 minutes. (It can be either soupy or thick.) Add salt and pepper to taste.

To serve, garnish with tomato wedges. If mixture is soupy, you can drink it or if thick, use the fingers of your right hand to scoop tuo zaafi *out of the container into your mouth. The left hand must never touch food; it is used only for personal grooming.*

CÔTE D' IVOIRE

Côte d' Ivoire (also known as Ivory Coast) is situated on the Atlantic coast, along the underside of the West African bulge. The neighboring countries are Liberia, Guinea, Mali, Burkina Faso, and Ghana. There are four major cultural groups in Ivory Coast, within which are 60 different ethnic groups. Each ethnic group has its own lifeways, rituals, and celebrations. Although the nation has two of the world's largest Roman Catholic cathedrals, only about 12 percent of the people are Christians, most of them Protestants. Muslims, living mostly in the north, make up a small minority of the population. Other Ivorians follow indigenous religions. (See Traditional African Life-Cycle Rituals, page xli.)

The Baoulés are the largest ethnic group. Baoulés trace kinship through their mother's family rather than their father's, and although Baoulé women live with their husband's family, women have superior authority in family matters. The land and power are passed down through a mother's family line to her sisters' sons, rather than to her own. Each Baoulé family line claims ownership of a ceremonial stool that represents the spirit of the founding ancestor of the mother's family. The male leader of the mother's family sits on this stool on important occasions, such as weddings.

Another large ethnic group in Côte d' Ivoire is the Sénoufo people, whose lifestyle, rituals, and customs are entirely different from those of the Baoulés. They believe a person's life is divided into seven-year phases, the most important being ages 14 through 21.

To prepare children for adulthood, the Sénoufo people have a secret society known as *lô*. Rigorous tests are part of the preparation for manhood, and each Sénoufo village has a "sacred forest" where these rituals take place in secret. The goal of *lô* is to preserve tribal traditions and folklore. The children are instructed over many years in the oral history and social mores of the Sénoufo people. Their education is divided into three seven-year periods ending with an initiation ceremony.

Sénoufo funerals are presided over by blacksmiths, even though they are of a low caste. Blacksmiths are believed to have a kinship with the earth that gives them special powers. During a funeral, the body is carried in a long procession through the village, while men in enormous grotesque masks follow along, chasing away the dead person's soul. Immune to evil spirits, the blacksmiths dig a hole and carefully position the body in the grave, after which they present the deceased his or her last meal. The funeral ends with a great communal feast and celebration.

One of the country's most celebrated special-occasion dishes is *kedjenou à la n'gatietro*. It is called "chicken-in-a-pot" because it is cooked in a *canari* (terracotta pot). In the Ivorian bush, the chicken is wrapped in banana leaves and cooked under the ashes of a fire instead of in a *canari*. Most dishes are served with rice and *attiéké* (recipe page 66), one of the country's best-liked specialties. *Kedjenou á la n'gatietro* can be prepared in a large electric slow cooker. Cook according to manufacturer's directions. Test for **doneness.**

Kedjenou à la N'Gatietro

Chicken-in-a-Pot

Yield: serves 6 to 8

3 to 4 pounds chicken, cut into serving-size pieces
salt and pepper to taste
4 onions, chopped
1 (16-ounces) canned chopped tomatoes
2 cloves garlic, **finely chopped**
1 tablespoon finely chopped fresh ginger, or 1 teaspoon **ground** ginger
1 bay leaf
1 cup water
1 cup peanut butter
ground red pepper, to taste
hot water, if necessary

Equipment: Large heatproof casserole with cover or **Dutch oven**, small bowl, mixing spoon, large serving platter

1. Sprinkle chicken pieces with salt and pepper to taste and layer in large heatproof casserole or Dutch oven. Add onions, canned chopped tomatoes, garlic, ginger, bay leaf, and salt and pepper to taste.

2. Put water in small bowl, and add peanut butter and ground red pepper to taste. Stir to mix well. Pour over chicken mixture and bring to boil over high heat. Reduce heat to **simmer**, cover, and cook for 1 to 1¼ hours, or until very tender. Add just enough hot water from time to time, if necessary, to prevent drying out. Test **chicken doneness**.

To serve, mound rice in center of large serving platter and arrange chicken pieces around the sides and spoon sauce over top of rice.

In Western African cooking, cassava is boiled and eaten as a vegetable; boiled and mashed into a porridge; or grated and dried for use as a staple food, similar to rice used in breads and dumplings. *Attiéké* is made with *gari* (also called *farina de manioca*), which is dried, coarsely ground cassava meal that has been toasted. You need to reconstitute *gari* to make *attiéké,* a grain-like dish resembling **couscous**.

Attiéké

Cassava Meal

Yield: 2 cups

1 cup **cassava** meal or gari (available at health food or Latin American food stores or multi-ethnic supermarkets)
cold water, as needed

Equipment: medium mixing bowl, whisk

1. Put cassava meal in medium mixing bowl. Stir in just enough water to completely cover cassava meal. Let stand for 10 minutes or until all water is absorbed.

2. Beat mixture with whisk until fluffy, 3 to 5 minutes.

Serve attiéké *as a side dish with* kedjenou á la n'gatietro *(recipe precedes) or any hot meat or fish dishes.*

Every feast includes assorted vegetables dishes, such as *jamma jamma*. Any combination of greens can be used to make this dish.

Jamma Jamma

Spiced Greens

Yield: serves 4 to 6

2 bunches **mustard greens**, **collard greens**, or spinach, or combination
3 tablespoons vegetable oil
1 onion, thinly sliced
3 cloves garlic, **finely chopped**
½ teaspoon **ground** red pepper, more or less to taste
¼ cup water
salt and pepper to taste

Equipment: Knife, paper towels, large skillet with cover, mixing spoon

1. Remove and discard stalks from mustard greens. If using collard greens or spinach, trim and discard stems. Rinse greens thoroughly under cold running water and shake to remove excess water. Pat dry with paper towels. Tear leaves into bite-size pieces. (You should have between 4 and 6 cups of greens.)

2. Heat oil in large skillet over medium-high heat. Add garlic and onion, and **sauté** until onion is soft, 3 to 5 minutes. Sprinkle in 1/4 teaspoon ground red pepper, more or less to taste. Stir constantly for about 30 seconds and add greens. Reduce heat to medium, cover, and cook until wilted, 3 to 5 minutes. Add broth and salt and pepper to taste and stir. Cover and cook until tender, 5 to 7 minutes. Remove from heat and serve immediately.

Serve jamma jamma *as a side dish with meat, chicken, or fish dishes.*

Sauces made with either palm nuts or peanuts are eaten to enhance the flavor of most dishes, much as Americans eat mustard or ketchup. This is a popular peanut sauce.

Sauce Arachide

Peanut Sauce

Yield: about 1 1/2 cups

- 1 cup unsalted peanuts, shelled and **roasted**
- 2 cups water
- salt to taste
- 1 teaspoon **ground** chili powder
- 2 tablespoons peanut oil
- 1 onion, **finely chopped**

Equipment: Electric **blender**, rubber spatula, small saucepan, mixing spoon, small skillet, small serving bowl

1. Put peanuts in blender and add enough water (1/2 to 1 cup) to **blend** into smooth paste.

2. Bring remaining water to boil in small saucepan over high heat. Reduce heat to **simmer** and stir in peanut mixture, salt to taste, and chili powder. Cook for 10 minutes.

3. Heat oil in small skillet over medium-high heat. Add onion and **sauté** until soft, about 3 minutes. Add onion to nut mixture, stir well, and continue to cook for 10 minutes more.

Serve sauce in small serving bowl and everyone uses it as they like. It is often poured over jamma jamma.

SIERRA LEONE

Sierra Leone is located on the Atlantic Coast of Africa, on the West African "bulge." It is one of the wettest countries in the region, with a rainy season that extends from May through November.

The two largest ethnic groups in Sierra Leone are the Temnes in the north and the Mendes in the south. The Temnes, who are Muslims, love pomp and pageantry, and they incorporate their own elaborate ceremonies in the life-milestone religious rites prescribed by the Koran. The Mende people are known for their secret societies, which are responsible for training children in matters of tribal law and cultural traditions. Like most Sierra Leoneans, they follow indigenous religious practices. The Creoles are a small group of Christians who are descendants of slaves who returned to Africa from Great Britain and North America. (See Protestant and Catholic Life-Cycle Rituals, page xlvi.)

In Sierra Leone, parents traditionally arrange marriages. In these arranged unions, the girls customarily have no say in whom they marry. Because brides have value and bring bride-price to the family, parents see to it that their daughters are attractive and well-trained. In some ethnic groups, girls of marriageable age go through a "fattening ceremony." They are kept in a special house for 2–12 months to be force-fed, in order to achieve a well-rounded figure. On the other hand, an educated women today may have a career and may be choosy about her husband. The bride-price in such a situation may be a sum of money to set the woman up in business.

Sierra Leoneans are always ready for a celebration. A wedding leads to days of visiting with friends, gift-giving, and feasting. The wedding feast day usually begins early in the morning and continues far into the night.

Another occasion for the gathering of friends and relatives is the naming of a child, usually on the 28th day of its life. Again, the celebration begins early in the day with singing, dancing, and feasting. Parents give their children such names as the season of their birth, the day of the week on which they were born, or weather conditions on the day of birth.

The Muslim wedding feast begins with *méchoui* (recipe page 75) or whole roasted lamb, such as *kabab barreh* (recipe page 141), vegetable dishes, and mountains of rice or *abala* (recipe page 70). The wedding and funeral feast for Christians and traditional practitioners would be *yassa* (recipe page 80), a specialty of most West African countries. It is made with lamb, fish, chicken, or even monkey. Serve with abala, ***couscous*** (cook according to directions on package), or *tuo zaafi* (recipe page 64). An added treat on the banquet table would be *ogede sise*. Allow 1 or 2 bananas per person.

Ogede Sise

Boiled Bananas

Yield: serves 3 to 6

- 6 cups water
- 6 bananas, with skin on

Equipment: Medium saucepan with cover, slotted metal spoon or metal tongs, paring knife, serving platter

1. Pour water into medium saucepan, and bring to boil over high heat. Add bananas with skin on, and bring water back to boil. Reduce heat to **simmer**, cover, and cook 15 minutes.

2. Remove bananas with slotted metal spoon or tongs and place on serving platter. Slit skins lengthwise with paring knife and serve at once.

To serve, place platter of bananas on the table. Each person eats the banana out of the skin, either by breaking it into bite-size pieces or scooping it out using only the fingers of the right hand. The left hand must never touch food; it is used only for personal grooming. The banana can also be eaten with a spoon or fork.

Sweets at celebrations are eaten as a symbol of prosperity and good luck. *Kanya* usually satisfies everyone's sweet tooth. The candy can be made into balls or bars, as in this recipe.

Kanya

Peanut Candy

Yield: about 15 pieces

- 1 cup smooth peanut butter
- 1 cup sugar
- 1 cup cream of rice or wheat cereal, more or less as needed

Equipment: 8-inch square cake pan, wax paper, food processor, rubber spatula, spoon, plastic food wrap, knife

Prepare pan: Line bottom of 8-inch square cake pan with wax paper.

1. Put peanut butter and sugar in food processor and process until well mixed. While running, slowly add just enough cream of rice or wheat cereal (about 1 cup) through feed tube to make firm dough.

Note: While processing, turn machine off once or twice and scrape down sides of container with rubber spatula.

2. Transfer mixture to prepared cake pan. Using your hand or back of spoon, press evenly to cover bottom of pan. Cover with plastic wrap and refrigerate to set and chill, at least 4 hours or overnight.

To serve, cut into small rectangular bars and eat as candy.

LIBERIA

Liberia was founded in 1821 by African American settlers from the United States whose ancestors had been taken from Africa as slaves. Liberia lies along the Atlantic coast, on the western "bulge" of Africa. It shares borders with Sierra Leone, Guinea, and Côte d' Ivoire. It is one of the last West African countries with a significant rain forest (an estimated 44 percent of the nation's land). Most Liberians are subsistence farmers.

The population is made up of 16 ethnic groups. About 5 percent of the people are descendants of freed slaves from the Americas. Twenty percent of the people are Muslims and almost an equal number are Christians, the majority of whom are Protestants. Other Liberians practice local religions. Indigenous beliefs and customs are part of all life-cycle celebrations in Liberia. (See Islam and Islamic Life-Cycle Rituals, page xlix; Protestant and Catholic Life-Cycle Rituals, page xlvi; and Traditional African Life-Cycle Rituals, page xli.)

The ethnic groups in Liberia have intermarried, and there is not the same strong sense of separation between groups as is found in most other parts of Africa. For example, there are secret societies in Liberia that are not restricted to a particular tribe—they are based on caste rather than on ethnicity. The men's society is called *poro* and the women's is called *sande*. Liberian secret societies have rites and ceremonies that are similar to those of most African tribes, but they are also involved in areas beyond religion and the education of the young; for instance, they control the activities of indigenous medical practitioners and they often judge disputes between members of high-ranking families.

Life-cycle celebrations in Liberia are communal, and they always involve music and dancing. Each community has its own drummers and musicians who play for weddings, school graduations, and other communal celebrations.

One of the most popular festive dishes is red nut stew, traditionally eaten with rice. Red nuts grow on oil palm trees, and although they are plentiful in Liberia, they are not easily available in the United States.

A soup with many variations that has traveled up and down the West African coast is pepper soup. It is cooked outdoors in a cauldron. Red nut stew or pepper soup are often eaten to restore health at the end of the wedding celebration. Meat is added when the soup is prepared for celebration feasts.

Pepper Soup

Note: Use care when handling peppers. Wrap your hands in plastic wrap or cover them with plastic sandwich bag. If you accidentally touch your eyes while handling peppers, rinse them out at once under cold running water.

Yield: serves 4 to 6

1 pound lean stewing beef, cut into bite-size pieces
8 cups water
2 hot green chili peppers (**jalapeños**), seeded and **finely chopped**, or **ground** red pepper to taste
1 onion, finely chopped
4 **new potatoes**, with skin on, washed, and cut into bite-size pieces
2 tomatoes, **peeled** and chopped
½ cup tomato paste
salt and pepper to taste
2 cups cooked rice (cooked according to directions on package), for serving

Equipment: Large saucepan with cover or **Dutch oven**, mixing spoon, ladle, individual soup bowls

Put meat, water, finely chopped peppers or ground red pepper to taste, onion, potatoes, tomatoes, tomato paste, and salt and pepper to taste in large saucepan or Dutch oven. Bring to boil over high heat. Stir well and reduce heat to **simmer**. Cover and cook until meat is very tender, 1 to 1½ hours.

To serve, divide cooked rice equally between 4 to 6 soup bowls and ladle hot soup over the rice.

Several rice dishes are always on the menu for life-cycle celebrations. In Sierra Leone and Liberia, banana leaves are used instead of foil to encase the rice mixture.

Abala

Savory Steamed Rice

Note: Use care when handling peppers. Wrap your hands in plastic wrap or cover them with plastic sandwich bag. If you accidentally touch your eyes while handling peppers, rinse them out at once under cold running water.

Yield: serves 6

1 cup cream of rice cereal (available at all supermarkets)
¾ to 1 cup boiling water
1 hot green chili pepper (**jalapeño**), **seeded** and **finely chopped**
1 onion, finely chopped
¼ cup vegetable oil
1 teaspoon salt

Equipment: Medium mixing bowl, mixing spoon, plastic food wrap, aluminum foil, work surface, **steamer pan**, metal tongs

1. Put cream of rice in medium mixing bowl. Stirring constantly, slowly add just enough boiling water (between ¾ to 1 cup) to make a smooth, firm mixture. Add finely chopped pepper, finely chopped onion, oil, and salt, and stir well. Cool to room temperature and cover with plastic wrap. Refrigerate for 1 hour to firm and chill.

2. Place 6 (8 or 9 inch square) pieces of foil on work surface. Mound equal amounts of mixture in the center of each square and enclose securely in foil.

3. Steam *abala*: Pour water into bottom of steamer, keeping it below, not touching, the rack or container that holds the food. Stack foil-wrapped packages on rack or in container and bring to boil over high heat. Reduce heat to **simmer**, cover, and steam until rice mixture is fully cooked and holds together, about 2 hours. Open foil package to check doneness.

Note: Check water level frequently during steaming to be sure there is at least 1 inch of water in bottom pan. Add more hot water, when necessary.

To serve, each person is given an abala. *Each guest opens their own and eats out of the wrapping, like eating a candy bar.*

Except in urban areas, most people in Africa don't have ovens—thus, few recipes call for baking. Cookies such as these can be made in homes with modern appliances or they can be bought at a bakery. These cookies would be served to guests who have come to a baby-naming party.

Kyekyire Paano

Toasted Cornmeal Cookies

Yield: about 24 pieces

1 cup yellow or white **cornmeal**
1½ cups all-purpose flour
½ teaspoon salt
½ teaspoon nutmeg
½ cup butter or margarine, at room temperature
½ cup sugar
2 eggs, beaten
1 teaspoon grated lemon rind

Equipment: Baking sheet, oven mitts, metal spatula, flour **sifter**, small bowl, large mixing bowl, electric mixer or mixing spoon, plate

Preheat oven to 350° F.

1. Spread cornmeal in baking sheet and place in oven or until lightly browned, about 20 minutes. Using oven mitts, stir with metal spatula so cornmeal toasts evenly. Remove from oven and cool to room temperature.

2. **Sift** flour, salt, and nutmeg into small bowl.

3. Put butter or margarine in large mixing bowl, add sugar, and beat with electric mixer or mixing spoon until fluffy and light, 1 to 2 minutes. Add flour, toasted cornmeal, salt, nutmeg, eggs, and lemon rind. Beat until well mixed. Leaving at least 1½ inches between, drop spoonfuls of dough onto baking sheet, making each cookie about the size of a Ping-Pong ball.

Increase oven to 375° F.

4. Bake in oven for 15 to 20 minutes, or until golden brown.

To serve, arrange cookies on a plate and set out as a snack with milk.

Cocoa was introduced to West Africa from Latin America and it is now a major export crop in such countries as Ghana, Côte d' Ivoire, and Sierra Leone. *Frejon* has an unusual combination of flavors. It often accompanies savory dishes at a wedding or funeral feast.

Frejon

Beans with Cocoa

Yield: serves 4

3 cups cooked **black-eyed peas**, homemade (cooked according to directions on package), or canned
½ cup coconut milk, homemade (recipe page 346), or canned (available at most supermarkets and Latin American food stores)
1 tablespoon cocoa powder, more or less to taste
2 tablespoons sugar, more or less to taste

Equipment: **Colander**, **blender**, rubber spatula, medium saucepan, mixing spoon, serving bowl

1. Drain cooked or canned black-eyed peas in colander and discard liquid. Put drained peas and coconut milk in blender and **purée**.

2. Transfer mixture to medium saucepan, and stir in 1 tablespoon cocoa powder, more or less to taste. Sprinkle in 2 tablespoons sugar, a little at a time, to get desired sweetness. Stirring fre-

quently, cook over medium heat for flavor to develop and to heat through, 7 to 12 minutes.

To serve, transfer to a serving bowl to eat as a side dish or sauce with meat or fish.

GUINEA AND GUINEA-BISSAU

The Republic of Guinea and its tiny neighbor Guinea-Bissau border the Atlantic Ocean on the west coast of Africa. Their closest neighbors are Senegal, Mali, Côte d'Ivoire, Liberia, and Sierra Leone.

In Guinea, more than 75 percent of the people are Muslims, and in Guinea-Bissau, about half are Muslims. Except for a few Christians in the urban areas, the rest of the people in both countries adhere to traditional local religions. (See Islam and Islamic Life-Cycle Rituals, page xlix, and Traditional African Life-Cycle Rituals, page xli.)

Muslims in Guinea and Guinea-Bissau combine local customs with general Islamic practices in all life-cycle celebrations. Traditionally, when a Muslim man in these countries is informed that his wife is pregnant, he must collect at least a three-month supply of firewood for the hot baths she will take after the delivery. Just after the birth, the mother drinks a spicy gruel made with potash. Four days after the birth, a soup made with the legs and jaw of a cow is prepared for the new mother.

Seven days after a birth, a naming ceremony is held for the baby. The father gives kola nuts to his parents, in-laws, friends, and neighbors. The ground in front of his house is thoroughly swept to set down carpets and mats for guests to sit on, and he must provide either a bull or ram to be sacrificed for this occasion. When the animal is being slaughtered, the *malaam* (Islamic religious leader) is told the name for the child. After the sacrifice, the *malaam* prays, blesses the child, and whispers the chosen name in its ear. A barber shaves the infant's head completely and—if it is the clan's tradition—he makes the desired tribal marks, called scarification, on the child. After the rituals are complete, there is a dancing, singing, and feasting celebration.

Circumcision of boys at seven years of age is required by Islamic law, although some put it off until the child is about nine. A group of boys who undergo circumcision at the same time often feel a bond with one another that lasts a lifetime. A barber trained in circumcision performs the procedure. The boys live together until they are healed; they are kept away from other people and fed only millet or corn porridge (recipes page 64 and 29). Once healed, the boys are washed, their heads are shaved, and they each receive a new *bante* (loincloth). They are then presented to the public at a celebration that includes a dance and a feast. A cow or lamb is slaughtered and roasted for the occasion.

When a Muslim dies in an urban area, he or she is buried in a communal cemetery. In rural areas, each family has its own burial area in their residential compound. The body is prepared according to specific religious rules. It is wrapped in a *kubba* (white cotton shroud) and carried to the burial site. The body is buried on its side with its face turned toward Mecca (the Islamic holy city).

After the burial, the bereaved family gives food to the poor, on behalf of the deceased: millet, corn or bean cakes similar to *tamiya* (recipe page 83), and millet porridge such as *tuo zaafi* (recipe page 64). A man has no designated mourning period after his wife dies, and he can remarry soon after her death. A woman is expected to mourn her dead husband for up to 4 months and 10 days. During the mourning period, widows do not comb their hair, nor do they wear jewelry or cosmetics.

Many dishes, especially stews, have crossed the borders from one African country to another. The dishes change somewhat since each cook adds a unique blend of spices and ingredients, which may be available in one country but not in another. Some dishes are similar to *kansiyé*, for instance Zimbabwe's *dovi* (recipe page 31).

Kansiyé

Guinean Goulash (Stew)

Yield: serves 4 to 6

3 tablespoons vegetable oil
1½ to 2 pounds beef or lamb cut into 1-inch cubes, or small chicken cut into serving-size pieces
1 onion, **finely chopped**
2 cloves garlic
½ teaspoon **ground** thyme
1 teaspoon ground clove
salt and pepper to taste
½ cup tomato sauce
3 tablespoons smooth peanut butter
3 cups water
4 to 6 cups cooked rice, for serving

Equipment: Large saucepan with cover or **Dutch oven**, mixing spoon, small bowl

1. Heat oil in large saucepan or Dutch oven over medium-high heat. Add meat or chicken and brown all sides, 7 to 12 minutes. Add onions and garlic, sprinkle in thyme, clove, and salt and pepper to taste.

2. In small bowl, combine tomato sauce and peanut butter with water. Stir until mixture is smooth, and pour over meat or chicken. Bring to boil. Reduce heat to **simmer**, cover, and cook for 1 to 1½ hours until very tender.

Serve over cooked rice.

Salt water and fresh water fishing are important industries in both Guinea and Guinea-Bissau. When properly **garnished**, this fish dish would be perfect to serve along with other dishes at a life-cycle celebration.

Poisson de Guinée

Guinean Fish

Yield: serves 4 to 6

2 to 3 pounds fish **fillets**, with skin on (trout, halibut, salmon, or red snapper)
8 tablespoons vegetable oil, divided
ground red pepper to taste
½ teaspoon ground cloves
salt and pepper to taste
1 onion, **finely chopped**
2 tomatoes, chopped
2 tablespoons tomato paste
1 tablespoon **ground** dried shrimp (available at Asian food stores)
1 onion, sliced into ¼-inch thick rings and separated, for **garnish**
1 plantain, sliced into ¼-inch thick circles, for garnish
4 cups cooked rice, kept warm, for serving
2 hard-cooked eggs, peeled and sliced, for garnish
1 green bell pepper, **trimmed**, **seeded**, and **julienned**, for garnish

Equipment: Paper towels, medium shallow baking pan, plastic food wrap, large skillet, mixing spoon, medium bowl, oven mitts, fork, large serving platter

1. Rinse fish fillets under cold running water, drain, and pat dry with paper towels. Put fish into medium shallow baking pan. **Drizzle** both sides of fish with 4 tablespoons oil. Sprinkle with ground red pepper to taste, cloves, and salt and pepper to taste. Cover with plastic wrap and refrigerate for 1 to 2 hours while preparing sauce and garnish.

2. Prepare sauce: Heat 2 tablespoons oil in large skillet over medium-high heat. Add chopped onion and **sauté** until soft, 3 to 5 minutes. Add chopped tomatoes, tomato paste, ground dried shrimp, and salt and pepper to taste. Stir to mix well. Reduce heat to **simmer**, and cook 3 to 5 minutes for flavor to develop. Transfer to medium bowl.

3. Prepare garnish: Heat remaining 2 tablespoons oil in large skillet over medium-high heat. Add onion rings, plantains, and salt and pepper to taste. Stir and sauté until lightly brown, 5 to 7 minutes.

Preheat oven to 350° F.

4. Remove plastic wrap from fish. Pour prepared sauce over fish. Bake in oven for 12 to 18 minutes until fish is opaque white and flakes easily when poked with a fork.

Serve by making a mound of cooked rice on large serving platter with raised edge. Lay fish on top of rice and spoon sauce over it. Garnish with sautéed onion rings and plantains. Arrange egg slices over the top and sprinkle with julienned green pepper.

SENEGAL AND GAMBIA

Senegal and Gambia are on the western "bulge" of Africa, along the Atlantic Ocean. Except for about 75 miles of coastline, English-speaking Gambia is entirely surrounded by French-speaking Senegal, which is bordered by Mauritania, Mali, Guinea, and Guinea-Bissau. The majority of people in both countries live in villages made up of compounds that house extended families

The majority of people in Senegal and Gambia are Muslims. Traditional local religions and customs are intermixed with Islam in both countries, especially in beliefs concerning death. Bad luck, childbirth deaths, and other sudden deaths are believed to be the work of witches, who steal people's souls immediately after birth or during circumcision, when a human is most vulnerable to attack. Also typical of the blending of Islamic and indigenous beliefs is the wearing of *jujus*. A juju is a leather amulet worn around the wrist, neck, waist, or ankle to bring good luck.

Much of African life centers around special events, such as weddings, baptisms, funerals, and village celebrations. Most celebrations in Senegal and Gambia include dancing, singing, and feasting.

Weddings are celebrated with great enthusiasm. On the day of the marriage, the legal and religious ceremonies are performed as early as possible so the day can be spent celebrating. The offering of kola nuts plays a special role in weddings, as well as on other special occasions. Biting into a kola nut is an age-old ceremony meant as a blessing. During a traditional wedding, the bride's grandmother and great-aunts take her to the marriage chamber where they lecture her about the pleasures and perils of marriage. If the first night of marriage goes well, the next morning, guests shower the bride with gifts. Senegalese and Gambian Muslim men may have up to four wives, if they can afford to support them.

Circumcision is an important rite for Muslim boys that is performed shortly after they reach puberty. Among some Gambian ethnic groups, before the procedure, the boys are dressed like women and wear shells and jewels in their long hair. Afterward, still wearing their costumes, they stay away from people and live in special huts until healed. On returning to their village, they are honored with a feast.

When affluent Senegalese and Gambian family and friends gather for a circumcision or wedding celebration, *méchoui*—roasted lamb (recipe follows) or goat—is prepared for the event. The meat is brushed with a mixture of hot pepper sauce, water, and peanut oil. As it roasts, the surface of the meat becomes crusty and spicy, and the inside stays moist and soft. For urban dwellers, *méchoui* is baked in the oven.

Many other dishes are served along with the meat. For those who cannot afford *méchoui*, a little meat is added to rice and vegetables, such as *gombos* (okra). Most dishes are served with "broken rice," rice that has been broken into tiny granules. Originally, broken pieces of rice were used because they were all that the Senegalese could afford—whole grains were reserved for export. Eventually, broken grains became a staple of Senegalese cooking, and now rice is grown and broken in order to supply the demand.

At feasts, family and guests assemble on the floor on a mat or cloth around platters of food. Eating is done only with the right hand (the left hand is used for personal grooming), although some city-dwellers use spoons.

Méchoui

Lamb Roast

Yield: serves 15 to 18

- 8 to 10 pounds lean lamb roast or baron (saddle and two legs) of lamb
- salt and pepper to taste
- juice of 2 lemons
- 2 tablespoons Dijon mustard

Equipment: Paper towels, large shallow roasting pan with rack, small bowl, mixing spoon, oven mitts, **bulb baster**, carving board, sharp knife, meat fork, large serving platter

Preheat oven to 450° F.

1. Wash lamb thoroughly and pat dry with paper towels. Place lamb on rack in large shallow roasting pan and sprinkle with salt and pepper to taste.

2. Put juice of two lemons, finely chopped garlic, and mustard in small bowl. Stir to mix well. Using your hand, rub mustard mixture over surface of lamb.

3. Place lamb in hot oven to **sear** for 35 to 45 minutes. Reduce heat to 325° F and continue to bake for 3½ to 4½ hours, or until meat thermometer registers about 150° F for medium. Allow 20 minutes per pound for rare meat and 35 minutes per pound for well done meat. While baking, **baste** occasionally with pan drippings using mixing spoon or bulb baster. Remove from oven and let rest at least 20 minutes before carving.

4. Transfer meat to carving board, and using sharp knife and holding meat in place with meat fork, cut across grain into thin slices and transfer to large serving platter. Set platter on the tablecloth set on the floor.

Serve mechoui *with North African* chlada felfel *(recipe page 90)*, thiebou nop niébé *(recipe follows), and* ***couscous*** *(cooked according to directions on package) seasoned with lamb drippings.*

This is one of many dishes served with lamb at a celebration feast. *Niébé* is made with beans called "the little eye of Senegal," similar to black-eyed peas.

Thiebou Nop Niébé

Black-eyed Peas and Rice

Note: This recipe takes 2 days.

Yield: serves 6 to 8

- 1 pound (about 2 cups) dried **black-eyed peas**

6 cups water
½ pound smoked ham hocks
1 onion, **chopped**
1 teaspoon **ground** red pepper, more or less to taste
1 cup cooked rice

Equipment: Medium bowl, **colander**, medium saucepan with cover, mixing spoon, tongs or slotted spoon, cutting board, sharp knife

1. In medium bowl, soak black-eyed peas in water over night.

2. Drain peas in colander and discard soaking water. Put peas in medium saucepan and cover with 6 cups water. Add ham hock, onion, and 1 teaspoon ground red pepper, more or less to taste, and bring to a boil. Reduce heat to **simmer** and stir. Cover and cook until the peas and meat are tender, 1 to 1 ½ hours.

3. Using tongs or slotted spoon, remove ham hocks and transfer to cutting board. Using a sharp knife, remove and discard skin from ham hock. Cut meat from bone and slice into small pieces. Return meat to saucepan with peas, stir in cooked rice, and heat through over medium heat, 5 to 7 minutes.

Serve as a side dish with lamb and salad.

Dem Saint-Louis is a specialty of Saint-Louis, a coastal town that was once the capital of Senegal. In Senegal, mullet is the fish used for this dish; however, any small, firm fish can be used. Rainbow trout is an excellent substitute.

Dem Saint-Louis

Stuffed Mullet, Saint-Louis Style

Yield: serves 4
4 whole mullet or rainbow trout, 10 to 12 ounces each, cleaned, with head and tail intact
1 cup onion, **finely chopped** and divided
½ cup green onions, finely chopped and divided
4 cloves garlic, crushed and divided
14 ounces canned chopped stewed tomatoes
salt and pepper to taste
4 ounces skinless fish **fillets, coarsely chopped** (cod, white fish, or tilapia)
2 eggs
½ cup tomato paste
¼ teaspoon **ground** red pepper, more or less to taste
1 cup fresh **bread crumbs**
1 tablespoon vegetable oil

Equipment: Paper towels, work surface, 12- x 9- x 1½-inch baking pan, mixing spoon, food processor, medium mixing bowl, rubber spatula, greased **pastry brush**, oven mitts

1. Place several sheets of paper towels on work surface. Rinse each fish under cold running water and drain on paper towels.

2. Put ½ cup onions, ¼ cup green onions, and 2 cloves garlic in baking pan. Add canned stewed tomatoes and salt and pepper to taste. Using mixing spoon, stir and spread mixture evenly over bottom of baking pan. Set aside.

Preheat oven to 350° F.

3. Prepare stuffing: Put coarsely chopped fish fillets in food processor. Add eggs and tomato paste and process until smooth and well mixed, about 1 minute.

Note: While processing, turn machine off once or twice and scrape down sides of container with rubber spatula.

4. Transfer mixture to medium mixing bowl. Add salt and pepper to taste, remaining ½ cup onion, ¼ cup green onions, and 2 cloves garlic. Add ¼ teaspoon ground red pepper, more or less to taste, and bread crumbs, and stir until well mixed. Stuff each whole fish with processed fish mixture and place side by side on tomato mixture in baking pan. Any leftover stuffing can be shaped into egg-shaped balls. Slightly flatten

leftover balls into patties and place in sauce around fish. Using pastry brush, brush top of each fish lightly with oil.

5. Bake in oven for 25 to 30 minutes, or until fish and stuffing are done.

To serve, cut each fish into 4 pieces and serve directly from the pan. In Senegal and Gambia most people pick up the food and eat it with the fingers of their right hand. (The left hand is used for personal grooming and must not touch the food.) Rice (recipe page 70), millet (recipe page 64), or ***couscous*** *(cooked according to directions on package) is served with this dish.*

Boulettes de Poisson

Fish Balls in Sauce

CAUTION: HOT OIL USED

Yield: serves 6 to 8

1 pound skinless fish **fillets** (cod, haddock, red snapper, or trout), cut in chunks
1 onion, chopped
1 tablespoon parsley, chopped
½ cup **bread crumbs**
1 egg
salt and pepper to taste
4 tablespoons oil, divided
1 onion, **finely chopped**
1 cup tomato paste
1 cup water
ground red pepper, to taste

Equipment: Food processor, rubber spatula, medium mixing bowl, mixing spoon, paper towels, 2 baking sheets, large skillet with cover, slotted metal spatula, serving platter

1. Put fish fillet chunks in food processor, add chopped onion, parsley, bread crumbs, and egg. Process until smooth. Transfer mixture to medium mixing bowl. Add salt and pepper to taste.

Note: While processing, turn machine off once or twice and scrape down sides of container with rubber spatula.

2. Prepare to skillet-fry: ADULT SUPERVISION REQUIRED. Place several layers of paper towels on baking sheet. Heat 2 tablespoons oil in large skillet over medium-high heat. Form fish mixture into egg-size balls, flatten slightly, and place in skillet. Lower heat to medium and fry on both sides, in batches, until lightly browned, 3 to 5 minutes on each side. Remove with slotted metal spatula and place on paper towel-covered baking sheet to drain.

3. Heat remaining 2 tablespoons oil in same large skillet over medium-high heat. Add finely chopped onion and **sauté** until soft, 3 to 5 minutes. Stir in tomato paste, water, salt and pepper to taste, and ground red pepper to taste. Cook for 5 minutes, until slightly thickened. Reduce heat to **simmer**, and add fish balls. Cover and cook for 30 minutes.

To serve, transfer to a serving platter and serve as finger food with other dishes.

This dish is frequently served on special occasions, and like many African dishes, it can be simple or very complex. *Thiakry* (also *chakrey*) can be eaten as dessert, but in Senegal and Gambia, everything is put on the table to eat at one time.

Thiakry (also Chakrey)

Sweetened Couscous with Yogurt

Yield: serves 6 to 8

2 cups water
½ teaspoon salt
10-ounce package **couscous** about 2¼ cups)
2 cups plain or vanilla yogurt
1 teaspoon vanilla extract
1 cup half & half
4 tablespoons granulated sugar, more or less to taste
fresh mint leaves, for **garnish**

Equipment: Medium saucepan with cover, mixing spoon, fork, medium mixing bowl, rubber spatula, small serving bowls

1. Pour water into medium saucepan and bring to boil over high heat. Add salt, slowly stir in couscous, and cover the pan. Immediately remove from heat and let stand undisturbed for 10 minutes, or until water is completely absorbed. Uncover, fluff with fork, and let cool.

2. In medium bowl, add yogurt, vanilla extract, and half & half, and stir to mix well.

3. Using rubber spatula, **fold in** couscous with yogurt mixture and **blend** well. Add 4 tablespoons sugar, more or less to taste.

To serve, spoon into small serving bowls and either eat with a spoon or pick the bowl up and sip.

BURKINA FASO

Burkina Faso is a landlocked country in West Africa, sharing borders with Côte d'Ivoire, Mali, Niger, Benin, Togo, and Ghana. The nation has more than 60 ethnic groups, the largest of which is the Mossi. For centuries, the Mossi resisted northern Muslim forces that tried to convert them to Islam. Today, most Muslims in Burkina Faso live in the north, and they account for about 40 percent of the population. (See Islam and Islamic Life-Cycle Rituals, page xlix.) About 50 percent of the population maintains indigenous religious beliefs. (See Traditional African Life-Cycle Rituals, page xli.) The nation's small number of Christians are predominantly Roman Catholics, mostly urban dwellers. (See Protestant and Catholic Life-Cycle Rituals, page xlvi.)

In Burkina Faso, no traditional life-milestone event takes place without sorcery and contacting the spirits. Among Muslims, as soon as a baby is born, an amulet is placed in the swaddling to ward off "the evil eye." The baby and mother are kept in seclusion until the naming ceremony, which occurs when the child is about three months old. If the baby is a boy, there is always a great celebration. The next important event in a Muslim boy's life is when he is circumcised at about seven years of age. Whole-roasted lamb (recipe page 141) is traditionally prepared for the feast.

Muslim marriages are arranged by parents, usually between first cousins. The rituals begin when a spokesman for the groom, usually an uncle, comes to negotiate the bride-price with the bride's father or a family elder. The bride-price is paid, and the local religious leader sanctions the union. Islamic law allows a man to have four wives.

Funerals among Burkina Faso's Bobo people can be dramatic events. When a person of wealth or importance dies, such as a village chief, a great funeral takes place about six months afterward. Dozens of masked dancers, each in the image of a different spirit, become increasingly energetic during the all-night ritual, performing spectacular acrobatics, taking giant leaps in the air, and looking for evil spirits that might prevent the deceased from going to paradise.

All life-cycle celebrations call for a feast, which must include meat, fish, or fowl. In rural areas, bush rodent is a tasty delicacy. In the cities, *broasheht* (recipe page 56) and grilled beef, chicken, rabbit, and goat are popular. Favorite beverages are nonalcoholic ginger beer and Senegalese *bissap*, a fruit juice drink.

If you grow your own sweet potatoes, you could use the green tops for this recipe—otherwise, substitute fresh spinach, collard greens, turnip greens, or mustard greens. West African dried smoked fish is a special ingredient added to many dishes because of its extremely strong flavor. It is available at African food stores and multi-ethnic supermarkets. Easily available dried **salt cod** makes a good substitute. ❂ ❂ ❂

Sauce aux Feuilles de Patates Douces

Fish with Sweet Potato Greens

Note: This recipe takes 2 days.

Yield: serves 4 to 6

- 1 pound dried **salt cod** (available at all Latin American food stores and some supermarkets)
- water, as needed
- 2 bay leaves
- 2 onions, chopped
- 2 cloves garlic, chopped
- 2 tomatoes, chopped
- 4 tablespoons tomato paste
- 1 teaspoon **ground** red pepper, more or less to taste
- 2 tablespoons vegetable oil
- 20 to 24 whole okra
- 10-ounces sweet potato leaves or other greens (see above), washed and **trimmed**
- ½ teaspoon ground nutmeg

Equipment: Medium bowl, work surface, medium saucepan, slotted spoon, plate, food processor, rubber spatula, large **heavy-based** skillet with cover, mixing spoon, medium saucepan with cover, **colander**

1. Put salt cod in medium bowl, and cover with cold water. Set on work surface to soak overnight. The next day, transfer fish to medium saucepan and discard soaking water. Cover fish generously with fresh cold water. Add bay leaves and bring to boil over medium-high heat. Reduce heat to **simmer** and cook 20 minutes. Using slotted spoon, remove fish and transfer to plate. Discard cooking liquid and bay leaves.

2. Put onions, garlic, chopped tomatoes, tomato paste, and 1 teaspoon ground red pepper, more or less to taste, in food processor. Process until smooth, about 30 seconds.

Note: While processing, turn machine off once or twice and scrape down sides of container with rubber spatula.

3. Heat oil in large heavy-based skillet over medium-high heat. Add tomato mixture, okra, and 2 cups water, stir, and bring to boil. Reduce heat to simmer, cover, and cook until okra is tender, 12 to 15 minutes.

4. Put greens in medium saucepan and add 2 cups water. Bring to boil over medium-high heat. Reduce heat to simmer, cover, and cook until tender, 10 to 15 minutes. Drain in colander.

5. Using your hands, flake cooked salt cod into tomato mixture. Add drained greens and sprinkle with nutmeg. Toss gently to mix. Cover and simmer for flavor to develop, 40 to 45 minutes. Stir occasionally.

Serve with putu *(recipe page 29). Use a chunk of* putu *to scoop up a morsel of fish mixture and pop it in your mouth. Also serve with cooked rice or millet.*

Yassa is the supreme West African party dish. It is a favorite for family gatherings, such as the party for a newborn or for the bride-price meeting. Spread a cloth on the floor and put the large serving platter of *yassa* in the center. Guests must remove their shoes outside before squatting to eat. All guests, having washed their hands, eat only from the section of bowl in front of them. It is rude to reach across into someone else's section.

Yassa

Chicken and Rice

Yield: serves 8 to 12

4 to 5 pounds chicken, cut into serving-size pieces
8 cloves garlic, **finely chopped**
8 onions, chopped
2 cups red wine vinegar
1 cup vegetable oil, more as needed
crushed dried chili pepper, to taste
salt and pepper to taste
8 to 12 cups rice, cooked according to directions on package and kept warm

Equipment: Paper towels, large mixing bowl with cover or plastic food wrap, mixing spoon, large skillet, metal tongs, large roasting pan with cover, oven mitts, deep serving platter

1. Wash chicken pieces and place on several layers of paper towels and pat dry.

2. Make **marinade**: Combine garlic, onions, vinegar, 1 cup oil, crushed chili peppers to taste, and salt and pepper to taste in large mixing bowl. Stir to mix well. Add chicken pieces and coat well with mixture. Seal bowl with cover or plastic wrap and refrigerate to **marinate** for at least 4 hours. Remove from refrigerator once or twice and toss to coat chicken pieces with marinade.

Preheat oven to 350° F.

3. Prepare to skillet-fry: ADULT SUPERVISION REQUIRED. Place large roasting pan near stove. Heat 2 tablespoons oil in large skillet over medium-high heat. Add chicken pieces, a few at a time, and fry until browned, 7 to 12 minutes on each side. Using metal tongs, transfer to large roasting pan and continue frying in batches.

4. Pour marinade over browned chicken pieces, cover, and bake in oven for 45 minutes. Remove cover and bake for another 30 to 40 minutes until chicken is very well done. Test **chicken doneness**.

To serve yassa, *cover bottom of deep serving platter with cooked rice and arrange chicken pieces over the top. Spoon tomato mixture from roasting pan over chicken and rice or serve in a separate bowl. To eat* yassa *as they do in Burkina Faso, gather a good amount of rice, chicken, and sauce in your right hand and form into a ball against the side of the platter. Squeeze it with your fingers until it's compact, then pop into your mouth. It is bad manners to start forming another ball while there is still food in your mouth. When you finish eating, clean off the part of the bowl in front of you with your hand and lick your fingers clean. If other people are still eating after you have finished, it is rude to watch them eat although you can sit and converse with them but keep your eyes focused on something else in the room.*

MALI

Mali is a landlocked country in the Saharan region of West Africa. Its neighbors are Guinea, Senegal, Mauritania, Algeria, Niger, Burkina Faso, and Côte d'Ivoire. Almost all Malians are Muslims, and in every ethnic group in the nation, life-milestone events combine Islamic practices with indigenous customs and beliefs. (See Islam and Islamic Life-Cycle Rituals, page xlix, and Traditional African Life-Cycle Rituals, page xli.)

Traditionally, when a Malian man wants to marry, he has a friend or male relative visit the girl's father to make the request for him. The suitor brings kola nuts to his prospective in-laws—to offer kola nuts as a gift signals respect. If the kola nuts are accepted, it indicates the father's consent to the marriage proposal.

Agreeing on a bride-price finalizes the marriage. Usually the bride-price is paid in installments over several years. The payment period is a time to strengthen the bond between families—or, if the bride doesn't fulfill her obligations to her husband, he can stop the payments, and she is returned to her father. It is not unusual for a father to offer another daughter or his unmarried sister or sister-in-law as replacement for a returned bride, who is felt to have disgraced the family.

Among Mali's Malinke people, a naming ceremony takes place on the eighth day after a baby's birth. Early in the morning, the villagers arrive for the day-long celebration. After saying a blessing over the infant, the religious leader shaves the child's head; he then shares kola nuts and says a blessing over the ritual food of rice, honey, and sour milk. He prays that the child will bring pride and honor to the family and community. The baby's name is a secret to all but the parents and officials. After the father whispers the name three times in the baby's ear, he announces it to everyone present. Then the music, dancing, and feasting begin.

The name of the feast dish whose recipe follows—two-sauce stew—is a little misleading. One sauce is made with a fish mixture and the other with cubed meat, then they are mixed together to make a one-sauce stew. Traditionally *le to* is eaten with cornmeal porridge, the same as *putu* (recipe page 29).

Le To

Two-Sauce Stew

Yield: serves 6

½ pound fresh skinless fish **fillets** (cod, catfish, or whiting), cut into 1-inch slices
½ pound lean **ground** meat
4 cups onions, **finely chopped** and divided
salt and pepper to taste
water, as needed
1 tablespoon cornstarch
1 tablespoon vegetable oil
½ pound lean beef, cut into bite-size cubes
3 tablespoons tomato paste
salt and pepper to taste
putu (recipe page 29), for serving

Equipment: Medium saucepan with cover, mixing spoon, cup, large skillet

1. Put fish pieces, ground meat, 2 cups chopped onions, and salt and pepper to taste in medium saucepan. Add enough water to cover and bring to boil over medium-high heat. Stir well and reduce heat to **simmer**. Cover and cook until the fish flakes easily when poked with a fork and the meat is lightly browned, 15 to 20 minutes.

2. Put cornstarch in cup and stir in about ¼ cup hot liquid from pan to make **slurry**. Gently stir slurry into fish mixture, and cook until smooth and thickened, 3 to 5 minutes. Remove from heat and keep covered.

3. Heat oil in large skillet over medium-high heat. Add cubed beef, stir, and **sauté** until browned on all sides, 7 to 12 minutes. Add remaining 2 cups chopped onions, stir, and sauté until soft, 3 to 5 minutes. Add tomato paste, salt and pepper to taste, and enough water to cover. Bring mixture to a boil. Reduce heat to simmer, cover, and stirring occasionally, cook until meat is tender, 35 to 45 minutes.

4. Prepare *putu.*

5. Add fish mixture to cubed beef mixture and gently stir to mix. Continue to cook, uncovered, over medium heat for 20 to 25 minutes, for flavor to develop and mixture to thicken.

To serve, put le to *in a bowl and the* putu *in a shallow dish. To eat, use only the fingers of the right hand, make a ball of the* putu, *and use it to scoop up the* le to. *According to Muslim tradition, the left hand must never touch food; it is used only for personal grooming.*

MAURITANIA

Mauritania is in northwestern Africa, bordering the Atlantic Ocean, Morocco, Mali, Algeria, and Senegal. The Moors, who make up 75 percent of the population, live in the northern part of the country. They are nomadic pastoralists of mixed Arab and Berber descent who herd camels, sheep, and goats, depending on the region. The remaining 25 percent of the people are black Africans living in the southern region. One of the major southern groups is the Fulani, cattle herders who live mainly on milk, milk products, and millet, eating meat only for special celebrations

Each group has its own traditions and customs, with one common bond: Islam. (See Islam and Islamic Life-Cycle Rituals, page xlix.) In some places, traditional indigenous practices are combined with Islamic rites.

In Mauritania, the main dish served for *kaliyoo*—the wedding or funeral feast— is whole roasted goat or lamb (recipe page 141), the saddle of lamb or lamb roast called *mechoui* (recipe page 75), or lamb kebabs called *meshwi* (recipe page 83).

Lakh-lalo

Fish Stew

Note: This recipe takes 2 days.

Yield: serves 6

2 pounds dried **salt cod** (available at all Latin American food stores and some supermarkets)
water, as needed
2 tablespoons vegetable oil
3 onions, **finely chopped**
16 fresh whole okra, chopped, or 10-ounce package frozen chopped okra, thawed
3 tomatoes, chopped, or 12 ounces canned stewed tomatoes
salt and pepper to taste
ground red pepper, to taste
putu (recipe page 29), for serving

Equipment: Medium bowl, work surface, medium saucepan with cover, slotted spoon, plate, large skillet with cover, deep serving bowl, ladle

1. Put salt cod in medium bowl and cover with plenty of cold water. Set on work surface to soak overnight. The next day, transfer fish to medium saucepan and discard soaking water. Cover fish generously with fresh cold water and bring to boil over medium-high heat. Reduce heat to **simmer**, cover, and cook 20 minutes. Using slotted spoon, remove fish and transfer to plate. Discard cooking liquid.

2. Heat oil in large skillet over medium-high heat. Add onions, stir, and **sauté** until soft, 3 to 5 minutes. Add 1 cup water, okra, and chopped tomatoes or stewed tomatoes. Stir well and bring to boil. Reduce heat to simmer, cover, and cook until okra is tender, 15 to 20 minutes.

3. Prepare *putu*.

4. Flake salt cod into okra mixture and gently toss to mix. Add salt and pepper to taste and ground red pepper to taste. Cover and cook for flavor to develop and to heat through, 15 to 20 minutes.

To serve, either put putu *in deep serving bowl and ladle* lakh-lalo *over it or serve separately.* Lakh-lalo *is also served over cooked rice.*

Fritters, patties, and balls made with dried beans, peas, lentils, and rice are popular throughout Africa and the Middle East. This recipe is made with dried yellow or green split peas or white beans.

Tamiya

Bean Balls

Note: This recipe takes 2 days.

CAUTION: HOT OIL USED

Yield: serves 6 or 8

- 2 cups (about 1 pound) dried yellow or green split peas or white beans, soaked in water overnight and drained
- 1 egg
- water, as needed
- 2 cloves garlic, **finely chopped**
- 1 onion, finely chopped
- ½ teaspoon **ground** turmeric
- ground red pepper, to taste
- salt and pepper, to taste
- vegetable oil, for deep frying

Equipment: **Blender**, rubber spatula, medium mixing bowl, plastic food wrap, **deep fryer, deep-fryer thermometer** or wooden spoon, paper towels, baking sheet, slotted spoon

1. Put drained split peas or white beans in blender, add egg, and **blend** until coarsely ground, not smooth, about 30 seconds. If necessary, add just enough water, about 1 or 2 tablespoons, to help mixture blend. (The mixture should be thick and coarse.) Transfer to medium mixing bowl.

2. Add finely chopped garlic, finely chopped onion, turmeric, ground red pepper to taste, and salt and pepper to taste. Cover with plastic wrap and refrigerate for at least 2 hours to thicken.

3. Prepare to deep-fry: ADULT SUPERVISION REQUIRED. Place several layers of paper towels on baking sheet. Heat oil to 375° F on fryer thermometer or oil is hot enough when small bubbles appear around a wooden spoon handle when it is dipped in the oil.

4. Form mixture into Ping-Pong balls and fry a few at a time until golden brown, 1 to 2 minutes. Remove with slotted spoon and drain on paper towels. Continue to fry in batches.

Serve warm as a starter or cold as a snack or use to scoop up stew, such as le to *(page 81).*

Traditionally, *meshwi* is made with lamb, goat, or antelope, but it also can be made with beef. When made with lamb, the dish is called *lahm meshwi*. Rice would be served with *meshwi* since it is regarded as special occasion food, especially when served with *sauce arachide* (recipe page 67).

Meshwi

Meat Kebabs

CAUTION: GRILL OR BROILER USED

Yield: serves 4

- 2 pounds lean lamb, goat, or beef, cut in 1½-inch cubes
- 1 cup olive oil
- salt and pepper to taste
- ½ teaspoon **ground** thyme
- 2 onions, **finely chopped**, for **garnish**

Equipment: Medium bowl, mixing spoon, plastic food wrap, 8 wooden or metal 8- or 10-inch skewers (if using wooden skewers, first soak in water for at least 30 minutes so they don't burn when cooked), charcoal **grill** or broiler pan, oven mitts, metal tongs, large platter

1. In medium bowl, combine oil, salt and pepper to taste, and thyme. Add **cubed** meat, and toss to coat. Cover with plastic wrap and refrigerate for about 4 hours to **marinate**, stirring frequently to coat.

2. Have an adult help prepare charcoal grill or preheat broiler.

3. Thread meat pieces tightly together on skewers. Place side by side on grill or broiler pan. Wearing oven mitts and using metal tongs, turn

skewered meat to brown on all sides, and cook 15 to 20 minutes, or to desired doneness.

To serve, arrange skewers on large platter, and sprinkle with finely chopped onions, for garnish. Serve with cooked rice.

NORTH AFRICA

The majority of people living in the North African countries of Morocco, Algeria, Tunisia, and Libya are Muslims, and as such the Islamic customs and laws dictate every facet of their lives and life-cycle events. (See Islam and Islamic Life-Cycle Rituals, page xlix.)

A *diffa* (feast) is part of most life-cycle celebrations, and it can be very elaborate or modest, depending upon the importance of the event. No amount of money is spared for the *diffa* that celebrates a Muslim's return from his pilgrimage to Mecca. A nonstop feast can go on for two or three days in celebration of the most important rite of passage in a Muslim's life. Making the pilgrimage not only assures a Muslim a place in heaven but he has the enviable title, *Hadji* (one who has made the pilgrimage to Mecca).

Strict Islamic modesty laws prevail throughout North Africa; however, exceptions are found in the chic Moroccan and Tunisian cities and resort areas. Exceptions are also found among the Berbers, the descendents of the pre-Arab inhabitants of North Africa, who make up a large part of the North African population. The Berbers eventually accepted Islam after the Arabs conquered North Africa in the seventh century A.D. The free-spirited Berbers enjoy a much more liberated lifestyle than their Arab neighbors do. They are known to infuse ancient pagan beliefs into their Muslim rituals.

When an Arab Muslim boy is born, the first words uttered to the child are the call to prayer. A week later this is followed by a ceremony in which the baby's head is shaved and an animal, such as a lamb or young calf, may be sacrificed. The sacrificial meat may be given to the poor.

Among the Berbers, the birth of a baby is a welcome addition to the family, whether it is a boy or girl, unlike the Arabs, who openly prefer boys. At birth, a Berber girl receives her first set of beads and a small amulet containing herbs and seeds believed to have magical powers to ward off evil spirits. At each stage of development a Berber girl receives jewelry befitting her age and social standing.

The major event of a Muslim boy's childhood is circumcision, which normally takes place sometime between the ages of 7 and 12. A feast is often prepared for family and friends to celebrate the event.

Dating is taboo, and a public show of affection is frowned upon in most of North Africa. Arranged marriages are the norm among Arab Muslim families.

A few days after the marriage proposal has been accepted and the first agreement, "the giving away" has been completed, the women of the groom's family traditionally pay a visit to the bride's family. This phase of the negotiating ritual is called *kèmletàtiya*. The women come to welcome their new daughter (or sister)-in-law into the family. The bride's mother traditionally serves everyone tea, a light repast and honey, which is provided for good luck.

Wedding rituals can take more than a week to complete. During that time the groom traditionally sends new clothes to his bride and she in return sends him trays piled with sugar, fresh butter, milk, a bunch of fresh mint leaves, dates (to signify wealth) and *kàb el ghzal* (recipe page 85).

Although the women and men are usually kept in separate quarters during wedding ceremonies, they are almost always colorful and noisy affairs. One custom among urbanites is for all the men to get in their cars and drive around the streets in a convoy making as much noise as possible. The men celebrate until the early hours of the morning, often ending at sunrise, with the day's first call to prayer.

For all Muslims the death ceremony is very simple, and there is no *diffa* (feast). A burial service is held at the mosque or the burial grounds. The body, wrapped in only a white cotton cloth, is simply buried in the ground without a casket.

MOROCCO

Morocco lies directly across the Strait of Gibraltar from Spain. On the east and southeast is Algeria; south of Morocco is the Western Sahara; and the Atlantic Ocean and Mediterranean Seas bound it on the west and north. The culture is a blend of Berber, Arab-Islamic, and African, with influences from France and Spain.

In the Berber culture, the Berber women are allowed to select their own husband, which is unheard of among Arabs, whose marriages are strictly prearranged according to the laws of Islam. As a matter of fact, in Imilchil, Morocco, high in the Atlas Mountains, an annual three-day festival is held every September where Berbers come to sell and trade camels, sheep and goats. Over the years it has become known as the Bridal Fair, due to the influx of Berber women of the Ait Hadiddu tribe looking for a husband. The young women parade around wearing full-length, black-hooded cloaks. They all look alike except for the different colored, narrow stripes running down the back of each garment. They decorate their hoods with brightly colored ribbon and yarn from which they hang small pieces of jewelry in the shape of animal paws, such as a jackal or turtle foot. They believe the symbolic animal paws possess magical powers.

On the last day of the festival couples make their choice, shake hands and declare themselves engaged. The couple then formalize their vows in front of a notary. Although a girl may meet her future husband at the fair she returns home with her father when it is over. Once home, a meeting is arranged between the families. When both families can agree about dowry and the marriage contract they give their consent. The marriage takes place about a year later.

Unlike the Muslim Arab women, who cannot remarry, divorced and widowed Berber women are free to remarry as often as they like and the fair is a good place to select a new husband. They wear decorative pointed hoods, called *aquilous,* to distinguish them from single girls.

European-style pastries are very popular throughout North Africa, especially Morocco. As you travel east through North Africa, the Middle Eastern-style pastries which are very syrupy and sweet become more popular. Delicious *kàb el ghzal,* a specialty of Morocco, are more like French pastries.

Kàb el Ghzal

Gazelle Horns (Cookies)

Yield: 34 to 36 pieces

3 cups all-purpose **flour**
1 pound (2 cups) unsalted butter, cut into pea-size pieces and refrigerated
½ teaspoon salt
6 to 8 tablespoons cold water

½ cup **blanched** slivered almonds, **toasted** and **finely ground**
1 cup **almond paste**, or 8-ounce package (available at all supermarkets), coarsely broken into pieces, at room temperature
4 tablespoons unsalted butter, at room temperature
1 tablespoon granulated sugar
1 egg
3 tablespoons orange-blossom water, divided (optional) (available at Middle Eastern food stores)
6 to 8 tablespoons confectioners' sugar

Equipment: Food processor, rubber spatula, lightly floured work surface, plastic wrap, medium mixing bowl, wax paper, 2 baking sheets, lightly floured rolling pin, ruler, paring knife, kitchen towel, oven mitts, wire cake rack, spray bottle for misting, fine-hole strainer, serving platter

1. Prepare pastry: Put flour, chilled butter pieces, and salt into food processor. Pulse off and on until mixture looks like coarse meal, about 1 minute. Transfer flour mixture to lightly floured work surface and sprinkle with 6 tablespoons cold water. Form dough into a ball. If dough crumbles and doesn't hold together, add remaining 2 tablespoons water, 1 tablespoon at a time, just until dough holds together. Divide the dough into 2 pieces, and using your hand, flatten each into squares, ½ inch thick. Wrap separately in plastic wrap and refrigerate for at least 1 hour.

Note: While processing, turn machine off once or twice and scrape down sides of container with rubber spatula.

2. Prepare filling: Put the ground almonds in the food processor. Add almond paste pieces, butter, granulated sugar, egg, and 1 tablespoon orange-blossom water. Process until smooth, about 1 minute. Transfer mixture to medium mixing bowl.

3. Roll 1 tablespoon almond mixture between the palms of your hands into a log shape, about 2 inches long and ½ inch thick. Continue making almond paste logs and placing them side by side on a wax-paper-covered baking sheet. Cover with plastic wrap and refrigerate until ready to use.

4. Cut pastry to size: For best results, remove only 1 piece of dough from the refrigerator at a time. Unwrap one piece of dough and on lightly floured work surface, using a lightly floured rolling pin, roll out into a square or rectangle about an 1/8 inch thick. Lay the ruler on the dough and using a paring knife, cut 17 or 18 pieces, each 3 inches square. Stack slightly overlapping on the work surface and cover with a towel. Continue to assemble the first batch before removing the second piece of dough from the refrigerator.

5. Assemble cookies: Work with 1 square of pastry at a time. Set the square on the work surface with a corner point facing you (diamond-shaped). Place 1 log of filling diagonally across the corner the corner nearest you, about ½ inch from the point. Tightly roll the pastry around the log, jellyroll fashion. Moisten your finger, lightly dab a little water under the end point, and press to seal. To seal the sides, dab a little water inside the opening, and pinch it together. Repeat with the second side, leaving the side points extended. Gently curve the dough into a crescent-shape and place on the baking sheet. Repeat making pastries, placing each about 1 inch apart on baking sheet. Lightly cover with plastic wrap and refrigerate until ready to bake. When the first batch is done take the second wrapped dough out of the refrigerator and repeat assembly process (Step 5. Assemble cookies). Refrigerate assembled pastries for at least 1 hour before baking.

Preheat oven to 375° F.

6. Bake in the oven until golden brown, 18 to 20 minutes. Transfer pastries to a wire cake rack.

Put 1 tablespoon orange-blossom water in spray bottle and lightly mist warm pastries. Put confectioners' sugar in a fine-hole strainer and sprinkle over pastries. Cool to room temperature to set.

To serve, stack decoratively on a serving platter and set out on the sweet table at a wedding celebration.

Bread is a staple, and no meal is complete unless great quantities of bread are on the table. Early each morning most households prepare their own dough, which they take to the local baker who bakes it for them.

Ksra

Moroccan Anise Bread

Yield: 2 small loaves

- 1 package dry active yeast
- 1½ cups **lukewarm** water, divided
- 1 teaspoon sugar
- 4 cups sifted all-purpose flour
- ½ cup whole wheat flour
- 2 teaspoons salt
- ½ cup lukewarm milk
- 1 tablespoon anise seed (available at supermarkets)
- ½ cup yellow **cornmeal**, more or less as needed

Equipment: Small bowl, mixing spoon, plastic wrap, large mixing bowl, wooden mixing spoon, lightly floured work surface, 2 greased dinner plates, greased baking sheet pan, kitchen towel, oven mitts

1. Place yeast in small bowl with about ¼-cup lukewarm water; stir to combine. Stir in sugar. Cover with plastic wrap and set aside in warm place for 10 minutes or until frothy.

2. In large mixing bowl, combine all-purpose flour, whole wheat flour, and salt. Using wooden mixing spoon, stir in yeast mixture and lukewarm milk. Gradually add just enough remaining 1¼-cups lukewarm water to make a stiff dough.

3. Transfer dough to lightly floured work surface and **knead** for 15 to 20 minutes or until dough is smooth and satiny. Knead in anise seed. (When necessary, lightly sprinkle flour on work surface to prevent sticking.)

4. Divide dough in half and shape each piece into a ball. Place each ball on a greased plate, cover with plastic wrap, and allow to rest for 10 minutes.

5. Using greased hands, shape balls into slightly flattened round loaves about 5 inches in diameter. Sprinkle cornmeal on greased baking sheet and set breads on top, allowing space between to rise. Cover with towel and set in warm place to double in bulk, 1 to 2 hours.

Preheat oven to 400° F.

6. Gently prick the top of each loaf in three or four places with fork. Bake in oven for 10 minutes, reduce heat to 300° F. for 35 to 40 minutes. (Test **bread doneness.**)

7. Cool on wire cake rack for 10 minutes to firm up.

Serving bread with each meal is essential in Morocco. Bread is used to transport food from the platter to the mouth and to help mop up the sauces and cooking juices. Bread is broken, never cut, into pieces. (Cutting requires both hands to touch the food, which is taboo.) Ksra *is delicious when eaten warm.*

Meals usually end with fresh fruit, such as this simple recipe for sliced oranges. This is probably the most popular way of eating fresh fruit throughout the Middle East and North Africa.

Fresh Oranges

Moroccan Dessert

Yield: serves 4

4 oranges, peeled
1 teaspoon **cinnamon sugar**
1 teaspoon **rose water** (available at Middle Eastern food stores and pharmacies)

Equipment: Paring knife, small bowl, spoon, individual plates

Using a paring knife, remove the white stringy membranes from the oranges and divide into segments. Place the orange segments, slightly overlapping on a plate and sprinkle with cinnamon sugar and rose water.

Serve immediately.

ALGERIA

Algeria is located in Northern Africa, bounding on the Mediterranean Sea, between Morocco to the west and Tunisia to the east. Most Algerians are of mixed Arab and Berber descent. Nearly all are Muslims.

Algeria belonged to France for nearly 130 years, finally gaining its independence in 1962. The cooking of Algeria has strong French influences, although most people follow family traditions that have been passed from mother to daughter for generations. In Muslim North Africa where pork products are taboo, sheep are the main source of meat, and a whole roasted lamb, *kabab barreh* (recipe page 141), or large lamb parts, such as saddle of lamb, *méchoui* (recipe page 75), are roasted on a spit which is the cornerstone of the cuisine. Lamb has been the main dish of weddings and other family celebrations for generations. Urbanites enjoy the lamb but they generally have it cut up before roasting over a charcoal grill.

The men traditionally eat first and apart from the women. To eat, the men sit on carpeted floors around a low table (*tbla* or *mida*). Before touching the food, which is eaten with the fingers of the right hand, a servant or young family member takes a bowl of perfumed water around to each diner. According to Muslim tradition, the left hand must never touch food, as it is used only for personal grooming. A little water is poured over their hands and then they are handed a towel (*ied ettas*) to dry them.

Chorba 'Dess

Lentil Soup

Yield: serves 6

2 tablespoons olive oil
¼ pound lean meat, (lamb, veal, or beef, or combination), **cubed**
1 large onion, chopped
2 teaspoons **ground coriander**
8 cups water
1 cup **lentils**
2 large potatoes, quartered
2 large carrots, quartered
salt and pepper to taste

Equipment: Large saucepan with cover, wooden mixing spoon

1. Heat oil in large saucepan over medium-high heat. Add cubed meat, onions, and coriander. Stir until meat is lightly browned on all sides, 5 to 7 minutes.

2. Add water and lentils, and stir. Increase heat to high and bring to a boil. Reduce heat to **simmer** and add potatoes and carrots. Stir, cover, and cook until lentils are soft and potatoes are tender, 30 to 40 minutes. Add salt and pepper to taste before serving.

Serve with plenty of bread to mop up the broth. Soups are eaten along with the main dishes, not before the meal as in western cultures.

In Algeria, *sferia* is a favorite dish served at celebrations. Add bread and this is a complete feast.

Sferia

Chicken and Chickpeas with Cheese Croquettes

Yield: serves 4-6

vegetable oil, as needed
3 to 3½ pounds chicken, cut into small serving-size pieces
1 onion, **finely chopped**
1 teaspoon **ground** cinnamon
salt and pepper to taste
2 cups water
2 cups canned chickpeas (garbanzo beans)
cheese croquettes (recipe follows)
1 **egg yolk**, for sauce
1 tablespoon lemon juice, for sauce
2 tablespoons fresh parsley, finely chopped for **garnish**

Equipment: Large saucepan with cover or **Dutch oven**, metal tongs, large baking pan, mixing spoon, large heatproof serving platter, slotted spoon, aluminum foil, oven mitts, small bowl, fork, whisk

1. Heat 3 tablespoons oil in large saucepan or Dutch oven over medium-high heat. Using metal tongs, add chicken and fry in batches until browned on both sides, 6 to 8 minutes per batch. Transfer browned pieces to baking pan. After all chicken is fried, add 2 tablespoons oil to same saucepan or Dutch oven. Stirring constantly, add onion and cinnamon, and fry until soft, 1 to 2 minutes. Return chicken pieces to large saucepan, and sprinkle with salt and pepper to taste. Add water and bring to a boil. Reduce heat to simmer, cover, and cook for 30 minutes. Add chickpeas, cover, and continue cooking until the chicken is tender, 30 to 40 minutes more. Test **doneness** of chicken.

2. Prepare *cheese croquettes* (recipe follows).

3. Arrange *cheese croquettes* in a ring around the edge of a large heatproof serving platter and place the cooked chicken pieces in a ring inside the croquettes. Using a slotted spoon, spoon a pile of the chickpeas in the center of the platter. Cover the platter loosely with foil and keep warm in 250° F oven while making the sauce.

4. Prepare sauce: In small bowl, beat egg yolk and lemon juice together with a fork. Beat in ½ cup hot pan juices to **temper** the egg mixture. Using a whisk, beat remaining pan juices constantly while slowly pouring them into egg mixture. Whisking constantly, cook over low heat until sauce lightly thickens to about the consistency of heavy cream. (Do not boil or sauce will curdle.) Adjust seasoning by adding salt and pepper to taste and pour sauce over the chickpeas and chicken.

To serve, sprinkle parsley over the entire dish.

Cheese Croquettes

Cheese Patties

Yield: serves 4 to 6

8 slices white bread
½ cup milk
1 whole egg
1 **egg yolk**
1 cup grated Gruyère or Swiss cheese (available at all supermarkets)
1 teaspoon orange-blossom water, optional (available at Middle Eastern food stores)
1 teaspoon **ground** cinnamon
¼ teaspoon salt
½ cup vegetable oil

Equipment: Bread knife, large mixing bowl, food processor, rubber spatula, 2 baking sheets, wax paper, paper towels, large **heavy-based** skillet, slotted metal spatula, paper towels

Preheat oven to 250° F.

1. Trim crusts off 8 slices of white bread and tear into small pieces to make about 4 cups. Put bread pieces and milk in large mixing bowl and using your hands, toss and squeeze bread to soak up milk. Crumble bread into food processor, add 1 whole egg and 1 egg yolk, cheese, orange-blossom water, cinnamon, and salt. Process until smooth and well blended, 1 to 2 minutes. Transfer bread mixture to large mixing bowl.

Note: While processing, turn machine off once or twice and scrape down sides of container with rubber spatula.

2. Make croquettes: Cover one baking sheet with wax paper and cover the other with several layers of paper towels. Moisten hands frequently with cold water. Shape 2 tablespoons bread mixture into 2 balls and slightly flatten on baking sheet. Place flattened balls side by side on wax paper until all the bread mixture is used.

3. In large heavy-based skillet, heat the oil over medium-high heat. TEST OIL HEAT: Drop a small piece of bread crust into the oil. It is ready for frying when it bubbles around the crust. Add croquettes in batches and fry on each side for 2 or 3 minutes until browned, turn with slotted metal spatula. When browned on both sides, transfer to paper towels to drain. Continue frying in batches.

Continue: Use with sferia *(recipe precedes: Step 3.)*

Salads and relishes are always served along with the meat dishes. This simple combination of vegetables is a typical Algerian salad.

Chlada Felfel

Tomato and Green Pepper Salad

Yield: serves 4 to 6

4 large yellow or red bell peppers, or combination
4 tablespoons olive oil
½ tablespoon wine vinegar
2 cloves garlic, **finely chopped**
salt and pepper to taste
2 large tomatoes, thinly sliced for **garnish**
6 pitted black olives, for garnish
6 stuffed green olives, for garnish

Equipment: Oven mitts, metal tongs, resealable plastic bag, medium serving platter, whisk, small bowl

Preheat oven broiler.

1. Set top oven rack about 4 inches under the broiler. Place whole peppers on the broiler pan and place under the broiler to blister all sides, 10 to 20 minutes. Wearing oven mitts and using metal tongs, turn peppers as they darken. When the skin has patches of black, remove from oven with metal tongs and place in plastic bag and seal tightly. (This is done so the peppers will sweat and the skin will easily peel off when they cool enough to handle.) Peel off skin, remove seeds, and coarsely chop peppers. Pile chopped peppers in the center of a serving platter.

2. Prepare dressing: Whisk olive oil, vinegar, garlic, and salt and pepper to taste in small bowl.

3. Arrange tomato slices around the peppers and drizzle with dressing. Garnish with black and green olives.

Serve as side dish with sferia *(recipe page 89) and use a chunk of* ksra *(recipe page 87) to sop up the dressing.*

El Maagoun

Almond Honey Balls (cookies)

Yield: about 25 balls

½ teaspoon **ground** cardamom
½ teaspoon ground nutmeg
½ teaspoon ground cinnamon
pinch ground red pepper

2 cups (about 1 pound) almonds, **blanched** and **ground**
1 cup seedless raisins
2 tablespoons candied ginger, **finely chopped** (available at most supermarkets)
½ cup honey
¼ cup butter or margarine
1 cup **sesame seeds**

Equipment: Food processor, rubber spatula, medium **heavy-based** saucepan, pie pan, wax paper, cookie sheet, serving platter

1. Put cardamom, nutmeg, cinnamon, red pepper, ground almonds, raisins, ginger, honey, and butter or margarine in food processor. Pulse until just mixed together, about 1 minute.

2. Transfer to medium heavy-based saucepan and, stirring frequently, cook over low heat until the mixture turns very thick, about 1 hour. (Watch carefully to prevent burning.) Let mixture stand until cool enough to handle.

3. Put sesame seeds in pie pan. Using your hands, form the nut mixture into walnut-size balls. Heavily coat the nut balls by rolling them in the sesame seeds. Place balls side by side on wax-paper-covered cookie sheet. Cover with wax paper and keep in cool, dry place.

To serve, stack balls on serving platter and place on sweet table.

Khchaf

Fruit Drink

Yield: serves 6 to 8
2 quarts water
2 sticks cinnamon
½ cup raisins
sugar, to taste

Equipment: Medium saucepan, mixing spoon, beverage glasses

1. Bring water with cinnamon sticks to a boil in medium saucepan. Add raisins, reduce heat to simmer, and cook for 15 minutes. Stir in sugar. Remove from heat and take out and discard the cinnamon sticks.

2. When liquid is completely cool, refrigerate for 30 to 40 minutes.

Serve in beverage glasses, adding a few raisins to each serving.

TUNISIA

Tunisia is the northernmost country in Africa. Its northern tip is only 85 miles from Sicily, in Italy. Tunisia is bounded on the north and east by the Mediterranean Sea. On the west, Tunisia is bordered by Algeria and on the south by Libya. Almost all Tunisians are Arabs and Muslims, and there is a heavy French influence, with many Tunisians speaking French as an additional language.

It is the custom for the women to serve the men, and they do not eat together. The men sit around a low table on carpeted floors, backed with an assortment of decorative pillows. The table is usually an etched, brass tray set on carved legs. Eating is done with the thumb and two fingers of the right hand, using chunks of bread for scooping and dipping. Muslims traditionally eat with the thumb, forefinger, and middle finger of the right hand. (The left hand is used for personal grooming and must never touch food.)

Tunisians prefer their food highly seasoned, and use *harissa* in almost everything except desserts. *Harissa* thinned with olive oil and tomato paste is spread on bread and fed to babies to ward off sickness and evil spirits.

Harissa (also Hrisa)

Fiery Red Pepper Seasoning

Yield: about 3/4 cup

1/2 cup **ground** red pepper
1/4 cup ground cumin
2 teaspoons salt

Equipment: Resealable plastic bag

Combine red pepper, cumin, and salt in resealable plastic bag. Seal top and shake bag to blend ingredients thoroughly. Refrigerate until ready to use.

Serve harissa *in a shaker or small dish and sprinkle it carefully as a hot seasoning.*

A wedding banquet menu includes soup, bread, salads, **couscous**, and more than one *tajine* or casserole. Everything is put on the table at the same time. Meat is a luxury in North Africa so using it in *tajine* makes a little meat go a long way. Sometimes camel meat is added to *tajine* but most are made with lamb, mutton, goat, or beef when rainfall is adequate and livestock plentiful. When the meat is left out, the *tajine* becomes a delicious vegetarian meal.

Tajine in Tunisia bears no relation to Moroccan *tajine*. The Tunisian version is like a quiche (a popular French savory pie made with eggs) and is normally served at room temperature.

Tajine Chakchouka

Tunisian Baked Lamb Casserole

Yield: serves 6 to 8

1 pound boneless lean lamb, cut into 1-inch cubes
1 teaspoon **ground** cinnamon
salt and pepper to taste
3 tablespoons olive oil
3 cups water
1 1/2 cups onions, **finely chopped**
3 large tomatoes, **peeled** and **coarsely chopped**
2 green bell peppers, stemmed, **seeded**, and coarsely chopped
1/4 teaspoon *harissa* (recipe precedes), more or less to taste
1/4 teaspoon ground **coriander**
1/2 cup grated Parmesan cheese
1/2 cup finely crumbled white bread
6 eggs, lightly beaten
2 tablespoons melted butter or margarine

Equipment: Large mixing bowl, large skillet with cover, metal spatula, 3-quart ovenproof casserole, wooden mixing spoon, oven mitts

1. Put lamb cubes in large mixing bowl, sprinkle with cinnamon, and salt and pepper to taste. Toss to coat.

2. Heat oil in large skillet over medium-high heat. Add meat, turning meat with metal spatula to brown all sides, 5 to 7 minutes. Add water and bring to boil. Reduce heat to **simmer**, cover, and cook for 45 minutes. Using slotted spoon, transfer lamb to ovenproof casserole, leaving juices in skillet. Add onions, tomatoes, green peppers, 1/4 teaspoon *harissa*, more or less to taste, coriander, and salt and pepper to taste to juices in skillet. Stir well and bring to boil over medium-high heat. Reduce heat to simmer, and cook for 15 minutes, until vegetables are tender.

Preheat oven to 350° F.

3. Transfer onion mixture to casserole dish of lamb and **fold in**. Gently fold in cheese, bread crumbs, and lightly beaten eggs.

4. Bake in oven for 45 minutes, or until top is golden brown. Just before serving drizzle melted butter over top.

Serve directly from casserole. To eat as they do in Tunisia, use only the fingers of your right hand, scoop up a portion and pop it in your mouth. According to Muslim tradition, the left hand must never touch food, it is used only for personal grooming.

Chunks of bread can be used instead of your fingers to scoop up the tajine.

Dates and pistachio nuts are plentiful and popular throughout North Africa. They are used in both savory and sweet dishes.

Tmar Mihchi

Pistachio-filled Candied Dates

Note: This recipe takes 24 hours.

Yield: about 4 dozen

- ½ pound unsalted, shelled pistachios (available at Middle Eastern food stores and health food stores)
- 3¾ cups sugar, divided, more as needed
- 2 tablespoons **rose water** or water
- 1 pound pitted dates
- 2 cups water
- **pinch** cream of tartar

Equipment: Medium saucepan, oven mitts, **colander**, 2 kitchen towels, work surface, baking sheet, food processor, rubber spatula, small bowl, paring knife, small saucepan, **candy thermometer** (optional), pie pan, wax paper, wooden skewer

Preheat oven to 350° F.

1. Remove skin from pistachios: Bring 4 cups water to boil in medium saucepan. Add pistachios and boil briskly for 2 minutes. Drain in colander and transfer to kitchen towel placed on work surface. Cover with second towel and rub pistachios until skin rubs off.

2. Spread pistachios on baking sheet and bake in oven until lightly golden brown, 8 to 10 minutes. Combine pistachios and ¾ cup sugar in food processor and process for 30 seconds. Add rose water or water and process into smooth paste, about 1 minute. Transfer pistachio paste to small bowl.

3. With paring knife, cut slits about 1 inch long and ½ inch deep in side of each date. Stuff ½ teaspoon pistachio mixture into slit and pinch edges together to seal in the filling. Place stuffed dates on work surface.

4. In small saucepan, combine water, remaining 3 cups sugar, and cream of tartar. Stirring constantly, bring to boil over medium-high heat. Stop stirring and cook until sugar mixture reaches 230° F on candy thermometer, or until a few drops spooned into cup of ice water immediately form coarse threads. Using oven mitts, carefully remove pan from heat.

5. Place 1 cup sugar in pie pan and place pie pan next to wax-paper-covered baking sheet. Poke wooden skewer into side of stuffed date. Dunk date on skewer into the saucepan of warm sugar syrup. Shake off excess over saucepan. Dip syrup-coated date in sugar in pie pan to coat on all sides. Slide coated date off skewer onto wax paper. Repeat coating dates. If it is necessary to stack dates, separate each layer with wax paper. Cover top layer with wax paper and set at room temperature for about 24 hours for flavor to develop and to keep soft and pliable for serving. (Do not refrigerate.)

Serve as a sweet treat for a wedding or other family celebration.

In Muslim countries alcoholic beverages are forbidden. Tea and coffee are served at all life-cycle celebrations. The ritual of preparing tea is as important as drinking the finished brew. Green leaf tea is combined with chunks of sugar chipped off a large cone. Many Moroccans use a **samovar** or urn called a *babour* for making tea, while others prefer to brew their tea in small brass pots. The traditional way to drink tea in Morocco is from narrow, 3-inch tall glasses.

Thé à la Menthe (also Etzai)

Mint Tea

Yield: serves 3 or 4

8 tablespoons green tea leaves
4 cups boiling water, divided
3 tablespoons sugar, more or less to taste
sprigs fresh mint to taste

Equipment: 2 six-cup teapots, 3 three-inch tall heatproof glasses, 3 or 4 teaspoons

1. Put green tea leaves in a teapot and pour in 1 cup boiling water; swirl liquid in pot for a minute, and then pour into second teapot. (This is called washing the tea.)

2. Add 3 tablespoons sugar, more or less to taste, and mint leaves to taste. Pour in remaining 3 cups boiling water. Carefully pour the tea mixture back and forth 3 or 4 times between the two teapots. (This is done to oxygenate the prepared tea.)

North Africans have a saying that goes along with the tea drinking ritual. "The first tea is bitter, like life, the second is sweet like love, and the third is gentle, like death." To drink the tea as they do in North Africa repeat the entire process two more times: repeat the recipe with the same amounts of water and sugar, but no more tea or mint. At the end, everyone will have had 3 glasses of tea, each milder than the one before.

LIBYA

Libya, in northeastern Africa, borders the Mediterranean and Tunisia, Algeria, Egypt, Sudan, Chad, and Niger. Once called the Desert Kingdom of Africa, most of the nation's land is desert. Over 90 percent of Libyans live on less than 10 percent of the land, primarily in cosmopolitan cities along the coast. The remaining population lives mostly in villages or small settlements. Libyans are mainly Arabs and Berbers, and almost all are Muslims. Islam, the state religion, provides the framework for both the secular and spiritual life of the nation. All life-cycle events are conducted and celebrated according to Islamic law and custom. (See Islam and Islamic Life-Cycle Rituals, page xlix.)

When a baby is born, the first words uttered to it are those of the call to prayer. A week later, there is a naming ceremony during which the baby's head is shaved and a goat or lamb is sacrificed for the occasion. The major event of a boy's childhood is circumcision, which normally takes place between the ages of 7 and 12; afterward, there is always a celebration feast.

For festive occasions, a goat or lamb is roasted, and as many as 40 other dishes are prepared for the feast. Diners sit on cushions on the floor and eat off a low table. They eat by dipping the fingers of the right hand into the food placed on the table. (The left hand is used for personal groooming and must never touch the food.) Traditionally, no plates or forks are used, but flat loaves of bread, such as *khobaz arabee* (recipe page 115), are broken into pieces and used to scoop up the food. Bowls of perfumed water are passed between courses so that diners may cleanse their fingers. There are often a dozen or so desserts and always a large fruit assortment, *fakha taza* (recipe page 97). Sweets from Turkey, Greece, North Africa, and the Middle East have crossed the borders into Libya—such desserts as honey-drenched *bureks* (recipe page 128), *tmar mihchi*, and *farareer* (recipe page 133) are very popular. Only water is served with food, and *kahve* (recipe page 139) is served after the meal.

A celebration feast always begins with the *mezze* (**appetizer**) table, with such dishes as *abrak* (stuffed grape leaves), which is the same as *yab-ra* (recipe page 136); pickled vegetables (available in jars at all supermarkets); black and green olives; cheeses; and plenty of bread. This recipe for *gibneh beydah* is another popular *mezze*. ۞ ۞ ۞

Gibneh Beydah

Cheese Dip

Yield: serves 4 to 6

¼ pound feta or goat cheese (available at all supermarkets)
3 tablespoons plain yogurt, more if necessary
juice of ½ lemon
1 tablespoons fresh dill or fennel, **finely chopped**
1 tablespoons fresh parley, finely chopped
olive oil, to taste, for **garnish**
crudités, for serving
crackers and/or chips, for serving

Equipment: Medium bowl, fork, small serving bowl, plastic food wrap

Crumble feta or goat cheese in medium bowl, and add 3 tablespoons yogurt and lemon juice. Using back of fork, mash until mixture is smooth and creamy. Add a little more yogurt, if necessary to obtain creamy consistency. Add dill or fennel and parsley, and stir to mix well. Transfer to small serving bowl, cover with plastic wrap, and refrigerate until ready to use.

*To serve, **drizzle** a little oil over the top of the dip as a garnish. Prepare a plate of crudités or a basket of crackers and/or chips to accompany the dip.*

Another easy-to-prepare mezze with an unusual combination of flavors is this recipe. Stuffed eggs are a symbol of fertility and life. They are prepared for most life-cycle celebrations.

Beid Mahshi

Stuffed Eggs

Yield: serves 4

1 cup plain yogurt
2 teaspoons sugar
1½ teaspoons **ground** cinnamon, divided
4 hard-cooked eggs, shelled
1 tablespoon olive oil
½ onion, **grated**
2 tablespoons chopped fresh parsley, or 1 tablespoon dried parsley flakes
½ teaspoon paprika
salt and pepper to taste

Equipment: Small bowl, mixing spoon, plastic food wrap, medium shallow bowl, work surface, fork, serving plate

1. Prepare sauce: Pour yogurt into small bowl, add sugar, and 1 teaspoon cinnamon. Stir well and cover with plastic wrap. Refrigerate until serving time.

2. Cut hard-cooked eggs in half lengthwise. Remove yolks and put into medium shallow bowl. Set whites cut-side up on work surface. Using fork, mash yolks in shallow bowl. Add olive oil, grated onion, parsley flakes, remaining ½ teaspoon ground cinnamon, paprika, and salt and pepper to taste. Stir to mix well.

3. Spoon egg yolk mixture equally into each egg white half and arrange them on a serving plate.

To serve, spoon yogurt sauce over tops of eggs and eat as a mid-day snack or appetizer.

It is not unusual for celebration feasts to take four or five hours. The meal is eaten in a leisurely manner, and every bite of food is savored. This fish dish can be set on the mezze table, or at a wedding banquet, it is often served to guests after the soup course and before eating the roasted lamb, *kabab barreh* (recipe page 141).

Sayadia

Fish with Lemon

Yield: serves 6

¼ cup olive oil
1 clove garlic, **finely chopped**
8 tablespoons lemon juice
4 cups water
1 teaspoons crushed chili peppers, or **ground** red pepper to taste
salt and pepper to taste
½ teaspoon turmeric
3½ tablespoons fresh parsley, chopped and divided
2½ pounds skinless fish **fillets**, fresh or frozen (thawed)
1 lemon, cut crosswise into thin slices, for **garnish**

Equipment: Large skillet with cover, mixing spoon, fork, wide slotted spatula, serving platter

1. Heat oil in large skillet over medium-high heat. Add garlic, stir, and **sauté** until soft, about 1 minute. Add lemon juice, water, crushed chili peppers or ground red pepper to taste, salt and pepper to taste, turmeric, and 3 tablespoons chopped parsley. Stir well, bring to boil, and add fish fillets. Bring back to boil. Reduce heat to **simmer**, cover, and cook until fish is opaque white and flakes easily when poked with a fork, 12 to 15 minutes. Remove from heat, uncover, and allow fish to cool in liquid.

2. Prepare to serve: Using wide slotted spatula, transfer fish to serving platter. Either discard cooking liquid or cover and refrigerate for another use.

To serve, garnish fish with lemon slices and sprinkle with remaining ½ tablespoon parsley. The fish is served at room temperature.

In this traditional Old World recipe, the rice is cooked in a muslin bag, which is set into the stew. As it cooks, the rice picks up the flavors of the cooking liquid. Instead of a muslin bag, use a more easily available knee-length nylon stocking. Cut off the elastic at the top before filling the stocking with the rice.

Gdra

Chicken with Chickpeas

Yield: serves 6

½ cup butter or margarine
4 saffron threads
2 onions, **finely chopped**
2½ to 3 pounds chicken, cut into serving-size pieces
12 ounces canned chickpeas (garbanzo beans)
2 or 3 sprigs fresh **cilantro** or 1 teaspoon **ground coriander**
¼ cup parsley, finely chopped
salt and pepper to taste
water, as needed
1½ cups rice
juice of 1 lemon

Equipment: Large saucepan with cover or **Dutch oven**, mixing spoon, clean lady's knee length nylon stocking with elastic removed (see above), metal tongs, heatproof bowl, scissors or paring knife, large platter

1. Melt butter or margarine in large saucepan or Dutch oven over medium-high heat. Crumble in saffron threads and chopped onions. Stir and **sauté** until onions are soft, 3 to 5 minutes. Add chicken, canned chickpeas with juice, cilantro or coriander, parsley, and salt and pepper to taste. Add enough water to cover chicken mixture by at least 2 inches, and bring to boil. Reduce heat to **simmer**, cover, and cook 45 minutes to 1 hour.

2. Put rice in a clean nylon stocking and knot the top allowing room in the stocking for the rice to expand as it cooks. Using back of mixing spoon, push down on rice bag to completely submerge in the cooking liquid. Cook rice for 25 to 30 minutes, until done. Using metal tongs, re-

move and set bag filled with rice in heatproof bowl. Keep bowl of rice warm until ready to use.

3. Prepare to serve: Place chicken pieces in center of a large platter. Using scissors or paring knife, cut open rice bag and spoon rice and chickpeas around the chicken.

To serve, sprinkle lemon juice over the entire dish. Ladle remaining pan juices either over the chicken or into a separate bowl for guests to spoon over each serving.

Throughout North Africa and Middle East, this dish is traditionally served with lamb at life-cycle celebrations.

Hunkar Begendi

Sultan's Pleasure

Yield: serves 6

2 eggplants (about 2 pounds total)
1 tablespoon lemon juice
¼ cup butter or margarine
1 cup half and half
½ cup **fresh white bread crumbs**
3 tablespoons grated Parmesan cheese
salt and pepper to taste
1 tablespoon chopped fresh parsley
1 green bell pepper, **trimmed**, **seeded**, and cut crosswise into thin rings

Equipment: Fork, baking sheet, oven mitts, knife, spoon, food processor, rubber spatula, mixing spoon, medium saucepan, serving bowl

Preheat oven to 450° F.

1. Poke eggplant skin with fork in about 8 places and set on baking sheet. Bake in oven until soft and tender, 30 to 40 minutes. Using oven mitts, remove from oven and cool enough to handle. When cool enough to handle, cut in half, scoop out pulp, and put into food processor. Discard eggplant skin. Add lemon juice to pulp in food processor and process until smooth, about 1 minute.

Note: While processing, turn machine off once or twice and scrape down sides of container with rubber spatula.

2. Transfer eggplant mixture to medium saucepan. Add butter or margarine and half and half, and cook over medium heat, stirring frequently, until butter or margarine melts. Stir in bread crumbs, salt and pepper to taste, and Parmesan cheese. Stir and continue to cook over medium heat until thickened, 5 to 7 minutes.

To serve, transfer to serving bowl, sprinkle with chopped parsley and garnish with green pepper rings. Serve as a vegetable side dish with meat.

A life-cycle feast usually includes dozens of different very sweet pastries and puddings, but nothing is more enjoyable to end a meal than platters of *fakha taza*. A combination of fruits is either set out on the buffet table for guests to peel and eat, or the fruits are made into a salad that is eaten at the end of the meal.

Fakha Taza

Fresh Fruit

Yield: serves 6 to 8

1 **pomegranate**
1 cantaloupe, peeled, **seeded**, and cut into ½-inch cubes
3 pears, **trimmed**, peeled, seeded, and cut into ½-inch cubes
1 mango, peeled and cut into bite-size chunks
2 oranges, peeled, **pith** removed, and cut into sections
2 cups strawberries, washed, drained, trimmed, and cut in half
juice of 2 lemons
2 bananas, peeled and sliced crosswise ¼-inch thick
12 pitted dates, cut in half

Equipment: Paring knife, teaspoon, small bowl, large serving bowl, salad tools, plastic food wrap

1. Cut pomegranate in half and work on one half at a time. Remove tough outer skin and white pith. Carefully pull out the edible seeds with your finger or a teaspoon and put in small bowl. Take care not to pierce the red seeds.

2. Put cubed cantaloupe, pears, mango chunks, orange sections, and strawberries into large serving bowl. Sprinkle with lemon juice. Using salad tools, gently toss to mix. Cover with plastic wrap and refrigerate until ready to serve.

To serve, add pomegranate seeds, sliced bananas, and dates, gently toss to mix, and serve at once.

MIDDLE EAST

Despite vast cultural, political and geographical differences that sets each Middle East country apart from the others, there are many similarities when it comes to the food that is prepared for life-cycle celebration feasts.

For Muslims, it's not a celebration feast unless there is lamb and unleavened wheat bread. In the Middle East, lambs and wheat date back thousands of years to when they were both domesticated to became humans' first controlled food supplies. By eating the grass and weeds that humans could not digest, the sheep turned into nourishing meat. Harvesting wild wheat became valuable to humans because it increased food supplies and it could be stored for a long time.

The favorite Middle East vegetable is eggplant, and yogurt is the preferred form of milk. The widespread religious taboo for both Muslims and Jews is against eating any meat from pigs.

For both Muslims and Israelis, the rituals of feasting not only include what food can be eaten but how it is processed, purchased, stored, prepared and cooked, in addition to the rituals and etiquette of eating. Israelis say a prayer over bread, and there are eating procedures and rituals for every occasion. Muslims likewise pray over food and the rituals carry over into the etiquette of eating.

Muslims traditionally eat with the thumb, forefinger and middle finger of the right hand. The left hand is considered unclean. To eat with one finger is considered a sign of hatred, to eat with two shows pride, three is in accord with the Prophet Mohammed, while to eat with four or five fingers is a sign of gluttony.

EGYPT

Egypt is located in the northeast corner of Africa. It is bordered on the west by Libya, on the south by Sudan, on the east by Israel and the Red Sea, and on the north by the Mediterranean Sea. Although Egypt is considered an Arab nation and most Egyptians are Arabs, they are proud of their own unique history and culture, which they consider different from the rest of the Arab world.

Egypt has a large rural population known as *fellahin*. The name is from the Arabic word *falaha*, which means "to labor" or "till the earth." Egypt also has a sizable Bedouin population. They are desert nomads who travel from one oasis to the next with their flocks.

Islamic beliefs and traditions form a common bond that unites most Egyptians and all life-cycle events are according to their religion. (See Islam and Islamic Life-Cycle Rituals, page xlix.)

In the cities the people have a very modern lifestyle often influenced by the Western world. About 10 percent of the population, mostly urbanites, belong to the Coptic Christian Church. They are descended from ancient Egyptians who converted to Christianity in the second or third centuries. Many Copts have a small cross tattooed on their wrists. Copts follow life-cycle events according to their religion. (See Eastern or Orthodox Church Life-Cycle Rituals, page xlviii.)

In the cities, Muslim baby boys are circumcised at birth, by a doctor, before they leave the hospital. In the countryside, families usually have the traditional circumcision done before the child is five years old. The circumcision is a very important event in a boy's life and there is always a celebration feast. On the day of the circumcision it is customary for the boy to ride around the village on a horse followed by his family and friends. Some of the men carry guns, which they fire in the air to announce the happy event.

One week after the birth of a child, many Egyptian families invite relatives and friends to see the newborn; this is called the Seven-Day Party. The guests bring gifts for the child, and they are served cookies, cakes, candies, and beverages.

Egyptian women have a great deal of freedom and there are few official restrictions. They are not required to wear veils or traditional Muslim clothing. They can vote, attend school, own property, drive cars and enjoy the same privileges as men. They probably enjoy more legal equality than women of other Arabic countries, and the government is encouraging women to take a more active roll in city and national affairs.

In the cities, young people can meet at work, in clubs, at social gatherings, and through friends. After a couple meets and dates, if they decide to marry, the boy should ask the girl's parents for permission. If everyone is agreeable there is an engagement party, which may be either small or elaborate. It is customary for the bride's parents to give a dowry, usually money, to the groom.

Most Muslim and all Christian brides living in the cities wear the Western-style long white wedding dress with veil. Urban Egyptians seem to favor grand wedding receptions held in a hotel ballroom with music, dancing, and great quantities of food and drink.

In rural areas it is the parents' responsibility to arrange the marriage of their children. The choices of mates are always made within the village, and often matches are made between cousins or other relations. Traditionally, in the country, newlyweds live with the groom's family. The young bride is subordinate to her husband and her mother-in-law, but when she has children, her status rises.

In Egypt, wedding ceremonies are very simple civil contracts rather than religious ones. All that is needed is the signing of a formal contract between the groom and the bride's male guardian, who is usually her father, but it could also be a brother or uncle. The contract is signed in front of witnesses. To make the marriage more "official," the wedding party visits the office of *Al Mazoun* (government witness). He oversees a special contract that guarantees a payment to the wife in the event of a divorce.

The wedding feast begins with *mazza* (appetizers) and the assortment includes black olives (*zeitoun*), plates of feta cheese (*gebna beida*), turnips and cucumber pickles (*torshi*), small boiled shrimp (*gambari*), fried **smelts** (*bissaria*), and Egyptian-style eggplant (*auberginen auf Ägyptische art*) (recipe page 103).

Egyptians love very sweet desserts, and a large assortment of sweet treats is always set out for guests and friends at parties and weddings. Stuffed dates and cookies are traditionally baked for religious feasts, birthdays, and weddings.

In villages and among the poor *fellahin* (farmers) the wife often saves for months before a celebration feast so that she is able to afford the ingredients to make feast cookies or *kahk el-eed*, such as *bel agwa* for her children. ۞ ۞ ۞

Kahk El-eed Bel Agwa

Feast Cookies with Date Filling

Yield: 30 to 40 pieces

- *date filling* (recipe follows)
- 3 cups all-purpose flour
- ¼ teaspoon salt
- 1½ cups melted **rendered** butter (recipe page 102), or melted margarine
- 1 teaspoon vanilla extract
- 1 package dry **yeast**
- ¼ cup **lukewarm** water
- 1 cup water
- 3 **egg yolks**
- 2 cups confectioners' sugar, for **garnish**

Equipment: Large mixing bowl, **pastry blender** (optional), 8-ounce cup, lightly floured work surface, kitchen towel, lightly floured rolling pin, baking sheet, oven mitts, wire cake rack, serving platter

1. Prepare *date filling* (recipe follows).

2. In large mixing bowl, mix together flour and salt and make a well (hole) in the center. Pour melted rendered butter or melted margarine in center, and add vanilla extract. Using your fingers or pastry blender, mix until mixture resembles crumbs.

3. In cup, dissolve yeast in lukewarm water, 5 minutes. Add yeast mixture to flour mixture and **knead** until very well blended, 3 to 5 minutes. Stir in enough water, ¼ cup at a time, to make firm dough. Knead dough until smooth, 5 to 7 minutes. Transfer to lightly floured work surface and knead for 5 more minutes. Add water, ¼ cup at a time, and knead constantly until all the water is incorporated and dough is satiny and **elastic**. Cover dough on work surface with towel and let rise for 1 hour.

Preheat oven to 350° F.

4. Divide dough into Ping-Pong-ball size pieces. On lightly floured work surface, roll a ball of dough out into a 3- x 4-inch rectangle using lightly floured rolling pin. Center a 3-inch long piece of date filling along the 4-inch edge and roll up. Dampen ends of dough with water and curve each end around to form into a ring, attaching the two ends together. Place on baking sheet. Repeat filling, shaping into rings, and placing on baking sheet.

5. Bake in oven until golden, 20 to 25 minutes. Remove and place cookies on wire cake rack. While still warm, dip cookies in confectioners' sugar to coat all sides.

To serve, stack cookies decoratively on a serving platter.

Date Filling

Yield: about 2 cups

1 pound pitted dates
3 tablespoons butter or margarine
½ teaspoon **ground** cinnamon
2 tablespoons water

Equipment: Scissors, medium skillet, mixing spoon, wax paper, serving tray

1. Using scissors, cut pitted dates into pea-size pieces. Rinse scissors under cold running water if it becomes sticky.

2. Melt butter or margarine in medium skillet over medium heat. Add dates and cinnamon. Stirring constantly, cook for 5 to 8 minutes. Stir in water and cook until mixture holds together, 3 minutes. Remove from heat and cool enough to handle.

3. Using wet hands, form mixture into log shapes, about ½ inch thick and 3 inches long. Place on wax-paper-covered serving tray.

Continue: Use in kahk el-eed bel agwa *(recipe precedes).*

In countries where most people do not have refrigeration, it is necessary to render butter to prevent it from turning rancid. Rendered butter keeps for months without refrigeration.

Samnah Baladi

Rendered Butter

1 pound unsalted butter
4 tablespoons coarse **bulgur,** or all-purpose **flour**

Equipment: Small saucepan, large spoon, small container with cover

1. Melt butter in small saucepan over low heat. Add bulgur or flour and cook on low heat until butter separates. (Clarified butter rises to the top and solids go to the bottom after about 5 to 7 minutes.) Remove from heat and cool to room temperature.

2. Carefully skim off clear rendered butter and put into small container. Rendered butter keeps for many months even without refrigerating. Either discard residue or refrigerate and use in soup.

Use over vegetables or in recipes calling for rendered butter.

Sugarless bitter coffee is served at wakes as a sign of deep grief. Drinking it is a show of sympathy for the bereaved. Egyptian coffee (*ahwa*) is brewed like *kahve* (recipe page 139). When making *ahwa*, a cardamom seed is added to the *kanaka* or metal coffee pot. *Ahwa* is served very hot, in small cups (*fengal*) or small glasses.

Serving great quantities of food at a banquet is a sign of a hospitable host and hostess. The meal must end with fresh fruit to refresh the mouth and cleanse the palate.

Khoshaf

Spiced Fruit Compote

Note: This recipe takes one or two days.

Yield: serves 6 to 8

1 cup dried figs (stems removed)
1 cup pitted prunes
1 cup dried apricots
5 cups warm water
½ cup seedless golden raisins
½ lemon, sliced thin and cut into half circles
½ cup sugar
1 cinnamon stick
½ cup **pine nuts**
juice of 1 lemon
heavy cream, for serving (optional)

Equipment: Medium bowl, **colander**, large saucepan, mixing spoon, medium bowl with cover, individual serving bowls

1. Put figs in medium bowl and cover with warm water. Soak for 1 hour. Drain in colander. Fill large saucepan a little more than halfway with water and add figs. Bring to boil over high heat. Reduce heat to **simmer**, and cook 10 minutes. Add prunes, apricots, raisins, sliced lemons, sugar, and cinnamon stick. Simmer for 5 minutes. Remove from heat and cool to room temperature. Transfer to medium bowl with cover.

2. Stir in pine nuts, lemon juice, and enough cold water to cover fruit by 2 inches. Cover and refrigerate at least 1 or 2 days for flavors to develop

To serve, spoon fruit mixture with juice into individual serving bowls. Serve with pitcher of cream to drizzle on top, if desired.

Eggplants have grown in the Middle East for more than 1,500 years. Unlike American eggplants, which are generally large and pear-shaped, Middle East eggplants are slim and small, resembling eggs, which is probably how they got their name. When buying eggplant, whatever its size or shape, look for uniform color and a firm, smooth skin. Arabs say they have over a thousand ways to cook eggplant. It's not unusual to find eggplant prepared several different ways for an Arabian wedding feast. This dish is served as an appetizer.

Auberginen auf Ägyptische Art

Egyptian-style Eggplant Salad

Yield: serves 8 to 12

2 eggplants (about 1 pound each), **trimmed**, discard stems, and cut crosswise into ½ inch thick circles
extra virgin olive oil, as needed
2 tomatoes, trimmed and **finely chopped**
1 onion, finely chopped
3 tablespoons fresh parsley, finely chopped
1 clove garlic, finely chopped
3 tablespoons red wine vinegar
salt and pepper to taste

Equipment: Pastry brush, 2 baking sheets, oven mitts, medium bowl, mixing spoon, serving platter

Preheat oven to 425° F.

1. Using pastry brush, brush both sides of eggplant slices with olive oil and place side by side on baking sheets.

2. Bake in oven for 20 to 25 minutes, or until browned and tender. Cool to room temperature.

3. Prepare tomato dressing: In medium bowl, combine chopped tomatoes, onion, parsley, garlic, red wine vinegar, and ¼ cup olive oil. Using mixing spoon, stir to mix.

4. Arrange eggplant slices in single layer on serving platter and spoon tomato dressing evenly over each slice. Add salt and pepper to taste.

Serve at room temperature for best flavor.

ISRAEL

Israel occupies a narrow land area bounded on the west by the Mediterranean Sea; on the southwest by Egypt; on the east by Jordan, the West Bank territory, and Syria; and on the north by Lebanon. Israel is a young country, having just celebrated 50 years as a Jewish state in 1998. Although some 17 percent of its residents are Arab Muslims, the vast majority are Jewish. At this time there is a major cultural clash between ultra-Orthodox Jews and the more secular (Conservative and Reform) Israelis. (See Judaism and Jewish Life-Cycle Rituals, page xlii.) Most ultra-Orthodox Jews (*haredim*) want Israel to be a religious state run by rabbis (Jewish religious leaders) and not politicians. The tough question facing the people of Israel is should the country be a liberal democracy, or a religious theocracy?

Within its borders, all issues relating to the life cycle—births, marriages, divorces and burials—are decided by the *haredim*. Rites-of-passage rituals must be performed according to strict orthodoxy to be recognized as legal by the Israeli government. They believe that in this way Jews will return to their religious and cultural roots. Rigid and inflexible interpretation of Jewish law dictates dress codes, the segregation of boys and girls in schools, and stringent observances of the Sabbath (from sundown Friday evening to sundown on Saturday), and Jewish dietary laws. They maintain the ritualistic laws of *kashruth* (kosher, also *kasher,* which means pure), the ritualistic slaughter of certain animals and fowl, no mixing of meat (*fleischig*) and milk (*milchig*), and separate utensils and dishes for these foods.

Secular couples resent the ultra-Orthodox bureaucracy at the ministry of religion where they must register to marry. Unless they marry according to the Orthodox traditions, an Israeli marriage is not legal. The Orthodox rituals are very complex, especially for women, who must take ritual baths (*mikvas*).

To marry, non-Orthodox couples have to travel out of the country, with nearby Cyprus a favorite location. The Israeli government accepts Cyprus certificates of marriage. To please their parents and friends and enjoy the traditions of a Jewish wedding, couples, on their return, often have a token second ceremony performed by a reform or conservative rabbi in a home, hotel, or community center.

A group of young Orthodox rabbis, interested in promoting Jewish unity and serving both the secular and religious communities, have started *Tzohar* (window), a movement to help the non-Orthodox Jews get married on Israeli soil. *Tzohar* rabbis respect the variations among Jews. They are reaching out to give couples a positive Jewish wedding experience, and one accepted as legal by the Israeli government. A *Tzohar* rabbi meets with the couples, before the wedding, and without imposing their standards of Orthodoxy, he explains the *kedushin* (sacredness) in marriage.

The half-million Ethiopian Jews living in Israel have their own marriage customs. Tradition forbids marriage within an extended family that can number thousands. If a marriageable Ethiopian woman wants to marry an Ethiopian man in Israel it is necessary to go to their council of elders for approval. If the family records show they shared a great-great-grandparent, marriage between the young couple is unacceptable. History shows that, by instinctively adhering to such strict rules, the tribe of Israelites that wandered into Africa almost 3000 years ago was able to maintain its religious and cultural identity without degrading its genetic pool.

Bread holds a sacred place in the Jewish home and at mealtime no one eats until prayer (*mitzvah*) is said over the loaf or loaves. The braided bread (*Challah*, also *Hallah*) is named for the manna (Biblical food) that fell from heaven for the Israelites during their Exodus from Egypt. On the Sabbath, a blessing is said over two loaves, representing the two portions of manna that fell on that day, instead of the single portion of manna that fell on other days.

When the Sabbath begins at sundown on Friday night, the loaves are placed under a special napkin at the head of the dinner table. The napkin covering the loaves symbolically represents the dew that collected on the manna in the morning.

In remembrance of her origin of creation, there is a ritual that a Jewish woman must perform when making the Sabbath loaf if she uses more than three pounds of flour to make her bread. It is the "separating *challah*" ritual. A small portion of the dough (not less than the size of an olive) is pinched off, which is called the small *challah*. She says the blessing (*mitzvah*) over it, and then she burns the piece of dough. Traditional *challah* must be made with unbleached white flour. ۞ ۞ ۞

Challah

Jewish Sabbath Bread

Yield: 1 loaf

1 package active dry **yeast**
¾ cup **lukewarm** water
2 tablespoons sugar
1 teaspoon salt
1 egg
1 tablespoon vegetable oil, more as needed
2½ to 2¾ cups unbleached or all-purpose **flour**, divided
egg wash, for **glaze**
1 tablespoon poppy or **sesame seeds**, for **garnish**

Equipment: Large mixing bowl, mixing spoon, lightly floured work surface, kitchen towel, lightly greased baking sheet, pastry brush, oven mitts, cloth napkin

1. In large mixing bowl, sprinkle yeast over lukewarm water and let stand until dissolved, 5 minutes. Stir in sugar, salt, egg, 1 tablespoon oil, and 1¼ cups flour, and beat until smooth. Stir in enough remaining 1¼ to 1½ cups flour to make dough easy to handle and no longer sticky.

2. Transfer to lightly floured work surface and **knead** until smooth and **elastic**, 5 to 7 minutes. Clean and lightly grease large mixing bowl. Place dough in lightly greased large mixing bowl and turn to grease all sides. Cover with towel and set in warm place to rise to double in bulk, 1½ to 2 hours. (Dough is ready if indentation remains when poked with your finger.)

3. **Punch down** dough, transfer to lightly floured work surface and divide into 3 equal parts. Roll each part into a rope, 14 inches long. Place each rope side by side on lightly greased baking sheet. Pinch ropes together at one end and braid them gently and loosely (do not stretch). When finished braiding, pinch ends of braid together and tuck both braided ends under the loaf to keep them in place. Brush braided loaf lightly with oil, cover with towel, and let rise to double in bulk, 40 to 50 minutes.

Preheat oven to 375° F.

4. Brush loaf lightly with egg wash and sprinkle with poppy or sesame seeds. Bake in oven for about 25 to 35 minutes, until golden. Test **bread doneness**.

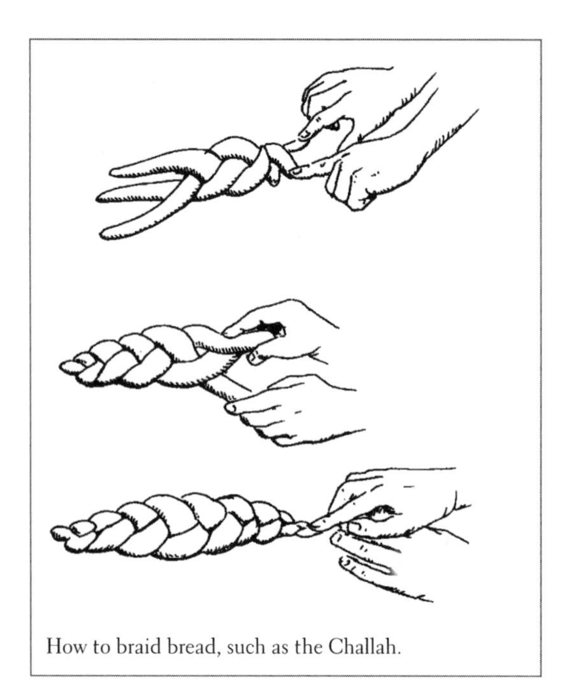
How to braid bread, such as the Challah.

To serve challah, *place the uncut loaf on the dinner table and cover with a large white napkin. Usually the host or a male guest will say the blessing as he cuts the first slice. He then cuts slices for everyone at the table and as each person breaks their bread to eat it, they repeat the prayer. A second loaf is often prepared and blessed to be eaten on the following day of the Sabbath.*

If there is a Jewish comfort food it would have to be chicken soup. When using this recipe for basic chicken broth alone, omit the dumplings (*kreplach*) and strain broth.

Hindel Zup (also Gilderne) mit Kreplach

Chicken Soup with Filled Dumplings

Yield: serves 8

2 to 3 pounds chicken, cut into serving-size pieces
1 gallon (16 cups) water
1 onion, quartered
2 carrots, **trimmed** and sliced
2 ribs celery with greens, chopped
salt and pepper to taste
16 *kreplach* (recipe follows), for serving
2 tablespoons fresh parsley flakes, for **garnish**

Equipment: Large **heavy-based** saucepan with cover or **Dutch oven**, slotted spoon, large bowl, **bulb baster** or mixing spoon, ladle, individual soup bowls

1. Prepare soup: Put chicken pieces in large heavy-based saucepan or Dutch oven and add water. Add onion, carrots, celery, and salt and pepper to taste, and bring to boil over high heat. Reduce heat to simmer, cover, and cook for 1 hour. Remove cover and cook to **reduce** liquid to about half, 30 to 40 minutes.

2. Using slotted spoon, remove onion, carrots, celery, and chicken pieces to large bowl and cool to room temperature. Cover and refrigerate for another use. Allow chicken broth to cool to room temperature and skim off and discard fat using bulb baster or mixing spoon.

3. Prepare *kreplach*.

4. Prepare to cook *kreplach*: Bring chicken broth to boil over high heat, add the *kreplach*, a few at a time so they don't stick together. Stir, reduce heat to simmer, and cook for 18 minutes, or until cooked through.

To serve, ladle soup, with 2 kreplach, *into individual soup bowls. Sprinkle each serving with fresh parsley flakes.*

Kreplach are simply dumplings or meat-filled squares of dough. This is a quick and easy recipe using prepared wonton skins (prepackaged paper-thin sheets of dough made from flour, eggs, and salt). They are available in small square or round shapes in the refrigerated or freezer section of all supermarkets and Asian food stores. Either shape can be used in this recipe.

Kreplach (also Kissonim)

Jewish Dumplings

Yield: 16 pieces

1 tablespoon vegetable oil
3 tablespoons onion, grated
1 cup (8-ounces) lean chopped beef
1 egg
salt and pepper to taste
16 wonton skins, if frozen, thawed (available at all supermarkets and Asian food stores)

Equipment: Medium skillet, mixing spoon, food processor, medium bowl, work surface, kitchen towel, cup with water, plate

1. Heat oil in skillet over medium-high heat. Add onion, stir, and **sauté** until soft, 3 to 5 minutes. Crumble chopped meat into the skillet, stir, and cook until browned, 3 to 5 minutes. Remove from heat and cool enough to handle. Transfer to food processor.

2. Process meat with egg until mixture forms smooth paste, 1 to 2 minutes. Transfer to medium bowl and add salt and pepper to taste.

Note: While processing, turn machine off once or twice and scrape down sides of container with rubber spatula.

3. Fill wonton skins: Unwrap skins and keep stack covered with damp towel so they don't dry out. Place one skin on work surface. Set 1 teaspoon meat mixture in center, moisten your finger with water in cup and rub it around the edge. Fold one side of skin over meat mixture to make a half moon (if skins are round), or triangle (if skins are square), and press edges together to seal in mixture. Repeat making dumplings and place on plate.

Continue with hindel zup mit kreplach *(recipe precedes: Step 4. Prepare to cook* kreplach:*).*

Prickly pears, a popular Israeli fruit, are called *sabra* in Hebrew, which means cactus. Native-born Israelis are called *sabra* because like the fruit they are bristly (show angry defiance) outside but are sweet on the inside. In Israel, the *sabra* are chilled, cut in half, and eaten right out of the skin, seeds and all. They are also peeled, sliced, sprinkled with lemon juice, and served as dessert. To remove the barbs or prickly coating that cover the skin, wear gloves and use a small paring knife to peel off the skin.

Mandelbrot is a classic recipe that has traveled through time and from one end of the world to the other, and survived. This is a twice-baked biscuit, similar to Italian *biscotti* (in Italian, *biscotti* means twice baked). *Kikar skadim* is a modern version of the old Israeli recipe.

Kikar Skadim (also Mandelbrot)

Twice Baked Biscuits

Note: This recipe requires more than one day

Yield: about 100 pieces

3 eggs
¾ cup sugar
1 cup vegetable oil
1 teaspoon vanilla extract
1 cup chopped walnuts
1 cup chocolate chips
2 cups all-purpose flour
2 teaspoons baking powder
¼ teaspoon salt
1½ cups corn flakes

Equipment: Large mixing bowl, wooden mixing spoon, small bowl, rubber spatula, plastic food wrap, baking sheet, aluminum foil, vegetable cooking spray, lightly floured work surface, oven mitts, metal spatula, **serrated knife**, wire cake rack, serving plate

1. Put eggs in large mixing bowl and add sugar and oil. Stir well using wooden mixing spoon.

Stir in vanilla extract, walnuts, and chocolate chips until well mixed.

2. In small bowl, combine flour, baking powder, and salt. Add flour mixture to egg mixture, a little at a time, stirring well after each addition. Using rubber spatula, stir in corn flakes. Cover with plastic wrap and refrigerate overnight.

Preheat oven to 350° F.

3. Prepare to bake: Line baking sheet with foil and spray with vegetable cooking spray. Divide dough into 3 equal balls. On lightly floured work surface, roll one ball into a rope, 1 inch wide and about 16 inches long. Place on prepared baking sheet. Repeat making 2 more ropes and place them side by side on baking sheet, allowing space between each dough rope to let rise. Bake in oven until golden, 25 to 30 minutes.

4. Remove from oven and while still warm, place on work surface. Using serrated knife, cut each rope diagonally into ½ inch thick slices. Lay pieces flat and close together on baking sheet. Return to oven for 5 minutes to lightly toast. Remove from oven and turn pieces over using metal spatula. Return to oven to toast other side for 3 minutes. Remove from oven and transfer to wire cake rack to cool.

To serve, stack on serving plate and eat as sweet snack with coffee or tea. Kikar skadim *keeps well in airtight container, refrigerated up to a week or frozen up to a month.*

Today, Jews from more than 70 countries call Israel home. This diversity of people is reflected in the way food is prepared for celebration feasts. The following *fleischig* (meat) wedding menu was served to some 500 guests at a *Kibbutz* (Israeli collective farm or settlement) and shows the cross-culturalism of present day Israel.

The reception began when the rabbi blessed the traditional *challah*, made extra large for the occasion. As he said the *mitzvah* over the loaf, and cut the first slice, this signaled the guests to eat.

The menu included huge baskets and bowls of assorted yeast breads, flat breads, rolls and an old favorite, Polish *piroshki* (recipe page 225). The buffet tables were laden with *forspeise* (appetizers) of international flavors: Russia's Mushrooms in *smetana* (recipe page 269), and eggplant Caviar (recipe page 261), and stuffed grape leaves (recipe page 136) from Eastern Europe and Mediterranean regions. Eggplant salad (recipe page 158), popular throughout the Middle East, and chicken soup with filled dumplings known as wontons in China, ravioli in Italy, and in Israel they are called *kreplach* (recipes page 107). The main dishes included Moroccan-style sweet *couscous* (also *couscousou*) (recipe page 109), Eastern European *fleischig tzimmes* (recipe page 110), Chinese stir-fry chicken, and *pashtida* (recipe page 109), an Israeli vegetarian casserole. The dessert table was covered with cakes, cookies, such as *kikar skadim* (recipe page 107) and candies. Honey cakes (recipe page 110) were prepared for the occasion to celebrate symbolically the sweetness of life.

Wine is the beverage for rituals and celebrations. Festivities include a round of toasts, where everyone drinks the wine, and says *"L'Chayim,"* (to life and good health). The non-wine drinkers enjoy Israel's national drink, *gazoz*, sweet syrups added to carbonated water. Other popular drinks are made from fresh fruit juices, pomegranates and *mitz* (made from clementines, which are tangerines that originated in Spain).

A typical Jewish wedding celebration includes circle dancing (the *hora*), where the bride and groom may be lifted above the circle. If either the bride or groom is the last child of the family to be married, another special dance may be performed for the parents to celebrate their success in marrying off all their children. In Orthodox communities, where dancing with the opposite sex is prohibited, dancing may be done with dance partners holding opposite ends of a scarf.

Pashtida

Vegetarian Casserole

Yield: serves 8

- 1 tablespoon butter or margarine
- 1 onion, **finely chopped**
- 2 cloves garlic, finely chopped
- 4 eggs, beaten
- 1 cup crumbled feta cheese
- 1 cup ricotta cheese
- 6 tablespoons grated Parmesan cheese, divided
- ½ cup green onions, finely chopped
- ¼ teaspoon **ground** nutmeg
- salt and pepper to taste
- 3 cups dry penne or rigatoni pasta (cooked according to directions on package), drained
- 10-ounce package frozen spinach, thawed

Equipment: Small skillet, mixing spoon, large mixing bowl, lightly greased 13- x 9- x 2-inch baking dish, aluminum foil, oven mitts

1. Heat butter or margarine in small skillet over medium-high heat. Add onion and garlic and **sauté** until onion is soft, 3 to 5 minutes. Remove from heat and set aside.

2. In large mixing bowl, combine eggs, feta and ricotta cheeses, 4 tablespoons Parmesan cheese, green onions, nutmeg, and salt and pepper to taste. Stir to mix well. Add sautéed onion mixture, cooked pasta, and thawed spinach, and toss to mix. Transfer to lightly greased baking dish. Sprinkle with remaining 2 tablespoons Parmesan cheese and cover with foil.

Preheat oven to 350° F.

3. Bake in oven for 35 minutes. Remove foil and bake until top is lightly browned, about 15 minutes.

Serve either warm or at room temperature. Place on the buffet table, cut into serving-size pieces, and have guests help themselves.

Israeli *couscousou* is quite different from North African ***couscous***. The North African variety is granule-size, smaller than rice. Israelis make small, round pearl-size noodles. Israeli *couscousou* (also called couscous) is available at some supermarkets and at most Jewish and Middle East food stores.

Sweet Couscousou

Sweet Noodle Pellets

Yield: serves 6

- 3 onions, chopped
- 6 kumquats, fresh or canned, chopped
- ½ cup seedless raisins
- ½ cup **pine nuts**
- 1 cup **blanched** sliced almonds, divided
- 1 pound **couscous** (cooked according to directions on package)

Equipment: Large **heavy-based** skillet, mixing spoon, serving bowl

Heat oil in large skillet over medium-high heat. Add onions, stir, and **sauté** until soft, 3 to 5 minutes. Reduce heat to medium. Add raisins, pine nuts, and ½ cup sliced almonds, and stir to mix. Add cooked couscous, stir to mix well, and cook to heat through, 5 to 7 minutes.

To serve, transfer to serving bowl and sprinkle with remaining ½ cup sliced almonds.

Brisket is a relatively inexpensive cut of beef that is easy to prepare and a favorite of East European Jews. For festive occasions *fleischig* (meat) is combined with prunes, carrots, and potatoes for the main course. There are no set rules, and every household has their own favorite combination of vegetables with the meat. A variation of this dish can be made vegetarian, without meat, and is called *tzimmes*. The Yiddish word *tsimmes* means to make a fuss over someone or something. This *tzimmes* recipe has a variety of ingredients mixed together.

Fleischig Tzimmes

Roast Brisket with Vegetable Medley

Yield: serves 6

2 tablespoons vegetable oil
4 onions, sliced
4 to 5 pounds **oven-ready** brisket of beef
6 tablespoons honey
juice of ½ lemon
1 teaspoon **ground** cinnamon
salt and pepper to taste
8 cups boiling water, more or less as needed
8 carrots, peeled and cut into chunks
6 potatoes, peeled and quartered
1½ cups (¾ pound) large pitted prunes, soaked, if necessary, according to directions on package

Equipment: Large roasting pan with cover, mixing spoon, oven mitts, **bulb baster** (optional), meat knife, small sauce bowl, serving platter, cutting board

Preheat oven to 325° F.

1. Heat oil in medium skillet over medium-high heat. Add onions, stir, and **sauté** until golden, 3 to 5 minutes. Spoon onions over bottom of large roasting pan and set meat on top. Spread honey over top of meat, sprinkle with lemon juice, cinnamon, and salt and pepper to taste. Pour 8 cups boiling water around meat, cover, and place in oven.

2. Bake in oven for 3 hours. Baste occasionally and add more boiling water to keep liquid to original level in pan.

3. Using oven mitts, remove from oven, add carrots, sweet potatoes, and prunes around sides of meat. Baste and add more boiling water, if necessary. Cover and continue baking for 1 to 1¼ hours more or until meat is fork tender.

To serve, transfer meat to cutting board. Let rest 20 minutes before slicing. Using meat knife, cut across the grain in thin slices and place on serving platter. Surround meat with potatoes, carrots, and prunes. Skim and discard fat from pan juices using bulb baster or mixing spoon. Pour pan juices over meat or in sauce bowl.

Honey plays an important role in all religious celebrations and cooking *mit lechig* (with honey) is a reminder of hope. To begin the new year, many Jews say a blessing over an apple dipped in honey: The evening meal ends with honey cake. Honey traditionally is served at the birth of a boy, at weddings, and at other happy occasions.

An old wedding custom among Eastern European Jews was to smear the doors of the homecoming newlyweds with honey. The honey symbolism has prevailed among Jews, according to Dov Noy, professor of folklore at Hebrew University of Jerusalem: "Thus the origin of the word honeymoon is derived because *isha* (woman or wife) has the value in Hebrew of *dvash*, "honey."

Lechig Cake

Honey Cake

Yield: 2 loaf cakes

3 cups all-purpose **flour**
1 teaspoon baking soda
½ teaspoon **ground** ginger
½ teaspoon ground cloves
½ teaspoon ground cinnamon
1 teaspoon salt
2 large eggs
½ cup sugar

1 cup clover honey
¼ cup vegetable oil
zest and juice of 1 lemon and 1 orange
½ cup apricot jam
½ cup dried apricots, soaked for 15 minutes in warm water, drained, and **finely chopped**
½ cup slivered almonds

Equipment: Flour **sifter**, medium bowl, electric mixer (optional), large mixing bowl, rubber spatula, wooden mixing spoon, 2 greased 9- x 5-inch loaf pans, oven mitts, toothpick, wire cake rack, serving platter

Preheat oven to 350° F.

1. **Sift** flour, baking soda, ginger, cloves, cinnamon, and salt in medium bowl.

2. Using electric mixer or mixing spoon, beat eggs in large mixing bowl. Add sugar, honey, oil, zests and juices of lemon and orange, and apricot jam. Beating egg mixture constantly, add flour mixture, a little at a time, alternately with water. Using rubber spatula or wooden spoon, **fold in** apricots and almonds. Transfer batter equally into 2 greased loaf pans.

3. Bake in oven for 40 to 50 minutes or until toothpick inserted in center comes out clean. Flip cake over onto wire cake rack to cool.

To serve, slice honey cakes into ½-inch thick slices and place on serving platter. Eat as dessert with fresh fruit.

LEBANON

Lebanon is a small country lying on the eastern end of the Mediterranean Sea. It is bordered on the north and east by Syria and to the south by Israel. Approximately 90 percent of the people living in Lebanon are Arabs, but they are almost equally divided between Christians and Muslims. Each group follows the life-cycle events according to their religion. (See Protestant and Catholic Life-Cycle Rituals, page xlvi, and Islam and Islamic Life-Cycle Rituals, page xlix.)

In Lebanon, Christians and Muslims are divided into different groups, or sects. There are at least 17 officially recognized sects. The largest Christian sect is the Maronite Catholics, a part of the Roman Catholic church. The Greek Orthodox is the next largest Christian sect. Although in business the Christians and Muslims often work together, they live in separate communities.

Both Christian and Muslim Lebanese have a high regard for family values. The mother is traditionally treated with respect, and she has a strong voice in family matters. Among the educated urbanite Christian and Muslim families, life is quite similar to the American way of life. It is acceptable, though not yet commonplace, for women to have careers, and most urban Muslim women wear Western fashions.

In the cities there are some families headed by Muslim husbands and Christian wives. Islamic law requires the children of such marriages to be brought up as Muslims. Marriage between a Christian man and a Muslim woman rarely happens, however, because it is forbidden by Islamic law.

SYRIA

Syria is a large country that lies south of Turkey and is bordered on the east by Iraq, on the south by Jordan, and on the west by the Mediterranean Sea, Lebanon, and Israel. The majority of Syrians are Arabs, and almost all of the people are Muslims except for a small Christian population who belong to the Orthodox Christian Church.

In Syria the Islamic modesty laws are less stringent than in other countries. Many urban Arabs keep strict Islamic rules at home for their family and follow a modern lifestyle in business. Muslim women can wear Western clothes if they like, without fear of punishment.

Women are publicly active in Syria and they have a prominent place in the urban work force. There are many well-educated Syrian Muslim women who have gone into business and the professions. In Syria, women doctors are free to set up practice and have male patients, which is unheard of in most other Muslim countries.

Pork is the favored meat for Christian religious holidays and life-cycle celebrations. Muslims select lamb, goat or camel; pork is forbidden. Celebration feasts are a time for large families living apart to come together. Whole roasted lamb (recipe page 141) is the favorite. The patriarch of the family purchases a live lamb from the market and fattens it for a week on malt and mulberry leaves. Neighbors and friends join in for the slaughtering of the lamb and to applaud the dressing and seasoning.

The ancient combination of lentils and rice is thought to be Esau's "mess of pottage" mentioned in the Bible. In Egypt and Saudi Arabia this same dish is called *ruz koshari*, where it is served with a side dish of tomato sauce. In Lebanon it is served with vegetable dishes and salad as part of the *mezze* (appetizer) table for a wedding celebration. ❂ ❂ ❂

Mujadarah (also Moudardara)

Rice and Lentils

Yield: serves 4

2 tablespoons olive oil or vegetable oil
2 onions, thinly sliced
3 cups water or chicken broth, homemade (recipe page 106), or canned
1 cup brown or green **lentils** (available at all supermarkets and health food stores)
½ cup white rice
1 teaspoon **allspice**
4 lemon wedges, for **garnish**
1 cup plain yogurt, for serving

Equipment: Large skillet with cover, slotted spoon, serving platter, small serving bowl

Heat 2 tablespoons oil in large skillet over medium-high heat. Add sliced onions and fry until soft, 3 to 5 minutes. Add water or chicken broth and bring to boil over high heat. Stir in lentils, rice, and allspice, and return to boil. Reduce heat to simmer, cover, and cook for 25 to 30 minutes, until rice and lentils are tender. Remove from heat and keep covered for 10 minutes.

To serve, place rice mixture on a serving platter and serve lemon wedges and a small serving bowl of yogurt on the side. To eat, sprinkle lemon juice over the rice mixture and spoon a little yogurt over each serving.

Shouraba il kuthra is fed to young Muslim boys to sooth them after their circumcision. It is also a favorite soup for breaking the fast of Ramadan. Christians serve the soup at the beginning of the wedding feast or to nourish a new mother.

Shouraba Il Kuthra

Vegetable Soup

Yield: serves 8

1½ pounds beef, including bone
3 quarts water
2 teaspoons salt
½ head cabbage, shredded

3 carrots, **trimmed** and sliced
1 onion, **finely chopped**
3 ribs celery, including leafy tops, sliced
2 cloves garlic, finely chopped
16 ounces canned whole tomatoes
¼ cup fresh parsley, finely chopped

Equipment: Large saucepan with cover, mixing spoon, ladle, individual soup bowls

1. Put beef with bone in large saucepan and add water and salt. Bring to boil over high heat. Remove and discard meat residue on the surface of the water. Reduce heat to simmer, cover, and cook 1 hour.

2. Add cabbage, carrots, onion, celery, garlic, and canned tomatoes. Stirring occasionally, increase heat to high and bring to boil. Reduce heat to simmer, cover, and cook 1 hour more.

To serve, ladle into individual soup bowls and serve with talamee *(recipe follows) for sopping.*

Freshly baked golden loaves of yeast leavened breads look and smell wonderful. There are many Syrian breads, but *talamee* is one of the best.

Talamee

Syrian Loaf Bread

Yield: 4 loaves
2 cups **lukewarm** water
1 package active dry **yeast**
2 teaspoons salt
¼ cup sugar
1 tablespoon vegetable oil
2 tablespoons melted butter
5 to 6 cups all-purpose flour

Equipment: Large mixing bowl, mixing spoon, lightly floured work surface, kitchen towel, knife, 1 or 2 greased baking sheet, oven mitts, napkin-lined bread basket

1. Pour lukewarm water into large mixing bowl, and add yeast to soften, 5 minutes. Stir in salt, sugar, oil, and melted butter. Beat in flour, 1 cup at a time, to make a stiff dough. When dough is no longer sticky, transfer to lightly floured work surface. **Knead** dough until smooth and **elastic**, 5 to 7 minutes. Transfer dough to lightly greased large mixing bowl and turn to grease all sides. Cover with towel and set in warm place for 1½ to 2 hours, to rise to double in bulk.

2. **Punch down** dough and cut into 4 equal pieces. Knead each piece until smooth and satiny. Form pieces into a ball. Place each about 4 inches apart on work surface, cover with towel and let rest for 30 minutes. Using the palm of your hands, flatten each ball to ½ inch thick, and place about 4 inches apart on 1 or 2 greased baking sheets. Cover with towel and let rise for 45 minutes.

Preheat oven to 450° F.

3. Bake in oven for 15 to 20 minutes, or until golden brown and baked through.

Serve warm, right from the oven for best flavor. Place loaves in napkin-lined bread basket to keep warm. Each person takes a loaf and uses it to sop up soup and stews.

Jaj mishwee is an easy way to prepare chicken. The chicken is very well cooked and it will please the most finicky eater. The broth should soothe the little guest of honor at his circumcision celebration.

Jaj Mishwee

Syrian Roast Chicken

Yield: serves 6
5 pound **oven-ready** whole chicken
water, as needed
salt and pepper, as needed
½ cup butter
¼ cup honey

1 teaspoon **ground** cinnamon
½ teaspoon ground nutmeg

Equipment: Large saucepan with cover, metal tongs, roasting pan, small saucepan, **pastry brush**, **bulb baster** (optional), oven mitts, serving platter

1. Remove bag with chicken gizzard from inside of chicken. Rinse chicken, inside and out, under cold running water. Put in large saucepan and cover with water. Add 1 teaspoon salt and bring to boil over high heat. Reduce heat to **simmer**, cover, and cook for 1 hour, or until tender. Using metal tongs, remove chicken from saucepan and place in roasting pan.

Preheat oven to 350° F.

2. Melt butter or margarine in small saucepan over medium heat. Add honey, cinnamon, nutmeg, and salt and pepper to taste, and stir to mix. Remove from heat. Using pastry brush, brush surface of chicken with honey mixture.

3. Bake chicken in oven for 1 hour, until golden brown. Combine remaining honey mixture with ¼ cup chicken broth from saucepan and use it to **baste** chicken frequently with bulb baster or mixing spoon.

To serve, set chicken on serving platter with rice or couscous (prepared according to directions on package). Serve with talamee *(recipe page 113).*

JORDAN

Jordan lies in the heart of the Middle East. It is bordered by Syria to the north, by Iraq to the east, by Saudi Arabia to the east and southeast, and the west by Israel and the West Bank territory. Almost all Jordanians are Muslim Arabs, and Arabic is the official language; however, English is used widely in commerce and government. Most of the population are urbanites and their lifestyle is very westernized. Women dress fashionably but conservatively. Women attend universities and have equality with men. Many women hold top-level jobs in the government and business and are well represented in the professions.

Jordanians feel strongly about their religion, and they follow Muslim life-cycle events accordingly (See Islam and Islamic Life-Cycle Rituals, page xlix). However the Muslim customs and practices in Jordan are less structured than in some of the other Muslim countries.

Men and women work together and meet at social gatherings. They are able to date, and when they marry they have a wedding reception with men and women together.

Muslim funerals are very simple and all burials must be within twenty-four hours. The religion requires the dead person to be washed by an authorized person, always women by women and men by men. The death is announced at the mosque by a holy man. Some words are read from the Koran (Islamic holy book), along with the dead person's name, funeral time and place.

The body is carried to the mosque but kept outside in the courtyard. After a short service the body is taken to the cemetery by a hearse followed by a convoy of men. Women are forbidden from attending funerals, but to show they are in mourning all female family members wear a white scarf over their head. The deceased is placed in the grave in only the shroud with the body. He is laid in the ground facing the direction of Mecca (the holy city in Saudi Arabia). The Imam's (Islamic holy man) prayers over the grave signify the end of the burial.

There is a memorial service for the deceased on the 7th and 52nd day of his death and includes Islamic readings. Sometimes big funerary meals or *halvah* (sweets) are offered to the poor to memorialize a death.

A religious or wedding feast often includes as many as 40 dishes followed by a dozen or so desserts and a profusion of fresh fruits. The preparations require the work of many people and are as much a part of the celebration as the feast itself.

As in other Arabic countries, the Jordanians traditionally sit on cushions on the floor and eat from dishes placed on low tables or on tablecloths spread out on the floor. Traditionally no plates or forks are used, but flat bread is broken into pieces and used to scoop up the food. Bowls of perfumed water are passed from time to time throughout the meal so diners may cleanse their carefully licked fingers.

Muslims are forbidden, by their religion, to drink wine. On special occasions, however, such as weddings, many drink the strong alcoholic *arack*, locally produced in most of the Arabic countries. *Arack* is a colorless drink made from fermented mash of rice and molasses, which is thought to be Chinese in origin. It is sipped from a small glass or may be mixed with water, which turns it milky. Bite-size *mezze* (appetizers) are usually served before a celebration meal with the *arack*.

Bamieh bi zayt can be served as a *mezze* (appetizer) or as one of the dozen vegetable dishes served with roasted lamb or goat.

Bamieh Bi Zayt

Okra in Olive Oil

Yield: serves 6

- 24 to 30 fresh whole okra
- ½ cup olive oil, divided
- 3 onions, chopped
- 4 cloves garlic, **finely chopped**
- 16 ounces canned stewed tomatoes
- ½ cup fresh **coriander**, chopped
- salt and pepper to taste
- water, as needed
- 2 lemons, cut in wedges, for serving

Equipment: Paring knife, **colander**, large saucepan with cover or **Dutch oven**, mixing spoon, serving bowl

1. Using paring knife, trim and discard cone-shaped portion from top of okra. Put okra in colander, rinse under cold running water, and set colander in sink to drain.

2. Heat half the oil in large saucepan or Dutch oven over medium-high heat. Add onions and garlic, stir, and **sauté** until onions are soft, 3 to 5 minutes. Add tomatoes, drained okra, coriander, and salt and pepper to taste. Add enough water to cover vegetables and bring to boil. Reduce heat to **simmer**, cover, and cook for 20 to 30 minutes, or until okra is tender.

To serve, transfer to serving bowl and serve either warm or chilled.

Bread is an essential part of a meal since it is used to scoop up the food.

Khobaz Arabee

Arab Bread

Yield: 8 thin loaves

- 2 cups **lukewarm** water
- 1 package active dry **yeast**
- 2 teaspoons salt
- 1 tablespoon vegetable oil
- 5 to 6 cups all-purpose flour, more as needed
- ½ cup yellow **cornmeal**

Equipment: Large mixing bowl, mixing spoon, lightly floured work surface, kitchen towel, knife, pie pan, wax paper, baking sheet, oven mitts, metal spatula, wire cake rack, napkin-lined bread basket

1. Pour lukewarm water into large mixing bowl, add yeast, and soften, 3 to 5 minutes. Stir in salt and oil. Beat in 5 cups flour, adding more if necessary to make a dough that does not stick to your hands. Transfer to lightly floured work surface and **knead** dough until smooth. Clean and grease large mixing bowl. Put dough in lightly greased large mixing bowl and turn to grease all sides. Cover with towel and let rise in warm place until double in bulk, 1½ to 2 hours.

2. **Punch down** dough and cut into 8 pieces. Knead each piece until dough is satiny. Shape each piece of dough into a ball. Put a little oil on your hands and rub each ball lightly with oil. Place on work surface, cover with towel, and let rise for 30 minutes.

Preheat oven to 450° F.

3. In pie pan, mix corn meal with ½ cup flour. Roll each ball in cornmeal mixture and flatten with palms of your hands to the size of a large pancake. Place on wax-paper-covered work surface and cover with towel.

4. Place one flat bread at a time on lightly floured work surface. Using your hands, gently stretch the bread into a thin round. Repeat stretching the remaining flat breads. Place two or three side by side on baking sheet.

5. Bake in oven for 7 minutes or until browned. Remove from oven and turn bread over with a metal spatula. Bake second side for 5 to 7 minutes more, until browned. Continue baking breads 2 or 3 at a time. Place baked breads on wire cake rack to cool.

To serve place 2 or 3 breads on baking sheet pan and place under broiler to heat through, 2 to 3 minute. Place in napkin-lined bread basket and set on buffet table.

Fruit is eaten at the end of a meal and sweets are eaten as between-meal snacks. Sweets are also served at most life-cycle celebrations, especially for weddings. Trays of *deser-e toot farangi* are especially liked in most Middle East countries.

Deser-e Toot Farangi

Strawberry Delight

Yield: about 3 pounds

2½ pounds strawberries, stems left on
2 cups sugar
½ cup water
2 tablespoons **rose water** (available at Middle Eastern food stores and pharmacies)

Equipment: Paper towels, work surface, 2 or 3 baking sheets, wax paper, small saucepan, **candy thermometer** (optional), fork or wooden skewer, dinner knife, serving platter

1. Place 3 or 4 layers of paper towels on the work surface. Rinse strawberries under cold water and place them in single layer on the paper towels to drain. Place a paper towel over the strawberries and gently pat dry.

2. Cover the surface of each baking pan with wax paper and place on the work surface next to the stove. Prepare **sugar syrup**: Put the sugar and water in a small saucepan and cook over medium heat, stirring constantly until sugar dissolves, 1 to 2 minutes. Add rose water and using a spoon, skim and discard any foam from the surface. When the syrup reaches the soft-ball stage, 234° to 240° F on the candy thermometer, reduce heat to warm. Poke a fork or wooden skewer in the stem end of a strawberry and carefully hold it over the pan of syrup. Spoon 1 teaspoon syrup over the strawberry. Let the excess drip back into the pan. Carefully place the coated strawberry on the wax paper. Repeat coating the strawberries and place them side by side, not touching, on the wax paper.

3. When the strawberries have cooled, loosen each one from the wax paper using the tip of a dinner knife.

To serve, arrange the strawberries decoratively on serving platter.

SAUDI ARABIA

Saudi Arabia is located on the Arabian Peninsula, bordered by Jordan and Iraq to the north, the Persian Gulf and the United Arab Emirates to the east, Oman and Yemen to the south, and the Red Sea to the west. In Saudi Arabia, Islam is not just a religion that can be separated from daily life and government, it is the framework for both secular and spiritual life. Every facet of life is governed by the Islamic religion. (See Islam and Islamic Life-Cycle Rituals, page xlix.) In their private lives the two most important family celebrations are the birth of a child, especially a boy, and weddings.

The holy city of Mecca where every Muslim man expects to make the *Hajj* (pilgrimage) is in Saudi Arabia. The *Hajj* to Mecca is without question the most important rite of passage any Muslim can experience. Regardless of where they live, family and friends always have a big feast to celebrate a person's *Hajj* to Mecca, upon his return home.

Saudis may give a boy as many as four names; his own name, his father's and grandfather's names, and a tribal or family name.

After kindergarten, girls are not allowed to go to school with boys. In later life they are not allowed to work with men, to drive cars, or to appear in public without being fully shrouded. The socially preferred role for Saudi women is to be in the home. If women or girls want to work it should be in medicine, education, or social work. They then should work only with female patients, students, and clients.

The long black outer cloak worn by women is called *abaaya* and they are not permitted out of their house without it.

The long, white garment worn by men is called a *thobe*. The subtle style differences and the fabric quality is a sign of wealth. The traditional cloth that is worn on the head was originally used to shield the face and neck from wind and sand storms. Now, however, it is highly fashionable for men to wear it with even Western-style business suits. The traditional men's dress is required for school, at the mosque during prayer, and at wedding celebrations.

A young woman almost always accepts the man her parents have chosen as her husband. Often the paternal or maternal grandmother plays an important role in the selection of a prospective mate. Her wedding is the most important day in the life of a Saudi woman, and it is an elaborate celebration. Wedding expenses can sometimes be exorbitant, but the cost is shared by both the groom and family of the bride.

At wedding celebrations, held in the evening at the home of the bride or in a hotel, male and female guests do not mix. The men never see the bride, since it is unacceptable for an unveiled Saudi woman to be seen by men who are not her close relatives.

Wedding photos, a new innovation, are taken only by female photographers and are never publicly displayed. The bride and groom make a formal appearance among the women guests to receive their congratulations. Male and female guests bring with them appropriate wedding presents for the newlyweds.

All meals, including the wedding feast, are eaten while sitting on the floor. There are no eating utensils since everyone eats with the fingers of the right hand. The left hand must never touch food, as it is used only for personal grooming. The soles of the feet are considered unclean, and it is offensive to point them at another person. It is also impolite to stare at other people while they are eating. Looking down at your own plate instead is considered good manners. (However, Saudis who have been educated or have traveled to the West may prefer to sit on chairs and use silverware, rather than sit on rugs and use their right hands to eat.)

Offering a large variety of food, in great quantities, is considered good manners. So is setting out the food on elegant silver platters on beautiful tablecloths, which have been decorated with bowls of fresh fruit and flowers. This lavish hospitality shows the generosity of the host and hostess.

The main dish of a wedding feast is likely to be whole roasted sheep (recipe page 141) or goat. The pieces of meat are piled on huge serving platters and surrounded by mounds of rice. The platters of food are often so big and heavy that it takes two servants to carry them to the male guests, who sit cross-legged on the rugs in the dining room.

The bride, along with her women wedding guests, eats apart from the men. Their feast is often as elaborate as that served to the men. In some households, the women must first serve the men before they can eat, which is often the leftovers.

The beverages are raisin tea, made with water in which raisins have been soaked; lemonade; "Saudi champagne" (a non-alcoholic carbonated fruit drink); and Arabic coffee flavored with cardamom. In Saudi Arabia alcoholic beverages are forbidden.

When the meal is over, the guests rinse their fingers in bowls of perfumed water brought to them by servants. Tea and coffee are served at the end of the feast, never with the food. Feasts can last far into the night.

When Saudis die, they must be buried within 24 hours. There are no elaborate funeral services nor are there cemeteries with monuments, even for very important people. A plain, small name plate is all one sees at a grave site.

Fruit is eaten throughout the meal and also at the end. This is just one of many fruit dishes that will be set out for guests during the wedding feast. ۞ ۞ ۞

Munkaczina

Zesty Orange Salad

Yield: serves 6

3 large oranges, peeled and thinly sliced
2 onions, **trimmed** and thinly sliced
3 tablespoons vegetable oil
3 tablespoons wine vinegar
ground red pepper to taste
salt to taste
12 ripe black olives, pitted and sliced

Equipment: Medium serving platter with raised lip, 8-ounce cup, mixing spoon

1. Arrange the orange and onion slices, alternately, slightly overlapping in medium serving platter.

2. In cup, combine oil, vinegar, ground red pepper to taste, and salt to taste. Stir and pour over orange and onion slices. Let salad **marinate** for 1 hour at room temperature. Sprinkle with sliced black olives before serving.

Serve as one of the side dishes with lamb or goat for a wedding feast.

Fouja djedad is a dish children especially like because it is sweet and easy to eat with just one hand.

Fouja Djedad

Chicken-stuffed Apples

Yield: serves 6

6 cooking apples (such as Granny Smith or Roman Beauty)
1 cup cooked chicken, **finely chopped**
¼ teaspoon **ground** cloves
½ cup melted butter or margarine, divided
¼ cup **bread crumbs**
6 teaspoons sugar

Equipment: Paring knife, small bowl, mixing spoon, buttered 8- or 9-inch baking pan, 8-ounce cup, **pastry brush**, aluminum foil, oven mitts, serving bowl, metal tongs

Preheat oven to 375° F.

1. Wash and core the apples. Using a paring knife, remove a portion of the center of the apple to allow space for the filling.

2. In small bowl, toss chicken with ground cloves. Fill each apple with the chicken mixture. Place stuffed apple in buttered 8- or 9-inch baking pan. Mix ¼ cup melted butter with bread crumbs in a cup and spoon over top of each apple. Brush remaining melted butter over the apples and sprinkle with sugar. Cover with foil.

3. Bake in oven for 45 minutes, or until apples are tender. Remove foil and bake for 5 minutes to brown bread crumbs.

To serve, using metal tongs, transfer apples to serving bowl and serve warm or at room temperature.

This is an important rice dish in the Middle East. The golden crust that forms on the bottom of the pan is placed on top of the rice when it is served. The brown crusted rice is a delicacy reserved for a special guest or the man of the house.

Chelou

Buttered Rice

Yield: serves 6 to 8

water, as needed
2½ cups (1¼ pounds) long-grain rice
1 tablespoon salt
6 tablespoons butter or margarine
½ cup milk
4 tablespoons melted butter or margarine
2 tablespoons hot water

Equipment: Medium saucepan, mixing spoon, **colander**, medium ovenproof **heavy-based** saucepan with cover, 2 small bowls, wooden spoon, oven mitts, heatproof surface, serving platter

1. Fill medium saucepan two-thirds with water and bring to boil over high heat. When water reaches rolling boiling, add rice and salt. Bring back to rolling boil, and cook for 10 minutes until rice is partly cooked.

2. Place colander in sink. Drain rice in colander and rinse under lukewarm running water and drain.

Preheat oven to 425° F.

3. Melt butter or margarine in medium ovenproof heavy-based saucepan over medium heat. Remove from heat and swirl pan to coat bottom and sides evenly. In small bowl, mix 1 cup of the drained rice with milk. Spread milk mixture evenly in bottom of pan to make a thin layer. Fill saucepan with remaining rice, mounding it up in center. With handle of a wooden spoon, make a deep hole in center of mound. Cover and bake in oven for 15 minutes. Using oven mitts, remove from oven and place on heatproof surface.

Reduce oven to 350° F.

4. Mix melted butter with hot water in second small bowl and sprinkle over rice. Cover, return rice to oven, and continue baking for 30

minutes longer. Using oven mitts, remove from oven and place on heatproof surface. Let sit for 10 minutes before uncovering. (This will make it easier to remove brown crust in bottom of pan.)

5. Uncover and stir rice gently. Transfer to serving platter in a mound and heap the brown crust from bottom of pan on top.

To serve, the brown crust is broken into pieces and eaten with the fingers of the right hand. According to Arab and Muslim tradition, the left hand must never touch food; it is used only for personal grooming.

IRAQ

Iraq is bordered on the north by Turkey, on the east by Iran, on the southeast by the Persian Gulf and by Kuwait, on the south by Saudi Arabia, and on the west by Jordan and Syria. Part of modern Iraq is situated on the ancient land known as Mesopotamia, where people first began to cultivate land and where cursive writing developed. Recent history has dealt less kindly with the Iraq government, which is unfortunate for the Iraqi people.

Iraq's largest ethnic group is the Arabs (approximately 75 percent), followed by a sizable Kurd population (approximately 20 percent). Both Arabs and Kurds are Muslims, but the Kurds differ from their Arab neighbors in language, dress and customs. All life-cycle celebrations are according to their religion. (See Islam and Islamic Life-Cycle Rituals, page xlix.)

For Muslims, the first important life-cycle celebration is the birth of a child, especially if it's a boy. Three days after the baby's birth, visitors come to pay their respects and bring gifts for the newborn. When the birth is a boy, superstitious rituals are performed to protect the child from harm. Childless women or guests with blue eyes, the sign of a non-Iraqi, are traditionally not allowed to see the child for fear they will bring him bad luck.

As in other Muslim countries, the next big celebration for a boy is when he is circumcised. In the cities the doctor often performs the operation in the hospital before the child is taken home. A small family dinner celebrates the event when the mother returns home with her son. In the countryside the traditional ceremony takes place when the boy is about seven years old. The child is usually paraded through the village and everyone is invited to a celebration feast.

The *al' Khatma* is the religious festival that celebrates the reading of the Koran (Islamic holy book) by children. Boys and girls have separate ceremonies for the *al' Khatma.* Each boy reads to men who hold a luncheon for them while women celebrate with an afternoon tea for each girl. After the reading, the young guest-of-honor is showered with gifts and money.

In Iraq, traditional families arrange the marriages of their children. The final decision as to whom her sons will marry is made by their mother. The new daughter-in-law usually moves in with her husband's parents.

Several days before the marriage ceremony the couple is fêted by relatives and friends. On her wedding day, the bride, dressed in her Western-style white wedding gown, spends the day in her parents' house receiving friends and relatives—female only. According to Muslim tradition, her hands and feet have been decorated with henna. She wears the gold jewelry given to her by her husband. Late in the day, the groom arrives with the Muslim religious leader to sign the Islamic contract; only immediate family and a few best friends are present.

After the contract is signed, a convoy of buses and cars carries the noisy horn-blowing and cheering family members and friends through the streets and then on to the groom's parents' home, a wedding hall, or a hotel ballroom for the official reception. In urban Iraq, Muslim men and women celebrate together and everyone has a great time singing, dancing, and feasting until the wee hours of the morning. In the countryside, wedding celebrations are segregated, with the men and women celebrating separately.

Roasted whole mutton or baby lamb (recipe page 141) is the traditional centerpiece of the wedding feast along with dozens of side dishes and great quantities of rice and fresh fruit.

This dish is prepared like a soup but the liquid is strained and served separately as a broth. The meat is sliced and the lentils and cabbage are served as a side dish. All dishes, including the soup, are placed in the center of the table and eaten at the same time.

Abgushte Adas

Lentil Soup

Yield: serves 6

2 pounds lean brisket of lamb or beef
2 cups brown or green **lentils**
1 onion, **finely chopped**
½ teaspoon **ground** turmeric
½ cup lemon juice
8 cups hot water, more as needed
2 cups cabbage, finely chopped
1 teaspoon salt
1 onion, thinly sliced, for serving
6 or 8 radishes, washed and **trimmed** for serving
6 or 8 fresh mint leaves, for serving

Equipment: Large saucepan with cover or **Dutch oven**, mixing spoon, carving board, strainer, small serving bowl, ladle, potato masher, meat knife, serving platter

1. Put meat and lentils in large saucepan or Dutch oven. Add chopped onion, turmeric, lemon juice, and 8 cups hot water. Bring to boil over high heat. Reduce heat to **simmer**, cover, and cook for 1 hour. Add cabbage and salt and pepper to taste. Add a little more hot water from time to time if needed to keep water level about the same. Cook for 45 minutes to 1 hour, or until meat is tender.

2. Transfer meat to a carving board. Strain cooking liquid and pour into small serving bowl with ladle. Mash lentils with cabbage using potato masher. Mound lentil mixture on serving platter. Thinly cut meat and place slices around lentils.

To serve, decorate lentil mixture with sliced onions and radishes and sprinkle with mint.

Qu'meh is served as a side dish at banquets. To eat *qu'meh,* use your right hand only, make a small ball of the meat or you can scoop it on a piece of bread and then pop it into your mouth. According to Arab and Muslim tradition, the left hand must never touch food; it is used only for personal grooming.

Qu'meh

Minced Meat

Yield: serves 6

4 tablespoons butter or margarine, more if necessary
1 onion, chopped
1 pound **ground** lamb or beef
½ teaspoon turmeric
salt and pepper to taste
1½ cups tomato juice

1½ cups hot water
½ cup dried yellow split peas
¼ cup lemon juice
1 cup canned pitted cherries, drained

Equipment: Medium saucepan, slotted spoon, paper towels, mixing spoon, serving bowl

1. Melt butter or margarine in medium saucepan over medium-high heat. Add onion, stir, and **sauté** until well browned, 7 to 12 minutes. Using slotted spoon, transfer to paper towels to drain.

2. Add more butter or margarine to medium saucepan, if necessary. Crumble in ground meat, stir, and sauté over medium-high heat until browned, 5 to 7 minutes. Stir in turmeric, salt and pepper to taste, tomato juice, hot water, split peas, and lemon juice. Bring to boil. Reduce heat to **simmer**, cover, and cook 45 minutes, or until peas are tender.

3. Add sautéed onions and cherries and stir. Cook to heat through, 3 to 5 minutes.

To serve, transfer to serving bowl and serve with chelou *(recipe page 119).*

A banquet ends with fresh fruit but during the celebration there is always a table with dozens of different cookies, cakes, and candies. Many cakes are made with dates and nuts, such as *tamriah.*

Tamriah

Date Cakes

Yield: 12 pieces
2 pounds pitted dates, **finely chopped**
½ cup walnuts, finely chopped
1 cup all-purpose **flour**
¼ cup melted butter or margarine
4 tablespoons butter or margarine, more as needed
1 cup plain yogurt, for serving

Equipment: Medium mixing bowl, mixing spoon, wax paper, work surface, large skillet, metal spatula, serving platter, small serving bowl

1. Put chopped dates, walnuts, and flour into medium mixing bowl. Using your hands, mix together. Stir in melted butter or margarine. Using your hands, divide date mixture into 12 balls. Shape each ball into ½-inch thick patty and place on wax-paper-covered work surface.

2. Melt 4 tablespoons butter or margarine in large skillet over medium-high heat. Fry cakes in batches, if necessary, until browned on both sides, 5 to 7 minutes. Add more butter or margarine as needed to fry each batch.

To serve, arrange cakes on serving platter around small bowl of yogurt placed in the center for dipping.

IRAN

Iran is bordered on the north by the U.S.S.R. and the Caspian Sea, and on the east by Afghanistan and Pakistan. To the south and southwest are the Indian Ocean and the Persian Gulf. The west and northwest borders are shared with Iraq and Turkey. In Iran the population is of many different ethnic and cultural groups who generally share one common bond—they are almost all Muslims. (See Islam and Islamic Life-Cycle Rituals, page xlix.) The largest ethnic group is the indigenous Persians (also known as Iranians). The other sizable ethnic groups—all Muslims—are the Turks, Kurds, and Arabs.

In the 1930s women were given the right to vote and freed from wearing the *chador,* a long black cloth that is draped over the head and body but does not cover the face. In 1979, however, the women voted for the Islamic restrictions limiting their freedom and then chose to wear the *chador.* During the 1990s the enforcement of some of the modesty law restrictions have relaxed.

Most Iranian Muslim families are not interested in Western ways and seem to prefer the customs and restricted traditions of the Islamic religion. Unmarried children live with their parents or relatives until married, and when they do marry it is usually arranged by their parents. If a son or daughter doesn't approve of the selected mate, parents seldom force the union.

The most important part of Muslim weddings is the *agd* (legal ceremony), where the contract is agreed upon and signed. In Muslim countries with stricter modesty laws, the groom and bride are separated by a door, and the holy man sits with the groom while marrying the couple. In Iran, segregated weddings were reinstituted in 1979, but before that time, the couple were together in the same room.

The holy man, chosen by the groom, reads the marriage contract and recites the traditional prayers. During the *agd*, which traditionally takes place in the home of the bride, only female relatives and friends are allowed, and they take part in several symbolic formalities. Today some couples have their *agd* in the private rooms of a hotel or marriage hall. The husband cannot join his wife until later at the *arusi* (reception) for women only. She is not allowed to mingle with the men at any time.

Traditionally after the *agd*, an *arusi* for men only takes place on the same night at the groom's home or hotel ballroom. Usually a convoy of buses and cars carries the noisy and cheering family members and friends to the *arusi*. According to strict Islamic law, at no time are men and women allowed to be together in the same room for any part of the wedding celebration.

The arusi is a grand celebration with feasting far into the night. The meal includes dozens of *mezze* (appetizers). Some appetizers have symbolic meaning: a platter of feta cheese, fresh herbs, and bread is served to bring happiness and prosperity; bowls of hard-cooked eggs in the shell and baskets with walnuts and almonds in the shell symbolize fertility. A bowl of honey is set out for a sweet future. The table is adorned with fresh flowers and herbs, all significant to the couple's future.

The feast includes whole roasted lamb (recipe page 141) and 40 or 50 different dishes, candies, and desserts.

Other *mezze* (appetizers) include bowls of olives and raw vegetables such as radishes, slices of cucumber, and *sebzi panier*. ۞ ۞ ۞

Sebzi Panier

Cheese and Herb Appetizer

Yield: serves 5 guests

5 slices rye or whole wheat bread
10 slices goat cheese or Greek feta cheese
10 walnut halves
10 leaves of fresh **coriander** or basil

Equipment: bread knife, work surface, large serving tray, 3 medium serving bowls

1. Using a serrated knife, cut each slice of bread lengthwise and crosswise into 4 equal pieces. (You will have 20 small pieces of bread.)

2. Place the cheese, walnuts, and herb leaves in separate bowls and place them on the serving tray. Arrange the slices of bread around the bowls on the tray. Place the tray on the dining table.

To serve, guests help themselves by sandwiching the ingredients between two pieces of bread. First place a slice of cheese on a piece of bread, and top it with a walnut half and a leaf of coriander or basil. Hold it in the fingers of your right hand to eat.

The Iranian meal is not served as a sequence of fixed courses. Instead, all the food is spread out at one time on the tablecloth-covered floor. *Bessara* is eaten as a dip with raw vegetables or with pieces of flat bread.

Bessara

Fava Bean Purée

Yield: serves 6 to 8

16 ounces canned fava beans (available at all supermarkets)
2 cloves garlic, **finely chopped**, divided
2 green onions (including green tops), **trimmed** and finely chopped
1 tablespoon fresh cilantro, chopped
1 teaspoon crushed dried mint
1 teaspoon **ground** cumin seed
salt and pepper to taste
ground red pepper, to taste (optional)
1 tablespoon extra virgin olive oil, more as needed
1 onion, sliced into rings, for serving
2 lemons, cut in wedges, for serving

Equipment: Electric **blender** (optional), rubber spatula, small bowl with cover, small skillet, mixing spoon

1. Put beans with juice in blender, add 1 clove chopped garlic, and **blend** until smooth.

Note: While processing, turn machine off once or twice and scrape down sides of container with rubber spatula.

2. Transfer to small bowl. Add green onions, cilantro, mint, cumin seed, and salt and pepper to taste, and stir to mix well. Stir in ground red pepper to taste if desired. Cover and refrigerate.

3. Heat 1 tablespoon olive oil in small skillet over medium-high heat. Add onion and fry until browned and crisp, 5 to 7 minutes.

To serve, sprinkle top of fava bean purée with fried onions and drizzle lightly with olive oil. Serve with lemon wedges and extra ground red pepper so everyone can season it to suit their taste. Serve with bite-size wedges of flat bread or crackers and raw vegetables.

There are always a variety of rice dishes for Iranian wedding banquets, and many have symbolic meaning. In this dish the raisins and nuts added to the rice look like wedding jewels, and so it is called *javaher polow* (jeweled rice).

Javaher Polow (also Shereen Polow)

Sweet Rice (also Jeweled Rice)

Yield: serves 8

2 cups **Basmati rice** (available at all supermarkets)
water, as needed
salt, as needed
3 oranges
1 cup sugar
1 cup shelled pistachios, divided
1 cup **blanched** sliced almonds, divided
1 cup seedless raisins, divided
12 tablespoons melted butter, divided

Equipment: Medium mixing bowl, vegetable peeler, plastic food wrap, paring knife, small saucepan, mixing spoon, strainer, medium saucepan, medium ovenproof casserole with cover, oven mitts, large serving dish

1. Put rice in medium mixing bowl, cover with cold water, and add 2 tablespoons salt. Let soak for 2 hours.

2. Using vegetable peeler, peel rind from oranges taking care to avoid the **pith**. Wrap orange pulp in plastic wrap and refrigerate for another use. Cut rind into small slivers with paring knife. Put rind slivers in small saucepan, cover with cold water, and boil for 30 minutes

to remove bitter taste. Drain water from orange rind into strainer in sink.

3. Combine sugar and 1 cup water in small saucepan. Cook over medium-high heat, stirring constantly to dissolve sugar. Stir in drained orange rind pieces, ½ cup pistachios, and ½ cup almonds. Reduce heat to **simmer** for 8 minutes. Remove from heat and set aside.

4. Drain rice in strainer and rinse under cold running water. Fill medium saucepan two-thirds with water and bring to boil over medium-high heat. Add drained rice and 1 teaspoon salt. Bring back to rolling boil and cook uncovered 10 minutes to partially cook rice. Drain rice in strainer and rinse under lukewarm running water. Transfer rice back to medium mixing bowl. Add orange rind sugar mixture and ½ cup raisins to rice, and gently stir to mix.

Preheat oven to 350° F.

5. Pour 6 tablespoons melted butter or margarine into medium ovenproof casserole and swirl to coat bottom and sides. Transfer rice mixture to casserole and mound it up in the center. Cover casserole dish.

6. Bake in oven for 45 minutes, until rice is tender. Using oven mitts, remove from oven and place on heatproof surface to let sit for 10 minutes before uncovering.

To serve, scoop rice out on large serving dish in a mound. Sprinkle with remaining ½ cup pistachios, ½ cup almonds, and ½ cup raisins. ***Drizzle*** *remaining 6 tablespoons melted butter over the top.*

Sweet desserts as we know them in the western world are never eaten at the end of an Iranian meal. Only fresh fruit is acceptable at the end of a meal. Any combination of fruit can be used in *paludeh*.

Paludeh

Persian Fruit Medley

Yield: serves 4

1 cup strawberries, stemmed and sliced
2 ripe peaches, peeled and sliced
½ cantaloupe or honeydew (or combination), **cubed** and peeled
granulated sugar, to taste
1 tablespoon **rose water** (available at Middle Eastern food stores and pharmacies)

Equipment: Medium bowl with cover, mixing spoon

Combine strawberries, peaches, and melon cubes in the medium bowl. Using a spoon, gently toss to mix. Add sugar to taste, toss, and sprinkle with rose water. Toss to mix well. Cover and refrigerate until ready to serve. Before serving, toss again to remix.

To serve, place the bowl in the middle of the table. Have guests help themselves from the bowl using only the fingers of the right hand to pick up the fruit. According to Muslim tradition, the left hand must never touch food; it is used only for personal grooming.

CYPRUS

Cyprus, an island in the Mediterranean Sea, is located to the south of Turkey and to the west of Syria. Approximately 80 percent of people in Cyprus are of Greek origin, and most of the remaining are of Turkish origin. The Greeks follow the Greek Orthodox life-cycle rituals (see Eastern or Orthodox Church Life-Cycle Rituals, page xlviii); see also discussion of Greek life-cycle celebrations (page 146). The Turks, who are Muslims, follow the life-cycle rituals according to their religion. (See Islam and Islamic Life-Cycle Rituals, page xlix.)

In the Greek communities, many traditions have grown around the village wedding ceremony. Everyone in the town is invited to the celebration, often lasting three days. One unusual custom is the "Filling the Mattress." The village women take bedding, blessed by the priest, to the reception and each holds an edge of it as they dance and sing. They then sew the covering to a mat, which they stuff and sew up. This is placed on the wedding bed.

The night before the wedding the groom is shaved by the best man in front of his friends to symbolize his giving up bachelorhood. A lovely local custom is the blessing of the bride by her father before she walks down the aisle.

Within the Greek Orthodox church the duties of the best man and bridesmaid are spelled out in detail. Following the ceremony they are expected to give financial assistance and even physical protection in times of crisis. They may later become godparents of the couple's first child, thereby entering into a virtual blood relationship, because their children are legally prohibited from marrying their godchildren.

On the day of the wedding, guests are invited into the new home immediately following the ceremony, and the best man pours each a glass of brandy and offers a piece of traditional seed cake (recipe page 128). Then the feasting and celebrating really begins, with music provided by a band composed of an accordion, a violin, and drums. Often the *aulos*, the shepherd's flute and the *bouzouki*, a stringed guitar-like instrument, are included in the group.

After a traditional wedding, the young couple starts the dancing, and during this time paper money is pinned to their clothes until the garments are completely covered. The party goes into high gear when groups of men challenge each other dancing the lively *pidiktos*, the ancient leaping dance performed only by men.

Over a two- or three-day period, the musicians lead the revelers as they move to and from the homes of different relatives and to the village square where dancing, singing, and feasting continues until everyone is exhausted.

Among the Turkish Cypriot communities, much of the wedding tradition is dictated by the presiding Muslim holy man of the village. In prominent families a *mullah*, or religious leader of high rank, may come from the Turkey mainland for the final blessing.

On special days, such as a religious holiday or birthday, an elaborate *klephtiko* (feast) is prepared. The feast includes spit-roasted whole lamb (recipe page 141) or mutton or goat roasted in the beehive clay ovens set out in the yard. Assorted breads and vegetables are served with the meat. This wonderful casserole-type pie is included in the *klephtiko*. The spinach filling can also be used for making little individual pastries. To make pastries, assemble according to *bureks* (recipe page 128, Steps 2. Cut phyllo: and 3. Assemble pastries:).

Tirópeta Tou Spetioú

Family-style Spinach Pie

Yield: serves 12 to 18

- 6 tablespoons extra virgin olive oil
- 2 onions, **finely chopped**
- 2 packages (10-ounces each) frozen chopped spinach, thawed and drained
- 1 pound feta cheese (available in dairy section of all supermarkets)
- 1½ cups cottage cheese, drained
- 6 eggs, well beaten
- salt and pepper to taste
- 1 cup (½ pound) melted butter or margarine, more if needed

20 sheets **phyllo** (available in freezer section of all supermarkets), thawed according to directions on package

Equipment: Large skillet, mixing spoon, large mixing bowl, potato masher or fork, rubber spatula, damp kitchen towel, **pastry brush**, buttered 9- x 12- x 2-inch baking pan, sharp knife, oven mitts

1. Heat olive oil in large skillet over medium-high heat. Add onions, stir, and **sauté** until soft, 3 to 5 minutes. Squeeze spinach to remove and discard liquid. Break up spinach clumps with your hands as you add it to onions. Stir well, reduce heat to simmer, and cook until liquid evaporates, 3 to 5 minutes. Remove from heat.

2. In large mixing bowl, mash feta cheese with cottage cheese, using potato masher or back of fork. Stir in eggs and salt and pepper to taste. Using rubber spatula, **fold in** spinach mixture.

Preheat oven to 350° F.

3. Assemble pie: While working with one sheet phyllo, keep remaining sheets covered with damp towel. Butter the top sheet of phyllo with melted butter or margarine and lay in buttered 9- x 12-inch baking pan. Continue to brush each sheet and place it on top of the last, covering the bottom layer of baking pan with 10 sheets of phyllo. Spoon spinach filling on top of the layer of phyllo in baking pan and spread smooth with rubber spatula. Brush a sheet of phyllo with melted butter and place over the spinach mixture. Repeat layering all the remaining sheets of phyllo, brushing each first with melted butter. Roll or push edges of phyllo down all around the pan to hold in mixture. Brush top and edges completely with melted butter. Lightly score top into pieces (3 lengthwise cuts and 4 or 6 across) with a sharp knife. (This will guide you when cutting after baking.)

4. Bake in oven 35 to 40 minutes, until golden brown. Using oven mitts, remove from oven and let rest 10 minutes before cutting into pieces.

Serve hot or at room temperature. Put on the buffet table and have guests help themselves.

Afelia is a Greek dish (Muslims do not eat pork), which would be served at a baptism or name day dinner along with *tirópeta tou spetioú* (recipe page 126) and salad.

Afelia

Pork with Coriander

Yield: serves 4 to 6

1 tablespoon vegetable oil
2 pounds lean boneless pork shoulder, cut into 1-inch chunks
1 cup dry white wine
1 tablespoon **ground coriander**
salt and pepper to taste
4 cups chicken broth
1 pound new potatoes, cut in quarters
2 cups sliced mushrooms

Equipment: Large saucepan with cover or **Dutch oven**, mixing spoon, serving bowl

1. Heat oil in large saucepan or Dutch oven over medium-high heat. Add pork, stir, and brown on all sides, 7 to 10 minutes. Reduce heat to medium. Add wine, coriander, and salt and pepper to taste, and stir to mix well. Cook for 10 minutes for flavors to develop and sauce to **reduce**.

2. Add chicken broth, new potatoes, and mushrooms. Increase heat to medium-high and bring to boil. Stir, reduce heat to **simmer**, cover, and cook 20 to 25 minutes, or until potatoes are tender.

To serve, transfer to serving bowl and serve with khobaz arabee *(recipe page 115).*

Bureks are popular throughout the Mediterranean and Middle East. Both Greek and Turk Cypriots prepare great quantities for family gatherings because they're easy to make and delicious. They can be made with different fillings and served on the *mezze* (appetizer) table for wedding receptions.

Bureks

Turkish Pastries

Yield: 36 pieces

1 cup (8-ounces) cream cheese, at room temperature
1 egg, lightly beaten
1 tablespoon chopped parsley
salt and pepper to taste
2 sheets **phyllo**, thawed according to directions on package
½ cup (¼ pound) melted butter or margarine

Equipment: Medium mixing bowl, mixing spoon, work surface, sharp knife, ruler, damp kitchen towel, pastry brush, buttered cookie sheet, oven mitts, serving plate

1. Prepare filling: In medium mixing bowl, beat cream cheese, egg, and parsley with mixing spoon until well mixed. Add salt and pepper to taste.

2. Cut phyllo: Stack 2 phyllo sheets on work surface and using sharp knife and ruler, cut the 18-inch length phyllo across into 6 (3-inch wide) strips. Cut each strip into 3 equal pieces. (Each piece will be almost square.) Keep stack of 36 pieces of phyllo under damp towel.

Preheat oven to 350° F.

3. Assemble pastries one at a time keeping others covered with damp towel. Place one piece of phyllo parallel with edge of table. Place 1 teaspoon cream cheese mixture on the phyllo about halfway between one edge and the center. Roll the cream cheese in the phyllo, leaving the two sides open. (As they bake the cheese spreads out toward the two open ends.) Place on buttered cookie sheet, seam side down. Brush with melted butter. Continue to fill and roll remaining phyllo pieces and place them close together on cookie sheet. Brush tops with melted butter. Bake in oven for 10 to 12 minutes or until lightly browned.

To serve, arrange on a serving plate so they are easy to pick up. Serve warm or cold as a finger snack.

The seeds in the cake represent many children, therefore everyone eats a piece immediately after the Greek wedding ceremony to wish the newlyweds a fruitful life.

Seed Cake

Yield: serves 10 to 12

2 or 3 thick-skinned oranges
1½ cups sugar, divided
½ cup water
2 cups all-purpose flour
½ teaspoon **ground** nutmeg
1 cup butter or margarine, at room temperature
1 cup sugar
5 **eggs, separated**
2 teaspoons caraway seeds
3 tablespoons brandy or 1 teaspoon brandy extract
6 to 8 sugar cubes, coarsely crushed for topping
confectioners' sugar, for **garnish**

Equipment: **Grater**, plastic food wrap, 2 small saucepans, spoon, strainer, 8-ounce cup, flour **sifter**, small bowl, electric mixer or large mixing bowl, mixing spoon, medium mixing bowl, whisk, rubber spatula, greased and floured 8-inch springform pan, oven mitts, toothpick, wire cake rack

1. Prepare candied orange peel: Using shredder side of grater, scrape off rind from 2 to 3 oranges, to get ½ cup rind. Take care to not

scrape down into the **pith** which is bitter. Wrap remaining oranges in plastic wrap and refrigerate for another use. Put rind in small saucepan and cover with cold water. Bring to boil over medium-high heat for 20 minutes to remove bitter taste. Drain orange rind into strainer in sink and let sit. Combine ½ cup sugar and ½ cup water in second small saucepan. Cook over medium-high heat, stirring constantly to dissolve sugar. Stir in drained orange rind. Reduce heat to simmer and cook for 8 minutes. Remove from heat and cool to room temperature. Drain excess liquid from orange rind mixture into strainer. Transfer candied orange rind to cup and set aside.

Preheat oven to 350° F.

2. Prepare cake: **Sift** flour and nutmeg into small bowl. In large mixing bowl, beat butter until creamy, using electric mixer or whisk. Gradually beat in remaining 1 cup sugar until mixture is fluffy and light, 2 to 3 minutes. Beat in egg yolks, one at a time alternately with 1 tablespoon flour mixture, beating well after each addition. Continue adding flour, 1 tablespoon at a time, beating well after each addition, until all flour is added. Stir in drained candied orange peel, caraway seeds, and brandy or brandy extract.

3. Put egg whites into medium mixing bowl and, using clean and dry electric mixer or whisk, beat whites until stiff, 3 to 5 minutes. **Fold in** egg whites with batter using rubber spatula. Transfer batter to greased and floured springform pan and sprinkle top with crushed sugar cubes.

4. Bake in oven for 1 hour and 45 minutes or until toothpick inserted in center comes out clean. Let cake cool to warm before removing from pan. Transfer to wire cake rack to cool completely.

To serve, sprinkle top with confectioners' sugar and cut into wedges.

TURKEY

Turkey occupies a unique geographic position, bounded partly by European countries and partly by Asian countries. It shares borders with, to the north and east, Georgia, Armenia, Azerbaijan, and Iran; to the south, Iraq, Syria and the Mediterranean Sea; and to the west, the Aegean Sea, Greece, and Bulgaria. To the north of Turkey is the Black Sea. Most of the people living in Turkey are Muslim, and unlike other predominantly Muslim countries, there is freedom of religion and a separation of church and state. Turkish Muslims are much more lenient about dietary and moral codes; the rules governing prayer, alcohol, and pork are not as formally followed. In an effort to share Islam with non-Muslims, anyone is permitted to visit a Turkish mosque. This is not permitted in strict, Islamic-ruled countries.

In 1926 the Turkish civil law was adopted, which suddenly changed the family structure. Polygamy was abolished along with religious marriages. Only civil marriages are recognized as legal. Divorce and child custody became the right of both parents. Child marriages were outlawed and the minimum age for marriage was fixed at 15 for girls and 17 for boys. Today the average marrying age is about 18 for girls and at least 20 for boys. In 1926 women gained equal rights with men in the field of education. Veiling was abolished as well as long garments that were required by the old religious beliefs. The right to vote was granted Turkish women in the early 1930s. Equal wages for both sexes was ratified by Turkey in 1966.

When a married woman announces her pregnancy, the excitement among family members grows. Upon hearing the good news, a golden bracelet comes immediately as a present from the mother-in-law. In rural areas a pregnant woman announces her pregnancy by embroidering a design, symbolic of a baby, on her clothing or her scarf. In some regions of Turkey, there is a custom of planting a tree in the name of a newborn child. Chestnut, mulberry, and apple trees are planted for girls, poplar or pine trees for boys.

Turkish names always have meanings. Some of the children's names may derive from the time in which they were born; *Bayram* (feast), *Safak* (dawn), *Bahar* (spring) or from events during the birth; *Yagmur* (rain), Tufan (storm); or to express the parents' feeling about the child, if they want him to be the last one, *Yeter* (enough). Sometimes the names of elder people in families are chosen as displays of respect. When the name is selected, it is given by an *imam* (Islamic holy man) or an elder person in the family by holding the child in the direction of Mecca and reading from the Koran into his left ear and repeating his name three times into his right ear.

In Turkey all Muslim boys are circumcised between the ages of 2 and 14 by licensed circumcision surgeons. The *sunnet* (circumcision) is the introduction of a child to his religious society as a new member. When a family determines a date for their circumcision feast, they send out invitations to relatives, friends, and neighbors. Depending upon the budget, feasts might take place in a ceremonial hall or a hotel instead of at home. They prepare a highly decorated room with streamers and balloons and a nice bed for the boy. The boys always wear special costumes for this event; a suit, a red cape, a scepter and a special hat with *Masallah* meaning "God preserve him" written on it.

On the morning of a traditional circumcision, the children of guests are all taken for a tour around in a big convoy with the boy either by horseback, horse cart, or automobile. This convoy is followed by musicians playing drums and clarinets.

On their return, the boy changes to a loose, long white dress. He is then circumcised by the surgeon while he is held by a person close to the family. It is a great honor to be selected as the person to hold the child. The *kirve* (honored person) will play an active role in the boy's life. He has nearly equal rights with the father regarding the boy's future. He is similar to a godfather in Christianity. Although there is no blood relation to his *kirve*, the boy will not be allowed to marry his *kirve's* daughter.

After the circumcision, the boy is kept busy opening presents while everyone hovers around singing and dancing and telling jokes to make him forget his pain. In the meantime, words from the Koran are recited and guests are taken to tables for the feast. There is always lamb; if not whole roasted baby lamb (see recipe page 141), then *baharatli kuzu* (recipe page 131) is the centerpiece for the occasion. There are many vegetable dishes and tables cover with sweets, such as *Eash-el-Asfoor* (Turkish Bird's Nests).

The marriage practices of the city and the countryside are often different. Many urban brides wear the long white Western-style dress with veil. In the country, brides wear traditional Muslim garments, and prearranged marriages are common. All Turkish brides prepare a complete trousseau so that once married they enter a house where nothing will be lacking. Traditionally, the groom's family pays for the wedding and pays a bride's price by giving money to her father.

On the day of the marriage, in order to protect the couple from poverty, wedding guests hang pieces of gold and jewelry on the clothing of the bride.

When couples marry, by law they must have a civil ceremony. Many couples have both the civil and religious ceremonies.

The wedding feast usually begins with the traditional *dügün çorbasi*. There are many old Turkish legends connected to *dügün çorbasi*, making it a very special soup. ❂ ❂ ❂

Dügün Çorbasi

Wedding Soup

Yield: serves 6 to 8

2 pounds meaty lamb or beef bones
1 onion, **finely chopped**
1 carrot, finely chopped
5 cups water
salt to taste
8 tablespoons butter or margarine, divided
½ cup all-purpose **flour**
2 egg yolks
juice from ½ lemon
½ tablespoon paprika
ground red pepper and black pepper to taste
croutons, as needed (available at all supermarkets)

Equipment: Medium saucepan with cover, mixing spoon, tongs, medium bowl, paring knife, two small bowls, large saucepan, whisk, measuring cup, teaspoon, ladle, individual soup bowls

1. Prepare broth: Put bones, onion, carrot, water, and salt in medium saucepan. Bring to boil over high heat. Reduce heat to **simmer**, cover, and cook until meat on bones is tender, about 1 hour. During cooking, using mixing spoon, occasionally skim off and discard any foam that collects on surface. Using tongs, remove bones and put in medium bowl.

2. When bones are cool enough to handle, using a paring knife or your fingers, pull off meat and shred into bite-size pieces. Put meat in small bowl and discard bones.

3. Melt 6 tablespoons butter or margarine in large saucepan over medium-low heat. Using whisk or mixing spoon, slowly stir in flour until mixture is well blended and smooth, 4 to 5 minutes. Whisking or stirring flour mixture constantly, slowly add hot broth mixture, a little at a time, until completely mixed. When all the broth is added, bring to a boil over medium-high heat and add shredded meat. Stir, reduce heat to simmer, and cook for 10 minutes. Reduce heat to warm.

4. Put eggs in small bowl, and whisking constantly, add lemon juice. Whisking egg mixture constantly, slowly add ½ cup hot soup to **temper** mixture. Stirring constantly, slowly add tempered egg mixture to pan of hot soup.

5. In small saucepan, melt remaining 2 tablespoons butter or margarine over medium-low heat. Stir in paprika, ground red pepper to taste, and black pepper to taste.

At serving time, ladle soup into individual soup bowls. Add a few croutons and drizzle about 1 teaspoon paprika mixture over top of each serving.

The hot soup is served as the first course of the wedding feast. The dinner will include *baharatli kuzu* (recipe follows) and *iç pilav* (recipe page 132).

The celebration is not complete unless lamb is prepared for the occasion. If whole roasted lamb is too expensive, the next best thing is *baharatli kuzu*.

Baharatli Kuzu

Spiced Leg of Lamb

Note: This recipe takes 24 hours.

Yield: serves 10

3 cups plain yogurt
½ cup olive oil
1 onion, **finely chopped**
1 tablespoon sweet marjoram
1 tablespoon rosemary
salt and pepper to taste

½ cup finely chopped fresh mint or 1 tablespoon dried mint
½ cup finely chopped fresh dill or 1 tablespoon dried dill
1 teaspoon **ground** thyme
4 cloves garlic, **crushed**
juice of 1 lemon
1 leg of lamb (about 6 pounds), **trimmed** of fat

Equipment: Medium mixing bowl, mixing spoon, paring knife, roasting pan with cover, oven mitts, **meat thermometer** (optional), **bulb baster** (optional), meat knife

1. Make **marinade**: In medium mixing bowl, combine yogurt, oil, onion, marjoram, rosemary, salt and pepper to taste, mint, dill, thyme, garlic, and lemon juice. Stir well to mix all ingredients.

2. Using the point of paring knife, make about 1-inch cuts all over the surface of meat. Place meat in roasting pan and completely cover with marinade. Cover and refrigerate overnight, turning meat several times to coat with marinade.

Preheat oven to 325° F.

3. Remove meat from refrigerator and leave at room temperature for 2 hours before baking, turning meat several times in marinade.

4. Bake in oven, covered, for 1 hour. Remove cover, insert meat thermometer, if using, in thickest part of meat. Continue baking, uncovered, for 2 to 2½ hours more, or until thermometer registers 145° to 150° F for medium doneness. (Bake 30 to 35 minutes per pound.) Using bulb baster or spoon, baste meat several times during baking. Remove from oven and allow to rest for 30 minutes before slicing.

Serve lamb with iç pilav *(recipe follows) and spinach pie (recipe page 126).*

Almost every religious holiday feast and life-cycle celebration in Turkey calls for one or more rice dishes. This one is especially delicious.

Iç Pilav

Rice with Chicken Livers

Yield: serves 8

½ pound chicken livers
water, as needed
6 tablespoons butter or margarine, divided
½ cup **pine nuts** (available at most supermarkets and all Asian and Middle East food stores)
1½ cups long grain rice
½ cup black currants (available at most supermarkets and all Middle East food stores)
1 teaspoon **ground allspice**
3 cups chicken broth, homemade (recipe page 106) or canned
salt and pepper to taste
6 green onions, white part only, **finely chopped**
¼ cup chopped fresh dill or 1 tablespoon dried dill

Equipment: Small saucepan, slotted spoon, paring knife, 2 small bowls, small skillet, large **heavy-based** saucepan, mixing spoon, kitchen towel, serving dish

1. Put chicken livers in small saucepan, cover with water, and bring to a boil over high heat. Reduce heat to **simmer** and cook for 5 to 8 minutes until done. They are fully cooked when lightly browned and firm to the touch. Remove from heat and let cool. When cool enough to handle, remove livers from liquid with slotted spoon. Using paring knife, cut into pea-size pieces and place in small bowl. Discard liquid.

2. Melt 2 tablespoons butter or margarine in small skillet over medium-high heat. Add pine nuts and **sauté**, stirring constantly, until lightly browned, 2 to 3 minutes. Remove from heat and transfer pine nuts to second small bowl.

3. Melt remaining 4 tablespoons butter or margarine in large heavy-based saucepan over medium-high heat. Add rice, currants, allspice, chicken broth, and salt and pepper to taste. Stirring constantly, bring to a boil. Reduce heat to simmer, cover, and cook for 20 to 30 minutes, until rice has absorbed all the broth. Remove from heat. Using mixing spoon, **fold in** green onions, dill, sautéed livers, and sautéed nuts. Place folded towel on top of pan. (This is done to keep moisture from falling back onto the rice.) Leave in warm place for 30 minutes for flavors to develop.

To serve, transfer rice to a serving dish, taking care not to mash rice.

The Turks have hundreds of very sweet pastries made with honey and nuts. These are easy and fun to make. Don't worry about getting them perfect; phyllo always looks great after baking.

Farareer

Bird Nests

Yield: 24 pastries

3½ cups walnuts, **finely chopped**
½ cup brown sugar
½ teaspoon **ground** cinnamon
24 sheets **phyllo** (14- x 18-inches each), thawed according to directions on package
2 cups melted butter or margarine
¾ cup honey
juice of ½ lemon

Equipment: Small bowl, spoon, barely damp kitchen towel, work surface, **pastry brush**, buttered baking sheet, spatula or dinner knife, oven mitts, heatproof surface, small saucepan, wire cake rack, serving platter

1. Prepare filling: In small bowl, mix finely chopped walnuts, brown sugar, and cinnamon.

Preheat oven to 400° F.

2. Assemble: While working with one sheet of phyllo, keep remaining sheets covered with barely damp towel. Place 1 phyllo sheet on work surface, and using pastry brush, brush top with melted butter or margarine. Fold in half lengthwise, making a half moon. Brush melted butter or margarine over top and sprinkle with 1 tablespoon walnut filling.

3. Tightly roll phyllo, starting at long folded edge. Roll until 1 inch from opposite edge. Bring both ends of the rolled phyllo together to make a ring, leaving about 1 inch open in the center of ring. Dab the outside end with melted butter or margarine and tuck under edge of ring. Place ring on baking sheet. Tuck unrolled 1-inch edge of phyllo under ring, folding it toward the middle, so some of it covers over bottom of 1-inch opening in center. Use spatula or dinner knife to help tuck unrolled portion under coil. Repeat procedure with remaining phyllo sheets. Fill center opening with 1 tablespoon walnut filling. Brush top with melted butter or margarine.

4. Bake in oven until crisp and golden brown, 35 to 40 minutes. Using oven mitts, remove from oven and place pan on heatproof surface.

5. Warm honey in small saucepan over low heat, about 3 minutes. Remove from heat, and stir in lemon juice. Brush honey mixture over warm pastries and sprinkle with remaining finely chopped walnuts. Place pastries to wire cake rack to cool.

To serve, place pastries on serving platter. Usually Turkish coffee accompanies the sweets. Turkish coffee (Türk kahvesi) *is similar to Middle East* kahve *(recipe page 139)*.

ARABIAN PENINSULA

Most people living in the Arabian Peninsula are Muslims. The non-Muslims are usually indentured workers from India, Pakistan, Bangladesh, and Sri Lanka, brought by wealthy landowners to Oman, Qatar, and United Arab Emirates. There is also a small Christian community in Kuwait and Catholics from the Philippines who are brought to United Arab Emirates as household servants.

All Muslim life-cycle ritual are celebrated according to the Islamic religion. (See Islam and Islamic Life-Cycle Rituals, page xlix.)

KUWAIT

Kuwait is bordered on the north and west by Iraq and to the south by Saudi Arabia, with the Persian Gulf to the west. The city of Kuwait is one of international banks, high-rise buildings, and air-conditioned homes. These days most men wear jeans or business suit and women wear Western outfits like jeans or mini-skirts underneath their robe-like *aba*.

Marriage is arranged by the parents in a very meaningful way. Marriage to a cousin is preferred, and marriage to a first cousin is considered to be the best possible match. The families know each other and the bride and groom would have met as children. Marriage outside of the clan is a last resort. Instead, a young woman might wait for an opportunity to become a cousin's second wife rather than marry out of the clan. Men are free to take up to four wives.

The degree to which women are consulted on their choice of husband varies with each family. A young person who marries without parental consent is expelled from the family and hence from the clan. A young girl brings wealth with her bride-price to her family in marrying and she knows her value in that sense.

In Islamic marriages in Kuwait, the couple must sign a contract before the marriage, and the woman can specify what is acceptable for her in the marriage. She can limit the number of additional wives her husband may take, and she can also have a large divorce settlement fee written into the contract, thereby making it less likely that her husband will divorce her. ۞ ۞ ۞

OMAN

Oman is bounded by the Gulf of Oman and the Arabian Sea to the north, east, and southeast and to the west by Yemen, Saudi Arabia, and the United Arab Emirates. Oman was an extremely poor country until the discovery of oil in the 1960s. Regardless of the new wealth and modernization in the cities, the people continue to follow the traditional lifestyle according to conservative Islamic values.

Among Muslims, there is great strength in the family unit. Families are very large, including two or three generations, uncles, several aunts for each uncle, and assorted cousins. In traditional families, they all live together in a compound with several mud brick houses built around an open courtyard.

Sometimes, the birth of the firstborn son means so much to the family that the parents may become known by the child's name. They are addressed as *abu* (father of) or *amm* (mother of) followed with the name of the child. Friends and family show a sign of respect and recognition of the couple's good fortune in having a son when they address them in this way.

While men and women are traditionally segregated outside the home, some work together in industry and government offices. In Oman, women have entered the professions and some even hold jobs on the police force. ۞ ۞ ۞

QATAR

Qatar lies on a peninsula, bounded to the north and east by the Persian Gulf, to the west by the Gulf of Bahrain, and to the south by Saudi Arabia. Since Sheik Hamad bin Khalifa Al-Thani took power in this sleepy country some three years ago, he is slowly changing Qatar's image as the region's most backward state. In a Muslim country where women have traditionally been homebodies, the young sheik leader has been hiring women to fill government jobs.

Qatar is struggling to modernize while retaining strict Islamic traditions. In the cities, traditional Arab and modern dress coexist. Many women wear long-sleeved, floor-length, Western-style dresses to work. Some may add the *hijab*, the traditional black headscarf. The young men prefer to wear jeans and T-shirts, while the older men prefer the long white dishdasha robe, the national dress of Qatar.

Most Qatari, including the working women, believe life-cycle rituals should follow strict Islamic law and traditions. There are separate schools for girls, socializing without a chaperone is forbidden and most marriages are arranged.

The religious part of a marriage takes place in the bride's family home. While the couple are in different rooms, a *mutawa* (holy man) asks the couple if they will take each other as husband and wife. The bride and groom sign the contract and are legally married though they will not join each other as man and wife until after the wedding ceremony. ۞ ۞ ۞

UNITED ARAB EMIRATES

The United Arab Emirates (UAE) are seven Arab states that gained their independence from the United Kingdom in 1971. The country is bounded by the Persian Gulf on the north and east, by Oman to the southeast, and by Saudi Arabia to the west. In a relatively short time the UAE has gone from a little-known desert country to an international business and vacation destination with five-star hotels. In recent years the discovery of oil has brought wealth and a new way of life to the small population. Today, the UAE is a federation of seven Arab states or emirates. Each emirate is named after its main town or city and is controlled politically and economically by its sheikh. *Emir* and *Sheikh* are words meaning prince.

The Arabs of the UAE usually have large families with up to four wives and numerous children. They have a strong alliance to all of their kin and the extended family often lives together in a compound with adjoining houses.

The people of the UAW not only eat three meals a day, but they also eat two other small meals called *fualah*. Traditionally, one *fualah* is between breakfast and lunch and the other *fualah* is between lunch and dinner. The *fualah* also becomes a ritualistic meal when there is an important event to celebrate or the need for a religious gathering. The morning *fualah* is a good time to view the newborn son, while the late afternoon *fualah* is the best time to celebrate the circumcision of a boy or a wedding. The food served includes a variety of fruits, sweets, nuts and *kahve* (recipe page 139). Perfumes and incense are also passed around as part of the ritual. Incense is placed in burners, lit and fanned until it is burning well enough to produce wafts of scented smoke. ֍ ֍ ֍

YEMEN

Yemen is located in the southwest corner of the Arabian Peninusula and is bounded on the north by Saudi Arabia, on the east by Oman, on the south by the Arabian Sea and the Gulf of Aden, and on the west by the Red Sea. Except for the language, which is Arabic, and the fact that most people are Muslims, there are great cultural differences among the regional groups in Yemen. The people living in the coastal lowland are racially and culturally influenced by the neighboring African countries (Eritrea and Djibouti) just across the strait of Bab el Mandeb. The people living in the cities and towns scattered over the rugged terrain of mountains and valleys of Northern Yemen live by strict Islamic laws.

On occasions of family feasts, female relatives and friends gather in the kitchen to help with the food preparations. Their job is to prepare and serve the food to the men who always eat separately from the women.

Boys and girls have different role models. Girls are taught to be subservient while still very young, and boys learn to be aggressive and decisive. Girls are kept at home with the women and small children. They do not have the freedom to come and go as boys do.

In the past, young boys were not considered culturally to have gone through an adolescent stage. As soon as they reached puberty they were accepted as adults, eligible for marriage and expected to help protect and provide for the family. Young women could be married after their menstruation began and have children while they were not yet grown themselves. This is slowly changing, but only in the cities, where education is making the difference.

Appetizers are an important part of every family celebration feast, and among the most popular throughout the Mediterranean region and the Middle East are stuffed grape leaves. In Greece they are called *dolmas*, in Turkey, *yalanci dolma* and in Libya, *abrak*. In Egypt, 1 tablespoon dry mint leaves are added to the meat mixture and they are called *wara enab mahshi*. In Armenia ground lamb added along with rice is called *misov derevapatat*. In Yemen stuffed grape leaves are called *yab-ra*. ֍ ֍ ֍

YAB-RA

STUFFED GRAPE LEAVES

Yield: about 6 dozen

16-ounce jar grape leaves (available at Middle Eastern food stores and some supermarkets)
1 pound chopped lean beef or lamb
½ cup long grain rice, uncooked
3 cloves garlic, **finely chopped**
salt and pepper to taste
½ cup lemon juice
3 cups chicken broth, canned or homemade (recipe p. 106), or water

Equipment: **Colander**, large mixing bowl, mixing spoon, work surface, paring knife, large saucepan with cover, heatproof dinner plate (slightly smaller than saucepan), serving platter

1. Prepare grape leaves: Remove leaves from jar and carefully separate them. Grape leaves are packed in a brine or salty solution so it is necessary to rinse them under cold running water. Stack leaves in a colander to drain. Set aside about 6 or 8 leaves to line bottom of saucepan.

2. Prepare filling: Combine chopped beef or lamb, rice, and garlic in large mixing bowl. Us-

ing clean hands, mix well and add salt and pepper to taste.

3. On work surface, spread out one grape leaf, with the dull side up, and stem end facing you. Using paring knife, cut off stem before stuffing leaf. Place about 1 teaspoon of the filling on the center of the leaf. (For larger leaves, use a little more.) Start to roll up the leaf from end where stem was. Tuck in the sides of the leaves to enclose the filling. Continue rolling, making little packages each about ¾ inch thick and about 2 inches wide. Place stuffed leaves seam side down on work surface. Repeat until all the leaves are filled.

4. Line bottom of large saucepan with 6 to 8 grape leaves. Place stuffed leaves on top and pack them close together, with seam sides down. When first layer is complete make a second layer, packing the stuffed leaves close together. Continue building layers until all the stuffed leaves are in the saucepan.

5. It is necessary to weigh down the stuffed grape leaves as they cook. Do this by placing a heatproof dinner plate, a little smaller than the diameter of the pot, upside down, on top of the stuffed leaves.

6. Add lemon juice and broth or water. Bring to a boil over high heat. Reduce heat to **simmer**, cover saucepan, and cook for 45 minutes. Remove from heat and cool to room temperature before removing from pan. Stuffed grape leaves keep well in covered container, refrigerated, for at least four days.

To serve as an appetizer, arrange stuffed grape leaves on serving platter. To eat, pick up with your fingers and pop into your mouth.

Lamb is always served for wedding celebrations, and *mozat bellaban* is a popular way of preparing it in Kuwait. Several different types of lamb dishes are traditionally served at weddings in Kuwait.

Mozat Bellaban

Braised Lamb Shanks in Yogurt Sauce

Yield: serves 6

6 lean lamb shanks
¾ cup vegetable oil, divided
water, as needed
1 onion, quartered
1 carrot, peeled and chopped
2 bay leaves
4 cloves
½ teaspoon peppercorns
2 quarts plain yogurt
2 **egg yolks**
¼ cup sifted cornstarch
½ cup chopped fresh mint
6 peeled hard cooked eggs, for **garnish**

Equipment: Large **heavy-based** skillet, metal tongs, large saucepan with cover or **Dutch oven**, medium enameled or stainless saucepan, small skillet, whisk, serving spoon, serving platter

1. Heat ¼ cup oil in large heavy-based skillet over medium-high heat. Brown lamb shanks well on all sides, 7 to 12 minutes. When browned, transfer to large saucepan or Dutch oven, and add water to cover. Add onion, carrot, bay leaves, cloves, and peppercorns. Bring to boil over high heat. Reduce heat to **simmer**, cover, and cook for 30 to 45 minutes, or until done.

2. Prepare yogurt sauce: While shanks are cooking, mix yogurt, egg yolks, cornstarch, and salt in medium enameled or stainless saucepan. Whisking constantly, bring to boil over medium heat. Reduce to low, and stirring frequently, cook for 5 to 7 minutes until thickened.

3. At serving time, heat remaining ½ cup oil in small skillet over medium-high heat. Add garlic and chopped mint, and stir constantly, until garlic is soft, 3 to 5 minutes. Remove from heat.

To serve, place braised lamb shanks on large serving platter, spoon over hot yogurt sauce, and top with garlic mixture. Decorate with wedges of hard-cooked eggs and serve with rice and flat bread.

Couscous is popular throughout North Africa and the Middle East. It would be one of the 30 or 40 dishes prepared for the wedding feast.

Maghrebia

Meat Stew with Couscous

Yield: serves 6 to 8

1 pound lamb or lean beef, cut into hearty chunks
1 bay leaf
1 teaspoon **ground** cinnamon
2 teaspoons salt
¼ teaspoon pepper
water, as needed
3 pounds chicken, cut into serving-size pieces
10 **boiling onions**, peeled
6 carrots, peeled and **coarsely chopped**
1½ cups canned chickpeas (garbanzo beans)
10-ounce package frozen green peas, thawed
2 boxes (5.8-ounces each) **couscous** (available at all supermarkets)
¼ cup parsley, **finely chopped** for **garnish**

Equipment: Large saucepan or **Dutch oven**, mixing spoon, large shallow serving platter, tongs, slotted metal spoon, large serving bowl, ladle, individual soup bowls

1. Place meat, bay leaf, cinnamon, salt, pepper, and 3 cups water in large saucepan or Dutch oven. Bring to boil over medium-high heat. Reduce heat to **simmer**, cover, and cook for 45 minutes.

2. Add chicken pieces, onions, carrots, chickpeas, and green peas. Add enough water to cover chicken and vegetables. Bring to boil over high heat. Reduce heat to simmer, cover, and cook for 40 to 50 minutes, until chicken and meat are very tender.

3. Prepare couscous according to directions on package, and keep warm.

4. Place warm couscous on large shallow serving platter. Make a well in the center and using tongs and slotted spoon arrange meat, chicken and vegetables in the center of the couscous. Sprinkle with parsley.

To serve, pour broth into a large serving bowl with ladle. Each person is given an individual soup bowl for the broth, which they drink.

All meals include several salads, and *fattoush* would be one of them.

Fattoush

Mixed Salad

Yield: serves 6

1 head romaine lettuce, **trimmed**, washed, and drained, separate leaves and break into bite-size pieces
3 tomatoes, trimmed and **coarsely chopped**
1 cucumber, peeled and **diced**
1 green bell pepper, trimmed and **finely chopped**
1 onion, finely chopped
4 tablespoons fresh parsley, finely chopped
1 tablespoon fresh mint, finely chopped or 2 teaspoons dried mint
½ cup extra virgin olive oil
¼ cup lemon juice
1 clove garlic, finely chopped
salt and pepper to taste
1 pita bread, toasted and cut into small bite-size pieces (available at most supermarkets and all Middle East food stores)

Equipment: Large salad bowl, salad tools, small bowl with cover, mixing spoon, plastic wrap

1. In large salad bowl, combine lettuce, tomatoes, cucumbers, bell pepper, onion, parsley, and mint flakes.

2. Combine oil and lemon juice in small bowl. Add garlic and salt and pepper to taste, and stir until well mixed. Pour over salad and toss well. Cover with plastic wrap and refrigerate for about 1 hour before serving.

To serve, uncover and add pieces of pita bread, toss them to mix through the salad.

A crown roast always makes a lovely presentation on the banquet table. When it is stuffed, it is even more special.

Kharoff

Stuffed Crown Roast of Lamb

Yield: serves 8

2 tablespoons vegetable oil
1 pound lean **ground** lamb
1 onion, **finely chopped**
1 cup water
½ teaspoons ground cinnamon
½ teaspoons ground cardamom
¼ teaspoon ground cloves
¼ teaspoon ground ginger
½ cup seedless raisins
½ cup sliced almonds, **blanched**
salt and pepper to taste
2 cups cooked white rice
4- to 5-pound **oven-ready** crown roast of lamb
3 hard-cooked eggs, peeled

Equipment: Large skillet, mixing spoon, medium mixing bowl, shallow roasting pan with rack, aluminum foil, oven mitts, meat **thermometer** (optional), large serving platter, carving knife

1. Heat oil in large skillet over medium-high heat. Crumble in ground meat and stir until lightly browned, 3 to 5 minutes. Stir in onions, water, cinnamon, cardamom, cloves, ginger, raisins, almonds, and salt and pepper to taste. Reduce heat to **simmer** and cook for 5 minutes for flavors to develop. Transfer to medium mixing bowl to cool to room temperature. Stir in cooked rice.

Preheat oven to 325° F.

2. Place lamb roast on rack in shallow roasting pan and fill center with half the rice mixture. Arrange 3 whole hard-cooked eggs on top and cover with remaining rice mixture, smooth top. Cover stuffing and top of roast with foil.

3. Roast in oven for about 2½ hours or until meat thermometer registers 175° to 180° for medium doneness (or 35 to 45 minutes per pound).

4. Remove foil during last 15 minutes of roasting. Allow to rest 20 minutes before carving.

To serve, bring the whole crown roast to the table on a large serving platter and carve in front of guests. Serve with salad, vegetables, and bread.

The ceremonial serving of coffee to guests expresses the importance of hospitality throughout the Middle East. Coffee is always freshly made, and often the beans are roasted and ground each day. Sugar is always added to the coffee while it cooks, so different brews must be served to please those who like different degrees of sweetness. The special long-handled pot for preparing coffee is called a *tanaka*. Coffee was discovered in Arabia about one thousand years ago and for many years the whole world's supply came from Yemen. (In Saudi Arabia a cardamom seed is added to the pot while the coffee is brewing.)

Kahve

Middle East Coffee

Yield: serves 4

2 cups water
4 teaspoons sugar, more or less to taste
4 teaspoons coffee, freshly ground to powder consistency or espresso grind (available at supermarkets and specialty coffee stores)

Equipment: Tanaka or small saucepan, teaspoon, 4 small cups (such as demitasse, Turkish coffee, or tea cups)

Put water in *tanaka* or small saucepan, and bring to boil over high heat. Stir in 4 teaspoons sugar, (1 teaspoon per serving gives average sweetness). Top the water with powdered ground coffee or espresso grind so it floats on the water. Bring water again to boil, remove from the heat and let the **froth** that has risen die down. Repeat boiling process once more. Bring to a boil and stir coffee well into the water, trying not to lose the froth. Pour at once into small cups, swirling the pot slightly as you pour so that a little froth is included in each cup.

Serve at once, the grounds will settle at the bottom of the cup and should not be drunk. Drink the coffee black as they do in Yemen. The coffee is served with pastries, such as farareer *(recipe p. 133) and* tamriah *(recipe p. 122).*

BAHRAIN

Bahrain is an archipelago (group of islands) in the Persian Gulf and the Gulf of Bahrain. It lies east of Saudi Arabia. Since the Middle East economic boom in the 1970s, Bahrain has done much to elevate the standard of living for its people by improving health care, education, and housing. Most of the population are urbanites, living in cities where ancient mosques and modern glass skyscrapers share the skyline and donkey carts and Rolls-Royce cars share the roads. Bahrain has one of the most modern communication systems in the world and is well established as a center in banking and commerce.

The majority of Bahraini are Muslims, and all life-cycle events are observed according to their religion. (See Islam and Islamic Life-Cycle Rituals, page xlix.)

At one time motherhood was the sole aim of the Muslim woman's life. Today, girls are getting a full education and finding jobs in government and business. In Bahrain, the women have a great many rights and privileges, but when it comes to family and children, they prefer to follow the strict Islamic traditions. While many Bahraini women are not completely veiled, most still prefer a head covering when in public. They dress modestly, preferring long-sleeved garments, even in the summertime.

The Middle Eastern families who adhere to ancient Muslim traditions follow rigid religious guidelines. When a Muslim woman marries, her loyalty is to the family she was born into. She is always a member of her father's family. For this reason, she does not change her name when she marries. A woman's children are members of her husband's family. Her wealth passes to her children upon her death and, thus, out of her father's family and into that of her husband. The ideal marriage then is between the children of two brothers. Muslims are aware of the genetic problems of such marriages but this has not yet altered this value.

Circumcision for boys at about seven or eight is a universal custom throughout Islam. In Bahrain, circumcisions are a family celebration, and the father often shoots off fireworks to celebrate the event. There is always a great feast and if it's for the first born son, whole roasted lamb would be prepared for the exciting event.

In Arab countries, a whole kid (baby goat) or lamb is roasted on a spit in celebration of feast days and weddings. The meat is presented on a huge tray, surrounded by large quantities of rice, and garnished with peeled, hard-cooked eggs.

If you are going to roast the whole baby lamb, be sure your oven is large enough to accommodate it. Otherwise you may have the butcher cut it up or roast it on the outdoor grill or pay to have it baked in a larger commercial oven at a local bakery or restaurant.

Kabab Barreh

Roasted Whole Baby Lamb

Yield: serves about 12

1 **oven-ready** 14 to 18 pound baby lamb
2 cups onions, **finely chopped**
salt and pepper to taste
2 tablespoons **ground coriander**
1 cup melted **rendered** butter (recipe page 102) or melted butter or margarine
10 to 12 cups cooked white rice, for serving
10 to 12 hard-cooked egg, peeled, for serving

Equipment: Paper towels, medium bowl, mixing spoon, pastry brush, large roasting pan, aluminum foil, oven mitts, meat **thermometer**, **bulb baster**, large serving tray

Preheat oven to 325° F.

1. Rinse lamb inside and out under running water and wipe dry with paper towels.

2. In medium bowl, mix chopped onions, salt and pepper to taste, coriander, and melted rendered butter or melted butter or margarine. Using pastry brush or your hands, rub the lamb inside and out with onion mixture. Place lamb in large roasting pan. If either end of the lamb overhangs the pan, make a shield of foil under the overhanging part to channel the drippings into the roasting pan.

3. Roast lamb in oven for 7 to 9 hours, or until meat is browned and very tender. Baste frequently with pan drippings using bulb baster or spoon. To keep from getting too dark, cover loosely with foil for the last hour or so of cooking. Meat thermometer inserted in thickest part of thigh should register 165° F for well-done meat. (Allow 30 to 35 minutes per pound.)

To serve, place the whole lamb on a large serving tray and surround with rice. Decoratively arrange the peeled hard-cooked eggs on top of the rice.

Assorted fruit and vegetable salads such as this one made with spinach are served along with the *kabab barreh*.

Borani Esf Anaj

Spinach Salad

Yield: serves 4

1 pound fresh spinach, washed and **coarsely chopped**
½ cup water
1 tablespoon extra virgin olive oil
1 onion, **finely chopped**
1 clove garlic, finely chopped
1 cup plain yogurt
salt and pepper to taste
2 tablespoons roasted walnuts, chopped
1 tablespoon fresh mint leaves, chopped

Equipment: Large saucepan with cover, metal tongs, **colander**, mixing spoon, medium serving bowl, mixing spoon

1. Put spinach in large saucepan and add water. Cover and cook over medium-high heat, for 10 minutes. Using metal tongs, toss occasionally. Drain spinach in colander.

2. Heat oil in large saucepan over medium-high heat. Add onion and garlic, stir, and **sauté** until onion is soft, 3 to 5 minutes. Add drained spinach, toss to mix, and cook 3 to 5 minutes to heat through. Transfer to medium serving bowl, toss with yogurt, and add salt and pepper to taste. Sprinkle with walnuts and mint.

Serve salad while still warm for best flavor with roasted lamb.

Muhallabieh is a favorite rice pudding prepared for little boys after their circumcision. It is soothing and easy to digest. This pudding is traditionally served to visitors and guests at the birth of a son. It is said that a family will serve it on the birth of a daughter only if she is the fifth child, after having four sons.

Muhallabieh

Rice Pudding

Yield: serves 4 to 6

- 2 cups uncooked **Basmati rice**
- 1 cup water, or 3/4 cup orange juice and 1/4 cup water
- 1 quart milk
- 3/4 cup sugar
- 1/2 cup chopped pistachio nuts, for **garnish**

Equipment: Electric **blender**, rubber spatula, medium bowl, mixing spoon, medium saucepan, individual serving bowls

1. Put uncooked rice in blender and **blend** until pulverized. Transfer pulverized rice to medium bowl, add 1 cup water or 3/4 cup orange juice and 1/4 cup water mixture, and stir to make a paste.

2. Put milk in medium saucepan and bring to boil over medium-high heat. Slowly stir in rice mixture and sugar. Reduce heat to **simmer**, and stirring frequently, cook until thickened, 45 minutes to 1 hour.

3. Pour into individual serving bowls and allow to cool to room temperature and refrigerate.

To serve, garnish each serving with chopped pistachio.

EUROPE

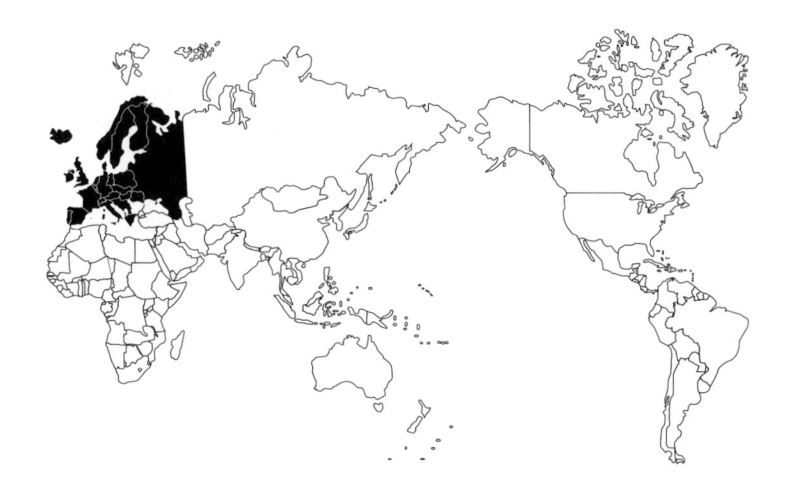

The majority of people living in Europe are Christians (see Protestant and Catholic Life-Cycle Rituals, page xlvi), although most countries have sizable Jewish and Muslim communities. Roman Catholics, who comprise the largest single Christian group, live mainly in Spain, Portugal, Italy, Ireland, Belgium, southern Germany, Hungary, and Poland. The greatest concentration of Protestant Christians is found in northern and central Europe—England, Scotland, northern Germany, the Netherlands, and the Scandinavian countries. The Orthodox church, the third major Christian group in Europe, has a strong following in Eastern Europe, primarily in Russia, Georgia, Greece, Bulgaria, Romania and the republics of the former Yugoslavia, except for Slovenia, which is mostly Roman Catholic.

Throughout the Christian world, many countries, cities, and towns, and every parish, diocese, and ecclesiastical province has its particular patron saints; many of which are unknown outside the country or local area. The custom of giving children the names of Christian saints dates from the first millennium. By the thirteenth century, this custom had spread across the continent of Europe. Today, when Christian parents are more likely to choose their children's names without regard to past traditions, the older European Christian churches strongly recommend that if the chosen first name is not of Christian origin or significance, a saint's name be bestowed at baptism as a middle name.

In Roman Catholic countries, the custom has been to celebrate the feast day of the saint whose name the person received at baptism instead of or in addition to the person's birthday. This "baptismal saint" is considered a special personal patron all through life. Children are made familiar with the history and legend of "their own" saint. They are inspired by his or her life and feel protected and bonded with their patron saint.

All Christian churches have rituals and customs for every stage of life, from the crib to the grave. Although the basic rituals of each Christian group remain much the same across Europe, how the rituals are celebrated varies from country to country, from region to region within a country, and between the urban and rural populations of a country or region.

GREECE

Located along the Mediterranean Sea in the southeastern corner of Europe, Greece has a recorded history that spans more than 2,500 years of struggles and accomplishments. Much of what we take for granted today in Western science, architecture, art, medicine, and theater has its origins in ancient Greece.

Most life-cycle events revolve around the Greek Orthodox church. (See Eastern or Orthodox Church Life-Cycle Rituals, page xlviii.) And most Greek celebrations, such as births, baptisms, and weddings, include roasted lamb and special breads decorated to commemorate the occasion and often blessed by a priest. Frozen bread dough can be used to make a decorative loaf. While still frozen, cut off a piece of dough to shape or cut into flowers, leaves and vines, or birds and religious symbols. (You might want to buy two packages of frozen dough, one to make into the loaf and one for the decorative pieces.) Follow the instructions on the package to thaw and prepare.

Be sure to shape the loaf before adding the decorative pieces of dough. Brush the back side of the decorative pieces lightly with water or **egg wash** to make them stick to the loaf. The loaf needs to rise according to the directions on the package. To give the decorations a shiny finish, brush their surface with egg wash before baking.

Besides lamb and breads, a traditional Greek menu can include vegetables—stuffed (recipe page 174)or baked into pies (recipe page 126) and casseroles (page 157)—as well as dishes of olives and pickles, tubs of *feta* (a crumbly white cheese); and bottles of *retsina* (a Greek ***apéritif***) and ouzo (a Greek ***liqueur***).

At the birth of a baby, relatives and friends come to pay their respects with gifts and money, and *kafés ellínikós* (Greek coffee) and a table of sweets are usually set out for the visitors. *Pasteli*, another favorite treat for guests, are small wrapped candies traditionally given out at the baptism. ❁ ❁ ❁

PASTELI

SESAME SEED AND HONEY SWEETS

Yield: 25 to 35 pieces

1½ cups honey

¾ cup water

3 cups **sesame seeds**

½ cup **blanched** almonds, finely **ground**

1 teaspoon grated orange rind (orange **zest**)

Equipment: Medium saucepan, wooden mixing spoon, **candy thermometer** (optional), aluminum foil, cookie sheet, large knife, pitcher, clear plastic food wrap

1. Put honey and water in medium saucepan. Stirring constantly, cook over medium-high heat until mixture comes to firm ball stage or reaches 250°F on candy thermometer. Remove from heat and add sesame seeds, almonds, and orange zest.

2. Cover a cookie sheet with aluminum foil and spread sesame mixture about ¼ inch thick on nonstick cookie sheet. While still slightly warm, cut the candy into squares using a large knife. To keep candy from sticking, dip knife into pitcher of hot water, shaking off any excess, before making each cut. When cool, wrap each individual square in plastic wrap.

Store in covered container. Serve at a name day party or set out dishes of Pasteli *at a wedding.*

Baptism is the first important life-cycle event in a Greek child's life. After the Greek Orthodox service, relatives, friends, and neighbors gather for the christening feast.

The traditional celebration includes plenty of food and drink, and the singing and dancing often continues well after the infant guest of honor has been put to bed.

Almonds, grapes, and honey, among the world's earliest cultivated foods, are usually included in Greek religious ceremonies for christenings, weddings, and memorial services. For instance, after the christening ceremony, godparents offer guests the pouches of coated Jordan almonds known as *koufeta* (recipe follows), either as the guests leave the church or later at the reception that follows. The custom of offering these candied coated nuts symbolizes a sweet life for the infant, with blue Jordan almonds in blue netting pouches for boys and pink Jordan almonds in pink netting for girls. At weddings, white Jordan almonds in white netting are passed out to the guests as they leave the church or reception.

Kouféta

Jordan Almond Pouches

Yield: about 28 pouches

2 pounds (about 144 pieces) candy-coated Jordan almonds (available at candy stores and Middle Eastern food stores)

Equipment: Pink, blue, or white netting, cut into 6- or 8-inch squares or circles (8-inch circles of netting are available in assorted colors at most handicraft shops); 28 feet of narrow, pink, blue, or white satin ribbon cut into 12-inch lengths; scissors

Put 5 Jordan almonds in the center of a square or circle of netting. Enclose the almonds in the netting and twist the unfilled portion of the netting around the almonds to form a pouch. (See drawing below.) Wrap a ribbon around the twisted area, tie tightly, and make a pretty bow. Repeat as necessary.

Arrange all the pouches in a basket or on a silver tray, and serve one to each guest.

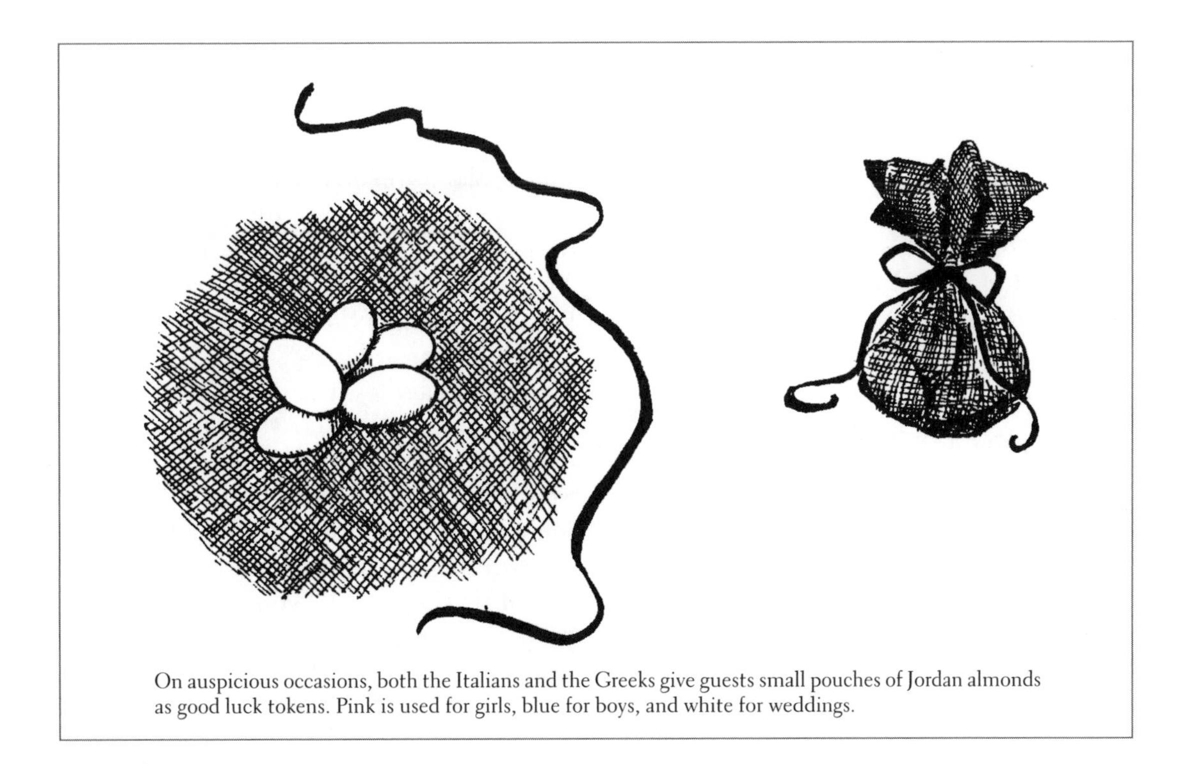

On auspicious occasions, both the Italians and the Greeks give guests small pouches of Jordan almonds as good luck tokens. Pink is used for girls, blue for boys, and white for weddings.

Instead of celebrating birthdays, Greek children often celebrate their name days. (See Eastern or Orthodox Church Life-Cycle Rituals, page xlviii.) The name day party includes a festive meal with plenty of sweets for gift-bearing relatives and friends. *Kourabiedes*, one of the most popular Greek desserts, appear at weddings, birthdays, name days, christenings, and all holidays.

Kourabiedes

Wedding Cookies

(White Shortbread Cookies)

Yield: about 40 cookies

- 1 egg yolk
- 1/4 cup strained orange juice
- 1 pound confectioners' sugar, divided
- 1 pound unsalted butter, melted and cooled to warm
- 1/4 cup finely ground almonds, **toasted** and **blanched**
- 4 cups all-purpose flour
- 1/2 cup cornstarch

Equipment: Electric **blender**, rubber spatula, flour **sifter**, large mixing bowl, mixing spoon, 2 nonstick cookie sheets, oven mitts, cardboard boxes, serving platter

1. Put egg yolk, orange juice, and 1/4 cup confectioners' sugar in blender, and **blend** for 2 to 3 seconds. Add melted butter and ground almonds, and blend for 5 to 7 seconds.

2. **Sift** flour and cornstarch into large mixing bowl. Add egg mixture from blender and, using a rubber spatula or mixing spoon, stir to form a soft dough. Transfer mixture to lightly floured work surface and **knead** for about 10 minutes until smooth and elastic. Wrap in plastic wrap and refrigerate for 1 hour.

Preheat oven to 350° F.

3. Form dough into balls about the size of a small egg; do not press or flatten them. (They do not rise during baking.) Place them about 1/2 inch apart from each other on cookie sheets.

4. Bake in oven for 30 to 35 minutes. These cookies do not brown easily, to test for doneness break one open and taste it. If there is a butter line in the middle of a cookie, continue baking for about 10 minutes more. Remove cookies from oven and allow to cool on cookie sheets.

5. Thickly coat the cookies with confectioners' sugar and leave them undisturbed for at least 6 hours. The easiest way to do this is line several large cardboard (canned soda flats) boxes with foil. Sift confectioners' sugar thickly over the foil. When the cookies are cool enough to handle, remove each one carefully from the baking sheet and place side by side, close together on the confectioners' sugar in the boxes. (Do not stack the cookies.) Sift all the remaining confectioners' sugar over the tops and sides of the cookies.

To serve, transfer cookies to serving platter. They can be stacked on the platter. The cookies will stay fresh for two to three weeks unrefrigerated.

The Greek wedding celebration is full of rituals and symbolism. The bride and groom exchange double rings and sip wine from a single golden goblet. Crowns of orange blossoms, joined together by ribbon, are crossed over the heads of the couple three times. The crowns symbolize their elevation to king and queen of the home they will share. Wearing their still joined crowns and holding tall lit candles, the couple follows the priest around the altar three times. This practice is referred to as the ceremonial wedding "dance" and it symbolically represents life as a continuous circle. According to tradition, the crowns are carefully preserved by the couple. When one of them dies, the crowns are buried with the body.

A member of the wedding party usually offers guests *kouféta* (recipe page 145) as the guests leave the church after the wedding, or as they arrive at the reception that follows. Because the wedding feast is a very important event for most Greeks, the main dish is usually spit-roasted lamb, the principal meat served for special occasions in Greece. However, the wedding feast is traditionally an elaborate affair and an endless array of other dishes is usually also included.

When the festivities are over, the bridal couple goes to the groom's family home. On their arrival, the groom's mother gives the bride a glass of honey mixed with water. The daughter-in-law sips this mixture so that from this day forward her words will sound as sweet as honey. The mother-in-law smears the overhead door frame with honey so that strife will never enter the couple's married life. A **pomegranate** is smashed on the threshold, its abundant seeds symbolizing future offspring. The couple may also share a quince to ensure that their life together will be as sweet as the taste of this fruit. The bittersweet taste of the quince also reminds them that they have taken each other "for better, for worse, the bitter with the sweet." Because Greece consists of a mountainous mainland and numerous islands scattered throughout the Aegean and Mediterranean Seas, many Greek rituals vary from region to region and island to island.

Moustalevria, one of the many desserts prepared for life-cycle celebrations, is made from grape must or unfermented grape juice. The dessert is traditionally prepared after the grape harvest, which is itself usually a Greek celebration feast. The following version of the recipe is easy and quick because it uses commercial grape juice instead of freshly squeezed juice.

Moustalevria

Grape Must Dessert

Yield: serves 4

4 tablespoons cornstarch
1 tablespoon sugar
3 cups grape juice
3 tablespoons **sesame seeds**, for **garnish**
ground cinnamon, for garnish

Equipment: Small bowl, whisk, small saucepan, individual dessert cups

1. Combine cornstarch and sugar in small bowl.

2. Pour grape juice into small saucepan and bring to boil over high heat. Remove from heat, and whisk about ½ cup hot grape juice into cornstarch mixture. Stir with whisk until smooth. Combine cornstarch mixture and remaining grape juice, and whisking constantly, cook over medium heat until thickened.

3. Remove from heat immediately after mixture thickens, and pour into individual dessert cups. Sprinkle with sesame seeds and cinnamon. Cool to room temperature, and refrigerate to set.

Serve as dessert.

A memorial (*mnemósinon*) and a memorial meal (*makaria*) follow a Greek burial service (cremation is forbidden by the Greek Orthodox Church). The *mnemósinon* and *makaria* are repeated 40 days, six months, one year, and three years after the death. The following fried fish recipe (*psari savoro*) is traditionally prepared for these feasts.

Psari Savoro

Fried Fish with Rosemary Sauce

Yield: 4 servings

rosemary sauce (recipe follows)

4 fish **fillets** (about 6 to 8 ounces each), cod, tilapia, or catfish are good choices
½ cup all-purpose flour, for **dredging**
salt and pepper to taste
2 to 4 tablespoons olive oil, for frying

Equipment: Large pie pan, mixing spoon, wax-paper-covered baking sheet, large-size skillet, metal spatula, serving platter

1. Prepare rosemary sauce and keep warm.

2. Put flour and salt and pepper to taste in pie pan, and stir to mix. Coat both sides of fish with flour mixture and shake off excess. Place floured fish fillets on wax-paper-covered baking sheet.

3. Heat 2 tablespoons oil in skillet over medium-high heat. Add fish fillets and fry until browned on both sides, 3 to 5 minutes each side. Using metal spatula, remove fish from skillet and place on serving platter.

To serve, spoon rosemary sauce over the fillets. Serve warm or at room temperature.

Saltsa Savoro

Rosemary Sauce

Yield: 1½ cups
½ cup olive oil
1 garlic clove, **finely chopped**
3 tablespoons all-purpose flour
¼ cup white vinegar
1 tablespoon tomato paste
2 cups water
2 sprigs fresh rosemary or 1 teaspoon dried rosemary
salt and pepper to taste

Equipment: Medium skillet, mixing spoon, small bowl

1. Heat olive oil in medium skillet over medium-high heat. Add garlic, stir, and fry for 1 minute. Remove from heat.

2. In small bowl, combine flour, vinegar, tomato paste, and water until smooth and lump-free. Return skillet with garlic oil in it to medium-high heat and stir in flour mixture. Stirring constantly, bring to a boil, and reduce heat to **simmer**. Add rosemary and stir until sauce thickens, 2 to 3 minutes. Add salt and pepper to taste. Keep warm.

Continue with psari savoro *(recipe precedes)*.

According to tradition, a tray of sweetened boiled wheat called *kólliva* is prepared and brought to church for the one year *mnemósinon*. After first being blessed by the priest, the *kólliva* is shared by parishioners attending the *mnemósinon*. Eating *kólliva* is a symbolic reminder that the dead are not forgotten.

Preparing *kólliva* takes two or three days; one day to soak the wheat, and one or two days to dry the wheat and prepare the presentation. When the ritual decorations are omitted the recipe is called *varvara*.

Kólliva

Memorial Wheat

Note: This recipe takes 24 hours.

Yield: serves 20 to 25
1¼ cups unpeeled whole wheat berries (sold in health food stores), soaked overnight in water
½ cup **sesame seeds**, **toasted**
½ cup chopped walnuts
½ cup seedless raisins
½ cup granulated sugar
½ tablespoon **ground** cumin
1½ teaspoon ground cinnamon, divided
½ cup graham cracker crumbs
1 cup confectioners' sugar, more if necessary
cinnamon sugar, as needed

20 to 30 white Jordan almonds, for **garnish** (available at candy and specialty food stores)

20 to 30 walnut halves, for garnish

Equipment: Large saucepan with cover, mixing spoon, **colander**, work surface, paper towels, clean pillow case, baking sheet, oven mitts, metal spatula, **mortar and pestle** or electric **blender**, large mixing bowl, 10- to 14-inch long oval or rectangular serving tray, wax paper, flour **sifter**, 8½ x 11 paper, pencil, scissors

1. Prepare grain: Put pre-soaked, drained wheat in large saucepan and cover with water, at least 3 inches above the kernels. Bring to boil over high heat, reduce heat to **simmer**, and cover, stirring occasionally to prevent sticking. During cooking, to keep the water level high, add more hot water when necessary. Cook 1 to 1½ hours, or until kernels begin to break open and are tender. Remove from heat. Drain thoroughly through colander placed in sink. Rinse kernels under warm running water and allow to drain well for an hour.

Preheat oven to 225° F.

2. Cover work surface with several layers of paper towels and spread out kernels. Pat dry with additional paper towels. Transfer kernels to clean pillow case, roll up pillow case, and squeeze to release any water. Transfer to baking sheet, and using your hands, spread out the kernels so that they are not stacked on top of each other.

3. Place in oven for 4 to 5 hours until kernels are completely dried. Turn frequently with spatula.

4. Crush toasted sesame seeds using mortar and pestle or in blender until pulverized; set aside.

5. In large mixing bowl, combine dried kernels, ground sesame seeds, chopped walnuts, raisins, granulated sugar, cumin, and ½ teaspoon cinnamon. Using your hands, toss to mix well.

6. Prepare for serving: Cover an oval or rectangular serving tray with wax paper. Using your hands, make wheat mixture into a 1-inch thick oval shape. Sprinkle graham cracker crumbs evenly over the mixture. **Sift** a ¼-inch thick layer of confectioners' sugar over the surface. Wrap a piece of wax paper around your hand and press down on the confectioners' sugar to make the top smooth and compact.

7. Add ritual decorating: To make a stencil in the shape of a cross, use a piece of paper about as large as the top of the *kólliva*. Fold the paper in half lengthwise and with a pencil, draw half of a cross that will cover the desired length. Cut out the half of a cross. Open the paper and center the cutout cross on top of the *kólliva*. Sprinkle remaining 1 teaspoon ground cinnamon over the cross-shaped opening in the paper to stencil the cross-shape on top of the powdered sugar. Carefully remove and discard paper stencil.

8. Using scissors, cut raisins in half. On the left side of the cross press the raisin pieces into the confectioners' sugar to form the initials of the deceased. On the right side of the cross, form the raisin pieces into the letters IC XC NIKA as shown here:

(The literal meaning of the letters is as follows: IC means Jesus Christ: XC means Nazarene; and NIKA means King of the Jews). Make a decorative border using the Jordan almonds and walnut halves. Lightly sprinkle with cinnamon sugar.

To serve: The priest should be notified several days in advance that you are bringing the kólliva *for the memorial service. Along with the* kólliva, *an envelope containing a donation and the name of the deceased should be brought to the church about an hour before the services begin. The* psalti *(the cantor or chosen church singer of liturgical music) places it on the sacramental table, between two tall candles* (lambathes)*, each tied with a black ribbon, signifying death. The candles are lit when the memorial service begins.*

At the end of the service an altar boy carries the tray to the back of the church where the *kólliva* is spooned into little plastic cups and given to the parishioners as they leave the church.

ALBANIA

The small country of Albania is part of the Balkan Peninsula of southeastern Europe; it lies on the east coast of the Adriatic Sea directly across the narrow Strait of Otranto from the heel of Italy. From the end of World War II until the early 1990s, Albania was a Communist country. In 1967, Albania's Communist government closed all places of worship, confiscated church property, and banned religious services. In 1990, the ban on religion was lifted and many churches and mosques have since reopened.

Albania is the only predominantly Islamic country in Europe. Although Albanian Muslims (see Islam and Islamic Life-Cycle Rituals, page xlix) aren't as rigid about following the Islamic modesty laws and traditional veiling practices of other Muslim countries, they do follow the dietary laws and do not eat pork. Muslim weddings and other celebrations call for a whole roasted lamb, when the budget allows, or a lamb stew made with mutton liver, entrails (intestines), or ground lamb patties.

For most life-cycle events, Albania's Orthodox and Roman Catholic minorities follow the traditional rituals of their churches. (See Eastern or Orthodox Church Life-Cycle Rituals, page xlviii, and Protestant and Catholic Life-Cycle Rituals, page xlvi.)

The difficult transition from Communist rule has brought many hardships, including shortages and high unemployment. In the past, the whole community celebrated events such as the birth of a baby or a wedding with great enthusiasm. Today the celebrations are simple family affairs. The old rural tradition at Christian weddings was for the bride to display extreme sorrow upon departing the family home. Amid tears and wailing, the bride, dressed in her wedding finery, bade her family goodbye. Anything less would have been an insult to her parents.

The wedding feasts of both Christian and Muslim Albanians usually include hot and cold *mézés* (little dishes of food or appetizers). Hot *mézés* are *fërgesa* (a mixture of fried food), *kordhëza* or *kukrec* (spit-roasted mutton or lamb insides), and *shishqebab* (kabobs). Cold *mézés* are various salads, *liptao* (cheese salad, recipe follows), sardines, seafood, and pickles. Mulberry-flavored brandy, known as *raki*, is usually served with the *mézés* on special occasions. ۞ ۞ ۞

LIPTAO

CHEESE SALAD

Yield: serves 4

5 tablespoons virgin olive oil
2 onions, **finely chopped**
5 cloves garlic, finely chopped
1 pound cottage cheese or drained yogurt
2 tablespoons chopped pimento (available in jars at all supermarkets)
salt and pepper to taste
suggested **garnish**es: 4 sliced dill pickles, 6 or 8 stuffed green olives, sliced carrots and celery, 4 or 6 slices rye or pumpernickel bread, 2 or 3 hard-cooked eggs, quartered

Equipment: Large skillet, mixing spoon, shallow serving bowl

Heat oil in large skillet over medium-high heat, add onion and garlic, stir, and **sauté** until onion is soft, 3 to 5 minutes. Reduce heat to medium, add cottage cheese or drained yogurt, and stir to mix. Add pimento and salt and pepper to taste, heat through, and remove from heat.

To serve, transfer to a shallow serving bowl and decoratively arrange the garnishes around the liptao: *sliced dill pickles, green olives* (ulinje), *carrot and celery slices, assorted breads, and quartered hard-cooked eggs. Use garnishes to scoop up the* liptao. *Cover and refrigerate leftover* liptao *for up to one week.*

When *quofte me mente* are made into small balls they are a favorite hot *mézé* at wedding banquets.

Quofte Me Mente

Minted Meat Balls

CAUTION: HOT OIL USED

Yield: serves 4 to 6

1 pound lean **ground** lamb or beef
2 eggs, lightly beaten
1cup stale **bread crumbs**
2 tablespoons chopped fresh mint or 1 teaspoon dried mint flakes
1 teaspoon ground cinnamon
salt and pepper to taste
vegetable oil for **deep frying**

Equipment: Medium mixing bowl, mixing spoon, 2 baking sheet, wax paper, work surface, **deep fryer** (see glossary for tips on making one), fryer thermometer (optional), paper towels, wooden spoon, metal tongs or **slotted spoon**

1. In medium bowl, combine ground meat, eggs, bread crumbs, mint, cinnamon, and salt and pepper to taste. Using mixing spoon or hands, stir to mix well. Let stand for 10 minutes.

2. Cover baking sheet with wax paper and place on work surface. Using your hands, roll small amounts of meat into Ping-Pong-size balls, and place side by side on wax paper.

3. Prepare to deep-fry: ADULT SUPERVISION REQUIRED. Have ready, several layers of paper towels on baking sheet. Heat oil to 375° F on fryer thermometer or until small bubbles appear around a wooden spoon handle when it is dipped in the oil.

3. Fry meatballs, a few at a time, carefully turning with metal tongs or slotted metal spoon to brown all sides, about 3 minutes per meatball. Transfer to paper towels to drain. Keep warm until ready to serve. Continue frying in batches.

To serve, arrange meatballs on platter. Guests eat the meatballs by picking them up with their fingers.

Albanian food is simple and hearty. For wedding feasts or Muslim circumcision celebrations, assorted stuffed vegetables and stuffed grape leaves (recipe page 136) are usually included in the menu. *Kabuni,* which is simply rice cooked according to the directions on package) became a dessert and a favorite party dish when sweetened with **cinnamon sugar** and raisins and sprinkled with walnuts or almonds. One or two different bean dishes, such as the following lima bean recipe (*fasule pllaqi*), may also be prepared for a celebration feast.

Fasule Pllaqi

Baked Lima Beans

Yield: serves 4

3 tablespoons olive oil
2 onions, sliced
3 cloves garlic, **finely chopped**
2 carrots, trimmed and sliced
1 cup canned stewed tomatoes, chopped

2 cups prepared lima beans, homemade (prepare according to directions on package), frozen (thawed), or canned
½ cup chicken broth, homemade (recipe page 106) or canned, or water
salt and pepper to taste
¼ cup **bread crumbs**
¼ cup grated Parmesan cheese

Equipment: Large skillet, mixing spoon, 9-inch baking pan, oven mitts

Preheat oven to 350° F.

1. Heat oil in large skillet over medium-high heat. Add onions, garlic, and carrot, stir, and **sauté** until onions are soft, 3 to 5 minutes. Stir in stewed tomatoes, reduce heat to **simmer**, and cook for 5 to 7 minutes to thicken.

2. Pour beans into buttered 9-inch baking pan, add chicken broth or water, and salt and pepper to taste. Pour tomato mixture over top and spread smooth with back of spoon. Sprinkle with bread crumbs and grated Parmesan cheese.

3. Bake in oven for 45 minutes to 1 hour or until lightly browned on top. Allow to set for 20 minutes for flavors to develop.

Serve warm or at room temperature. Serve right from the baking pan placed on the table and have guests help themselves. Serve beans with quofte me mente *(recipe page 151).*

Albanian feasts often include extra sweet pastries and desserts. Greek and Middle Eastern pastries are favorite endings to the Muslim circumcision feasts or Christian baptism celebrations. *E matur* is one of the few Albanian pastries that is not doused in honey or sugar syrup. It is important to use unsalted butter in this recipe.

E Matur

Almond Pastry

Yield: 16 pieces
2 cups unsalted butter
2 cups sugar
1 cup water
2 teaspoons almond extract
1½ cups all-purpose flour, sifted
16 **blanched** whole almonds, for **garnish**

Equipment: 8-inch square cake pan, 8-inch square parchment paper, large **heavy-based** saucepan, wooden mixing spoon, rubber spatula, knife, oven mitts, serving plate

Prepare cake pan: Grease bottom and sides of 8-inch square cake pan. Set 8-inch square parchment paper in the bottom and grease paper.

Preheat oven to 400° F.

1. Melt butter in large saucepan over medium-high heat. Add sugar and water, stir, and bring to boil for 2 minutes. Add almond extract. Stir in flour all at once, reduce heat to low, and beat until mixture leaves sides of pan and forms a ball. Stirring constantly, cook 1 minute longer. Transfer flour mixture to prepared cake pan and spread smooth. Using a knife, mark off 16 squares (*4 equally spaced cuts, horizontally and vertically*) and place a blanched almond in the center of each square.

2. Bake at 400° F for 15 minutes, then reduce heat to 300° F and bake for 20 minutes more. Using oven mitts, remove from oven and allow to cool to room temperature in pan.

To serve, cut along marked lines and place pastries on serving plate.

BULGARIA

Situated in the heart of the Balkan Peninsula, Bulgaria borders the Black Sea on the east, Romania to the north, Serbia and

Macedonia to the west, and Greece and Turkey to the south. Due to its mountainous terrain, most of the population works and lives in urban areas.

After 40 years of religious restrictions imposed by the Communists, Bulgaria acquired freedom of worship in the late 1980s. Today, more than 90 percent of the people have returned to the Bulgarian Orthodox Church. (See Eastern or Orthodox Church Life-Cycle Rituals, page xlviii.) Bulgaria also has sizable Muslim and Roman Catholic communities. Each group follows the life-cycle customs and rituals of its church. (See Islam and Islamic Life-Cycle Rituals, page xlix, and Protestant and Catholic Life-Cycle Rituals, page xlvi.)

Bulgaria is particularly identified with yogurt, which was discovered by ancient Bulgarians. In 1908, the Russian microbiologist Ilya Metchnikoff isolated the lactic acid microbes in yogurt. He found that the microbes were the prime factor in promoting the unusual longevity found in some regions of Bulgaria, where it was claimed that a daily diet of natural yogurt containing **acidophilus** aided digestion and promoted good health and long life. Metchnikoff, who won the Nobel Prize in medicine for his discoveries, named the microbes *Bacillus bulgaricus*, in honor of the Bulgarian octogenarians that he studied.

Since the end of Communist rule, more Bulgarian weddings are being performed in churches. The long and solemn Orthodox wedding rituals are usually followed by a festive Bulgarian wedding meal, which is today often held at a restaurant and is traditionally paid for by the groom's family. Big or small, wedding receptions are usually noisy, exciting events with much music and dancing. Favorite beverages for wedding receptions are *boza*, made from fermented grain; *mastika*, a grape brandy; and *slivovitza*, a strong plum brandy; both brandies are used for making the wedding toast.

The Bulgarian wedding table might include suckling pig (recipe page 162) for Christian celebrations and spit roasted lamb (recipe page 141) for Muslims. Wedding dishes enjoyed by all Bulgarians, regardless of religion, include *rengha*, smoked herring (recipe follows); *sarmi*, stuffed grape leaves (recipe page 136); *agneski drebulijki*, shish kebab (recipe page 154); *shopska salata*, cucumber salad (recipe page 154); and breads of all sizes, shapes, and grains.

Bulgarian food is known for its strong flavors and extensive use of seasoning and garlic. For instance, the appetizer *rengha* (recipe follows) has a particularly distinctive taste. *Rengha* on toast is best eaten with a dab of yogurt or with the refreshing, nonalcoholic yogurt drink, *lassi*. A favorite beverage throughout the Balkans and Middle East, *lassi* is made simply by mixing equal amounts of yogurt and water in a glass of ice. ۞ ۞ ۞

Rengha

Smoked Herring Fillets (also Kipper Herring)

Yield: serves 4

- 3½-ounce canned smoked herring fillets (also called kipper snacks) (available at all supermarkets)
- juice from ½ of a lemon
- 3 tablespoons virgin olive oil
- 3 slices white bread, for serving
- 2 teaspoons minced fresh parsley or 1 teaspoon dried parsley flakes, for **garnish**
- ½ cup yogurt, for serving

Equipment: Knife, small bowl with cover, spoon, toaster, small side dish, small serving plate

1. Cut smoked herring into 1- to 2-inch pieces and put into small bowl. Sprinkle pieces with lemon juice and oil and stir to coat. Cover, and **marinate** for several hours or overnight.

2. At serving time, toast bread slices, **trim** off crusts, and cut each into 4 square pieces.

To serve, mound herring in center of small serving plate, sprinkle with parsley, and surround with toast squares. Serve with a side dish of yogurt. To eat, put one or two pieces of herring on the toast and add a dab of yogurt.

Shopska Salata

Cucumber Salad

Yield: serves 4

2 cloves garlic, **finely chopped**
1 cup shelled walnuts
2 tablespoons vinegar
½ cup virgin olive oil
salt and pepper to taste
1 or 2 cucumbers, peeled and finely chopped
2 lettuce leaves, washed and drained

Equipment: Electric **blender**, rubber spatula, small bowl with cover, shallow serving bowl

1. Put garlic, walnuts, and vinegar in blender. Cover, and **blend** on high speed for about 12 seconds. Run at slow speed and slowly pour oil through feed hole in cover until blended, about 10 seconds. Transfer to small bowl and add salt and pepper to taste. Cover and refrigerate.

2. At serving time, line shallow serving bowl with lettuce leaves, spoon chopped cucumber on top, and **drizzle** with walnut sauce.

Serve with basket of crackers or as a relish or topping with lamb or suckling pig.

Shish kebabs are a favorite meat dish throughout the Balkans and the Middle East. The origins of the dish can be traced back to nomads who, during their migrations, killed wild game, stuck it on their swords, and roasted it over the fire.

Agneski Drebulijki

Shish Kebab

Note: This recipe takes 24 hours.

CAUTION: GRILL OR BROILER USED

Yield: serves 4

2 pounds lean lamb or beef, cut into 2-inch cubes
6 cloves garlic, **finely chopped**
1 onion, finely chopped
1 cup yogurt, more as needed
½ cup olive oil
1 teaspoon *each*: salt and pepper
1 teaspoon dried oregano leaves
3 green bell pepper, trimmed and quartered
3 medium tomatoes, quartered
3 medium onions, peeled and quartered
12 mushrooms, rinsed and wiped dry
½ cup melted butter

Equipment: Medium bowl with cover, mixing spoon, 6 wooden or metal 10- or 12-inch skewers (if using wooden skewers, first soak in water for at least 30 minutes so they don't burn), charcoal **grill** or broiler pan, baking sheet, **pastry brush**, metal tongs, oven mitts, serving platter, small side dish

1. Put meat, chopped garlic, and chopped onion into medium bowl. Add 1 cup yogurt, oil, salt and pepper, and oregano. Mix well to coat meat, cover, and refrigerate for at least 24 hours. Stir occasionally.

2. Prepare to **grill** or broil: ADULT SUPERVISION REQUIRED. Have an adult preheat broiler or prepare charcoal grill at least 30 minutes before you want to cook.

3. Thread meat cubes on skewers, alternating them with pieces of green pepper, tomato, on-

ion, and whole mushroom. Place on baking sheet and brush on all sides with melted butter. Place side by side on grill or broiler pan. Using metal tongs, turn to brown all sides and cook through, 15 to 20 minutes.

To serve, transfer to serving platter and serve with bowl of yogurt for dipping.

ROMANIA

Bordered on the east by Moldova and the Black Sea, on the north by Ukraine, on the west by Hungary and Serbia, and on the south by Bulgaria, Romania was under Communist rule from the end of World War II until late 1989. The majority of Romanians belong to the Romanian Orthodox Church. (See Eastern or Orthodox Church Life-Cycle Rituals, page xlviii.) Roman Catholics comprise the largest minority group. (See Protestant and Catholic Life-Cycle Rituals, page xlvi.)

Under the Communist regime, religious observances were strongly discouraged, and most Romanian weddings were civil services conducted at the local mayor's office. Since the end of Communism, couples have been returning to the tradition of elaborate church weddings.

Romanian weddings, which usually occur on Sunday, are the focus of many traditions and rituals involving food and drink. The cooks know exactly when to bring out the food, and special "cup-bearers" are charged with maintaining a steady flow of drinks. *Tuica*, a plum brandy, is the main drink at weddings. The day before the wedding, a large loaf of bread is baked especially for the wedding ceremony and blessed by the priest. To complete the ceremony, the bride and groom, sharing the same plate and spoon, take bites out of the wedding loaf, while friends sprinkled them with water and grains of corn. Sprinkling the couple with these basics of life is a symbolic ritual that blesses them and wishes them a joyful life together.

The *székely* people, a predominately Hungarian group living in the Transylvania region of Romania, have wedding customs that differ from those practiced in other parts of either Romania or Hungary. *Székely* wedding couples traditionally have the *menyasszonykalácsfa*, a bridal cake tree also called a life tree or *életfa*. Each item placed on the *prémes* (furry twigs) of the tree symbolically expresses a good wish for the couple. The unusual name—furry twigs—probably comes from the elaborate items decorating the tree, which are copies of the embroidered decorations on the bride's wedding dress.

Preparing the *menyasszonykalácsfa* begins with selecting branches of the right size and shape, a task always performed by the men. The important thing is to select a sturdy central branch with many branches going upwards. The men clean the branches and remove the bark. The women then prepare the dough, the *csöröge* (recipe page 156), to cover the branches, or the branches are dipped into thick pancake batter (*palacsinta appareil*). With either coating, the branches are put into the oven to bake. (It might be best to work with smaller branches that can fit in the oven. After the branches are baked, **florist wire** can be used to wire them together.)

A large cake serves as the base of the tree. (Setting the branch in a block of Styrofoam covered with foil would make a more secure base. Conceal the foil with sheet cake, then frost.) Adults and children have a hand in making decorations, which can be crafted from colored ribbons; small fresh fruits, such as cherries, plums, apricots, or grapes; or cookie dough cut into the shapes of birds, frogs, flowers, leaves, and butterflies and then baked and hung from the tree. A pouch is often hung on the tree and filled with money intended for the bride.

The finished *menyasszonykalácsfa* is brought to the bride's house on the morning of the marriage together with all the wedding gifts. Along with the large decorated tree, a lucky bride may receive as many as 15 or 20 extra decorated *prémes* (furry twigs). The *prémes* are carried as symbols of good fortune in a procession to the new home of the newlyweds. At the end of the wedding dinner, guests break off twigs and eat the crusty coating. The bride usually sets aside the prettiest *prémes*, which she keeps for many years. The following pastry dough recipe can be used to coat the *prémes* or can be made into cookies to be placed around the *menyasszonykalacsfa* or hung from the branches of the tree.

Csöröge

Cookie Pastry Dough for Covering Branches

Yield: about 16 cookies or enough to cover a branch about the size of one to two coat hangers

- Prepare tree branches for covering (see preceding directions)
- 1 cup all-purpose flour
- 4 egg yolks
- ½ teaspoon sugar
- 1 teaspoon rum extract
- 1 tablespoon sour cream
- ¼ teaspoon salt
- confectioners' sugar, for **garnish**

Equipment: Food processor, rubber spatula, lightly floured work surface, lightly floured rolling pin, knife or cookie cutter of desired shapes, baking sheet, oven mitts, serving platter (if making cookies)

1. Put flour, egg yolks, sugar, rum extract, sour cream, and salt into food processor. Process until mixture pulls away from sides of container and forms a ball. Transfer to lightly floured work surface and **knead** into firm dough, 3 to 5 minutes. Let dough rest for 15 minutes.

Note: While processing, turn machine off once or twice and scrape down sides of container with rubber spatula.

Preheat oven to 350° F.

2. Using lightly floured rolling pin, roll dough about 1/8 inch thick.

3. To make *premes:* Place prepared branches on work surface. Cut dough into 1½-strips and wrap around branches completely covering them (like wrapping with bandages), and place on baking sheet.

4. To make cookies: Using cookie cutters, cut dough into desired shapes and place on baking sheet. If they are to be hung from the *menyasszonykalácsfa*, punch a hole in each cookie.

5. Bake in oven for 25 to 35 minutes, until golden. Carefully remove from oven and allow to cool to room temperature.

6. If you made cookies, sprinkle with confectioners' sugar.

The prémes *would be fun to make for birthday or anniversary celebrations. The cookies can be wired onto the branches or placed on a serving platter.*

The national dish of Romania is *ghiveci*, a medley of vegetables cooked in a special casserole dish called *guvens*. *Ghiveci* is traditionally made with whatever vegetables are available. Meat is often cooked with the vegetables, especially for baptism and wedding feasts.

Ghiveci

Medley of Vegetables Casserole

Yield: serves 6 to 8

water, as needed
2 potatoes, peeled and **cubed**
2 carrots, trimmed and sliced
2 celery ribs, trimmed and sliced
2 cups **cauliflowerets**, fresh or frozen (thawed)
½ pound green beans, trimmed and cut into 1-inch pieces or frozen (thawed) cut beans
2 tablespoons vegetable oil
2 onions, **finely chopped**
2 cloves garlic
4 tomatoes, chopped
salt and pepper to taste
1 teaspoon dried thyme leaves
1 zucchini, trimmed and sliced
1 green bell pepper, trimmed, seeded, and chopped

Equipment: Large saucepan with cover, **colander**, large skillet with cover, mixing spoon, greased medium casserole with cover or baking pan with cover, oven mitts

Preheat oven to 350° F.

1. Fill large saucepan with 1 to 2 inches water, add potatoes, carrots, celery, cauliflower, and green beans. Bring to boil over high heat, reduce heat to **simmer**, cover, and cook 10 minutes. Remove from heat and drain in colander. Discard liquid or cool, cover, and refrigerate liquid for another use.

2. Heat oil in large skillet over medium-high heat and add onions and garlic. Stir and **sauté** until soft, 3 to 5 minutes. Add tomatoes, salt and pepper to taste, and thyme. Stir, reduce heat to simmer, cover, and cook 5 minutes for flavors to develop. Remove from heat and keep covered.

3. Spread potato mixture over bottom of greased medium casserole or baking pan. Add salt and pepper to taste, and spread half the tomato mixture over top of potato mixture. Layer zucchini slices and chopped green pepper over tomato mixture. Top zucchini and green pepper with remaining tomato mixture.

4. Bake in oven, covered, for 50 to 60 minutes, until vegetables are tender.

Serve the casserole along with bors de pui *(recipe page 159) and* tocana cartofi *(recipe page 158). Be sure there is plenty of rye and pumpernickel bread on the table.*

Romanians are fond of *mezelicuri* (appetizers). A celebration meal always begins with a glass of *tuica* (plum brandy), wine, and assorted small snacks to satisfy the guests' hunger before the main meal. Some popular appetizers are *mititei*, grilled beef (recipe follows); fresh caviar and *icre* (carp roe), olives; green onions eaten with salt; *ayvar*, eggplant salad (recipe page 158); and slices of dark bread.

Mititei

Grilled Beef

Note: This recipe takes 24 hours.

CAUTION: GRILL OR BROILER USED

Yield: serves 6

1 pound **ground** beef
½ pound ground pork
1 teaspoon baking soda
½ teaspoon ground thyme
½ cup canned beef broth or water
4 cloves garlic, **finely chopped**
salt and pepper to taste
½ cup melted butter or margarine

Equipment: Food processor, rubber spatula, medium mixing bowl, baking sheet, wax paper, plastic food wrap, charcoal **grill** or broiler pan, metal tongs, oven mitts, **pastry brush**, serving platter

1. Put ground beef and pork, baking soda, thyme, water or beef broth, and garlic in food processor and process until well mixed and smooth. Transfer to medium mixing bowl and add salt and pepper to taste.

Note: While processing, turn machine off once or twice and scrape down sides of container with rubber spatula.

2. Cover baking sheet with wax paper. Using your hands, roll ½ cup meat mixture into a sausage shape about 4 inches long. Place on wax paper. Moisten your hands frequently with water to prevent meat from sticking as you work. Repeat making sausage shapes and place side by side on wax paper. Cover with plastic wrap and refrigerate for 8 hours or overnight for flavors to develop.

Prepare to grill or broil: ADULT SUPERVISION REQUIRED. Have an adult help prepare charcoal grill or preheat broiler.

3. Using pastry brush, brush sausages with melted butter. Place sausages side by side on grill or broiler pan. Using metal tongs, turn to brown all sides and cook through, about 7 to 10 minutes.

To serve, transfer to serving platter and serve warm, as an appetizer.

Ayvar

Eggplant Salad

Yield: about 2 cups

- 1 eggplant about 1 to 1½ pounds
- 2 cloves garlic, **finely chopped** or ½ teaspoon garlic granules
- juice from 1 lemon
- 2 tablespoons virgin olive oil, more as needed
- salt and pepper to taste
- 1 or 2 cucumbers, trimmed and sliced, for **garnish**

Equipment: Fork, 9-inch baking pan, oven mitts, spoon, small bowl, electric **blender**, rubber spatula, medium bowl with cover

Preheat oven to 400° F.

1. Poke eggplant skin with fork in about 8 or 10 places. Put in baking pan and bake until soft and tender, 30 to 40 minutes. Using oven mitts, remove from oven and when cool enough to handle, cut in half. Using spoon, scoop out insides of eggplant, and put in bowl. Discard eggplant skin.

2. Put insides of eggplant, garlic, lemon juice, and 2 tablespoons oil in blender and **blend** until smooth. If mixture is too dry, add ½ to 1 tablespoon more of oil and blend. Using rubber spatula, scrape eggplant mixture into medium bowl, add salt and pepper to taste, and stir. Cover and refrigerate for at least 2 hours for flavor to develop.

Serve as an appetizer dip with cucumber slices or eat as a spread on bread.

Potatoes are a much-loved Romanian vegetable. *Tocana cartofi* is a favorite way of preparing them.

Tocana Cartofi

Creamed Potatoes

Yield: serves 6

- 2 tablespoons vegetable oil
- 2 tablespoons flour
- 1 tablespoon paprika
- 2 cups canned beef broth
- 6 potatoes (2½ to 3 pounds), peeled and cubed
- ½ cup heavy cream
- salt and pepper to taste

Equipment: Large **heavy-based** skillet with cover, mixing spoon, serving bowl

1. Heat oil in large heavy-based skillet over medium heat, stir in flour until smooth. Slide skillet off heat and slowly stir in beef broth until smooth. Stir in paprika until well mixed. Return to heat and stir constantly until thickened, 3 to 5 minutes. Add potatoes, toss to coat, and cover. Cook for 20 to 25 minutes, until tender. Add cream, gently toss, cover, and cook for 5 minutes.

To serve, put into serving bowl to eat with bors de pui *(recipe follows).*

The following dish is typical of Romanian cooking, simple but full of flavor. Sauerkraut juice is often added instead of lemon juice to sharpen the flavor of food.

Bors de Pui

Poached Chicken

Yield: serves 6

- 3 to 4 pounds chicken, cut into serving pieces
- 4 cups water
- 4 onions, chopped
- 1 celery rib, sliced
- 2 leeks, white part only, well washed and sliced
- 1 carrot, trimmed and sliced
- salt and pepper to taste
- 2 cups sauerkraut juice, or juice from 2 lemons mixed with 2 cups water
- 3 **egg yolks**
- 1 cup sour cream
- 1 tablespoon fresh or dried dill, or tarragon leaves, for **garnish**

Equipment: Large **heavy-based** saucepan with cover or **Dutch oven**, mixing spoon

1. Put chicken into large heavy-based saucepan or Dutch oven. Add water, onions, celery, leeks, carrot, and salt and pepper to taste. Bring to boil over high heat, reduce heat to **simmer**, and cover. Cook for 45 minutes, until chicken is tender. Add sauerkraut juice or lemon juice mixture, stir, increase heat to medium-high, and bring to boil. Remove from heat.

2. Beat egg yolks with sour cream. **Temper** egg mixture, stir in ½ cup chicken broth. Return to pan with chicken mixture and stir to mix through.

To serve, transfer to serving bowl and sprinkle with dill or tarragon. Serve with side dishes of tocana cartofi *and* ghiveci. *Dessert is often* fructa crude *(fresh fruit). A bowl of apples, plums, peaches, and pears is put on the table with small plates and special fruit knifes for peeling the fruit. Peeling and eating fresh fruit is an art in Romanian culture. Using the fruit knife, one can carefully peel the fruit from the bottom, working up and around, keeping the peel in one long snake-like coil. To eat fruit, cut into bite-size pieces, never put the whole fruit in your mouth, that's considered crude and bad manners.*

FORMER YUGOSLAVIA—SERBIA, MONTENEGRO, SLOVENIA, CROATIA, BOSNIA-HERZEGOVINA, AND MACEDONIA

In 1991, Yugoslavia, a nonaligned Communist republic located on the eastern side of the Adriatic Sea in southeastern Europe, began to break up into a series of ethnically defined successor states. By the late 1990s, this complex patchwork of ethnic and religious groups included the countries of Serbia and Montenegro (which formed a loose federation still calling itself Yugoslavia), Slovenia, Croatia, Bosnia-Herzegovina, and Macedonia. Besides a collision of cultures, which has led to extensive warfare and violence in the 1990s, these neighboring states are troubled by friction arising from a diversity of religious groups, including Roman Catholics, Orthodox Christians, and Muslims.

Each group observes life-cycle celebrations according to its religion. (See Protestant and Catholic Life-Cycle Rituals, page xlvi, and Islam and Islamic Life-Cycle Rituals, page xlix.) The majority of people in Serbia and Montenegro are Serbian Orthodox, while the overwhelming majority of people in Croatia and Slovenia are Roman Catholic. Bosnia-Herzegovina is almost equally divided among Muslim Slavs, Orthodox Serbs, and Roman Catholic Croats. Most of the people of Macedonia belong to the Orthodox Church.

Although many religious and ethnic differences divide these Balkan states, food serves as a unifying thread. Slow cooked vegetable soups and stews, with meat added whenever the budget allows, are favored dishes. Christian celebration feasts call for lamb or *prebranac peceno prase* (roasted **suckling pig** with baked lima beans, recipes pages 162 and 163); Muslim feasts traditionally serve roast lamb or goat (recipe page 141). Fruits and vegetables and breads and pastries doused in honey are prepared much the same way in every Balkan kitchen—only the name of the dish changes depending on the language of the householder.

Soups, a favorite beginning to a Balkan meal, are hearty and thick, and are included in most life-cycle celebration feasts. The combination of vegetables depends upon the season, the cook, or (at a wedding feast) the preferences of the bride and groom. Soup is always eaten with bread. ❂ ❂ ❂

Kisela Corba

National Soup of Serbia

Yield: serves 6 to 8

- 4 tablespoons vegetable oil
- 2 pounds chicken, pork, or lamb, cut into small pieces
- 2½ quarts water
- 1 parsnip, trimmed and chopped
- 2 carrots, trimmed and chopped
- 2 celery ribs with leafy tops, chopped
- 2 onions, chopped
- ½ cup white rice
- 1 teaspoon paprika
- salt and pepper to taste
- 1 cup sour cream
- 2 **egg yolks**, beaten
- 2 tablespoons cider vinegar

Equipment: Large saucepan with cover or **Dutch oven**, mixing spoon, small saucepan, small mixing bowl, individual soup bowls

1. Heat oil in large saucepan or Dutch oven over medium-high heat. Add chicken or meat, and brown on all sides, 5 to 7 minutes. Add water, bring to boil over high heat, reduce heat to **simmer**, cover, and cook 1 hour.

2. Add parsnip, carrots, celery with leafy tops, onions, rice, paprika, and salt and pepper to taste. Bring to boil, reduce heat to simmer, stir, and cover. Cook for ½ hour, until chicken or meat and vegetables are tender.

3. Stir ½ cup hot soup into egg yolks to **temper.** Stirring constantly, slowly return tempered egg yolks to hot soup. (Egg yolks slightly thicken the soup.) Remove from heat. In small bowl, beat together sour cream and vinegar, and stir into soup until well mixed.

To serve, ladle soup into individual bowls with chunks of chicken or meat. When eating soup, bread is often broken into bite-size pieces and dropped into the bowl. Allow the bread to soak up the rich broth before eating.

Bread is eaten at every meal and special breads are baked and blessed by the priest for christenings and weddings. Adding eggs to the dough makes the bread special. The Macedonian rich egg bread *pogacha* is the same as Jewish *challah* (recipe page 105). For weddings, the *pogacha* is braided, like the *challah*, but the ends are pinched together making a large braided wreath. After brushing the braided wreath with **egg wash** but before putting it in the oven, sprinkle 2 tablespoons of sesame seeds over the top.

For many Balkan Christians, baptism is the most important event in a child's life. The church baptismal service is usually followed by a feast, either at home or in a restaurant. If the celebration is at home, family puts the *Bosanski lonac* (Bosnian meat pie, recipe follows) in the oven to slow cook. In some villages, the sealed container is taken to the baker who bakes it for the family.

Bosanski Lonac

Bosnian Meat Pot

Yield: serves 6

1 cup shredded cabbage
3 potatoes, peeled and **cubed**
salt and pepper to taste
2½ pounds pork, beef, or lamb, or any combination, cubed
8 cloves garlic, peeled
1 cup water
2 cups canned stewed tomatoes, divided
1 cup pearl onions, peeled, fresh, frozen, or canned (drained)
1 cup **diced** carrots
1 cup diced celery
3 sprigs fresh parsley, finely chopped or 2 teaspoons dried parsley flakes

Equipment: Greased medium heat-proof earthenware casserole with cover or **Dutch oven**, heavy-duty aluminum foil, oven mitts, trivet

Preheat oven to 325° F.

1. Spread shredded cabbage over bottom of greased medium heat-proof earthenware casserole or Dutch oven. Layer potatoes over cabbage, and sprinkle with salt and pepper to taste. Add meat, whole garlic cloves, water, and 1 cup stewed tomatoes. Add onions, carrots, celery, and remaining 1 cup stewed tomatoes. Sprinkle with salt and pepper to taste and parsley flakes. Cover and seal with heavy-duty foil so no steam can escape while cooking.

2. Cook in oven for 3½ hours. Using oven mitts, carefully remove from the oven. Allow to rest 15 minutes before serving.

To serve, take the pot to the table and place on a trivet. Using oven mitts, remove foil and lid in front of the guests, releasing all the appetizing aromas.

Cabbage is a staple in most European kitchens, especially when made into sauerkraut. The following unusual but simple recipe would be served as a side dish with *Bosanski lonac*. After much eating and drinking at a wedding celebration, sauerkraut juice, considered a digestive aid, is often consumed to quiet the stomach.

Podvarak

Baked Sauerkraut

Yield: serves 6 to 8

4 cups (2 pounds) canned sauerkraut
3 tablespoons bacon drippings or vegetable oil
2 onions, **finely chopped**
2 tart apples, peeled, cored, and **diced**
½ cup brown sugar
1 potato, peeled and grated
salt and pepper to taste
1 cup sour cream
6 ounces canned tomato paste

Equipment: Strainer, medium bowl, mixing spoon, large skillet, 2 forks, greased medium casserole or baking pan, oven mitts

Preheat oven to 350° F.

1. Drain sauerkraut in strainer, discard juice or cover and refrigerate juice for another use. Rinse sauerkraut under cold running water, press out water with your hands, and transfer to medium bowl.

2. Heat bacon drippings or oil in large skillet over medium-high heat. Add onions and apples, stir, and **sauté** until soft, 3 to 5 minutes. Separate sauerkraut with your hands as you add it to onion mixture, so it doesn't lump. Reduce heat to **simmer**. Add brown sugar, grated potato, and salt and pepper to taste. Using 2 forks, toss to mix. Cover and cook for 10 minutes for flavors to blend.

3. In small bowl, mix sour cream and tomato paste. Transfer sauerkraut mixture to greased medium casserole or baking pan. Pour sour cream mixture over top of sauerkraut, toss to mix.

4. Bake in oven for 30 to 40 minutes, or until golden and bubbly.

To serve, put casserole or baking pan on the table and serve as a side dish with Bosanski lonac.

If the wedding is in winter, Serbs roast a 50- or 60-pound hog for the reception; if it's in the summer, lamb is the preferred meat. The roasting is done out of doors, snow or sunshine, non-stop, day and night, for perhaps 20 to 30 hours. Even children take turns working the hand crank that rotates the pig over the fire for even roasting. The *razhan* (rod or spit), which is rammed through the length of the animal, rests on steel tripods on either side of the fire. A drip pan is usually employed to catch the pig grease. Toward the end of the roasting, loaves of bread are set in the pan to absorb the grease. This grease-soaked bread is a delicacy that is served with the meat. *Prebanac* (lima beans, recipe follows) are almost always served with the pig.

Peceno Prase

Roast Suckling Pig

Yield: 10 to 12

10- to 15-pound **oven-ready** suckling pig
kosher salt to taste
1 lemon
1 cup vegetable oil
12-ounce bottle light beer or 1½ cups apple cider
small apple, for **garnish**

Equipment: Aluminum foil, large roasting pan with rack, **bulb baster** or large mixing spoon

Preheat oven to 400° F.

1. Rub inside of pig with kosher salt. Wrap a lemon with foil and place in the mouth of the pig to keep the mouth open during baking. Set the pig in an upright position on the rack in the roasting pan. Rub oil over the entire outside of pig. Cover ears and tail with foil to prevent burning.

2. Bake pig in oven for about 5 hours, basting frequently with beer or apple cider and pan drippings, using bulb baster or large mixing spoon.

Serve the pig at room temperature with prebanac *(recipe follows),* pogacha *(Macedonia Egg bread; the recipe is the same as* challah, *page 105), and salad.*

Prebanac

Baked Lima Beans

Note: This recipe takes 24 hours.

Yield: serves 6 to 8

4 cups large dried lima beans
2 bay leaves

1 cup vegetable oil
4 red onions, **finely chopped**
2 tablespoons paprika
salt and pepper to taste

Equipment: Large bowl, **colander**, large saucepan with cover, mixing spoon, greased **Dutch oven** or greased large oven-proof casserole, oven mitts

1. Soak beans overnight in water. When ready to cook, drain beans in colander. Transfer to large saucepan and add water to reach at least 2 inches above top of beans. Add bay leaves, bring to boil over high heat, and stir. Reduce heat to **simmer**, cover, and cook 1½ hours, or until soft. Remove and discard bay leaves.

2. Heat oil in large skillet over medium-high heat. Add onions and **sauté** until soft, 3 to 5 minutes. Sprinkle in paprika and salt and pepper to taste, and stir to mix well. Add onions and pan drippings to cooked beans and stir. Transfer beans to greased Dutch oven or greased large oven-proof casserole.

Preheat oven to 350° F.

3. Bake in oven for 35 to 45 minutes, or until top is golden brown.

To serve, put pot of beans on the table and serve warm with peceno prase (recipe precedes).

Every Balkan country has its own version of strudel, the famous pastry made with thin layers of **phyllo** dough, which is used for both sweet and savory dishes. When made sweet, a dish called *zeljanica* is filled with fruits, nuts, or soft cheese, and is sometimes doused with honey. The same dish is known in Cyprus as *tirópeta tou spetioú* (recipe page 126). The following apple-filled pastry recipe (*triglav strudel*) is often used by Serbian Christians to make a festivity cake that is part of the celebration of the Festival of Holy Petkovica on October 27, the feast of Saint Petka, the patron saint of Serbian women.

Triglav Strudel

Apple Filled Pastry

Yield: serves 8

1 pound cooking apples, peeled, cored, and chopped
¼ cup sugar
1 teaspoon **ground** cinnamon
½ teaspoon **allspice**
½ cup seedless raisins
4 sheets (14- x 18-inches) frozen **phyllo** pastry, thawed (according to directions on package)
½ cup melted butter
1 cup fresh **bread crumbs**, divided
confectioners' sugar, for **garnish**

Equipment: Work surface, clean damp kitchen towel, medium bowl, mixing spoon, 16- x 20-inch sheet heavy-duty aluminum foil (join 2 pieces together), **pastry brush**, greased baking sheet, oven mitts

Preheat oven at 375° F.

Unwrap phyllo according to directions on package, place on work surface, and cover with damp towel to keep from drying out.

1. In medium bowl, mix apples, sugar, cinnamon, allspice, and raisins.

2. Lay 1 phyllo sheet on 16- x 20-inch piece of foil, and brush phyllo with melted butter. Repeat layering 3 more sheets, brushing each with melted butter before covering with next sheet. Brush top sheet with melted butter.

3. Sprinkle bread crumbs over the pastry, leaving about 1½-inch border on all sides. Spread apple mixture over bread crumbs. Fold over border, then roll up the long side of the phyllo, jelly roll-style, to enclose the apple mixture. (Strudel should be about 15 inches long.) Pull up on the foil to help roll up the strudel. On greased baking sheet, remove foil as you carefully turn strudel over seam-side down. Discard foil. Brush pastry with remaining melted butter.

4. Bake in oven for 30 to 40 minutes, or until golden. While still warm, sprinkle with confectioners' sugar, for garnish.

To serve, cut crosswise into two-inch thick slices. Eat strudel with a fork, while it is still warm.

HUNGARY

Hungary, a small landlocked country in central Europe, is bordered on the east by Romania, the north by Slovakia, the west by Austria, and the south by Croatia and Serbia. Hungary is predominantly a Roman Catholic country with a large Protestant minority. From the end of World War II to the 1970s, Hungary's Communist government strictly controlled religion. However, at the end of the latter decade, relations between the Hungarian government and the Roman Catholic Church improved. Today, Hungarians observe most religious life-cycle celebrations according to their church. (See Protestant and Catholic Life-Cycle Rituals, page xlvi.)

Although life-cycle celebrations, especially weddings, vary from region to region and from city to village, a day-long round of feasting and dancing before and after the wedding ceremony is common. In the past, appetizers (*elöételek*) were only served in the dining halls of the aristocracy, not by the peasants. Appetizer dishes would not be eaten first by most Hungarians, but with the meal. The following cheese spread recipe would be used on bread or eaten with fruit at the end of the meal. It is from the north Hungarian region of *Liptó*. Neighboring Austrians make a popular substitute called *liptauer* (available at all supermarkets), which many people think is Hungarian, but it is not. When the recipe combines authentic *Liptó* cheese with butter, it is called *körözött júhtúró*, and when cottage cheese is combined with cream cheese it is called *liptauer garniert*.

KÖRÖZÖTT JÚHTÚRÓ (ALSO LIPTAUER GARNIERT)

CHEESE SPREAD

Note: This recipe takes 24 hours.

Yield: about 2½ cups

- 1 cup large-curd cottage cheese or *Liptó* (sheep's-milk cheese, available at most cheese shops and some specialty food stores)
- 1 cup butter or cream cheese, at room temperature
- 2 tablespoons anchovy paste (available at all supermarkets)
- 2 teaspoons prepared mustard
- 4 tablespoons grated onion
- 2 teaspoons caraway seeds
- 1 tablespoon Hungarian paprika

Equipment: Food processor, rubber spatula, small bowl with cover

1. Combine large-curd cottage cheese or *Liptó* cheese and butter or cream cheese in food processor. Add anchovy paste, prepared mustard, grated onion, caraway seeds, and paprika. Process for about 1 minute, until smooth.

Note: While processing, turn machine off once or twice and scrape down sides of container with rubber spatula.

2. Transfer cheese spread to small bowl, cover, and refrigerate for at least 24 hours for flavors to develop.

Serve as a spread for bread or crackers, or a dip for raw vegetables such as carrot, celery, and zucchini sticks.

Although stuffed cabbage is prepared in all Balkan countries, few recipes are better than the *töltött kaposzta* made in Hungary. Cabbage, whether as little stuffed cabbages for appetizers or as whole heads filled with ground meat, is prepared for most Hungarian life-cycle celebrations.

TÖLTÖTT KAPOSZTA

STUFFED CABBAGE

Yield: serves 8

water, as needed
salt and pepper, as needed and to taste
1 large green cabbage
3/4 pound *each*: **ground** beef and pork
1 onion, **finely chopped**
1 egg
1 cup raw white rice
3 cups canned stewed tomatoes with juice
2 cups water
1 tablespoon Hungarian paprika, for serving
1 cup sour cream, for serving

Equipment: Paring knife, work surface, large **heavy-based** saucepan with cover, oven mitts, metal tongs, large pan, medium bowl, large mixing bowl, large serving bowl, small side dish

1. Prepare cabbage: Using paring knife, cut out and discard the core at the bottom of cabbage. Fill large saucepan more than halfway with water, add 1 teaspoon salt, and bring to boil over high heat. Reduce heat to **simmer,** add whole cabbage with head facing down. **Blanch cabbage** until leaves soften, 4 to 5 minutes. Use metal tongs to press down on cabbage to keep submerged in water. Using oven mitts and metal tongs, lift cabbage out and transfer to large pan. When cool enough to handle, carefully peel cabbage leaves off, leaving them whole. Place cabbage in medium bowl. If leaves become difficult to peel off, put cabbage back into boiling water for 3 or 4 minutes until you have 8 to 10 separated leaves. Cut out and discard any tough, fibrous vein at the bottom end of each leaf. (The leaves should be soft and flexible.) Discard water in large saucepan. Chop small leaves from center of cabbage, and spread over bottom of large saucepan.

2. Prepare stuffing: Put beef, pork, onion, egg, salt and pepper to taste, and raw rice in large mixing bowl. Using your hands, mix thoroughly.

3. Stuff cabbage leaves: Place a cabbage leaf on work surface with leafy top edge toward center of table or counter. Place 2 or 3 tablespoons meat mixture in center of leaf. Fold over sides, covering filling, and roll up, beginning at the bottom edge of the leaf. Place stuffed cabbage, seam-side down on top of cabbage leaves in large saucepan. Repeat stuffing until all meat mixture is used. If there are extra leaves, coarsely chop them and spread over top of cabbage rolls. Pour stewed tomatoes and water over top of stuffed cabbage.

4. Bring to boil over high heat, reduce heat to simmer, cover, and cook for 1½ hours.

5. Prepare for serving: Transfer cabbage rolls to serving bowl. Pour cooking liquid into small bowl, and stir in paprika and sour cream to make a sauce to drizzle over cabbage rolls.

Serve cabbage rolls as an appetizer or main course at the wedding banquet. Serve plenty of Macedonian pogacha *(recipe [same as Jewish challah—recipe page 105]) for sopping up juices and Romanian* tocana cartofi *(recipe page 158).*

The word *kalác* comes from the Slavic word *kolo* meaning circle. *Kalács* are sweet cakes, plain or stuffed with raisins, candied fruit, and nuts made of yeast dough. There are special shaped *kalács* for weddings, holidays, name days, and other life-cycle events. For funeral feasts, woven or braided *kalács* signify the hair sacrifice placed on a fresh grave. Among some groups, *kalác* is baked in the shape of a small ring and placed on the arm of a stillborn baby, so the infant will have something to nibble on and play with when arriving in the hereafter.

Ostor Kalács

Braided Coffeecake

Yield: 1 large loaf

- 1 cup milk
- ½ cup butter or margarine
- 1 package dry **yeast**
- ½ cup sugar
- 2 eggs, beaten
- 4 to 5½ cups all-purpose flour
- ½ teaspoon salt
- 1 cup confectioners' sugar, more as needed, for icing
- 3 teaspoons water, more as needed, for icing
- 8 to 12 walnut halves, for **garnish**
- 8 to 12 candied cherries, for garnish

Equipment: Small saucepan, mixing spoon, flour **sifter**, large mixing bowl, lightly floured work surface, clean kitchen towel, greased baking sheet or large pizza pan, oven mitts, toothpick, wire cake rack, dinner knife or **icing** spatula, **pastry brush**

1. Warm milk in small saucepan with butter until melted, then cool to lukewarm. Sprinkle yeast on top and leave for 5 minutes or until dissolved. Stir in sugar and eggs.

2. **Sift** flour and salt into large mixing bowl. Make a well (hole) in flour mixture, add yeast mixture, and stir to form smooth dough. Mix with your hands until dough pulls away from sides of bowl. Transfer to lightly floured work surface. **Knead** for 5 minutes, or until dough is smooth and elastic. Transfer to large greased mixing bowl and turn to coat all sides. Cover with towel and set in warm place to rise to double in bulk, ¾ to 1 hour.

3. Knead dough lightly in bowl to knock out air bubbles. Pull sides to the center, turn dough over, and cover with towel. Let dough rise again for 30 minutes.

4. Transfer dough to lightly floured work surface and divide into 3 equal parts. Shape dough into ropes about 14 inches long. Pinch the 3 ropes together at one end and braid them together. When finished braiding, pinch the other end of the braided dough together. Transfer braided dough to greased baking sheet or large pizza pan. Shape braided dough into a ring, and join ends smoothly together. Cover lightly with towel and let rise a third time in warm place 30 to 40 minutes, or until almost double in bulk.

Preheat oven to 375° F.

5. Bake in oven for 25 to 35 minutes, or until golden brown and toothpick inserted in center comes out clean. Remove from oven and transfer to wire cake rack to cool.

6. Decorate cake: Put 1 cup confectioners' sugar into small bowl and stir in 3 tablespoons water to make soft icing. If too thin, add little more confectioners' sugar. If too thick, add more water. Using dinner knife or icing spatula, spread icing over top of ring while still warm. Garnish with walnuts and cherries, and lightly brush them with icing.

To serve, place on table as the centerpiece of the wedding feast. A candle can be set into the center of the ring. To eat, cut into 2-inch thick slices.

Szalámi (sausage-shaped) candy is popular in Hungary. The candies are made with different shelled nuts, candied cherries, and even poppy seeds and honey. *Szalámi* are often coated with crushed nuts.

Mandulás Szalámi

Chocolate Marzipan Candy

Yield: about 24 pieces

- 1 tube (8 ounce) **almond paste** (available at all supermarkets)
- 2 squares (1 ounce each) semisweet chocolate, melted and cooled
- ¼ cup almonds, **finely chopped**

confectioners' sugar, as needed

Equipment: Food processor, rubber spatula, work surface, serving plate

1. Put almond paste, melted chocolate, and almonds in food processor and process until well mixed, 1 or 2 minutes.

Note: While processing, turn machine off once or twice and scrape down sides of container with rubber spatula.

2. Transfer almond mixture to work surface sprinkled with 1 or 2 tablespoons confectioners' sugar. Using your hands, **knead** into a log about 6 inches long. Sprinkle almond mixture with more confectioners' sugar to coat. Wrap in plastic wrap and refrigerate for at least 12 hours. Unwrap and cut roll crosswise into ¼-inch slices.

To serve, place slightly overlapping on serving plate and serve as a sweet treat for a baptism or name day party.

CZECH REPUBLIC AND REPUBLIC OF SLOVAKIA

In 1993, after years of internal ethnic rivalry, the Central European nation of Czechoslovakia split into two independent states—the Czech Republic and the Republic of Slovakia. The division, initiated by the Slovaks, was amiable. Although most Czechs regretted the separation, the Czech Republic has become the most stable former Communist state in Europe. Many citizens from the less-developed Republic of Slovakia have moved west to the Czech Republic where they can find greater economic and cultural opportunities. Thousands of mixed marriages have occurred between the Czech and Slovak peoples and the two groups have made progress in resolving their differences.

Both countries are predominantly Roman Catholic and most life-cycle celebrations are conducted according to their religion. (See Protestant and Catholic Life-Cycle Rituals, page xlvi.) As in all Christian countries, baptism is a special family event. After a baptism, many urban Czechs and Slovaks prefer dining in a restaurant while relatives in the country prefer to hold their baptism celebration meal at home. The national dish for both Czechs and Slovaks, whether urban or rural, is *knedliki s vepová a zeli* (dumplings, sauerkraut, and roast pork) (recipe page 168). ❂ ❂ ❂

SAUERKRAUT

FERMENTED CABBAGE

Yield: serves 6 to 8

2 pounds finely shredded cabbage
2 teaspoons **kosher salt**

Equipment: Work surface, clean kitchen towel, large saucepan, 1 quart Mason jar with 2-part dome lid, oven mitts, metal tongs

Sterilize jar: Prepare clean work surface and cover with a clean towel. Fill large saucepan ¾ full with water. Bring to boil over high heat, lay jar on its side in the water, add lid, and boil for 5 minutes. Wearing oven mitts and using metal tongs, carefully remove jar from water, dump out water, and place upside down to drain on towel. Remove 2-part dome lid and place on towel.

1. Tightly pack jar halfway with shredded cabbage. Add 1 teaspoon salt. Tightly pack remaining cabbage, filling to shoulder of jar. Add remaining 1 teaspoon salt. Add cold water up to rim of jar. Set lid loosely on top of jar.

2. Let stand at room temperature for 9 days, adding more cold water each day as water level

drops. Screw lid tight and refrigerate until ready to serve.

Serve sauerkraut as a side dish or condiment or make knedliki s vepová a zeli *(recipe follows).*

Knedliki s Vepová a Zeli

Dumplings, Sauerkraut, and Roast Pork

Yield: serves 6 to 8

- 2 pounds sauerkraut, homemade (preceding recipe) or 32-ounce canned sauerkraut
- 2 cups water, more as needed
- 3½- to 4½-pound **oven-ready** boned pork roast
- salt and pepper to taste
- 1 teaspoon paprika
- ½ cup vegetable oil
- 3 cloves garlic, **finely chopped**
- 7.5-ounce tube ready-to-bake homestyle or buttermilk biscuits, for dumplings (available in refrigerated section of all supermarkets)

Equipment: **Colander**, large roasting pan with cover, large skillet, mixing spoon, metal tongs, **meat thermometer (optional)**, **bulb baster** or mixing spoon, oven mitts, medium saucepan, scissors, slotted spoon, medium bowl, serving platter

1. Drain sauerkraut in colander and rinse under cold water. Spread drained sauerkraut over bottom of large roasting pan, and add 2 cups water.

Preheat oven to 325° F.

2. Rub pork with salt and pepper and paprika.

3. Heat oil in large skillet over medium-high heat. Add garlic, stir, and **sauté** 1 to 2 minutes to release flavor. Add pork roast and brown on all sides, 5 to 7 minutes. Using metal tongs, put browned pork roast on top of sauerkraut in roasting pan, and pour pan drippings from skillet over top.

4. Bake, covered, in oven 2¼ to 3 hours (allow 35 to 45 minutes baking time per pound). Check doneness: Meat thermometer inserted into meat registers 175° to 185° F, roast is well done. Using bulb baster or spoon, **baste** pan drippings over meat once or twice during baking. Remove from oven and allow meat to rest about 20 minutes before slicing.

5. Prepare dumplings: Fill medium saucepan halfway with water, add 1 teaspoon salt, and bring to boil over high heat. Open tube of ready-to-bake biscuits and separate biscuits. Using scissors, cut each biscuit in half and drop into boiling water. Cook in batches, if necessary to avoid crowding pan. Reduce to rolling boil, turning over once or twice. Cook about 10 minutes, or until dumplings come to surface, and then cook for 3 to 5 minutes longer. Taste for doneness and adjust cooking time accordingly. (When dumplings are light and airy and no longer taste doughy, they are done.) Remove with slotted spoon and place in medium bowl.

To serve, place slices of meat in center of serving platter, surround with sauerkraut, and spoon dumplings over meat. Serve at once.

Special breads are baked for baptisms, name day celebrations, weddings, and funeral feasts. For baptisms, the *houska* (a braided raisin bread) is blessed by the priest and at the celebration feast the godparents are given the honor of cutting the first slice from the loaf.

Houska

Two Tier Braided Raisin Bread

Yield: 1 loaf

- 1 envelope active dry **yeast**
- ¼ cup **lukewarm** water
- 1 teaspoon sugar
- 4½ cups all-purpose flour, divided
- 1 teaspoon salt

1 teaspoon grated lemon rind
1 cup milk
½ cup butter
½ cup sugar
½ cup *each:* seedless raisins and sultanas (golden raisins)
1 whole egg
2 **eggs, separated**
½ cup sliced **blanched** almonds

Equipment: Small bowl, flour **sifter**, large mixing bowl, mixing spoon, small saucepan, kitchen towel, well floured work surface, knife, greased baking sheet, **pastry brush**, oven mitts, bread basket

1. In small bowl, **proof** yeast in lukewarm water with 1 teaspoon sugar for 10 minutes.

2. **Sift** 3 cups flour and salt into large mixing bowl, and add grated lemon rind.

3. **Scald milk** in small saucepan over medium-high heat. Add butter or margarine, stir until melted. Remove from heat, add sugar, raisins, and sultanas, and cool to lukewarm. Put 1 whole egg and 2 egg yolks in cup, and lightly beat with fork. Stir eggs into lukewarm milk mixture. Pour yeast mixture into milk mixture and stir. Pour the mixed yeast and milk combination into flour mixture, and stir until smooth. Cover with towel and let rise in a warm place for 1 to 1½ hours, or until double in bulk.

4. Transfer dough to floured work surface. **Knead** in about 1½ cups flour, ½ cup at a time, until dough is smooth and satiny, 10 to 15 minutes. Cut dough into 7 equal pieces.

5. Roll pieces into 13-inch long ropes. Place 4 ropes side by side, and pinch them together at one end. Braid ropes together and pinch finished ends when finished. Place braided loaf on greased baking sheet and pinched tuck ends under. Braid remaining 3 ropes together, pinch ends, and tuck under. Place center of larger braided loaf on top of smaller loaf, with both loaves running in same direction. Beat 2 **egg whites** in small bowl until frothy, 1 minute. Using pastry brush, brush loaf with egg white. Cover with towel and let rise in warm place for 1 hour, or until double in bulk. Using a pastry brush, gently brush again with egg white, and sprinkle with sliced blanched almonds.

Preheat oven to 425° F.

6. Bake in oven 35 to 40 minutes, or until golden brown.

To serve, slice and place in bread basket with other breads for the celebration feast.

After a Czech or Slovak funeral, a small reception for mourners, with food and beverages, is held at the house of the deceased. After a final farewell toast to the deceased, everyone eats a light meal that usually includes a fruit dumpling called *ovocné knedlíky* (recipe follows), bread such as *houska* (recipe precedes), and cheeses, fruits, and cakes with brandy, as well as schnapps (an alcoholic beverage) and hot tea.

Ovocné Knedlíky

Fruit Dumplings

Yield: serves 6
1 tablespoon butter
½ cup cottage cheese
1 **egg yolk**
salt, as needed
4 tablespoons milk
1 cup all-purpose flour, **sifted**
12 *fresh, pitted*: plums, apricots, peach halves, or prunes
6 teaspoons **cinnamon sugar**
¼ cup melted butter
granulated sugar, for **garnish**

Equipment: Food processor, rubber spatula, large mixing bowl, plastic food wrap, lightly floured rolling pin, lightly floured work surface, knife, large saucepan with cover, slotted spoon, serving bowl

1. Put butter, cottage cheese, egg yolk, ½ teaspoon salt, and milk in food processor. While processor is running, add flour through feed tube. Pulse until flour mixture leaves sides of container, about 1 minute. Transfer to large mixing bowl, cover with plastic wrap, and let rest 30 minutes.

Note: While processing, turn machine off once or twice and scrape down sides of container with rubber spatula.

2. Using lightly floured rolling pin, roll dough on lightly floured work surface into a 9- x 12-inch rectangle, about ¼ inch thick. Using a knife, cut twelve 3-inch square pieces. Place pitted fruit in center of each square, and sprinkle with ½ teaspoon cinnamon sugar. Wrap dough into a ball around fruit.

3. Fill large saucepan halfway with water. Add 1 teaspoon salt for each quart of water and bring to boil over high heat. Drop dumplings into boiling water, a few at a time. Cover and cook about 8 to 10 minutes, or when dumplings rise to the top. reduce heat to **simmer**, and cook 3 to 5 minutes longer. Use slotted spoon to remove and drain well. Taste a dumpling and adjust cooking time for doneness. When done, put into serving bowl, pour melted butter over, and sprinkle with sugar.

Serve hot as dessert.

AUSTRIA

For more than 600 years, until the end of World War I in 1918, Austria was the heart of a powerful empire that included Hungary and Czechoslovakia and stretched from southern Poland to the Adriatic. Its capital, Vienna, was one of the most exciting cities in Europe—an international center of great music and fine cuisine.

Although present-day Austria is only a tiny remnant of the old Austro-Hungarian Empire, its geographic position on the southeastern approach to Western Europe and on the north-south routes between Germany and Italy gave it great strategic importance during World War II and the Cold War.

Most Austrians are of German decent and the majority belong to the Roman Catholic Church, celebrating most life-cycle events according to the Church's rites and traditions. (See Protestant and Catholic Life-Cycle Rituals, page xlvi.)

To Austrians, eating is serious business and great care is taken to provide the finest fare for life-cycle celebrations. Austrian christenings, first communions, weddings, wedding anniversaries, and funerals are usually memorable events. Austrians eat not only well, but often. The day begins with coffee, milk, and wonderful rolls. *Gabelfrühstück* (fork breakfast) is a hearty mid-morning meal. The big meal of the day is at noon and usually includes soup, meat, vegetables, potatoes, and rich dessert. Celebration feasts usually take place at the midday meal, and often expand the menu to include fish or the much-prized venison from the Austrian Alps. Late afternoon is the time for *jause*, a coffee and dessert break, and evening supper is usually light, often just soup, salad, and bread. A pastry or cake, for which Austria is world famous, is usually eaten as a bedtime snack.

Austrian cooking has been enriched by neighboring influences—paprika dishes from Hungary; dumplings from Germany; and pasta, tomato cookery, and *schnitzel* (which started out as *piccata alla Milanese*) from Italy. The Turks, who besieged Vienna twice, get credit for Austria's heavenly coffees: *melange* (coffee with milk), *melange mit schlag* (coffee with milk and whipped cream), *Wiener eiskaffee* (Viennese Iced Coffee) (recipe page 173), and *mokka* (black coffee). Whatever the dish, in Austrian kitchens it has been refined, enriched, and generally improved, assuming a new, uniquely Austrian character.

A typical Austrian celebration meal begins with *vorspeise* (appetizer), *suppe* (soup), *hauptspeise* (main course) and *beilagen* (several raw and cooked side dishes). Also included are either *kuchen* or *torte* (cake) or *mehlspeise* (any baked specialty made with flour). A warm or cold after-meal sweet treat, *nachspeise,* is served during the dancing part of the celebration. With a fine meal, Austrian adults favor drinking beer, wine, or *sekt* (sparkling wine). Children drink fruit flavored waters and wine spritzers (wine mixed with sparking water).

Often, more than one kind of soup is prepared for a celebration feast. *Geröstete brotsuppe* is an unusual and popular soup made with bread. When stale white bread is used, *geröstete brotsuppe* is called *panadisuppe.*

Geröstete Brotsuppe

Bread Soup

Yield: serves 6

- 5 or 6 slices (about 5 ounces) Jewish rye bread, cut into **cubes**
- 2 tablespoons finely chopped fresh parsley or 2 teaspoons dried parsley flakes
- 3 tablespoons all-purpose flour
- 6 tablespoons butter or margarine
- 1 onion, **finely chopped**
- 3 cloves garlic, finely chopped
- 3 cups water
- 3 cups canned beef broth
- salt and white pepper to taste
- 2 eggs
- 2 tablespoons heavy cream
- ½ teaspoon **ground** nutmeg

Equipment: Medium bowl, mixing spoon, large saucepan or **Dutch oven**, metal spatula, small bowl, ladle, electric **blender**, rubber spatula, fork

1. Put bread cubes in medium bowl, sprinkle in parsley and flour, and toss to coat.

2. Melt butter or margarine in large saucepan or Dutch oven over medium-high heat. Add onions and garlic, and **sauté** for 2 to 3 minutes or until onions are soft, stirring constantly. . Using metal spatula, add bread cube mixture and toss to brown bread cubes, 3 to 5 minutes. Remove 4 tablespoons browned bread cubes, put in small bowl, and set aside to use for garnish. Reduce heat to medium, and stir water and broth into remaining bread cubes. Cook until bread has absorbed liquid and is soft, 3 to 5 minutes. Remove from heat.

3. Using ladle, transfer bread mixture, in batches, to blender and **purée** for about 1 minute or until smooth. Return mixture to large saucepan or Dutch oven, and add salt and white pepper to taste. Cook bread soup over medium heat for 5 to 7 minutes to heat through.

4. Using a fork, beat eggs with heavy cream. Add nutmeg to soup mixture, and beat to thicken, 3 to 5 minutes.

*Serve immediately, **garnishing** each serving with a few browned bread cubes.*

Perhaps the most famous Austrian dish is *schnitzel* (a word meaning "little cut" of meat). The beloved Austrian delicacy *Wiener schnitzel* is enjoyed at many life-cycle celebrations. If made with chicken instead of veal, the dish is called *backhendi* and when made with pork, *schweinsschnitzel.*

To make *Wiener schnitzel,* choose top quality veal from the center of the rump. Have the butcher slice it ¼ inch thick and **trim** all fat. Allow about 4 to 6 ounces per person. Have the butcher pound each slice as thin as possible (about ⅛ inch) making them **oven-ready** or you can do it yourself (instructions follow). Follow the same directions if making *schnitzel* with chicken breast or boneless pork cutlet.

Wiener Schnitzel

Viennese Veal Cutlets

Yield: Serves 6

6 (4 to 6 ounces each) veal slices
½ cup milk
3 eggs
salt and pepper to taste
1 cup all-purpose flour, for dredging
1 cup **bread crumbs**
6 tablespoons butter or margarine, more as needed
6 lemon slices, for **garnish**
1 tablespoons parsley, **finely chopped**

Equipment: Plate, plastic food wrap, wooden chopping block, wooden meat mallet or small **heavy-based** skillet, paring knife or scissors, 3 pie pans, fork, baking sheet, large heavy-based skillet, metal spatula, serving platter

1. Prepare and pound cutlets: Place 10- or 12-inch sheet of plastic wrap on wooden chopping block. Place a cutlet on top, cover with another sheet of plastic wrap. Using either a wooden mallet or the bottom surface of a small heavy-based skillet, carefully flatten cutlet to about ⅛ inch thick. Remove plastic wrap. Using paring knife or scissors, make small vertical cuts (about 1/16th inch deep and 1 inch apart) all around the edges of the meat to keep it from curling up as it fries. Repeat preparing cutlets and stack on plate.

2. Prepare pans for breading cutlets: In first pie pan, put all of the flour. In second pie pan, put milk, eggs, and salt and pepper to taste, and using a fork, beat to mix well. In third pie pan, put bread crumbs.

3. To bread cutlets: First dredge cutlet in flour, coat both sides, and shake off excess. Next dip cutlet in egg mixture, coat both sides, and shake off excess. Finally coat both sides with bread crumbs. Press bread crumbs onto cutlet with your hands. Place cutlet on baking sheet covered with plastic wrap. Repeat breading remaining cutlets and place side by side on baking sheet with a sheet of plastic wrap between layers.

4. Melt 6 tablespoons butter or margarine in large skillet over medium-high heat. Fry one or two cutlets at a time, do not crowd pan. Fry 3 to 5 minutes on each side until golden brown and crisp. Using tongs, carefully transfer cutlet to serving platter and keep warm, but do not cover or breading will get soggy. Continue frying cutlets, adding more butter or margarine when needed to prevent sticking.

To serve, place a slice of lemon on top of each cutlet and sprinkle with parsley. Boiled potatoes and spätzle *(recipe follows) are served with the cutlets.*

Spätzle is one of Austria's comfort foods. *Spätzle,* tiny dumplings, are included in the menu for christening feasts, weddings, and funerals. Almost every household has a *Spätzle* maker which looks something like a flat shredder. It is placed over a pot of boiling water and a flat sliding box filled with batter is pushed back and forth along runners at the sides of the grater. The batter is forced through the holes to form teardrop-shaped dumplings, which cook in seconds. A good substitute is a colander; push the mixture through the colander holes with a rubber spatula. The mixture separates into small teardrop shapes as it drops into the boiling water.

Spätzle

Tiny Dumplings

Yield: serves 4

water as needed

salt and pepper to taste
2 eggs
1½ cups all-purpose flour, more if necessary
¼ teaspoon baking powder
½ cup milk
¼ teaspoon **ground** nutmeg
2 cups ice cubes
vegetable oil, as needed
½ cup butter or margarine
½ cup onions, **finely chopped**
2 tablespoons grated Parmesan cheese, more as needed for **garnish**
1 tablespoon chopped fresh parsley, or 2 teaspoons dried parsley flakes, for garnish

Equipment: Large saucepan, food processor or large mixing bowl, mixing spoon, large bowl, *spätzle* maker (see above) or **colander**, rubber spatula, strainer or slotted spoon, large skillet, 2 forks, serving bowl

1. Fill large saucepan two-thirds full with water, add 1 teaspoon salt and bring to boil over high heat. While water is heating, put eggs, 1½ cups flour, baking powder, milk, and nutmeg in food processor or large bowl. Process or beat with mixing spoon until well mixed. If the mixture is sticky, add a little more flour, ½ tablespoon at a time, until smooth.

2. Prepare to cook: Fill large bowl halfway with water, add ice cubes, and place near stove. Fill *spätzle* maker or colander with egg mixture. Cooking in batches, press about half the mixture through the *spätzle* maker into boiling water or using a rubber spatula, push through holes of colander Boil dumplings for 2 to 3 minutes, or until they swell and rise to the surface, stirring often to prevent sticking together. Using strainer or slotted spoon, remove dumplings and transfer them to bowl of ice water to stop cooking action. Cook remaining dough. When all dough is cold, drain thoroughly and sprinkle with just enough oil to prevent sticking together.

3. At serving time, prepare sauce: Melt butter or margarine in large skillet over medium-high heat. Add onions and **sauté** for 2 to 3 minutes, until soft. Add dumplings and using 2 forks, toss to heat through, 3 to 4 minutes. Transfer to serving bowl and sprinkle with 2 tablespoons grated cheese and parsley.

Serve with extra cheese to sprinkle over the dumplings. Spätzle *makes a great side dish with* Wiener schnitzel.

Austrians consider a meal incomplete unless it ends with dessert. Cakes and pastries are the crowning glory of Viennese cuisine. *Apfelstrudel* (apple strudel) is the same as *triglav strudel* (recipe page 163). Traditionally, pastry is eaten with a cup of coffee.

Wiener Eiskaffee

Viennese Iced Coffee

Yield: serves 1
1 scoop rich vanilla ice cream, softened
1 cup strong black coffee
2 tablespoons prepared whipped cream
confectioners' sugar, for **garnish**

Equipment: Tall heat-proof glass, spoon

Place ice cream in tall heat-proof glass and fill with coffee. Put a dollop whipped cream on top and sprinkle with confectioners' sugar.

To serve, stir as you drink the coffee.

SWITZERLAND

Situated in the middle of Europe, Switzerland has survived as an independent nation for more than 700 years. The Swiss remained neutral during both world wars and have become known for helping victims of wars. The International Red Cross was founded in Switzerland in the mid-1800s. Switzerland is greatly influenced by the neighboring countries of Italy, France, Germany, and Austria. Many cultures, customs, and foods have spilled over the borders making the various regions of Switzerland different from one another even in language and religion. The tastes of the 23 cantons (states) can easily be divided along their linguistic lines. The Swiss Germans have their own dialect; the Swiss living along the French border have a different dialect known as *Les Suisses Romandes*, and the *Graubunden Romansh* is the language spoken by the Swiss living along the Austrian and Italian borders.

The Swiss population is almost equally divided between Protestants and Roman Catholics and all life-cycle celebrations are conducted according to the religious tradition of the region. (See Protestant and Catholic Life-Cycle Rituals, page xlvi.)

In Switzerland, many traditions have grown out of cheese and cheese making. One such ancient tradition among the cheese-making families is to set aside, upon the birth of a child, a great wheel of cheese. It is marked with the baby's name, birth date, and other vital statistics. The cheese is eaten only during the person's life-cycle celebrations, such as christening, graduation, promotions, new jobs, betrothal, wedding, and anniversaries. The last of the cheese would be eaten, as a final tribute, by mourners at the individual's funeral.

This following recipe, originally from the French region of Switzerland, is popular all over the country. It is often prepared for a wedding banquet. ❁ ❁ ❁

Tomates au Fromage

Stuffed Tomatoes with Cheese

Yield: serves 4 to 6

4 to 6 tomatoes, **peeled**
salt and pepper to taste
3 **shallots, finely chopped**
1 cup grated cheese (preferably half Parmesan and half Gruyère) (available in the deli section of all supermarkets)
½ cup **fresh white bread crumbs**
4 to 6 tablespoons melted butter

Equipment: Paring knife, teaspoon or **melon baller**, small bowl with cover, greased 8- or 9-inch square or round baking pan, small bowl, oven mitts, serving platter

Preheat oven to 375° F.

1. Using paring knife, cut about 1 inch off top of each tomato. Using teaspoon or melon baller, scoop out about 3 teaspoons from inside tomato shell. Put scooped out tomato and tops of tomato in small bowl, cover, and refrigerate for another use. Set tomatoes, cut side up, in 8- or 9-inch square or round greased baking pan. Sprinkle each tomato with salt and pepper and chopped shallots.

2. Mix cheese and bread crumbs in small bowl. Fill each tomato equally with bread crumb mixture. Carefully spread 1 tablespoon melted butter over the top of each stuffed tomato.

3. Bake in oven for 10 to 12 minutes, or until cheese is melted and tomatoes are tender but still hold their shape.

To serve, transfer to serving platter and eat while still warm.

With all the rich dairy products in Switzerland, it is no surprise that some Swiss pastries and desserts have become world famous. In Switzerland, most children have both a birthday and name day celebration with cake and ice cream; the following recipe for *aargauer rüebli torte* (carrot cake) is a favorite for these celebrations.

Aargauer Rüebli Torte

Carrot Cake

Yield: serves 10 to 12

1 tablespoon butter
1 cup dried **bread crumbs**, divided
¾ cup **grated** raw carrots
1½ cups **ground** almonds
½ teaspoon ground mace
½ teaspoon ground cinnamon
1 teaspoon ground ginger
1 teaspoon ground baking powder
6 large **eggs, separated**
1¼ cups sugar
1 tablespoon grated lemon peel
3 tablespoons lemon juice
confectioners' sugar icing (recipe follows), for **garnish**
mixed chopped candied fruits, for garnish (available at all supermarkets)

Equipment: 8-inch springform pan, wax paper, pencil, scissors, mixing spoon, medium bowl, small bowl, 2 large mixing bowls, electric mixer or whisk, rubber spatula, oven mitts, toothpick, wire cake rack, dinner knife or **icing spatula,** airtight storage container

1. Place springform pan on sheet of wax paper, use pencil to trace around bottom and cut out with scissors. Butter bottom and sides of inside of springform pan, and coat with ¼ cup dried bread crumbs. Shake out excess bread crumbs. Place wax paper circle in bottom of pan, butter, and sprinkle with bread crumbs.

Preheat oven to 350° F.

2. In medium bowl, mix grated raw carrots and ground almonds.

3. In small bowl, mix remaining ¾ cup bread crumbs with mace, cinnamon, ginger, and baking powder. Transfer bread crumb mixture to carrot mixture, and stir to mix well.

4. In large mixing bowl, using electric mixer or whisk, beat egg yolks until thick and lemon-colored, 3 to 5 minutes. Beating constantly, add sugar, grated lemon peel, and lemon juice, a little at a time. Using rubber spatula, **fold in** carrot mixture.

5. Put **egg whites** into second large mixing bowl, and using clean, dry electric mixer or whisk, beat whites until stiff, 2 to 3 minutes. Using rubber spatula, fold egg whites into carrot mixture. Transfer to prepared 8-inch springform pan.

6. Bake in oven for 1 hour, or until toothpick inserted in center comes out clean. Remove sides of pan and place on wire cake rack to cool to room temperature.

7. Prepare confectioners' sugar icing.

8. Frost cake: Using dinner knife or icing spatula, spread confectioners' sugar icing over top and sides of cake. Sprinkle top with mixed chopped candied fruits to garnish.

To serve, cut in wedges. Store in airtight container. Cake flavor improves on the second day.

Confectioners' Sugar Icing

Yield: about 1 cup

1 cup confectioners' sugar, sifted
1 tablespoons water
½ teaspoon vanilla extract

Equipment: Medium bowl, mixing spoon

In medium bowl, mix confectioners' sugar and water until smooth. Stir in vanilla extract and mix well.

Continue with aargauer rüebli torte *(recipe precedes: Step 7. Frost cake:).*

The following recipe for *totenbeinli* (almond cookies) is baked for All Souls' Day, November 2, in memory of the dead.

Totenbeinli

Almond Cookies

Yield: about 40 pieces

½ cup butter
1 cup sugar
1 teaspoon **ground** cinnamon
3 eggs
1 tablespoon **rose water** (available at Middle East food stores and pharmacies)
½ teaspoon salt
2½ to 3 cups all-purpose flour
2 cups sliced almonds, **blanched**
egg wash, for **garnish**

Equipment: Large mixing bowl, electric mixer or wooden mixing spoon, lightly floured work surface, plastic food wrap, lightly floured rolling pin, paring knife, ruler, buttered and floured baking sheet, **pastry brush**, oven mitts, metal spatula, wire cake rack, serving platter

1. In large mixing bowl, using electric mixer or wooden mixing spoon, cream butter with sugar and cinnamon until fluffy, 2 to 3 minutes. Add eggs, one at a time, beating well after each addition. Add rose water and salt to beaten eggs, and mix well.

2. Beating constantly, add 2½ cups flour, ½ cup at a time, beating well after each addition. Dough will be sticky, but if too sticky to handle, beat in remaining ½ cup flour, a little at a time. Transfer dough to lightly floured work surface. **Knead** in almonds and, using your hands, shape dough into ball and flatten to ½ inch thick. Wrap in plastic wrap and refrigerate for 2 hours.

Preheat oven to 375° F.

3. Unwrap dough on lightly floured work surface, and using lightly floured rolling pin, roll dough into rectangle, about ¼ inch thick. Using paring knife and ruler, cut dough into 40 finger-length pieces, about 1 inch long and 3 inches wide. Place dough pieces about ½ inch apart on buttered and floured baking sheet. Using pastry brush, brush dough with egg wash.

4. Bake in oven for 12 to 18 minutes, or until golden brown. Cool for 2 minutes on baking sheet, remove cookies with metal spatula, and place on wire cake rack to cool completely.

Serve cookies by stacking them on a serving platter.

The one thing the different cultural and linguistic regions of Switzerland have in common is a passion for salads, cheese, wine, and excellent breads. Breaded *Berne oder emmentaler zopf* (rich egg bread from Berne) is similar to Jewish *challah* (recipe page 105).

Swiss chocolate is the finest in the world and the Swiss consume about 23 pounds of it per person, per year. They are, without question, the chocolate eating champions of the world. It's almost impossible to set up a celebration buffet table without one of Switzerland's famous chocolate cakes. *Schokoladen torte* originated from a famous Swiss chocolate factory.

Schokoladen Torte

Chocolate Cake

Yield: serves 10 to 12

1 cup all-purpose flour
1 teaspoon baking powder
½ pound dark sweet chocolate
½ cup butter or margarine, at room temperature
1 cup sugar
5 eggs, separated
1 teaspoon vanilla extract
sifted confectioners' sugar, for **garnish**
1 cup prepared whipped cream, for serving

Equipment: 9-inch **springform pan**, buttered wax paper, pencil, scissors, flour **sifter**, small bowl,

grater, work surface, **double boiler**, large mixing bowl, electric mixer or mixing spoon, medium mixing bowl, whisk, rubber spatula, oven mitts, toothpick, wire cake rack, 9-inch lace paper doily, small side dish

Place 9-inch springform pan on sheet of wax paper, use pencil to trace around bottom and cut out with scissors. Butter bottom and sides of inside of springform pan and line bottom of pan with buttered wax paper circle.

Preheat oven to 350° F.

1. **Sift** flour and baking powder into small bowl.

2. Coarsely grate chocolate on piece of wax paper on work surface. Transfer grated chocolate to top pan of double boiler. Fill bottom pan halfway with water, and bring to boil over high heat. Set pan with grated chocolate on top of other pan, add butter, and stir until melted and smooth, 7 to 10 minutes. Add sugar, stir until melted, 2 to 3 minutes. Transfer chocolate mixture to large mixing bowl. Using electric mixer or mixing spoon, add egg yolks, one at a time, beating well after each addition. Add vanilla extract to chocolate mixture and mix well.

3. Put **egg whites** in medium mixing bowl, and using clean, dry mixer or whisk, beat until stiff. Using rubber spatula, **fold in** egg whites with chocolate mixture. Transfer to prepared springform pan.

4. Bake for 40 to 50 minutes, or until toothpick inserted in center comes out clean. Cool on wire cake rack, remove sides of pan.

5. Place a 9-inch lace paper doily on top of cake. Sift confectioners' sugar over it. Remove doily; there will be a lacy pattern on the cake.

Serve the cake with side dish of whipped cream. Cut into wedges.

ITALY

Italy, the boot-shaped peninsula that extends into the Mediterranean from Central Europe, has given the world some of its finest architecture, art, literature, and music, particularly opera. Italy is also among the world's leading wine producers. The majority of Italians are Roman Catholic and most life-cycle events are observed according to Catholic traditions. (See Protestant and Catholic Life-Cycle Rituals, page xlvi.)

Italian celebrations are loaded with symbolism, such as the giving of *bomboniera* as a memento to guests at baptisms and wedding celebrations. The *bomboniera* can be small elaborate ceramic or painted wooden boxes or simply netting (tulle) or lace fabric tied like a pouch and filled with three Jordan almonds representing the Holy Trinity or five representing the five letters in the Italian word *amore* (love). Jordan almonds, called *confetti*, are not tiny bits of paper, but rather candy-coated nuts. When made with netting and filled with *confetti*, the custom of giving *bomboniera* is exactly the same custom as the Greek *kouféta* (see instructions page 145). The Italians also use white netting for weddings and pink or blue for the birth of girls or boys.

Italian life-cycle events, especially weddings, are generally lively affairs. They are celebrated with great quantities of *nutrimento* (food) which is the focal point of the festivities. Wedding soup is popular in southern Italy where **escarole**, a slightly bitter green leafy vegetable is the traditional ingredient; spinach is a good substitute. The meatballs for wedding soup can be made ahead of time and refrigerated for up to two days or frozen for up to one month. ۞ ۞ ۞

Zuppa di Nozze

Wedding Soup

Yield: serves 8

1 egg
1 pound lean **ground** meat (combination beef and veal is recommended)
½ cup **fresh white bread crumbs**
2 tablespoons flat-leaf parsley (also called Italian parsley), **finely chopped**
1½ teaspoons grated lemon rind
1 teaspoon grated nutmeg
½ teaspoon salt
8 cups canned beef broth
3 cups escarole leaves, washed, drained, and chopped into bite-size pieces
grated Parmesan cheese, as needed, for serving

Equipment: Large mixing bowl, **whisk** or fork, baking sheet, oven mitts, medium storage container with cover, large-size saucepan with cover, mixing spoon, ladle, individual soup bowls

1. Prepare meatballs: Put egg in large mixing bowl and using whisk or fork, beat lightly. Add ground meat, bread crumbs, parsley, lemon rind, nutmeg, and salt. Using clean hands, mix together for 2 to 3 minutes.

2. Using wet hands, form meat mixture into small marble-size balls. Keep your hands moistened while making meatballs and set them in a single layer on baking sheet. Cover loosely with plastic wrap and refrigerate for 1 hour to firm.

Preheat oven to 350° F.

3. Bake in oven for 30 minutes or until browned on the outside and no pink is showing on the inside when cut open. Cool to room temperature, transfer to medium container, cover, and refrigerate until ready to serve.

4. Prepare soup: Put beef broth in large saucepan, and bring to boil over high heat. Add the escarole, stir, and bring to a boil. Reduce heat to medium-high, cover, and cook 5 minutes more until escarole is tender. Add the meatballs and **simmer**, uncovered for 5 to 7 minutes or until meatballs are heated through.

To serve: put 2 or 3 meatballs in each soup bowl and ladle escarole broth over them. Pass grated cheese for sprinkling.

Torta di biscotti originated around Naples in the Campania region and is mostly prepared for baptisms and name day celebrations. When it is prepared for weddings, it's called *torta di biscotto di nozze* (wedding cookie cake). The cookies are decoratively stacked in a pyramid to look like a multicolored, multi-layered round or rectangular cake. For the finishing touch, a small cluster of flowers is often placed at the top. At traditional southern Italian weddings, the table holding the *torta di biscotto di nozze* is placed on the dance floor. The guests dance the *tarantella* (Italian folk dance) around the cake table before eating the cookies.

Torta di biscotti should be made with at least six different kinds of cookies plus assorted candies to give it interesting color, texture, and design. Place the firmest cookies on the bottom, such as *biscotti*, which is the same as Israel's *kikar skadim* (recipe page 107). The most delicate cookies can be added near the top. When the *torta* is prepared for girls, pink candies are inserted among the cookies; blue candies are added for boys and white candies for weddings. The cookies can be both store-bought and homemade, such as *biscotti di nozze* (recipe page 179). Some cookies can be made up to a month ahead of time and frozen until the day before the party when the *torta di biscotti* is assembled. Thaw cookies before assembling. The number of cookies you need will vary according to the size of *torta* you want to build and the size of the cookies you are using.

Torta di Biscotti

Celebration Cookie Cake

Yield: serves 40 to 50

2 to 3 dozen biscotti, homemade (follow Israel *kikar skadim*, recipe page 107) or commercial (available at all supermarkets)
butter cream icing (recipe page 361)
5 to 6 dozen assorted cookies homemade (see index) and/or commercial
1½ to 2 pounds assorted firm and/or hard candies
fresh, silk or dried flowers, greenery, ribbons and bows, for garnish

Equipment: Round piece of Styrofoam 8 to10 inches in diameter and 1 to 2 inches thick, aluminum foil, large serving tray at least 14 inches in diameter, **serrated knife**, table knife or **icing spatula**

1. Prepare *biscotti*.

2. Prepare *butter cream icing*.

3. Wrap Styrofoam with foil to use as the base and place in center of tray.

4. Form the bottom layer: If using *biscotti* that are 5 to 6 inches long, cut the long side in half using a serrated knife. Each *biscotti* usually has a flat bottom and slightly rounded top. Either stand the *biscotti* upright, setting the flat bottom on the tray, or lay them on their sides, all facing the same direction. Place the *biscotti* close together against the Styrofoam form, but first dab the side that will be on the bottom with icing. (The icing "glues" the *biscotti* in place.) Repeat icing and placing *biscotti* side by side around the Styrofoam. Place small cookies of contrasting colors between the wedge-shaped spaces at the outer perimeter of the *biscotti*.

5. Repeat building, one layer at a time, with a variety of cookies, dabbing each cookie with a little icing before setting it in place. Continue to stack layers until the entire piece of Styrofoam is covered.

6. Place candies; fresh, silk, or dried flowers; greenery; and ribbons and/or bows in spaces between cookies.

To serve, place the torta di biscotti *on the buffet table as the centerpiece. If it's for a wedding, place it next to the traditional wedding cake. To eat, each person removes their selected cookie and candy from the pyramid, usually from the top down.*

Italians have different cookies specially baked for almost every occasion and celebration. For wedding receptions, large trays of *biscotti di nozze* are set out for guests to munch on.

Biscotti di Nozze

Wedding Cookies

Yield: about 66 pieces

6 eggs, beaten
1¼ cups sugar
¾ cup vegetable oil
5 teaspoons baking powder
½ teaspoon salt
½ teaspoon **ground** anise
5 to 6 cups all-purpose flour
confectioners' sugar, as needed for **garnish**

Equipment: Electric mixer or whisk, large mixing bowl, dough hook for mixer or wooden mixing spoon, lightly floured work surface, ruler, pizza cutter or paring knife, 1 or 2 nonstick cookie sheets, oven mitts, wire cake rack

Preheat oven to 350° F.

1. Using electric mixer or whisk, beat eggs until **frothy**. Add sugar, oil, baking powder, salt, and ground anise, beating well after each addition. Beat in 3 cups flour, a little at a time until soft dough forms. Using the electric mixer with dough hook or wooden spoon, beat in just enough of the remaining 2 or 3 cups remaining flour, a little at a time, to make nonsticky dough.

Knead until smooth and satiny. Transfer to lightly floured work surface and using your hands, shape and pat dough into a 12-inch square, about ½ inch thick and as even as possible. Using ruler and pizza cutter or paring knife cut 12-inch strips 1-inch wide. Cut strips across into 2-inch lengths and place about ½-inch apart on 1 or 2 nonstick cookie sheets.

2. Bake in oven for 25 to 30 minutes, until edges turn brown. Transfer to wire cake rack and while still warm, sprinkle with confectioners' sugar.

To serve, arrange cookies on serving platter and set on buffet table at the wedding reception. Wedding cookies can also be used for the torta di biscotti *(recipe page 179).*

Amaretti

Famous Italian Cookies

Yield: about 20 pieces

- 1 cup **almond paste**, (available at all supermarkets)
- 1 cup granulated sugar
- 2 **egg whites**
- ½ cup **pine nuts** (available at all supermarkets and specialty food stores)

Equipment: Food processor, rubber spatula, medium mixing bowl, greased baking sheet, oven mitts, metal spatula, wire cake rack, ruler, pencil, assorted colors of waxed tissue (available at craft and bakery supply shops), scissors, medium bowl or basket

Preheat oven to 325° F.

1. Using your fingers, break almond paste into small pieces and put in food processor. Add sugar and egg whites, and process to a smooth paste, 1 to 2 minutes. Transfer to medium mixing bowl. Form mixture into walnut-sized balls, and place on greased baking sheet, about 1 inch apart. Flatten each ball slightly with your hand. Sprinkle each ball with pine nuts and press in slightly with your hand again to make the pine nuts stick.

Note: While processing, turn machine off once or twice and scrape down sides of container with rubber spatula.

2. Bake in oven for 10 to 15 minutes, or until cookies are pale golden. Using metal spatula, transfer cookies to wire cake rack to cool.

3. Using ruler and pencil, mark off ten 6-inch squares on the assorted colors of waxed tissue. Using scissors, cut out the squares. Place two cookies in a square of tissue with bottoms touching, and wrap tissue around them like a pouch. Twist tissue just above the cookies to secure.

To serve, place wrapped cookies in a medium bowl or basket and set out for guests to help themselves. Or don't wrap them and use for torta di biscotti *(recipe page 179).*

According to tradition, in some parts of Italy and Sicily, children are given gifts of toys and sweets on All Souls' Day, November 2. Legend has it that the dead leave their tombs on the night between All Saints' Day, November 1, and All Souls' Day to pilfer the best pastry shops and toy stores for sweets and toys for their descendants. When the children awake on November 2, they search for the hidden goodies and shout with joy and thanks to their dead ancestors when they find them.

Italians eat *fave dei morte* (tiny cookies shaped to look like fava beans) on All Souls' Day. Fava beans and chestnuts were symbols of the dead in ancient Greece and Rome. In some parts of Italy, all Souls' Day is celebrated with village festivals at which people eat huge bowls of fava bean soup along with roasted chestnuts to celebrate the memory of their dead ancestors.

Fave dei Morte

Dead Men's Beans

Yield: about 24 "beans"

1 cup **ground** almonds, **blanched**
¾ cup all-purpose flour
1 teaspoon ground cinnamon
¼ cup butter or margarine, cut into small pieces and chilled
¾ cup sugar
grated rind of 1 lemon
1 egg, beaten

Equipment: Food processor, rubber spatula, greased cookie sheet, oven mitts, wire cake rack, serving plate

Preheat oven to 350° F.

1. In food processor, combine ground almonds, flour, and cinnamon, and pulse to mix, 2 to 3 seconds. Add butter and pulse until mixture resembles coarse crumbs, about 1 minute. Add sugar, lemon rind, and egg, and process to form smooth dough, about 1 minute.

Note: While processing, turn machine off once or twice and scrape down sides of container with rubber spatula.

2. Transfer dough to medium mixing bowl and pinch off small walnut-size pieces. Shape each into an oval, resembling the shape of fava beans. Place on greased cookie sheet about 1 inch apart.

3. Bake in oven for 15 to 20 minutes, or until lightly browned. Transfer to wire cake rack to cool.

To serve, decoratively arrange on serving plate. Eat in memory of an ancestor.

PORTUGAL

The Pyrenees mountains are a massive natural barrier separating the Iberian peninsula from the rest of Europe. Perhaps that is why the Portuguese and Spanish people who live on the peninsula sailed out into the Atlantic in the late fifteenth and sixteenth centuries. It was easier to explore to the west by ship than trying to scale the mountains. Of course, this is no longer true and the Iberian Peninsula at the end of the twentieth century is very much a part of the European community.

The majority of Portuguese are Roman Catholic and most life-cycle celebrations center around the Catholic Church. (See Protestant and Catholic Life-Cycle Rituals, page xlvi.)

Codfish, both fresh and salt, is a popular Portuguese food. Cooks speak lovingly of cod as *o fiel amigo* (faithful friend). They claim 365 ways to cook it, one for each day of the year. Salt codfish cakes are on the appetizer menu for most celebration feasts. Portuguese salt codfish cakes (*Bacalhau*) are similar to Dominican Republic *bacalaitos* (recipe page 370).

If Portugal has a national soup, it must be *caldo verde*. This green soup, a specialty of the north region, is a favorite in even the most sophisticated Lisbon homes. It is often served for the family celebration meal after a christening ceremony in church. ⁂

Caldo Verde

Green Soup

Yield: serves 6 to 8

3 tablespoons olive oil
3 cloves garlic, **finely chopped**
8 cups water
2 potatoes, peeled and shredded
1 pound greens: kale, spinach, or collard greens, or combination, fresh, rinsed and trimmed, or frozen (thawed)

½ pound sausage (either Portuguese *linguiça* or *chouriço* or Polish *kielbasa*), sliced in ½-inch pieces
salt and pepper to taste

Equipment: Large saucepan with cover or **Dutch oven**, mixing spoon, potato masher, individual soup bowls

1. Heat oil in large saucepan with cover or Dutch oven over medium-high heat, add garlic, **sauté,** and stir until soft, 2 to 3 minutes. Add water and potatoes, bring to boil over high heat. Reduce heat to **simmer**, cover, and cook for 15 to 20 minutes, or until potatoes are soft. Using potato masher, mash potatoes so liquid becomes creamy.

2. Add greens, sausage, and salt and pepper to taste to potato mixture, and stir. Bring to boil over medium-high heat, stir, reduce heat to simmer, cover, and cook until greens are done, 15 to 20 minutes.

Serve in soup bowls with plenty of bread for dipping.

Meat is always the centerpiece of a Portuguese celebration feast. It can be kid (goat), lamb, pork, or, if the budget allows, beef. Pot roast is called *alcatra*, which comes from *alcatre*, the Portuguese word for rump, the preferred cut of meat for pot roast, which is a style of cooking, not a cut of meat. Boneless rump, heel of round, and Boston-cut are good cuts of beef to use in this recipe.

Alcatra

Portuguese Pot Roast

Yield: serves 6 to 8

4 tablespoons olive oil
4 to 5 pounds **oven-ready,** boned, and rolled beef rump
1 onion, chopped
3 cloves garlic, **finely chopped**
1 carrot, trimmed and chopped
2 red bell peppers, trimmed, seeded, and chopped
6 fresh **cilantro** leaves or 1 tablespoon dried **coriander** flakes
4 cups dry red wine or chicken broth (homemade, recipe page 106) or canned, more if needed
1 bay leaf
salt and pepper to taste
5 potatoes, peeled and thickly sliced
2 strips bacon, chopped
2 tablespoons fresh chopped parsley, for **garnish**

Equipment: Large roasting pan with cover, metal tongs, plate, mixing spoon, oven mitts, **bulb baster** (optional), carving board, medium skillet, whisk, strainer, sauce bowl, meat knife, medium serving bowl, serving platter

1. Heat oil in large roasting pan over medium-high heat. Add meat and brown on all sides, 7 to 12 minutes. Remove meat with metal tongs and set on plate. Add onions, garlic, carrot, red bell peppers, and cilantro or coriander to roasting pan. Stir and **sauté** until onions are soft, 3 to 5 minutes. Return meat to roasting pan and pour wine or chicken broth over it. Add bay leaf and salt and pepper to taste. Bring to boil, reduce heat to **simmer**, cover, and cook for 20 minutes.

Preheat oven to 375° F.

2. Put roasting pan in oven and bake, covered for 1½ hours, basting occasionally. Using oven mitts, remove from oven, add potatoes, and sprinkle them with chopped bacon. Cover and bake for 45 minutes more. Reduce oven to 325° F, and using bulb baster or mixing spoon, **baste** meat and potatoes. Bake, uncovered, for 30 minutes more, until meat and potatoes are fork-tender and browned. Add more wine or chicken broth when necessary. The bottom of the pan should be generously covered with pan juices so the meat doesn't dry out.

3. Remove potatoes from roasting pan, put into medium serving bowl, and keep warm. Transfer meat to carving board and let rest for 20 minutes before slicing. Using bulb baster or mixing spoon, skim off and discard most fat from pan juices. Transfer pan juices to medium skillet. Discard bay leaf.

4. Prepare gravy: For each cup of pan juices, combine 2 tablespoons flour with 1/2 cup water to form a paste, and quickly whisk in to prevent lumping. Cook and whisk over medium heat until gravy thickens, 3 to 5 minutes. Add salt and pepper to taste. Strain into sauce bowl.

To serve, slice meat across the grain, using meat knife. Place sliced meat on serving platter and surround with potatoes. Serve with gravy to spoon over each serving.

All special occasions and all religious holidays call for special breads. Some holidays are created around bread, such as the yearly *Festa dos Tabuleiros* in the city of Tomar. Girls are adorned with headdresses made of loaves of bread stacked more than five feet high. *Massa sovada* are special rolls prepared for christenings, weddings, and anniversaries. They are eaten throughout the meal, with the soup or the main course, or at the end of the meal.

Massa Sovada

Sweet Bread Buns

Yield: 12 rolls

1 package active dry **yeast**
1/4 cup cool water (70° F)
5 tablespoons sugar, divided
1 teaspoon salt
2 tablespoons melted butter or margarine
1 egg
1 cup milk or half & half
3 1/2 to 3 3/4 cups all-purpose flour
egg wash, for **garnish**

Equipment: Large mixing bowl, wooden mixing spoon, rubber spatula, lightly floured work surface, lightly buttered 9- x 13-inch baking pan, clean kitchen towel, **pastry brush**, oven mitts, napkin-lined bread basket

1. In large mixing bowl, sprinkle yeast over water. Let yeast stand until dissolved, 3 to 5 minutes. Using wooden mixing spoon, stir in 3 tablespoons sugar, salt, melted butter or margarine, egg, and milk or half-and-half, and mix well. Stir in 3 1/2 cups flour to form a smooth dough.

2. Scrape dough onto lightly floured work surface. Sprinkle in flour, and **knead**, until dough is no longer sticky but smooth and elastic, 8 to 10 minutes. Shape dough into 12 equal balls and evenly space in lightly buttered 9- x 13-inch baking pan. Cover with towel and place in warm place to rise until double in bulk, 45 minutes to 1 hour.

Preheat oven to 350° F.

3. Brush egg wash over tops of rolls and sprinkle with remaining 2 tablespoons sugar. Bake in oven 25 to 30 minutes, or until golden brown.

To serve, separate rolls and transfer to napkin-lined bread basket.

Portuguese nuns in the Catholic convents are famous for making wonderful pastries, candies, cookies, preserves, and elaborate wedding cakes. For christenings, name-day celebrations, and weddings, the nuns sell little pastry creations, such as the delightfully named *orelbas de abade* (abbot's ears), *papos de anjo* (angel's breasts), and the following recipe, *barrigas de freiras* (nuns' bellies). Many of the dishes prepared by the nuns are made with simple ingredients like those used in this recipe.

BARRIGAS DE FREIRAS

NUNS' BELLIES

Yield: serves 4

1 cup sugar
¾ cup water
2 tablespoons unsalted butter
4 cups fresh white **bread crumbs**, best made from French or Italian bread
8 **egg yolks**, beaten
ground cinnamon, for **garnish**
slivered almonds, for garnish

Equipment: Medium **heavy-based** saucepan, wooden mixing spoon, candy **thermometer** (optional), serving dish

1. Make **sugar syrup**: Pour water into medium heavy-based saucepan, add sugar, and stir to dissolve. Bring to boil over medium-high heat, stirring frequently. Reduce heat to **simmer**, cook until mixture thickens to syrup and reaches soft-ball stage or registers 234°-236° F on candy thermometer. Remove from heat and stir in butter until melted. Add bread crumbs and stir well to mix.

2. Return syrup mixture to low heat and stir in egg yolks, one at a time, beating well after each addition. Continue cooking over low heat, stirring constantly until syrup thickens, 5 to 10 minutes. Do not increase heat. Transfer to serving dish and sprinkle with ground cinnamon and toasted almonds.

Serve this dessert in very small portions because it is extremely sweet. It will be enjoyed best with a cup of tea or coffee at the end of a meal.

SPAIN

Because of its location, Spain has been linked for centuries to the cultures of both Europe and North Africa. Although situated in southwestern Europe, Spain's southern tip is only eight miles from Africa, across the straits of Gibraltar. Due to the mountainous terrain separating the different regions within the country, Spain has a diversity of cultures. Each region has its own language, customs, and cuisine. One thing most Spaniards have in common is their religion, the Roman Catholic Church. Spain became a secular state in 1978 and religious freedom is a constitutional right for all citizens; however, the influence of the Catholic Church remains strong and most life-cycle celebrations are conducted according to the Roman Catholic traditions. (See Protestant and Catholic Life-Cycle Rituals, page xlvi.)

First Communion is an important event in Spain, and families will spend heavily for the finest clothes and an elaborate celebration for their children. Usually several parents join together and share expenses for the First Communion celebration in a *merendero* (small restaurant). They each invite their relatives and friends to the celebration, which involves singing, dancing, and feasting on *cocido* (meat stew), Spain's national dish. Each cook, village, and region makes it differently but the classic one-pot recipe, *cocido Madrileño,* is from Madrid (recipe page 185).

Spanish weddings are usually followed by a big feast. In the cities, it is usually at a restaurant, hotel, or inn. In the country, the feast is at the groom's parents' house or an inn. Wealthy Spanish families often have the reception in one of the many restored castles or monasteries called *paradores* (literally, "halting places") that can be found in every region of the country.

Great quantities of food and wine are important to the success of all Spanish celebrations, especially weddings. Depending upon the region and the budget, the menu can include roasted goat or **suckling pig** (recipe page 383); seafood, such as mussels, shrimp, and fish, especially eel; and meat stews (*cocidos*). The celebration meal also often includes *tapas* (appetizers) and a variety of side dishes, cheeses, and breads, such as *pan mistura* (recipe page 187). The *tapas* can be simply bowls of salted almonds, olives, pickled vegetables, hard-cooked eggs with a sauce such as *ali-oli* (recipe page 186), *banderillas* (recipe follows), or platters of thinly sliced ham. Fresh fruit is eaten at the end of a meal while a variety of sweet pastries, cakes, and candies are always available to eat during the celebration.

This following recipe is one of the many *tapas* dishes. Most ingredients are available in the deli section of supermarkets.

Banderillas

Miniature Kebabs

Yield: serves 6

- 12 to 18 pitted black olives
- 12 to 18 pitted green olives
- 10-ounce jar marinated artichoke hearts (available in all supermarkets)
- 12 *each*: cooked shrimp and cooked scallops (available in the seafood section of all supermarkets)
- 6 (½-inch) cubes boiled ham
- 6 pieces cooked sausage, cut in ½-inch slices
- 12 (½-inch) cubes cheese
- 1 cup *ali-oli*, for serving (recipe page 186)

Equipment: 12 (6-inch) wooden skewers, serving platter

Thread any combination of ingredients on wooden skewers.

Prepare *ali-oli* and put in small serving bowl.

Serve kebabs on a serving platter with a side dish of ali-oli *as a sauce to spoon over or use as dip.*

Despite regional differences, Spaniards have several things in common—their religion, the heavy use of garlic, and *cocido* (one-pot stew). There are as many ways of making *cocido* as there are cooks in Spain. The way it is served remains constant—the broth is strained and served as a soup for the first course, while the vegetables are served separately, often before the meat and chicken, which are served as the third course.

Cocido Madrileño

Madrid Stew

Yield: serves 6

- ½ pound piece bacon or salt pork
- 1½ pounds *chorizo* or Italian sausage
- water, as needed
- 2 pound piece eye of round or sirloin tip of beef
- 2½ to 3 pounds frying chicken, cut into serving-size pieces
- 3 cloves garlic, **finely chopped**
- 2 onions, thinly sliced
- 4 **leeks**, white part only, sliced
- 4 carrots, sliced
- 6 small new potatoes, scrubbed
- 1 cup drained, canned *garbanzos* (also called chickpeas)
- 16 ounces canned chopped tomatoes (with liquid)
- salt and pepper to taste
- 1 cup uncooked small noodles (shells, bows, or elbow macaroni)

Equipment: Medium saucepan, slotted spoon, large saucepan with cover or **Dutch oven**, mixing spoon, tongs, cutting board, meat knife and fork, strainer, large serving platter, serving bowl, individual soup bowls

1. Put bacon or salt pork and sausage in medium saucepan, and cover with water. Bring to

boil and cook for 10 minutes. Drain meat and discard liquid. Set aside sausage.

2. Put drained bacon or salt pork in large saucepan or Dutch oven. Add beef, chicken, garlic, and 3 quarts (12 cups) water. Bring to boil over high heat. Using mixing spoon, skim off and discard top foam. Reduce heat to **simmer**, cover, and cook 1 to 1½ hours, or until beef is tender and chicken is done. (See glossary for tips on **chicken doneness**.)

3. Add onions, leeks, carrots, potatoes, *garbanzos*, tomatoes, drained sausage, and salt and pepper to taste. Bring to boil over high heat, reduce heat to simmer, and cover. Cook 20 to 25 minutes until potatoes are tender.

4. Using slotted spoon or tongs, remove bacon or salt pork and beef, and place on cutting board. Place chicken pieces on large serving platter and keep warm. Using meat knife and fork, cut beef and bacon or salt pork into serving-size slices, place on platter with chicken, and keep warm. Using slotted spoon, remove vegetables from broth, place in serving bowl, and keep warm. Set strainer over medium saucepan and strain broth. Spoon any residue in strainer over the vegetables.

5. Cook broth over medium-high heat, bring to boil, and reduce heat to simmer. Add noodles, stir, and cook 6 or 7 minutes, or until tender.

To serve, ladle soup into individual soup bowls for the first course. After eating the soup, guests help themselves to vegetables, and then the meats. Serve with plenty of bread and coliflor con ali-oli *(recipe follows).*

Vegetables are eaten in great quantities at most Spanish meals. Garlic is the all-pervasive seasoning in Spain. Garlic mayonnaise is a favorite sauce used on vegetables, fish, and even meats. The following recipe is a safe and an easy way of making *ali-oli* using commercial mayonnaise. The original recipe calls for uncooked eggs, which can develop harmful bacteria.

Coliflor con Ali-oli

Cauliflower with Garlic Mayonnaise

Yield: serves 6

water, as needed
1 teaspoon salt
1 cauliflower, divided into **florets**
garlic mayonnaise, for serving (recipe follows)
1 tablespoon chopped fresh parsley or 1 teaspoon dried parsley flakes, for **garnish**
6 pitted black olives, for garnish

Equipment: Medium saucepan, slotted spoon, **colander**, serving spoon, small serving bowl

1. Fill medium saucepan two-thirds full with water, add salt, and bring to boil over high heat. Add cauliflower, bring back to boil, and reduce heat to **simmer**. Cook for 8 to 10 minutes until cauliflower is tender. Drain in colander and cool to room temperature.

2. Prepare garlic mayonnaise.

3. Assemble: Arrange cooled cauliflower on serving platter and spoon some garlic mayonnaise over the top. Sprinkle with parsley flakes and place black olives around platter for garnish.

Serve as a side dish with cocido Madrileño *(recipe page 185) or as one of the little dishes on the* tapas *table. Serve remaining garlic mayonnaise in small serving bowl for guests to add as needed.*

Ali-oli

Garlic Mayonnaise

Yield: about 1 cup

¼ cup extra virgin olive oil
3 cloves garlic, **finely chopped**
1 cup prepared mayonnaise

Equipment: Electric **blender**, rubber spatula, spoon, small bowl with cover, small jar with cover

Put olive oil and chopped garlic in blender, and **blend** on high until garlic is fully blended into oil and there are no visible garlic pieces. Put mayonnaise in small bowl, stir in about 1 teaspoon garlic oil mixture and set aside for at least 5 minutes for flavor to develop. Taste mayonnaise and add more garlic mixture if you like a stronger garlic flavor.

Continue to use in coliflor con ali-oli *(recipe precedes: Step 3. Assemble:), or cover and refrigerate to use in recipes calling for* ali-oli. *Put leftover olive oil mixture in a small jar, cover, and refrigerate. It can be used in recipes calling for oil and garlic.*

A Spanish meal usually includes bread, and *pan mistura* is a type of bread that is both delicious and nourishing.

Pan Mistura

Spanish Cornbread

Yield: 1 loaf

- 1 package dried active **yeast**
- 1½ cups **lukewarm** water
- 2¾ cups all-purpose flour
- 1½ cups yellow **cornmeal**
- 1½ teaspoons salt

Equipment: Small bowl, mixing spoon, large greased mixing bowl, lightly floured work surface, plastic food wrap, paring knife, greased baking sheet, clean kitchen towel, oven mitts, wire cake rack

1. In small bowl, dissolve yeast in lukewarm water until bubbly, 5 to 10 minutes.

2. In large mixing bowl, mix flour, cornmeal, and salt. Make well (hole) in center of flour mixture and pour in yeast mixture. Stir flour into yeast mixture to make soft dough. Transfer dough to lightly floured work surface and **knead** 3 to 5 minutes, until smooth. Place dough in greased large mixing bowl and turn to coat all sides of dough with grease. Grease one side of plastic wrap and place with greased side down over bowl of dough. Let rise in warm place until double in bulk, 1 to 1½ hours.

3. Transfer dough to lightly floured work surface, **punch down,** and knead again for 3 to 5 minutes. Shape dough into a flattened disk about 6 inches wide. Cut an X in the top and place on greased baking sheet. Cover loaf with towel and leave in warm place to rise again until almost double in bulk, 45 minutes to 1 hour.

Preheat oven to 450° F.

4. Bake at 450° F for 15 minutes then reduce heat to 350° F and bake for 20 minutes more. Test for bread **doneness**. Remove from oven and cool on wire cake rack.

Serve bread while slightly warm from the oven with cocido Madrileño *(recipe page 185).*

In Spain, candy and other sweets are prepared for special occasions and holidays.

Turrón

Candy Nougats

Yield: serves 8 to 10

- 1 tablespoon confectioners' sugar
- 1 tablespoon cornstarch
- 1¼ cups sugar
- 10 tablespoons honey, divided
- 2 tablespoons milk
- 3 tablespoons **almond paste**, (available at supermarkets)
- 1 pound sliced or whole almonds, **blanched**

Equipment: Small strainer, aluminum foil, baking sheet, medium **heavy-based** saucepan, wooden mixing spoon, **serrated knife**, pitcher, small candy dish

1. Put confectioners' sugar and cornstarch in small strainer, and sprinkle lightly over foil-covered baking sheet. Set aside.

2. Put sugar and 8 tablespoons honey in medium heavy-based saucepan. Stirring constantly, cook over medium heat until sugar melts and mixture is golden, 3 to 5 minutes. Stir in remaining 2 tablespoons honey and milk, and using your hand, crumble in almond paste. Remove from heat, and beat with wooden mixing spoon until smooth. Pour ½-inch thick layer of mixture onto prepared foil-covered baking sheet. Smooth top of candy mixture. Using serrated knife dipped in pitcher of warm water, cut candy into 1-inch squares.

To serve, stack candy squares on small dish to eat as a sweet snack.

FRANCE

France, the largest country in Western Europe, has long been a world leader in both fashion and food. In a sense, Paris, the French capital, became the world capital of good eating because of the French Revolution that began in 1789. Ignited in part by the excessive social and economic privileges enjoyed by the nobility, the Revolution, in its most violent phase in the early 1790s, led to death on the guillotine for many French aristocrats. With their livelihoods gone, many fine chefs who had been in noble service went to Paris and opened restaurants specializing in what they knew best, haute cuisine. Thus, in the last two centuries, other countries have come to look to France for inspiration in what to eat.

The majority of French are Roman Catholic and most life-cycle celebrations are conducted according to the Catholic Church. (See Protestant and Catholic Life-Cycle Rituals, page xlvi.) A family's financial and social status also determines how they will celebrate life-cycle events and whether the celebration will be *haute cuisine* or *cuisine bourgeoisie*. *Haute cuisine* is refined, elegant French cooking prepared by highly trained cooks, called chefs. Weddings or other special occasions serving *haute cuisine* are always spectacular and expensive events. On the other hand, *cuisine bourgeoisie*—French country cooking—includes many classic dishes that are hearty, and also well within the budget of most French couples. One such dish is *poulet Marengo* (recipe follows).

Most French life-cycle celebrations are followed by a meal. After a baptismal ceremony, for instance, the family group either goes to a restaurant or holds a family dinner at home. French church weddings, which are generally held in the morning, are usually followed by a brunch or luncheon reception that takes place in the bride's family home or in a wedding hall, restaurant, or hotel banquet room. At the reception, it is customary for newlyweds to toast using a *coupe de mariage* filled with champagne. This special two-handled cup is often a family heirloom that has been passed down through generations.

Hors d'oeuvres (**appetizers**) are part of all celebration feasts regardless of social status. *Hors d'oeuvres* are eaten anytime and anywhere, from a simple farmer's lunch to an affluent wedding or birthday celebration. The farmer or working person's *hors d'oeuvres* might be simple platters of sliced fresh tomatoes **drizzled** with olive oil and a sprinkle of parsley or anchovy fillets on slices of toast, or sausage with assorted cheeses served with freshly baked bread. When *haute cuisine* is followed, the *hors d'oeuvres* are presented to guests on silver trays by formally attired waiters. The selection would be *pâtés* (the word means "pie" but they are a loaf made of a mixture of meat, seafood, or vegetables), *les* *crudités* (decoratively cut assorted raw vegetables, such as tiny baby carrots, celery hearts, and radishes), and expensive lobster or filled pastries, such as the following recipe for *chausson aux champignons* (mushroom pastries). ۞ ۞ ۞

Chausson aux Champignons

Mushroom Pastries

Yield: serves 8 to 10

- 1/4 cup butter
- 2 cups fresh mushrooms, **finely chopped**
- 1 onion, finely chopped
- 2 cloves garlic, finely chopped or 1 teaspoon garlic granules
- 4 1/2-ounce can deviled ham (available at all supermarkets)
- salt and pepper to taste
- nutmeg cheese pastry (recipe follows)

Equipment: Large skillet, wooden mixing spoon, medium mixing bowl, teaspoon, cup of water, lightly greased baking sheet, fork, oven mitts, large serving platter

1. Melt butter in large skillet over medium-high heat. Add finely chopped mushrooms, onion, and garlic. Stirring frequently, **sauté** for 3 to 5 minutes, or until onion is soft and mushrooms are golden. Remove from heat. Transfer to medium mixing bowl. Stir in deviled ham and salt and pepper to taste.

2. Prepare nutmeg cheese pastry (recipe follows).

Preheat oven to 425° F.

3. Assemble: Place a heaping teaspoonful of mushroom mixture in center of a pastry circle. Lightly moisten your finger with water and brush it along the edge of the pastry circle. Fold pastry shell over mushroom mixture to encase filling, making pastry into a half moon. Press edges of pastry shell together to seal in the mushroom mixture. Place on lightly greased baking sheet. Prick pastries 2 or 3 times with fork to allow steam to escape while cooking.

4. Bake in oven for 10 to 15 minutes, or until golden.

To serve, place warm pastries on a large serving platter. To eat pastries, pick one up from the tray with your fingers. Cocktail napkins should be provided for guests.

Pâtisserie Fromage avec Muscade

Nutmeg Cheese Pastry

Yield: 20 to 24 pieces

- 2 cups all-purpose flour
- 1/2 cup grated cheddar cheese
- 1/4 teaspoon salt
- 1/2 teaspoon **ground** nutmeg
- 3/4 cup vegetable shortening
- 1/4 cup water

Equipment: Large mixing bowl, **pastry blender** or 2 forks, plastic food wrap, lightly floured work surface, rolling pin, 3- or 4-inch round cookie cutter, clean kitchen towel

1. Put flour, cheese, salt, and nutmeg in large mixing bowl. Using a pastry blender or two forks, cut in shortening until mixture is crumbly. Add water, a little at a time, and using your hands, mix until smooth. Form into a ball, flatten to about 1-inch thick disk, wrap in plastic wrap, and refrigerate for 30 minutes.

2. On lightly floured work surface, using a rolling pin, roll pastry out to 1/8 inch thickness. Using 3- or 4-inch cookie cutter, cut 20 to 24 circles. Stack, slightly overlapping, on work surface and cover with towel.

Continue with chausson aux champignons *(recipe precedes: Step 3. Assemble:) or pastries can be refrigerated overnight in an airtight container or frozen for up to 1 month. Thaw before using.*

Pain de mariage (wedding bread) is wrapped in a napkin and taken to church to be blessed by the priest. The bread is then taken to the wedding breakfast where the bride and groom cut it together and share the first slice. The sharing of bread symbolizes their unity as husband and wife. Some couples have the *brioche* (rich egg bread) baked for their wedding bread. *Brioche* is the same as Belgium's *coûque de vise* (recipe page 197), except that the Belgians, unlike the French, add crushed sugar cubes or rock candy crystals.

Pain de Mariage

Wedding Bread

Yield: 1 large loaf

- 1½ cups all-purpose flour
- 1 cup rye flour
- 2 tablespoons baking powder
- ½ teaspoon baking soda
- 1 teaspoon salt
- ½ teaspoon **ground** cardamom
- ½ teaspoon black pepper
- 2 eggs
- ½ cup honey
- ½ cup orange juice
- 1 cup melted butter or margarine
- 1 teaspoon almond extract
- 1 tablespoon grated orange peel
- 1 cup chopped or sliced almonds

Equipment: Flour **sifter**, medium bowl, large mixing bowl, electric mixer, mixing spoon or rubber spatula, greased 9 x 5 loaf pan, oven mitts, toothpick, wire cake rack

Preheat oven to 350° F.

1. **Sift** all-purpose flour, rye flour, baking powder, baking soda, salt, cardamom, and black pepper into medium bowl.

2. In large mixing bowl, beat eggs, using electric mixer, until thick and yellow, 2 to 3 minutes. Beating constantly, add honey, orange juice, melted butter or margarine, almond extract, and orange peel. Beat until well mixed, 1 to 2 minutes. Using mixing spoon or rubber spatula, **fold in** flour mixture, 1 cup at a time, blending well after each addition. Fold in almonds. Pour batter into lightly greased 9 x 5 loaf pan.

3. Bake for 45 to 50 minutes, or until toothpick inserted in center comes out clean. Allow to cool for 10 minutes before turning onto wire cake rack.

Serve the bread either warm or cold. After the bride and groom slice the bread, it is shared with grandparents, parents, and the wedding party. Each guest then gets a slice.

The first decorated wedding cakes were really wedding breads with icing on them.

During the seventeenth century, French pastry chefs created the forerunners of today's elaborate tiered wedding cakes. The cake was heavily spiced, much like the English wedding cake and coated with **marzipan**, similar to the Caribbean black wedding cake (recipe page 360).

In France, the *croquembouche* (meaning "crisp in mouth") is not only a great wedding cake, but is also made for other auspicious occasions, such as birthdays, saints' days, and anniversaries. The *croquembouche* is an assembly project of tiny custard-filled cream puffs. Traditionally the cream puffs are dipped in **sugar syrup**, which hardens and "glues" them together as they are stacked.

The following recipe is much easier to make than traditional *croquembouche*; the cream puffs hang on toothpicks around a foil-covered, cone-shaped piece of Styrofoam. Prepare the cone first and have everything ready to assemble. The decorations can be anything you like. Some ideas are listed as garnishes in the recipe.

Croquembouche

Wedding Cake of Cream Puffs

Yield: Serves 30 to 40

choux à la crème (recipe follows)

2 (8-ounces each) canned buttercream icing (available at all supermarkets)

Candied cherries, fresh strawberries or fresh or dried flowers, for **garnish**

Equipment: 18-inch cone-shaped Styrofoam (available at craft and hobby stores), **serrated knife**, aluminum foil, double-sided mounting tape (available at all supermarkets or office supply stores), large round tray or platter, toothpicks, paring knife, rubber spatula or mixing spoon, **pastry bag** fitted with ¼-inch plain tip, 1 or 2 baking sheets

1. Prepare Styrofoam: Using a serrated knife, cut off about 5 inches from the top pointed end of the cone. Completely cover Styrofoam cone with foil, tucking it under the bottom about 1 inch. Attach several strips of double-sided mounting tape to large round tray or platter, set the cone on top, and press down to secure. Cover surface of the cone with toothpicks, spaced about 1 inch apart and sticking out halfway.

2. Prepare *choux à la crème* (cream puffs): To make a larger *croquembouche* you will need to make 3 or 4 batches of *choux à la crème* (cream puffs, recipe follows).

4. Assemble: Open cans of butter cream icing, and using small knife, put a thick dab of icing on flat bottom-side of each cream puff and press onto toothpicks around the bottom of the cone. Complete each row, fitting cream puffs close together and working toward the top. (See illustration.)

Continue to decorate the croquembouche *by poking candied cherries, fresh strawberries, or fresh or dried flowers into spaces between the cream puffs. At the top, put a small bouquet of flowers, ribbons, or decorations of your choice.*

Choux à la crème are cream-filled pastries that puff-up during baking. *Choux* is the pastry and *la crème* is the pudding-like filling.

Choux à la Crème

Cream Puffs

Yield: 3 to 4 dozen

1 cup water

½ teaspoon salt

½ cup unsalted butter

1 cup bread flour or all-purpose flour, sifted

4 eggs, at room temperature

egg wash

French cream filling (recipe follows) or 1 to 2 boxes vanilla pudding mix (available at all supermarkets)

Equipment: Medium **heavy-based** saucepan, wooden mixing spoon, medium mixing bowl, 1 or 2 baking sheets, parchment paper, teaspoon or **pastry bag** fitted with 1/4-inch plain tip, **pastry brush**, wire cake rack

Preheat oven to 400° F.

1. Prepare *choux* pastry: Heat water and salt in medium heavy-based saucepan over medium-high heat. Stir until butter melts and mixture comes to a boil; remove from heat. Add flour all at once and beat briskly with wooden spoon for 2 or 3 minutes until mixture pulls away from sides of pan. Return pan to heat for about 30 seconds, beating vigorously to dry out pastry. Cool for 5 minutes. Beat in eggs, one at a time, beating briskly after each addition until mixture is glossy and very smooth. After eggs are added, continue to beat for 3 minutes more. The mix-

ture should cling to sides of pan and to the mixing spoon.

2. Prepare to bake: Line baking sheets with parchment paper. Make the *choux* pastry the size of Ping-Pong balls. (The balls puff up as they bake.) If using a spoon to make small mounds, leave 2-inch space between each. For more uniform results, pipe *choux* dough through the pastry bag. Fill pastry bag fitted with ¼-inch tip. Hold the bag with the tip almost touching the parchment paper. Do not move the tip as you gently squeeze the bag from the top. Allow the desired amount of dough to bubble up around the tip of the pastry bag and quickly lift the bag to finish making the ball. The small point formed when you lift the tip can be pressed down with a moistened finger. Repeat making pastries, spacing them 2-inches apart on baking sheets. Brush each *choux* pastry lightly with egg wash.

3. Bake in hot oven for 15 minutes. Reduce heat to 325° F for 15 minutes and bake 20 to 25 minutes longer, until firm and golden brown. Remove from oven, and transfer to wire cake rack.

4. Prepare *French cream filling* (recipe follows), or 2 boxes vanilla pudding (prepared according to directions on package). Keep covered and refrigerated until ready to use.

5. Fill *choux* pastries: Using a paring knife, make a ½-inch slit in the side of each pastry. Uncover and stir French cream filling, or if using prepared pudding mix, do the same. Use rubber spatula or mixing spoon, fill pastry bag fitted with ¼-inch plain tip with filling. Squeeze about 1 teaspoon filling into each slit. Place filled shells side by side on baking sheet.

Unfilled baked choux *pastries can be refrigerated up to one week in an airtight container or frozen*

The French *croquembouche* is a tower of tiny cream puffs. For easy assembly, hang the cream puffs on toothpicks inserted halfway into a foil-dovered Styrofoam cone.

for about one month. Place in 275° F. oven for 3 to 5 minutes to crisp and freshen.

Two boxes of vanilla pudding (available at most supermarkets and prepared according to directions on package) can be used instead of the following *French cream filling*.

French Cream Filling

Yield: about 2 cups
- ½ cup sugar
- 2 tablespoons cornstarch
- ¼ cup sifted all-purpose flour
- ¼ teaspoon salt
- 2 egg yolks, slightly beaten
- ¼ cup milk, at room temperature
- 2 cups **lukewarm** half & half
- 1 tablespoon unsalted butter
- 1 teaspoon vanilla or almond extract

Equipment: Medium heavy-based saucepan, mixing spoon, small bowl, plastic food wrap

1. In medium heavy-based saucepan, mix sugar, cornstarch, flour, and salt. In small bowl, mix egg yolks with milk, and stir into sugar mixture until smooth. Continue to stir, adding warm light cream to sugar mixture, a little at a time, until well mixed.

2. Cook over medium heat, stirring constantly, until thickened, 8 to 10 minutes. Reduce heat to low and stir constantly for 5 minutes. Remove from heat and stir in butter to dissolve. Cool to room temperature, stirring frequently to keep smooth consistency and to prevent crust from forming on top. When cool, stir in vanilla or almond extract. When finished mixing, lay plastic wrap directly onto the top of mixture to prevent a film from forming. You must refrigerate for 3 or 4 hours before using.

Traditionally, French weddings are morning affairs requiring a brunch or lunch-type menu. A large platter of *beignets soufflés* set out for hungry guests is a welcome treat. The *beignets soufflés* offer a way of using up any puff pastry dough that might be leftover from making the *croquembouche*.

Beignets Soufflés

Deep Fried Puff Pastry (also Fritters)

CAUTION: HOT OIL USED

Yield: serves 6 to 10
- *choux* pastry (recipe page 191)
- vegetable oil for **deep frying**
- granulated sugar, for **garnish**
- assorted fruit jams or marmalades, for serving

Equipment: Teaspoon, wax paper, baking sheet, **deep fryer** (see glossary for tips on making a deep fryer), **deep-fryer thermometer** or wooden spoon, paper towels, baking sheet, metal tongs or **slotted metal spoon**

1. Prepare puff pastry dough (recipe precedes; use only step 1.

2. Divide dough into heaping teaspoonfuls on wax-paper-covered baking sheet.

3. Prepare to deep-fry: ADULT SUPERVISION REQUIRED. Heat oil to 375° F on deep-fryer thermometer or when small bubbles appear around a wooden spoon handle when it is dipped in the oil. Have ready several layers of paper towels on baking sheet. Fry pastries, a few at a time, carefully turning with metal tongs or slotted metal spoon to brown all sides, about 3 minutes. Transfer to paper towels to drain. Keep warm until ready to serve. Continue frying in batches.

4. Sprinkle *beignets* generously with sugar, for garnish.

Serve at once while still warm with side dishes of assorted fruit jams or marmalades.

According to legend, on the night of June 14, 1800, after defeating Austrian troops at Marengo in Italy, Napoleon wanted to celebrate with a fine dinner. However, his Swiss chef, Dunand, had lost his food wagons during the battle, so he was forced to scrounge for whatever he could find in the vicinity. Coming up with a few chickens, eggs, tomatoes, olive oil, and garlic, he concocted what became a *bourgeoisie* classic—*poulet Marengo*. The dish is perfect for a French wedding luncheon when garnished with heart-shaped *croûtes* and eggs, the symbol of fertility. Today, a few more ingredients, such as mushrooms, are added to make the recipe more interesting.

Poulet Marengo

Chicken Marengo-style

Yield: serves 4 to 6

1 tablespoon vegetable oil
10 tablespoons butter or margarine, divided
$2\frac{1}{2}$ to $3\frac{1}{2}$ pound roasting chicken, cut into serving-size pieces
3 cloves garlic, **finely chopped**
2 cups mushrooms, fresh or canned (drained), sliced
2 tomatoes, **peeled**, **seeded,** and finely chopped
1 tablespoon tomato paste
$1\frac{1}{2}$ cups canned beef broth
salt and pepper to taste
4 to 6 slices white bread, for **garnish**
4 to 6 eggs, for garnish
2 tablespoons finely chopped parsley, for garnish

Equipment: Large **heavy-based** saucepan with cover or **Dutch oven**, metal tongs, baking pan, mixing spoon, work surface, paring knife or heart-shaped cookie cutters, large skillet with cover, metal spatula, paper towels, saucer

Preheat oven to 250° F.

1. Heat oil and 4 tablespoons butter or margarine in large **heavy-based** saucepan or Dutch oven over medium-high heat. Add chicken pieces and fry, in batches, until golden brown on both sides, 5 to 7 minutes on each side. Remove chicken with metal tongs leaving the juices in the saucepan, put in baking pan, and keep warm in oven while frying remaining pieces.

2. Stir garlic into juices leftover in saucepan or Dutch oven used to fry chicken. Add mushroom, tomatoes, tomato paste, beef broth, and salt and pepper to taste, and stir well. Return fried chicken pieces to saucepan or Dutch oven, cover, and cook over medium heat for 45 to 50 minutes, or until tender and cooked through. Test for **chicken doneness**.

3. Prepare ***croûtes***: Place bread slices on work surface and, using paring knife or heart-shaped cookie cutter, cut each slice into a heart shape. Melt 4 tablespoons butter or margarine in large skillet over medium-high heat. Add heart-shaped bread slices and fry until golden brown, 2 to 3 minutes on each side. Remove with metal spatula and drain on paper towels.

4. Just before serving, melt remaining 2 tablespoons butter or margarine in large skillet over medium heat. Break eggs, one at a time, into a saucer, and transfer to skillet. **Baste** eggs, cover, and cook until whites are set and yolks are done, 3 to 5 minutes.

To serve, arrange the chicken pieces on a large platter and spoon sauce over top. Place the croûtes around the edge of the platter with the pointed ends facing out. Arrange fried eggs either between or on each heart-shaped croûte. *Sprinkle with parsley and serve at once.*

BELGIUM

Located in northwestern Europe between the Netherlands on the north and France on the south, Belgium contains two major linguistic groups—French-speaking Walloons in the south and the Flemish-speaking Flemings in the north. A German-speaking minority lives close to the eastern border with Germany. Each region has its own separate educational administration and children are taught their regional language.

Belgium is predominantly Roman Catholic and religion plays an important part in the nation's culture. The country has many Catholic schools where children get religious instruction along with their regular studies. Belgium is the last country in northern Europe to have a Catholic monarch, and most national holidays are still based on religious occasions, particularly Christmas and Easter. The people traditionally turn to the Catholic Church for important life-cycle events. (See Protestant and Catholic Life-Cycle Rituals, page xlvi.)

Although church attendance is low, most Belgians see to it that their children are baptized, make first communion, and go to Sunday school. Baptisms are conducted according to Catholic ritual and the ceremony is usually followed by a family dinner, either at home or at a local restaurant. The big occasion for most children is when they make their First Communion at age 12. This life-cycle event marks the child's passing into young adulthood. The celebration usually includes a big family party with plenty of sweets and children receive gifts from relatives and friends.

Belgian endive is originally from Belgium where it is called *whitloof* (white leaf) due to its delicate whitish-green color. The color is a result of the vegetable being grown in complete darkness to prevent it turning deep green; the endive also turns bitter if it is exposed to light.

Whitloof Farci au Fromage

Belgian Endive with Ham in Cheese Sauce

Yield: 6 or 8

water, as needed
salt and pepper, as needed
6 or 8 fresh Belgian endives
6 or 8 boiled ham slices
1 cup dry white wine or chicken broth, homemade (recipe page 106) or canned
1 cup milk
2 tablespoons butter or margarine
¼ pound Gruyere or Emmentaler cheese, coarsely chopped (available in refrigerated section of most supermarkets)
¼ teaspoon nutmeg

Equipment: Medium saucepan, **colander**, 1 or 2 buttered 8- or 9-inch square baking pan, small **heavy-based** saucepan, mixing spoon, oven mitts

Preheat broiler.

1. **Blanch** endives: Fill medium saucepan halfway with water, add 2 teaspoons salt, and bring to boil over high heat. Add endives, and continue to boil for 3 minutes. Drain endives in colander until cool enough to handle.

2. Wrap a slice of boiled ham around each endive and place seam-side down in buttered 8- or 9-inch baking pan, do not stack. Place remaining endive in a single layer on second baking pan.

3. Pour white wine or chicken broth into small heavy-based saucepan. Add milk and butter or margarine. Bring to boil over medium-high heat, stir to melt butter or margarine. Reduce heat to medium-low, add cheese, and stir to melt cheese and thicken sauce. Stir in nutmeg and salt and pepper to taste. Pour cheese sauce over wrapped endives in baking pan.

4. Place in oven under broiler for 12 to 18 minutes, or until heated through, and sauce is bubbly and lightly browned.

Serve as the first course for the wedding reception luncheon. Each person is served a ham-wrapped endive.

In Belgium, *poussins aux chicons en cocotte* (chicken and Belgian endive stew) is made with young chickens not available in this country; use Cornish hens instead.

Poussins aux Chicons en Cocotte

Chicken and Belgian Endive Stew

Yield: serves 6

10 Belgian endives, trimmed, washed, and drained
6 Cornish hens, fresh or frozen (thawed) (available at all supermarkets)
salt and pepper to taste
½ cup vegetable oil, divided
1½ cups water
1 cup heavy cream

Equipment: Work surface, paring knife, large bowl, meat knife, paper towels, large skillet, metal tongs, large plate, large saucepan with cover or **Dutch oven**, mixing spoon, serving platter

1. On work surface, cut endives crosswise into about ¼-inch slices and put in large bowl. Set aside.

2. Place hens on work surface and using meat knife, split each in half lengthwise. Rinse under cold running water and pat dry with paper towels. Sprinkle all sides with salt and pepper to taste.

3. Heat ¼ cup oil in large skillet over medium-high heat. Add hens in batches and fry until browned on both sides, 7 to 12 minutes each side. Reduce heat to medium, if necessary to avoid burning. Using metal tongs, transfer hens to large plate.

4. Pour remaining ¼ cup oil into large saucepan or Dutch oven and swirl to coat bottom. Spread sliced endives over bottom of pan and layer fried hens on top. Add water and pan drippings from skillet.

5. Cover and cook over medium heat for 1 hour, until hens are done. (*See* **chicken doneness.**) Using metal tongs, remove hens, place around edge of serving platter, and keep warm. Add heavy cream to cooked endives in saucepan or Dutch oven and stir. Cook over medium heat 5 to 7 minutes to **reduce** and thicken. Spoon endive mixture into center of serving platter.

To serve, each person gets two halves (Cornish hens are small). Spoon creamed endive on the dinner plate. Serve with potatoes or noodles and salad.

Southern Belgium grows particularly fine asparagus, which is a favorite vegetable throughout the country. The following easy-to-prepare dish would be served for a family celebration dinner.

Asperges de Malines

Asparagus with Egg Sauce

Yield: serves 4

2 hard-cooked eggs, coarsely chopped
1 tablespoon fresh parsley, **finely chopped**
salt and pepper to taste
¾ cup melted butter, cooled
2½ to 3 pounds fresh asparagus

Equipment: Small bowl with cover, fork, paring knife or vegetable peeler, large saucepan, metal tongs, spoon, large serving platter

1. In small bowl, mash chopped hard-cooked eggs with fork. Add parsley and salt and pepper

to taste, and stir to mix well. Stirring constantly, slowly pour in melted butter in a thin stream. Cover and set aside.

2. Using paring knife or vegetable peeler, **trim** off tough fibrous bottom part of each asparagus spear and discard. Wash asparagus under cold running water.

3. Fill large saucepan two-thirds full with water and bring to boil over high heat. Add 2 tablespoons salt and asparagus, and boil for 8 to 10 minutes (depending upon thickness of spears), or until tender. Do not overcook. Using tongs, transfer asparagus to large serving platter and arrange neatly so all lay in same direction. Carefully spoon sauce in a ribbon across the middle of asparagus.

Serve asparagus while still warm as a side dish with poussins aux chicons en cocotte *(recipe page 196).*

The Walloons have many of the same lifecycle customs as neighboring France (see France page 188). Some Belgian brides prefer *coûque de visé,* a sugar crusted egg-rich bread for the wedding celebration feasts in place of *pain de mariage* (recipe page 190). *Coûque de visé* is the same as French *brioche* except the French do not add the coarsely crushed sugar cubes or rock candy crystals.

Special *brioche* pans are available at kitchenware stores. They range in size from 4 to 9½ inches in diameter. For this recipe, you can use either an 8-inch *brioche* pan or 8-inch springform pan that is at least 4 inches deep.

The original recipe for *coûque de visé* calls for homemade rock candy crystals that take at least one to two weeks to crystallize. In this recipe, you can substitute crushed sugar cubes or commercial rock candy crystals.

Coûque de Visé (also French Brioche)

Belgian Egg Bread

Note: This recipe takes 24 hours.

Yield: 1 loaf

6 tablespoons coarsely crushed sugar cubes or rock candy crystals, homemade (recipe follows) or commercial (available at candy stores or some supermarkets)
1 package active dry **yeast**
3 teaspoons sugar, divided
3 tablespoons **lukewarm** water
½ cup milk
½ cup butter or margarine, at room temperature
½ teaspoons salt
3 cups sifted all-purpose flour
2 eggs, beaten
egg wash, for **garnish**

Equipment: Small bowl, small spoon, small saucepan, candy **thermometer** (optional), greased large mixing bowl, mixing spoon, lightly floured work surface, greased plastic food wrap, 8-inch greased *brioche* or 8-inch springform pan, **pastry brush**, oven mitts, aluminum foil (optional), wire cake rack

1. If adding homemade rock candy crystals, prepare at least 1 to 2 weeks ahead.

2. In small bowl, dissolve yeast and ½ teaspoon sugar in lukewarm water and let stand until foamy, 5 to 10 minutes.

3. Bring milk to boil in small saucepan over medium-high heat. Add butter or margarine, remaining 2½ teaspoons sugar, and salt, and stir until dissolved. Remove from heat and set aside to cool to lukewarm.

4. Put 1¾ cups flour in large mixing bowl. Add beaten eggs, yeast mixture, and milk mixture, beat until well mixed and smooth. Beating con-

stantly, add remaining 1¼ cups flour, a little at a time, to form soft dough. Transfer to lightly floured work surface and **knead** until smooth and satiny, about 3 to 5 minutes. Shape dough into a ball and put into greased large mixing bowl, and turn dough to grease all sides. Grease one side of plastic food wrap and place, greased-side down, over bowl of dough. Leave dough in warm place to rise to double in bulk, 1½ to 2 hours.

5. Transfer dough to lightly floured work surface, **punch down,** and knead for 3 to 5 minutes. Knead half the crushed sugar cubes or crushed rock candy crystals into the dough. Shape into a ball, place in greased large bowl, and turn dough to grease all sides. Cover with greased plastic wrap and refrigerate overnight.

6. Next morning, remove dough from refrigerator and bring to room temperature, about 1 hour. Pull off a piece of dough about the size of an egg. Shape remaining dough into a ball and place in 8-inch greased *brioche* or springform pan. Using your finger, poke a hole about 1 inch deep into the top center of loaf. Form the egg-size piece of dough into a light bulb shape, and set small bottom end into the hole, making a top knob on the loaf. Cover with greased plastic wrap and leave in warm place to rise until double in bulk, 1 to 1½ hours.

Preheat oven to 375° F.

7. Using pastry brush, gently brush loaf with egg wash and sprinkle with remaining 2 tablespoons crushed sugar cubes or crushed rock candy crystals.

8. Bake in oven for 40 to 45 minutes or until golden brown. If top knob of dough looks like it might be getting too brown, cover it with small piece of foil. Test **bread doneness** and adjust cooking time accordingly. Using oven mitts, remove from baking pan and cool on wire cake rack.

Serve this bread the same day it is baked for best flavor and texture.

Making rock candy crystals is an interesting project in crystallization that takes about 1 to 2 weeks.

Rock Candy Crystals

Yield: about 1 cup
3 cups sugar
1 cup water

Equipment: 20 inches kitchen string, 6-inch pencil or stick, 2 small metal washers to use as weights, wide-mouth pint-size canning jar, medium saucepan, mixing spoon, candy **thermometer**

Prepare processing container: Cut string in half, making two 10-inch pieces of string. Tie one end of each string around the middle of a pencil or stick. Leave space between strings so they do not touch each other or sides of container. Tie a metal washer as a weight on the bottom end of each string to keep it in the water. Adjust the length of strings so the washer pulls it taut to the bottom of the jar. The finished string lengths will be about 4 to 5 inches long.

1. Prepare **sugar syrup**: Stir sugar in water in medium saucepan to dissolve. Bring to boil over medium-high heat. Reduce heat to **simmer** and cook without stirring until mixture registers 247° to 252° F on candy thermometer. Remove from heat.

2. Pour hot sugar syrup into the processing container. Rest the pencil or stick across the top of the jar and lower the strings into the syrup. Set the jar in a safe place in easy view. Do not disturb for about 2 weeks when rock candy should form on the strings. If any crystals cover the top of the syrup solution carefully break up the crust with a spoon to let evaporation continue.

3. Remove strings from solution and rinse quickly under cold water. Hang to dry at room temperature for about 12 hours.

Coarsely crush rock candy crystals, discard string, and use in recipe for coûque de visé *(recipe precedes: Step 5.) or eat as candy.*

UNITED KINGDOM

A constitutional monarchy comprising England, Scotland, Wales, and Northern Ireland, the United Kingdom (UK) is located on an archipelago (i.e., a cluster of islands) that is separated from northwestern Europe by the English Channel, the North Sea, and the narrow Straits of Dover. Great Britain, the largest of the British Isles, contains the main constituent parts of the United Kingdom—England in the south, Scotland in the north, and Wales in the west. The United Kingdom also encompasses Northern Ireland, the northeastern corner of Ireland, second largest of the British Isles; the small Isles of Man and Wight; and the Shetlands, Orkneys, and Hebrides, island chains off Great Britain. Although the term "Great Britain" is sometimes employed to refer to the United Kingdom, the name England should never be used to describe the UK as a whole, for England is only one part of the modern united monarchy. ۞ ۞ ۞

ENGLAND

In modern England, the population is largely urban and suburban and has in recent years become more ethnically diverse, with many persons of Asian and African descent living in London, the capital, and the other large cities of the country. The Church of England (Episcopal Church in the U.S.) is the national church and the largest denomination, but virtually all major world religions can be found in the UK. People celebrate most life-cycle events according to their particular religion. (See Protestant and Catholic Life-Cycle Rituals, page xlvi.)

English families often come together to share a home-cooked meal, especially on Sunday. Although the midday Sunday meal is a hearty feast, it is called "lunch." Even when children marry and have their own families, they often return with their children for the weekly Sunday lunch reunion at their parent's home. This tradition is especially practiced in farming communities where family members usually live close to one another.

English weddings are often held in the early afternoon. Wedding rehearsal dinners, which are popular in the United States, are virtually unheard of in England. After an English wedding ceremony, guests are usually served a hearty sit-down dinner or buffet. Later in the evening, cold cuts, cheeses, condiments, salads, and assorted breads are set out for guests to munch on as the celebration continues.

The wedding reception is generally in a rented hall, hotel, inn, or family home. In past generations, the wedding cake was a simple wheat cake or bread-like biscuit. It was broken and the first pieces were eaten by the bride and groom. The remainder of the cake was broken over the bride's head and the guests gathered up the crumbs and ate them. The cake was a symbol of fertility and the earth's abundance. It supposedly guaranteed the bride and groom a life of prosperity and many children.

For many generations, the traditional English wedding cake has been the *English fruitcake* (recipe page 202), which is still a favorite today. The top tier, called the "christening cake," is saved for the christening of the couple's first child. When the top is used for a christening, it decorated on top with a crib or cradle. The christening is a joyous occasion and is often followed with a large party at either a rented hall or at the family home.

The English usually end formal and informal dinners and buffets with the *cheese board,* an assortment of cheeses with crackers served with coffee and port (sweet wine). Sometimes a light savory course is served after dessert. These course generally consists of such simple dishes as stuffed mushrooms (recipe follows), *spiced prawns* (recipe page 200), *Welsh rarebit* (recipe page 211), or trout with bacon (recipe page 210). Most savories make excellent appetizers.

Brandy Butter Stuffed Mushrooms on Toast

Yield: *Serves 4 to 6*

- ½ cup butter or margarine, more as needed
- 1 clove garlic, **finely chopped**
- 1 **shallot**, finely chopped
- 2 teaspoons parsley, finely chopped
- 1 teaspoon brandy-flavored extract or 1 tablespoon brandy
- 1 cup **bread crumbs**
- salt and pepper to taste
- 16 fresh medium mushrooms, stems removed, rinsed, and dried with towel
- ½ cup shredded Swiss cheese
- 4 slices bread, crusts removed

Equipment: Medium skillet, mixing spoon, 8–10 inch baking pan, plastic food wrap, oven mitts, serving platter or individual appetizer plates

1. Prepare brandy butter: Melt ½ cup butter or margarine in medium skillet, over medium heat. Add garlic and shallot, stir, and sauté until soft, about 1 minute. Remove from heat, add parsley, brandy extract or brandy, and bread crumbs, and stir to mix well.

2. Stuff mushrooms: Using your hands, rub outside of each mushroom cap with butter or margarine, and place side by side, top-side down in baking pan. Fill caps equally with brandy butter and sprinkle each with shredded cheese. Cover with plastic wrap and refrigerate until serving time.

Preheat oven to 350° F.

3. At serving time: Bake in oven for 10 to 12 minutes, or until mushrooms are just tender and cheese is melted. Toast bread and cut each slice diagonally to form 2 triangular pieces. Set on a serving platter or individual plates. Set 2 mushrooms on each piece of toast and spoon pan drippings over each serving.

Serve warm as an appetizer or savory (after dinner item). It is best to use a fork and knife to eat this dish.

Spiced prawns is another popular English appetizer or savory that is elegant and easy to make.

Spiced Prawns

Spiced Shrimp

Yield: serves 4

- 2 tablespoons butter or margarine
- 2 tablespoons all-purpose flour
- 1 cup milk
- ½ teaspoon curry powder
- 1½ cups (about ½ pound) small shrimp, cooked, **peeled, and deveined**
- salt and pepper to taste
- 4 slices white toast, crusts removed and buttered on one side
- 2 tablespoons grated Parmesan cheese, for **garnish**

Equipment: **Heavy-based** medium skillet, **whisk**, mixing spoon, medium bowl with cover, greased baking sheet, oven mitts, metal spatula, individual appetizer plates

1. Prepare sauce: Melt 2 tablespoons butter or margarine in heavy-based medium skillet over medium-high heat. Remove from heat, and whisk in flour until smooth. Reduce heat to medium and return skillet to heat. Whisking constantly, slowly add milk until sauce is smooth and thickened. Stir in curry powder. Remove from heat and cool to warm.

2. Using mixing spoon, **fold in** shrimp. Add salt and pepper to taste. At this point the shrimp mixture can be transferred to medium bowl, covered, and refrigerated until serving time.

At serving time, preheat broiler.

3. Place toast, buttered side up, on greased baking sheet. Divide shrimp mixture equally on each slice of toast, and sprinkle with grated cheese. Broil until golden brown and bubbly, 3 to 5 minutes. Remove from baking sheet using metal spatula and place on individual appetizer plates.

Serve at once while still hot. Forks and knives are needed for eating spiced shrimp.

Tea is more than just a warming, stimulating liquid to the English. Drinking tea is a ritual that has been part of English life since about 1700. The English drink tea at all hours of the day, beginning first thing in the morning. A designated "tea" can be prepared for many different occasions: afternoon tea, funeral tea, high tea, and Christmas tea, to mention a few. "Tea" is also the name of a meal. In rural areas, where the heartiest meal is at midday, the lighter evening meal is called "high tea" (also "meat tea"). In the cities, where dinner is served late in the evening, "tea" is an afternoon snack. Afternoon tea should be a relaxing and pleasant break from work and the pressures of the day.

Traditional fare for afternoon tea includes bread and butter; a special bread, such as scones; biscuits (cookies); a selection of cakes; and two or three different thin sandwiches. Fresh fruit, cookies, and nut candies are also welcome. A children's tea or nursery tea is usually a simple affair. The menu might include tiny sandwiches spread with butter, jam, honey, or mashed banana; gingerbread or *ginger cat cookies* (recipe page 202); or some kind of cake served with *cambric tea*, which is warm milk with sugar to which a drop or two of tea is added.

An English funeral usually includes a funeral tea prepared by the widow or other family members of the deceased. Besides tea, assorted sandwiches, cakes, biscuits, cookies, and candies are provided; alcoholic beverages are also usually available for the mourners.

Whether in times of stress and sorrow or in moments of joy, the English turn almost automatically to their favorite beverage. Tea is a great comforter; it relaxes people and encourages friendship. To drink tea English-style, some people prefer to pour the desired amount of milk in the cup before adding the tea, while others add the milk after the tea is in the cup. A debate raged for months in The London *Times* newspaper whether to add milk before or after the tea is added to the cup. Opinions were divided, although everyone agreed that one should never add hot milk to the tea

English Tea

Hot Beverage

boiling water

loose black tea leaves (Allow 1 teaspoon tea leaves for each cup to be served and 1 teaspoon for the pot)
cold milk, for serving
sugar, for serving

Equipment: Tea kettle, teapot, tea cozy (insulated cloth cover for the teapot) or thick kitchen towel, tea strainer

Add a little boiling water to the teapot, swirl the water to warm the pot, and pour it out. Put proper amount of tea leaves in the pot, add 1 cup boiling water for each serving. Put the lid on and cover the teapot with a tea cozy or a thick towel. Let the tea brew for 5 minutes before serving. Pour tea through a strainer into the cup.

Serve tea with something to munch on, preferably something sweet.

Ginger Cat Cookies

Yield: 25 to 35 pieces
2¼ cups all-purpose flour
2 teaspoons **ground** ginger
¼ teaspoon ground cinnamon
½ cup sugar
½ cup (¼-pound) butter or margarine
½ cup hot water, more or less as needed
1 (4.25 ounce) tube blue decorating icing, for **garnish** (available at all supermarkets)
1 (4.25 ounce) tube pink or red decorating icing, for garnish (available at all supermarkets)

Equipment: Flour **sifter**, large mixing bowl, mixing spoon, lightly floured work surface, lightly floured rolling pin, cat-shaped cookie cutter, greased baking sheet, oven mitts, wire cake rack, 4 plastic decorating tips to screw on 4.25 ounce tubes of decorating icing (optional) (available at all supermarkets)

Preheat oven to 325° F.

1. **Sift** flour, ginger, cinnamon, and sugar into large mixing bowl. Add butter or margarine, and using your hands, **blend** until mixture resembles fine bread crumbs. Add hot water, a little at a time, to make a firm dough. Transfer to lightly floured work surface and shape into a flat square.

2. Using lightly floured rolling pin, roll dough to ¼ inch thick. Using cat-shaped cookie cutter, cut out cookies. Place cookies on greased baking sheet.

3. Bake in oven for 15 to 20 minutes until edges are lightly browned. Transfer to wire cake rack to cool.

4. Using tube of blue decorating icing fitted with writing tip (small, round tip), pipe 2 blue dots for the eyes. Using tube of pink or red decorating icing fitted with either writing tip or leaf tip (narrow, tear-drop-shaped tip), make a bow around the neck of each cat cookie. Set aside to dry, 1 to 2 hours.

Serve children ginger cat cookies *with* English tea.

The traditional English wedding cake takes more than a month to prepare. The fruitcake can be rich, such as the *black wedding cake* of the Caribbean (recipe page 360) or it can be made according to the following recipe. To make a three **tiered wedding cake**—10-inch bottom layer, 8-inch middle layer, and 6-inch top layer—requires three batches of this recipe. ***Note***: *Making the recipe three times is easier than trying to triple it.* After making three batches, distribute batter among three prepared cake pans.

English Fruitcake

English Wedding Cake

Note: this recipe requires a month to finish.

Yield: 8-inch cake
3 cups seedless golden raisins
2 cups seedless raisins

2 cups chopped mixed candied fruits
1 cup slivered almonds
2 cups all-purpose flour
½ teaspoon salt
½ teaspoon **ground** cinnamon
½ teaspoon ground nutmeg
¾ cup butter or margarine
grated rind of ½ lemon or orange
¾ cup dark brown sugar
4 eggs, beaten
2 tablespoons brandy or rum or 1 tablespoon frozen orange juice concentrate
marzipan, (available at all supermarkets) for **garnish**

Equipment: Buttered 8-inch springform pan, scissors, parchment paper, small bowl, flour **sifter**, medium mixing bowl, large mixing bowl, electric mixer, mixing spoon, rubber spatula, spray bottle with misting nozzle, oven mitts, aluminum foil, toothpick, wire cake rack, large plastic bag, work surface, rolling pin

Prepare baking pan: Cut parchment paper to fit bottom of buttered 8-inch springform pan, place in pan, and lightly butter top surface of paper.

Preheat oven to 350° F.

1. Put golden raisins, raisins, chopped mixed candied fruit, and almonds in small bowl.

2. **Sift** flour, salt, cinnamon, and nutmeg into medium mixing bowl. Scoop out 1 cup flour mixture and sprinkle over mixed fruit mixture. Toss well until fruit mixture is thoroughly coated with flour.

3. In large mixing bowl, beat butter or margarine, using electric mixer or mixing spoon, until creamy, 1 to 3 minutes. Add lemon or orange rind and brown sugar, continue beating until well mixed. Beat in eggs, one at a time, beating well after each addition and continue beating for 1 minute. Using rubber spatula, **fold in** about ½ cup flour mixture and floured fruit mixture, and mix well. Stir in remaining flour mixture, brandy, rum, or orange juice concentrate until well blended. Pour cake mixture in prepared pan and smooth top. Using spray bottle filled with water, spray air about 12 inches above pan to lightly mist surface of cake. ***Note:*** *The little amount of steam from the misting prevents the top of the cake from forming a hard crust during the long baking.*

4. Bake at 350° F for 1 hour. Reduce heat to 325° F and cover top of cake with foil. Bake 1 hour longer, or until toothpick inserted in center comes out clean. Cool cake in pan for 30 minutes, release side ring, and turn cake upside down on wire cake rack to cool completely. Remove pan bottom and peel paper from bottom of cake.

5. To age fruit cake: Put about ½ cup brandy or rum in spray bottle and lightly mist cake all over. Put cake in large plastic bag and seal to make airtight. At least once a week, for one month, unwrap and spray cake with brandy or rum. Rewrap each time for flavor to develop.

Continue: After one month cover cake with marzipan (instructions follow), or wrap in plastic wrap and refrigerate or freeze to use at another time.

The top surface of fruitcakes are seldom smooth so it is a good idea to turn the cake upside down before covering with **marzipan**.

Marzipan Topping for Fruitcake

1 cup smooth apricot jam
2 to 3 (8 ounces each) tubes marzipan (available at all supermarkets)
granulated sugar, as needed
English Fruitcake (recipe precedes)

Equipment: Small saucepan, mixing spoon, work surface, rolling pin, 8-inch springform pan (to use for pattern) **pastry brush**, dinner knife

1. Put apricot jam in small saucepan and warm over medium-low heat until melted, 3 to 5 minutes.

2. Sprinkle work surface and rolling pin with granulated sugar to prevent sticking. Using rolling pin, roll 1 tube marzipan into a circle about 1/8 inch thick. Use 8-inch springform pan bottom as a pattern, place it on top of rolled out marzipan to get exact cake size. Cut out marzipan circle with a knife.

3. Brush cake surface with melted apricot jam. Place marzipan circle on top of jam and carefully press in place.

4. Sprinkle work surface and rolling pin again with granulated sugar. Roll remaining marzipan in a strip, the length and width to completely cover sides of cake. Use the side ring of the springform pan for a pattern. It may be easier to work with shorter lengths to wrap around the cake then pinch them together.

5. With wet fingers, pinch the top and side edges of the marzipan together. Smooth over all seams with wet dinner knife. Cover with plastic wrap and refrigerate for 2 or 3 days for marzipan to dry and harden.

Continue: Cover prepared fruitcake with whipped icing *(recipe follows).*

Cover the English wedding cake with whipped icing. For a three **tiered wedding cake**: 10-inch bottom, 8-inch middle, and 6-inch top layers require three batches of this recipe.

Whipped Icing

Yield: 3 to 4 cups

prepared fruitcake (recipe page 202) covered with **marzipan** (recipe page 203)
4 tablespoons all-purpose flour
1 cup milk
½ cup: solid shortening, at room temperature
½ cup unsalted butter, at room temperature
1 cup granulated sugar
1 teaspoon vanilla extract

Equipment: 8-inch **cake board**, medium **double boiler, whisk**, large mixing bowl, electric mixer, rubber spatula, serving tray, wax paper, **icing** spatula

1. Place prepared fruitcake on cake board.

2. Fill bottom pan of double boiler halfway with water, and bring to boil over high heat. Put flour in top pan of double boiler, and whisk in milk until lump-free. Set over boiling water, mixing frequently, and cook until thickened, 12 to 15 minutes. Cool to room temperature.

3. Put solid shortening and butter in large mixing bowl, and using electric mixer, beat until creamy. Beating constantly, add sugar, a little at a time, and continue beating for 3 to 5 minutes, until light and fluffy.

4. Beating constantly, slowly add cooled flour mixture and beat for 3 to 5 minutes more. Add vanilla extract and beat 1 minute more.

5. Icing the fruitcake: Place prepared cake on serving tray. To keep tray clean, cover with wax paper that is easy to remove after icing cake. Spread icing over top of cake with icing spatula. Work down over the sides until cake is completely covered.

To serve, allow cake to firm three or four hours. Today, decorating cakes, especially wedding cakes, with fresh flowers and greenery, especially English ivy, is very popular. Simply have the flowers and greenery cascade over the cake in a natural way.

When someone wants special individualized candies or treats to commemorate a life-cycle event, *rout biscuits*, a form of **marzipan**, are often tinted with food coloring and made into the desired shapes. In the following recipe, instructions are given for making heart-shaped designs, popular for weddings.

English Rout Biscuits

English Marzipan

Yield: makes 25 to 30 pieces

- 8-ounce package **almond paste** (*Look for almond paste that does not contain glucose or syrups, as it may be too soft to shape.*)
- ¼ cup butter or margarine
- 1½ to 2 cups confectioners' sugar, sifted
- 1 tablespoon rum or orange juice
- 2 teaspoons corn syrup
- food coloring, for **garnish** (*For richer-colored* ***marzipan****, use paste food coloring instead of the liquid form.*)
- walnut halves, as needed, for garnish (optional)
- granulated sugar, for garnish (optional)

Equipment: Medium mixing bowl, electric mixer, work surface, baking sheet or tray, heart-shaped candy molds (optional), 1-inch heart-shaped cookie cutter (optional),

1. Crumble almond paste into medium mixing bowl. Add butter or margarine. Beat with an electric mixer on medium speed until combined. Add 1 cup sifted confectioners' sugar, rum or orange juice, and corn syrup. Beat until thoroughly combined.

2. Shape mixture into a ball. Transfer to work surface and **knead** in as much of the remaining confectioners' sugar as needed until mixture is firm enough to hold its shape and forms a flexible paste for modeling consistency.

3. Divide into small portions to make into various shapes and colors, and place on baking sheet to firm.

The following are just a few suggestions for decorating the biscuits or use your own creative talents:

For walnut bonbons: Tint marzipan to desired color by adding a few drops of food coloring to mixture, and using your hands, **blend** in. Roll colored marzipan into ½-inch balls. Stick a half walnut on either side, press lightly together on baking sheet or tray, and set aside to firm.

For preparing heart shapes: Color portion of marzipan pink with food coloring and follow one of these 2 different methods: A.) Using heart-shaped candy molds: Press marzipan into heart-shaped molds; allow to set over night on baking sheet or tray. Remove by inverting filled molds on work surface, causing candies to fall out. B.) Use a 1-inch heart-shaped cookie cutter: Sprinkle work surface with granulated sugar. Place each 1-inch ball of marzipan on the sugar, and using your hands, flatten it into a disk slightly larger than the 1-inch cookie cutter. Cut each disk with the 1-inch heart-shaped cookie cutter. Place on baking sheet or tray and allow to firm up overnight.

For a baby shower, shape biscuits into rattles, cribs, tiny teddy bears, or babies. For birthdays, shape into numbers or flowers to put on the cake. *Rout biscuits* can be shaped into fruits, bugs, worms, or small animals and used as edible cake decorations.

Serve decorative rout biscuits *with* English Tea *(recipe page 201).*

SCOTLAND

Scotland, one of the constituent parts of the United Kingdom, occupies the northern third of the island of Great Britain. Originally, the clan, a group of related families with one head (*laird*), was an important fighting force and the foundation of Scottish society. Over time, the solidarity of clan lineage has developed into a strong point of Scottish national pride. In Scotland, many important family events, such as births, christenings, weddings, and burials, have their origins in ancient Celtic rituals that predate Christianity. The favorite time of year for weddings in Scotland is between the November term day (*Martinmas*, on November 28) and the New Year. Many old customs and rituals are still observed at Scottish weddings.

The Scottish wedding celebration is a joyous and sometimes riotous affair—a grand excuse for feasting, drinking, and merrymaking. This practice is in direct contrast to the hardness and frugality that characterized Scottish life during various periods in the past. In the sixteenth century, for instance, a law was passed restricting extravagant eating because of food shortages, although exemptions were granted for certain feast days and special celebrations.

Scottish weddings are usually held in a church, most Scots being members of the national church, the Church of Scotland (Presbyterian), or of another Protestant denomination. A small number of Scottish weddings are held in hotel ballrooms, at home, or in a castle rented for the occasion. Whether the wedding food is just a light repast or a full dinner, shortbread is sure to be on the menu. The following recipe is called *Petticoat Tails* for the frilly-looking border around the edge of the shortbread.

Petticoat Tails

Scottish Shortbread

Yield: 8 to 12 pieces

1¼ cups all-purpose flour
3 tablespoons cornstarch
¼ cup sugar, more as needed
½ cup chilled butter or margarine, cut into small pieces

Equipment: Large mixing bowl, lightly greased 8- or 9-inch springform pan, fork, oven mitts, knife, serving platter

Preheat oven to 325° F.

1. In large mixing bowl, combine flour, cornstarch, ¼ cup sugar, and butter or margarine. Using your hands, rub mixture together until it is crumbly. Form into a ball (it is still crumbly) and transfer to springform pan. Using your fingers, press dough to evenly cover bottom of pan and pat smooth. Press into dough with back of fork to make decorative border, about 1 inch wide all around the edge.

2. Bake in oven for 35 to 40 minutes, until golden brown. Remove from oven and while still warm, sprinkle with 1 tablespoon sugar, and cut into 8 to 12 wedges. Cool to room temperature and remove sides of pan.

To serve, decoratively place wedges on serving platter. Eat as a cookie.

Each region of Scotland has its own version of gingerbread, which is almost always included in celebration feasts. In past centuries, gingerbread was a luxury; it contained hard-to get, expensive spices and only the rich were able to afford it.

Parkin (also Yorkshire Parkin)

Oatmeal Gingerbread

Yield: serves 12 to 16

½ cup butter
½ cup honey
½ cup dark brown sugar, firmly packed
1 egg
6 tablespoons milk
1 cup **self-rising flour**
1 teaspoon **ground** ginger
1 teaspoon ground cinnamon

½ cup regular oatmeal
confectioners' sugar, for **garnish**

Equipment: Small saucepan, mixing spoon, flour **sifter**, large mixing bowl, greased 7-inch square cake pan, oven mitts, toothpick

Preheat oven to 350° F.

1. Melt butter in small saucepan over medium heat. Add honey and brown sugar, and stir until sugar dissolves. Cool to room temperature and beat in egg and milk.

2. **Sift** flour, ginger, and cinnamon into large mixing bowl. Stir in oatmeal and egg mixture, and mix well. Transfer batter to greased baking pan and smooth top.

3. Bake in oven for 1 to 1½ hours or until toothpick inserted in cake comes out clean and cake has pulled away from sides of pan. Cool in pan for 15 minutes and turn out on wire cake rack. This is best served the following day for flavors to develop, sprinkle confectioners' sugar over the top.

To serve, slice and spread with softened butter or cream cheese.

Scottish salmon is a prized fish around the world. Few Scottish wedding receptions would be complete unless poached whole salmon were on the buffet table. Traditionally, whole fish is cooked with the head on in a special poaching kettle. The following recipe is an easy way to get the same end result.

Poached Salmon

Yield: serves 10 to 12

butter or margarine, as needed
6 to 8 pound **oven-ready** whole salmon with head and tail attached (available at most supermarkets and all fish markets)
½ cup chicken broth, homemade (recipe page 106) or canned
salt and pepper to taste
fresh parsley as needed, for **garnish**
10 to 12 lemon wedges, for garnish
lettuce leaves, as needed, for cold garnish
5 to 6 hard-cooked eggs, shelled and cut in half, for cold garnish
10 to 12 tomato slices, for cold garnish
prepared Hollandaise sauce or mayonnaise, for serving (Hollandaise sauce mix is available at all supermarkets, prepare according to directions on package)

Equipment: Aluminum foil, scissors, paring knife, large roasting pan or baking sheet, oven mitts, meat **thermometer**, small bowl, large serving platter, kitchen towel, small serving bowl

Preheat oven to 350° F.

1. Using scissors, cut foil large enough to generously enclose fish and place on work surface. Rub butter or margarine thickly over foil, and set fish in the center. Using paring knife, make 3 or 4 diagonal slits, 2 to 3 inches long, in fish skin. (The skin shrinks during cooking; cutting slits keeps fish from curling up). Bring ends of foil together above the fish so juices can't leak out. Pour chicken broth over the fish, and sprinkle with salt and pepper to taste. Pinch ends of foil together so there is airspace above the fish (about an inch or two of air). This allows room for steam to collect during cooking. Place in roasting pan or on baking sheet.

2. Bake in oven for 1½ to 2 hours, depending on size. (Fish is done when meat thermometer registers 145° when inserted in the thickest part of the flesh, or when fish flakes easily when poked with a fork.)If fish is to be served warm, do not open foil for 10 minutes. If fish is to be served cold, cool to room temperature before removing foil.

3. Open foil and drain fish juices into small bowl. Slide fish onto serving platter. Using par-

ing knife, peel off and discard skin only from top of fish. Leave head and tail intact.

4. If serving fish warm, pour fish juice over fish, and garnish with parsley and lemon wedges. Serve with small bowl of Hollandaise sauce to spoon over each serving.

5. If serving fish cold, place lettuce leaves around cooled fish. Garnish with parsley, lemon wedges, sliced hard-cooked eggs, and sliced tomatoes. Pour fish juices over fish. Serve with small bowl of mayonnaise to spoon over each serving.

Serve fish, either warm or cold, with thinly sliced dark bread and butter.

The Scottish wedding feast often includes some sort of game dish, usually partridge or quail, but if there is no hunter in the family, *howtowdie* (roast chicken) will do just fine. Traditionally, the bird is stuffed with *skirlie* (recipe follows). For this recipe, *skirlie* is made as a dressing or side dish and baked in a casserole.

Howtowdie

Roast Chicken

Yield: serves 6

3- to 4-pound chicken, **oven-ready**
6 onions, quartered
½ cup melted butter or margarine
2 cups hot water, more as needed
salt and pepper to taste
skirlie, for serving (recipe follows)

Equipment: Shallow roasting pan, **pastry brush**, oven mitts, paring knife, carving board, **bulb baster** or mixing spoon, small saucepan, **whisk**, strainer, serving bowl, serving platter

Preheat oven to 375° F.

1. Place chicken, breast side up, in shallow roasting pan. Arrange onions around chicken. Brush chicken and onions with melted butter or margarine. Add 2 cups hot water to roasting pan.

2. Roast in oven for 1 to 1¼ hours. Test for **doneness**: Pierce thickest part of chicken with knife, if juices trickle out clear, not pinkish in color, the chicken is done. Transfer chicken to carving board and let rest 15 minutes before slicing. Using bulb baster or mixing spoon, skim off and discard most fat from pan juices.

3. Prepare gravy: For each cup of pan juices combine 2 tablespoons flour with ½ cup water to form a paste, and quickly whisk to prevent lumping. In small saucepan, cook and whisk over medium heat until gravy thickens. Add salt and pepper to taste, and strain gravy into serving bowl.

To serve, place the chicken pieces in the center of the serving platter and surround with onion wedges. Each person gets a piece of chicken, a wedge of onion, a spoonful of skirlie, *and a* ***drizzle*** *of gravy.*

Skirlie

Oat Dressing

Yield: serves 6

1 cup butter or margarine, divided
1 onion, **finely chopped**
1 cup regular oats
½ teaspoon: salt and pepper
½ teaspoon **ground coriander**
¼ teaspoon ground nutmeg
1½ cups chicken broth, homemade (recipe page 106) or canned

Equipment: Large skillet, mixing spoon, buttered medium oven-proof casserole with cover, oven mitts

Preheat oven to 350° F.

1. Melt ½ cup butter or margarine in large skillet over medium-high heat. Add onion, **sauté,** and stir until soft, 2 to 3 minutes. Stir in oats, salt and pepper, coriander, and nutmeg. Reduce heat to **simmer**, stir, and cook until oats are golden brown, 3 to 5 minutes. Transfer to buttered medium oven-proof casserole and pour over 1 cup chicken broth. Dot top with remaining ½ cup butter.

2. Cover casserole and bake in oven for 40 to 45 minutes. Remove cover, add remaining ½ cup chicken broth, and bake, uncovered for 15 to 25 minutes more, until golden.

Continue with howtowdie *(recipe precedes).*

The *Dundee cake* is one the most popular cakes to grace the Scottish tea table, especially for christening and birthday celebrations. Neighbors often bring *Dundee cakes* to feed mourners at a wake.

Dundee Cake

Light Fruitcake

Yield: serves 10-14

- 1 cup butter or margarine, at room temperature
- 1 cup sugar
- 4 eggs
- 2½ cups cake flour, divided
- 1 teaspoon baking powder
- ½ teaspoon salt
- 3 tablespoons lemon juice
- ½ cup seedless raisins, **finely chopped**
- ½ cup dried currants, finely chopped (available at most supermarkets)
- ½ cup **glacé cherries**, finely chopped (available at most supermarkets)
- grated rind of 1 lemon
- 2 tablespoons grated orange rind
- 1¼ cups sliced almonds

Equipment: Large mixing bowl, electric mixer, rubber spatula, mixing spoon, flour **sifter**, medium mixing bowl, small bowl, greased 10- x 5- x 3-inch loaf pan, oven mitts, toothpick, wire cake rack, aluminum foil, serving plate

1. Put butter and eggs into large mixing bowl, and using electric mixer, beat until fluffy, about 2 minutes. Using rubber spatula, scrape down sides of bowl. Beat in eggs, one at a time, until well mixed.

Preheat oven to 325° F.

2. **Sift** 2¼ cups flour, baking powder, and salt into medium mixing bowl. With electric mixer on low speed, add flour mixture, a little at a time, alternately with lemon juice, beat until smooth.

3. In small bowl, mix raisins, currants, glacé cherries, lemon and orange rinds, and sliced almonds. Add remaining ¼ cup flour and toss to coat. Using mixing spoon or rubber spatula, **fold in** raisin mixture with batter. Transfer to greased loaf pan.

4. Bake in oven for 1 to 1½ hours or until toothpick inserted in middle comes out clean. Using oven mitts, remove from oven, allow to cool 15 minutes in loaf pan, and turn out on wire rack to cool completely. Wrap in foil to keep fresh and allow 2 or 3 days for flavors to develop before eating.

To serve, cut into ¼- to ½-inch slices and place, slightly overlapping, on serving plate. Wrapped in foil, Dundee cake *freezes well for up to one month.*

Old-fashioned wakes are still held in many parts of Scotland, although how the wake is celebrated varies with each region. After the deceased is buried, mourners go to the home of a family member for tea and sandwiches or a home cooked meal. Most urbanites prefer to take the mourners to a hotel for a prearranged sit-down dinner.

WALES

Wales, the two-pronged western peninsula of the island of Great Britain, is the third major component of the United Kingdom. The Welsh, like the Scots, are of Celtic origin. The majority of Welsh people are Protestants, mainly Methodists, and they follow life-cycle celebrations according to their church. (See Protestant and Catholic Life-Cycle Rituals, page xlvi.) The Methodist religion grew out of the Anglican Church (Church of England) and became popular among the Welsh.

Welsh weddings are often short and simple and nowadays need not take place in church. Castles, hotels, and wedding halls are often rented for the occasion. Breads, often filled with currants or other dried fruit, are basic to Welsh meals and usually included in wedding and other Welsh life-cycle feasts.

Bara Brith

Speckled Bread

Note: This recipe takes 24 hours.

2 cups chopped mixed candied fruit
1 cup brown sugar
1 cup hot tea
4 cups **self-rising flour**
1/4 teaspoon salt
1/4 cup butter or margarine
1 egg, well beaten

Equipment: Small bowl with cover, mixing spoon, large mixing bowl, **pastry blender** (optional), greased 9- x 5- x 3-inch loaf pan, oven mitts, wire rack

1. Put chopped mixed candied fruit and brown sugar into small bowl, stir, and pour over hot tea. Cover and let stand at room temperature overnight. (Do not refrigerate.)

Preheat oven to 350° F.

2. **Sift** flour with salt into large mixing bowl. Add butter or margarine and, using a pastry blender or your fingers, work butter or margarine into flour. Make a well (hole) in the center of flour, add egg and candied fruit mixture. Using mixing spoon, stir to mix well. Transfer to greased loaf pan.

3. Bake in oven for 1½ to 2 hours, or until toothpick inserted in center comes out clean. Cool bread in pan for 30 minutes then transfer to wire cake rack to cool to room temperature.

To serve, cut in slices and serve with fruit and cheeses. This is a popular bread to serve with afternoon tea or at a bridal shower.

The Welsh love freshwater fish, especially when cooked or served with bacon. Such dishes are often served for baptism lunches after church or are part of the buffet table at the wedding receptions.

Brythyll a Chig Moch

Trout with Bacon

Yield: serves 6

12 slices bacon
6 **oven-ready** whole trout (10 to 12 ounces each)
2 tablespoons fresh parsley flakes or 1 tablespoon dried parsley flakes
salt and pepper to taste

Equipment: Paper towels, baking sheet, large skillet, metal spatula or metal tongs, shallow roasting pan, aluminum foil, oven mitts, fork

1. Place several layers of paper towels on baking sheet. Fry bacon in large skillet over medium-high heat, until soft and **render**ed, but not crisp, 3 to 5 minutes on each side. Transfer bacon to paper towels to drain. Lay bacon strips side by side in shallow baking pan. Save rendered bacon fat.

Preheat oven to 350° F.

2. Rinse fish under cold running water and pat dry with paper towels. Using pastry brush, brush skin and inside of fish with rendered bacon fat. Sprinkle inside of fish with parsley flakes and salt and pepper to taste. Place fish on top of bacon in shallow baking pan. Cover with foil.

3. Bake in oven for 15 minutes, uncover, and continue to bake for 10 to 12 minutes more or until fish flakes easily when poked with a fork.

Serve as the first course at a wedding feast or as the main dish for a baptism luncheon. Allow one whole fish and two slices bacon for each serving.

In the past, appetizers were known in the British Isles as "fore bits" because they were eaten before the main meal. An old tradition among English aristocrats was to have a savory dish served after dessert at formal banquets. The savory was referred to as "rear bits" because it was served at the end or rear of the meal. Some food historians believe the word rarebit could have been a form of the word "rear bits" since rarebit was often served as an after dinner savory.

Caws Pobi

Welsh Rarebit (also Welsh Rabbit)

Yield: serves 4

1½ tablespoons butter
1 cup sharp cheddar cheese, grated
2 tablespoons milk
1 teaspoon prepared mustard
ground red pepper to taste
4 to 6 slices hot toasted white bread, buttered on one side for serving

Equipment: **Double boiler**, mixing spoon, baking sheet, oven mitts

1. Fill bottom pan of double boiler halfway with water, and bring to boil over high heat. Set the other pan over the pan with boiling water, add butter, and melt. Reduce heat to **simmer**, and add cheese, stirring occasionally until melted. Stir in milk, mustard, and ground red pepper to taste, and mix well.

Preheat broiler or toaster oven.

2. At serving time, place slices of toast, butter side up, on baking pan. Spoon cheese mixture onto the toast. Place under the broiler or in a toaster oven to lightly brown, 3 to 5 minutes.

Serve immediately while hot. To serve as a savory or "rare bit" after the wedding feast, cut in half and ***garnish*** *with a sprig of parsley.*

Leeks, the national emblem of Wales, are often eaten on the feast day of Wales's patron saint, St. David. *Tatws rhost* (oven-fried potatoes) are a favorite old Welsh recipe and often served along with *brythyll a chig moch* (recipe page 210) at a baptism luncheon.

Tatws Rhost

Oven-Fried Potatoes

Yield: serves 6

4 leeks, trimmed, white part only
8 slices bacon, coarsely chopped
6 potatoes, peeled and thinly sliced
6 green onions, with tops, trimmed and chopped
½ cup water
salt and pepper to taste

Equipment: Knife, work surface, **colander**, large skillet, mixing spoon, greased 9- x 13- x 2-inch baking pan, aluminum foil, oven mitts, serving platter

Preheat oven to 400° F.

1. Slice leeks on work surface, transfer to colander, and rinse carefully under cold running water to remove any sand particles. Drain well.

2. Fry bacon in large skillet over medium-low heat until **rendered**, 3 to 5 minutes. Add leeks, stir, and sauté for 3 to 5 minutes, until leeks are soft, not browned.

3. Arrange potato slices in greased baking pan. Spoon over bacon, leeks, and pan drippings. Pour water over potatoes, sprinkle with green onions, and add salt and pepper to taste. Cover with foil.

4. Bake in oven for 35 minutes. Uncover and bake until potatoes are tender and bacon is crispy but not burned, 15 to 20 minutes.

To serve, transfer to serving platter and serve hot.

In the past, most Welsh homes did not have ovens. For name-day, baptism, and wedding celebrations, sweet cakes and biscuits were usually made on the griddle. The following recipe for *ffrois* (Welsh crepes) is typical of griddle-style desserts.

Ffrois

Welsh Crepes

Yield: serves 4 to 6

- 6 tablespoons dried currants
- 1 cup all-purpose flour
- 1/4 teaspoons salt
- 3 eggs
- 1 3/4 cups milk
- vegetable oil, as needed, for pan frying
- confectioners' sugar, for **garnish**

Equipment: Large cup, large mixing bowl, electric mixer or whisk, kitchen towel, paper towels, work surface, **heavy-based** 6- or 8-inch skillet

1. Put dried currants in cup, cover with water to soak for 10 minutes, and drain well.

2. Put flour, salt, eggs, and milk in large mixing bowl, and using electric mixer or whisk, beat until smooth, 2 to 3 minutes.

3. To pan-fry: Have ready paper towels spread out on work surface. Using a paper towel dipped in oil, lightly grease bottom and sides of heavy-based 6- or 8-inch skillet.

4. Heat skillet over medium-high heat until hot, about 1 minute. Add 1/4 cup batter and swirl in pan to completely coat bottom of pan with thin layer of batter. Quickly add a little more batter, if necessary, to cover bottom of pan. When edges pull away from sides of pan and surface turns dull, slide crepe onto towel to remove from skillet, 2 to 3 minutes. Return crepe to skillet, bottom-side up, and quickly fry second side, about 1 minute. Remove from skillet and place on towel. Repeat making crepes, grease skillet each time before adding batter, and adjust heat as necessary if skillet becomes too hot. Slightly overlap crepes on towel.

5. To assemble: Sprinkle each crepe with 1/2 teaspoon currants and confectioners' sugar, and roll the crepe up around the currants. Or you can stack the sprinkled crepes in layers and cut into wedges, like a cake.

Serve stacked cakes with candles for a birthday or name-day party. Serve rolled crepes on a serving platter for a dessert table at tea time or as dessert at a wedding banquet.

IRELAND

Ireland lies west of Great Britain across the Irish Sea. Ireland is divided into two countries, the Republic of Ireland, which makes up more than 80 percent of the island, and Northern Ireland, which is part of the United Kingdom. Most of the people in the Irish Republic are Roman Catholic, while the majority of the people in Northern Ireland are Protestant. Most Irish life-cycle events center around the dominant church in the region. (See Protestant and Catholic Life-Cycle Rituals, page xlvi.)

January pudding is an old Irish dessert many mothers and grandmothers enjoyed when they were little children. To keep traditions alive, they often prepare it as a special treat for their children or grandchildren on a birthday or name-day celebration. ✺ ✺ ✺

January Pudding

Yield: serves 6 to 8

½ cup unsalted butter, at room temperature
½ cup brown sugar
2 eggs, lightly beaten
2 heaping tablespoons raspberry jam
1 cup all-purpose flour
½ teaspoon baking soda
raspberry jam sauce, for serving (recipe follows)

Equipment: Medium mixing bowl, electric mixer or mixing spoon, flour **sifter**, small bowl, rubber spatula, buttered steamed pudding mold (1 quart-size) with cover or 1-quart stainless mixing bowl, scissors, wax paper, aluminum foil, kitchen string, **steamer pan**, oven mitts, serving plate

1. Put butter and brown sugar in medium mixing bowl, and using electric mixer or mixing spoon, beat until light and fluffy, 1 to 2 minutes. Beat in eggs and raspberry jam.

2. **Sift** flour and baking soda into small bowl. Using rubber spatula, fold the flour mixture into the egg mixture. Spoon the batter into buttered pudding mold or buttered 1-quart stainless mixing bowl. Cut a piece of wax paper to fit over the top of the mold or bowl and butter one side of it. Place the circle of wax paper, buttered-side down on top of the pudding batter. If using the mold, close the cover. If using the bowl, cut a piece of foil large enough to cover the top and at least 2 inches down the sides of the bowl. Place foil over the top of bowl and press firmly against the sides. Tie foil in place with string just under the ledge of the bowl.

3. Place mold or bowl on rack in the steamer pan. Fill mold or bowl with boiling water to reach about two-thirds up the sides of the pudding container. Bring to boil over high heat and cover the steamer pan. Reduce heat to **simmer** and cook for 2 hours. From time to time, check water level. Add more boiling water when level drops below halfway up the sides of the pudding container.

4. While pudding is cooking, prepare raspberry jam sauce.

5. Using oven mitts, remove mold from the water and place on heat-proof surface. Remove the cover and wax paper. Let the pudding cool for 30 minutes before removing from mold or bowl. To remove pudding from mold or bowl, place the serving plate upside down over top of pudding container. Holding both firmly together, flip plate and mold or bowl together so pudding drops onto plate. Carefully lift off empty container.

To serve, cut the warm pudding into wedges. Put raspberry jam sauce *in a small bowl to spoon over each serving.*

Raspberry Jam Sauce

Yield: serves 6 to 8

½ cup raspberry jam
¼ cup water
juice of 1 lemon

Equipment: Small saucepan, mixing spoon, small serving bowl, serving spoon

Put raspberry jam, water, and lemon juice in small saucepan. Stir and heat over low heat until heated through and well blended, 2 to 3 minutes.

To serve pour into small serving bowl. Serve as sauce for January pudding *(recipe precedes).*

Traditionally, Catholic weddings take place in the church following a long engagement. New Year's Day is considered the luckiest day of the year to be married. If the wedding is held in the country, the reception is most likely to be at the bride's family home or a pub (i.e., a public house or bar where food is also served). In the cities, the reception would probably be in an inn or hotel ballroom. The traditional Irish wedding cake is a fruitcake, similar to the *English wedding cake* (recipe page 202).

The traditional Irish wake for the dead, with several nights of drinking, reminiscing, and storytelling, is now only a remembrance of Ireland past. The Catholic Church has discouraged it in recent years because it had become too social, too expensive, and the butt of too many jokes. The present procedure is to wake the body for only one night at home before it is taken to the church for a brief rosary service (a Roman Catholic devotion) on the second evening. The funeral occurs on the following morning.

During the long wake-keeping time of the past, relatives and neighbors sat with the casket. Because shame attached to any person who fell asleep, a kettle of soup or stew was kept simmering on the stove so the all-night mourners could revive themselves when the need arose.

Dried peas are popular in rural Ireland, where, until the twentieth century, few fresh vegetables beyond potatoes, onions, cabbage, and carrots were available. *Pea and ham soup* could keep mourners nourished during a wake.

Pea and Ham Soup

Yield: serves 8

- 4 slices bacon, coarsely chopped
- 2 onions, chopped
- 9 cups water
- 2¼ cups (about 1 pound) dried green split peas
- 1½ to 2 pounds smoked ham hocks, cut into 2- or 3-inch lengths
- 1 bay leaf
- ½ pound cooked ham, cut into bite-size chunks
- salt and pepper to taste
- milk, if needed

Equipment: Large skillet, mixing spoons, large saucepan with cover or **Dutch oven**, ladle, large soup bowls

1. **Render** bacon in large skillet over medium-low heat, 3 to 5 minutes. Add onions, increase heat to medium-high, and **sauté** until soft, 3 to 5 minutes.

2. Transfer sautéed onions and pan drippings to large saucepan or Dutch oven. Add water, split peas, ham hocks, and bay leaf. Bring to boil over medium-high heat, stir, and reduce heat to **simmer**. Cover and cook for 1½ to 2 hours, until peas are soft yet tender. Add ham and salt and pepper to taste, cover, and continue to simmer for 30 minutes. If soup is too thick, add a little milk to thin. Bring the soup to simmer and heat through, do not boil. Remove and discard bay leaf.

To serve, ladle into large soup bowls and serve with soda bread *(recipe follows).*

Many Irish women still make soda bread every day. There is no waiting for it to rise nor does it require extensive kneading. The less handling of the dough, the better the bread will be. It is important to use buttermilk when making soda bread because its reaction with baking soda helps the bread rise. If buttermilk is not available, substitute either sour milk or sour cream. You can make sour milk or sour cream by adding one tablespoon of white vinegar to each cup of fresh milk or heavy cream.

Soda Bread

Yield: 2 loaves

4 cups cake flour
1/4 teaspoon salt
2 tablespoons baking soda
1 1/2 teaspoons cream of tartar
1/4 cup sugar
1 tablespoon caraway seeds
3 tablespoons raisins
1/4 cup solid vegetable shortening
1 1/4 cups buttermilk

Equipment: Flour **sifter**, large mixing bowl, **pastry blender** (optional), lightly floured work surface, lightly floured baking sheet, sharp paring knife, oven mitts, wire cake rack, napkin-lined bread basket

Preheat oven to 400° F.

1. **Sift** flour, salt, baking soda, cream of tartar, and sugar into a large mixing bowl. Using your fingers or pastry blender, rub in shortening until mixture resembles coarse meal. Add raisins, caraway seeds, and buttermilk, and using your hands, mix the dough until it holds together.

2. Transfer to lightly floured work surface, **knead** for 20 seconds, and divide dough in half. Use your hands to shape each piece into a round loaf. Place each loaf on lightly floured baking sheet with at least 3-inch space between the loaves. Using paring knife, cut a deep X in top of each loaf and sprinkle lightly with flour.

3. Bake for 30 to 35 minutes, until lightly browned and firm. Test for **bread doneness**. Transfer to wire cake rack to cool.

Serve while warm from the oven and place loaves in napkin-lined bread basket. Serve with pea and ham soup (recipe page 214) or Dublin coddle *(recipe follows).*

Dublin coddle is a filling and nourishing stew traditionally served to restore one's health after too much partying, especially on Saturday night.

Dublin Coddle

Dublin Stew or Sausage & Potato Stew

Yield: serves 6 to 8

1 cup all-purpose flour
2 pounds pork sausage, cut into 2- or 3-inch pieces
4 slices bacon, coarsely chopped
2 onions, sliced
2 cloves garlic
2 carrots, thickly sliced
4 potatoes, thickly sliced
9 cups water or apple cider
salt and pepper to taste
1 tablespoon chopped fresh parsley or 1 teaspoon dried parsley flakes

Equipment: Pie pan, large skillet, slotted spoon, plate, large saucepan with cover or **Dutch oven**, deep plates or soup bowls

1. Put flour in pie pan. Dip each piece of sausage in the flour to coat.

2. **Render** bacon in large skillet over medium-low heat, 3 to 5 minutes. Increase heat to medium-high, add flour coated sausage pieces, and fry on all sides until browned, 5 to 7 minutes. Using slotted spoon, remove sausage from skillet and place on plate. Add onions and garlic to skillet, and sauté until soft, 3 to 5 minutes.

3. Put sausage, onion mixture, pan drippings, carrots, and potatoes in large saucepan or Dutch oven. Add water or apple cider and salt and pepper to taste. Bring to boil over high heat, and reduce heat to **simmer**. Cover and cook for 1 hour. Sprinkle parsley over the top, for **garnish**.

To serve, spoon into deep plates or soup bowls and serve together with soda bread.

Many Irish cakes, bread, and tarts are made with fruit and *kerry cake* is easy to make and an Irish favorite.

Kerry Cake

Apple Cake

Yield: serves 9 to 12

- ¾ cup butter or margarine
- ½ cup granulated sugar
- 3 eggs
- grated rind of 1 lemon
- 3 apples, pared, cored, and **diced**
- 1 ½ cups cake flour, sifted
- ¼ teaspoon salt
- 1½ teaspoon baking powder
- 1 teaspoon **ground** cinnamon
- confectioners' sugar, for **garnish**

Equipment: Large mixing bowl, electric mixer, mixing spoon, flour **sifter**, medium mixing bowl, rubber spatula, greased 8- or 9-inch square or round cake pan, oven mitts, toothpick, wire cake rack

Preheat oven to 350° F.

1. In large mixing bowl, using an electric mixer, beat butter with sugar until creamy. Add eggs, one at a time, beating well after each addition. Using a mixing spoon, stir in lemon rind and diced apples.

2. **Sift** flour, salt, baking powder, and cinnamon into medium mixing bowl. Using mixing spoon or rubber spatula, **fold in** flour mixture with egg mixture, a little at a time, and **blend** well. Pour into greased 8- or 9-inch square or round cake pan.

3. Bake in oven for 30 to 35 minutes, until golden, and when toothpick inserted in center comes out clean. Cool on wire cake rack. While still warm, sprinkle top with confectioners' sugar, for garnish.

Serve slightly warm, cut into squares or, if made in a round pan, cut into wedges.

NETHERLANDS

Wedged into the northwestern corner of Europe between Belgium and Germany, and lying across the English Channel from Great Britain, the Netherlands is a small, flat, low-lying country that has for centuries faced the threats of inundation by the North Sea and invasion by more powerful European neighbors. Both threats became reality in the twentieth century. The Netherlands was invaded by Nazi Germany in 1940 and occupied until 1945. In 1953, a great flood cost many Dutch lives; to prevent the recurrence of such a tragedy, the Dutch built the Delta Project, a storm-surge barrier of massive dams and dikes that took 33 years to complete.

The Netherlands has a Catholic majority, living mainly in the southern part of the country and an almost equal number of people who claim no religious affiliation. Dutch Protestants are divided into several groups, with the largest being the Dutch Reformed Church. In the Netherlands, church and state are separate, and everyone is guaranteed religious freedom by the constitution. Life-cycle celebrations are either secular or according to religious beliefs. (See Protestant and Catholic Life-Cycle Rituals, page xlvi.)

A very old custom, especially in the country, is for families to dress their newborn in christening clothes and show the child to relatives and friends. The baby is again dressed in christening clothes at about five to seven months for his or her baptism, which is usually followed by a family dinner. Friends drop in with gifts for the baby during the afternoon and enjoy a light repast of sweets, cakes, and candy with either hot or cold beverages, depending upon the weather.

Birthdays are celebrated more elaborately in the Netherlands than in any other country in Europe, for the Dutch do not have name days. Most homes prominently display a calendar listing each family member's birthday. On the morning of someone's birthday, family members come into the bedroom with gifts and candy and sing a birthday song. Later in the day or in the evening, friends and relatives come with presents. A Dutch birthday celebration does not have one birthday cake, but a variety of cakes, cookies, and other sweet treats. Adult guests drink *candeel.* The beverage is generally made with white wine but apple cider also works well.

Candeel

Warm Beverage

Yield: serves 4 to 6

- 4 eggs
- 1 cup sugar
- 1 teaspoon grated lemon rind
- juice of 1 lemon
- 1 quart dry white wine or apple cider
- 1 stick cinnamon

Equipment: Medium mixing bowl, **whisk**, medium saucepan, individual beverage cups

1. In medium mixing bowl, using whisk, beat eggs with sugar until light and fluffy. Add the lemon rind and lemon juice.

2. Pour dry white wine or apple cider into medium saucepan, and whisk in egg mixture. Beating constantly, heat over medium heat until bubbles appear around the edge of pan. Add cinnamon stick and **simmer** for 3 minutes, stirring frequently. Remove cinnamon stick before serving.

Serve warm, in individual cups.

When they marry, Dutch couples often have a civil ceremony at city hall that is then followed by a wedding ceremony in their church. The wedding is followed by a reception at the bride's parents' home, a restaurant, an inn, or a hotel ballroom, depending upon budget.

Many Dutch entertain with the *rijsttaffel* (rice table) of Indonesian origin. For 300 years, Indonesia, formerly known as the Netherlands East Indies, was a colony under Dutch control. Many Dutch settlers in the spice-rich colony had leisure time and money and employed many Indonesian servants. They turned *rijsttaffel,* the simple indigenous style of eating, into an ostentatious display of food and a form of entertainment. Often anywhere from 10 to 100 white-coated servants formed a procession bringing one dish after another to diners during the three- or four-hour meal.

To Indonesians, *rijsttaffel* simply meant rice meal, not rice table. Because many Indonesians subsisted on rice and fish, with a little meat or chicken for special occasions, they resented the wasteful display of food by the Dutch settlers. Since the Dutch left the country, Indonesians say there are no rice tables, but there is rice on every table.

Today in the Netherlands, the *rijsttaffel* remains a popular form of entertaining. The presentations are much simpler than past years; there are usually no servants, and the hot and cold dishes vary with each Dutch chef or hostess. For instance, in the Netherlands, unlike in Indonesia, bread is served with the *rijsttaffel,* and it is not unusual for Dutch Jews, on the Sabbath and some religious feasts, to serve the kosher meal *rijsttaffel*-style. At weddings, this hearty feast is followed by the Western-style tiered wedding cake, champagne, and dancing.

A sweet table is usually provided at Dutch baptisms, birthdays, and weddings. *Roomborstplaat* (brown sugar candy) is an old Dutch recipe that mothers and grandmothers have been making for their children for many years.

Roomborstplaat

Brown Sugar Candy

Yield: 20 to 24 pieces
1½ cups granulated sugar
1½ cups dark brown sugar
½ teaspoon salt
½ teaspoon cream of tartar
1 cup milk
¼ cup butter or margarine, at room temperature, more as needed
1 teaspoon vanilla extract
2½ cups **coarsely chopped** walnuts

Equipment: Medium **heavy-based** saucepan, wooden mixing spoon, candy **thermometer** (optional), baking sheet, wax paper

1. Put granulated sugar, brown sugar, salt, cream of tartar, and milk into medium heavy-based saucepan. Stir and cook over medium heat until sugars dissolve, 3 to 5 minutes. Continue to cook until candy thermometer registers 236° to 238° F, 12 to 15 minutes. Remove from heat and cool to 220° F, about 10 to 20 minutes. Stir in ¼ cup butter or margarine, vanilla extract, and walnuts. Using wooden mixing spoon, beat until creamy, 2 to 3 minutes.

2. Cover baking sheet with wax paper and lightly coat surface of wax paper with about 1 tablespoon butter or margarine. While still soft, drop spoonfuls of candy batter onto wax paper about 1 inch apart from each other. Cool to room temperature.

Serve the same day for best flavor, but the candy may be stored in airtight container, with wax paper between layers, for several days.

Great quantities of sugar are not only used in candy but in cooking and baking.

Koggetjes

Caramelized Sugar Drop Cookies

Yield: about 3 dozen
caramelized sugar (recipe follows)
¾ cup butter or margarine, at room temperature
½ cup sugar
½ teaspoon vanilla extract
1½ cups all-purpose flour
½ teaspoon baking powder
2 tablespoons water

Equipment: Large mixing bowl, electric mixer, mixing spoon, flour **sifter**, small bowl, nonstick or well-greased cookie sheet, oven mitts, spatula, wire cake rack, serving plate

Preheat oven to 325° F.

1. Prepare *caramelized sugar.*

2. In large mixing bowl, beat butter or margarine, sugar, and vanilla extract using electric mixer or mixing spoon until creamy, 2 to 3 minutes.

3. **Sift** flour and baking powder into small bowl. Beat or stir flour mixture into sugar mixture alternately with water. Stir in crushed caramelized sugar. Drop rounded teaspoonfuls of dough about 2 inches apart onto nonstick or well-greased cookie sheet.

4. Bake in oven for 12 to 15 minutes, until edges are lightly browned. Let cool on baking sheet for 1 minute. Using spatula, transfer to wire cake rack and cool completely.

To serve cookies, arrange decoratively on serving plate.

Caramelized Sugar

½ cup sugar

Equipment: 10- to 12-inch square buttered aluminum foil, heat-proof work surface, small **heavy-based** saucepan, paring knife, electric **blender**

1. Place buttered foil on heat-proof work surface. Put sugar in small heavy-based saucepan over medium-high heat. Cook until sugar melts and becomes an amber (brownish-yellow) color, 3 to 5 minutes. Immediately pour melted sugar onto buttered foil. Let stand until cool and hardened.

2. Using your hands or paring knife, break caramelized sugar into pieces. Put in electric blender and **blend** until coarsely crushed, about 30 seconds.

Continue with koggetjes *(recipe precedes: Step 3).*

In the Netherlands, when fresh fruits are not in season or are too expensive, many cooks turn to dried fruits. A compote is fruit cooked in syrup; it is often served along with the cake and cookies at an afternoon birthday party.

Gedroogde Abrikozen

Apricot Compote

Note: This recipe takes 24 hours.

Yield: serves 6

1½ cups water
½ cup sugar
3 cups dried apricot halves, soak according to directions on package and drain
3-inch stick of cinnamon
3 or 4 whole cloves
½ cup **toasted** sliced almonds
1 cup prepared whipped cream, for serving

Equipment: Medium saucepan with cover, mixing spoon, medium bowl with cover

1. Pour water into medium saucepan and bring to boil over medium-high heat. Stir in sugar to dissolve. Add drained apricots, cinnamon stick, and cloves, and bring to a boil. Stir, reduce heat to **simmer**, cover, and cook for 20 to 25 minutes, or until apricots are tender. Stir in almonds and cool to room temperature.

2. Transfer apricot mixture to medium bowl, cover, and refrigerate at least 24 hours for flavor to develop. Remove and discard cinnamon stick and cloves.

Serve in individual dessert dishes and top each serving with whipped cream.

Eggs, especially when hard-cooked, are a popular snack food or appetizer in most countries. The Dutch make *gehaktnestjes,* which are similar to the Scotch eggs of Scotland. *Gehaktnestjes* are easy to make and always a welcome treat.

Gehaktnestjes

Meatball Nests

Yield: *serves* 6

1 pound bulk seasoned pork sausage or finely ground beef
6 hard-cooked eggs, peeled
1 cup all-purpose flour
1 cup **bread crumbs**
2 raw eggs
3 tablespoons water
2 cups vegetable oil

Equipment: Work surface, small bowl, fork, 2 pie pans, large plate, plastic food wrap, paper towels, baking sheet, large **heavy-based** skillet, wooden spoon, slotted spoon, serving platter

1. On work surface, divide sausage or beef into 6 equal portions. Flatten a portion in your hand and place a peeled hard-cooked egg in the center. Wrap sausage or beef completely around the egg to encase it, and pat smooth. Repeat this process to encase all the eggs with sausage or beef.

2. Put raw eggs in small bowl, add water, and beat well with fork. Put flour in one pie pan and bread crumbs in the other. Dip an encased hard-cooked egg in flour to coat completely, and shake off excess. Cover encased egg with beaten eggs, and roll it in bread crumbs to make a thick coating. Repeat coating remaining encased hard-cooked eggs. Place on plate, cover with plastic wrap, and refrigerate for 1 hour to firm.

3. Prepare to skillet-fry: ADULT SUPERVISION REQUIRED. Have ready several layers of paper towels on baking sheet. Pour oil in large heavy-based skillet and heat over medium-high heat. Oil is hot enough when small bubbles appear around a wooden spoon handle when it is dipped in the oil. Carefully put prepared hard-cooked eggs into oil, and fry on all sides until golden brown, 5 to 7 minutes. Remove with slotted spoon and drain on paper towels.

To serve, cool the eggs to warm before cutting in half, lengthwise. Arrange on serving platter, with cut side up. Serve warm or cold as an appetizer or light snack.

GERMANY

Located in the heart of Europe, Germany became a unified state only in 1871. The country experienced hardship and defeat in both World Wars and was divided into Communist East Germany and democratic West Germany from 1945 until 1990. Although reunification created some economic difficulties, Germany at the end of the twentieth century is one of the wealthiest and most industrialized nations of Europe.

The German population is almost equally split between Roman Catholics and Protestants, with the great majority of the latter being Lutherans. Most Germans turn to their church when conducting celebrations surrounding baptisms, first communions, weddings, funerals, and important religious holidays. (See Protestant and Catholic Life-Cycle Rituals, page xlvi.)

In Germany, the *Verlobung* (engagement) is as binding as the wedding. It is often announced in the local paper or an engagement notice is mailed to friends and relatives. After learning the good news, friends can casually drop in to congratulate the family or a *Verlobungsfeier* may be planned by the bride-to-be's family. Such guests often enjoy a simple late morning repast of punch with cheese and crackers. Many parents also prepare a cold buffet that includes assorted salads; cold meats; poached fish, such as Scottish *poached salmon* (recipe page 207); and assorted breads.

The *Verlobungsfeier* (formal engagement party) is often given by the parents of the bride, usually in their home or a restaurant. The party is generally an elegant sit-down dinner followed by speeches praising the upcoming marriage.

A German wedding reception of traditional fare can take place at a local restaurant, inn, or hotel, or at the home of the bride's parents. Guests are usually provided with mountains of food and plenty to drink, with choices varying according to region and season. Meat is almost always served—wild game or bird are the most popular, followed by suckling pig (recipe page 162) and veal or beef. *Spitzkraut* (cabbage) is made into sauerkraut (recipe page 167), and dozens of other dishes.

Sauerbraten (marinated pot roast) is a classic German meat dish. For flavors to develop, begin this recipe three days prior to serving. ❂ ❂ ❂

SAUERBRATEN

MARINATED POT ROAST

Note: This recipe takes 3 days

Yield: *serves 6 to 8*

3 to 4 pounds beef rolled rump roast, boneless chuck or top round
5 cups water, more as needed
2 cups red wine vinegar
2 onions, finely sliced
2 bay leaves
6 whole cloves
4 black peppercorns
1 teaspoon salt
4 tablespoons vegetable oil
8 gingersnaps (available in cookie aisle at all supermarkets)
2 tablespoons brown sugar
3 tablespoons all-purpose flour

Equipment: Fork, large plastic, glass or ceramic bowl with cover, medium saucepan, mixing spoon, paper towels, strainer, small bowl, large saucepan with cover or **Dutch oven**, metal tongs, large baking pan, 3 or 4 cup-size measuring cup, **bulb baster** or mixing spoon, large skillet, whisk, chopping block, meat knife, small sauce bowl

1. Prick beef roast all over with fork and place in large plastic, glass, or ceramic bowl. Set aside.

2. Prepare marinade: Pour 5 cups water and wine vinegar into medium saucepan. Add onions, bay leaves, cloves, peppercorns, and salt. Bring to boil over high heat, stir, and remove from heat. Cool to warm and pour over meat. Add more cold water, if necessary, to completely cover meat. Cover and refrigerate for 3 days, turning meat daily.

3. On serving day: Remove meat from marinade, pat dry with paper towels. Strain and save marinade in small bowl.

4. Heat oil in large saucepan or Dutch oven over medium-high heat. Add meat and brown on all sides, 25 to 30 minutes. Add marinade, bring to boil, reduce heat to **simmer**, cover, and cook 1½ hours. Turn meat, cover, and simmer 1 to 1½ hours longer, or until tender. Transfer meat to large baking pan and keep warm. Pour pan drippings into 3 or 4 cup measuring cup. Skim off grease, using bulb baster or spoon. Allow meat to rest 15 to 20 minutes before slicing.

5. Prepare gravy: Add water to pan drippings if necessary, to make 2½ cups of liquid for gravy, pour into large skillet. Or, if you have more than 2½ cups pan drippings, transfer excess to covered container, and refrigerate or freeze for another use. Bring liquid to boil over medium-high heat. Stir in crumbled gingersnaps and brown sugar until well mixed, and reduce heat to simmer.

6. Make **slurry**: Stir flour into ½ cup water to make smooth paste. Whisk slurry into gingersnap mixture and continue to whisk until smooth and thickened, 3 to 5 minutes.

*To serve, slice meat on chopping block, using meat knife. Place slices, slightly overlapping, on serving platter, **drizzle** about ½ cup gravy on slices, and pour remaining gravy into sauce bowl to spoon over each serving.* Sauerbraten *is usually served with plain boiled potatoes and horseradish (recipe follows). Just a touch of horseradish is eaten with each bite of the meat.*

Horseradish is one of the favorite German condiments; it is served with everything from sandwiches to banquet meats.

Homemade Horseradish

Yield: *about 2 cups*

½ pound fresh horseradish, washed, peeled, and chopped (available at most supermarkets)
½ cup white vinegar
½ cup water
1½ teaspoons sugar, more if necessary

Equipment: Electric **blender**, mixing spoon, rubber spatula, 1-pint jar with cover

Put chopped horseradish, vinegar, water, and 1½ teaspoons sugar in blender, and **blend** on high until finely ground. Turn off machine once or twice, use rubber spatula to scrape down sides of container. Adjust seasoning, adding a little more sugar if necessary. Transfer to pint jar, cover tightly, and refrigerate.

Serve horseradish as condiment, as dip with meat or seafood, or in sauce recipes.

In Germany, funerals are simple. In the Catholic tradition, Requiem Mass and burial is followed by a *beerdigung feier* (funeral feast). If the funeral is in the countryside, the feast is usually given in the home of the deceased; in the city, the feast is often held in a local restaurant. The noontime menu could include *sauerbraten* (recipe page 221) with boiled potatoes and *erbspüree* (recipe follows).

Erbspüree

Stewed Yellow Peas

Yield: *serves 4 to 6*

6 slices lean bacon, **diced**
1 onion, **finely chopped**
1 cup *each:* carrots and celery, finely chopped
2 leeks, finely chopped, rinsed, and drained
2 cups dried yellow peas
6 cups water
¼ teaspoon ground marjoram
salt and pepper to taste

Equipment: *Large skillet, slotted spoon, paper towels, plate, large saucepan with cover or* ***Dutch oven****, mixing spoon, serving bowl*

1. Fry bacon in large skillet over medium heat to **render**, 3 to 5 minutes. Using slotted spoon, remove bacon pieces, and transfer to paper-towel-covered plate to drain. Add onion to skillet and stir to coat with bacon fat. Increase heat to medium-high and **sauté** until soft, 3 to 5 minutes. Set aside.

2. Put carrots, celery, leeks, and dried peas into large saucepan or Dutch oven. Add water, bring to boil over high heat, and stir. Reduce heat to **simmer**, cover, and cook for 35 to 45 minutes, until peas are soft yet tender and have absorbed all the liquid. Stir occasionally to prevent sticking. Stir in marjoram and salt and pepper to taste.

To serve, transfer cooked peas to serving bowl and sprinkle with bacon. Serve hot as a side dish with sauerbraten *(recipe page 221).*

Germany's culinary history is identified with sweet and savory breads of all sizes and shapes. For religious holidays, such breads were baked in a variety of shapes, from rings, hearts, and animals, to saints, especially St. Nick. *Kugelhopf* is the traditional name-day sweet bread.

Kugelhopf (also Bundt Kuchen)

Sweet Bread

Yield: *serves 8 to 10*

1 package active dry yeast
1 cup **lukewarm** milk

3 cups all-purpose flour, divided
½ cup butter, at room temperature
1 cup sugar
4 eggs
¼ teaspoon salt
grated rind of 1 lemon
½ teaspoon ground nutmeg
1 cup seedless raisins, soaked in warm water for 10 minutes and drained
½ cup sliced almonds, **blanched**
confectioners' sugar, for **garnish**

Equipment: Small mixing bowl, mixing spoon, kitchen towel, large mixing bowl, electric mixer, rubber spatula, greased **bundt pan**, oven mitts, wire cake rack, serving platter

1. Make yeast sponge: In small mixing bowl, dissolve yeast in lukewarm milk, 5 to 10 minutes, until bubbly. Stir in 1 cup flour, cover with towel, and let rise in warm place until double in bulk and spongy looking, about 1 hour.

2. In large mixing bowl, using electric mixer or mixing spoon, beat butter until creamy. Add sugar and eggs, one at a time, beating well after each addition. Add salt, lemon rind, and nutmeg, and beat to mix well. Use rubber spatula to scrape down sides of bowl.

3. Using mixing spoon or rubber spatula, gently stir in yeast sponge, remaining 2 cups flour, and drained raisins. Mix well. Sprinkle bottom of bundt pan with almonds, add dough, and spread evenly in pan. Cover with towel and let rise in warm place until almost double in bulk, ¾ to 1 hour.

Preheat oven to 350° F.

4. Bake in oven for 45 minutes to 1 hour, until golden brown. Wearing oven mitts, remove from oven. Flip pan to remove bread and place on wire cake rack to cool. While still warm, sprinkle with confectioners' sugar.

To serve, slice in wedges and place on serving platter.

POLAND

Located in northeastern Europe, Poland is bordered by Germany on the west, the Czech Republic and Slovakia on the south. Belarus and Ukraine on the east, and the Baltic Sea on the north. From the eighteenth century to the end of World War I, Poland was controlled by Russia. An independent republic between the World Wars, Poland was invaded by Nazi Germany in 1939, an act that began World War II. Poland was a Communist state under the domination of the Soviet Union from 1945 until 1989, when Communist rule ended.

Most Poles are Roman Catholic with strong attachments to church and family. Most life-cycle celebrations are conducted according to the Roman Catholic Church. (See Protestant and Catholic Life-Cycle Rituals, page xlvi.)

Poles believe the success of a marriage depends on the lavishness of the hospitality and the gaiety of the wedding celebration. It's not unusual for Polish weddings to go non-stop for three or four days and invited guests often take off work to attend. Many old Polish customs are brought to life with music and dancing. The *czepek* (money dance) has a long history; it allows guests to pay money for the privilege of dancing with the bride. The money is looked upon as a wedding gift to the couple. When the groom pays for the privilege of a dance with his new wife, it is a signal to the guests that the wedding couple are exiting the festivities. The dancing and feasting continues, with more food and drink, after they depart. The late night repast is usually pastries and fruit.

Decorated wedding bread and wedding cake are both prepared for Polish weddings, depending upon the region, village, city, or family preference. The first Polish wedding breads date back to the thirteenth century. This was a sweet bread made with yeast. It was called *korowaj*, which comes from the Polish word for circle. The baking of the wedding bread is important, with special rules and procedures. The godmother of the bride is responsible for baking the bread with the help of selected women. Clumps of dough are shaped into birds, flowers and ivy, chickens, and other barnyard animals. The wedding bread is similar to Ukrainian wedding bread (instructions page 266) and *Krendel* (recipe page 267).

The first pieces of wedding bread are cut for the bride and groom, then for parents and grandparents, next for the attendants and all the guests, including children. The sharing of bread is a symbol of abundance and goodwill.

Wedding feasts are considered the grandest of family celebrations and no expense is spared to give guests the very best and the most food the family can afford. Today the Polish wedding feast begins with *zakqski* (small bites or appetizers). The tradition probably originated centuries ago with the aristocracy. The *zakqski* generally included pickles, pickled herring, *salatka z piklowanymi jajkami* (recipe follows), smoked meats and sausages with mustard and horseradish (recipe page 222), *sauerkraut* (recipe page 167), cheeses, *piroshki* (recipe page 225), and *pierogi* (recipe page 226), baskets of hearty breads and rolls, and bowls of nuts, figs and raisins. Bowls of *smetana*, either homemade (recipe page 263) or commercial, are usually provided for guests to spoon over dumplings. *Zakqski*, either hot or cold, are supposed to stimulate the eye and thus whet the appetite so it is important to make the presentations as attractive as possible. ۞ ۞ ۞

Salatka z Piklowanymi Jajkami

Polish Salad with Pickled Eggs

Yield: serves 6

- pickled eggs (recipe follows)
- 1/4 cup virgin olive oil
- 2 tablespoons lemon juice
- salt and pepper to taste
- 1 head romaine lettuce, rinsed, drained, and torn into bite-size pieces
- 1 red onion, thinly sliced and separated into rings

Equipment: Small bowl, whisk, medium salad bowl, salad tools, individual salad plates

1. Prepare pickled eggs.

2. Prepare dressing: Pour oil into small bowl, whisk in lemon juice and salt and pepper to taste, and set aside.

3. Assemble salad: Put lettuce and onions into medium salad bowl. Whisk oil dressing, **drizzle** over salad mixture, and toss to coat. Cut pickled eggs into wedges and arrange on top of the salad.

Serve as zakqski *with salad plates for guests to help themselves. Provide plenty of bread.*

Pickled Eggs

Yield: serves 6

- 2 (14 to 16 ounces each) cans beets with juice
- water, as needed
- 3/4 cup vinegar
- 1 cup sugar
- 2 bay leaves
- 10 whole cloves
- 6 hard-cooked eggs, peeled

Equipment: 2 cup-size measuring cup, small container with cover, small saucepan, mixing spoon, large plastic resealable bag

1. Drain beet juice from cans of beets and pour into 2 cup-size measuring cup. Put beets in small container, cover, and refrigerate for another use. Add water to the beet juice, if necessary to make 2 cups of liquid, and pour into small saucepan. Add vinegar, sugar, bay leaves, and cloves. Bring to boil over medium-high heat, and stir to dissolve sugar. Reduce heat to **simmer**, and cook 5 minutes. Cool to warm.

2. Put peeled, whole hard-cooked eggs into large plastic resealable bag, and pour in warm beet juice mixture. Close bag securely and refrigerate for at least 12 hours for flavor and color to develop. Turn bag once or twice to make sure all eggs are developing color from the beet juice mixture.

Continue with salatka z piklowanymi jajkami *(recipe precedes: Step 3. Assemble salad:) or put drained eggs in a bowl and eat as a snack. Pickled eggs keep well for 1 week if covered and refrigerated.*

There are many fillings for *piroshki*, such as cottage cheese, finely chopped hard-cooked eggs, mashed potatoes, and cooked fish. Any leftover vegetables or meat can be finely chopped and used as filling.

Piroshki

Filled Pastries

Yield: about 3 dozen

beef filling (recipe follows)
3½ cups all-purpose flour
½ teaspoon salt
¾ butter or margarine
2 eggs, beaten
3 tablespoons sour cream
egg wash

Equipment: Food processor, rubber spatula, lightly floured work surface, plastic food wrap, lightly floured rolling pin, 2- to 2 ½-inch cookie cutter or water glass, pastry brush, fork, lightly greased baking sheet, oven mitts, wire cake rack

1. Prepare beef filling.

2. Put flour, salt, and butter or margarine in food processor, and pulse until mixture resembles fine crumbs, about ½ minute. Add beaten eggs and sour cream, and pulse to mix about 1 minute, until mixture pulls away from sides of container and forms a ball. Transfer to lightly floured work surface and **knead** 1 to 2 minutes until smooth and satiny. Divide dough into 2 pieces and shape each into ½-inch thick disk. Cover each disk of dough separately in plastic wrap and refrigerate 30 minutes.

Note: While processing, turn machine off once or twice and scrape down sides of container with rubber spatula.

3. Work with one piece of dough at a time, and keep the other refrigerated. On lightly floured work surface, roll dough with lightly floured rolling pin to about ¼ inch thick. Use 2- to 2½-inch cookie cutter or rim of water glass to cut out circlesin the dough. Sprinkle lightly with flour, stack, and cover with plastic wrap. (It's easier to roll dough very thin when pieces are small.) Using lightly floured rolling pin, roll each circle into a thinner 3-inch circle. Lightly sprinkle the circles with flour, stack, and cover with plastic wrap.

Preheat oven to 400° F.

4. Fill pastry circles: Place 1 tablespoonful of filling in center of each circle and brush edges with egg wash. Fold dough over into a half circle, encasing filling, and press edges togetherwith a fork. Poke the top of each 2 or 3 times with fork to make vent holes in pastries. Place on lightly greased baking sheet, and brush tops with egg wash.

5. Bake in oven for 15 to 20 minutes, until golden brown. Remove from oven and transfer pastries to wire cake rack to cool.

6. While first batch is baking, repeat process with remaining dough in refrigerator.

Serve at room temperature with soup or set out on the zakqski *table as a light snack.*

Beef Filling for Piroshki

Yield: about 3 cups

2 tablespoons butter or margarine
1 onion, **finely chopped**
1 clove garlic, finely chopped
1½ pounds **ground** lean beef
salt and pepper to taste

Equipment: Large skillet, mixing spoon

Melt butter or margarine in large skillet over medium-high heat. Add onion and garlic, stir, and **sauté** until onion is soft, 2 to 3 minutes. Crumble ground meat into skillet, stir, and cook until browned, 5 to 10 minutes. Add salt and pepper to taste.

Continue to make piroshki *(recipe precedes: Step 4. Fill pastry circles:)*

Dumplings of all sizes and shapes, with savory and sweet fillings, are probably the most popular finger food in Eastern Europe. It would be hard to find a wedding feast that did not provide great quantities of dumplings for guests to munch on.

Pierogi

Boiled Filled Pockets

Yield: serves 6 to 8

cheese filling (recipe follows)
4 cups all-purpose flour
1 teaspoon salt
5 eggs, well beaten
1 teaspoon water, more if needed
egg wash
1 cup melted butter or margarine, for **garnish**
4 tablespoons dry **bread crumbs**, for garnish

Equipment: Food processor, rubber spatula, large mixing bowl, plastic food wrap, lightly floured rolling pin, lightly floured work surface, 2- to 2½-inch cookie cutter or water glass, tablespoon, dinner fork, wax paper, baking sheet, large saucepan, slotted spoon

1. Prepare cheese filling (recipe follows).

2. Place flour, salt, and eggs in food processor, and pulse until mixture is very coarse and grainy; it should not form a ball. The mixture should pack easily when a small amount is pressed together in the palm of your hand. If mixture is too dry and doesn't hold together, add water, 1 teaspoon at a time, to reach correct consistency. If it gets too wet, add a little more flour. Transfer dough to large mixing bowl and form into a ball. Cover with plastic wrap and let rest for 10 minutes.

Note: While processing, turn machine off once or twice and scrape down sides of container with rubber spatula.

3. Divide dough into 3 equal pieces. Work with one piece at a time, keeping the others covered with plastic wrap. Using lightly floured rolling pin, roll dough as thin as possible on lightly floured work surface. Using 2- to 2½-inch cookie cutter or rim of water glass, cut out circles. Sprinkle lightly with flour, stack, and cover with plastic wrap. (It's easier to roll dough very thin when pieces are small.) Using lightly floured rolling pin, roll each 2- or 2½-inch circle into a 3-inch circle by rolling it thinner. Sprinkle lightly with flour, stack, and cover with plastic wrap. Repeat cutting pastry circles with remaining dough.

4. Fill pastries: Place 1 tablespoon filling in center of each circle. Using finger, brush edges with egg wash, and fold dough over into a half circle to encase filling. Press edges of circle to-

gether and seal using fork. Place side by side on wax-paper-covered baking sheet.

5. Fill large saucepan two-thirds full with water, add 2 teaspoons salt, and bring to boil over high heat. Add dumplings, a few at a time, so they don't stick together. Cook 7 to 10 minutes until tender. To test doneness, taste a dumpling; if it is soft, it is done. If it is doughy tasting and hard, it is undercooked and needs more time. When done, remove with slotted spoon and place in serving bowl. **Drizzle** each batch with melted butter or margarine to prevent sticking together and keep warm. Before serving, sprinkle with bread crumbs.

Serve dumplings as a side dish or a zakqski *(appetizer).*

Cheese Filling for Pierogi

Yield: about 2½ cups

- 2 cups ricotta or cream cheese, at room temperature
- 4 tablespoons seedless raisins
- 1 egg
- 4 teaspoons sugar

Equipment: Medium mixing bowl, mixing spoon

Put ricotta or cream cheese, raisins, egg, and sugar into medium mixing bowl and stir to mix well.

Continue to make Pierogi *(recipe precedes: Step 4. Fill pastries:)*

Kielbasa (Polish sausage) is the most traditional food at Polish weddings. Everyone expects it and loves it, especially when it is cooked with purple cabbage. This delicious sausage dish can be served as an appetizer or side dish.

Kielbasa z Kapustoy

Sausage with Cabbage

Yield: serves 4 to 6

- 2 tablespoons butter or margarine
- 1 to 1½ pound head purple cabbage, shredded
- 2 cups canned beef broth
- salt and pepper to taste
- 2 tablespoons dark brown sugar
- 1 tablespoon cornstarch
- ½ cup lemon juice
- 1 pound kielbasa or other smoked sausage, thinly sliced

Equipment: Large saucepan with cover, mixing spoon, small bowl, serving bowl

1. Melt butter or margarine in large saucepan over medium-high heat. Add cabbage, stir, reduce heat to **simmer**, and cook for 5 minutes. Add beef broth, stir, cover, and simmer 45 minutes.

2. In small bowl, stir dark brown sugar, cornstarch, and lemon juice with ½ cup cooking liquid from saucepan. Add brown sugar mixture to cabbage mixture, and stir until thickened, 3 to 5 minutes. Add sausage, stir, cover, and simmer 30 minutes.

To serve, transfer to serving bowl and serve with thick slices of bread.

Today in Poland, many couples are having smaller weddings with family and a few close friends. Many years ago, the Polish aristocracy often entertained with the *cukrowa kolacja* (sweet supper) and now it's popular for small wedding receptions. The menu is an assortment of sweets; cakes; pastries; cookies; tarts, such as this recipe for *mazurki bakaliowe* (fruitcake tart); *nalesniki*, which is the same as Estonian *pannkoogid* (recipe page 255); candy; and fresh fruit. Champagne, sweet liqueurs, and tea and coffee are the usual beverages at a sweet supper. *Mazurki bakaliowe* is a simple cookie-type sweet tart that goes well with a cup of tea.

Mazurki Bakaliowe

Fruitcake Tart

Yield: *24 to 32 pieces*
- 2 cups all-purpose flour
- ½ teaspoon salt
- ½ cup chilled butter or margarine, cut into small chunks
- 1½ cups sugar
- 3 eggs, divided
- 3 tablespoons light cream
- 1 cup seedless raisins
- 1 cup chopped dates
- 1 cup chopped mixed candied fruit
- 1 cup chopped walnuts
- juice of 2 lemons

Equipment: Large mixing bowl, **pastry blender (optional)**, small bowl, mixing spoon, 4 (6-inch size) greased or nonstick pizza pans or pie pans with 6-inch bottoms, oven mitts

Preheat oven to 350° F.

1. In large mixing bowl, mix flour, salt, and butter or margarine, and using fingers or pastry blender, **blend** until mixture resembles coarse crumbs. Add 1 cup sugar and blend well until mixture resembles fine crumbs.

2. In small bowl, beat 1 egg with cream. Add egg mixture to flour mixture, and using your hands, form into smooth dough. Divide dough into 4 balls. Pat each ball out to cover bottom of 4 greased or nonstick 6-inch pizza pans or pie pans with 6-inch bottoms.

3. Bake in oven for 20 minutes, until set. Remove from oven. Set aside.

4. Prepare topping: In medium mixing bowl, mix remaining ½ cup sugar, remaining 2 eggs, raisins, dates, mixed candied fruit, nuts, and lemon juice until well blended. Spread evenly over baked crusts. Return to oven and continue baking for about 20 minutes.

5. Using oven mitts, remove from oven and while still warm, cut each into 6 or 8 wedges.

Serve as sweet snack. Store in airtight container.

SCANDINAVIA

Scandinavia is a region of northern Europe that includes the countries of Norway, Sweden, Denmark, Finland, and the island country of Iceland. It is a cold area with long, dark winters and short summers. Most Scandinavians have the same or similar life-cycle celebrations because the majority of the people belong to the Lutheran Church. (See Protestant and Catholic Life-Cycle Rituals, page xlvi.)

Over time, rituals, customs, and foods have crossed the borders of Scandinavia. While the customs and foods are similar throughout these countries, each country has its own names for these things. For example, a popular cake the Norwegians call *kransekake* (recipe follows), is called the *kransekage* by the Danes and *kranskaka* by the Swedes. The name means wreath cake, and it is a pyramid of baked cookie rings, each layer a little smaller than the previous one. This festive pastry is drizzled with butter cream icing (recipe page 361) and decorated with miniature trinkets, flags, flowers, or greenery appropriate to the celebration—weddings, anniversaries, landmark birthdays, and even national holidays.

Although the recipe for this wreath cake is similar throughout Scandinavia, each country has its own traditions for serving it. When it is made for a wedding in Finland, for example, a bottle of champagne is placed in the center of a large round serving tray, and the baked rings are stacked to completely cover the bottle. The cake is eaten by breaking off the rings and serving pieces to guests. When the champagne bottle is exposed, it is opened and everyone drinks a toast to the bride and groom.

The Scandinavians use a special set of pans to make the *kransekage*. The pans consist of ring-shaped grooves in graduating sizes. The pans are available at kitchenware and bakery supply stores, but they are a little expensive. The following instructions for the preparation of the **cake boards** can be used instead of purchasing the special pans needed for making the cookie rings used in *kransekage*.

Cardboard cake boards cut into circles are called **cake circles,** and they can be used for making the 18 cookie rings for the *kransekage*. The rings range in size from 12 inches in diameter for the bottom cookie to 3½ inches at the top. The cake circles are available at most craft and hobby shops and kitchenware and bakery supply stores in packages of 12 (either 12, 10, 8, or 6 inches).

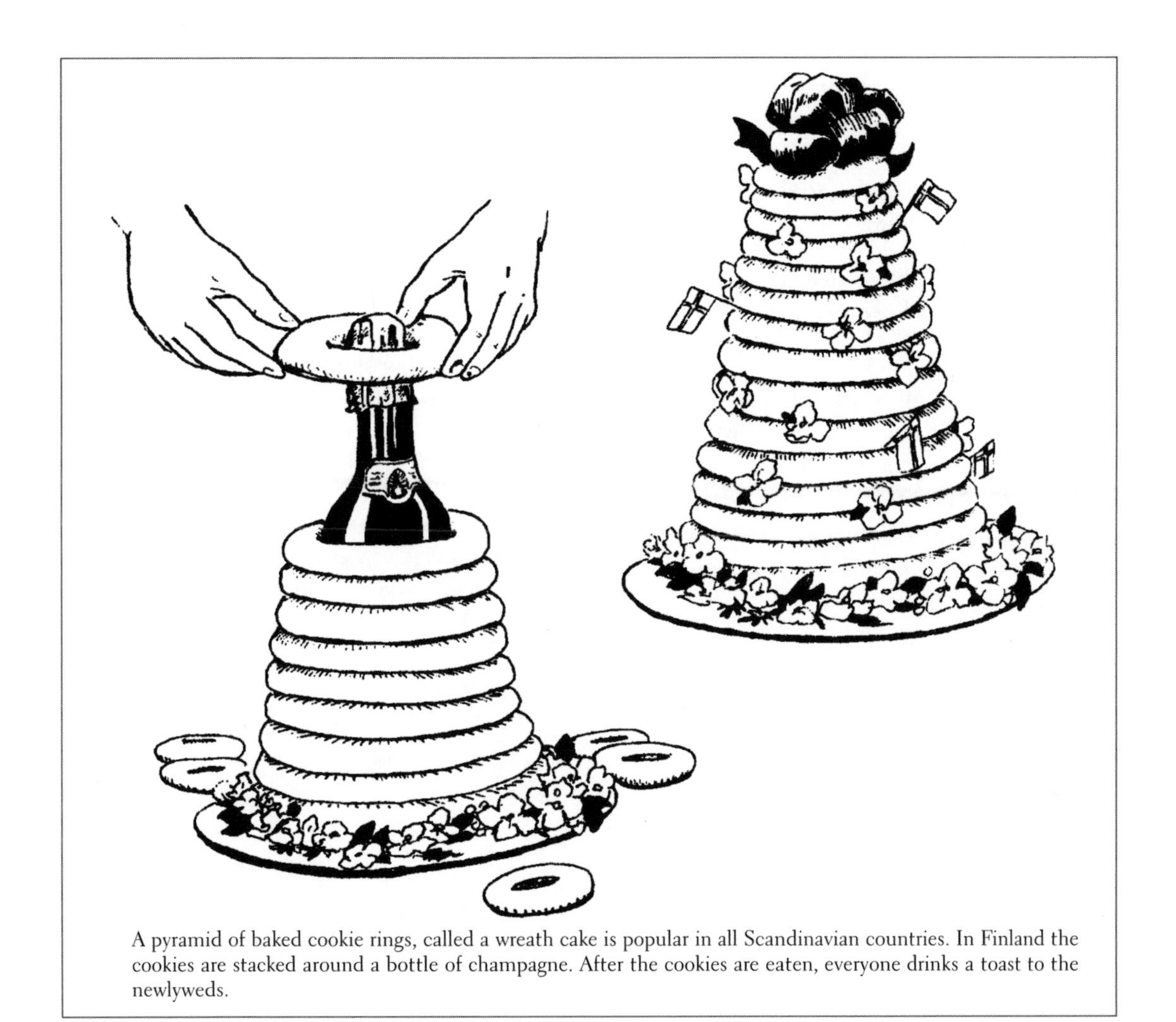

A pyramid of baked cookie rings, called a wreath cake is popular in all Scandinavian countries. In Finland the cookies are stacked around a bottle of champagne. After the cookies are eaten, everyone drinks a toast to the newlyweds.

Cake Circles for Kransekage

Equipment: Eighteen 12-inch cake circles, a compass with a pencil, scissors or a sharp pallet knife, dark permanent marker, heavy-duty aluminum foil

1. Using the compass and pencil, mark-off the boards that need to be trimmed smaller. Each board will be ½-inch smaller than the last. As you are measuring each cake board, using marker, write the number of each cake circle in the center of the board, with the size of each board under the number. The sizes of the boards are as follows: #1 (12 inches); #2 (11½ inches); #3 (11 inches); #4 (10½ inches); #5 (10 inches); #6 (9½ inches); #7 (9 inches); #8 (8½ inches); #9 (8 inches); #10 (7½ inches); #11 (7 inches); #12 (6½ inches); #13 (6 inches); #14 (5½ inches); #15 (5 inches); #16 (4½ inches); #17 (4 inches); and #18 (3½ inches). Stack the boards in numerical order.

2. Cut the cake boards to size using the scissors or pallet knife. Keep the boards in numerical order.

3. Cover the unnumbered side of the boards with foil, leaving the numbers visible on the other side. Directions to cover the board with foil are in the glossary under **cake boards** (cake circles). Keep the boards stacked in numerical order and begin making the *kransekage*.

If you are using a standard size food processor, you will need to process this dough recipe in two batches to make an 18-layer *kransekage*.

Kransekage (also Kransekake or Kranskaka)

Wreath Cake (Scandinavian Wedding Cake)

Yield: serves 25 to 35

- 1 pound (2 cups) unsalted butter, at room temperature
- 2 cups confectioners sugar, **sifted**
- 2 cups (16 ounces) **almond paste** (available at supermarkets)
- 2 whole eggs
- 2 **egg yolks**
- 2 teaspoons almond extract
- 5 cups all-purpose flour, sifted
- nonstick cooking spray
- *butter cream icing* (recipe page 361), for assembling

Equipment: Food processor, rubber spatula, mixing spoon, medium mixing bowl, plastic wrap, 18 prepared **cake circles** (instructions precede), lightly floured work surface, wide spatula, 2 baking sheets, oven mitts, wire cake rack, large tray or serving platter with at least a 14-inch flat surface, **pastry bag** with fine writing tip

1. Put 1 cup butter and 1 cup confectioners' sugar in food processor and process until creamy and well mixed, 30 seconds. Continue to process on medium speed. Break 1 cup almond paste into small pieces and add through the feed tube a few pieces at a time. Process until mixture is smooth. Add 1 egg, 1 egg yolk, and 1 teaspoon almond extract. Process until well mixed. Add 2 ½ cups flour, a little at a time, and process until thoroughly mixed, 3 to 4 minutes. Do not over process.

Note: While processing, turn machine off once or twice and scrape down sides of container with rubber spatula.

2. Transfer dough to medium mixing bowl. If dough seems too soft to roll between the palms of your hands, cover with plastic wrap and refrigerate for about 1 hour to firm up.

3. Cover cake boards: Lightly coat foil-side of 1 cake board with nonstick cooking spray. Work only with the amount of dough you can easily handle at one time. Using your hands, roll it into a 1-inch thick rope on lightly floured work surface. Place the rope along the outer edge of the foil-covered board. Continue making short lengths of rope and join them together into a smooth ring along the outer edge of the cake board. Using your hands or wide spatula, press gently on the cookie ring to flatten it evenly to about ½-inch thick. Taper the cookie ring gently along the outer edge so it is smooth and even with the edge of the cake board. The inside edge of the cookie rings can be uneven; they do not show. Continue making the remaining cookie rings. As each cookie ring is finished, lightly cover with plastic wrap and refrigerate until ready to bake.

Preheat oven to 350° F.

4. Prepare to bake: Remove only the cake boards you can bake at one time, keeping the others refrigerated. Place cake boards on baking sheets about ½-inch apart.

5. Bake cookie-covered cake boards in batches in oven until lightly golden, 30 to 40 minutes. Remove cake boards from baking sheets and place on wire cake rack to cool, about 30 minutes. With cookie rings still on cake boards, carefully flip cookie onto wire cake rack to set, 1 hour. Wrap cookies and boards in plastic wrap and refrigerate for at least 4 hours or overnight to firm up. Do not remove the boards until ready to assemble. The numbers on the back of the cake boards make it easy to stack in proper order.

6. Prepare *butter cream icing* (recipe page 361).

7. To assemble: Beginning with cake board #1, transfer cake board to tray or serving platter. Keeping the cookie ring attached to the cake board, dab the bottom-side of the board with icing to make it stick to the tray or platter. Carefully remove the cookie ring from cake board #2, taking care not to break it. Turn the cookie ring over and spread icing on the bottom to act as glue. Set ring #2 on top of ring #1. Repeat icing and stacking cookie rings in numbered sequence. If necessary, dab extra icing under a ring to keep the layers level. If any rings break, use a dab of icing to glue them back together as you stack them.

8. Decorate *kransekage*: Spoon icing in a pastry bag fitted with a fine writing tip. Make icing loops, dots, or any design you like. If icing seems too thick to pass through writing tip, add a little water to thin before filling pastry bag.

To serve, let the kransekage *stand for at least 1 hour, until the icing sets. Add the decorations of your choice. To assemble at a later date: freeze individual rings, wrapped in plastic wrap or foil for up to one month. When ready to use, unwrap and thaw before assembling.*

Note: *If using the* kransekage *pans: Directions come with the pans or use the following directions. Coat pans with nonstick cooking spray. Spoon dough into a large pastry bag fitted with a plain ½-inch tip. (Don't use a larger tip or the cookie rings may expand too much.) Pipe dough out in a long rope into the ring-shaped grooves of the pans. Press rope ends or any breaks in the dough together to form smooth, unbroken rings. Continue to bake. (See step 5, above.)*

DENMARK

The country of Denmark, sharing a border with Germany on the south, consists of a peninsula and small island in the Baltic Sea. It is the smallest of the Scandinavian countries, and even though it lacks many natural resources, Denmark has a strong economy and industry. The Danes are admired worldwide for their education and science, craftsmanship and culture, industry and commerce.

Most Danes belong to the Lutheran Church and observe all life-cycle celebrations according to the Christian doctrine. (See Protestant and Catholic Life-Cycle Rituals, page xlvi.) The christening of a newborn is an important day for most Danish families. Family, relatives, and friends come before the minister for the solemn ceremony of introducing the infant to the Lutheran faith. Traditionally, the infant wears a christening gown that has been in the family for many generations. Afterwards a family dinner is served with a cake honoring the newly baptized child.

The Danes celebrate many life-cycle events with generous feasts, setting out platters, bowls, and trays of food. The Danish *smørrebrød* (literally, "bread and butter") is world famous. Open-faced sandwiches, made from a choice of hundreds of local delicacies, are prepared for the feast, along with *fyldt svinemørbrad* (recipe follows) and *frikadeller* (recipe page 233), assorted cheeses, fresh fruits, and marvelous puddings. If it is a wedding, the *kransekage* (recipe page 230) will be the centerpiece on the buffet table. Whatever the occasion, the Danes' favorite beverages are beer and fruit juices.

Throughout Scandinavia, but particularly in Denmark, pork is served on special occasions. The Danes are very fond of combining dried fruits with meat, as is the case in the following recipe, *fyldt svinemørbrad*, a wonderful dish to serve at a christening dinner or a wedding banquet. In Sweden, a similar dish is called *fläskkarre*. ❂ ❂ ❂

Fyldt Svinemørbrad

Danish Pork Tenderloins

Yield: serves 6 to 8

- 2 pork loins (3/4 to 1 pound each), have butcher **butterfly** the loins lengthwise
- salt and pepper to taste
- 3 cooking apples, **finely chopped**
- 12 pitted prunes, soaked in 2 cups hot water for 1 hour and drained
- 2 cups water, more as needed
- 2 tablespoons all-purpose flour

Equipment: Work surface, kitchen string, knife, shallow roasting pan with rack, oven mitts, meat **thermometer** (optional), cutting board, aluminum foil, metal spatula, medium saucepan, measuring cup, small mixing bowl, small spoon, whisk, small serving bowl

Preheat oven to 325° F.

1. Place the loins, cut-side up, on work surface. Sprinkle with salt and pepper to taste. Place half of the chopped apples and 6 prunes down the center of each tenderloin. Roll up each loin, jelly-roll style, and tie with string to securely close. Place them side by side, seam-side down, on rack in shallow roasting pan. Pour 2 cups water into the bottom of the pan to catch the fat drippings. If necessary, to prevent drying out, add more water, 1 cup at a time, to keep the same 2-cup water level during the baking.

2. Bake in oven for 1½ to 1¾ hours, or until meat thermometer registers 160°F. Remove from oven and transfer meat to cutting board. Cover with foil to keep warm until ready to serve.

3. Prepare gravy: Remove rack from roasting pan. Scrape up brown bits of pan drippings with metal spatula from the bottom of the roasting pan. Put pan drippings in measuring cup. There should be about 2 cups; if not, add more water. Transfer drippings to medium saucepan. Bring to boil over medium-high heat. In small mixing bowl, stir together 1/4 cup water with flour to make **slurry**. Pour slurry into the pan drippings

and whisk until thickened, 3 to 5 minutes. Add salt and pepper to taste and cook 1 minute longer.

To serve, remove string and slice meat crosswise into 1- or 2-inch thick slices. Serve gravy in a small serving bowl and spoon a little gravy over each serving.

A popular appetizer at a Danish wedding banquet is *frikadeller med citronsovs.*

Frikadeller med Citronsovs

Danish Meat Balls with Lemon Sauce

Yield: 25 to 30 pieces

½ pound **ground** veal
½ pound ground lean pork
½ cup fine dry white **bread crumbs**
2 tablespoons grated onion
½ cup light cream
½ cup water
salt and pepper to taste
1 bay leaf
citronsovs, for serving (recipe follows)

Equipment: Medium mixing bowl, wax paper, baking sheet, large shallow saucepan, slotted metal spoon, medium baking pan, serving bowl or **chafing dish**

1. Put veal, pork, bread crumbs, and grated onion in medium mixing bowl. Using your hands, mix well. Add light cream, water, and salt and pepper to taste. Continue to mix with your hands until mixture holds together and comes away from sides of bowl.

2. Form meatballs: Dampen your hands and roll about 1 tablespoon of mixture into a Ping-Pong size ball. Place on wax-paper-covered baking sheet. Dampen your hands each time and continue to make meatballs, using up all the meat mixture.

3. **Poach** meatballs: Fill large shallow saucepan with at least 2 inches of water. Add bay leaf and ½ teaspoon salt. Bring to boil over high heat. Reduce heat to **simmer**, and drop in a few meatballs at a time, don't crowd the pan. Poach meatballs for 4 to 5 minutes. Remove with slotted metal spoon and drain over the pan. Place in medium baking pan. Continue poaching all the meatballs.

4. The cooked meatballs can be served immediately or covered and refrigerated to be served later. To serve later, reheat meatballs in boiling water for 1 to 2 minutes or place in the oven or microwave until heated through, 2 to 5 minutes.

To serve, transfer meatballs to a serving bowl or chafing dish and pour citronsovs *(recipe follows) over them.*

Citronsovs can be used over fish or other meat dishes. This sauce is what makes *frikadeller* distinctly Danish, setting it apart from Sweden's *kjottboller* (meatballs).

Citronsovs

Danish Lemon Sauce

Yield: about 2½ cups

2 tablespoons unsalted butter
2 tablespoons all-purpose flour
1 ½ cups chicken broth, homemade (recipe page 106), or canned
½ cup light cream
juice of ½ lemon
salt and white pepper to taste
2 **egg yolks**
¼ cup heavy cream

Equipment: Medium saucepan, whisk, mixing spoon

1. Melt butter in medium saucepan over low heat. Whisk in flour to make a smooth paste. Increase heat to medium. Whisking constantly, slowly add chicken broth, then light cream. Con-

tinue whisking until mixture is smooth and glossy, with the consistency of heavy cream. Stir in lemon juice and salt and white pepper to taste. Turn heat to low.

2. Stir egg yolks with heavy cream in cup until well mixed. Stir about ¼ cup butter mixture into egg mixture, to **temper**. Whisking butter mixture constantly, return egg mixture to the pan. Increase heat to medium and whisk constantly until sauce thickens to consistency of heavy cream. Do not let it boil or it will curdle and become inedible.

Continue with frikadeller *(recipe precedes).*

Beets are a favorite vegetable in all Scandinavian countries. *Syltede rødbeder* is served as one of the little dishes on the *smørrebrød*. The pleasant, tangy taste of the beets goes well with *fyldt svinemørbrad* (recipe page 232).

Syltede Rødbeder

Danish Pickled Beets

Note: This recipe takes 8 or more hours.

Yield: serves 4 to 6

14 ounces canned sliced beets, drained
¾ cup white or cider vinegar
½ cup water
2 to 3 tablespoons sugar
salt and pepper to taste
2 teaspoons caraway seed

Equipment: Medium bowl with cover, small saucepan, mixing spoon, serving dish

1. Put drained beets into medium bowl.

2. Prepare pickling juice: Put vinegar, water, and 2 tablespoons sugar into small saucepan. Bring to boil over high heat, and cook for 2 minutes. Taste to adjust the sweetness, adding the remaining 1 tablespoon sugar if necessary.

3. Pour pickling juice over beets. **Fold in** salt and pepper to taste and caraway seeds. Cool to room temperature. Cover and refrigerate for at least 8 hours.

To serve, drain beets and transfer to serving dish. The beets can be kept covered and refrigerated for up to 2 weeks. Syltede rødbeder *is served cold.*

NORWAY

Norway is a mountainous country that is bordered by the North Sea on the southwest, Sweden on the east, Finland and Russia on the northeast, and the Barents Sea on the north. Its long coastline, 1,700 miles, has many islands and fjords or narrow sea inlets. Thanks in part to the discovery of large oil and gas reserves in the North Sea, Norway is one of the world's richest countries.

The majority of Norwegians are Lutheran and follow the life-cycle events prescribed by the Lutheran Church. (See Protestant and Catholic Life-Cycle Rituals, page xlvi.) In recent years, though, Norway has become home to increasing numbers of immigrants. The government has opened the country to foreign workers and the asylum-seekers from various parts of the world. Complete religious freedom is assured them, even though the state religion is the Evangelical Lutheran Church.

In Norway, urbanites have more sedate Western-type weddings, while country weddings are more colorful and raucous. Often the traditional country wedding is a three-day celebration with a big meal served each day. The wedding party and guests begin eating about mid-afternoon and continue celebrating far into the night with plenty of singing and dancing and all-around good fun. Roasted pig, home-cured ham, smoked pork and sausages, *dyresteg* (venison or reindeer roast, recipe page 236), Norwegian sauerkraut with caraway seeds, cauliflower, sweet peas and carrots, and an assortment of cakes and puddings are some of the foods prepared for these meals.

Wedding cakes are often regional, such as the labor-intensive *brudlaupskling*. This cake is made of dozens of pancake-like layers, cooked on an iron griddle and smeared with butter and a mixture of cheese, heavy cream, and syrup. Each layer is then folded and cut into small, square cakes. The easier to make *kransekake* (recipe page 230) is preferred by many couples.

The first big meal is held after the church nuptials, when guests are treated to a late night feast beginning with nourishing *spinatsuppe* (recipe follows), sour-cream porridge (recipe page 236), and a concoction called *dravle*, made of curds and whey sweetened with syrup. As a show of unity, everyone drinks from a communal bowl filled with beer.

In the morning, guests refresh themselves with coffee and cakes. The party continues through the second day and night, and on the third day things start to wind down and slowly life returns to normal.

Spinatsuppe

Spinach Soup

Yield: serves 4 to 6

- 2 pounds fresh spinach, washed, drained, and **coarsely chopped**, or 2 (16-ounce) packages of frozen chopped spinach, thawed and drained
- 2 quarts chicken broth, homemade (recipe page 106), or canned
- 3 tablespoons butter or margarine
- 2 tablespoons all-purpose **flour**
- 1 teaspoon salt
- ¼ teaspoon **ground** nutmeg
- ¼ teaspoon ground white pepper
- 2 hard-cooked eggs, sliced

Equipment: Large saucepan, mixing spoon, food processor, ladle, small **heavy-based** saucepan, medium saucepan with cover, whisk, individual soup bowls

1. Put spinach in large saucepan and add chicken broth. Bring to a boil over high heat and stir. Reduce heat to **simmer** and cook for 8 to 10 minutes, until spinach is well cooked. Remove from heat and set aside to cool to warm.

2. **Purée** spinach mixture in two batches to avoid overfilling processor. Ladle half the spinach mixture into food processor and purée until smooth and lump-free. Repeat with second batch. Pour both batches into medium saucepan.

3. In small heavy-based saucepan, melt butter or margarine over medium-low heat. Remove pan from heat and whisk in flour. Return pan to heat and continue whisking until mixture is smooth. Whisk in 1 ladle of puréed spinach mixture to butter mixture. Pour back into medium saucepan with the rest of the puréed spinach mixture in it. Cook over medium-high heat until small bubbles appear around edge of pan. Reduce heat to low. Add salt, nutmeg, and white pepper. Stir, cover, and cook 5 minutes.

To serve, ladle into individual soup bowls and ***garnish*** *each serving with a few slices of hard-cooked egg.*

At country weddings, the dish most anticipated by the guests is *rømmegrøt* (recipe follows). According to tradition, the bride's mother is supposed to make it for the groom and serve it to him on their wedding night. *Rømmegrøt* is considered the national dish of Norway and is often eaten as the evening meal.

Norwegians use cultured heavy cream to make *rømmegrøt*. You can make your own by adding buttermilk to heavy cream (recipe follows *rømmegrøt* recipe). Allow two or three days for the sour cream to develop before making *rømmegrøt*. A good substitute for Norwegian sour cream is **crème fraîche.**

Rømmegrøt

Norwegian Sour Cream Porridge

Note: This recipe takes 2 or 3 days.

Yield: serves 8

2 tablespoons all-purpose **flour**
1 tablespoon sugar
2 cups milk
1 cup *Norwegian sour cream* (recipe follows) or **crème fraîche**
2 tablespoons cornstarch
2 tablespoons water
seedless raisins, to taste, for serving
cinnamon sugar, to taste, for serving

Equipment: Medium saucepan, whisk, cup, small bowl with cover, small dessert bowls

1. Put flour and sugar in medium saucepan. Slowly whisk in milk and *Norwegian sour cream* or crème fraîche . Place pan over medium-high heat and whisking constantly, bring to boil. Reduce heat to **simmer**, and cook, whisking frequently, until mixture is **reduced** to about 2¾ cups, 15 to 20 minutes.

2. Mix cornstarch and water in cup until well blended. Whisk cornstarch mixture into milk mixture. Whisking constantly, bring to boil over medium-high heat. Reduce heat to low and cook until thickened, 3 to 5 minutes. Remove from heat. Cool to room temperature. Transfer porridge to small bowl, cover, and refrigerate overnight.

Serve either cold or reheat and serve warm. Sprinkle with raisins and cinnamon sugar. Individually serve in small dessert bowls.

Norwegian Sour Cream

Note: This recipe takes 2 or 3 days.

1 cup heavy cream
1 tablespoon buttermilk

Equipment: Small saucepan or microwave-safe bowl, cooking **thermometer** (optional), spoon, small bowl with cover

Warm heavy cream over medium heat to 100° to 110° F on thermometer in small saucepan (2 to 3 minutes) or in a microwave-safe bowl in a microwave oven (about 1 minute). Remove from heat and stir in buttermilk. Transfer to small bowl, cover, and store at room temperature until mixture is thick enough to just hold its shape (like yogurt) when scooped onto a spoon, 24 to 30 hours.

You need to allow two or three days for Norwegian sour cream to develop before using. Keep covered and refrigerated for up to a week.

Roasted venison (or reindeer) is often included in the Norwegian wedding feast. If you don't have a hunter in the family, your butcher can often special-order a venison-roast from his purveyor.

Dyresteg

Roasted Venison

Yield: serves 6 to 8

4 to 6 pounds boneless haunch of venison or reindeer
3 tablespoons butter or margarine, at room temperature
salt and pepper to taste
2 to 3 cups canned beef broth
1 tablespoon **flour**
1 tablespoon red currant or raspberry jelly
½ cup sour cream

Equipment: Kitchen string, paring knife, shallow roasting pan with rack, oven mitts, heatproof surface, **bulb baster** or large spoon, meat thermometer (optional), baking sheet, aluminum foil, measuring cup, small **heavy-based** saucepan, whisk, serving platter, small serving bowl

Preheat oven to 475° F.

1. Tie roast up neatly at ½-inch intervals with string so it will hold its shape while cooking. Using your hand, spread the softened butter evenly over the meat. Place the roast on a rack in a shallow roasting pan.

2. Bake roast in hot oven to **sear** for 20 minutes, or until browned.

Reduce heat to 375° F.

3. Using oven mitts, remove roast from oven and place on heatproof surface. Sprinkle the roast with salt and pepper to taste. Carefully pour 2 cups beef broth into the bottom of the roasting pan and return to oven. Allow about 20 minutes per pound. Cook 1¼ to 1½ hours for rare; 1¾ to 2 hours for well done. During the baking, use the bulb baster or large spoon to baste about every 30 minutes, adding more beef broth if the pan gets dry. To test doneness for meat insert meat thermometer into thickest part of the roast; it should register about 160° F. for medium doneness and about 170° F. for well done.

4. Remove roast from oven and transfer to baking sheet. Pour pan juices into measuring cup, cover roast with foil, and return to turned-off oven to keep warm while making sauce.

5. Prepare sauce: Skim and discard the fat from the pan juices. Add water, if necessary, to make 1 cup of liquid. In small heavy-based saucepan, melt butter over medium-low heat. Pull pan off heat and whisk in flour. Return pan to heat and continue whisking until mixture is smooth. Whisk in pan juices and increase heat to medium. Whisk until mixture thickens, 3 to 5 minutes. Remove from heat. Whisk in jelly, sour cream, and salt and pepper to taste.

To serve, remove the strings from the roast, thinly slice the meat, and place on serving platter. Pass the sauce separately in a small serving bowl. Spoon sauce over each serving.

SWEDEN

Sweden is a country dominated by rivers and over 100,000 lakes, which make up nearly a third of the total land area. It is bordered by Norway on the west, Finland on the northeast, and the Baltic Sea on the southwest.

The Swedish people enjoy the highest standard of living in Europe. An overwhelming majority of the population belong to the Evangelical Lutheran Church, the state religion, and follow life-cycle events prescribed by the Church. (See Protestant and Catholic Life-Cycle Rituals, page xlvi.) Despite the presence of a state religion, Sweden has complete religious freedom making it a secure haven for the many Muslims, Jews, Hindus, and Buddhists who live there. They each follow life-cycle celebrations according to their religion.

Besides the traditional Christian life-cycle celebrations, the Swedes celebrate the birth of a baby and birthdays. Most Swedish babies are christened, and the parents usually have their immediate family and godparents to a small Sunday dinner after the church service, forgoing large christening parties. A child's birthday (*kalas*) is celebrated with young friends who bring gifts and stay to play games and eat home baked cake which could be the Finnish *Kermakakku* (recipe page 246). A special day for children, usually in their early teens, is their confirmation in the Church of Sweden. It is followed by a family celebration with cake and gifts.

Wedding ceremonies are held mostly in the church, followed by a dinner and dancing afterwards. In the countryside, weddings are community affairs in both the preparation and the celebration. In the urban areas, like in other European cities, the celebration often includes champagne, flowers, and the traditional bridal waltz to start the dancing.

For many Swedes, the wedding events begin before the actual ceremony. Prior to the wedding, it is customary for friends of the bride to surprise her with a hen night (*möhippa*) and for the groom's friends to surprise him with a stag night (*svensexa*); both are rowdy affairs with practical jokes and lots of beer drinking.

On the Sunday before the wedding, the couple may have a *lysning*. The *lysning* is an afternoon party, after church, with a light meal and drinks. The couple receives presents from the guests at this afternoon party, not at the wedding.

On the day of the wedding, the bride's family traditionally welcomes the guests to the church. During the service, the bride and groom walk up the aisle together. Couples exchange two rings at their engagement, so at the official ceremony, the bride usually receives a second gold band. At the end of the service, the couple generally exits the church first. They stand just outside the entrance to receive good wishes and congratulations from departing guests.

The reception is usually held at a community hall or restaurant. According to Swedish tradition, a bridal arch of flowers designates the place of honor in the banquet hall. The arch is like a canopy of flowers, either fresh or dried, that frames the seated newlywed couple as they eat. During the festive meal, it is customary for guests to raise their glasses many times to toast (*skål*) the newlyweds.

The buffet table is the most important form of entertaining in Sweden, including at wedding celebrations. The formal buffet (*kalas*) is not the same as the better-known *smörgåsbord*, which is really a sandwich buffet. (*Smör* refers to butter and *bord* is bread.) Whether the buffet is *kalas* or *smörgåsbord* depends upon the budget. For both types of buffet, the centerpiece is often a decorated pig's head or perhaps a whole suckling pig (see recipe page 162). Herring dishes are generally served in several forms—pickled, jellied, baked, smoked, and poached; other foods prepared include assorted pork and beef dishes, often reindeer meat (recipe page 236); breads; potatoes; cheeses; salads; and cakes. These dishes are laid out onto a long table or several tables for self-service. Important eating etiquette is to never pile lots of food on the plate at one time; it is eaten in several courses. The standard order of eating is to start with the fish, move on to the meat and then the hot dishes, and finish with cheeses. Guests usually take a break before turning to the desserts with coffee. Separate plates are provided and guest get a fresh plate each time they go to the buffet. It is considered rude and bad luck to take the last bit of food in the serving dish.

As with wedding traditions throughout the world, cakes are often part of the celebration. An unusual regional wedding cake called *spettekaka* is so complicated only commercial bakers can make it. It is made by beating sugar and scores of eggs for hours on end. The concoction is baked by drizzling batter onto a rotating spit in front of an open fire. The batter clings to the spit as it rotates and the finish cake ends up about 12 inches wide at the base and about 2 feet tall. A popular Swedish wedding cake that is much easier to make is the *kransekage* (recipe page 230).

The following recipe for pea soup with pork, *ärter med fläsk*, is typical of the types of dishes that would be served on the buffet table. ۞ ۞ ۞

Ärter med Fläsk

Pea Soup with Pork

Yield: 6

- 1 pound (2 cups) yellow split peas
- 10 cups water
- 1 pound lean salt pork in one piece
- 2 onions, **finely chopped**
- 1 whole onion, peeled and studded with 4 cloves
- ½ teaspoon **ground** marjoram
- 1 teaspoon salt, more or less to taste

Equipment: Medium saucepan, mixing spoon, cutting board, meat knife, serving dish, tureen or covered casserole dish, ladle, soup spoons, soup bowls

1. Put yellow peas in medium saucepan, add water, salt pork, chopped onions, clove-studded onion, and marjoram. Bring to boil over high heat. Stir, reduce heat to **simmer**, cover, and cook until peas are tender, 1 to 1½ hours. Remove and set aside the clove-studded onion and salt pork.

2. Transfer pork to cutting board. Slice the pork and place it on a serving dish. Pour the hot soup into a tureen or casserole dish and cover it to keep warm.

Serve pea soup with plenty of crusty bread for dunking and sopping. Place soup on the kalas *or* smörgåsbord *table with soup bowls and soup spoons next to it. Each person ladles soup into a bowl and eats it with a spoon.*

Fresh salmon is one of Sweden's favorite foods. Poached salmon served cold with mustard sauce is traditionally on the *kalas* or *smörgåsbord* tables. Prepare the Scottish poached salmon (recipe page 207) and serve it with a side dish of this delicious *Swedish mustard sauce*.

Swedish Mustard Sauce

Yield: about 1½ cups

- 2 tablespoons Dijon mustard
- 1 tablespoon sugar
- 1 tablespoon vinegar
- ½ cup olive oil
- ½ cup sour cream
- 2 tablespoons **finely chopped** fresh dill, or 1 tablespoon dried dill

Equipment: Small mixing bowl with cover, whisk, small serving bowl

Whisk mustard, sugar, and vinegar in small mixing bowl. Whisking vigorously, add the oil in a slow, thin stream. The sauce will thicken rapidly but continue to whisk until all the oil is incorporated. Whisk in the sour cream and finely chopped dill. Cover and refrigerate.

To serve, transfer to small serving bowl and place beside the poached salmon on the buffet table.

The Scandinavians love pork stuffed with dried fruits. *Fläskkarre* (Swedish loin of pork) is just like the Danish *fyldt svinemørbrad* (recipe page 232) except for the filling; dried apricots are combined with prunes instead of the apple. Prepare the meat in the same way. Soak the 12 pitted dried apricots and 12 pitted prunes in 2 cups hot water for 1 hour to plump and soften, drain and continue to stuff and bake the loin of meat according to directions for *fyldt svinemørbrad*.

The Scandinavian people have hundreds of different sandwich combinations. *vårsörgåsar* are finger sandwiches that can be whipped up in no time for a birthday party or to add to the buffet table at other celebrations.

VÅRSÖRGÅSAR

FINGER SANDWICHES

Yield: 24 pieces

12 slices day-old white bread
10 anchovy **fillets**, **finely chopped**, or 1 tube anchovy paste
4 tablespoons butter or margarine, at room temperature
2 tablespoons prepared mustard
4 hard-cooked eggs, peeled and **coarsely chopped**
¼ cup fresh dill or fresh parsley, finely chopped
2 tablespoons vegetable oil
2 tablespoons butter or margarine

Equipment: Work surface, **serrated knife**, food processor, rubber spatula, small mixing bowl, plastic food wrap, paper towels, baking sheet, large skillet, metal spatula, serving platter

1. Stack bread slices on work surface and using serrated knife, trim off crusts.

2. Put anchovies, butter or margarine, mustard, coarsely chopped hard-cooked eggs, and dill or parsley in food processor. Process until smooth, about 1 minute. Transfer to small mixing bowl.

Note: While processing, turn machine off once or twice and scrape down sides of container with rubber spatula.

3. Thickly spread egg mixture onto 6 slices of bread. Top each slice with a remaining slice of bread and lightly press them together. If not using right away, wrap each sandwich in plastic wrap and refrigerate up to 3 days or freeze up to 2 weeks. Defrost frozen sandwiches before frying.

4. Prepare to fry: Place several layers of paper towels on baking sheet. Heat oil and melt 2 tablespoons butter or margarine in large skillet over medium heat. Add the sandwiches, 1 or 2 at a time. Fry each sandwich for 2 to 3 minutes on each side, until golden brown and crisp. Drain on paper towels. Cut each diagonally, from corner to corner, into 4 triangular pieces.

To serve, stack the finger sandwiches on a serving platter and place on the buffet table.

Another popular Swedish appetizer or side dish is *lökdolmar.* This dish can be prepared a day or two in advance, covered, refrigerated, and baked on the day of the dinner.

LÖKDOLMAR

STUFFED ONIONS

Yield: serves 6 to 8

4 yellow onions, (about 4 to 5 ounces each)
salt and pepper to taste
1 pound **finely ground** lean beef
½ cup fresh white bread, finely crumbled
4 tablespoons heavy cream, more if needed
1 egg
3 tablespoons dried **bread crumbs**
¼ cup melted butter or margarine
white sauce (recipe follows), for serving

Equipment: Large saucepan, slotted spoon, baking sheet, medium mixing bowl, small mixing bowl, mixing spoon, work surface, paring knife, buttered 10- or 12-inch baking pan, aluminum foil, oven mitts, small serving bowl

1. Fill large saucepan with 12 cups water and add 1 teaspoon salt. Bring to boil over high heat. Put whole onions, with skin on, into boiling water. Bring water back to boil. Reduce heat to **simmer** and cook for 40 minutes. Remove onions with slotted spoon and place on baking sheet to cool for at least 2 hours. Discard water.

2. Prepare stuffing: Put meat into medium mixing bowl. In small mixing bowl, combine crumbled fresh white bread and cream. Stir until cream is soaked up into the bread, adding a little more cream if bread seems dry. Add egg and salt and pepper to taste to meat mixture. Using your hands or mixing spoon, mix meat mixture until it holds together, about 2 minutes.

3. Take apart the onions: Place an onion on the work surface. Using a paring knife, cut off about ½ inch from each end of onion. Make a lengthwise slit, from top to root end, and cut just to the **core**. Peel off and discard the skin. Put your finger in the vertical slit and carefully separate the layers by peeling them off, one at a time. Each layer curls up as it is peeled off. You should have about 4 to 6 usable layers from each onion. The center core of the onions is not used in this recipe. Discard it or refrigerate for another use.

Preheat oven to 375° F.

4. Assemble: Uncurl 1 onion layer and place a heaping tablespoon of stuffing in the center and roll it up again. (When rolled up, it looks like a little football.) Place it, seam side down, in well buttered 10- or 12-inch baking pan. Continue to fill the remaining onion layers and place them seam side down, side-by-side in the baking pan. Sprinkle with bread crumbs and **drizzle** with melted butter. Cover with foil.

5. Bake in oven for 20 minutes. Remove from oven and remove foil. Return to oven, uncovered, to finish baking until golden, 10 to 12 minutes more.

To serve, transfer to serving dish and either cover with white sauce *or put the sauce in a small serving bowl.* Lökdolmar *can be an appetizer or a side dish with* dyresteg *(recipe page 236).*

White Sauce

Yield: about 1½ cups

2 tablespoons unsalted butter
2 tablespoons all-purpose flour
1 cup heavy cream
salt and white pepper to taste

Equipment: Small **heavy-based** saucepan, **whisk**

Melt butter over medium-low heat in small heavy-based saucepan. Remove from heat and whisk in flour. Return to heat and continue whisking until mixture is smooth. Whisk in heavy cream and increase heat to medium. Whisk until mixture thickens, 3 to 5 minutes. Add salt and white pepper to taste. Remove from heat.

Continue with lökdolmar *(recipe precedes). This is a multipurpose sauce and it can be used in many other recipes.*

Herring is the favorite fish in the Scandinavian countries, and the buffet table often has several different herring dishes. This dish is made up of bits of food always available in most Swedish kitchens. The name "save the family" refers to the vital role herring has played in the Scandinavian diet. When times were hard, a family could always beg, borrow, or fish for a little herring. It was tasty, nourishing, and plentiful and saved many families from starvation.

Familjens Räddning

"Save the Family" Herring Platter

Yield: serves 2

2 to 4 lettuce leaves, washed and patted dry
4 to 6 pieces pickled herring, drained (available at all supermarkets)
1 small cucumber, peeled and finely sliced
½ cup pickled beets, homemade (recipe page 234), or canned
2 hard-cooked eggs, each cut into 4 or 6 wedges
½ cup sour cream
2 tablespoons parsley, **finely chopped** for **garnish**

Equipment: Large round dinner plate, mixing spoon

Cover the large dinner plate decoratively with 2 to 4 lettuce leaves. Mound the herring in the center and surround with a ring of cucumber slices. Next make a ring of pickled beets. Border the plate with a sunburst of egg wedges. **Drizzle** with sour cream and sprinkle with parsley flakes, for garnish.

To serve, place the herring plate on the buffet table. This is wonderful nibbling food to leisurely enjoy with rye or pumpernickel bread and butter.

FINLAND

Situated in the northeastern tip of Europe, Finland is a land of pristine lakes (over 60,000) and thick forests of dark pine and silver birch. It is bordered by Sweden on the west, Norway on the north, Russia on the east, and the Gulf of Finland and the Baltic Sea on the south.

Much like the other Scandinavians, the majority of Finns belong to the Lutheran Church and follow the life-cycle traditions of the Church. (See Protestant and Catholic Life-Cycle Rituals, page xlvi.) Although these events are similar to those celebrated in other Christian countries, the Finns add their own distinctive touches.

One of those touches involves weddings and the summer solstice, the longest day of year, on June 21. In Finland, the summer solstice is called Midsummer Day. Celebrations begin on Midsummer Eve and end on the eve of the Feast of St. John the Baptist, June 23. The customs and rituals attached to the three-day festival, especially when it comes to marriage, blend Christian symbolism with ancient pagan beliefs.

In Finland, more couples marry during the Midsummer celebration than any other time of the year. On the morning of the wedding, it is the tradition for the bride and her girlfriends to congregate in the sauna. (Most Finnish homes have saunas, a steam or dry heat bath, usually in a room or cabinet.) The most painful part of the sauna ritual comes when the bride's hair is cut very short in front of her friends. Everyone present sobs crocodile tears to show their sorrow; this haircut represents her loss as a single woman. After the haircut, the bride puts on the *tzepy,* the traditional headdress worn by married women. The *tzepy* is a close fitting cap, with either a hard or soft crown, and it is trimmed with lace and embroidery.

In Helsinki, thousands of people gather to watch a solemn ceremony in which a newly married couple, chosen to represent all the men and women married that day in Finland, is rowed across the water to a small island. On the island, a huge tower has been built of fir trees and the hulls of old boats, and together the bride and groom set it ablaze. The tradition symbolizes hope for a bright future for all of the newlyweds and a request for eternal light and warmth from the sun.

During the Midsummer celebrations, eating, music, singing, dancing, swimming, and sitting in the sauna are all important elements of the festivities. Traditionally, Finns participate in a Midsummer sauna and then enjoy a lavish feast. The table is usually decorated with birch branches and flower garlands. The menu includes assorted herring and other fish dishes, cheeses, both smoked and fresh fish, shellfish and meats, wild mushrooms, assorted berries, and melon dishes. No Midsummer meal is complete unless there are assorted cakes such as *kermakakku* (recipe page 246), and breads, among them, *pulla* (recipe follows).

In addition to weddings and the Midsummer Day events, the birth of a child is an exciting event for Finns. When the mother and baby return home, friends and relatives come to visit, and they bring gifts for the infant and a covered dish or baked goods for the family.

One to three months after the baby's birth, a christening ceremony is held in the church, followed by a family celebration at home or in a restaurant. According to tradition, the infant will wear the christening dress that has been worn by other family members. This may include the baby's mother or father and siblings whose names are embroidered on the garment.

Another unique tradition the Finnish people have developed is a distinctive style of hospitality known as coffee-table entertaining. For an occasion, such as a birthday, name day, anniversary, wedding, christening, and funeral, it is an old custom to serve guests seven items from the coffee table. The assortment always includes a bread, such as *pulla* (recipe follows), or, if it's a name day party, it would be *hieno nimipäivärinkilä* (recipe page 244). Usually two cakes and four kinds of cookies round out the seven items. The Finnish people are great coffee drinkers, and with each piece of pastry, they have another cup of coffee.

Precise rules govern coffee table etiquette regarding what is eaten and in what order. A bread is eaten with the first cup of coffee. The second cup of coffee is sipped along with *kermakakku* (recipe page 246) and cookies, including *ruiskakut* (recipe page 244). A rich and gooey cake is always eaten last along with the third cup of coffee. A favorite is *mansikkakakku* (see recipe page 245).

PULLA

CARDAMOM BREAD

Yield: 2 loaves

1 package active dry **yeast**
1/4 cup **lukewarm** water
1 cup canned evaporated milk
1/2 cup sugar, more as needed
1/2 teaspoon salt
1/2 teaspoon **ground** cardamom
2 eggs, slightly beaten
4 to 4 1/2 cups all-purpose flour
1/4 cup melted butter or margarine
egg wash (made with milk), for **garnish**
1/4 cup sliced almonds, for garnish
sugar, as needed, for garnish

Equipment: Large mixing bowl, mixing spoon, kitchen towel, lightly floured work surface, greased baking sheet, **pastry brush**, oven mitts, wire cake rack, bread knife, serving platter or bread basket

1. Dissolve yeast in lukewarm water in large mixing bowl. Stir in evaporated milk, 1/2 cup sugar, salt, cardamom, 2 eggs, and 2 cups flour. Beat in melted butter until mixture is smooth and glossy. Stir in enough of the remaining, 2 to 2 1/2 cups flour, 1/2 cup at a time, to make dough easy to handle. Cover with towel and let rest for 15 minutes.

2. Turn dough out onto lightly floured work surface. **Knead** until smooth and **elastic**, 8 to 10 minutes. Wash, dry, and grease large mixing bowl. Place dough in bowl and turn to grease all sides. Cover with kitchen towel and let rise in warm place to double in bulk, about 1 hour. **Punch down** dough. Cover and let rise for the second time until double in bulk, about 1 hour. Dough is ready if impression remains when poked with your finger.

3. Divide dough in half. Divide each half into 3 parts. On lightly floured work surface, roll each part into a rope, 1 inch thick. Braid 3 ropes together to make straight loaf. Pinch ends of

braided dough together and fold the pinched ends under the braid. Repeat braiding with remaining three ropes. Place each braided loaf on lightly greased baking sheet. Cover with towel and let rise to double in bulk, 30 to 45 minutes.

Preheat oven to 375° F.

4. Brush loaves with egg wash and sprinkle with almonds and sugar to taste. Put breads in oven and bake until lightly browned, 20 to 25 minutes. Test **bread doneness**. When done, cool on wire cake rack.

To serve, slice and place on platter or in bread basket. Set on the coffee table. Munch on a slice of pulla *while sipping on the first robust cup of brew.*

Hieno nimipäivärinkilä is made with *pulla* dough (recipe precedes) and shaped into a ring instead of a braid. Cookies are usually stacked in the center of the ring and birthday candles are poked around the top.

Hieno Nimipäivärinkilä

Fancy Name Day Sweet Bread

Yield: 1 large loaf

pulla dough, (recipe precedes)
egg wash, for **garnish**
½ cup chopped or sliced almonds, for garnish
12 sugar cubes, for garnish

Equipment: lightly greased large cookie sheet or lightly greased 12- to 16-inch pizza pan, **pastry brush**, small plastic resealable bag, hammer, oven mitts, wire cake rack, large serving tray, bread knife

1. Prepare *pulla* dough: Follow steps 1 to 3 of preceding recipe.

2. After *Pulla* dough has risen the second time and an impression remains when poked with your finger, turn dough out onto lightly floured work surface. Form into a rope 24 to 27 inches long and pinch the ends together to form into an oval or circular ring. Place on lightly greased cookie sheet or lightly greased 12- to 16-inch pizza pan. Let rise to double in bulk, for 30 to 45 minutes.

Preheat oven to 400° F.

3. Using pastry brush, brush dough with egg wash and sprinkle with sliced almonds. Put sugar cubes in small plastic bag. Coarsely crush the cubes by gently tapping the bag with a hammer. Sprinkle the crushed sugar over the bread.

4. Bake in oven for 20 to 25 minutes, or until lightly browned and sounds hollow when tapped on the bottom. Cool on wire cake rack before serving.

To serve, place the uncut bread ring on a large serving tray and place on the coffee table. Provide a bread knife for slicing.

Ruiskakut are almost always included in the cookie selection on the coffee table. These cookies, made with rye flour, are very popular in Finland and are great for dunking.

Ruiskakut

Rye Cookies

Yield: about 3 dozen

½ cup butter or margarine, at room temperature
¾ cup sugar
1 to 1½ cups rye **flour**
½ cup all-purpose flour
1 egg, slightly beaten

Equipment: Food processor, rubber spatula, lightly floured work surface, lightly floured rolling pin, 2-inch circular cookie cutter, wash and dry small bottle cap (such as from water or soft drink), greased cookie sheet, fork, oven mitts, wire cake rack, serving tray

Preheat oven to 400° F.

1. In food processor, process butter or margarine with sugar until light and fluffy. Processing constantly, add rye and all-purpose flour through the feed tube. Add egg through feed tube. Pulse off and on until well mixed. Transfer to lightly floured work surface.

Note: While processing, turn machine off once or twice and scrape down sides of container with rubber spatula.

2. Using a lightly floured rolling pin, roll to about 1/8 inch thick. Using 2-inch cookie cutter, cut into circles. Place 1 inch apart on greased cookie sheet. Using clean bottle cap as small cookie cutter, cut a hole, slightly off center, in each cookie. Add the cutout centers to the dough to make more cookies. Pierce each cookie 4 or 6 times with fork.

3. Bake in oven until lightly brown, 5 to 7 minutes. Remove from oven and cool on wire cake rack.

To serve, place on serving tray or arrange in the center of the hieno nimipäivärinkilä.

The showpiece of the coffee table is always a deliciously gooey cream cake, such as *mansikkakakku*. It is eaten last with the third cup of coffee.

Mansikkakakku

Strawberry Cream Cake

Yield: serves 12

1 cup all-purpose flour
1 teaspoon baking powder
2 teaspoons cornstarch
¼ teaspoon salt
4 eggs
1 cup sugar, more as needed
2 tablespoons water
1 teaspoon vanilla extract
2 cups heavy cream
¾ cup raspberry jam, seedless or strained to remove seeds
2 cups strawberries, halved, fresh or frozen (thawed)

Equipment: Flour **sifter**, large mixing bowl, medium mixing bowl, whisk, electric mixer, rubber spatula, 3 greased and floured 8-inch round cake pans, oven mitts, toothpick, wire cake rack, medium metal mixing bowl, serving platter, small saucepan, spoon, metal spatula or dinner knife

Preheat oven to 375° F.

1. **Sift** flour, baking powder, cornstarch, and salt into large mixing bowl.

2. Put eggs in medium mixing bowl and using electric mixer or whisk, beat until foamy, about 2 minutes. Add 1 cup sugar and beat until thick and bright yellow, 2 to 3 minutes. Beat in 2 tablespoons water and vanilla extract. Using rubber spatula, fold flour mixture into egg mixture, and **blend** well. Divide batter equally between 3 greased and floured 8-inch round cake pans.

3. Bake in oven for 10 to 15 minutes, or until toothpick inserted into center comes out clean. Cool in pans for 10 minutes. Remove from pans and cool completely on wire cake rack.

4. Assemble cake: Put medium metal mixing bowl and clean, *dry* beaters in freezer to chill about 10 minutes before whipping the cream. Pour heavy cream into chilled bowl and using chilled electric beaters, beat cream until soft peaks form. Beating constantly, sprinkle in 2 tablespoons sugar, and continue beating until stiff peaks form again. Place one cake layer on serving platter and using the spatula, spread 2 tablespoons raspberry jam over the top. Spread whipped cream about ¼ inch thick over jam. Place second cake layer on top, repeat spreading with same amount of jam and cream on top. Top with third cake layer. Cover and refrigerate remaining whipped cream to keep chilled until needed.

5. Arrange strawberries over top of cake, cut-side down, leaving about 1-inch border around the edge. Put remaining 8 tablespoons raspberry jam in small saucepan and stir. Cook over medium heat until dissolved, 3 to 4 minutes. Spoon jam over strawberries to **glaze** (coat) them.

6. Spoon dollops of whipped cream around the top edge of cake. Using a metal spatula or dinner knife, spread remaining whipped cream around the side. Cover and refrigerate until ready to serve.

To serve, remove the cake from the refrigerator, just before serving. Place on the coffee table with a cake spatula or dinner knife for serving.

A Midsummer tradition, baking a "silent cake," is supposed to foretell the future. According to custom, several unmarried women get together to bake a cake without talking. They each take a small piece of the baked cake and sleep with it under their pillow to dream of the man in their future. The *kermakakku*, a popular name day and birthday cake, can easily be baked without speaking.

Kermakakku

Cream Pound Cake

Yield: serves 12

1 cup heavy cream
2 eggs
1 teaspoon vanilla
1 ½ cups all-purpose flour
1 cup granulated sugar
2 teaspoons baking powder
½ teaspoon salt
confectioners' sugar, for **garnish**

Equipment: Large mixing bowl, electric mixer, rubber spatula, small bowl, **sifter**, medium mixing bowl, greased 9-cup **bundt pan**, oven mitts, serving platter, cake knife

Chill large mixing bowl in freezer at least 1 hour.

Preheat oven to 350° F.

1. Pour heavy cream into chilled large mixing bowl and using electric mixer, beat until stiff peaks form, 3 to 5 minutes.

2. In small bowl, beat eggs and vanilla until light and fluffy. Using the rubber spatula, **fold in** egg mixture with whipped cream.

3. **Sift** flour, granulated sugar, and baking powder into medium mixing bowl. Using rubber spatula, fold in flour mixture with whipped cream mixture. Pour batter into greased bundt pan.

4. Bake in oven until cake pulls away from sides of pan, 50 to 60 minutes. Cool in pan 10 minutes. Flip onto wire cake rack and cool completely.

To serve, set upright on serving platter and sprinkle with confectioners' sugar. Cut into wedges at serving time.

ICELAND

Iceland is often considered one of the Scandinavian countries even though it is an island in the North Atlantic sitting some 600 miles to the west of Europe. Iceland is known as the land of "fire and ice." The fire refers to the numerous volcanoes that cover vast areas with molten lava and the thousands of geysers erupting steaming water; at the other extreme of the landscape are ice fields and glaciers. The steaming hot water spewing out of geysers is harnessed and piped into homes in Reykjavik, Iceland's capital city. Greenhouses heated by the *hver* (hot springs) are able to grow bananas, oranges, and pineapples.

The first settlers arriving about A.D. 900 were Norwegian Vikings, exiled from their mother country. They were seafaring people, and today their descendants have the most modern fleet of fishing boats and fish processing plants in the world.

Most Icelanders belong to the Evangelical Lutheran Church, the state religion, and celebrate life-cycle events according to their religion. (See Protestant and Catholic Life-Cycle Rituals, page xlvi.)

Newborns are baptized at around 6 months of age, and a family dinner follows. Many babies are born out of wedlock since numerous couples do not marry until they can afford their own apartment or home. They often live together, and perhaps have a child or two, before marrying. When the couple does decide to marry, the children walk down the aisle with them and take part in the ceremony. Weddings follow Western traditions, a white wedding dress with veil for the bride, business suit for the groom; the ceremony is usually in church. The wedding cake could be *kransekake* (recipe page 230) or the English fruit cake (recipe page 202) or the basic white cake with white icing.

Funerals are similar to those in the United States, and the body is buried or cremated. After the burial, a meal is served for mourners, usually a *smørrebrød* table at the family home. Food is prepared and covered dishes are brought in by neighbors and friends. While others go to the funeral, the neighbors and friends stay to help set up the feast. Pots of coffee and alcoholic beverages are made ready for the bereaved family and hungry mourners on their return.

The main course of a celebration feast is usually lamb or pork or both and a variety of fish dishes. Because of Iceland's seafaring tradition, fish is a mainstay of Icelandic cooking and is processed and cooked every way imaginable. At a celebration feast a great variety of fish dishes are served. *Fiskbudingur* might be one of the selections.

Fiskbudingur

Fish Soufflé

Yield: serves 6 to 8

10 tablespoons butter or margarine, divided
8 tablespoons dry **bread crumbs**, divided
1 pound skinless fish **fillets** (such as cod or haddock)
water, as needed
½ cup all-purpose flour, **sifted**
1 cup milk
salt and white pepper to taste
6 **eggs, separated**

Equipment: 1½- to 2-quart ovenproof casserole or soufflé dish, 2 medium saucepans, fork, colander, small bowl, whisk, large mixing bowl, rubber spatula, medium mixing bowl, electric mixer (optional), oven mitts, serving spoon

Prepare ovenproof casserole or soufflé dish: Coat bottom and sides with 2 tablespoons butter or margarine and sprinkle 3 to 4 tablespoons bread crumbs over bottom and sides to cover well. Shake out excess.

Preheat oven to 375° F.

1. Put fish in medium saucepan and cover with water. Bring to boil over high heat. Reduce heat to **simmer** and cook for 5 to 7 minutes, until fish flakes easily when poked with fork. Place colander in sink and drain fish. Cool enough to handle, break fish into bite-size pieces, and put in small bowl.

2. Melt remaining 8 tablespoons butter or margarine in second medium saucepan over medium heat. Remove from heat and whisk in flour until smooth. Return to medium heat. Whisking constantly, slowly add milk, and **blend** well. Cook, whisking constantly until very thick, 5 to 7 minutes. Add salt and white pepper to

taste. Transfer milk mixture to large mixing bowl and set aside to cool to warm.

3. Using whisk, beat egg yolks together. Add beaten yolks to milk mixture and mix well. Using rubber spatula, **fold in** fish pieces.

4. Put egg whites in medium mixing bowl. Using electric mixer, beat egg whites until stiff, 2 to 3 minutes. Using rubber spatula, fold egg whites into milk mixture. Transfer to prepared casserole or soufflé dish and sprinkle remaining 4 to 5 tablespoons bread crumbs over top.

5. Bake in oven for 20 to 25 minutes, until golden brown and set.

To serve, set baking container on the table with serving spoon. Fiskbudingur *can be eaten either warm or cold. Serve with boiled potatoes and* agurkesalat *(recipe page 249).*

Cold left-over soufflé can be cut into 1-inch thick slices, sautéed in butter, and served for breakfast.

Sheep are an important part of Icelandic farming, and every part of the animal is eaten at celebrations. Lamb spareribs are very popular and often eaten at weddings and other life-cycle celebrations. They are every bit as delicious as those from the pig; this recipe can be made with either.

Golden Glazed Lamb Spareribs

Yield: serves 4

3 pounds lean lamb spareribs (breast of lamb)
1 cup peach preserves
½ cup pineapple juice
½ teaspoon **ground coriander**
½ teaspoon ground cinnamon
½ teaspoon ground **allspice**
1 teaspoon salt
1 orange, peeled and sliced

Equipment: Large shallow roasting pan with rack, small bowl, mixing spoon, oven mitts, heatproof surface, **pastry brush**, large knife

Preheat oven to 325° F.

1. Place slabs of ribs on rack in large shallow roasting pan. Bake in oven for 1 to 1½ hours.

2. In small bowl, stir together peach preserves, pineapple juice, coriander, cinnamon, allspice, and salt. Using oven mitts, remove lamb from oven and place on heatproof surface. Using pastry brush, brush ribs generously with peach mixture to **glaze** meat. Arrange orange slices on the ribs. Return to oven and bake 35 to 45 minutes longer, or until tender. Let meat rest at least 10 minutes before cutting ribs apart.

Serve as one of the many dishes on the buffet table. Ribs are best eaten with the fingers, so provide plenty of napkins.

Iceland was under Danish rule until fairly recently (1944), and so it is only natural the cooking in Iceland is basically Danish. The Danish *smørrebrød* (literally, "bread and butter") table is the preferred way to entertain at home for birthday, anniversary, or baptism celebrations or to feed mourners after a funeral. Open-faced sandwiches are made from hundreds of local delicacies. The open face sandwiches can be any size and made of just about anything. In Danish the fixings are called *paalaeg,* literally "something laid on" the bread.

The bread for open face sandwiches is rye or pumpernickel, and it is heavily spread with butter before adding the *paalaeg.* The sandwiches should be decoratively arranged so they are inviting to eat. Cold cuts and sausages, cheeses, all sorts of herring and smoked fish, eel, shrimp and vegetables, hard-cooked eggs, and pickles are used for making *paalaeg.* Other standard items on the *smørrebrød* table are *syltede rødbeder* (recipe page 234) and *agurkesalat.*

AGURKESALAT

PICKLED CUCUMBER SALAD

Yield: serves 4

2 or 3 cucumbers (6 to 8 inches long), washed and patted dry
1 cup white vinegar
1 tablespoon sugar
2 tablespoons chopped fresh dill or 1 teaspoon dried dill
salt and white pepper to taste

Equipment: Fork, paring knife, small bowl with cover, small saucepan, mixing spoon

1. Score cucumber skins lengthwise with fork . With paring knife, cut cucumbers crosswise in thin slices, and put into small bowl.

2. Pour vinegar into small saucepan and add sugar. Bring to boil over high heat, stir to dissolve sugar, and remove from heat. Cool to room temperature. Pour vinegar mixture over cucumber slices. Sprinkle with dill and salt and white pepper to taste. Toss to mix, cover, and refrigerate for 2 to 3 hours for flavor to develop.

Serve in a small bowl as a salad or use as garnish on open-faced sandwiches.

For weddings, a platter of heart-shaped *sykur kaka* are often set out for guests to munch on while eating *skyr*, a popular yogurt-like sauce, similar to *rømmegrøt* (recipe page 236), which they sprinkle with **cinnamon sugar**. Cookie cutters of different sizes and shapes are available at kitchenware stores and many supermarkets.

SYKUR KAKA

LITTLE SUGAR CAKES

Yield: about 40 pieces

2½ cups all-purpose flour
½ teaspoon baking powder
¼ teaspoon baking soda
¾ cup unsalted butter
¾ cup granulated sugar
1 egg
1¼ teaspoons almond extract
food coloring, for **garnish**

Equipment: Flour **sifter**, medium bowl, large mixing bowl, electric mixer, rubber spatula, mixing spoon, plastic food wrap, work surface, wax paper, rolling pin, 2- to 3-inch cookie cutters (any shape), wide metal spatula, 2 greased or nonstick cookie sheets, oven mitts, wire cake rack, serving tray

1. **Sift** flour, baking powder, and baking soda in medium bowl.

2. In large mixing bowl, using electric mixer, beat butter until creamy, about 1 minute. Beat in sugar, a little at a time, until fluffy. Beat in egg and almond extract and continue beating to mix well, 1 to 2 minutes. Using rubber spatula, scrape down sides of bowl. Beating constantly, add flour mixture, ½ cup at a time, beating well after each addition. Beat in 2 or 3 drops of desired food coloring. Cover with plastic wrap and refrigerate to firm, about 30 minutes.

Preheat oven to 350° F.

3. Cover work surface with 16- or 18-inch length of wax paper and lightly sprinkle with flour. Using your hands, spread half the dough as flat as you can on wax paper, staying well within the edges. Lightly sprinkle flour over dough and place a second piece of wax paper on top. Using a rolling pin, roll dough between sheets of wax paper to ¼ inch thick. Peel off and discard top sheet of wax paper. Lightly sprinkle rolled-out dough with flour. Using a cookie cutter dipped in flour, cut out desired shapes. Using wide metal spatula, transfer cookies to cookie sheet, set about 1 inch apart. Repeat making cookies with remaining dough.

4. Bake in oven for 8 to 12 minutes, or until golden brown at the edges. Remove from oven

and allow to firm for at least 8 minutes before using metal spatula to transfer to wire cake rack to cool completely. Bake in batches.

To serve, arrange cookies, slightly overlapping on serving tray. Store cookies in airtight container for up to one week or freeze up to one month.

BALTIC NATIONS

The three Baltic nations—Lithuania, Latvia, and Estonia—are all bordered by Russia and Belarus on the east and the Baltic Sea on the west. After years of being under the control of the Soviet Union, the three Baltic countries became independent in 1991, several months before the Soviet empire formally dissolved. Today all three nations are working toward establishing economic, political, and cultural stability. ۞ ۞ ۞

LITHUANIA

Lithuania, the most westerly Baltic republic, is also the largest in area and population. Most Lithuanians live in urban areas, and the majority belong to the Roman Catholic Church. All life-cycle celebrations center around the Church. (See Protestant and Catholic Life-Cycle Rituals, page xlvi.)

Most Lithuanian children are baptized and then they have their first communion according to Church doctrine. Currently many of the old wedding traditions are being revived, although somewhat modified or simplified.

Years ago, every wedding began with a matchmaker responsible for getting the families together. After the match was set, the families would meet to discuss the dowry. For the dowry, parents provided daughters with one or more chests made of wood from trees inhabited by storks in the belief they would bring good luck and lots of babies. The chests became known as "hope chests"; girls kept jewelry, letters, money, clothing for their future first-born, candles, medicinal herbs and linens, blankets, and personal clothing they made for married life. The number, size, and beauty of the dowry chests was the indication of the bride's wealth, taste, and qualities as a future wife and mother.

When dowry carriers came to take the chests away to the groom's home, relatives of the bride sat on them and pretended they were unwilling to give them away. To make it look like the bride had more possessions, stones were sometimes put inside the chests to make them heavier.

Today, weddings are simpler, but many of the traditions have survived in modified form. Dowries are mostly symbolic and the ritual of sending dowry carriers adds to the merriment of the wedding celebration. Weddings used to be four days long, but now two days is the customary length.

On the morning of the wedding day, the bride says good-bye to her parents and siblings. After the ceremony in the church or Registrar's office (for non-Catholics), it is customary for the matchmaker, if one was used, and bridegroom's friends to drive in the wedding car. From the back seat, the newlyweds throw candy to children along the way. Somewhere on the car route, friends and relatives of the bride often block the road with a rope of flowers. Those in the car have to buy their passage with candy and bottles of brandy or wine.

When the wedding party arrives at the home of the bride's parents, the newlyweds are greeted at the threshold with a loaf of bread sprinkled with salt and wine glasses of pure water, symbols for a rich full life and good fortune.

Roast whole suckling pig (recipe page 162) is the preferred meat for a Lithuanian wedding celebration. If it's more than the family can afford, stuffed cabbage (recipe page 165), assorted soups and stews, and vegetable dishes, such as this well-loved *kugelis*, are served for all celebration meals.

Kugelis

Potato Pudding

Yield: serves 8 to 10

8 slices bacon, **finely chopped**
8 potatoes for grating
1 onion, peeled
5 ounces canned evaporated milk
6 eggs, beaten
salt and pepper to taste

Equipment: Medium skillet, mixing spoon, food processor fitted with **grater** attachment or hand grater, rubber spatula, large mixing bowl, well buttered 9- x 13- x 2-inch baking pan, oven mitts, knife

Preheat oven to 425° F.

1. Fry chopped bacon in medium skillet over medium-high heat. Stir and fry until crisp, 3 to 5 minutes. Remove from heat.

2. Using food processor with grater attachment or hand grater, grate potatoes and onion. Drain off and discard excess liquid from potato mixture and transfer to large mixing bowl. Add fried bacon with pan drippings, milk, eggs, and salt and pepper to taste. Beat to mix well. Transfer to well buttered baking pan and spread smooth.

Note: While processing, turn machine off once or twice and scrape down sides of container with rubber spatula.

3. Bake in oven 30 minutes. Reduce heat to 375° F and cook for 30 to 40 minutes more, or until pudding is set and top is golden brown

Cut into serving-size pieces and serve from baking pan while still warm.

A favorite dish of Lithuanians is jellied pork, which they call *koseliena saltiena.* It is served at almost all celebration feasts. *Koseliena saltiena* is not much different from the Caribbean jellied pork (*pudding and souse*) (recipe page 362), which can be used as a substitute.

Bread is an indispensable part of every meal, and Lithuanians have hundreds of bread recipes. *Bulvinis ragaisis* is a favorite that is taken to the church to be blessed by the priest on many life-cycle occasions.

Bulvinis Ragaisis

Potato Bread

Yield: 1 loaf

1/4 cup **lukewarm** water
1 package active dry **yeast**
1/2 teaspoon sugar
3/4 cup **lukewarm** milk
1 medium baking potato, peeled and grated
3 to 3 1/2 cups all-purpose flour
2 teaspoons salt
1 egg, beaten
2 tablespoons sour cream
egg wash, for **garnish**

Equipment: 2 small bowls, wooden mixing spoon, large mixing bowl, kitchen towel, lightly floured work surface, buttered 9- x 5- x 3-inch loaf pan, **pastry brush**, oven mitts, wire cake rack, napkin-lined bread basket

1. In first small bowl, sprinkle lukewarm water with yeast and sugar. Stir, let stand 5 to 10 minutes, until bubbly and doubled in volume. Pour milk into second small bowl and stir in grated potato.

2. In large mixing bowl, stir to combine 3 cups flour and salt. Make a well in the center and pour

in yeast mixture and potato mixture. Stir to mix well. Stir in egg and sour cream until well mixed. Using mixing spoon, beat flour with liquid until dough forms into a ball, 3 to 5 minutes. Transfer to lightly floured work surface and **knead**, adding up to ½ cup more flour if necessary to make a smooth, non-sticky dough. Clean and grease large mixing bowl or use a new large mixing bowl. Place dough in lightly greased large mixing bowl and turn to coat all sides. Cover with towel and let rise in warm place until double in bulk, 1 to 1 ½ hours.

3. Gently **punch down** dough to release air, and put in buttered loaf pan. Cover with towel and set in warm place to rise to double in bulk again, about 1 hour.

Preheat oven to 375° F.

4. Using pastry brush, brush loaf with egg wash and bake in oven for 35 to 40 minutes, or until loaf has a hollow sound when tapped on the bottom. Test bread for **doneness**. Flip loaf onto wire cake rack to cool.

Serve in napkin-lined bread basket with other breads and rolls.

LATVIA

Latvia, traditionally known as the "workshop of the Baltic," is the middle country of the Baltics. The majority of Latvians belong to the Lutheran Church, although a large Roman Catholic population resides in the country. People of both religions follow the life-cycle traditions of their respective churches. (See Protestant and Catholic Life-Cycle Rituals, page xlvi.) Latvians, or Letts as they are called, represent only about half of the population; Russians, Belarusians, Ukrainians, and Poles make up the rest.

In Latvia, most people set the food out and let people help themselves buffet-style for weddings, baptisms, name day celebrations, or funeral meals. In Eastern Europe, people in neighboring countries share many of the same recipes, each adding their own special touch or ingredients. For example, a dish may be called Russian-style, Minsk-style, or Romanian-style. Such dishes as Belarus-style *kolbasa z kapustov* (recipe page 263) and Ukraine-style *zulynez gribnoy* (recipe page 269) have crossed borders. To complete the bountiful buffet, plenty of bread is prepared; *undens klinger* and *saldskabmaize* (recipe page 253) are among the assortment. ۞ ۞ ۞

Undens Klinger

Pretzel Rolls

Yield: 10 or 12 pieces

- 1½ cups **lukewarm** water
- 3 teaspoons dark brown sugar, divided
- 1 package active dry **yeast**
- 3 tablespoons salt, divided
- 4 cups all-purpose flour
- ½ cup **cornmeal**, for baking

Equipment: Large mixing bowl, mixing spoon, kitchen towel, lightly floured work surface, knife, wax paper, greased baking sheet, metal spatula, large saucepan, slotted spoon, wire cake rack, oven mitts

1. Pour lukewarm water into large mixing bowl. Stir in 1½ teaspoons dark brown sugar and sprinkle with yeast. Let set until bubbly, 5 to 10 minutes. Stir in remaining 1½ teaspoons sugar and 1 tablespoon salt. Gradually add flour, 1 cup at a time, and use your hands to mix dough until flour is well incorporated.

2. **Knead** the dough in the bowl until smooth, about 5 to 7 minutes. The dough should be shiny. Cover with towel and set in warm place to rise to double in bulk, about 1 hour.

3. Transfer dough to lightly floured work surface and divide into 10 or 12 equal pieces.

4. Form into pretzel-shaped rolls: Place piece of wax paper on work surface. Roll a piece of dough between the palms of your hands, into a thin rope about 8 inches long. Loop ends over each other to make into a pretzel-shape. To keep pretzel from coming apart, dampen ends with water and pinch them in place. Place on wax paper and repeat making pretzel-shaped rolls. Leave them set until they begin to rise, about 10 minutes.

Preheat oven to 425° F.

Lightly sprinkle cornmeal on greased baking sheet.

5. Fill large saucepan two-thirds full with water. Add remaining 2 teaspoons salt and bring to boil over high heat. Carefully add rolls, a few at a time, and boil on one side for 2 minutes. Turn over and boil on second side for 1½ minutes. They should become firm and puff up. Carefully remove with slotted spoon and drain on wire cake rack for 1 minute. Place on prepared baking sheet.

6. Bake in oven for 12 minutes. Using oven mitts, remove pan from oven. Using metal spatula, turn rolls over, return to oven, and bake 7 to 10 minutes more, until golden brown. Transfer to wire cake rack to cool.

Serve with soup or appetizers at the life-cycle celebration. Mothers often hang a undens kinger *on a string and use it for their baby's teething ring.*

Breads prepared for Catholic life-cycle celebrations are always blessed by the priest. Baking breads and cakes is an important part of wedding preparation rituals in all Eastern European countries.

Saldskabmaize

Sweet-Sour Bread

Note: This recipe takes 10 to 12 hours.

Yield: 1 loaf

- 4 cups **sift**ed all-purpose **flour**, divided
- 1¼ cups warm water (about 200° F)
- 1 package active dry **yeast**
- 1 teaspoon sugar
- 3 tablespoons **lukewarm** milk
- 1 teaspoon salt
- 2 to 3 teaspoons caraway seeds

Equipment: Large metal mixing bowl, kitchen towel, wooden mixing spoon, electric mixer (optional), cup, small spoon, floured work surface, plastic food wrap, greased baking sheet, small spray bottle, oven mitts

1. Rinse large metal mixing bowl under hot water to warm and wipe dry with towel. Put 2 cups flour into warm bowl and gradually stir in the warm water. Cover with towel and let stand 10 minutes.

2. Using wooden spoon or electric mixer, beat flour mixture for 3 to 5 minutes, until cooled to room temperature. Cover with towel and leave in a warm place overnight or for 10 to 12 hours for flavor to develop.

3. In cup, sprinkle yeast and sugar over lukewarm milk. Stir and set aside in warm place for 5 to 10 minutes until **frothy**.

4. Using a wooden spoon, stir yeast mixture into flour mixture. Add remaining 2 cups flour, salt, and caraway seeds. Using your hands, mix well. Transfer to floured work surface and **knead**, sprinkling flour on work surface and your hands, until dough is no longer sticky. Clean and grease large mixing bowl or use new large mixing bowl. Form dough into a ball and place in greased large mixing bowl. Turn dough to grease all sides. Cover with plastic wrap and leave in warm place to rise to double in bulk, 1 to 1½ hours.

Preheat oven to 400° F.

5. Transfer dough to lightly floured work surface, **punch down** and knead until smooth and **elastic**, 5 to 10 minutes. Shape into rectangular loaf about 10 inches long. Place on greased baking sheet and using a spray bottle filled with cold water, lightly spray air around, but not directly on, the loaf.

6. Bake in oven for 45 minutes to 1 hour, until golden brown and sounds hollow when tapped on the bottom. Test **bread doneness**.

To serve, break into chunks. Throughout most of Eastern Europe, it is considered bad luck to cut bread with a knife at weddings. The superstition holds that to cut the wedding loaf is to sever the marriage.

ESTONIA

The northernmost of the three Baltic republics, Estonia is linked with neighboring Finland, just 50 miles to the north across the Gulf of Finland. Like the Finns, most Estonians belong to the Lutheran Church. All life-cycle events are celebrated according to their religion. (See Protestant and Catholic Life-Cycle Rituals, page xlvi.)

Even though the various Christian groups have their own traditions for funerals, including Estonians, some traditions are fairly similar. If the funeral is for a young wife, she is often buried in her wedding dress. Women in mourning wear black or dark clothes, while men usually wear a black ribbon on the lapel of their coats. Coffins are built of wood and have six sides and are narrow at the foot end. Estonians have preserved the tradition of kissing the dead as a way of saying the last goodbye.

In Estonia, mourners sing hymns every evening, followed by prayers for dead relatives from the past three generations. After each evening's prayers, a special meal is served, prepared by the best cook of the neighborhood. If the family has a pig, it is killed and eaten on this occasion.

A new tradition that has developed, in both villages and cities, is throwing flowers into the grave. Funerals usually last three days in villages, and in cities, two at the most. After the burial, mourners are invited to the funeral repast at the home of the deceased if it is in the countryside or possibly to a restaurant if it is in the city.

Before eating, a toast is given in memory of the deceased; wine or brandy is the chosen beverage. Usually the meal begins with assorted appetizers, similar to the Russian *zakuska* table (recipes p. 259). Breads, such as *saldskabmaize* (recipe p. 253), and rolls, *undens klinger* (recipe page 252), are also served. If a pig is prepared, it is accompanied by many side dishes, including *kugelis* (recipe p. 251).

Beets and potatoes are probably the most important vegetables in Eastern European cooking. In Estonia, no meal would be complete if it didn't have more than one potato or beet dish on the table. *Rossol'ye,* a hearty appetizer salad, is an Estonian specialty.

Rossol'ye

Potato Salad

Yield: serves 8 to 10

2 cups sour cream
1 tablespoon prepared horseradish
2 tablespoons prepared mustard
2 teaspoons sugar
salt and pepper to taste
1 cup canned pickled beets, drained and chopped
2 apples, peeled, **cored**, and **cubed**
6 new potatoes, boiled, peeled, and cubed

2 Polish or Kosher dill pickles, drained and cubed (available at all supermarkets)
½ cup drained pickled herring, cut into bite-size pieces, (available in refrigerated section of most supermarkets)
½ pound lean cooked beef or ham, chopped
8 lettuce leaves, for **garnish**
4 hard-cooked eggs, peeled and chopped, for garnish

Equipment: Medium mixing bowl with cover, mixing spoon, large mixing bowl, salad tools, plastic food wrap, large salad bowl, small serving bowl

1. Prepare dressing: Put sour cream into medium mixing bowl. Add horseradish, mustard, and sugar and stir. Add salt and pepper to taste. Stir, cover, and refrigerate.

2. In large mixing bowl, combine chopped pickled beets, apples, potatoes, pickles, herring, and beef or ham. Toss carefully with salad tools. Cover with plastic wrap and refrigerate until ready to serve.

3. At serving time: Line large salad bowl with lettuce leaves. Uncover salad mixture, and pour over half of the prepared sour cream dressing. Using salad tools, toss to mix. Transfer to prepared salad bowl. Sprinkle with chopped hard-cooked eggs, for garnish. Serve remaining sour cream dressing in a separate small serving bowl to spoon over.

Serve as a first course on the appetizer table. Rossol'ye *is eaten with bread and butter.*

Many life-cycle feasts end with *pannkoogid*, a plate-size pancake eaten for dessert.

Pannkoogid

Dessert Pancakes with Fruit Marmalade

Yield: serves 6
3 eggs, well beaten
1½ cups milk
1 cup all-purpose flour
½ teaspoon salt
2 teaspoons vanilla extract, divided
2 tablespoons melted butter or margarine
butter or margarine, as needed for frying
1 cup sour cream, for serving
confectioners' sugar to taste, for serving
2 cups raspberry, blueberry, or lingonberry marmalade, for serving

Equipment: Large mixing bowl or electric **blender**, whisk or mixing spoon, plastic food wrap, kitchen towel, work surface, **heavy-based** nonstick 8- or 9-inch skillet, baking sheet, oven mitts, small bowl, small serving bowl

1. In large mixing bowl or electric blender, combine eggs and milk. Add flour, salt, 1 teaspoon vanilla extract, and melted butter or margarine. **Blend** or beat 1 to 2 minutes, until smooth. Cover with plastic wrap and refrigerate for 1 to 2 hours. (The batter will be thin.)

Preheat oven to warm

2. Prepare to fry: Spread a kitchen towel out on work surface. Melt 1 tablespoon butter or margarine in heavy-based nonstick 8- or 9-inch skillet over medium-high heat, and swirl in pan to coat. Remove from heat and pour in ½ cup batter, tilting pan to spread evenly over bottom. Return to heat and fry 2 to 3 minutes, until golden brown and dull on top. Remove from heat and flip onto kitchen towel. Return pancake, bottom side up, to skillet and fry second side for about 1 minute. Transfer pancakes to baking sheet and keep in warm oven until ready to serve. Repeat making pancakes, using all the batter. Add butter or margarine, 1 tablespoon at a time, to recoat pan, as needed.

3. In small bowl, mix sour cream with remaining 1 teaspoon vanilla extract and confectioners' sugar to taste.

Serve each pancake flat on the guest's dinner plate. Put marmalade in small serving dish. Eat the pancake by putting a spoonful of marmalade on the surface, folding over, and cutting into bite-size pieces. Add a dollop of sweetened sour cream.

THE INDEPENDENT STATES OF THE FORMER SOVIET UNION

On December 25, 1991, Soviet president Mikhail S. Gorbachev resigned, bringing an end to the Soviet Union. Minutes after his resignation, the red Soviet flag was replaced with the Russian tricolor flag. The 15 nations (including the Russian Federation, see page 257, and the three Baltic countries, see page 250) that had been union republics under the Soviet system were now independent. Although many people thought of the Soviet Union as being Russia, the area it controlled encompassed many different nationalities, and with the removal of Soviet power, many of these groups have re-established local traditions.

Because the area of the former Soviet Union was so large, many of the countries have more in common with neighboring countries and regions than with Russia. For example, many of the foods served in Central Asia and the Caucus regions are very similar to dishes served in the Middle East and the Mediterranean. Other regions, including Russia, Ukraine, and Belarus, share foods with other Eastern European nations. For example, a Greek recipe for stuffed grape leaves, *dolmas*, is called *yarpakh dolmasy* in Armenia and Georgia. A similar dish is called *yafrak* in Israel and *yab-ra* (recipe page 136) in Yemen. Despite these differences, some common dishes are served throughout the countries of the former Soviet Union. Filled dumplings, fritters, dark breads, sour cream and/or yogurt, and sticky pastries are popular in all the former Soviet countries and are prepared for the life-cycle celebration feasts. The cow's milk sour cream (*smetana*), popular on Russian tables, becomes *matsoni* in Georgia, *matsun* in Armenia, *katyk* in Azerbaijan, and *egurt* in Turkmenistan; all are made with ewe's milk.

In much of what was the USSR, including Russia, Belarus (also Belorussia), Ukraine, Moldavia, and Georgia, the majority of the people are Orthodox Christians. (See Eastern or Orthodox Church Life-Cycle Rituals, page xlviii.) Armenia, which was the first nation to accept Christianity as the state religion (A.D. 301), has its own national church. The central Asian republics—Kazakhstan, Krygzystan, Tajikistan, Turkmenistan, and Uzbekistan—and Azerbaijan are predominantly Muslim. (See Islam and Islamic Life-Cycle Rituals, page xlix.) Since the fall of Communism, religious life-cycle rituals and celebrations are being revived.

In the Christian countries, christening, name day, birthday, weddings, anniversary, and funeral celebrations can go on from several hours to all day, with huge amounts of food served. Several days in advance of the event, family members and friends get together to prepare the food. The preparation and cooking is as much a joyous social occasion as the feast that follows. Sharing great amounts of food with family and friends, even on sad occasions, is the way people in Eastern Europe celebrate life. Mourning the death of a loved one is celebrated with a bountiful funeral repasts.

Funerals are important social events. After the burial everyone returns to the home of the deceased to partake in a lavish feast where the atmosphere of mourning changes to one of celebration.

In many of the former Soviet states, along with several Eastern European and Mediterranean countries, sweetened **wheat berries** have a significant association to life and death. A mixture of wheat berries with honey and nuts is an ancient dish, eaten by Roman Catholics and Orthodox Christians on Christmas Eve and at funerals and memorial services. In Poland, a similar dish, *kutya,* is traditionally eaten on Christmas Eve. The Italians make a wheat berry Easter pie, and in Greece, they serve a wheat berry recipe called *kólliva* (recipe page 148). Turkish *hedik* and Armenian *hadig* (recipe page 272) are similar, both are eaten for life-cycle celebrations, as is the Georgian *korkoti* (recipe page 274).

THE RUSSIAN FEDERATION

Despite the loss of the newly independent Soviet republics, the Russian Federation is still the largest country in the world, stretching from the Baltic Sea in the west to the Pacific Ocean in the east. Although ethnic Russians form a large majority of the population, people of other nationalities can be found throughout Russia. Many of these groups have their own life-cycle celebrations and rituals, but for the purposes of this book, the focus will be on celebrations of the Russian Orthodox Church.

In 1988, the Russian Orthodox Church, the largest Eastern Orthodox Church in the world, celebrated one thousand years of Christianity in Russia. Once the state religion of Russia, the Russian Orthodox Church, along with all religions, suffered under the anti-religious policies of Communism.

Starting with reforms of Mikhail Gorbachev (glasnost) in 1985 and continuing with the fall of the Communist empire in 1991, the restrictions against religious freedom have been slowly fading away. Under the current Russian government, Christian holidays are once again official state holidays. In addition, the christening of children is on the rise, religious funerals are more common, and church weddings are becoming fashionable. (See Eastern or Orthodox Church Life-Cycle Rituals, page xlviii.)

Marriage practices vary considerably among the nationalities and between urban and rural areas. Country weddings usually follow old traditional Russian *usviats* (wedding rituals). They are a three-day marathon, Friday through Monday, with breaks for sleep and work.

In the cities, civil ceremonies usually take place in a municipal "wedding palace." A member of the local council quickly performs the rite and pronounces the couple husband and wife while family and friends look on. Many couples find the civil ceremonies sterile and cold and hold a church service after the civil ceremony with candlelight and vestments, chanting and incense, and organ music.

In the Soviet era, it was customary for Moscow newlyweds to take a crepe-paper-draped taxi to the Lenin Mausoleum in route to their reception. On arrival, wedding couples were ushered to the front of the line, where according to tradition, the bride tossed her flowers on Lenin's casket for good luck. In other Soviet cities, couples went to the tomb of the war heroes for this ritual. Communism is dead, but the flower tossing lives on.

After the ceremony the wedding guests usually pile into vehicles, and with horns blaring, they form a procession to the bride's parents' house. Relatives bundle up the belongings of the bride in a sheet and carry them back to the procession. This symbolizes the bride's move to her new home.

The groom's parents wait for the wedding party at the entrance of their house with symbolic offerings. Outside the entrance to the house, a wooden bowl of salt and a freshly baked loaf of beautifully decorated bread, Russian symbols for good luck, have been set out on a table. The bread is sliced by the host and dipped in the salt. He offers it to the newlyweds and says *Khleb da sol'*, literally translated as "bread and salt" but meaning "good luck and have a wonderfully rich, full life."

Before entering the house, the newlyweds each raise a glass of vodka, drink half, and fling the rest over their shoulder. When the groom smashes his glass on the ground, it signals the beginning of the festivities. The party generally lasts late into the night with plenty to eat and drink.

An important phase of the celebration is the *nadel* (gift-giving) ritual, held on the second day. Well-wishers bring gifts to the newlyweds and cheer and applaud as the gifts are opened. A special wedding bread called *karavai* is traditionally served at the *nadel*.

The baking of the *karavai* is the responsibility of the bride's godmother. She supervises the work of the *karavainitsy* ("wedding loaf women"), her female helpers. The *karavai* is a round white loaf decorated with pine cones, flowers, leaves, and images of children, birds, and animals made out of dough. The decorations are symbols of good health, wealth, happiness, and many children. ۞ ۞ ۞

Karavai

Wedding Loaf

Yield: 1 decorated loaf

2 or 3 packages frozen bread dough

egg wash

Equipment: Lightly floured work surface, cookie cutters (any shapes), large baking sheet, pizza pan, or roasting pan

1. Follow the directions on the package to prepare the dough for baking. Shape the dough into a loaf or wreath.

2. Decorate uncooked dough with pieces of dough in various shapes. You can use cookie cutter shapes or mold the dough into shapes like working with clay. Remember to allow room for the dough to rise. Brush the decorated loaf with egg wash to make the bread shiny. The bread can be baked on a large baking sheet, pizza pan or roasting pan.

The bride's friends may also bake sweet *klubtsy*, a pastry in the form of intertwined rings, while the groom's party brings *baranki*, ring-shaped rolls. The breads symbolize the joining together of two people.

Great quantities of food and drink are important to the success of the wedding. The beverages are milk, soda, seltzer, hot tea, and *kvas* (recipe page 262), a cold beer-like beverage made from black bread and honey. Vodka is also very popular.

A wedding feast would be unthinkable without the *zakouska* (appetizer) table. Dozens of *zakouski*, "little dishes," are prepared for nibbling. The variety of *zakouski* is endless, with many items readily available from the delicatessen section of a supermarket. A variety of flavors, colors, and textures are important.

Zakouska Table

Appetizer Table

pickled herring in wine sauce and in sour cream
sauerkraut sprinkled with caraway seeds
assorted cheeses
green and black olives
pickled hot peppers, pickled beets, pickled mushrooms (*selenyia gribi*), and pickled green tomatoes
anchovy on sliced hard-cooked egg (*kilki croutyia yaitza*)
assorted cold cuts
mustard, horseradish, butter or margarine and sour cream
assorted breads and rolls

Equipment: Cloth tablecloth, serving platters and bowls, serving forks, spoons and knives, napkins, appetizer plates and flatware

Cover the dinner table with a freshly pressed tablecloth. Place a centerpiece on the table. (Fresh flowers and candles are always lovely.) Place salt and pepper shakers on the table. Fill the appropriate platters and serving bowls with the food. Always include the proper serving utensil for each item. Bread and rolls look nice in a basket lined with a napkin. Place appetizer plates, napkins, and eating utensils on the table or on the sideboard.

Easy to prepare *zakouski* include such dishes as freshly boiled new potatoes tossed with dill and seasoned with salt and pepper, deviled eggs, sliced cucumber sprinkled with salt and mixed with sour cream, and *stolichnyi salat*. Many salads are called Russian salad but *stolichnyi salat* shows the Russian flare for an unusual mix of ingredients.

Stolichnyi Salat

Russian Salad

Yield: serves 8 to 10
4 potatoes, washed
1 orange, peeled, **pith** removed, and cut into bite-size pieces
½ pound cooked chicken, cut into bite-size pieces
2 apples, cored and cut into bite-size pieces
2 carrots, peeled, **trimmed**, and cut into circles about ¼ inch thick
1 cup frozen peas, thawed
2 green onions, trimmed and thinly sliced crosswise
3 hard-cooked **egg yolks**
3 tablespoons olive oil, divided
3 tablespoons white wine vinegar, divided
1 cup mayonnaise, divided
1 cup sour cream, divided
salt and pepper to taste
sprigs of fresh parsley, for **garnish**

Equipment: Medium saucepan, fork, tablespoon, work surface, paring knife, large mixing bowl, plastic food wrap, mixing spoon, small mixing bowl with cover, serving platter

1. Put potatoes in medium saucepan and cover generously with water. Bring to boil over high heat. Reduce heat to **simmer** and cook for 20 to 30 minutes, or until just tender when poked with a fork. Remove potatoes from water and cool to warm. Using paring knife, peel, place on work surface, and cut into ½-inch chunks. Put potatoes in large mixing bowl and add orange, chicken, apples, carrots, peas, and green onions. Toss to mix.

2. Prepare salad dressing: In a small mixing bowl, mash hard-cooked egg yolks using back of fork. Stir in 2 tablespoons olive oil to smooth paste. Stir in 2 tablespoons vinegar, ½ cup of mayonnaise, and ½ cup sour cream. Add salt and pepper to taste. Stir dressing, pour over chicken

mixture, and toss to mix well. Cover with plastic wrap and refrigerate until ready to serve.

3. Prepare garnish dressing: In small mixing bowl, mix together remaining 1 tablespoon olive oil, 1 tablespoon vinegar, ½ cup mayonnaise, and ½ cup sour cream. Add salt and pepper to taste. Cover and refrigerate until ready to serve.

4. At serving time, transfer salad mixture to serving platter. Stir prepared dressing and pour over salad. Garnish with sprigs of fresh parsley.

To serve, place on table with other zakuski *on the* zakouska *table.*

When the family can afford it, caviar, the eggs of Caspian Sea's Beluga sturgeon, will be on the *zakouska* table. Caviar is eaten with *blini* (recipe follows).

Russian caviar is extremely expensive and not easily available in the United States. Small jars of domestic black and red caviar are available at most supermarkets, and although they may seem expensive, a little goes a long way. To serve, place the small jar of caviar, with a teaspoon, on the *zakouska* table. Place a small pitcher of warm melted butter and a bowl of sour cream next to it. *Blini* can be made of either all-purpose flour (recipe follows) or buckwheat flour or a combination of the two.

Blini

Russian Pancakes

Yield: serves 6 to 8

1 package dry **yeast**
½ cup water
1 cup milk, at room temperature
1½ cups all-purpose **flour, sifted**
3 **eggs, separated**
½ teaspoon salt
¼ teaspoons sugar
6 tablespoons melted butter, cooled to room temperature
1 cup butter or margarine, more as needed, divided

Equipment: Cup, mixing spoon, electric **blender**, rubber spatula, large mixing bowl, kitchen towel, medium mixing bowl, electric mixer (optional), large skillet, ladle, metal spatula, baking sheet, aluminum foil

1. Dissolve yeast in ½ cup warm water for 5 minutes. Pour yeast mixture into blender and add milk, flour, egg yolks, salt, sugar, and 6 tablespoons melted butter. **Blend** at high speed for about 30 seconds. Turn off the machine and using a rubber spatula, scrape down the flour clinging to the sides of blender. Blend a few seconds longer, then pour batter into large mixing bowl. Cover loosely with a towel. Let batter rise for 2 hours in a warm place. (After 2 hours the batter will have risen and bubbles will cover the top.)

2. Put egg whites in medium mixing bowl. Using electric mixer or mixing spoon, beat egg whites with a pinch of salt until stiff, 3 to 5 minutes. Using rubber spatula, gently **fold in** egg whites with batter.

3. Melt 4 tablespoons butter or margarine in large skillet over medium heat. Swirl to coat bottom of pan. Using ladle, scoop 2- to 3-inch wide pancakes into skillet, leaving space between each to easily turn over. Lightly brown on each side, 1 or 2 minutes. Remove with metal spatula and place, slightly overlapping, on baking sheet. To keep them warm and crisp, cover loosely with foil. Continue making in batches, adding more butter or margarine to skillet, as needed to keep pancakes from sticking.

To serve, place the blini *on the* zakouska *table. To eat* blini, *place one or two on a small plate, moisten the top with melted butter or margarine, and add a little sour cream and a dab of caviar.* Blini *are either picked up and eaten with the fin-*

gers or a fork. Blini *are also eaten with jellies, marmalades, or herring in sour cream (available in deli section at most supermarkets).*

The Russians, who are often unable to afford fish roe caviar, have come up with an affordable substitute, *baklazhannaya ikra* (eggplant caviar), often referred to as "poor man's" caviar.

Baklazhannaya Ikra

Eggplant Caviar

Yield: serves 6 to 10

1½ to 2 pounds large eggplant
2 tablespoons olive oil
2 onions, **finely chopped**
1 green pepper, **trimmed** and finely chopped
4 cloves garlic, finely chopped
3 tomatoes, **peeled** and finely chopped
1 tablespoon honey
juice of one lemon
salt and pepper to taste

Equipment: Baking sheet, oven mitts, paring knife, small bowl, medium skillet, mixing spoon, food processor, rubber spatula, medium serving bowl with cover

Preheat oven to 375° F.

1. Put eggplant on baking sheet and bake in oven until tender, 35 to 45 minutes. Remove from oven and set pan aside to cool. After baking, the eggplant skin easily peels off using paring knife. Put the eggplant insides in a small bowl. Discard skin.

2. Heat 2 tablespoons oil in medium skillet over medium-high heat. Add onions, green pepper, and garlic and stir. **Sauté** until soft, 3 to 5 minutes. Add eggplant and tomatoes, stir, and bring to boil. Reduce heat to **simmer**, cover, and cook 30 minutes, stirring occasionally. Stirring frequently, remove cover and continue to simmer for 15 to 20 minutes, until most of the liquid is evaporated and mixture has thickened. Cool enough to handle and transfer to food processor container.

3. Add honey, lemon juice, and salt and pepper to taste. Process until smooth, about 1 minute. Transfer to medium serving bowl, cover, and refrigerate for about 4 hours for flavors to develop.

Note: While processing, turn machine off once or twice and scrape down sides of container with rubber spatula.

Serve eggplant caviar on the zakouska *table. It can be spread on crackers or bread or used as dip for raw vegetables, such as carrot, celery, cucumber, and zucchini.*

The Russians love potatoes so much they call them *vtoroi khleb,* which means the second bread. A potato dish is almost always prepared for the wedding feast, and a favorite way to fix them is in the *zapekanka* (casserole).

Kartofel'naya Zapekanka

Casserole of Mashed Potatoes

Yield: serves 4 to 6

2 pounds potatoes, peeled and quartered
water, as needed
5 tablespoons butter or margarine, divided
1 cup milk
salt to taste
2 eggs, lightly beaten
2 tablespoons vegetable oil
3 onions, thinly sliced
½ cup sour cream

Equipment: Medium saucepan, **colander**, large mixing bowl, potato masher or electric mixer, mixing spoon, large skillet, greased 2-quart casserole, oven mitts

1. Put potatoes in medium saucepan and cover generously with water. Bring to boil over high heat. Reduce heat to **simmer**, and cook until tender, 15 to 20 minutes. Drain potatoes in colander. Transfer to large mixing bowl. Add 3 tablespoons butter or margarine, milk, and salt to taste. Using potato masher or electric mixer, mash until smooth. Beat in eggs.

2. Heat oil and remaining 2 tablespoons butter or margarine in large skillet over medium-high heat. Add onions, stir, and **sauté** until soft, 3 to 5 minutes.

Preheat oven to 350° F.

3. Assemble: Place half the mashed potatoes in greased casserole and smooth top. Spread onions over potatoes and cover with remaining mashed potatoes. Spread sour cream over the top.

4. Bake in oven for 30 minutes, or until top is lightly browned.

To serve, place the casserole on the table and have guests help themselves.

Russians drink *kvas* as a cold beverage and they also use it as a soup stock for making cold soups.

Kvas (also Kvass)

Mint-Flavored Bread Drink

Note: This recipe takes 4 to 6 days.

Yield: 6 cups

1 pound day-old Russian or Danish pumpernickel bread, sliced, (available at many bakeries and supermarkets)
10 cups water
2 packages dry **yeast**
1 cup sugar
¼ cup **lukewarm** water
2 tablespoons fresh mint leaves or 1 tablespoon crumbled dried mint
2 tablespoons raisins

Equipment: Work surface, **serrated knife**, baking sheet, oven mitts, large saucepan, mixing spoon, kitchen towel, strainer, 10-15 coffee filters, medium bowl, funnel, 2 half-gallon bottles with cap, tall beverage glasses

Preheat oven to 200° F.

1. On work surface, using a serrated knife, cut bread into 1-inch cubes and spread out evenly on baking sheet. Place in oven for 1 to 2 hours, or until thoroughly dry.

2. Pour water into large saucepan, and bring to boil over high heat. Add dried bread, and press down with mixing spoon to immerse in water. Remove from heat. When the bread mixture is cool enough to handle, cover loosely with towel and set at room temperature for at least 8 hours or overnight for flavors to develop.

3. Place strainer lined with overlapping coffee filters over medium bowl. Strain bread mixture, squeezing soaked bread with your hands to release all the liquid. Discard all bread left in strainer.

4. Add yeast and ¼ teaspoon sugar to lukewarm water. Stir to dissolve yeast completely. Set aside in warm, draft-free place (such as an unlighted oven) for about 10 minutes, or until the yeast mixture almost doubles in volume.

5. Stir yeast mixture, remaining sugar, and mint into strained bread liquid. Cover with towel and set at room temperature for at least 8 hours or overnight.

6. Line a funnel with a coffee filter and place in neck of half-gallon bottle. Pour bread liquid through the filter into the bottle. Remove funnel and drop raisins into the bottle. Screw cap on the bottle and set in cool, but not cold place for 3 to 5 days, or until the raisins have risen to the top and the sediment has sunk to bottom.

7. Strain bread liquid again through coffee filter-lined strainer and rebottle in clean bottle. Refrigerate until ready to use.

To serve kvas, *pour into tall beverage glasses, over ice. Russians drink* kvas *at life-cycle celebrations.*

BELARUS

One of the former Soviet Republics, Belarus is small country in the northern part of Eastern Europe. It is bordered on the east by Russia, on the south by Ukraine, and on the west by Poland, Latvia, and Lithuania. It is often referred to as "White Russia," which is a translation of the Russian name, Belarus. Despite its recent independence, Belarus maintains many ties with Russia, and approximately 13 percent of the Belarus population is Russian.

Most Belarusians belong to the Eastern Orthodox Church, although a great many Roman Catholics (nearly 15 percent) live in the country. The basic life-cycle rituals are similar for all Christians in Eastern Europe and Russia. (See Eastern or Orthodox Church Life-Cycle Rituals, page xlviii.) The same or similar foods are served at celebration feasts, especially bread. Bread, blessed by the priest, is the center of religious and life-cycle rituals. Preparing the food and baking the bread, as it has been done for generations, is an important part of the total observance.

Smetana (sour cream) is used liberally in Eastern European cooking. It is difficult to imagine cooking in this region without *smetana*. Homemade sour cream has a richer flavor than the commercial product, and it will not clump when added to hot soups. ❂ ❂ ❂

SMETANA

HOMEMADE SOUR CREAM

Note: This recipe takes over 24 hours.

Yield: about 4 cups

4 cups heavy cream
2 tablespoons buttermilk

Equipment: Medium glass bowl, mixing spoon, plastic food wrap

1. Pour heavy cream into medium glass bowl, and stir in buttermilk. Cover with plastic wrap and let stand for 24 hours in warm place to develop.

2. Uncover and stir to **blend**. Cover with plastic wrap and refrigerate.

To serve, use in recipes calling for sour cream or use as a sauce.

Sausage and cabbage are often called the comfort foods of Eastern Europe. This traditional recipe, made with both ingredients, would be served as an appetizer or side dish on the banquet table in a wealthy home. Most everyone else eats it as the main dish with side dishes of *kartofel'naya zapekanka* (recipe page 261), *zulynez gribnoy* (recipe page 269), and *stolichnyi salat* (recipe page 259).

KOLBASA Z KAPUSTOV

SAUSAGE AND CABBAGE

Yield: serves 4 to 6

1 pound lean kielbasa (Polish sausage) or other lean smoked pork sausage, cut across into 1-inch pieces (available at all supermarkets)
1 onion, **finely chopped**

1 pound head cabbage, **shredded**, or 16-ounce package shredded cabbage (available at most supermarkets)
½ teaspoon salt
2 cups canned beef broth
3 tablespoons dark brown sugar
1 tablespoon cornstarch
2 tablespoons water
juice of 1 lemon

Equipment: Medium saucepan with cover or **Dutch oven**, mixing spoon, small bowl

1. Put sausage pieces into medium saucepan or Dutch oven, over medium-high heat. **Sauté**, tossing constantly, until browned on all sides, 5 to 7 minutes. Add chopped onions and stir. Cook for 3 to 5 minutes to soften. Add shredded cabbage and salt. Reduce heat to medium, cover, and cook for 5 to 7 minutes to wilt cabbage. Add beef broth, increase heat to medium-high, and bring to boil. Reduce heat to **simmer**, cover, and cook for 35 to 45 minutes.

2. Stir brown sugar and cornstarch with water in small bowl until smooth. Stir brown sugar mixture into cabbage mixture, and add lemon juice. Stirring frequently, simmer, uncovered, for 15 to 20 minutes to thicken.

Serve hot as a side dish or main course with plenty of bread to soak up juices.

Meat cutlets (also meat patties) are a favorite way of making a little meat go a long way, and they are very popular for family dinner parties and other social events.

Kotlety Pojarski

Meat Cutlets (also Meat Patties)

Yield: serves 6
1½ pounds **ground** lean pork or chicken, or combination
2½ cups **fresh white bread crumbs**, divided
½ cup heavy cream
½ teaspoon ground nutmeg
salt and pepper to taste
2 eggs
2 tablespoons butter or margarine, more if necessary
2 tablespoons vegetable oil, more if necessary
1 cup sour cream, for serving

Equipment: Food processor, rubber spatula, medium mixing bowl, mixing spoon, wax paper, baking sheet, plastic food wrap, small shallow bowl, pie pan, large skillet, metal spatula, medium baking pan, serving platter, small serving bowl

1. Put ground pork or chicken or combination in food processor. Add 1 cup fresh white bread crumbs, heavy cream, nutmeg, and salt and pepper to taste. Process to smooth paste, about 1 minute. Transfer meat mixture to medium mixing bowl.

Note: While processing, turn machine off once or twice and scrape down sides of container with rubber spatula.

2. Divide meat into 6 equal portions and form each into an oval patty, less than ½ inch thick. Place on wax-paper-covered baking sheet. Cover with plastic wrap and refrigerate for at least 2 hours to firm.

3. Put eggs in small shallow bowl and beat with a fork. Set bowl on work surface next to pie pan with remaining 1½ cups fresh bread crumbs. Dip each patty into beaten egg, shake off excess, and press into bread crumbs, coating each side well. Place back on wax-paper-covered baking sheet and cover with plastic wrap. Refrigerate for 1 hour to set.

4. To pan-fry: Heat 2 tablespoons butter or margarine and 2 tablespoons oil in large skillet over medium-high heat. Fry patties in batches, for 5 to 7 minutes on each side, or until golden brown and cooked through. If necessary, add a little more of equal amounts butter or marga-

rine and oil. Transfer to medium baking pan and keep warm until serving time.

To serve, put meat patties on a serving platter and ***drizzle*** *with 2 or 3 tablespoons sour cream that has been heated to warm in small pan. Pour the remaining sour cream into a small serving bowl to serve on the side.*

In Eastern Europe, offering guests a glass of tea is the sign of a good host. Tea drinking is a beloved ritual, and the samovar is an important part of the tradition. The samovar, which means self-cooker, is used strictly for heating water. Contrary to popular belief, the tea itself is not made in the samovar. *Zavarka* (strong tea concentrate) is brewed in a tiny pot that is kept warm on top of the samovar.

To make tea, a small amount of *zavarka* is poured into each glass or cup, and then hot water is added from the samovar's spigot. Spoonfuls of sugar are added to the tea as needed for taste. A favorite tradition among peasants is to sip tea with a cube of sugar clenched between the teeth. Children drink their tea from a saucer to avoid burning their lips. Adding jam to tea is another tradition.

Chai

Russian Tea

Yield: serves 6

- 8 cups water
- 8 teaspoons black tea
- strawberry or raspberry jam, for serving (optional)
- lump sugar, for serving

Equipment: Tea kettle or **samovar**, 2 to 3 cup teapot, tea strainer, oven mitts, heatproof beverage glasses

Bring water to boil in the tea kettle or samovar. Pour a little boiling water into teapot, swish around to warm it, and discard water. Spoon tea leaves into teapot, add 1½ cups boiling water, cover, and let **steep** 3 to 5 minutes. This is called *zavarka* (tea concentrate).

To serve, pour about ¼ cup zavarka *(tea concentrate) through a tea strainer into each heatproof glass or cup and fill with boiling water. To drink tea Russian style, stir a spoonful of jam into the tea.*

UKRAINE

Except for Russia, Ukraine is the largest country in Europe and is blessed with mineral and agricultural wealth. Located north of the Black Sea, Ukraine shares borders with Moldova, Romania, Hungary, Slovakia, Poland, and Belarus. As with other former Soviet republics, a large Russian population remains in Ukraine, about 22 percent.

Although most Ukrainians belong to the Orthodox Church, the Church itself has split into several factions with the removal of Russian power. These differences notwithstanding, Ukrainians celebrate life-cycle rituals in much the same way as their Orthodox brethren. (See Eastern or Orthodox Church Life-Cycle Rituals, page xlviii.)

Since the fall of Communism and Ukrainian independence in 1991, more and more couples are exchanging vows in the various branches of the Orthodox Church, though first they must have the mandatory civil ceremony at the Palace of Rituals (a fancy name for the government marriage bureau).

Village weddings are simple civil ceremonies followed by a colorful procession to the church. The wedding celebration then often goes on for two or three days. The ideal menu for a village wedding feast includes assorted appetizers (recipe page 259), great loaves of different breads, mountains of both savory and sweet filled pastries and dumplings (recipes pages 271 and 226), roasted **suckling pig** (recipe page 162), *koulibiac* (recipe page 267), sweet breads and cookies (recipes page 267 and 269), strudel (recipe page 163), candies (recipe page 274), and nuts. Most urbanites have shorter receptions, with fewer people, less food, and pork roast or *kotlety pojarski* (recipe page 264) replaces suckling pig.

One of the old traditions that is being revived since independence is the Ukrainian wedding bread, blessed by the priest. The breads are gigantic and stout, and some are sweet tasting, almost like cake. Some breads are so large and ornate that it takes a couple of strong attendants to carry one into the wedding hall. The wedding breads are decorated with birds, flowers, leaves, and butterflies made out of baked dough, which symbolize long life, happiness, wealth, and fertility. At the reception, the guests get a piece of wedding bread; the bride saves hers for good luck and to eat on the birth of her first child.

Thawed, frozen dough can be used to make *korovai z peremyshlia* (Ukrainian wedding bread). To give it a sweet, cake-like taste, **glaze** or sprinkle the bread with confectioners' sugar mixed in a little water after it is baked. Buy two or more loaves for the bread (follow directions on package) and an extra loaf or two to make the decorations. Working with the dough to make the decorations is like working with clay (see illustrations), except you need to allow the dough to rise after finishing the different shapes (follow rising and baking directions on package). Cookie cutters can also be used to make the decorations. Flatten dough on a lightly floured work surface and cut out the desired shapes, allowing the dough to rise. To decorate the loaf, touch the backside of each decoration with a dab of water and then gently attach it to the loaf of bread before baking in the oven. Or the decorations can be baked separately on a cookie sheet and attached to the baked bread with toothpicks, wooden skewers, or **florist wire**.

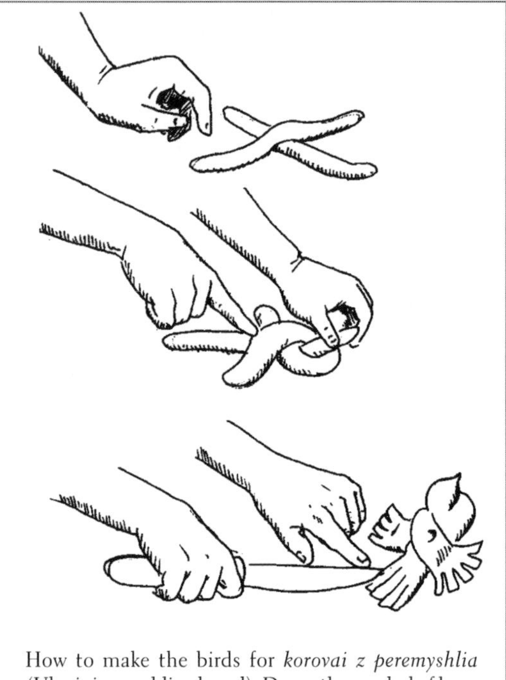

How to make the birds for *korovai z peremyshlia* (Ukrainian wedding bread). Doves the symbol of love, decorate the *kovovai*. Often a miniature *kovovai* is made as a keepsake for the newlyweds.

Krendel is a very popular sweet bread in many of the countries of the former Soviet Union. The bread is made into a pretzel or figure-8 shape as the centerpiece for birthdays and name day celebrations. Double or triple the recipe if it is being used for a large, decorative wedding loaf.

Krendel

Sweet Bread

Yield: 1 loaf

3 tablespoons **lukewarm** water
1 package dry **yeast**
½ cup sugar, divided
3 cups all-purpose flour, divided
½ teaspoon salt
¼ cup cold butter or margarine, **coarsely chopped**
2 eggs, lightly beaten
½ cup light cream
egg wash
confectioners' sugar, for **garnish**

Equipment: Small bowl, mixing spoon, flour **sifter**, large mixing bowl, well-floured work surface, kitchen towel, greased baking sheet, **pastry brush**, oven mitts, wire cake rack, cloth napkin

1. Pour lukewarm water into small bowl, sprinkle in yeast and 1 teaspoon sugar. Leave for 10 minutes to become foamy and almost double in volume.

2. **Sift** 2 cups flour, salt, and remaining ½ cup sugar into large mixing bowl. Using your hands, work cold butter into flour mixture until it becomes crumbly. Add beaten eggs and stir well. Add cream and yeast mixture, and stir to mix. If dough is sticky add flour, ½ cup at a time, until smooth. Form dough into a ball. Transfer to well-floured work surface and using lightly floured hands, **knead** for 5 minutes, or until smooth and **elastic**. Form into ball, place in lightly greased bowl, and turn to grease all sides. Cover with towel and let rise to double in bulk, 1 to 1½ hours.

Preheat oven to 350° F.

3. Shape into loaf: **Punch down** dough and on lightly floured work surface shape into long rope, about 2 inches thick. Place dough on greased baking sheet and shape into whatever shape you like. Cover with towel and let rise in a warm place until double in bulk, 30 to 45 minutes. Using pastry brush, brush top of dough with egg wash.

4. Bake in oven for 30 to 35 minutes, or until golden. Using oven mitts, remove from oven and transfer to wire cake rack. While warm, sprinkle with confectioners' sugar.

To serve sweet bread, cut into slices or place on a cloth napkin and have guests break off a chunk. Spread with butter or jam.

The centerpiece for a wedding banquet is frequently the *koulibiac* (**poached** salmon baked in puff pastry). It can be prepared simply, shaped as a large rectangle, or more decorative, shaped like a large, round-bodied fish, resembling an angelfish.

To make the pattern for fish-shaped pastry you need 9- x 15-inch paper, 9-inch round dinner plate, pencil, and scissors. Lay the dinner plate upside down in the center of the paper, and trace around it with a pencil. Draw the fish tail on one side of the circle and the head on the opposite side of the circle, making the overall fish length about 15 inches. Using scissors, cut out the fish pattern. The fish-shaped presentation is worth the little extra effort. Directions for both pastry shapes are given below. Follow step 3 if making the rectangular shape and step 4 if the fish shaped is being attempted.

Koulibiac (also Coulibiac)

Salmon in Puff Pastry

Yield: serves 10 to 12

2 pounds fresh skinless salmon **fillet**, about 1 inch thick
2 cups chicken broth, homemade (recipe page 106), or canned

water, as needed
1 bay leaf
4 tablespoons butter or margarine
1 onion, **finely chopped**
2½ cups (about 1 pound) mushrooms, finely sliced
1 cup long-grain rice (cooked according to directions on package)
juice of 1 lemon
3 tablespoons parsley, finely chopped
salt and pepper to taste
1½ packages (total of 3 sheets) frozen **puff pastry**, thawed and unwrapped
4 hard-cooked eggs, shelled and chopped
egg wash

Equipment: Large skillet with cover, fork, wide metal spatula, large plate, large skillet, mixing spoon, large mixing bowl, lightly floured work surface, paring knife, lightly floured rolling pin, baking sheet, paper fish pattern (see instructions above),damp kitchen towel, **pastry brush**, oven mitts, scissors

1. Put salmon fillet in large skillet and add chicken broth and enough water to cover. Add bay leaf and bring to boil over high heat. Reduce heat to **simmer**, cover, and cook 20 minutes, or until the fish flakes easily when poked with fork. Remove from heat. Using wide metal spatula, remove fish from pan and set on large plate to cool. Discard liquid or cover and refrigerate for another use. When fish is cool enough to handle, using your fingers, flake into large chunks. Feel for small bones in fillets as you flake and discard.

In the Ukraine the *koulibiac* (also *coulibiac*) is often made in the shape of an angel fish and used as the centerpiece on the buffet table. To simulate fish scales, small cuts are made with a scissors, before the fish-shaped pastry is baked in the oven.

2. Prepare filling: Melt butter or margarine in large skillet over medium-high heat. Add onions, stir, and cook until soft, 3 to 5 minutes. Add mushrooms and reduce heat to medium. Stirring frequently, cook 10 to 15 minutes until mushrooms soften and are fully cooked. Transfer to large mixing bowl. Add the cooked rice, lemon juice, parsley, and salt and pepper to taste. Toss gently to mix.

3. Prepare rectangular pastry: On lightly floured work surface, unfold 3 pastry sheets and cut one sheet in half with paring knife. Overlap matching edges of a full sheet and half sheet by 1 inch and lightly dab between them with a moistened finger. Press moistened sheets together so they stick to each other. Using lightly floured rolling pin, roll out to 10 x 16 inches. Repeat with second whole pastry sheet and second half sheet. To transfer pastry to baking sheet, carefully fold over 3 or 4 times (to keep from tearing) and unfold in baking sheet. Repeat folding over second pastry but do not remove from work surface. Cover with damp towel until ready to assemble.

4. Prepare fish-shaped pastry: Place the fish pattern on top of 10- x 16-inch pastry sheet and cut around it with paring knife. Sprinkle lightly with flour. Carefully fold over 3 or 4 times and unfold in baking sheet. Repeat folding over second pastry but do not remove from work surface. Cover with damp towel until ready to use.

5. Save pastry scraps to decorate top pastry. Use scraps to cut out an eye, thick fish lips, and fins. Using scissors, cut little ½-inch nips (>>>)

facing in the same direction, over top pastry to resemble fish scales. When pastry bakes, the nips puff up.

Preheat oven to 400° F.

6. To assemble: Cover bottom pastry (on baking sheet) with half the rice mixture and stay about 1 inch inside the edges. Cover rice with salmon chunks and chopped eggs. Top with remaining rice, piled high in the middle. Using pastry brush, lightly brush water around 1-inch edge of bottom pastry. Unfold second pastry over the filling, line up the edges, and press together. Using your fingers or the back of fork, press down on edges to seal pastry together. After pastry is assembled, decorate with cut out pieces. Lightly dab the backside of each cutout with water to make it stick. Brush pastry and decorative pieces with egg wash. Using knife, cut 3 or 4 vent slits in top pastry to let steam escape when cooked.

7. Bake in oven for 25 to 35 minutes, or until golden brown. Using oven mitts, remove from oven and allow to rest 10 minutes before cutting.

To serve, place the whole, uncut koulibiac *as the centerpiece on the buffet or dinner table so everyone can enjoy the beautiful presentation. Serve warm or at room temperature with a side dish of sour cream* (smetana) *to spoon over each serving.*

Life-cycle celebration feasts almost always include two very popular Ukrainian foods, mushrooms and sour cream, as in the following recipe.

Zulynez Gribnoy

Baked Mushrooms in Sour Cream

Yield: serves 6

4 tablespoons butter or margarine
1 onion, **finely chopped**
2½ cups (about 1 pound) sliced fresh mushrooms
1 tablespoon all-purpose flour
½ cup milk
1 cup sour cream
salt and pepper to taste
½ cup **bread crumbs**
½ cup shredded mozzarella cheese

Equipment: Large skillet, mixing spoon, buttered shallow 8-inch baking pan, 2 small bowls, oven mitts

1. Melt butter in skillet over medium-high heat. Add onions and **sauté** until soft, 3 to 5 minutes. Add mushrooms and reduce heat to medium. Stir and cook until soft, 10 to 15 minutes. Remove from heat. Transfer to buttered shallow baking pan.

Preheat oven to 350° F.

2. In small bowl, stir flour into milk until smooth. Stir in sour cream and salt and pepper to taste. Spoon over mushrooms and **fold in**. In second small bowl, mix bread crumbs and shredded cheese together. Sprinkle bread crumb mixture over top mushrooms.

3. Bake in oven for 20 to 30 minutes until top is golden brown.

Serve warm or at room temperature as an appetizer or a side dish.

Sweets are always popular, and assorted cakes, pastries, and cookies are typical of Ukrainian life-cycle celebrations.

Paliushky

Walnut Finger Cookies

Yield: about 40 pieces

½ cup butter or margarine
2½ tablespoons solid vegetable shortening
1 cup confectioners' sugar, divided, more if necessary
¼ teaspoon salt

1 **egg yolk**
2 tablespoons sour cream
zest of 1 lemon, **grated**
½ cup walnuts, chopped
2 cups all-purpose flour

Equipment: Medium mixing bowl, electric mixer, wooden mixing spoon, rubber spatula, plastic food wrap, lightly greased cookie sheet, oven mitts, metal spatula, wire cake rack, small bowl, serving platter

1. In medium mixing bowl, using an electric mixer or wooden mixing spoon, beat butter or margarine and vegetable shortening until light and fluffy. Beat in ½ cup confectioners' sugar, salt, egg yolk, sour cream, and lemon zest, beating well after each addition. Using wooden mixing spoon or rubber spatula, **fold in** walnuts and flour. Cover bowl with plastic wrap and refrigerate for 1½ to 2 hours until firm.

Preheat oven to 350° F.

2. Shape cookies: Using your hands, pull off about 3 tablespoons dough at a time and shape into a round rope about 2½ inches long and ½ inch thick. Continue making cookies and space them about 1 inch apart on lightly greased cookie sheet.

3. Bake in oven for 10 to 12 minutes, or until brown around the edges. Using oven mitts, remove baking sheet from oven. Let stand about 3 minutes to firm before using metal spatula to transfer to wire cake rack to cool enough to handle.

4. Roll warm cookies, one at a time, into small bowl with remaining ½ cup confectioners' sugar. Return to wire cake rack to cool completely. Add more confectioners' sugar if necessary.

To serve, stack paliushky *on serving platter. Store in airtight container for up to one week.*

MOLDOVA REPUBLIC

Moldova is in the most southwesterly corner of the former Soviet Union. The tiny country is sandwiched in between Ukraine to the northeast and Romania to the west. The Moldavians share a common heritage with their Romanian neighbors. Although significant numbers of Ukrainians and Russians live in Moldova (about 13 percent each), most people in Moldova speak Moldavian, which is very similar to Romanian, and belong to the Moldavian Orthodox Church, which has ties to both the Romanian and Russian Orthodox Churches.

Life-cycle celebrations, in accordance with the custom of the Church, begin with the baptism of newborns. The parents select three couples to act as sponsors for their infant and to participate in the baptism rituals. One of the sponsors' more interesting tasks comes after the baby has been dipped in a basin of water (the font) and returned to its mother's arms. Each of the three couples in turn go through the motions of spitting three times over their shoulders. The spitting signifies the baptized baby was purged of the devil. After the baby is dressed in new clothes, they join the congregation, carrying icons and banners from the church, and they parade around the church grounds or through the village with other worshippers. The singing and chanting procession is lead by two or three men ringing a large bell which they carry suspended from poles. The baptism is announced by the revelers and a celebration feast follows.

Baked, boiled, or fried, dumplings or filled pastries are staples of a life-cycle celebration. They are eaten as appetizers, in soup, as the main meal, or filled with jam or fruit for dessert. The following recipe for *kartophelnye vareniky* (stuffed potato dumplings) is a typical dish served.

Kartophelnye Vareniky

Stuffed Potato Dumplings

Yield: 18 to 20 pieces

18 to 20 pitted prunes, soaked in warm water for 10 minutes and drained
½ cup walnuts, **finely chopped**
¾ cup sugar, divided
3½ cups mashed potatoes, cooled to room temperature
1 egg, beaten
salt to taste
½ cup all-purpose flour, more if necessary
1 tablespoon cornstarch
1 cup butter or margarine
1½ cups **bread crumbs**
1 cup sour cream, for serving

Equipment: Work surface, knife, small bowl with cover, mixing spoon, food processor, rubber spatula, lightly floured work surface, damp kitchen towel, lightly floured rolling pin, large saucepan, slotted spoon, large heatproof platter, small saucepan, small serving bowl

1. Prepare filling: On work surface, finely chop prunes and place in small bowl. Add finely chopped walnuts and ¼ cup sugar. Stir, cover, and refrigerate.

2. Prepare dough: Put mashed potatoes in food processor, add egg, salt, ½ cup flour, and cornstarch. Pulse and process until mixture pulls away from sides of container and forms a ball, 1 to 2 minutes.

Note: While processing, turn machine off once or twice and scrape down sides of container with rubber spatula.

3. Transfer to lightly floured work surface and **knead** until smooth, 3 to 5 minutes. If dough is sticky add a little more flour. Using lightly floured rolling pin, roll dough ¼ inch thick. Using knife, cut into 2½-inch squares. Place squares slightly overlapping on work surface and cover with damp towel to prevent drying out.

4. Assemble dumplings: Place a heaping teaspoon prune filling in center of each dough square. Enclose filling in dough and shape into a ball. Repeat making dumplings, using up all the dough.

5. Fill large saucepan halfway with water, add ½ teaspoon salt, and bring to boil over high heat. Drop dumplings, a few at a time, in boiling water. When water comes back to boil, reduce heat to **simmer**, and cook for 15 to 20 minutes, or until dough is cooked. (It should taste tender and airy when done.) Using slotted spoon, transfer dumplings to large heatproof platter and keep warm.

6. Prepare topping: Melt butter in small saucepan over medium heat. Add bread crumbs, stir to coat, and heat through, 3 to 5 minutes.

To serve, spoon breadcrumb mixture over dumplings, sprinkle with remaining ½ cup sugar, and serve at once. Serve with small serving bowl of sour cream to spoon over dumplings.

Many recipes from neighboring regions have crossed into Moldova. The banquet feast might include *zulynez gribnoy* listed in the Ukrainian section(recipe page 269) and *kolbasa z kapustov* described in the Belarus section (recipe page 263), eaten along with the potato dumplings.

ARMENIA

Situated in the Transcaucasian region between the Black and Caspian Seas, Armenia is surrounded by Turkey, Iran, and the other Transcaucasian nations, Georgia and Azerbaijan. It is the smallest of the former Soviet republics.

Armenia was the first country in the world to establish Christianity as its official religion in A.D. 301. After years of Communist oppression, most citizens are openly showing loyalty to their Church in the years since independence in 1991. Almost all babies born in Armenia are baptized by the Armenian Apostolic Church. Other life-cycle events are similar to those celebrated by the Eastern Orthodox Churches. (See Eastern or Orthodox Church Life-Cycle Rituals, page xlviii.)

Bread is eaten with every meal, and special breads are baked for religious holidays. Great quantities of bread are prepared for life-cycle celebration feasts.

Churek

Armenian Flat Bread with Sesame Seeds

Yield: about 10 pieces

1 package active dry **yeast**
3 teaspoons sugar, divided
2½ cups **lukewarm** water, divided
6 cups all-purpose **flour**
½ cup melted butter or margarine
1 teaspoon salt
2 to 3 tablespoons **sesame seeds**

Equipment: Small bowl, mixing spoon, large mixing bowl, kitchen towel, lightly floured work surface, lightly floured rolling pin, nonstick baking sheet, spray bottle, oven mitts, wide metal spatula, wire cake rack, napkin-lined bread basket

1. Sprinkle yeast and 1 teaspoon sugar into ½ cup lukewarm water in a small bowl. Let stand 5 minutes and stir to dissolve yeast completely. Set the yeast mixture in a warm, draft-free place (such as an unlighted oven) for 5 to 10 minutes, or until almost doubled in volume.

2. Put flour into large mixing bowl and make well (hole) in center. Pour in yeast mixture, remaining 2 cups lukewarm water, melted butter, remaining 2 teaspoons sugar, and salt. Using a mixing spoon, beat flour into water mixture until soft, spongy dough is formed, 3 to 5 minutes. Cover with towel and set in warm, draft-free place to rise to double in bulk.

Preheat oven to 350° F.

3. Place dough on lightly floured work surface and divide into 10 equal pieces. Shape into balls and using lightly floured rolling pin, roll each ball into a disk, as thin as possible (less than ¼ inch). Place 2 or 3 disks on nonstick baking sheet. Using spray bottle filled with cold water, lightly mist each disk with water and sprinkle with sesame seeds.

4. Bake in oven for 20 to 25 minutes until the loaves are golden brown. Allow to firm up for 10 minutes before transferring to wire cake rack with wide metal spatula. Continue baking remaining loaves in batches.

To serve, place churek *in napkin-lined bread basket and spread with butter or margarine. This bread keeps well for several days, at room temperature, when wrapped in foil.*

Wheat berries are eaten to celebrate religious holidays, the harvest, and at funerals. Each country has its own combination of ingredients, such as this Armenian recipe called *hadig*.

Hadig

Wheat Berries with Pomegranate and Raisins

Yield: serves 4

2 cups water

1 cup **wheat berries**
¼ teaspoon salt
½ cup sugar
1 teaspoon **ground** cinnamon
seeds of 1 **pomegranate**
1 cup seedless raisins
¼ cup sliced almonds, for **garnish**

Equipment: Medium **heavy-based** saucepan with cover, wooden mixing spoon, strainer, medium bowl, serving bowl

Bring water to boil over high heat in medium heavy-based saucepan. Slowly stir in wheat berries and salt. Reduce heat to **simmer**, cover, and cook just until the skins begin to burst, but not until mushy, 30 to 40 minutes. Remove from heat and pour into strainer to drain. Transfer to medium bowl. Stir in sugar, cinnamon, pomegranate, and raisins.

Serve either warm or at room temperature. Spoon hadig *into a china serving bowl and smooth top. Sprinkle with almonds, for garnish. Eat as a dessert.*

GEORGIA

Mountainous Georgia is the westernmost country of the Transcaucasian region between the Black and Caspian Seas. Bounded on the west by the Black Sea, Georgia shares borders with Russia, Turkey, Armenia, and Azerbaijan.

Despite the difficult years under Soviet rule, most Georgians refused to leave their homeland, and today more than 90 percent of the Georgians in the world still live in Georgia. The Georgians are very proud of their national traditions and the traditions of the Georgian Orthodox Church. The Orthodox life-cycle events—baptisms, communions, name days, weddings, and funerals—are important family celebrations centering around a lavish feast in the home.

Ritual celebrations, both great and small, take place around the *supra* (food laden table), an important part of Georgian culture. For life-cycle celebrations, except for the most casual, a *tamada* (toastmaster) oversees the proceedings at the *supra*. The *tamada* is always a man, more often an elder who knows most of the people present. He guides the party through a series of toasts, each followed by a downing of wine. A *merikipe* (server) is selected to make sure no one is holding an empty wine glass. Wine is not simply a drink to accompany food, but it is part of the ritual—to welcome the newborn, to say farewell to the dead, and to impart good wishes to newlyweds.

Walnuts, a specialty of Armenia and Georgia, are added to everything, from soup to candied nuts. This recipe for *satsivi*, made with walnuts, is a typical meat dish served frequently at the *supra* for life-cycle and holiday feasts. ❂ ❂ ❂

SATSIVI

CHICKEN WITH SPICY WALNUT SAUCE

Yield: serves 6
4 tablespoons vegetable oil, divided
6 boneless, skinless chicken breasts
1 cup chicken broth, homemade (recipe page 106), or canned
1 onion, **finely chopped**
1 cup walnuts, finely chopped
1 cup unsweetened pomegranate juice (available at Middle East food stores)
1 cup water
1 teaspoon **ground** cinnamon
salt and pepper to taste
¼ teaspoon ground **coriander**
¼ teaspoon ground **allspice**

Equipment: Large skillet with cover, metal spatula, medium skillet, mixing spoon, slotted spoon, serving platter

1. Heat 2 tablespoons oil in large skillet over medium-high heat. Add chicken breasts and **sauté** on each side for about 5 to 7 minutes, until lightly browned. Add chicken broth and reduce heat to **simmer.** Cover and cook for 15 to 20 minutes.

2. Prepare walnut sauce: Heat remaining 2 tablespoons oil in medium skillet over medium-high heat. Add onion, stir, and sauté until soft. Stir in walnuts, pomegranate juice, water, cinnamon, salt and pepper to taste, coriander, and allspice. Stirring frequently, bring to boil. Pour walnut mixture over chicken breasts in large skillet. Cover and simmer for 20 to 25 minutes until chicken is fully cooked. Check **chicken doneness**.

3. Using slotted spoon, transfer chicken breasts to serving platter and keep warm. Continue to simmer walnut mixture in large skillet. Stirring occasionally, cook until thickened, 10 to 15 minutes. Spoon sauce over chicken.

Serve with bulgur plov *(recipe page 280) and* churek *(recipe page 272).*

Wheat berries hold a special place in Eastern European Christian life-cycle rituals. In Georgia, very sweet and chewy *korkoti* is traditionally made in celebration of a baby's first tooth.

Korkoti

Wheat Berries with Honey and Nuts

Yield: serves 4

3 cups water
1 cup **wheat berries**
1/4 teaspoon salt
1/4 cup sugar
1/4 cup honey
1/2 cup finely **ground** walnuts

Equipment: Medium **heavy-based** saucepan with cover, wooden mixing spoon, strainer, medium bowl, small serving dish

Bring water to boil over high heat in medium heavy-based saucepan. Gradually stir in wheat berries and salt. Reduce heat to **simmer**, cover, and cook for 30 to 40 minutes, or just until the skins begin to burst, but not until mushy. Remove from heat and pour into strainer to drain. Transfer to medium bowl, and while still warm, stir in the sugar, honey, and nuts.

Serve either warm or at room temperature. Korkoti *is put in a small serving dish and eaten with a spoon.*

The origin of *churchkhela*, an unusual candy made with two important products of Georgia, walnuts and grapes, is shrouded in mystery and folklore. The candy is a string of shelled walnuts that is dipped repeatedly into thickened, concentrated grape juice (*badagi*). It is often left hanging in a dry place, such as an attic or pantry, for as long as 3 years. We are speeding up the process by using grape jam. Although time-consuming, *churchkhela* is fun to make and good to eat.

Churchkhela

Grape and Walnut Candies

Note: This recipe takes over one week.

Yield: serves 3 or 4

20 shelled walnut halves
1 cup grape jam
1/2 cup cornstarch
confectioners' sugar, as needed

Equipment: Kettle at least 8-inches deep and 8 to 9-inches wide, aluminum foil, heavy-duty thread, scissors, heavy-duty sewing needle, small saucepan, wooden spoon, tongs, long handled wooden spoon or 10- to 12-inch long stick at least 1/4-inch thick

Line inside bottom of large kettle with foil.

1. String walnuts: Cut a length of thread about 14 inches long. Thread through the eye of a heavy duty sewing needle and tie a thick knot at the end. Thread through the center of shelled walnut halves, just like stringing beads or popcorn. When finished threading the length of the thread, push walnut halves tightly together in the middle of the string and tie ends together, like a necklace.

2. Put jam in small saucepan, and stirring constantly, cook over medium heat until the jam has a smooth, thick, lump-free consistency, about 3 to 5 minutes. Stir in cornstarch and simmer about 5 minutes, stirring continuously until mixture thickly coats mixing spoon. Remove from heat and allow to cool to warm, 15 to 20 minutes.

3. To coat walnuts: Hold the knotted end of the string with tongs or your fingers and dip the walnuts at the other end into the jam mixture. Using the back of a spoon, push down on the nuts to coat well.

4. To dry coated nuts: Slip the long wooden spoon handle or stick through the string and carefully pick up the necklace of coated nuts. Place the spoon handle or stick across the top of the kettle so coated nuts dangle undisturbed inside the kettle. The coated walnuts should not touch sides or bottom of the kettle allowing excess jam to drip on the foil.

5. Let nuts hang to dry over night. Repeat dipping and drying 1 or 2 more times to thicken the coating of grape jam on the nuts. Allow nuts to dry for at least a week for flavor to develop. Cover and refrigerate remaining jam mixture each time to use for repeated dipping. To use each time, reheat over medium-low heat to make jam mixture spreadable, 5 to 7 minutes.

Roll in confectioners' sugar and keep in dry, airtight container.

To serve, cut the sausage-shaped candies crosswise into 1-inch pieces. Remove and discard pieces of thread.

Georgia is famous for growing wonderful grapes, and besides the ubiquitous wine, celebrations generally include a dish or two made from grapes. *Pelamushi* is an unusual combination of two simple ingredients—cornmeal and grape juice.

Pelamushi

Grape-Flavored Cornmeal Squares

Yield: about 30 pieces

1 1/2 cups fine white **cornmeal**
3 cups frozen grape juice concentrate, thawed
2 cups water

Equipment: Food processor, rubber spatula, medium saucepan, mixing spoon, 8-inch baking pan, sharp knife, serving platter

1. Put cornmeal in food processor and process to flour consistency, 2 to 3 minutes.

Note: While processing, turn machine off once or twice and scrape down sides of container with rubber spatula.

2. Pour thawed grape juice concentrate and water into medium saucepan. Stir and bring to boil over medium-high heat. Reduce heat to **simmer**. Slowly stir in processed cornmeal and continue stirring until well mixed. Reduce heat to low, and stirring frequently to prevent sticking, cook for 15 minutes, until thickened and cornmeal is cooked. Rinse 8-inch baking pan with cold water and pour in cornmeal mixture. Smooth top with rubber spatula. Cool to room temperature.

To serve, cut into 2-inch squares or diamonds, using a knife rinsed under cold running water.

Arrange pieces on a serving platter. Eat as dessert or as snack with cup of chai *(recipe page 265).*

AZERBAIJAN

Although Azerbaijan is considered a Transcaucasian country like Georgia and Armenia, it is different is some key ways. The most important of these differences is that it is a Muslim state, and most Azerbaijanis, like neighboring Iranians, belong to the Shi'ite branch of Islam. Most of the Muslim people of the former Soviet Union belong the Sunni branch of Islam. (See Central Asia Republics, pp. 277.) Even before independence in 1991, the Muslim mosques, which had closed since the 1930s, were reopened in the mid-1980s. Today Muslim traditions are being restored, and life-cycle events are celebrated according to the Islamic tradition. (See Islam and Islamic Life-Cycle Rituals, page xlix.)

In Azerbaijan, *piti*, a lamb stew, is slow baked in a clay pot. It is a perfect dish to serve for family get-togethers and social gatherings and life-cycle celebrations, such as weddings.

Piti

Lamb Stew with Apricots and Prunes

Yield: serves 4 to 6

½ cup dried apricots, chopped
½ cup pitted prunes, chopped
1 cup warm water
6 tablespoons butter or margarine, divided
1 onion, chopped
1½ pounds lean **ground** lamb or any lean ground meat
½ pound green beans, cut into 1-inch lengths (either fresh or frozen, thawed)
½ teaspoon ground turmeric
½ teaspoon ground cinnamon
juice of ½ lemon
salt and pepper to taste
12 ounces wide egg noodles, cooked, (according to directions on package) drained, and kept warm
3 tablespoons grated Parmesan cheese
1 cup plain yogurt
2 cloves garlic, **finely chopped**

Equipment: Small bowl, **colander**, large skillet with cover, mixing spoon, buttered ovenproof medium casserole, oven mitts, electric **blender**, rubber spatula, small serving bowl with cover

Preheat oven to 350° F.

1. Put chopped apricots and prunes in small bowl and add warm water. Let stand 10 minutes to soften. Drain into colander and discard water.

2. Heat 4 tablespoons butter or margarine in large skillet over medium-high heat. Add onion, stir, and **sauté** until soft, 3 to 5 minutes. Using your hands, crumble ground meat into skillet. Stir and sauté until meat looses pink color, 5 to 7 minutes. Add apricot mixture, green beans, turmeric, and cinnamon. Stir, reduce heat to **simmer**, and cover. Stirring frequently, cook until flavors are blended, 10 to 12 minutes. Remove from heat and stir in lemon juice and salt and pepper to taste.

3. Toss cooked noodles with remaining 2 tablespoons butter or margarine. Transfer to buttered medium casserole and spread evenly. Spread meat mixture over noodles and sprinkle with Parmesan cheese.

4. Bake in oven until meat mixture is bubbly and top is golden, 30 to 35 minutes.

5. Prepare sauce: **Blend** yogurt and garlic in electric blender until smooth. Using rubber spatula, scrape down sides of container once or twice during blending. Transfer to small serving bowl.

Serve with side dish of room temperature garlic sauce *to spoon over each portion.*

CENTRAL ASIAN REPUBLICS

The majority of people living in the southern and southeastern regions of the former USSR are Muslims. Because of their cultural similarities and shared history, Kazakhstan, Uzbekistan, Tajikistan, Kyrgyzstan, and Turkmenistan are grouped together as the Central Asian Republics. In these countries, life-cycle rituals and religious observances are followed according to Islamic law. (See Islam and Islamic Life-Cycle Rituals, page xlix.)

Traditional cooking includes stews and soups—ways of making a little meat go a long way. Meat is precious and reserved for special occasions. When roast chicken or mutton is on the table, it is a good bet it is for a celebration. ۞ ۞ ۞

KAZAKHSTAN

Located at the crossroads of Europe and Asia, Kazakhstan is the second largest state of the former Soviet Union after Russia. It extends from the Caspian Sea in the west to China in the east, and is bordered on the north by Russia and shares its southern border with all of the other Central Asian states, except Tajikistan.

More than a hundred different national groups make their home in Kazakhstan; even though the largest group is the Kazakhs, European Slavs actually outnumber Kazakhs if counted together. These demographics are changing rapidly, however, because Europeans have been leaving Kazakhstan and because the Kazakhs have a much higher birthrate. Once a nomadic people, the Kazakhs were forced, under Communism, to settle in collective state run farms or small villages. Historically, the Kazakhs have been Muslim and have returned to Muslim practices, including life-cycle rituals, since independence in 1991. (See Islam and Islamic Life-Cycle Rituals, page xlix.)

Because of the long Russian presence, Kazakhs combine Russian cooking with local foods, especially in urban areas. For a wedding celebration, for example, they may have the *zakouska* table (see page 259) with *baklazhannaya ikra* (recipe page 261), sliced onions sprinkled with vinegar and sugar, and boiled mushrooms with yogurt. The feast might also include *kartofel'naya zapekanka* (recipe page 261) and *stolichnyi salat* (recipe page 259). Large loaves of unleavened bread, similar to *chapatis* (recipe page 285), are eaten along with Russian black bread. Bread is torn into chunks and eaten with each mouthful of food.

Nothing is better for the celebration feast than *plov* (rice pilaf), prepared with mutton, beef, or *kazy* (horse meat) and enriched with fruits and nuts. When the family can afford it, a whole lamb is slaughtered and roasted over an open spit for the wedding feast. The lamb is accompanied by side dishes of noodles and smoked sausages made of *kazy*, a Kazakh specialty. *Alma-Ata Plov* (a pilaf) is prepared when family and friends gather for the circumcision celebration. ۞ ۞ ۞

Alma-Ata Plov

Pilaf with Meat and Fruit

Yield: serves 6

6 tablespoons vegetable oil, more or less as needed
1 pound lean lamb or beef, **cubed**
2 onions, thinly sliced
2 carrots, **trimmed** and **julienned**
10 or 12 dried apricots, **coarsely chopped**
½ cup seedless raisins
1 cooking apple, cored and coarsely chopped
2 cups long-grain rice
4 cups chicken broth, homemade (recipe page 106), or canned
salt and pepper to taste
½ cup slivered almonds, **blanched** and **roasted**

Equipment: Large skillet, mixing spoon, slotted spoon, large ovenproof casserole with cover, oven mitts, medium saucepan

Preheat oven to 350° F.

1. Heat 2 tablespoons oil in large skillet over medium-high heat. Add meat cubes and **sauté**, stirring constantly, for 6 to 8 minutes, or until well browned. Add remaining 2 tablespoons oil if necessary to prevent sticking. Using slotted spoon, transfer meat to large ovenproof casserole.

2. Heat 2 tablespoons oil in same large skillet over medium-high heat. Add onions and sauté until soft, 3 to 5 minutes. Add carrots, apricots, raisins, apple, and rice. Stir to coat rice with oil, and cook for 2 minutes. Add 1 tablespoon oil, if necessary. Pour rice mixture over meat in casserole.

3. Pour chicken broth into medium saucepan and bring to boil over high heat. Pour hot broth over rice mixture in casserole and add salt and pepper to taste.

4. Bake in oven, covered, for 40 to 50 minutes, or until rice is tender. Using oven mitts, carefully uncover casserole and taste for doneness. Return to oven to cook uncovered for 10 to 15 minutes to brown top. Sprinkle roasted almonds over the top.

Serve alma-ata plov *from the casserole with* churek *(recipe page 272) for sopping.*

Another popular Kazakh dish is meat pancakes served with *kumys* (mare's milk yogurt) to spoon over the cakes. Commercial yogurt can be used.

Kartophelnye Piroshki z Baraninoy

Lamb and Potato Cakes

Yield: serves 6 to 8

6 potatoes, peeled and **grated**
1 onion, peeled and grated
3 eggs
1 pound lean **ground** lamb or beef
3 tablespoons all-purpose flour
salt and pepper to taste
4 to 6 tablespoons vegetable oil, as needed
1 cup yogurt or sour cream, for serving

Equipment: **Colander**, large mixing bowl, mixing spoon, wax paper, work surface, baking sheet, paper towels, large skillet, wide metal spatula, baking pan, oven mitts

1. Put grated potatoes in colander, rinse, and drain. Using your hands, squeeze out as much liquid as possible and transfer to large mixing bowl. Add grated onion, eggs, lamb or beef, and flour. Using your hands, mix together until well blended. Add salt and pepper to taste. Roll ½ cup meat mixture between your hands into a ball. Repeat making balls using all the meat mixture. Place on wax-paper-covered work surface.

Preheat oven to 250° F.

2. Prepare to pan fry: Cover baking sheet with several layers of paper towels. Heat 2 tablespoons oil in large skillet over medium heat. Add 3 or 4 meatballs at a time, do not crowd pan. Using back of spatula, flatten each ball into a pancake. Fry on each side 5 to 7 minutes, until browned. Remove with slotted spatula and place on paper towels to drain. Continue making pancakes, a few at a time. Transfer to baking pan and slightly overlap each cake. Keep in warm oven until finished frying all cakes.

Serve warm with side dish of yogurt or sour cream to spoon over the pancakes.

UZBEKISTAN

Located right in the middle of the Central Asia region, Uzbekistan is bordered by Kazakhstan on the north and Turkmenistan on the south. It also shares borders with Afghanistan, Tajikistan, and Kyrgyzstan. As with the other Central Asian countries, the Uzbeks are primarily Muslims, and while religion was officially discouraged during the Soviet period, independence has left Uzbeks to celebrate life-style events according to Islamic traditions. (See Islam and Islamic Life-Cycle Rituals, page xlix.)

The fertile region surrounding Uzbekistan is famous for fruit and nut orchards. Dried fruit and nuts are used in everything from soups to candy. This easy-to-make tart is one of the many desserts served for religious holidays, family gatherings, and life-cycle celebrations.

Tort iz Sushyonykh Fruktov i Orekhov

Dried Fruit and Nut Tart

Yield: serves 10 to 12

tart pastry (recipe follows)
1 cup apple juice, divided
1 cup honey, divided
18 dried apricots or peaches, or combination
1 teaspoon grated orange rind
3 eggs
1 teaspoon vanilla extract
2 tablespoons melted butter
1 cup whole almonds
1 cup chopped walnuts
2 cups whipped cream or whipped topping, for **garnish**
cinnamon sugar, to taste, for garnish

Equipment: Small saucepan, wooden mixing spoon, medium mixing bowl, whisk, rubber spatula, lightly greased 10-inch springform pan, oven mitts, knife

1. Prepare *tart pastry* (recipe follows) and refrigerate.

2. Prepare fruit: Pour ½ cup apple juice and ½ cup honey into small saucepan. Stir and bring to boil over medium-high heat. Add dried fruit and orange rind and reduce heat to low. Cook for 20 to 25 minutes, stirring frequently, until fruit is soft and puffed. Remove from heat and cool to room temperature.

3. Prepare topping: Put eggs in medium mixing bowl and using a whisk beat in the remaining ½ cup apple juice, ½ cup honey, vanilla, and melted butter. Using rubber spatula, **fold in** whole almonds, chopped walnuts, and dried fruit mixture.

Preheat oven to 350° F.

4. Assemble: Unwrap pastry and place in lightly greased 10-inch springform pan. Using your hand, press pastry evenly over bottom and about ¾ inch up sides of pan. Spread egg mixture evenly over pastry.

5. Bake in oven 40 to 50 minutes, or until crust is golden brown. Cool to room temperature before removing sides of springform pan.

To serve, cut into wedges and serve with dollop of whipped cream or whipped topping and sprinkle with cinnamon sugar.

Tart Pastry

1 1/4 cups all-purpose flour
1/4 cup sugar
1/2 cup cold unsalted butter, cut into small pieces
1/4 teaspoon salt
1 **egg yolk**

Equipment: Food processor, lightly floured work surface, plastic wrap

1. Prepare crust: Put flour, sugar, butter, and salt in bowl of food processor. Process until mixture resembles bread crumbs. Drop egg yolk through feed tube, and process until pastry dough pulls away from sides of container and forms ball, about 30 seconds. Remove from container and transfer to lightly floured work surface.

Note: While processing, turn machine off once or twice and scrape down sides of container with rubber spatula.

2. Form pastry dough into ball and press to about 1/2-inch flat. Wrap in plastic wrap and refrigerate for 30 minutes.

Continue: Tort iz sushyonykh fruktov i orekhov*(recipe precedes)*.

TAJIKISTAN

Sometimes referred to as the "Rooftop of the World" because of its rugged mountainous terrain, Tajikistan is the southernmost of the Central Asian countries. It is the poorest and most underdeveloped of the former Soviet republics. The difficult terrain and harsh weather, along with constant threats of earthquakes make this a difficult place to live.

Despite the years of official atheism under the Soviet regime, virtually all Tajiks are Muslims and celebrate life-cycle events according to Islamic traditions, which have been revived since independence in 1991. (See Islam and Islamic Life-Cycle Rituals, pp. xlix.)

Pilafs, such as the recipe for *bulgur plov* below, are popular throughout the Central Asian republics and could accompany the main dish in life-cycle and other feasts.

Bulgur Plov

Bulgur Pilaf

Yield: serves 4 to 6

2 tablespoons butter or margarine
1 onion, chopped
1 1/4 cups **bulgur** (available at most supermarkets and health food stores)
1 3/4 cups water or chicken broth, homemade (recipe page 106), or canned
salt to taste

Equipment: Medium saucepan with cover, mixing spoon, kitchen towel

1. In medium saucepan, melt butter or margarine over medium-high heat. Add onion, stir, and **sauté** until soft, 3 to 5 minutes. Add bulgur, and stirring constantly, cook for 3 minutes. Add water, chicken broth, and salt to taste. Bring to boil and stir. Reduce heat to **simmer**, cover, and cook, stirring occasionally, until bulgur is tender, 20 to 25 minutes.

2. Remove from heat, remove cover, and stretch a towel over the pan. Replace cover over the towel and set aside for 10 to 15 minutes until serving time. (The towel absorbs moisture from the steam and keeps it from dropping into the bulgur pilaf.)

Serve plov *with* piti *(recipe page 276)*, salat *(recipe page 281), and* chapatis *(recipe page 285)*.

KYRGYZSTAN

Kyrgyzstan is a highly mountainous country located in the eastern part of Central Asia. It is bordered by China on the east and shares borders with Tajikistan, Uzbekistan, and Kazakhstan.

Like other Central Asian Republics, the majority of people living in Kyrgyzstan are Muslim. (See Islam and Islamic Life-Cycle Rituals, page xlix.) Under Communism religious practices were officially discouraged. Since gaining independence in 1991 the Kyrgyz Muslims have been free to observe life-cycle customs of Islam. In addition to the Muslim population, Kyrgyzstan still has a large Russian minority, particularly in the cities, and these Russians celebrate life-cycle rituals of the Russian Orthodox Church. (See Eastern or Orthodox Church Life-Cycle Rituals, page xlviii.)

The food of Kyrgyzstan is simple and hearty, similar to neighboring countries. Rice, noodles, or potatoes and both yeast and flat breads are eaten at almost every meal. For special occasions and life-cycle feasts, mutton, beef, or goat are added to the pot. Pigs are raised in the region, but the pork is only eaten by the Christian or Chinese foreigners who live in the country. Other dishes served at a celebration feast are *kartophelnye piroshki z baraninoy* (recipe page 278), *baklazhannaya ikra* (recipe page 261), and *salat* (recipe follows), assorted cheeses, and breads.

In Muslim countries, salads are not eaten as a separate course but rather all food is placed on the table and eaten at the same time.

SALAT

TOMATO, CUCUMBER, AND YOGURT SALAD

Yield: serves 4

2 large tomatoes, sliced ¼ inch thick
2 small cucumbers, thinly sliced diagonally
1 red onion, thinly sliced
¼ cup virgin olive oil
salt and pepper to taste
¾ cup plain yogurt

Equipment: Medium serving platter, spoon, plastic food wrap

1. Arrange tomato and cucumber slices alternately, slightly overlapping on medium serving platter. Separate onions into rings and spread over top. Sprinkle with oil and salt and pepper. Cover with plastic wrap and let stand at room temperature for about 2 hours for flavors to develop.

2. Prepare to serve: Uncover and spoon dollops of yogurt over the vegetables.

Serve at room temperature as a salad.

Tea is the favorite beverage in Kyrgyzstan, especially when it is made with rhubarb as in this recipe.

CHAI IZ REVENYA

RHUBARB TEA

Yield: serves 4 to 6

2 cups frozen rhubarb, thawed and chopped, or 2 cups fresh rhubarb, **trimmed** and chopped
6 cups water
sugar to taste
1 lemon, cut in 4 or 6 wedges
4 or 6 fresh mint leaves, for **garnish**

Equipment: Medium saucepan, mixing spoon, strainer, wide-mouth pitcher, spoon, beverage glasses

1. Put rhubarb and water into medium saucepan and bring to boil over medium-high heat. Reduce heat to **simmer** and cover. Stirring occasionally, cook until rhubarb is mushy and fully cooked, 30 to 40 minutes.

2. Strain rhubarb liquid into wide-mouthed pitcher. Using back of spoon, press on residue in strainer to release all liquid. While liquid is hot, stir in sugar to taste. Cool to room temperature and refrigerate. Discard rhubarb residue or cover and refrigerate for another use.

To serve, pour rhubarb liquid over ice cubes in glasses, and garnish with wedge of lemon and sprig of mint.

TURKMENISTAN

Located in the southwestern part of Central Asia, Turkmenistan is bordered on the south by Iran and Afghanistan. The Caspian Sea forms the western border, and Kazakhstan and Uzbekistan are to the north. It is a dry country dominated by the Kara Kum Desert, one of the largest sand deserts in the world.

Most Turkmen are Sunni Muslims who speak various dialects of the Turkmen language. Since the break-up of the Soviet empire, the Turmen are free to follow the customs of Islam, including celebrating life-cycle events.

Central Asians are fond of very sweet pastries and candies, usually made with nuts. Sweet candies are reserved for special occasions, such as *Lailat al-Qadr*, the "Night of Power," a celebration for children who have learned all 114 chapters of the Koran, the Islamic holy book, and when boys are circumcised. (See Islam and Islamic Life-Cycle Rituals, page xlix.)

Sladkoye Pyechenye Iz Gryetskikh Orekhov

Walnut Brittle

Yield: serves 6

1 cup sugar
1 teaspoon **ground** cinnamon
1 cup walnuts, **coarsely chopped**

Equipment: Baking sheet, aluminum foil, medium skillet, wooden mixing spoon, knife, candy dish

1. Cover baking sheet with foil and using your hand, coat with butter. Set aside.

2. Melt sugar in medium skillet over medium heat. When sugar turns golden brown, reduce heat to low. Stir in cinnamon and nuts and cook about 2 minutes.

3. Transfer to foil covered baking sheet and spread out to cool to room temperature. When cool enough to handle, break or cut with knife into bite-size pieces.

To serve, arrange pieces in a candy dish. Store in airtight container.

ASIA

Asia is a vast region of the world where many of the major religions of the modern world evolved. (See Religious Life-Cycle Rituals and Customs, page xl.)From birth through death, most Asian cultures continue rituals and customs that have remained unchanged for centuries. Today, however, signs of change between ancient and modern ways appear everywhere. As the Asian nations and territories move into the future, they are plagued with such problems as scarce resources and exploding population growth.

In most Asian countries, rice is a symbol of life and fertility, and it figures strongly in many rituals. (The Western ritual of throwing rice at newlyweds, for example, is inherited from India). Special rituals and prayers are said at the time rice is planted and again when it is harvested. In China it is bad luck to overturn a bowl of rice, and to have a bad experience might be referred to as "breaking one's rice bowl." In some Asian countries, rice is placed on the family altar and dedicated to the ancestors as a symbol of thanksgiving for a fruitful previous year and a desire for a successful coming year.

INDIAN SUBCONTINENT

India, Pakistan, Afghanistan, Bangladesh, Sri Lanka, Nepal, and Bhutan are all countries within the region known as the Indian subcontinent. Hinduism is the principal religion in India, while the majority of people living in Pakistan, Afghanistan, and Bangladesh are Muslims. Sri Lanka contains a mix of the four major religions: Hinduism, Buddhism, Islam, and Christianity. The majority of people living in the remote country of Bhutan are Buddhist, and in Nepal, Hindu.

There are great diversities among the people living in this is part of the world, but they have a few food-related things in common, for instance, *ghee* (recipe follows), unleavened breads, and the finger-and-bread-scoop method of eating.

Hindus often use *ghee* in religious rituals. *Ghee* keeps well indefinitely, even when not refrigerated. ۞ ۞ ۞

GHEE

CLARIFIED BUTTER

Yield: about 1 cup

1 pound unsalted butter or margarine

Equipment: Small saucepan, large spoon or bulb baster, small bowl with cover

1. In small saucepan, melt butter or margarine over very low heat, undisturbed, for 45 to 50 minutes, until it separates; solids on the bottom and clear oil (*ghee*) on the top. Do not let it brown.

2. The *ghee* on the top can be carefully spooned off or removed with a bulb baster into a small bowl. Either discard solids or cover and refrigerate for another use. Allow *ghee* to cool to room temperature, cover, and refrigerate.

Serve ghee *over vegetables, spread on bread, or use in cooking instead of butter.*

Chapatis, *parathas*, *puris*, *phulkas* (recipes follow in this section), or *poppadums* (recipe page 307) are the popular breads of the region. They are used to scoop up food, making them indispensable to a meal. *Chapatis* are made on a *tawa*, a slightly concave, thin metal disc, 8 to 9 inches in diameter. The *tawa* is placed over an open fire.

CHAPATIS

INDIAN BREAD

Yield: 9 to 10 pieces

2 cups **atta** (**chapati flour**) (available at Indian and Middle Eastern food stores and some health food stores) or fine **ground** whole wheat flour
1 teaspoon salt
3 tablespoons *ghee*, homemade (recipe this page or available in a jar at Indian and Middle Eastern food stores) or vegetable oil
lukewarm water, as needed

Equipment: Work surface, kitchen towel, rolling pin, nonstick griddle, wide metal spatula, tongs, oven mitts

1. Mix flour and salt on work surface. Make a well (hole) in the center and add *ghee* or oil. Using your fingers, mix until mixture resembles crumbs. Add ½ cup water, a little at a time, to make a pliable dough. Add more water, 1 tablespoon at a time, as needed. **Knead** the dough thoroughly for 8 to 10 minutes. Cover with a damp towel and let rest for 2 hours.

2. Divide dough into 9 or 10 pieces and roll them into balls. On floured work surface, roll out the balls, using a rolling pin, to a very thin disk about 8 to 9 inches across. Stack the completed disks, slightly overlapping on the work surface. Keep them covered with the damp towel.

3. Heat the griddle over medium heat. Place 1or 2 disks on the griddle and grill for 2 or 3 minutes. Using the metal spatula, press down lightly until brown spots appear on the bottom side. Turn over and brown the other side.

4. Just before serving, place the *chapatis* under the oven broiler or in a toaster oven for about 1 minute, until they puff up in patches. Remove hot *chapatis* from oven with tongs. For safety wear oven mitts.

Serve chapatis *as soon as they are cooked.*

Parathas

Pan Fried Breads

Yield: 4 to 5 pieces
chapatis dough, (recipe precedes)
ghee, as needed, homemade (recipe p. 285 or available in a jar at Indian and Middle Eastern food stores) or vegetable oil, as needed

Equipment: Lightly floured work surface, knife, rolling pin, **pastry brush**, kitchen towel, large skillet, metal spatula, aluminum foil

1. After *chapatis* dough has rested for 2 hours (see *chapatis* step 1, preceding recipe), roll the dough into a rope about 1 inch in diameter on lightly floured work surface. Cut the rope into 1-inch lengths. Using your hand or a rolling pin, flatten each into a 2- to 3-inch disk.

2. Using pastry brush, brush *ghee* or oil on one side of each disk and stack them, 4 or 5 high. Do not brush oil on the top disk of each stack, it should be plain.

3. Place one stack of disks on a lightly floured work surface and using a rolling pin, flatten the stack out and roll it to 9 to 10 inches in diameter. Repeat rolling out the other stacks. Place them, slightly overlapping on work surface and cover with a damp towel until ready to fry.

4. To fry: Heat 1 tablespoon of *ghee* or oil in a large skillet over medium heat and fry each bread for 2 minutes. Do not let them brown or they will be tough and hard. Turn and fry on the other side, turn again and fry 1 minute longer. All the *ghee* or oil will be absorbed and the breads should be crisp and flaky. Wrap the *parathas* in foil to keep warm, while frying the remaining breads.

Serve while still warm for the best flavor.

Puris

Deep Fried Breads

CAUTION: HOT OIL USED

Yield: 9 to 10 pieces
chapatis dough, (recipe p. 285)
vegetable oil, as needed for deep frying

Equipment: Lightly floured work surface, rolling pin, towel, paper towels, baking sheet, **deep fryer** or large saucepan, deep-fryer **thermometer** or wooden spoon, slotted metal spatula or metal tongs, aluminum foil

1.After *chapatis* dough has rested for 2 hours (see *chapatis* recipe, step: 1, page 285), continue: Divide dough into 8 or 9 pieces. On lightly floured work surface, roll dough into 8- to 9-inch disks, using a rolling pin. Cover with damp towel.

2. Prepare to deep fry: ADULT SUPERVISION REQUIRED. Have ready several layers of paper towels on a baking sheet. Fill deep fryer with oil according to manufacturer's directions or fill a large saucepan with about 3 inches of vegetable oil. Heat oil to reach 375° F on deep-fryer thermometer or place the handle of a wooden spoon

in the oil, if small bubbles appear around the surface, the oil is ready for frying.

3. Fry disks, one at a time: Carefully slip one disk into oil and using the metal spatula or metal tongs, press down to keep it submerged for about 30 seconds, or until puffy. When golden brown, turn over and fry second side, 1 to 2 minutes each side. Remove and place on paper towels to drain. Wrap *puris* in foil to keep warm while frying the remaining disks.

Serve at once while still crisp and warm.

Most people throughout the Indian subcontinent have small 5-inch *tawas* for cooking *Phulkas*.

Phulkas

Small Flatbreads

Yield: 16 to 18 pieces
chapatis dough, (recipe page 285)

Equipment: Lightly floured work surface, rolling pin, kitchen towel, nonstick griddle, metal spatula, oven mitts, aluminum foil

1. After *chapatis* dough has rested for 2 hours (see *chapatis* recipe, step 1, page 285), divide the dough into 16 to 18 pieces and roll into balls. On lightly floured work surface, using a rolling pin, roll the balls into very thin disks about 5 inches across. Stack the completed disks, slightly overlapping, on the work surface. Keep covered with the damp towel.

2. Heat the griddle over medium heat and grill the disks in batches. Using a metal spatula, press down lightly until brown spots appear on the bottom side and cook 2 to 3 minutes. Turn over and brown the other side, 2 to 3 minutes.

3. Just before serving, place the *phulkas*, a few at a time, under the oven broiler or in a toaster oven for about 1 minute, until they puff up. Wrap in foil to keep warm while heating the remaining breads.

Serve phulkas *as soon as they are cooked.*

AFGHANISTAN

Afghanistan is a mountainous country that is split from east to west by the Hindu Kush mountain range, which has peaks as high as 24,000 feet. It is bordered on the north by Turkmenistan, Tajikstan, and Uzbekistan; on the northeast by China; on the south and east by Pakistan; and on the west by Iran.

Afghanistan's population, consisting of hundreds of different ethnic groups, has one common bond: the Islamic religion. (See Islam and Islamic Life-Cycle Rituals, page xlix). Ninety-nine percent of Afghans are Muslims, with two-thirds of the country is controlled by Islamic fundamentalists known as the Taliban.

Family structure is often considered the backbone of Afghan society, and it is the custom, among both villagers and nomads, for several generations to live together. The head of the household is the oldest man, or patriarch. In the villages, families generally live in mud-brick houses or in a walled compound containing several such houses. The same family structure is common among the nomads, except that black wool tents replace the mud-brick structures.

In Afghanistan, as in other Islamic countries, the birth of a son is celebrated with festivities. An important event in a young boy's life is his circumcision, which takes place between the ages of five and 10. A feast is part of the circumcision celebration.

In Afghanistan, men and women attending a wedding celebrate in separate quarters or even different locations. In southeastern Afghanistan, the *pashai* (farmers) men often perform a traditional wedding dance, accompanied by musicians playing the *zuma* (oboe) and the *dûl* (double-headed drum), ancient instruments unique to the region. A whole lamb or two might be roasted for the wedding feast, or the male guests might be served *kebabs* (recipe page 83). Everything is put on the table at one time, including *maushauwa* (recipe page 289), a stew-like soup. Vegetable dishes are important at every meal. Bowls of *chaka* (recipe page 289) are set out to drizzle in soup, smear on bread, or pour over vegetables.

Great quantities of bread are usually eaten at each meal. Afghan *naan* is famous, and while the small breads (this recipe) are usually made at home, large breads, 16–18 inches long, are made in bakeries. ۞ ۞ ۞

Naan

Afghan Teardrop-shaped Bread

Yield: makes 6

- 4 cups all-purpose flour
- ½ teaspoon salt
- 1 tablespoon baking powder
- ¼ teaspoon baking soda
- 1 teaspoon sugar
- 2 eggs
- 1 cup milk

Equipment: Large mixing bowl, mixing spoon, lightly floured work surface, 2 nonstick baking sheets, oven mitts, heatproof surface

1. Put flour, salt, baking powder, baking soda, and sugar in large mixing bowl. Stir with a mixing spoon (or use your fingers) until well mixed. Make a well (hole) in the center of the mixture and drop in the eggs, stirring them into the flour. Slowly stir in the milk and stir constantly until all the ingredients are well combined.

2. Transfer the dough to a lightly floured work surface. Sprinkle flour on your hands and the work surface. **Knead** the dough for about 10 minutes or until it is smooth and can be gathered in a soft ball; sprinkle more flour on your hands and the work surface as needed from time to time.

3. Lightly grease the large mixing bowl and place the ball of dough inside, turning the ball over to coat all sides. Cover the bowl with plastic wrap and let the dough rest in a warm, draft-free place for about 3 hours.

Preheat oven to 450° F.

Put 2 nonstick baking sheets into the oven to get them hot.

4. Prepare for baking: Divide the dough into 6 equal portions. Lightly oil or butter your hands. Place one portion of dough on the lightly floured work surface. Using your hand, flatten it into a teardrop shape, about 6 inches long by 3½ inches wide at the base and tapered at the top. Repeat making the remaining portions of dough.

5. Using oven mitts, carefully remove the preheated baking sheets from the oven and place on a heatproof surface. Place the breads side by side on the pans and bake them in the oven for 6 minutes, until they are firm to the touch.

6. Remove from the oven. Change oven temperature to broiler heat. Place the pans, one at a time, on the top rack under the broiler to lightly brown the breads, 2 to 3 minutes.

Serve the breads hot or at room temperature.

At an Afghan feast, all the food is set out and eaten at the same time; there are no separate courses. The food is put out on low trays, and everyone sits around on the beautiful carpets that the Afghan craftsmen are famous for. Tea is the favorite drink.

If Afghanistan has a national dish it is probably *chaka*, which is spread over everything they eat. A bowl of *chaka* is usually set out on the table.

Chaka

Afghan Yogurt Sauce

Yield: about 1 cup
1 cup plain yogurt
3 cloves garlic, **finely chopped**
2 tablespoons finely chopped fresh mint, divided
salt to taste

Equipment: Small bowl, mixing spoon

Put yogurt into small bowl. Add garlic, 1 tablespoon chopped mint, and salt to taste. Stir to mix. Cover and refrigerate. Sprinkle the remaining 1 tablespoon of chopped mint on top.

To serve, place the bowl on the table. Each person can either add a dollop to their soup, use as a sauce for meat or fish dishes, or serve as a dip for fresh vegetables.

Meat is expensive and it is often necessary to make a little go a long way, such as adding tiny meatballs to soup as in this recipe.

Maushauwa

Meatball Soup

Yield: serves 6 to 8
½ cup lentils
½ cup green or yellow split peas
¼ cup long-grain rice
8¼ cups water, divided
1 (14-ounce) can red kidney beans
8 ounces lean **ground** beef or lamb
1½ teaspoons ground cinnamon
½ teaspoon ground red pepper, more or less to taste
salt and black pepper, to taste
½ cup **bread crumbs**
2 tablespoons vegetable oil
1 onion, **finely chopped**
1 (14 ounce) can stewed tomato pieces
1 to 2 cups *chaka* (recipe precedes), for serving
¼ cup chopped fresh mint leaves, or 1 tablespoon dried mint, for serving
salt to taste

Equipment: Large saucepan with cover, mixing spoon, baking sheet, wax paper, large mixing bowl, large skillet, metal spatula

1. Put lentils and split peas in large saucepan and cover with 6 cups water. Bring to a boil over high heat. Stir, reduce heat to **simmer**, cover, and cook for 10 minutes. Add rice and continue cooking 15 to 20 minutes longer, or until lentils, peas, and rice are tender. Set aside.

2. Prepare meatballs: Cover baking sheet with waxed paper. Put meat in large mixing bowl, add cinnamon, ½ teaspoon ground red pepper (more or less to taste), bread crumbs, ¼ cup water, and salt and black pepper to taste. Using your hands, mix well. Pinch off about 1 tablespoon meat mixture and roll between your hands into a walnut-size ball. Continue making balls, using all of the mixture, and place side by side on wax paper.

3. Prepare sauce: Heat the oil in a large skillet over medium-high heat. Add chopped onions, stirring constantly, and **sauté** until soft, 2 to 3 minutes. Add meatballs and fry in batches if necessary. Cook until firm and browned on all sides, 3 to 5 minutes. Use metal spatula to turn meatballs. When all of the meatballs have been cooked, place all of them back into the skillet, adding stewed tomatoes and remaining 2 cups water. Gently stir, bring to boil, reduce heat to simmer, cover, and cook for 10 minutes.

To serve, ladle the hot soup into 6 or 8 bowls and add an equal number of meatballs with the sauce to each. Place a bowl of chaka *and a small bowl of chopped fresh mint on the table. To eat, each person spoons 1 or 2 tablespoons of* chaka *over their soup and sprinkles lightly with mint.*

As in other Indian subcontinent countries, sweets play an important role in Afghan life-cycle celebrations. This easy-to-make *halvah* is popular in most Muslim and Hindu countries.

Sesame Halvah

Sesame Candy

Yield: about 24 pieces

4 cups **sesame seeds**
2 cups **bulgur** (available at most supermarkets and health food stores)
3 cups water
1 tablespoon vanilla extract
¾ cup sorghum molasses (available at most supermarkets and health food stores)

Equipment: Strainer, large skillet, wooden mixing spoon, electric blender or food processor, greased 12- x 16-inch baking pan, oven mitts, knife

1. Put sesame seeds in strainer and rinse under cold running water. Drain well and transfer to large nonstick skillet. Dry roast the sesame seeds over medium-high heat. Shake the pan and stir with a wooden mixing spoon until the seeds turn tan in color and begin to pop. Remove at once from the heat.

2. Place seeds in blender or food processor. Grind the seeds to a fine texture, then transfer to large mixing bowl. Place bulgur in the blender or food processor and grind until bulgur resembles coarse flour. Add bulgur to the **ground** sesame seeds. Add water, vanilla, and sorghum and stir with a wooden spoon until well mixed. Pour sesame batter into baking pan and smooth out to cover bottom of pan.

Preheat oven to 375° F.

3. Bake in oven for 25 to 30 minutes or until sides are nicely browned. Remove from oven using oven mitts. Using a knife, cut into 24 rectangular pieces by equally dividing 4 cuts lengthwise and 6 cuts crosswise. Cool to room temperature.

To serve, place pieces of halvah *on a serving plate and set out with other sweets for guests to eat at a life-cycle celebration.*

PAKISTAN

Pakistan, located between Afghanistan and India, consists of four regions containing not only differences in climate and terrain, but in lifestyle, language, and dress. Pakistani peoples are identified by their region; for instance, those living in the Baluchistan region are known as Balochi and those in the Sindh region are known as Sindhi. But despite many regional differences, the majority of the Pakistani population have a strong unifying sense of being Pakistani. Most Pakistanis are Muslim, but a small portion of the population is Hindu.

After centuries of living in close proximity, the Hindus and Muslims of Pakistan have adopted many of each others' rites and customs. Muslim Pakistanis, for instance, have adopted the dowry system, the shaving off of a newborn's hair, and burning incense at holy places, while many Hindu brides perform the Muslim *mehndi* (henna) ceremony.

The birth of a male heir is generally a happy event. The father rushes off to buy candy, packed in colorful boxes, which he distributes to relatives and friends to announce the birth. In return for receiving the *luddus*, family and friends give money to the child. Also a favorite infant gift is a sacred charm (*ta'weez*), given to protect the child against all evil.

Sweets, such as *badam pistaz barfi* (recipe p. 299), hold an important place in life-cycle rituals. They can be given as an offering to the gods and goddesses by the Hindus, or as a gesture of goodwill and friendship. The art of making candies is a family business passed down from one generation to the next. Every village, no matter how small, will have a *halwai* (a sweetmeat seller).

In rural areas, by tradition, circumcisions take place when the boy is between the ages of two and five. It is usually done by the local barber, who also prepares the feast following the circumcision (the barber prepares feasts for other life-cycle occasions as well). The most important life-cycle event for Pakistani Muslim boys is the circumcision between the ages of eight and 12. Those in urban areas are likely to arrange a party at home, while in the countryside the whole village attends. The child, dressed in fancy clothes specially made for this occasion, receives small gifts of money from the guests. In some rural communities, such as among the Balochi farmers, the father, escorted by a couple of drummers, assorted musicians, neighbors, and friends, carries his infant son in a procession to show him off.

The extended family, with many relatives living together or nearby, is a source of strength for most Pakistani, and most seldom marry outside their clan. It is common and acceptable among Muslim families in Pakistan for first cousins or even an uncle and a niece to marry. Marriage is considered more of a bond between families than a personal undertaking, and it is not unusual for families to arrange marriages for their yet-to-be-born children. Quite often the couple to be married meet for the first time on their wedding day; however, in urban areas today, once an engagement is formally announced, the couple may date, usually accompanied by a chaperone.

According to tradition, the bride's family is expected to pay for the largest and most expensive wedding feast they can afford. Marriage ceremonies often last for three days, during which time the father of the bride must feed and accommodate hundreds of guests. He not only buys the wedding clothes for the groom and the groom's parents and siblings, but is expected to give expensive gifts of clothing and jewelry to senior in-laws.

In Pakistan, most of the ceremonies associated with a marriage are not Muslim, but traditional to the Indian subcontinent. In a traditional celebration, the bride remains in seclusion for two weeks before the wedding, while her family and friends prepare for the big event. The formal coming together of the families unfolds in two stages. The first day, the bride remains home while her family visits the groom's house; the next day, the groom remains home while his family visits the bride's house where the *mehndi* ceremony takes place. In the *mehndi*, a symbolic expression of joy, the groom's sister or mother applies henna to the hands and feet of the bride-to-be.

A few days before the wedding celebration, the legal aspects of the marriage, such as signing dowry documents, takes place in a Muslim civil ceremony (*nikah*). The wedding (*shadi*) is a lavish celebration with invited guests, great quantities of food, traditional dancers, and musical entertainment. In Pakistan, popular music known as *qaw-wali* is often played at weddings. The newlyweds remain formally seated throughout the festivities, and then leave to eat in a secluded area apart from the guests. At some point during the festivities the couple departs the wedding reception for the groom's house.

A day or two after the wedding, the groom's parents hold the *walima*, a reception honoring the married couple. The seated bride and groom greet throngs who come to pay their respects and partake in a lavish feast. In rural villages, the barber traditionally prepares the *walima* feast.

The height of Pakistani hospitality is to offer a fine *paan* to guests after dinner. For weddings, hundreds of *paan* are prepared and decorated with edible silver foil (*vark*). They are decoratively placed on the buffet table where guests can help themselves.

The more important the celebration, the more elaborate the menu, and the more dishes and accompaniments are served. Great quantities of rice are always included, either plainly boiled or cooked with other ingredients, such as the *murgh biryani* (recipe page 293). A wedding feast includes assorted Indian breads (recipes pages 285–88) as well as this very delicious Pakistani bread made with locally grown almonds and apricots. ۞ ۞ ۞

Kimochdun

Almond and Apricot Bread

Yield: 1loaf

1 package active dry **yeast**
1 teaspoon sugar
1 cup **lukewarm** water
4 cups all-purpose flour, divided, more if needed
1 cup **scalded** milk
2 tablespoons butter, at room temperature
2 tablespoons honey
1 tablespoon salt
2 cups whole wheat flour
1 cup dried apricots, quartered, with skin on
whole almonds (about 3 ounces)

Equipment: Medium mixing bowl, wooden mixing spoon, plastic wrap, large mixing bowl, kitchen towel, measuring cup, lightly floured work surface, rolling pin, greased 10- to 12-inch round baking pan 2- to 3-inches deep, paring knife, oven mitts

1. Make the yeast sponge: In medium mixing bowl, dissolve yeast and sugar in warm water. Add sugar and using a mixing spoon, beat in 2 cups of all-purpose flour to make a smooth batter. Cover with plastic wrap and let rise in a warm place until double in bulk, about 1 hour.

2. Make the dough: In large mixing bowl, pour the hot milk over the butter, honey, and salt, stir to melt butter, and cool to lukewarm. Add the yeast sponge and stir in remaining 2 cups of all-purpose flour and 2 cups of whole wheat flour, ½ cup at a time, until soft dough forms. Transfer to a lightly floured work surface and **knead** until smooth and **elastic**, 8 to 10 minutes. If dough is sticky, knead in additional all-purpose flour, 1 tablespoon at a time.

3. Rinse and dry large mixing bowl and lightly grease sides and bottom. Place the dough in the greased bowl and turn it so the entire surface of the dough is lightly greased. Cover with towel and let rise in a warm place until double in bulk, about 1to 1½ hours. To test if doubled in bulk: poke fingers into dough; if the dent remains, the dough is ready. Uncover and gently **punch down** dough and knead on lightly floured work surface for 3 minutes until smooth.

Preheat oven to 350° F.

4. Using the heel of your hands, flatten dough out until it is 1 inch thick. Sprinkle the apricots and almonds over the dough and roll up jellyroll fashion. Shape the dough into a ball and gently knead in the apricots and nuts to distribute them throughout the dough. Transfer dough to prepared baking pan and press out to fit in the pan. Cover lightly with dry towel, set in warm place to double in bulk, 45 minutes to 1 hour. Transfer dough to greased baking pan. Using a paring

knife, cut a ½-inch deep X, centered, on the surface of the dough.

5. Bake in oven for 35 to 45 minutes, until light golden brown and bread sounds hollow when tapped.

To serve kimochdun *as they do in Pakistan, cut it into wedges and serve warm.*

There are many different ways of making *biryani*. *Biryani* is usually served at weddings and other life-cycle family celebrations, as it is a dish easy to prepare for a large group of people. *Murgh biryani,* a specialty of the Shindh region, is popular all over the country. The Shindh region is where the famous rich and nutty-flavored basmati rice is grown. (Basmati rice is available at all supermarkets.) The secret to a good *biryani* is for the chicken and the rice to be partially cooked before combining and cooking further.

Murgh Biryani

Chicken Pilaf

Yield: serves 4 to 6

- 1 cup water
- 2 cups **basmati** or other long-grain rice, soaked in cold water for 1 hour and drained
- *ghee* (recipe page 285 or available in a jar at Indian and Middle Eastern food stores), butter, or margarine, divided, as needed
- salt, to taste
- 1 cup yogurt
- ¼ cup *masala* (recipe page 294)
- 1 teaspoon **ground** cinnamon
- 6 to 8 serving-size chicken pieces
- 2 cups chicken broth, homemade (recipe page 106), or canned
- 2 onions, thinly sliced, for **garnish**
- 1 cup sliced almonds, **roasted,** for garnish
- 2 hard-cooked eggs, quartered, for garnish

Equipment: Medium saucepan with cover, wooden mixing spoon, large mixing bowl, plastic food wrap, large buttered casserole with cover, tongs, oven mitts

1. **Parboil** rice: Pour water into medium saucepan, add rice, 2 tablespoons of *ghee* or butter or margarine, and salt, stir with wooden spoon, and bring to a boil over high heat. Reduce heat to **simmer**, cover, and cook for 5 minutes. Remove from heat, keep covered, and set aside.

2. Put yogurt in large mixing bowl. Using a mixing spoon, stir in *masala* and cinnamon. Add salt to taste and stir until well mixed. Cover with plastic wrap and refrigerate.

3. Heat 7 tablespoons of *ghee* or butter or margarine in large skillet over medium-high heat. Add chicken pieces and fry in batches for 5 to 7 minutes, until golden brown on each side. (The chicken will finish cooking in the oven.) Turn chicken pieces with tongs. When all the chicken pieces are browned, add to yogurt mixture and coat well. Cover with plastic food wrap and refrigerate for 2 hours, turning chicken pieces frequently.

Preheat oven to 350° F.

4. Spread half of the rice over the bottom of a large buttered casserole and place chicken pieces on top. Pour the yogurt mixture over the chicken and cover with the remaining rice and smooth top with back of spoon. Pour the chicken broth over the rice. Cover the casserole and bake in the oven for 40 minutes. Uncover the casserole and continue cooking until all the liquid has been absorbed, 15 to 20 minutes.

5. For garnish: Heat 3 tablespoons *ghee,* butter or margarine in medium skillet, over medium-high heat. Add sliced onions and fry until soft and golden, 3 to 5 minutes.

To serve, heap the biryani *on a serving platter and sprinkle with fried onions and roasted, sliced almonds for garnish. Place hard-cooked egg wedges decoratively over the* biryani.

Sai gosht, a specialty from the Sindh region, is now a favorite throughout Pakistan. Although a special red spinach called *kulfa* is used for this dish in Pakistan, any variety of spinach will do. This is one of the many dishes prepared for life-cycle celebrations.

SAI GOSHT

SPINACH WITH MEAT

Yield: serves 6 to 8

½ cup *ghee* (recipe p. 285 or available in a jar at Indian and Middle Eastern food stores), butter or margarine
2 onions, **finely chopped**
4 cloves garlic, finely chopped
1½ tablespoons *masala* (recipe follows) or garam *masala* (available at Middle Eastern and Indian food stores)
2 pounds lean boneless lamb, cut into 1-inch cubes
2 pounds fresh spinach, washed, drained, and chopped or 2 boxes frozen chopped spinach, thawed, drained, and squeezed to remove excess water
salt to taste
1 cup yogurt

Equipment: Large saucepan with cover, mixing spoon

1. Heat *ghee* or melt butter or margarine in large saucepan over medium heat. Add onions and garlic, and **sauté** for 2 to 3 minutes until soft. Add the *masala* or garam *masala,* stir, and cook for 2 minutes. Add the meat and stir to coat. Cover and cook 20 minutes, stirring frequently.

2. Add the spinach and salt to taste to the meat mixture, stir, and cook for 2 minutes. Reduce heat to **simmer**, stir in the yogurt, cover, and cook until meat is tender, 30 to 45 minutes. Stir occasionally to prevent sticking.

To serve, transfer meat mixture to large serving platter. Serve along with peela chaaval *(recipe page 295).*

Garam *masala* is a mixture of hot dry spices available at Middle Eastern and Indian food stores. In most Indian and Pakistani kitchens, the spices are ground by hand using a **mortar and pestle.** Each household makes their own special blend of spices on a daily basis. This is a recipe for *masala* in the paste form.

MASALA

HOT SPICE PASTE

Note: Use care when handling peppers. Wrap your hands in plastic wrap or cover them with plastic sandwich bag. If you accidentally touch your eyes, rinse out at once under cold running water.

Yield: about ¾ cup

1 onion, **finely chopped**
2-inch piece fresh ginger, peeled and finely chopped
3 cloves
1 teaspoon cumin seeds
1 teaspoon **coriander** seeds
1 teaspoon salt
1 teaspoon black peppercorns
3 cloves garlic, finely chopped
4 fresh mint leaves
1 sprig fresh **coriander** leaves
1 fresh **jalapeño**, finely chopped
1 teaspoon salt
2 tablespoons water

Equipment: Electric blender, rubber spatula, small jar with cover

Put chopped onion, ginger, cloves, cumin seeds, coriander seeds, salt, black peppercorns, garlic, fresh mint leaves, fresh coriander leaves, jalapeño, and water in blender and blend until mixture forms a **purée**.

Note: While processing, turn machine off once or twice and scrape down sides of container with rubber spatula.

Put masala *in a small jar and cover. Keep refrigerated and use within 3 to 4 days.*

Peela Chaaval

Yellow Rice with Garnishes

Yield: serves 8 to 10

1 1/2 cups **basmati rice** or any long grain rice
1/2 teaspoon ground turmeric
2 tablespoons *ghee* (recipe p. 285 or available in a jar at Indian and Middle Eastern food stores), butter or margarine, at room temperature
1 onion, thinly sliced, for **garnish**
1 cup **toasted** sliced almonds
1 cup toasted cashew nuts, for garnish
1 cup seedless raisins
8 pieces (about 2 x 3-inches each) edible **silver leaf** (available at Middle Eastern and Indian food stores)

Equipment: Medium saucepan, wooden mixing spoon, medium (about 9 inches across x 3 1/2 inches deep) rounded-bottom metal mixing bowl, large serving platter, plastic food wrap

1. Cook rice in medium saucepan according to directions on package and add turmeric to the water at the same time you add the rice. Set aside.

2. Coat inside of metal bowl with butter or margarine. Line the greased bowl with plastic wrap and press it as smooth as possible against the greased surface. Lightly grease surface of plastic wrap with butter or margarine. Pack cooked rice into bowl.

3. To unmold: Invert a large serving platter over the top of the bowl and holding both tightly together, flip them over so the bowl of rice will be upside down on top of the platter. Carefully remove the bowl and peel off the plastic wrap.

4. Heat 2 tablespoons of *ghee* or melt butter or margarine in small skillet over medium-high heat. Add onions and **sauté** until golden brown, 3 to 5 minutes.

5. Garnish the dome of rice: Sprinkle with sautéed onions, toasted almonds, cashews, and raisins. Decoratively place the pieces of edible silver leaf over the surface of the rice.

Serve the dome of rice, at room temperature, as the centerpiece on the buffet table.

The candies unique to India and the Subcontinent are extremely sweet. For auspicious life-cycle celebrations the candies are usually decorated with edible **silver leaf** (*vark*).

Badam Paprh

Almond Sweetmeat

Yield: serves 6 to 8

1 1/2 cups **blanched** almonds
1/2 cup firmly packed brown sugar
1/2 cup confectioners' sugar
edible **silver leaf** (***vark***), for **garnish**

Equipment: Food processor, rubber spatula, work surface, wax paper, rolling pin, pie pan, baking sheet

1. Put almonds in the food processor and grind them until they are finely ground and form an oily mass. Add the brown sugar and process until the mixture is smooth and soft, 2 to 4 minutes.

Note: While processing, turn machine off once or twice and scrape down sides of container with rubber spatula.

2. Divide the almond mixture into 6 or 8 portions and using your hands, form each into a ball. Put confectioners' sugar in pie pan and roll each ball around to lightly coat. Place a 10-inch piece of wax paper on the work surface and place

a ball in the center. Cover with another piece of wax paper. Using a rolling pin, flatten the ball into a thin disk. Remove the top piece of wax paper and place the thin disk, still on the bottom piece of waxed paper, on a baking sheet. Repeat making the thin candy disks and place them side by side on the baking sheet. Set aside, at room temperature, to dry out 6 to 8 hours.

To serve, place on a serving platter and garnish each piece with a dab of edible silver leaf (vark). Badam paprh *are eaten as a sweet snack, especially popular at birthday parties. Store up to 2 weeks, between pieces of waxed paper, in an airtight container.*

INDIA

India is the largest country of the subcontinent of south Asia. It is bordered by Bangladesh, Bhutan, Burma, China, Nepal, and Pakistan, and has over 7,000 miles of coastline.

India's vast population, mostly Hindu, live in a country of overwhelming diversity. To understand how Indians observe life-cycle events it is necessary to know something about their country, their religion (see Hinduism and Hindu Life-Cycle Rituals, page li), their lifestyle and habitat, and how they relate to one another.

India is divided into 25 states and seven union territories; each has its own culture, language, dress, religious rituals, arts and crafts, and food. Within each region there are many different sects and branches of the Hindu religion, each following their own rituals and ceremonies. To add to the diversity, the Hindus were, for centuries, segregated by a very complicated caste system. The caste system doctrine states that each person is born to perform a specific job, marry a specific person, eat certain food, and have children who will continue the never-changing cycle. In 1949, the Indian constitution abolished the caste system, making all men equal under the law, but discrimination by caste continues to be an issue in modern India. For most Hindus, a totally casteless social system is contrary to their religious beliefs. The caste system was woven into every fiber of life, and to change this ancient religious practice seems to some an unattainable feat. In some rural areas, disobeying caste rules is still punished by death.

The most basic ceremonies for Hindus are those that involve the life cycle (*samskaras*). The *samskaras* include directions for carrying out the necessary rituals for each life-cycle event, for both high and low castes. These ancient ceremonies are often complex and minutely detailed; today they are not followed as closely in urban areas as they were in the past.

The hair-cutting ritual for baby boys is a very important occasion and a feast is prepared for friends and relatives. The most auspicious coming-of-age event for boys is the "thread ceremony" (see Hinduism and Hindu Life-Cycle Rituals, page li), which includes a celebration feast for family and friends.

A coming-of-age ceremony for girls is still celebrated in some villages and tribal areas, signaling to the community that the girl is available for marriage. In the cities, the event may be marked by a change of dress; the girl may go from skirt or school uniform to Indian dress. The style of clothing she wears is restricted by region, religion, and caste.

The biggest and most important life-cycle celebration in India is the wedding. About 95 percent of all Indians who marry have an arranged marriage, including university educated, "foreign-returned" young men and women. (In some families a young man or woman may exercise a right of veto after meeting the potential partner.) Wedding customs vary, even within a community, but the arrangements are usually as extravagant as the bride's family can afford. It is not unusual for a father to go heavily in debt to give his daughter an expensive wedding; including the dowry, gifts to the groom's family, and a reception for hundreds of people or the whole village.

On the morning of the wedding, the bride arrives at the temple or wedding hall after having been elaborately dressed and adorned with makeup and jewels by her female relatives. The day before, she would have had intricate designs painted on her hands and legs with henna in the *mendhi* ceremony, a Muslim custom that Hindus have adopted. The bridal gown is usually a *sari*, beautifully decorated with gold brocade. Popular colors worn by brides are red for happiness, light green for purity and new life, or gold for wealth and good fortune.

Wedding receptions are elaborate affairs, and it is the sign of a gracious host and hostess to provide great quantities of *paan*, decorated with edible **silver leaf (*vark*)**. At one time, the preparation of *paan* after dinner was an elaborate ritual performed by the woman of the house. Today many hostesses buy the *paan* already prepared.

In India, Hinduism influences every aspect of life. The rituals and customs extend to not only what food is cooked and how it is prepared, but how and where it is served. Meals are eaten in the kitchen; dining rooms are nonexistent. The person preparing the meal sits on the floor, as do those who eat it. Shoes are never worn in the kitchen, and before eating there is a ritual of hand and feet washing. In all classes of society, both urban and rural, food is eaten with the fingers of the right hand alone. (The left hand is used for personal grooming and must never touch food.) The finger-and-bread-scoop method is acceptable; knives, forks, and spoons and men and women dining together are taboo at the traditional Hindu table. (Some urban families now eat at a table in the kitchen, occasionally using spoons.) In south India, banana leaves often replace the *thalis* (the trays food is eaten from). In many parts of India, even in the large cities, banana leaves are often used to serve hundreds of guests at a wedding banquet or reception. Meals generally consist of a great many dishes of different tastes, colors, and textures. The more important the occasion, then the more numerous and elaborate the foods will be that are served to guests.

Most Hindus do not eat meat, or eat it only for special celebrations. Those that eat meat never eat beef or veal. In India, the cow, useful to every aspect of life, is sacred. Bullocks are the beasts of burden; they pull the plow, the water wheel, and the wagon. Cow dung is burned for fuel, used for fertilizer and flooring, and plastered on the walls of houses. Cow's milk and curd and buttermilk are essential nutrients. The cows are so revered there is cow protection legislation; to kill a cow is considered the same as murdering a human being. ۞ ۞ ۞

Simia belati is a dish often included in the wedding feast; the red tomato color is symbolic for good luck and happiness.

Simia Belati

Stuffed Tomatoes

Yield: serves 4

4 tomatoes

3 tablespoons *ghee* (recipe page 285 or available in a jar at Indian and Middle Eastern food stores) or vegetable oil, divided

2 onions, sliced
1 teaspoon canned, **finely chopped** green chilies, more or less to taste
1 teaspoon **ground** cumin
salt to taste
½ cup **roasted** cashew nuts, **coarsely chopped**

Equipment: Sharp knife, teaspoon, strainer, small bowl, paper towels, work surface, medium skillet, mixing spoon, 8- or 10-inch baking pan or pie pan, oven mitts

1. Using a sharp knife, cut ½ inch off top of each tomato and set aside. Using a teaspoon, scoop pulp out of tomatoes and put into a strainer placed over a small bowl. Place several layers of paper towels on work surface and turn tomato shells upside down on paper towels to drain. Reserve tomato juice and tomato pulp.

2. Heat 2 tablespoons *ghee* or oil in medium skillet over medium-high heat. Add onions, stir, and fry until golden brown, 3 to 4 minutes. Stir in tomato pulp, chilies, cumin, and salt to taste. Reduce heat to **simmer** and cook for 3 minutes. Remove from heat, stir in cashews. Using your hands, rub the skin of the tomato shells with the remaining 1 tablespoon oil; fill with onion mixture and place side by side in baking or pie pan. Replace the tops on each stuffed tomato shell. Spoon any leftover onion mixture and the reserved tomato juice in the pan around the stuffed tomatoes.

3. Bake in 350° F oven for 10 to 15 minutes, just until tomatoes are cooked through and still hold their shape.

Serve either warm or at room temperature. Transfer stuffed tomatoes to serving dish and spoon pan drippings around them.

Sweets and rice hold a special place in India's social and religious life. Every joyous occasion or holiday, every arrival or departure, new baby or new job, promotion or award is celebrated with great quantities of sweets, many made with rice.

It is the belief that the Western practice of throwing rice at the wedding couple originated in India. During some Hindu ceremonies, the groom throws three handfuls of rice over the bride as a symbolic desire for many children. In other ceremonies, the bride and groom throw rice over each other. Sometimes the rice is colored to look like confetti.

Usually several different savory and sweet rice dishes are served for the same meal. This sweet rice dish is popular at wedding banquets. Its sweetness and yellow color are symbols of gold and good fortune.

Meeta Pilau

Sweet Saffron Rice

Yield: serves 4 to 6
2 ½ cups water
salt, as needed
1 cup rice
3 tablespoons *ghee* (recipe page 285 or available in a jar at Indian and Middle Eastern food stores) or butter or margarine
¼ cup crushed cardamom seeds
¼ teaspoon **ground** cloves
1/4 teaspoon ground cinnamon
1½ cups milk, more as needed
½ cup sugar
3 saffron threads (available at supermarkets) or ½ teaspoon ground turmeric
½ cup seedless raisins
¼ cup slivered almonds

Equipment: Medium saucepan with cover, mixing spoon, **colander**, medium **heavy-based** saucepan with cover, small saucepan, fork

1. Pour water in medium saucepan. Add ½ teaspoon salt and bring to a boil over high heat.

Add rice, stir, reduce heat to **simmer**, cover, and cook for 6 minutes. Drain rice in colander.

2. In heavy-based medium saucepan, heat *ghee* or melt butter or margarine over medium heat. Add drained rice, stir constantly, and cook for 2 to 3 minutes, until the *ghee* is absorbed. Add cardamom, cloves, cinnamon, 1½ cups milk, and sugar. Stir frequently, bring to boil over medium-high heat, reduce heat to **simmer**, cover, and cook for 20 to 25 minutes, or until rice is tender and all the milk is absorbed. (If rice mixture gets too dry before the rice is tender, stir in ¼ cup warm milk at a time to complete the cooking process.) The rice mixture should be creamy, not soupy or dry.

3. In a small saucepan, heat ¼ cup milk over high heat until small bubbles appear around the edge of the pan. Remove from heat and add the saffron or turmeric, stir, and set aside for 30 minutes. Using a fork, stir the raisins and saffron or turmeric milk into the rice.

To serve, transfer to serving dish and sprinkle almonds over the top.

Panch armit, the "five immortal nectars"—sugar, milk, honey, yogurt, and *ghee*—are included in most Hindu life-cycle rituals and celebration feasts. This sweetmeat, made with three of the "five immortal nectars," is served for life-cycle celebrations.

Badam Pistaz Barfi

Almond and Pistachio Candy

Yield: about 24 pieces

1 quart milk
1 cup granulated sugar
1 cup **ground** almonds
1 cup unsalted, ground pistachios
3 teaspoons *ghee* (recipe page 285 or available in a jar at Indian and Middle Eastern food stores) or butter or margarine, at room temperature
1 teaspoon almond extract

Equipment: Heavy-based medium saucepan, wooden mixing spoon, buttered 8-inch square baking pan, metal spatula

Pour milk into heavy-based medium saucepan and bring to a boil over high heat. Reduce heat to **simmer** and using wooden mixing spoon, stir frequently and cook for 35 to 40 minutes, or until the milk thickens to the consistency of heavy cream. Stir sugar into the milk and continue stirring for 10 minutes. Add ground almonds and pistachios and continue stirring frequently 10 minutes longer. Stir in *ghee* or butter and almond extract. Continue stirring until mixture thickens to a solid mass and pulls away from sides of the pan. Remove from heat and quickly spread out in the buttered 8-inch baking pan. Smooth the top with a metal spatula.

To serve, let candy cool for about 30 minutes and using a paring knife, cut into 24 small squares or diamond shapes. When cool, the candy hardens to the consistency of fudge.

Only the best and most expensive food the family can afford is served for auspicious occasions in India. *Durbar* means a formal gathering, such as a wedding. This lamb dish is served on such an occasion. In India, the labor-intensive job of grinding the spices is considered an essential and important part of the total dining experience. This recipe has been simplified with ground spices easily available at supermarkets.

Korma Durbari

Roast Lamb for a Banquet

Note: Use care when handling peppers. Wrap your hands in plastic wrap or cover them with plastic sandwich bag. If you accidentally touch your eyes, rinse out at once under cold running water.

Yield: serves 4 to 6

2 tablespoons curry powder (available at supermarkets)
3 tablespoons white wine vinegar
1½ to 2½ pounds lean lamb, cut into 2-inch cubes
3 tablespoons *ghee* (recipe page 285 or available in a jar at Indian and Middle Eastern food stores) or butter or margarine
1 onion, **finely chopped**
4 cloves garlic, finely chopped
1-inch piece of fresh ginger, peeled and finely grated
1 cup water
¼ cup tomato paste
1 or 2 fresh **jalapeño** peppers, stemmed, **seeded**, finely chopped (optional or add peppers according to your preference)
2 tablespoons finely chopped fresh **cilantro** leaves
salt to taste

Equipment: Medium bowl with cover, mixing spoon, **Dutch oven** or large saucepan with cover, small bowl

1. In medium bowl, stir curry powder into vinegar. Add meat cubes and using clean hands, rub the curry mixture on the meat. Cover and refrigerate for at least 4 hours or overnight.

2. In Dutch oven or large saucepan, heat *ghee* or melt butter or margarine over medium-high heat. Add onions, stir, and fry until soft, 2 to 3 minutes. Stir in garlic and ginger and fry for 1 minute more. Add the meat cubes, stir, and cook until all sides are browned, 4 to 6 minutes.

3. Pour water into small bowl, stir in tomato paste and blend well. Add the tomato paste mixture to the meat mixture, stir, and bring to a boil over medium-high heat. Reduce heat to **simmer**, cover, and cook until meat is tender, 30 to 40 minutes.

4. Stir in jalapeños (optional), chopped cilantro, and salt to taste. Stir and cook 2 to 3 minutes.

To serve, mound the lamb attractively in a deep platter. Serve with one or more Indian breads (recipes pages 285–88). To eat, break off a piece of bread, using only your right hand, and use it to scoop a cube of meat out of the platter. Enclose the meat in the piece of bread and eat. Never use the left hand for eating, as it is used for personal grooming.

SRI LANKA

An island in the Indian ocean, Sri Lanka is a multiethnic, multireligious, and multilinguistic country, where for centuries, the four major world religions have been firmly established among several ethnic groups. The largest ethnic group, the Sinhalese, make up about three-quarters of the population. Other significant ethnic groups are the Tamils, most of whom are Hindus; the Moors of Arabic ancestry; and the Burghers (which means "town dwellers"). The Burghers are mostly Christian and are descendants of Portuguese, Dutch, and British colonists.

Distinctions between the Buddhists, Hindus, Muslims, and Christians in Sri Lanka are not always clear-cut. Sri Lankans have been mixing and borrowing religious rituals and symbols from one another for generations. For example, most Sinhalese are Buddhists, yet they follow the stratified caste system of the Hindus. It is not unusual to see Sri Lankan Muslims wearing the *thali*, a symbolic marriage necklace of Tamil Hindus. Because of Sri Lanka's diverse population, life-cycle rituals vary not only by racial and religious differences, but by intermarriage, mixed heritage, region, or whether one is a villager or urban dweller.

In Sri Lanka, the anticipated birth of a baby is regarded as an exciting event that families look forward to with great enthusiasm. When the baby is born it is customary for visiting family and friends to bring gifts for the infant.

Among the Sinhalese and Tamil the first important event in the baby's life comes at around eight months old, when, for the first time, the baby is given solid food (usually boiled rice with milk). For Hindus, the first mouthful of solid food is such an important occasion it is fed to the baby in the *kovil* (the Hindu temple). Whenever decisions have to be made concerning the child, the family consults an astrologer, which they do when the child reaches the age of two years. The astrologer chooses an auspicious hour for the child to be given its first lesson by a scholarly relative, head schoolmaster, or temple monk.

A Sri Lankan girl is eligible for marriage when she reaches puberty, and the family celebrates her coming of age. Followers of traditional Tamil and Sinhalese rituals keep the young girl in seclusion for about 16 days. It is considered bad luck for the girl to look upon a male, even her own brother, during her seclusion. Again an astrologer is consulted and an auspicious date for the "coming out" ritual is selected. A *dboby* (washerwoman) comes to the house to prepare the girl; all jewelry and clothes the girl was wearing when she started her first menstruation are discarded by the *dboby*. The *dboby* then bathes the girl by pouring water over her from a clay pot. To complete the bath ritual, the *dboby* smashes the pot on the ground. Once the girl comes out of seclusion, the family throws a big party in her honor where she receives gifts, often jewelry and money. Many families today are ignoring the rituals and opting for just the celebration party.

Most marriages in Sri Lanka are arranged. At one time a marriage broker, the *magul kapuwa*, brought eligible people together. Today the marriage broker has been replaced by a go-between, which might be an aunt, colleague, parent, or friend. The go-between usually consults with an astrologer throughout the entire marriage negotiation process. Horoscopes come in the form of a chart written on paper or an *ola* (a scroll made of a cured piece of talipot palm leaf). Good and bad periods of each person's life are listed on these charts. When a marriage is proposed, the horoscopes of both the man and the woman are compared, and if more than half of 20 "conditions" are favorable, the nuptial arrangements continue.

For Sinhalese Buddhists, the astrologer first decides whether the couple's birth dates are compatible, then he or she charts an auspicious time for every step of the ceremony. The couple marries in a decorative house-like structure called a *poruwa*. It is usually up to the bride's maternal uncle to arrange the ritual proceedings.

Dowries are a part of the arranged marriage, and the bride's parents must come forth with property, cash, jewelry, and a house for the groom. A Tamil custom allows the groom's family to take part of the dowry and add it to the dowry they are preparing for their own daughter. It is up to the go-between to not only ask for a substantial dowry from the bride's parents, but also to do the proposing.

Weddings are often lavish celebrations, especially among those living in cities, taking place in a wedding hall or hotel. Brides are generally beautifully dressed in rich silks embroidered with gold thread. Tamils can either have the marriage ceremony in a temple and the reception elsewhere, or if the wedding ceremony and reception takes place in a hotel, a priest comes to perform the marriage rituals before the guests. Muslims have an evening celebration, which can be very elaborate, in the bride's home or in a hotel. Most Christian Burghers prefer church ceremonies followed by the reception in either a hotel or the bride's family's home.

A charming ritual performed during the Tamil marriage ceremony is when the little fingers of the bride and groom are tied to each other with gold thread, and water from a silver urn is poured over the knot to symbolize sharing. Adding to the happy occasion, a chorus of girls sing *jayamangala gatha* (songs of good wishes and celebration).

Following the wedding celebration, the tradition is for the bridal couple to spend the wedding night at the groom's family home. The following day they are visited by the bride's parents and other family members. If the couple take a honeymoon journey, the groom's parents welcome them back with a homecoming party.

The rituals for the dead in Sri Lanka vary according to religious beliefs. Hindus and Buddhists cremate their dead. According to the *Koran* (Islamic holy book), Muslims must bury their dead within 24 hours. Muslim mourners carry their dead to the cemetery on a covered stretcher and place them in the ground without a coffin. Most Christians prefer the traditional coffin burial for their deceased, though cremation has become common. In Sri Lanka, a paper *stupa* (Buddhist monument) may be placed on the cremation pyre, and at intervals after the funeral, meals are offered to monks in honor of the departed.

Rice is the most important food in Sri Lanka. Rice curries made with cooked vegetables in coconut milk are popular and are included in life-cycle celebration feasts.

Yogurt, known throughout the world, is an important ingredient in Sri Lankan cooking. This popular yogurt sauce is used to spoon over raw, boiled, or steamed vegetables or to use as a dip for chips or Indian flat breads, such as *chipati* (recipe page 285) or *poppadums* (recipe page 307).

Kadhi

Yogurt Sauce

Yield: 2 cups

½ teaspoon **ground** turmeric
½ teaspoon ground mustard seeds
1 teaspoon ground cumin
1 teaspoon ground **coriander**
red pepper flakes, to taste (optional)
1 tablespoon vegetable oil
2 cloves garlic, **finely chopped**
2 cups plain yogurt

Equipment: Small skillet, mixing spoon, small bowl with cover, rubber spatula

In small skillet over medium heat, add turmeric, mustard seeds, cumin, coriander, and red pepper flakes. Stir constantly and cook until mustard seeds begin to pop, about 1 minute. Add oil and garlic, stir, and **sauté** until garlic is soft, about 2 minutes. Stir in yogurt and cook to heat through, 2 to 3 minutes. Cool to room temperature, transfer to small bowl, cover, and refrigerate for up to 5 days.

Serve kadhi *as a dip or as a sauce over vegetables.*

Samosa are favorite savory filled pastries that definitely would be prepared for life-cycle celebration feasts. This is a vegetarian treat.

Samosa

Vegetarian Pastries

Yield: 20 pieces

2 cloves garlic, **finely chopped**

½ teaspoon **ground** ginger
½ teaspoon ground turmeric
½ teaspoon ground **coriander**
½ teaspoon ground cumin
3 tablespoons vegetable oil, divided
1 onion, finely chopped
1 carrot, **trimmed** and finely chopped
1 potato, peeled and finely chopped
½ teaspoon salt
½ cup water
½ cup fresh or frozen green peas
juice of 1 lemon
2 sprigs fresh coriander (also called **cilantro**), finely chopped or 1 tablespoon ground dried coriander leaves
5 sheets (14 x 18-inch) **filo** (also phyllo) pastry (available in 1 pound boxes in the freezer section of supermarkets)
½ cup melted butter or margarine

Equipment: Mixing spoon, medium skillet with cover, work surface, knife, ruler, damp kitchen towel, 2 cups, **pastry brush**, baking sheet, oven mitts

1. In cup, mix garlic, ginger, turmeric, coriander, and cumin with 1 tablespoon of oil and stir until mixture forms a paste.

2. Prepare filling: Heat remaining 2 tablespoons of oil in medium skillet over medium-high heat. Add finely chopped onion and **sauté** until soft, 2 to 4 minutes. Reduce heat to medium, stir in spice paste and cook 1 minute. Add finely chopped carrot and potato, salt, and water. Stir, cover, and cook for 12 to 15 minutes, or until potato is tender. Stir in peas, lemon juice, and coriander. If mixture seems watery, cook uncovered for 5 to 10 minutes to **reduce**.

3. Cut pastries: On work surface, neatly stack the 5 sheets filo. Using a sharp knife and a ruler, mark the 18-inch length into 4 equal strips, each 4½-inches wide. Cut through the 5 sheets; you will have 20 strips of filo, each 4 ½ x 14 inches. Keep covered with damp towel and work with one strip at a time.

Preheat oven to 375° F.

4. Fill pastries: Place a cup with melted butter and a pastry brush near work surface. Put one strip of filo on work surface, lightly brush with melted butter or margarine, and place a tablespoon of filling at one end, 2-inches up from bottom edge. Fold a corner of the bottom edge diagonally over the filling to meet the other side, forming a triangle (two edges are 4½ inches long and folded diagonal side is about 6 inches long). Press edges together to seal in filling. Repeat folding the pastry strip up and over (like folding a flag) to make a small triangular package with the filling wrapped inside. Brush with melted butter, gently press edges to seal package, and place on baking sheet. Repeat assembling and place about 1 inch apart on baking sheet.

5. Bake in oven for 12 to 15 minutes, or until golden, puffy, and crisp.

Serve either warm or at room temperature.

Vadas are a favorite party treat and especially popular with children.

Vadas

Fried Lentil Puffs

CAUTION: HOT OIL USED

Yield: 12 pieces

2 cups cooked lentils (cook according to directions on package)
1 onion, **finely chopped**
1 clove garlic, finely chopped
ground red pepper to taste
½ teaspoon ground ginger
salt and pepper to taste
all-purpose flour, as needed
4 cups vegetable oil, for frying

Equipment: Food processor, rubber spatula, baking sheet, wax paper, paper towels, **deep fryer** or large saucepan, cooking **thermometer** or wooden spoon, tongs, slotted metal spatula

1. Put lentils in food processor. Add onion, garlic, red pepper to taste, ginger, and salt and pepper to taste. Process into a thick smooth paste.

Note: While processing, turn machine off once or twice and scrape down sides of container with rubber spatula.

2. Cover baking sheet with wax paper and sprinkle lightly with flour. Divide the lentil mixture into 12 balls. Using floured hands, shape the balls into patties about 2- to 3-inches across.

3. Prepare to **deep fry**: Place two or three layers of paper towels on baking sheet. Heat oil in large saucepan or deep fryer to 375° F. Use cooking thermometer or deep the handle of a wooden spoon into the hot oil. When small bubbles appear around the handle at the surface of the oil, the oil is ready for frying.

4. Using your finger, poke a small hole in the center of the patty, smooth the edges, and using tongs, carefully slide into the oil. Repeat poking holes in the patties and fry in small batches. Fry on each side for 2 to 4 minutes, or until browned. Use slotted metal spatula to turn over. Remove with spatula and drain on paper towels.

Serve vadas *with* kadhi *(recipe page 302).*

BANGLADESH

On the northern coast of the Bay of Bengal, Bangladesh is surrounded by India except for a small border with Myanmar (Burma). It is a low-lying land of many rivers.

The majority of people living in Bangladesh are Muslim, while the remaining population are mostly Hindu. Bangladesh struggles with overpopulation and a weak economy and is often inundated by tropical cyclones, monsoons, floods, and tidal waves. Many Bangladeshis live in rural areas, chiefly in small villages, and most place importance on religion, prayer, family, and life-cycle celebrations. Among the Muslim majority, Islam dominates social, political, and religious life, and all life-cycle rituals are done according to Islamic law. (See Islam and Islamic Life-Cycle Rituals, page xlix.) The Hindus of Bangladesh follow many of the same rituals and customs as neighboring India. (See Hinduism and Hindu Life-Cycle Rituals, page li.)

Both Muslim and Hindu Bangladeshis generally put great importance on having a male child. Only a son can continue the family line, and a Hindu son brings dowry. Muslim men have traditionally followed the Persian system of paying a bride-price, but the Hindu dowry system is becoming popular among Muslims. Also, in the Hindu culture, only a son can perform the funeral rites that will ensure his father's soul safe passage into the afterlife.

Rice, the chief agricultural product of Bangladesh, and fish are the most popular foods for Bangladeshis, and tea is the most popular drink. (Alcoholic beverages are forbidden according to Islamic law.) Many different rice and fish dishes are served at wedding banquets, along with great quantities of sweets.

Both Muslim and Hindu parents choose their children's marriage partners. Muslims consult a religious person for an auspicious wedding day, and Hindus call upon an astrologer. Both Muslim and Hindu brides attend a *mehndi* ceremony before the wedding, in which henna is painted on their hands and feet.

Weddings are generally big noisy affairs with great quantities of food. During traditional Muslim weddings, the women and men celebrate in separate quarters. At the Muslim wedding feast, *brindaboni* is a very popular dish, often served as one of many side dishes with roasted lamb or goat. When made with **snow peas** and sweet potatoes and the unusual blend of spices, *brindaboni* becomes a very flavorful vegetarian dish for a Hindu wedding banquet. ❂ ❂ ❂

Brindaboni

Snowpeas and Sweet Potatoes

Yield: serve 4 to 6

2 tablespoons vegetable oil
1 teaspoon **ground** cumin
1 teaspoon ground **coriander**
1 teaspoon ground turmeric
2 bay leaves
2 sweet potatoes, peeled and thinly sliced
½ pound **snow peas**, **trimmed**, sliced crosswise in half

Equipment: Large skillet with cover, wooden mixing spoon

1. Heat oil in large skillet over medium-high heat. Add cumin, coriander, turmeric, and bay leaves. Stir and cook for about 1 minute to develop the flavors. Add sweet potato slices and toss to coat. Pour in water and bring to a boil. Reduce heat to **simmer**, cover, and cook for 10 to 12 minutes, or until tender but not mushy.

2. Add snow peas, gently toss to mix, cover, and simmer for 3 to 5 minutes, or until heated through. Remove and discard bay leaves.

To serve, transfer to serving platter and serve as a side dish with lamb, rice, and other vegetable dishes.

Kichri (also *khitcherie*) is a famous rice dish. The Hindustani word *kichri* (or *khitcherie*), means "mishmash" or "hodgepodge." This is a vegetarian dish which is also called Indian white *kedgeree*. The English version of *kedgeree* is traditionally made with *finnan haddie* (recipe page 306).

Kichri (also khitcherie)

Indian Rice with Vegetables

Yield: serves 4

2 tablespoons vegetable oil
1 onion, **finely chopped**
1 clove garlic, finely chopped
1 teaspoon **ground** cumin
1 teaspoon fresh ginger, finely chopped or ½ teaspoon ground ginger
1 bay leaf
½ cup **basmati** or other long-grain rice
1 cup skinless mung beans (*mung dal*) (available at Asian and Indian food stores)
1 potato, peeled and **diced**
3 cups water
½ teaspoon salt
1 cup finely chopped cauliflower
½ cup frozen peas, thawed

Equipment: Medium saucepan, wooden mixing spoon

1. Heat oil in medium saucepan over medium-high heat. Add onions and **sauté** until golden, 3 to 5 minutes. Stir in garlic, ginger, cumin, and bay leaf and cook for about 1 minute for flavors to develop.

2. Add rice, beans, and potato, stirring to coat. Add water and salt, stir, bring to a boil, and reduce heat to **simmer.** Cover and cook for 20 to 25 minutes, or until rice, beans, and potato are tender. Add cauliflower and peas, stir, cover, and cook 3 to 5 minutes until tender. Remove and discard bay leaf.

Serve warm, with plenty of flatbread for scooping and soaking up the juices.

Kedgeree is a Bangladeshi dish the English made popular while the region was under British colonial rule. For this *kedgeree* recipe you can either add the *finnan haddie* after it is prepared according to the following recipe, or you can use more easily available fresh salmon, cod, or other firm skinless fish

fillets. In India yellow *kedgeree* is an ideal dish for occasions such as weddings. The eggs are symbolic of fertility, and the yellow turmeric symbolizes richness and good fortune.

Kedgeree

Yellow Rice with Smoked Haddock or Fresh Fish

Yield: serves 4 to 6

½ cup butter or margarine
Boiled ***finnan haddie***, flaked (recipe follows) or 1 pound fresh skinless fish **fillet**, cut into bite-size pieces
1 cup heavy cream
1 teaspoon **ground** turmeric
4 cups cooked rice (cooked according to directions on package)
4 hard-cooked eggs, shelled and chopped
¼ cup chopped parsley
salt and pepper to taste
1 lemon, cut into wedges, for **garnish**

Equipment: Medium saucepan, mixing spoon, 2 forks

1. Melt butter or margarine in medium saucepan over medium-high heat. If using *finnan haddie* (recipe follows): Stir in flakes and cook to heat through, 2 to 3 minutes. If using bite-size pieces of fresh fish: Stir constantly and **sauté** until opaque and cooked through, 3 to 5 minutes.

2. Stir in cream and turmeric. Cook until small bubbles appear around edge of pan. Reduce heat to **simmer**, add cooked rice, chopped eggs, chopped parsley, and salt and pepper to taste. Gently toss to mix using 2 forks, and cook until heated through, 5 to 8 minutes.

To serve, pile kedgeree *into a large serving bowl and garnish with wedges of lemon around the edge. Sprinkle lemon juice on each serving.*

Boiled Finnan Haddie

Boiled Smoked Haddock

1 pound ***finnan haddie***
milk as needed

Equipment: Medium skillet, metal spatula

Put the fish in medium skillet and add milk to cover. Soak for 1 hour. Bring to boil over medium-high heat, reduce heat to **simmer,** and cook for 20 minutes. Drain and discard milk. When cool enough to handle, flake fish, removing and discarding the skin and bones; put flaked pieces into small bowl.

Continue with kedgeree *(recipe precedes) or cover and refrigerate or freeze for another use. The flaked* finnan haddie *is delicious added to salad or omelet.*

NEPAL

The tiny, landlocked country of Nepal is located on the southern slopes of the Himalayan mountains between India on the south and the Tibetan region of China on the north. Nepal is home to numerous ethnic groups, each with their own language, customs and culture. Most Nepalese are Hindus, the official religion of Nepal.

The Hindus, along with the country's Buddhist minority, have, over the centuries, interwoven many of their rituals with local traditions of animism (the belief that all things have a soul) and shamanism (sorcery or magic). This blending has formed many unusual and complex religious practices. In ceremonies performed by the Hindu temple priest (*pujaari*), the Buddhist monk (*lama*), or the village shaman (*jhaakri*), some form of worship (*pujaa*) will focus on all things in nature. Rites of passage, especially funerals, and curing ceremonies are interwoven with animists' and shamans' concerns for placating local spirits and natural forces. Cows are sacred to Hindus and are protected and not eaten. Even trees are given offerings of flowers and colored rice by the people of Nepal.

Hindus have a very important ceremony for boys of the higher castes (see Hinduism and Hindu Life-Cycle Rituals, page li), known as the "thread ceremony." During the ritual, the young men receive a sacred "thread" (a three-strand rope or cord), which symbolizes their transition into manhood and officially welcomes them into their religion. In Nepal, the thread ceremony (*janal purniama*) is held during the month of *Saaun* (July-August). Men wear the thread, which is looped over the left shoulder and tied under the right arm, for the rest of their lives, changing it only if it is damaged or defiled.

Among most Nepalese, marriages are prearranged by parents. The wedding ceremony usually takes place on an auspicious date selected by an astrologer. Most weddings are held in mid-winter, especially during January and February, well after the harvest and before the spring planting. Wedding ceremonies vary with each ethnic group, and some can be very complicated affairs, lasting up to a week. Very important to all celebrations are the groups of professional musicians referred to as "wedding bands," who travel around the country providing music for weddings. At different stages of the ceremony, the wedding procession, led by a wedding band, moves back and forth between the bride's and groom's houses.

Among the upper Hindu castes, the weddings are loud, musical affairs accompanied by much drumming and horn blowing as the bride's and groom's parties travel to and from each other's villages, sometimes over a period of several days. Solemn rituals, with aspects of the Hindu fire ceremony (see Hinduism and Hindu Life-Cycle Rituals, page li), take place in the evening, usually at the home of the bride's parents. Food is important to wedding celebrations, and there is often more than one great feast, depending upon the family's wealth. In Nepal, as in a number of other Asian countries, red is a happy color and worn for weddings (white is the color for funerals and mourning). During the ceremony, to denote marriage, women have the traditional Hindu application of vermilion (red dye) applied in the parting of their hair.

Bread, an important staple, is eaten at every Nepalese meal. Life-cycle celebration feasts include several different breads (recipes pages 285–88), among them *poppadums*. *Poppadums* are crisp, paper thin flatbreads about 6-inches in diameter, made from beans or lentils. They are sold in dried form in Asian and Indian food stores and are either roasted, grilled, or fried at home. Traditionally *poppadums* are deep-fried at 375° F for about 1 minute, until puffed and crisp, then drained on paper towels. They are easier to prepare, delicious, and fat-free when baked in a toaster oven. They are done when they turn puffy, brown, and crisp. They can also be baked in a conventional oven (directions follow). ❁ ❁ ❁

Poppadums

Bean or Lentil Flatbread (Wafers)

1 package *poppadums* (available at most Asian, Indian, and Middle Eastern food stores)

Equipment: Kitchen towel, nonstick baking sheet, tongs or metal spatula, oven mitts

1. Separate the *poppadums* from the package, and keep covered with damp towel until ready to bake.

Preheat oven to 350° F.

2. To bake in batches: Place 2 or 3 flatbreads side by side on nonstick baking sheet and bake for 4 to 6 minutes on each side, or until puffed, brown around the edges and crisp. Use tongs or metal spatula to turn over.

To serve, stack in a napkin-lined basket to keep warm. Break the breads into manageable pieces and use each to transport the food to your mouth.

In Nepal, people eat with the fingers of their right hand. (The left hand is used for personal grooming and must not touch food.) Food is either eaten from communal bowls or served on green leaves sewn together to make plates. For most Nepalese, the main dish of a meal is a heavy porridge made from maize, **millet,** and wheat flour boiled in water. Sauce (*tyun*) made with dried beans (*simi*) or vegetables (*tarkaari*) is added to the porridge. Dishes such as lentils mixed with vegetables and rice (recipe follows) are reserved for special occasions, such as the wedding feast. The mixed vegetables for this dish can be carrots, potatoes, peas, green beans, or whatever you have on hand.

Daal Bhaat Tarkaari

Lentils and Rice with Curried Vegetables

Yield: serves 4

4 tablespoons vegetable oil, divided
1 onion, **finely chopped**
2 cloves garlic, finely chopped
2 teaspoons grated, fresh ginger or 1 teaspoon ground ginger, divided
½ teaspoon **ground** turmeric
1 cup red lentils
5 cups water, divided
salt and pepper to taste
½ teaspoon ground red pepper
1 teaspoon ground **coriander**
1 teaspoon ground cumin
2 cups finely chopped, fresh mixed vegetables or frozen mixed vegetables, thawed (see above for vegetable selections)
2 cups rice (cooked according to directions on package) kept warm, for serving

Equipment: Medium saucepan with cover, mixing spoon, large skillet with cover

1. Prepare lentils: Heat 2 tablespoons oil in medium saucepan over medium-high heat. Add onions and garlic, stir, and **sauté** until soft but not browned, 2 to 3 minutes. Add 1 teaspoon fresh ginger or ½ teaspoon ground ginger, turmeric, and lentils, stir to combine and cook for 1 minute more. Add 4 cups of water and bring to a boil over high heat. Reduce heat to **simmer**, stir, cover, and cook for 20 to 25 minutes until lentils are tender. Add salt and pepper to taste and keep warm until ready to serve.

2. Prepare vegetables while lentils are cooking: Heat remaining 2 tablespoons of oil in large skillet over medium-high heat. Add ground red pepper, remaining 1 teaspoon of fresh ginger or ½ teaspoon ground ginger, ground coriander, and ground cumin. Stir constantly, cooking for about 1 minute to let flavors develop. Add the vegetables and using a mixing spoon, toss gently to coat with spices. Add remaining 1 cup of water. Reduce heat to simmer, cover, and cook for 10 to 15 minutes, or until vegetables are tender.

To serve, put the lentils in a serving bowl and cover with vegetable mixture. Serve with side dish of rice.

Most Hindu, Buddhist, and Muslim life-cycle celebrations, with the exception of funerals, include great quantities of sweets. Throughout the Indian subcontinent, candy making is a family tradition passed from one generation to another. *Halvais* (candy makers) sell their specialties in bazaars and small shops. *Rasgulla* are a popular sweet treat made with *paneer* (recipe follows).

Rasgulla

Cheese Balls in Syrup

Yield: serves 10 to 12

paneer tikki (firm cheese) (recipe follows)
½ teaspoon crushed cardamom seeds
1 tablespoon farina (available at most supermarkets and Middle Eastern food stores)
2 cups sugar
1 ¾ cups water
1 tablespoon **rose water** (available at Middle Eastern food stores and pharmacies)

Equipment: Food processor, rubber spatula, medium bowl, mixing spoon, wax paper, baking sheet, medium saucepan, candy **thermometer**, slotted spoon, raised-edge serving dish

1. Put firm cheese in food processor. Add cardamom and farina and process until smooth, about 1 minute. Using spatula, scrape cheese mixture down from sides of bowl and process for 30 seconds more. Transfer cheese mixture to medium bowl. Using clean hands, form cheese mixture into walnut-size balls and place on wax paper-covered baking sheet.

2. Put sugar into medium saucepan, add water, stir, and bring to a boil over medium-high heat. Stir, reduce heat to medium, and cook until syrup forms a thread when a little is lifted on a spoon or the syrup registers 230° to 240°F on a candy thermometer. Reduce heat to low.

3. Gently drop cheese balls, a few at a time, in syrup and **simmer** 8 to 10 minutes, or until balls are puffy. Carefully lift balls out of syrup with slotted spoon and place in raised-edge serving dish. Pour remaining syrup over the balls and sprinkle with rose water.

Serve warm or at room temperature. Nepalese eat by dipping the fingers into the bowl and scooping out a cheese ball; a spoon would be more helpful.

Paneer (Indian cheese) is easy to make and is eaten throughout the Indian subcontinent. When the cheese is soft and fresh, it is called *paneer cheena*, and when it is firm, it is called *paneer tikki*. The soft cheese is used in desserts and some savory dishes. The firm cheese is cut into wedges and even when heated it keeps its firmness, rather than melting. Firm cheese is used for *rasgulla* (recipe precedes).

Paneer cheena (soft) and Paneer tikki (firm)

Indian Cheeses

5 cups milk
juice of 2 lemons

Equipment: Noncorrosive medium saucepan with cover, wooden mixing spoon, **colander**, 3 layers of cheesecloth about 14-inches square, large bowl, heavy duty rubber band

1. Heat milk in medium saucepan over medium-high heat until small bubbles form around the edge of the pan. Cook 2 to 3 minutes, stirring with wooden mixing spoon to prevent a film from forming on the top. Remove from heat and stir in lemon juice. Cover and let stand until milk separates, about 1 minute.

2. Place a colander lined with the layered cheesecloth over a large bowl. When the thick white curd separates from the pale greenish whey, pour it into the cheesecloth lined colander. Gather the edges of the cheesecloth together to make a pouch and gently squeeze out the whey. (Discard the whey or cover and refrigerate for another use. In Nepal and many other countries, the whey is considered a healthy, re-

freshing drink. It is also used as a soup stock instead of water.) Wrap a heavy duty rubber band around the top of the pouch and hang over the sink faucet so the bag contents will drain into the sink.

3. For a soft cheese (*paneer cheena*), remove from bag in 1 hour. For a firm, dry cheese (*paneer cheena*), drain overnight. Use for making *rasgulla* (recipe precedes).

Both the soft and firm cheeses are used in cooking or simply sprinkled with assorted spices, such as turmeric, mint, ground red pepper, or cumin and eaten with bread.

BHUTAN

The Himalayan kingdom of Bhutan has been isolated for most of its history both by geography and by choice. The country is currently ruled by King Jigme Singye Wangchuck, also known as "the Precious Ruler of the Thunder Dragon People." Most Bhutanese are followers of Buddhism. (See Buddhism and Buddhist Life-Cycle Rituals, page liii). Bhutan also has a minority population of Hindus.

Although more than a dozen native languages are spoken in this tiny country (which is only a little larger than Pennsylvania), English, the official working language, is taught in schools. Communities are clustered in fertile valleys around gigantic monasteries (*dzongs*), which can be four or five stories high. The *dzongs* are central to each town, and for centuries have served as administrative as well as religious centers. Community celebrations and festivals take place in and around the *dzong*.

Bhutan has no set rules about marriage, and polygamy is acceptable (the current king has four wives). Bhutanese Buddhists have no one ritual for weddings. Though an auspicious wedding date is usually selected by an astrologer, Bhutanese are not particularly rigid about the calendar, and they might latch on to one auspicious date, making it several days long.

In Bhutan, marriages are traditionally prearranged by the couple's parents. Everyone in the community is generally expected to attend the wedding ceremony, which can be held in the home or in a Buddhist temple. The bride and groom wear new clothes; symbolic of a new beginning. An important part of wedding rituals is the white ceremonial scarf (*chata*). The person officiating puts a *chata* around the shoulders of the couple as they sit on meditation cushions. The meaning of marriage is then discussed: kindness, consideration, and affection toward one another. Many couples prepare an offering tray that contains items vital to life: a bowl with three fruits (usually a pear, apple, and orange); three jewels that represent the three jewels of Buddhism (the teacher [*Buddha*], teaching [*dharma*], and spiritual community [*sangha*]; burning incense (an offering to Buddha as well as a purifier); a piece of silk brocade cloth that represents a precious possession; two carefully folded *chatas* (one from each person), symbols of good luck; flowers; and an envelope with money). At the end of the service the couple toast each other with fruit juice that has been provided for the occasion. As the newlyweds leave the temple, the guests shower them with rice (*chaamal*), symbolically sprinkling good wishes over them. Depending upon the family's wealth, a wedding feast may be provided for guests.

Masala can be a simple or very complex blend of spices, depending upon the cook and the dish being prepared. For this recipe the blend is very simple.

Masala

Spice Blend

Yield: serves 4

1 teaspoon poppy seeds
1 teaspoon **finely chopped** fresh ginger or **ground** ginger
1 tablespoon ground **coriander**
1 tablespoon **coarsely chopped** almonds
1 teaspoon ground cloves

Equipment: **Mortar and pestle**

Combine poppy seeds, finely chopped fresh ginger or ground ginger, ground coriander, coarsely chopped almonds, and ground cloves in mortar and using the pestle, press down on the spices to grind them together.

Use in the following recipe for paneer kari *or transfer to a small jar, cover tightly, and refrigerate to use in recipes calling for* masala.

Paneer Dhuai Kari

Fried Cheese with Yogurt Curry Sauce

Yield: serves 6 to 8

4 tablespoons vegetable oil, divided
paneer tikki (firm cheese) (recipe page 309) cut into ¼-inch squares
1 onion, **finely chopped**
2 cloves garlic, finely chopped
½ teaspoon finely chopped fresh ginger or **ground** ginger
masala (recipe precedes)
3 tablespoons unsweetened *shredded or grated coconut*, homemade (recipe page 346), or frozen (available in the freezer section of most supermarkets and Asian food stores)
1 cup plain yogurt
½ cup water
salt and ground red pepper to taste
5 or 6 sprigs fresh mint, finely chopped, for **garnish**

Equipment: Large skillet, slotted mixing spoon, plate

1. Heat 2 tablespoons oil in large skillet over medium-high heat. Add cheese cubes, in batches. Reduce heat to medium and fry until golden, 10 to 12 minutes. Remove with slotted mixing spoon and set on plate. Add remaining 2 tablespoons oil to skillet and fry onions over medium heat until soft and all sides are golden, 3 to 5 minutes. Add garlic, ginger, *masala*, and coconut. Reduce heat to low, stir constantly, and cook for about 2 minutes for flavors to develop.

2. Stir in yogurt and water to make a smooth, creamy sauce. Add salt and ground red pepper to taste. Add fried cheese and gently toss to coat. Cook until heated through, 3 to 5 minutes.

To serve, garnish with chopped fresh mint and eat either hot or at room temperature. Use poppadums *or other flatbread to scoop the cheese cubes out of the bowl.*

PEOPLE'S REPUBLIC OF CHINA & TAIWAN

The People's Republic of China in southern Asia has the largest population in the world. Taiwan, an island off the coast of China, was a Chinese province until 1895, when it was captured by Japan. Taiwan was returned to China in 1945, until nationalists, fleeing Communist rule in China, set up a separate government in Taiwan. Today, life-cycle events are still important in both countries, though many rituals are no longer performed or are done in moderation in mainland China, which is a Communist regime. Although officially atheist, China retains elements of its traditional religions—Confucianism, Taoism, and Buddhism.

To most Chinese, food and friendship are inseparable, and any gathering without food is considered incomplete. Weddings, birthdays, funerals, holidays, and public ceremonies are celebrated with appropriate feasting. The more important the event, the more dishes are prepared for the occasion. The preparation of food holds special meaning; for instance, if fish is served, it is always the whole fish, including the head, to symbolize unity and togetherness. Red is the color of happiness, and many foods are colored red. Soups are usually served with a meal, and to serve shark-fin soup is a symbol of status and wealth.

Noodles are a symbol of longevity, and they are served at all birthday celebrations, which are celebrated on New Year's Day, not the date of birth. The older the person is, the longer the noodles; sometimes they can reach 30 inches in length. In Northern China, on a woman's 66th birthday, her oldest daughter is expected to prepare 66 tiny dumplings for her mother. The dumplings can be stuffed with meat or other stuffings such as *jien dui* (red bean paste), *buchu mandoo* (finely chopped vegetables), and *hom soi gok* (pork, shrimp, bamboo shoots, and mushrooms).

In Taiwan, traces of centuries-old Chinese wedding rituals are still included in modern-day weddings. The groom's *pinjin* ("bride's wealth") is often used by the bride-to-be to buy her trousseau as well as furnishings for the home the newlyweds plan to share. In both mainland China and Taiwan, the wedding date is chosen from the Chinese almanac that coincides with the eighth month of *Zhong Qiu Jie*, the period of time in which the "moon is at its fullest and the flowers at their best." Cakes and sweets, such as peanut brittle or toffee, wrapped in red paper, are sent to friends and relatives to inform them of the forthcoming wedding.

An old ritual, performed more often in Taiwan than in mainland China, is the wedding tea ceremony held at the bride's future in-law's home. According to traditional Chinese wedding rituals, the tea ceremony formalizes the marriage. All relatives from both families are expected to be present. During the ceremony both the bridegroom and bride offer each parent a cup of tea; if, for instance, the future mother-in-law refuses to accept the cup of tea from her daughter-in-law-to-be, this means she refuses to accept her into the family.

In mainland China, funerals are family affairs, conducted by the eldest son. In Taiwan the Taoist priest presides over the rituals. In both Taiwan and China the body of the deceased is cremated. The casket is decorated with paper flowers, and paper money is burned with the body. After incense and ceremonial candles are burned, fireworks are shot off, which, according to tradition, intimidates evil sprits.

The most important dish for special occasions in China or Taiwan is Peking duck. Not only the preparation, but the serving and eating follows a set pattern. ❂ ❂ ❂

Pei-ching-k'ao-ya

Peking Duck

Yield: serves 4 to 6

- *Po-ping* (Mandarin pancakes, recipe page 314), for serving
- 6 quarts or more water
- 2 cups honey, plus 1 to 2 tablespoons
- 10 thin slices peeled fresh ginger root, about 1 inch in diameter, or 2 tablespoons ground ginger

4½- to 6-pound oven-ready duck (if frozen, thaw according to directions on package)
16 to 20 green onions, including green tops, trimmed, and cut into 4-inch lengths for **garnish**
¼ cup hoisin sauce (available at Asian food stores and most supermarkets)
1 tablespoon water
1 teaspoon sesame-seed oil (available at Asian food stores)
2 teaspoons sugar

Equipment: 8- to 12-quart kettle, wooden mixing spoon, small plastic bag, **colander**, paper towels, kitchen string, oven mitts, large baking pan, sharp paring knife, large roasting pan with rack, work surface, **pastry brush**, medium bowl, small saucepan, small serving bowl, carving board, sharp meat knife, large serving platter

1. Prepare *po-ping*: keep refrigerated until ready to serve.

2. Prepare ahead: Fill an 8- to 10-quart kettle two-thirds full with water. Add 2 cups honey and ginger, stir to mix, and bring to boil over high heat.

3. Remove the bag of innards from inside the bird, put in plastic bag, and refrigerate for another use. Wash the duck thoroughly under cold running water, and drain well in colander, about 10 minutes. Using paper towels, pat inside the cavity and on the outside of the duck until most excess water is removed. The skin on the bird should no longer be shiny. Wrap the middle of a 3- to 4-foot length of string around the neck of the duck and loop it under the wings. Make a handle of the string, extending above the neck, by tying the two ends together. The string must be strong enough to hold the bird without breaking.

4. **Note: Adult supervision required:** When water is at a full boil, wearing oven mitts, hold the duck by the string handle and carefully lower it into the boiling liquid. Dunk the bird up and down 6 to 8 times, and then completely submerse the bird in the boiling liquid for 10 minutes. (The skin becomes very firm.)

5. Have a colander ready in a large roasting pan. Carefully remove the duck from boiling liquid and drain over the sink. Place duck in the colander to drain at least 30 minutes. Using a wad of paper towels, wipe out the duck cavity. With fresh paper towels, wipe off the duck skin. Discard boiling liquid when it cools enough to handle.

Preheat oven to 225° F.

6. Dry-out duck: Remove and discard string. Place duck, breast side up, on rack set in large roasting pan and place in warm oven for 1 hour. Remove from oven. Lift the rack and duck together from the roasting pan and set on work surface. Set roasting pan aside to use again. Allow duck to rest 30 minutes on rack and then wipe out inside of duck with wad of paper towels. Use fresh paper towels to wipe off fat oozing from skin. Allow to rest 1 hour on the rack and repeat wiping duck inside and out several times. Using a pastry brush, coat the duck's skin completely with 1 to 2 tablespoons honey.

7. While duck is drying out, make green onion brushes: Fill a medium bowl with ice water. Using a sharp paring knife, make 4 cuts 1-inch deep in each end of the green onion. Put onions in ice water and refrigerate until time to serve so that cut ends will spread out and curl up.

8. Prepare sauce: In small saucepan, combine hoisin sauce, 1 tablespoon water, sesame-seed oil, and sugar. Cook over medium heat and stir until sugar dissolves, about 3 minutes. Reduce heat to low and cook for 5 minutes more for flavor to develop. Cool to room temperature and transfer to small serving bowl.

Preheat oven to 450° F.

9. Return honey-coated duck on the rack to roasting pan and set in hot oven to bake for 35 minutes. Lower heat to 275° F and bake for 1 hour. Wearing oven mitts, remove from oven and

turn duck breast-side-down and roast 1 hour longer. The skin becomes very dark and crisp. Remove from oven and transfer duck to carving board. Allow to rest 20 minutes before carving duck.

10. Using a sharp meat knife and your fingers, remove crisp skin from breast, sides and back of duck. Cut skin in serving-size pieces about 1 x 3 inches and arrange slightly overlapping around edge of a serving platter. Cut wings and drumsticks from duck and cut all the meat away from the breastbone and carcass, slicing it into strips about 1 x 3 inches, and pile in the middle of the serving platter.

In China, it is not only what you eat, but also how it is eaten. There is a procedure and ceremony to every part of the meal. *Po-ping* are an important part of the total *Pei-ching-k'ao-ya* experience. To serve, heat foil-wrapped *po-ping* in a 350° F oven for 5 to 10 minutes or until heated through. Unwrap *po-ping*, fold in half and place on serving platter. Place bowl of hoisin sauce on plate and surround with green onion brushes. All platters are placed in the center of the table. Traditionally, each guest spreads a *po-ping* flat on their plate, dips a green onion in the sauce, using it as a brush to coat the *po-ping* with sauce. The green onion is placed in the middle of *po-ping* with a piece of duck skin and a piece of duck meat on top. *Po-ping* is rolled up enclosing the green onion, skin, and duck. The *po-ping* package is picked up and eaten with the fingers.

PO-PING

MANDARIN PANCAKES

Yield: about 24 pieces

2 cups all-purpose flour, **sifted**
¾ cup boiling water
1 to 2 tablespoons sesame seed oil

Equipment: Large mixing bowl, wooden mixing spoon, damp towel, lightly floured work surface, rolling pin, 2 ½-inch cookie cutter or water glass, **pastry brush**, dry towel, **heavy-based** 8-inch skillet, metal spatula, aluminum foil

1. Put flour in large mixing bowl, make a well (hole) in the center, and pour in boiling water. Using wooden spoon, mix flour and water together until a soft dough forms. Transfer to lightly floured work surface and **knead** gently for 10 minutes or until smooth and **elastic**. Cover with damp towel and allow to rest for 15 minutes.

2. On lightly floured work surface, roll dough to about ¼ inch thick. With 2½-inch cookie cutter or rim of glass, cut as many circles as possible from the dough. Knead scraps together and roll out again and cut more circles until you have about 24 pieces. Place circles side by side on work surface and keep covered with a damp towel.

3. Using a rolling pin, flatten each into a 6-inch circle, rotating the circle so it keeps its round shape. With pastry brush, lightly brush one side of each circle with sesame seed oil. Cover with a dry towel and continue until all circles are rolled out and brushed with oil.

4. Prepare to fry: Have a dry towel spread out on work surface. Place a heavy-based 8-inch skillet over high heat for about 30 seconds. Reduce heat to medium and cook pancakes, one at a time, in the ungreased skillet. Using a metal spatula, turn pancakes over when brown flecks appear on the surface, about 1 minute on each side. Remove from skillet and place on towel to cool to room temperature. Cut a piece of foil large enough to wrap around the stack of pancakes. Wrap up pancakes and refrigerate until ready to serve.

Po-ping are eaten with pei-ching-k'ao-ya *(recipe precedes).*

Meals often end with fruit and the following watermelon shell is frequently decorated with hand carved designs on the rind.

Shib-chin-kuo-pin

Watermelon Shell filled with Fruit

Yield: serves 6 to 8

- 1 medium watermelon (about 10 pounds)
- 2 cups canned litchis, drained (available at Asian food stores and some supermarkets)
- 1 cup canned loquats, drained (available at Asian food stores)
- 1 cup preserved canned kumquats, drained (available at Asian food stores)
- 2 cups water-pack canned kumquats, drained (available at Asian food stores and some supermarkets)
- 1 cantaloupe or honeydew melon
- 6 to 8 bunches purple and green grapes, for **garnish**
- 1 to 2 pounds strawberries, for garnish

Equipment: Work surface, paper towels, large knife, **melon baller**, large mixing bowl, plastic food wrap, sharp paring knife

1. Place the watermelon on the work surface and wipe it off with paper towels. Using a large knife, cut about one-third off the top of the melon, leaving two-thirds of the melon intact to use as a container.

2. Using the melon baller, scoop out melon balls, taking care not to cut into white pulp lining inside shell of melon. By scooping out the watermelon fruit, it creates a hollow watermelon bowl. Put melon balls in large mixing bowl and add drained litchis, loquats, and both kinds of kumquats.

3. Cut cantaloupe or honeydew in half, remove and discard seeds. Using melon baller, cut melon into balls and add to fruit mixture. Cover with plastic wrap and refrigerate until ready to serve.

4. If desired, cut a design in the outer rind of the watermelon container with a sharp paring knife or scallop the top edge.

To serve, drain fruit very well before transferring to watermelon bowl. When setting on buffet table, place green and purple grapes around the base of the watermelon to keep it from tilting. Garnish with strawberries. Add a large spoon for serving.

MYANMAR (BURMA)

Myanmar, located in southeast Asia and bordered by Thailand, China, India, and Bangladesh, is made up of many different cultures. It is customary in Myanmar for people to live in communities and compounds with others of the same ethnic heritage. Most Burmese are Buddhists. (See Buddhism and Buddhist Life-Cycle Rituals, page liii.)

Among Buddhists, the occasion for a feast may be a christening, a birthday, a Buddhist initiation or ear-piercing ceremony, a wedding or wedding anniversary, or a celebration held in honor of deceased parents. A feast can take place in one's home or in a monastery and usually includes offerings of food and other items to the monks.

Almost all Burmese eat with their fingers. Both soup and salad are served with the main dishes, not as separate courses. Appetizers and desserts are reserved for ceremonial occasions. Otherwise the final course is tea, without milk or sugar, and fresh fruit.

In Myanmar, birth is an auspicious occasion in every family, and before the child is born, the expectant mother is closely guided by astrology. Each day of the week is designated by a different animal and significant to the infant's horoscope. After the baby is born, the mother receives many gifts and good wishes from family and friends.

The month of *Tabodwe* (usually falling near February) is not only the time to celebrate the rice harvest, but also the time that young boys of seven years or more enter a monastery for a brief time and devote themselves to prayer. At the same time, young girls participate in a formal ear-piercing ceremony called *shinpyu*. The foods served at a *shinpyu* ceremony vary, depending upon the wealth of the celebrants. The more wealthy enjoy a meal that can consist of as many as four meat and four fish and shellfish dishes, plus vegetable soup and rice. A middle-class family will sit down to fewer dishes, and the poor honor the day with a meal of rice and pickled vegetables.

Myanmar marriages involve only the mutual consent of the two parties concerned. Living and eating together is enough to constitute marriage, and traditionally, the marriage is valid if neighbors recognize it as such. But, if desired, weddings can be as elaborate as the couple's wishes and the parents' financial position can make them. The simplest wedding is held at the home of the bride-to-be. Parents of both parties and relatives are present along with a gathering of elders. The bride and groom sit together on a smooth mat as they pay obeisance to parents and the "triple gems": the Buddha, the *dharma* (also dhamma) (which means "truth" or "law"), and the *sangha* (which refers to Buddhist monks).

The marriage ceremony is performed by a master of ceremonies dressed like a Brahmin (a Hindu of priestly caste). During the ceremony, the hands of bride and groom are tied with a silk scarf and dipped in a silver bowl of water. This ritual signifies that they are now joined together as one. At the end of the ceremony, silver coins and paper confetti are showered on guests as symbols of wealth and hopes for many children for the newlyweds. The refreshments served after the ceremony can range from simple tea with cakes to an extensive buffet laden with beautifully garnished delicacies.

According to Buddhist beliefs, death is accepted as just one stage in the endless cycle of existence. (See Buddhism and Buddhist Life-Cycle Rituals, page liii.) The body of the deceased remains behind while the soul moves on to a new rebirth. No formal periods of mourning are designated by the Buddhist religion. On the day a person dies, a monk from the family's monastery is brought to the home of the deceased. Family members make a feast offering to the monastery. The deceased is bathed and fully dressed in favorite garments. Candles, incense sticks, water, and token offerings of food are placed at his or her head. An earthen water pot is placed under the bed on which the body is laid.

At the funeral, the height of each family member is measured with string. The lengths of string are then put into the coffin as a reminder, to the deceased, of his or her earthly family. A coin, 25 *pya* (about 4 cents), is placed in the mouth of the deceased. This is used as payment to the navigator guiding the soul across to the land of the dead. The water pot is then broken. At this time the grieving family is expected to show their emotions; loudly wailing (crying is considered healthy and cathartic for the mourners).

A week-long wake then takes place to appease the spirit of the dead, who according to legend, stays in the house for up to a week after its demise. Doors and windows are kept open to make it easy for the spirit of death to exit the premises. A week later, monks are again invited to the house to pray and to remind the spirit of the deceased that it is no longer a member of the household and must go on its way.

Special occasions, such as weddings, usually call for large quantities of steaming coconut rice. ۞ ۞ ۞

Ohnhtamin

Coconut Rice

Yield: serves 4

2 cups rice
2 cups coconut milk, homemade (recipe page 346), or canned
1 onion, thinly sliced
1 tablespoon vegetable oil
½ teaspoon sugar
½ teaspoon salt
1 cup water

Equipment: Medium saucepan with cover, wooden mixing spoon

Put rice, coconut milk, onion slices, oil, sugar, and salt in medium saucepan. Add water, stir to mix well. Bring to a boil over high heat, stir, and immediately reduce heat to very low. Cover and cook for about 30 minutes until rice is tender.

Serve at once with vegetables.

In rural areas, curry is served only on special occasions. Each person is served boiled rice, and a little food is taken from each accompanying dish to eat with it.

Weta Hin

Curried Pork

Yield: serves 4

1 onion, **finely chopped**
5 cloves garlic, finely chopped
1 tablespoon finely chopped ginger root
1 teaspoon **ground** turmeric
½ teaspoon dried red pepper flakes
2 tablespoons vegetable oil
2 pounds boneless lean pork shoulder, cut into 2-inch cubes
1 teaspoon sesame oil (available at Asian food stores)
16-ounce can of whole tomatoes, drained
1 stalk fresh **lemon grass** (use about 4 to 6 inches off the tender, whitish end and discard tougher green top) and, finely chopped (available at Asian food stores)
1 tablespoon fish sauce (*nuoc mam*) (available at Asian food stores)
cooked rice, kept warm for serving

Equipment: Electric **blender**, rubber spatula, **Dutch oven** or large saucepan with cover

1. Put onion, garlic, ginger root, turmeric, and red pepper flakes in blender. Cover and **blend** until smooth, about 1 minute.

Note: While blending, turn machine off once or twice and scrape down sides of container with rubber spatula.

2. Heat vegetable oil in Dutch oven or large saucepan over medium-high heat. Add cubed pork, blended onion mixture, sesame oil, tomatoes, lemon grass, and fish sauce. Using a fork, break up tomatoes. Bring to boil and stir. Reduce heat to **simmer**, cover, and cook until meat is tender, about 1½ hours.

To serve, transfer cooked rice to serving bowl and either cover with weta hin *or serve it in separate bowls.*

The number of dishes is important (more is better) so it is not unusual for several rice dishes to be served at the same meal.

Thorebut Htamin

Buttered Rice with Raisins and Roasted Cashews

Yield: serves 4

2 cups rice
4 cups water

¼ teaspoon salt
1 cup butter or margarine, cut into small pieces (about the size of walnuts)
1 cup golden raisins
1 cup **roasted** cashews

Equipment: Medium saucepan with cover, mixing spoon

1. Put rice in saucepan. Add water, salt, and butter or margarine. Bring to a boil over medium-high heat and stir. Reduce heat to **simmer**, cover, and cook for 20 minutes. Remove from heat, keep covered for 5 minutes.

2. Add raisins and cashews, and stir to mix thoroughly. Let stand, covered, 15 minutes for flavor to develop before serving.

To serve, transfer to serving bowl and serve with weta hin *(recipe page 317).*

THAILAND

Thailand is located in southeast Asia, southeast of Myanmar (Burma). Nearly 95 percent of all Thais are Buddhist (see Buddhism and Buddhist Life-Cycle Rituals, page liii), but elements of Hinduism and other beliefs are often blended with Buddhist belief. Mystics, mediums, and astrologers are often consulted by members of every social and economic class.

In rural areas many people believe the spirit *phi* is responsible for babies. A few days before the infant's birth, food offerings are left out to appease the *phi* spirit in hopes for the child's safe delivery. The infant, for the first month of birth, is not considered a family member. At the end of 30 days, the family holds a special rite to accept the child into the family. Baby boys are often given names that mean "strength" or "honor," while girls are named for feminine qualities, such as beauty and purity, or after flowers, plants, and fruits.

Astrology is taken seriously in Thailand, especially when selecting the prospective marriage partner. Most Thai marriages take place in an even-numbered lunar month. This is because weddings involve two people, therefore the wedding months should be multiples of two, the best being the second, fourth, sixth, and eighth.

As many as nine Buddhist monks can officiate at a traditional Thai wedding. The ceremony begins in the morning with the couple kneeling inside a semicircle: Both the bride and groom wear headdresses of looped white yarn called *mongkols*. The two *mongkols* are joined by a string to symbolize the uniting of the man and woman as husband and wife. Monks place a white cord (*sai sin*) around the area where the couple is kneeling, marking it off as a sacred zone. A half-hour of chanting and blessings follow and the senior monk, using a sprig of Chinese gooseberry, sprinkles the couple with holy water. Later at the wedding reception, guests take turns pouring purified water over the joined hands of the bride and groom.

The next event is a trip to the bride's house. In former times, the groom was required to build a house for himself and his bride in his father-in-law's compound. Today, he simply presents gifts to the bride's family. Traditionally, the party must pass through "toll gates" erected by the children at the bride's house. The bride and groom must give the children money to be allowed to pass.

Thai Buddhists believe in an afterlife and reincarnation. Funerals are looked upon as celebrations, and beautifully designed structures are built for the cremation and are burnt along with the body, three to seven days after death.

Ethnic minorities, such as Muslims and nearly all hill tribal groups, bury their dead rather than cremate them. Village funerals can be very elaborate, with everyone taking part in the activities. Some tribes dress in gaily decorated costumes that are worn only during funerals. Water buffalo and cattle are slaughtered and the meat divided among either the clan of the deceased or the entire village.

The Thai words for rice and food are synonymous. Rice represents life and is revered as such. To cook rice in the Thai manner, choose a long-grain variety of polished white rice. Rice is soaked overnight, then drained and steamed. This takes longer than cooking it directly in the water, but it gives a very fluffy and grainy result. It must be served as soon as it is cooked; it will go hard and dry if left to stand.

A Thai meal is based on rice, but the number and variety of dishes served with rice is limited only by the chef's time, imagination, patience, and budget. It is customary to have soup, two or more *kaengs* (dishes with sauces), and as many *krueng kieng* (side dishes) as possible. Other than the rice, which is served hot, food is generally served at room temperature.

Some Thais eat mostly with spoon and fork, while many eat with their fingers. Everything is served at once and diners choose according to individual taste, combining each dish separately with a little rice.

Meat is the highlight of most Thai meals and always served on special occasions. This is a festive way of preparing pork. ۞ ۞ ۞

Kao Hom Moo

Thai Pork and Fragrant Rice

Note: Use care when handling peppers. Wrap your hands in plastic wrap or cover them with plastic sandwich bag. If you accidentally touch your eyes, rinse out at once under cold running water.

Yield: serves 10 to 12

- 12 cups cooked rice (cook according to directions on package), at room temperature
- 1½ cups carrots, **trimmed** and **finely chopped**
- 1½ cups green onions, trimmed and thinly sliced
- 3 tablespoons fresh **cilantro**, finely chopped
- 4 cloves garlic, finely chopped
- 2 **jalapeño** peppers, trimmed, **seeded**, and finely chopped
- 10 tablespoons *nam pla* (fish sauce) or soy sauce, more or less to taste, divided (fish sauce is available at Asian food stores)
- 4 tablespoons lime juice, divided
- 2 tablespoons sugar
- 6 pounds boneless pork loin (have butcher **butterfly** meat and pound into ½ thick rectangular piece suitable for stuffing)
- 1½ cups brown sugar, firmly packed
- 1 cup water
- *peanut sauce* (recipe follows), for serving

Equipment: Large mixing bowl, mixing spoon, work surface, kitchen string, paring knife, large roasting pan with wire rack, plastic food wrap, small bowl, **bulb baster**, meat **thermometer**, oven mitts

Preheat oven to 325° F.

1. In large mixing bowl, combine rice, carrots, green onions, cilantro, garlic, jalapeños, 8 tablespoons fish sauce or soy sauce (more or less to taste), 2 tablespoons lime juice, and sugar. Stir to mix well.

2. Place prepared pork loin, cut-side up, on work surface. Spread about half rice mixture onto surface of meat and roll up, jelly roll fashion, to enclose rice filling. Using string, tie roast in 3 or 4 places to secure filling. Place fat side up on wire rack in roasting pan. Cover remain-

ing rice mixture with plastic wrap and refrigerate until ready to serve.

3. In a small bowl, combine brown sugar, remaining 2 tablespoons lime juice, remaining 2 tablespoons fish sauce or soy sauce, and water. Stir to mix well. Spread over pork. Insert meat thermometer in center of meat.

4. Roast in oven until meat thermometer reaches 160 degrees, 2½ to 3 hours. Using bulb baster, **baste** frequently to moisten meat. Let stand 20 minutes before carving.

5. Remove rice from refrigerator and let sit at room temperature at least 1 hour before serving.

To serve, cut pork into ¼-inch thick slices. Mound reserved rice in the center of a large serving platter. Surround rice with slightly overlapping slices of pork. Serve with bowl of nam tua *(recipe follows) to spoon over each serving.*

Nam tua

Peanut Sauce

Yield: about 3 cups

1 cup crunchy peanut butter
1 cup plain lowfat yogurt
¼ cup chopped green onions
¼ cup lemon juice
¼ cup honey
2 tablespoons soy sauce
1 teaspoon **ground** ginger
½ teaspoon ground red pepper

Equipment: Medium mixing bowl, mixing spoon

In a medium bowl combine peanut butter, yogurt, onion, lemon juice, honey, soy sauce, ginger, and red pepper. Stir until smooth.

To serve, put sauce in small bowl. To eat, each person spoons sauce over their serving of pork.

The literal translation of this appetizer called *ma ho* is "galloping horses." It is often served at wedding banquets. The combination of fruit and meat gives interesting contrast in both color and texture.

Ma Ho

Pork and Pineapple

Yield: serves 6 to 8

1 tablespoon vegetable oil
4 cloves garlic, **finely chopped**
1 pound lean **ground** pork
1 to 2 **jalapeño** peppers, **trimmed**, **seeded**, and finely chopped
2 tablespoons sugar
½ cup dry roasted peanuts, finely chopped
1 head leaf lettuce, separated, washed, and drained well
1 16-ounce can of sliced pineapple, drained, for serving
fresh mint or **coriander** leaves, for **garnish**

Equipment: **Wok** or large skillet, mixing spoon

1. Heat oil in wok or large skillet over medium-high heat. Stir-fry garlic until soft, 3 to 5 minutes. Crumble in pork and stir-fry until browned, 5 to 7 minutes. Add peppers and sugar and stir-fry for 2 minutes. Add peanuts, stir in thoroughly, and remove from heat.

2. Dry lettuce leaves by gently patting with paper towels and arrange them decoratively on a serving platter. Place a well drained pineapple slice on each leaf. Mound spoonfuls of meat mixture equally in the center of each slice of pineapple. Garnish with either sprigs of fresh mint or coriander leaves.

To serve as an appetizer, chill for about 1 hour before serving. To eat, pick up the lettuce leaf and wrap it around the pineapple-meat mixture.

Wood mushrooms used in this recipe are a dried variety that look like burnt paper. When soaked in water they turn a delicate brown.

Gai Pad Khing Hed Hoo Noo

Stir-fry Chicken with Wood Mushrooms

Yield: serves 8

3 tablespoons peanut oil
2 onions, cut into ¼-inch thick slices
2 cloves garlic, **finely chopped**
2 pounds boneless, skinless chicken breasts, cut into ½- x 2-inch strips
6-inch piece fresh ginger, peeled and finely sliced
8 large wood mushrooms, soaked in warm water about 10 minutes, drained, and **coarsely chopped** (available at Asian food stores)
1 tablespoon dried red pepper flakes, more or less to taste
½ cup chicken broth, homemade (recipe page 106), or canned
½ cup oyster sauce (available at Asian food stores and some supermarkets)
3 teaspoons sugar
8 green onions, cut into 1-inch pieces
2 tablespoons white vinegar
fresh **coriander** leaves, for **garnish**

Equipment: **Wok** with cover or large skillet, mixing spoon

1. Heat oil in wok or skillet over medium-high heat. Add onions and garlic, stir, and cook until soft, 3 to 5 minutes. Add chicken pieces, increase heat to high, and stir-fry 3 to 5 minutes until no longer pink. Add ginger, mushrooms, and 1 tablespoon pepper flakes, more or less to taste. Toss well and cook about 1 minute.

2. Add chicken broth, oyster sauce, sugar, green onions, and vinegar. Toss and cook for about 1 minute more to heat through.

To serve, transfer to large platter and sprinkle with coriander, for garnish.

LAOS/CAMBODIA

Laos and neighboring Cambodia are located on the Indochinese peninsula of southeast Asia, between Thailand and Vietnam. The people in both countries have suffered from many years of oppression and wars, which have left them mostly impoverished. As a result, the people, who are mostly farmers, can barely eke out a living. The majority of people in both countries follow the teachings of Buddha and celebrate life-cycle events accordingly. (See Buddhism and Buddhist Life-Cycle Rituals, page liii.)

In Laos, the naming ceremony (*baci*) of a newborn baby is the first big event in a person's life. The celebration feast is held for family members, friends, and neighbors or the entire village, depending upon the family's wealth. During the celebration, money is tied to the baby's arm with red string. A Buddhist monk is asked to choose a name for the child, one that is astrologically correct for that child.

Boys go through a coming-of-age ceremony around the age of 13. Only close relatives are invited to the ceremony, which involves cutting the boy's hair. In some areas, a boy receives a tattoo to symbolize his manhood that is also supposed to ward off evil spirits.

In Cambodia, it is customary for an engaged couple to exchange gifts. Among the gifts is a box of **betel nuts** from the future groom to his bride-to-be. When she accepts the betel nuts, it seals their commitment to marry. Once engaged, the groom accepts his responsibilities to his in-laws by taking a vow of servitude, known as *thvo bamro. Thvo bamro* can last from one month to two years, during which the groom works for his future in-laws. If he shows disrespect, complains, or fails to impress them they can cancel the engagement.

Many city weddings follow Western customs, and couples choose their own partners. In the country, however, parents still choose their children's marriage partners. Each family appoints a marriage broker to investigate the other family and to make certain that their social and economic standing is good. Once the two families agree to the marriage, they consult an astrologer to select the wedding day, and exchange gifts, food, and plants.

The wedding ceremony takes place in the bride's home, where wedding rings and gifts are exchanged. The couple's wrists are tied together with red thread that has been soaked in holy water. The Buddhist priest delivers a sermon, and married guests pass around a candle to bless the newlyweds. After the ceremony, there is a grand feast with traditional music.

In both Laos and Cambodia, the most important life-cycle event is the funeral. A Buddhist funeral is generally regarded as a festive occasion, since it represents the rebirth of the soul rather than the end of life. In both countries, the body can be cremated in an elaborate ceremony, depending upon the wealth of the family. After the body is washed and dressed, it is placed in a coffin. In Cambodia, the body is transported to a public crematorium to be burned. In Laos, the body is placed in a shelter in the garden or yard. The family holds a series of feasts and ceremonies before the body is taken to a cremation pyre on a river bank, or to a field where it is washed, exposed to the sky, and then cremated. Depending upon family wealth, the funeral pyre can be a magnificent work of art or, for the less wealthy, the body can simply be buried in the forest. Family members traditionally show their grief by wearing white clothing and shaving their heads.

Rice is the mainstay of both the Laos and Cambodian diet, and no meal is complete unless rice is on the table. Soups are eaten with the meal.

Sweet and Sour Soup

Yield: serves 6 to 8

- 2 quarts chicken broth, homemade (recipe page 106), or canned
- ½ pound boneless chicken breasts or thighs, finely sliced
- 1 cup fresh pineapple, peeled, **cored**, and **finely chopped**
- 1 tomato, **trimmed** and **coarsely chopped**
- 1½ cups zucchini, cut in half lengthwise and sliced crosswise ¼ inch thick
- 3 tablespoons white vinegar
- 3 tablespoons fish sauce (*nuoc mam*) (available at Asian food stores)
- 1 teaspoon sugar
- ½ pound headless medium shrimp, **peeled and deveined**
- salt and pepper to taste

Equipment: Large saucepan, wooden mixing spoon, large serving bowl

1. Pour chicken broth into large saucepan, add finely sliced chicken, chopped pineapple, chopped tomato, sliced zucchini, vinegar, fish sauce, and sugar. Bring to a boil over medium-high heat. Stir, reduce heat to **simmer**, cover, and cook 1 hour.

2. Add shrimp, stir, and cook until shrimp are cooked through and they turn an opaque pinkish-white. Add salt and pepper to taste.

To serve the soup, transfer to large serving bowl and have guests help themselves by pouring their serving into an individual bowl which they pick up and drink. The shrimp and vegetables can be picked out of the bowl with their hand or a spoon.

A favorite rice dish for weddings and other auspicious occasions is *phoat khsat*.

Phoat Khsat

Royal Rice

Yield: serves 6

6 tablespoons vegetable oil, divided
3 **shallots**, peeled and **finely chopped**
5 cloves garlic, finely chopped
2 sprigs fresh fennel, **coarsely chopped**
1 cup finely chopped boneless, skinless chicken
1 cup finely chopped boneless, lean pork
8 cups boiled rice (cooked according to directions on package)
1 cup **crayfish**, cooked, peeled, and finely chopped
1 tablespoon vinegar
1 tablespoon sugar
1 tablespoon fish sauce (*nuoc mam*) (available at Asian food stores)
salt and pepper to taste
1 egg, beaten, for **garnish**
1 green pepper, finely sliced, for garnish
juice of 1 lemon, for serving

Equipment: **Wok** or large skillet, mixing spoon, small skillet, metal spatula, plate, paring knife

1. Heat 5 tablespoons oil in wok or large skillet over medium-high heat. Add shallots, garlic, and fresh fennel. Reduce heat to medium and stir-fry until soft, 3 to 5 minutes. Add chicken and pork, and stir-fry until cooked through, 5 to 7 minutes.

2. Add cooked rice and cooked crayfish. Continue to stir-fry until heated through. Add vinegar, sugar, *nuoc mam,* and salt and pepper to taste.

3. Heat remaining tablespoon of oil in small skillet over medium-high heat. Add beaten egg and swirl around to coat pan to make a flat omelet. Sprinkle with green peppers and fry until done, about 3 minutes. Using metal spatula, remove omelet to plate. Using a paring knife, shred omelet into strips and sprinkle over rice mixture, for garnish

To serve, transfer rice mixture to large serving bowl. Just before serving, sprinkle with juice of 1 lemon.

Njum is an easy-to-make Laos salad that is more like a condiment. It is eaten with rice and meat dishes.

Njum

Bamboo Shoot Salad

Yield: serves 4

2½ cups canned sliced bamboo shoots, drained and **blanched** (available at supermarkets)
1 clove garlic, **finely chopped**
1 tablespoon lime or lemon juice
1 tablespoon sugar
1 tablespoon fish sauce (*nuoc mam*) (available at Asian food stores)
1 cup coconut milk, homemade (recipe page 346), or canned
3 green onions, **trimmed** and finely sliced
1 tablespoon finely chopped fresh basil
1 tablespoon finely chopped fresh mint
dried red pepper flakes, to taste
salt and pepper to taste

Equipment: Medium salad bowl, mixing spoon, small bowl, plastic food wrap

1. Put blanched bamboo shoots in medium salad bowl.

2. Prepare dressing: In small bowl, combine garlic, lime or lemon juice, sugar, fish sauce, and coconut milk.

3. Pour dressing over bamboo shoots. Sprinkle green onions, basil, and mint on top, and toss to mix well. Cover with plastic wrap and refrigerate until ready to serve.

To serve, put salad on table and eat as a condiment with other dishes for the wedding feast.

VIETNAM

Vietnam is located in southeast Asia just south of China. The religion most Vietnamese embrace is referred to as *Tam Giao*, the "triple religion" or "Vietnamese Buddhism." It combines elements of Buddhism, Confucianism, and Taoism with ancestor worship. In the countryside, animist belief (everything has a soul) is added to *Tam Giao*. About 10 percent of the Vietnamese population are Roman Catholics.

With such a variety of religions in Vietnam, there are no shortages of life-cycle celebrations. Significant events in life, birth, marriage, and death were once marked by elaborate ceremonies. After the war years in the late twentieth century, ceremonies became simpler under Communist rule, but lately, there has been a return to more elaborate rituals, especially for weddings and funerals.

The Vietnamese family is likely to have a small party when a baby is one month old. After the first year, birthdays are not celebrated on the date of birth; instead all birthdays are celebrated on *Tet*, the first day of the New Year.

Traditionally, a family asked the help of a matchmaker to choose a marriage partner for their son or daughter. Today, couples generally select their own mates and usually consult fortune-tellers to see if they are compatible and to choose an auspicious day for the wedding. The wedding ceremony itself consists of two parts. On the first day, the groom, with his parents and a small group of family members and friends, goes to the bride-to-be's home to seek permission to marry her. Often, the groom presents the traditional offering of **betel nuts** to the bride's family.

On the second day, there is a celebration after the bride and groom have performed ancient rituals at an altar set up for the occasion. At this ceremony, held at the groom's house, the "guardian god of marriage" is traditionally asked to bless and protect the couple. Three tiny cups are filled with rice wine and placed on the altar. The elder who leads the ceremony bows before the altar, takes a sip from one of the cups, and passes it to the groom. The groom takes a sip then passes the cup to the bride, who also sips from it. The groom then takes a piece of ginger and rubs it in salt, and both bride and groom eat a little of it to signify their lasting love. Only then are they ready to exchange wedding rings and drink the remaining two cups of wine. Once the solemnities are over, it is time for a feast with family and friends.

Wedding banquets are a group affair. The food, such as rice, is placed on the table in large bowls; guests then fill their individual bowls with rice. Using chopsticks, they pick out pieces of fish, meat, and vegetables from other large bowls and add it to the rice.

Pork or beef is eaten at weddings and other auspicious occasions. Larger animals, such as water buffalo, are prepared and eaten when someone dies. Funerals are elaborate affairs. To ensure a comfortable afterlife, the family provides colorful paper model houses, "spirit money," and other necessities to be burned along with the body. Relatives take turns guarding the coffin during the night. Traditionally, a coin is placed in the mouth of the deceased for luck, and a bowl of rice left in the coffin. In some parts of Vietnam, a knife is rested on the stomach of the dead person to ward off evil spirits.

Exhumation is common practice in Vietnam. Three years after burial, the family exhumes the body from the grave site and collects the bones. The bones are cleaned and placed in a smaller earthen coffin for reburial. A photograph of the dead is usually placed on the family altar at home and sometimes also in a temple. Offerings of food or burning incense are made to the spirit of the deceased on special occasions or on the death anniversary.

This fragrant sweet and sour dish is typical of Vietnamese cooking.

Thit Ga Xao Dam Gung Sa

Chicken with Lemon Grass

Yield: serves 4

1 stalk **lemon grass, trimmed** (use about 4 to 6 inches off the tender, whitish end) and cut in 1-inch lengths, or 2 strips lemon peel
2 tablespoons fish sauce (*nuoc mam*) (available at Asian food stores), divided
6 boneless and skinless chicken thighs (about 2 pounds), cut into 1-inch pieces
3 tablespoons vegetable oil
1 onion, finely sliced
2 cloves garlic, **finely chopped**
3 green onions (with tops), cut into 1-inch pieces
1/4 cup water
1 teaspoon cornstarch
1 teaspoon sugar
2 tablespoons vinegar
1 tablespoon finely chopped ginger root
dried red pepper flakes, to taste
hot cooked rice, for serving

Equipment: Large resealable plastic bag, **wok** or large skillet, wooden mixing spoon, cup

1. Prepare **marinade**: In large resealable plastic bag, combine 1 tablespoon fish sauce and lemon grass or lemon peel. Seal shut and shake to mix well. Open bag, add chicken, re-seal, and shake to coat well. Refrigerate for at least 1 hour. Turn bag once or twice to coat chicken pieces.

2. Prepare to stir-fry: Remove chicken pieces from marinade. Pick out and discard pieces of lemon grass or lemon peel. Heat oil in wok or large skillet over medium-high heat. Add onion and garlic, and stir-fry for 1 minute. Add chicken and green onions, and stir-fry for 5 minutes. Reduce heat to medium, cover, and cook, stirring occasionally, for 2 minutes.

3. Put water in a cup and stir in cornstarch until dissolved. Stir cornstarch mixture into chicken mixture until thickened. Sprinkle in sugar, vinegar, ginger, remaining 1 tablespoon of fish sauce, and dried red pepper flakes to taste. Stir, cover, and cook for 1 minute for flavor to develop.

To serve, transfer to large serving bowl and serve with individual bowls of rice. To eat, spoon a little chicken mixture over your bowl of rice.

All banquets begin with appetizers, such as *cha-gio*.

Cha-Gio

Pork Rolls

CAUTION: HOT OIL USED

Yield: serves 8

vegetable oil, as needed
2 cloves garlic
1/2 pound lean **ground** pork
1/4 pound shrimp, cooked, peeled, **and coarsely chopped**
4 green onions, **trimmed** and **finely chopped**
1/2 cup daikon radish (available at Asian food stores and some supermarkets)
2 tablespoons fish sauce (*nuoc mam*) (available at Asian food stores)
2 ounces *sai fun* (cellophane) noodles, soaked in warm water 15 minutes and drained well (available at Asian food stores)

8 (10-inch square) *lumpia* wrappers, frozen (available at Asian food stores)

Equipment: **Wok** or large skillet, wooden mixing spoon, work surface, **deep fryer** (see glossary for tips on making a deep fryer), paper towels, baking sheet, **deep-fryer thermometer** (optional), slotted spoon or metal tongs

1. Heat 2 tablespoons of oil in wok or large skillet over medium-high heat. Add garlic and stir for about 30 seconds. Crumble in pork and stir-fry for 3 minutes. Add shrimp, green onions, radish, fish sauce, and drained noodles. Stir-fry for 2 to 3 minutes for flavors to develop. Remove from heat and cool to room temperature.

2. Spread *lumpia* wrappers on work surface and spoon equal amounts of pork mixture in the center of each. Roll up to completely enclose filling. Seal the end flap with a dab of water.

3. Prepare deep fryer: ADULT SUPERVISION REQUIRED. Have several layers of paper towels ready on a baking sheet. Heat oil to 375° F on fryer thermometer (or oil is hot enough when small bubbles appear around a wooden spoon handle when it is dipped in the oil). Deep fry 2 or 3 at a time, until golden brown, 3 to 5 minutes. Remove with slotted metal spoon or metal tongs and drain on paper towels.

To serve, each person receives a cha-gio. *It is usually cut diagonally in 3 or 4 pieces and set on a plate. It is eaten with* nuoc cham *(recipe follows). Before each bite, dip the* cha-gio *in dipping sauce.*

Nuoc Cham

Vietnamese Dipping Sauce

Yield: about 2½ cups

½ cup fish sauce (*nuoc mam*) (available at Asian food stores)
2 tablespoons rice wine vinegar (available at Asian food stores)
2 teaspoons sugar
1 cup water
¼ cup grated carrots
1 clove garlic, **finely chopped**
juice of ½ lime
ground red pepper, to taste

Equipment: Small bowl with cover, mixing spoon

1. Put fish sauce, rice wine vinegar, water, grated carrots, garlic, juice of ½ lime, and ground red pepper to taste into small bowl, stir well. Cover and refrigerate until ready to serve. To serve, spoon a little into individual small dipping containers. Each person has their own dish of dipping sauce.

KOREA

Korea has been divided into two countries since 1948—North Korea (the Democratic People's Republic of) and South Korea (Republic of Korea). The majority of South Koreans are Christian or Buddhist; often the ideas and rituals of these religions are mixed with shamanism (the belief that the spirits of nature inhabit both living and nonliving things).

South Korea is the only country in the world where intra-clan marriages are banned. According to Confucian scholars, the ban originated in China thousands of years ago, and its purpose was to prevent birth defects due to the marriage of close relatives.

Giving birth to a son is considered a great event in the life of a Korean woman. Because of its importance, women offer prayers and follow rituals in the hopes of giving birth to a boy. Often, offerings are made for 100 days to Taoist shrines, to Buddhist shrines, and to various things in nature, such as rocks, trees, streams, and mountains. The grandmother spirit, *samshin halmoni*, is the main spirit involved with childbirth. Her shrine is kept inside the house, and is represented by a piece of folded paper or clean straw hung in one corner of the room. The spirit traditionally guides the child in its growth and well-being throughout its young life. Seaweed soup and rice are offered to the grandmother spirit morning and evening for one week, and the same foods are eaten by the new mother.

In Korea, a baby's 100th day (*paegil*), its first birthday (*ortol*), and an adult's 60th birthday (*hwangap*), are all very special life-cycle celebrations. The 100th-day party marks the baby's survival of a critical period in infancy. Gifts are given to the baby, and offerings of food are made to the grandmother spirit. Family and friends celebrate with wine, rice cakes, and a grand feast. The first birthday celebration is enjoyed in much the same way, but is regarded as a more important event. As guests leave the celebration, the child's parents give them each a package of rice cakes. Sharing their rice cakes is a symbol of good health and happiness for the child.

Koreans traditionally use the Chinese lunar calendar, which is based on 60-year cycles—when people reach their 60th year, the cycle returns to the year of their birth. For the *hwangap* (60th birthday), the family usually throws a lavish party, and loved ones visit to honor the celebrant. Rituals involve bowing and drinking wine to honor the celebrant, while traditional Korean music plays throughout the festivities. Rice cakes and fresh fruit are part of the feast.

In Korea, wedding rituals (*shingei*) follow rules set down by Confucius in his book of rites. There are two types of marriage: love marriage (*yonae*) and arranged marriage (*chungmae*). The favorite season for marrying in Korea is in the fall, after the harvest moon, and the date is based on the couple's horoscopes. A fun betrothal event is the prearranged delivery of a large box of gifts for the bride. The box (*ham* or *hahm*) is usually delivered by friends of the groom. It contains an assortment of items: fabric for the traditional Korean dress (*banbok*), jewelry, and some symbolic items, such as stalks of ripened **millet**, which represent a wish for many children. As the group comes within earshot of the house the deliverers begin shouting, "*hahm* for sale!" Family members toss the group money, and the box is given to the bride in exchange for food and drink.

In Korea, the betrothal is an important part of the nuptials. The families of the couple gather in the bride's family home to meet and eat. According to ancient traditions, the couple is seated at the head of a long table, with the bride-to-be's family sitting down on one side and the groom's family seated across from them. After each family member is formally introduced, the meal is served.

The traditional wedding ceremony is held in the bride's home. Most brides wear Western-style wedding dresses, though some prefer to wear the traditional Korean dress (*banbok*), which has a long full skirt (*chima*) made of silk. The wedding ceremony begins with an exchange of bows and drinks. The bride and groom face one another across a table filled with objects symbolic of many aspects of the life they are about to begin together. This ceremony is followed by another called the *pyebaek*, which is the bride's first greeting to her husband's family. It is at this time that the bride presents the groom's family with their gifts.

An altar is set up, and on it are placed items of Korean symbolism, such as a wooden or live goose, which symbolized fidelity. The groom, while holding the goose, may *kowtow* (bow low) to his bride as a display of his sincerity and faithfulness. Other altar items include *otsuka* (symbolic shapes and figures woven from straw), dried pheasant, a gourd-bottle of rice wine tied in blue and red thread, rice cakes, chestnuts, dates, and fruits.

The groom's kinfolk, after being bowed to, receive a cup of "bride's wine" (also called "cup of the wine of mutual joy") and small portions of pheasant. The in-laws pelt the bride on the long white sleeves of her wedding gown with dates and chestnuts, wishing her good fortune as a mother. On leaving they may discreetly deposit *kowtow* money for the bride in a white envelope on a tray.

The Korean wedding banquet known as "noodle banquet" (*kook soo sang*) is much less formal and elaborate than other Asian wedding feasts. The banquet gets its name from the noodle soup (*kook soo*) served with the meal. Noodles represent a wish for a long and happy life. ۞ ۞ ۞

Kook Soo

Noodle Soup with Meatballs

Yield: serves 6

8 ounces **ground** beef
1 small onion, **finely chopped**
1 teaspoon **sesame seeds**
½ teaspoon ground ginger
salt and pepper to taste
½ cup all-purpose flour
1 egg, beaten
2 tablespoons vegetable oil, more as needed
8-ounce package thin egg noodles (cooked according to directions on package and drained) (available at Asian food stores and most supermarkets)
1 teaspoon sesame oil
6 cups canned beef broth
1 clove garlic, finely chopped
2 green onions, finely sliced
3 tablespoons soy sauce, more or less to taste
1 teaspoon rice vinegar
ground red pepper, to taste

Equipment: Large mixing bowl, 2 small shallow bowls, large skillet, slotted spoon, large serving bowl with cover or tureen (covered casserole dish), mixing spoon, large saucepan

1. Prepare meatballs: In large mixing bowl, combine ground beef, onion, sesame seeds, ginger, and salt and pepper to taste. Using your hands, mix well. Form into tiny ¾-inch meatballs (makes about 20).

2. Prepare to pan fry: Put flour in one small shallow bowl and beaten egg in another small shallow bowl. Heat 2 tablespoons oil in large skillet over medium heat. Dip each meatball in flour, shake off excess, then dip in egg mixture, and put in skillet. Fry a few meatballs at a time for 5 to 7 minutes until cooked through and browned on all sides. Using slotted spoon, transfer to large serving bowl or tureen. Continue frying meatballs, adding more oil as needed.

3. Sprinkle cooked, drained noodles with sesame oil to prevent them from sticking together and add to serving container with meatballs. Cover to keep warm.

4. In a large saucepan, bring beef broth to boil over medium-high heat. Add garlic, green onions, soy sauce, rice vinegar, ground red pepper to taste, and salt and pepper to taste. Reduce heat to **simmer** for 5 to 7 minutes for flavor to develop. Pour over noodle mixture in serving container, stir, and cover.

To serve, set soup on the table with a ladle and small bowls for portioning out individual serving. In Korea, soup is eaten with the meal, not first as an appetizer as in Western cultures.

Kimchi is so much a part of Korean life that it is considered a national treasure by the South Korean government. Many different types of *kimchi* are prepared for the wedding feast. The ultimate *kimchi* for special celebration feasts is *possam kimchi*. It is very complicated and added to the vegetables are such items as octopus, salted shrimp juice, and oysters. The following *kimchi* is made with easily available ingredients. Daikon radishes are long white tubular radishes popular in many Asian countries.

Daikon Kimchi

Pickled Radishes

Note: This recipe takes over 2 days.

Yield: serves 8 to 10

2 pounds daikon radishes (available at Asian food stores and some supermarkets), peeled and cut into 1-inch cubes
1 tablespoon Kosher salt
3 tablespoons dried red pepper flakes
3 cloves garlic, **finely chopped**
1 tablespoon rice vinegar
1 tablespoon soy sauce
1 tablespoon **sesame seeds**
½ teaspoon salt
1/2 teaspoon sugar

Equipment: **Colander**, large mixing bowl, 2-quart food container with tight fitting lid

1. Put cubed daikon radishes in colander set in sink and sprinkle with Kosher salt. Toss to mix well and let drain for 5 minutes. Using your hands, squeeze out excess water. Transfer radishes to large mixing bowl. Add red pepper flakes, garlic, rice vinegar, soy sauce, sesame seeds, regular salt, and sugar. Toss to mix well.

2. Transfer to 2-quart container. Cover loosely with lid so as the *kimchi* ferments the gas can escape. Leave at room temperature overnight or up to 2 days for flavor to develop. Cover leftovers tightly with lid and refrigerate up to one week.

To serve, put kimchi *in a small serving bowl. To eat, take a little* kimchi *with each bite of food.*

Beef is the favorite meat for Korean banquets, which include great quantities of rice, several *kimchi* dishes, and a great many vegetable side dishes (*panchan*). Something as simple as bean sprouts makes a tasty and unusual side dish.

Kongnamul

Cooked Bean Sprouts

Yield: serves 6

6 cups fresh bean sprouts
2 tablespoons **sesame seeds**
3 green onions, **trimmed** and finely sliced
3 tablespoons soy sauce
2 teaspoons sesame oil
1 teaspoon dried red pepper flakes
salt to taste
water, as needed for cooking

Equipment: **Colander**, medium saucepan, 2 mixing spoons or tongs

1. Put bean sprouts in colander, place in sink, and rinse under running water. Drain well.

2. Fill medium saucepan with water halfway and bring to boil over medium-high heat. Add bean sprouts, stir, reduce heat to **simmer**, and cook for 5 to 7 minutes until soft. Drain well in colander.

3. Return bean sprouts to saucepan and add sesame seeds, green onions, soy sauce, sesame oil, and red pepper flakes. Using 2 mixing spoons or tongs, toss to mix well. Add salt to taste. Place over medium heat, stir frequently until heated through and flavors are developed, 5 to 7 minutes.

To serve, transfer to large serving bowl. Serve either hot or cold as a side dish.

JAPAN

Japan is a series of islands separated from the east coast of Asia by the Sea of Japan. Most Japanese are Shintoist or Buddhist, often blending different elements from both religions. In Japan, many life-cycle events, especially for children, are national celebrations. In the most popular, *Shichi-Go-San*, in November (see Shintoism and Shinto Life-Cycle Rituals, page liv) parents take children ages three, five, and seven to shrines to pray for their future. Another annual festival is Boy's Day (*Tango No Sekku*) on May 5. Symbolic items are displayed by parents in hopes that their sons will grow up healthy and strong. Warrior dolls (*Hina*), are displayed, iris leaves are placed under the eaves of homes to ward off evil, and large carp-shaped banners fly on poles over the houses where young boys live.

Girl's Day (*Hina Matsuri*) on March 3, is a national event honoring young girls. Traditionally, imperial court dolls dressed in the costumes of ancient court ladies as well as peach blossoms are displayed, and a sweet drink made with fermented rice, called *shirozake* is served.

This easy-to-prepare shrimp recipe is a specialty for *Hina Matsuri*. ❂ ❂ ❂

ONIGARI-YAKI

BROILED SHRIMP IN SOY SAUCE

Yield: serves 4

24 (about one pound) large shrimp, **peeled and deveined**
½ cup Japanese soy sauce (available at most supermarkets and Asian food stores)
½ cup water
2 tablespoons sugar
cooked rice, for serving

Equipment: 8 (6 to 8 inches long) bamboo skewers, 1 gallon-size resealable plastic bag, small saucepan, indoor **grill** or oven broiler, metal tongs, **pastry brush**, oven mitts

1. Thread 3 shrimp on each skewer and place in resealable plastic bag. Seal top and refrigerate.

2. In small saucepan, heat soy sauce, water, and sugar over high heat, stirring constantly to dissolve sugar. Cook for 1 minute. Cool to room temperature and pour into plastic bag with shrimp. Close top and rotate bag several times to coat shrimp with liquid. Refrigerate for 30 minutes.

Connect indoor grill or preheat oven broiler.

3. Broil shrimp over an indoor grill or place the shrimp on an oven broiler pan and set it under the broiler heat. Using the indoor grill, cook for 2 to 4 minutes on each side over medium heat or 3 to 5 minutes on each side under the broiler heat in the oven. Use pastry brush to coat shrimp with soy sauce mixture after turning them over with the metal tongs.

Serve hot, 2 skewers per person over bed of rice.

Hikicha manju are served on auspicious occasions. The buns are eaten at banquets, or they are often given as gifts for the guests to take home at the end of a wedding feast.

HIKICHA MANJU (ALSO KOHAKU MANJU)

RED BEAN PASTE BUNS

Yield: 12 buns

½ cup sugar
¼ cup water
2¼ cups all-purpose flour
3½ teaspoons baking powder
¼ cup milk
2 tablespoons vegetable shortening

18 ounces (about 1½ cups) canned sweetened red bean paste (available at Asian food stores)

Equipment: Small saucepan, mixing spoon, flour **sifter**, lightly floured work surface, tablespoon, kitchen towel, wax paper, **steamer pan** or **wok** with bamboo steamer basket, oven mitts

1. In small saucepan, stir and dissolve sugar in water over low heat, about 30 seconds. Cool to room temperature.

2. Using flour sifter, **sift** flour and baking powder into a mound on work surface. With your hands, make a well (hole) in the center and pour in sugar-water and milk. Using your fingers, mix the liquids into the flour mixture a little at a time and mix in shortening. (If the dough is too dry, add 1 tablespoon of water at a time and if dough is too wet, sprinkle the work surface and your hands lightly with flour.) **Knead** for 12 to 15 minutes until dough becomes smooth and **elastic**. Cover dough with damp towel and allow to rest for 1 hour.

3. Divide dough into 12 equal portions. Using your hands, roll each portion into a ball, and place on lightly floured work surface. Using your hands, flatten each ball into a 3½- to 4-inch disk. Spoon 1 tablespoon bean paste in the center of the disk. Wrap dough around filling and pinch edges tightly together to seal in filling. Rub bun lightly with oil. Repeat filling the buns.

4. Prepare to steam buns: Cut 12 squares of waxed paper, slightly larger than each bun, and rub each square lightly with oil. Set each bun, seam-side down on wax paper square and set about ¾-inch apart in steamer basket, allowing space to rise. The wax paper prevents buns from sticking to steamer basket. Don't crowd the steamer basket; it will be necessary to steam in batches.

5. To steam buns: Pour 4 cups water into the lower pan of the steamer pan or wok and bring to boil over high heat. Place either the perforated top pan with the buns or the bamboo steamer with the buns over the boiling water, cover, and steam for 15 to 20 minutes, until springy to the touch and well risen. Wearing oven mitts, remove basket with buns. Remove buns from basket; peel off wax paper, and place buns on wire rack. Continue steaming buns in batches. Add more water and bring to boil, if necessary to continue steaming.

Serve immediately for best flavor and texture. Leftover buns can be refrigerated in covered container and reheated in a microwave oven or resteamed.

Until the 1950s, Western-style courting or dating was not part of Japan's social scene, and arranged marriage was the custom throughout Japan. The Star Festival (*Tanabata*), a national event, was held on July 7 to celebrate the coming together of couples planning to marry.

From ancient times, *kagami-biraki* has been one of the essential Japanese wedding rituals to celebrate the beginning of a marriage. The rituals take place around the *butsudan* (the family shrine), found in many homes. The bride and groom break open a container of saké with a special mallet amidst cheers of congratulations from the guests. The saké is then served to all the guests.

The central feature of the Japanese wedding ceremony is the *sansankudo* (also *sakazukigoto*). Meaning "three-three nine times," *sansankudo* refers to a precise ritual of drinking saké. *Sansankudo* is an ancient custom (used in weddings as early as the Heian period [A.D. 794-1185] and appearing in the fourteenth-century *Samurai Rules of Etiquette*), and is used in many Japanese functions to create or reinforce social bonds. As with all Japanese rituals, the *yuino*, the seating arrangement for *sansankudo*, is exceedingly precise and essential to the ritual itself. The drinking from the same cup is a symbolic agreement that the couple will share a lifetime of joy and sorrow. The Japanese regard three (*san*) as an extremely auspicious number; in earlier days there were three people present at the wedding ritual, a fire was maintained for three nights, and three trays of food were served.

Most food served at the wedding feast is selected because of its symbolic connection to happiness, prosperity, long life, or hopes for many children. Sea bream (*tai*), kelp (*kombu*), and *sekiban* (recipe page 335) are essential to the traditional wedding feast and almost all other celebration feasts.

The wedding banquet can be simple, or very artistic and formal (*kaiseki*). For the *kaiseki*, there can be as many as 15 different dishes, and each one is a work of art. For formal occasions, food must be pleasing to the eye as well as to the mouth. The *kaiseki* banquet follows a set order of courses: first appetizers, then a clear soup, then *sashimi* or *sushi* (recipe page 333). A grilled dish is followed by a boiled dish, a deep-fried dish, a steamed dish, and then salad. The meal ends with rice served with pickles and miso soup, which is garnished with such things as cooked shrimp, bean curd, chunks of cooked fish, button mushrooms, chicken, and pork meatballs. Several different garnishes are often added to each serving of miso. Instant miso soup mix is available at all Asian food stores. Prepare according to directions on package and add garnishes of choice.

The wedding feast will often include a broth (*tai no tsumire wan*), made with two meaningful ingredients: sea bream (*tai*) and kelp (*kombu*). When the broth is served to the bride and groom, the stems of the green garnish are made into a knotted ring to symbolize their union. Guests may have their garnish knotted, or chopped fresh parsley can be sprinkled over the soup to symbolize spreading good wishes for the couple. Sea bream is also known as porgy, a popular fish in Japan. Red snapper is very similar and makes a good substitute.

Tai No Tsumire Wan

Clear Broth with Fish Dumplings

Yield: serves 6

- 1 pound skinless fish **fillets, coarsely chopped** (about 1 cup)
- 1 egg
- 1 teaspoon grated fresh ginger, or ½ teaspoon **ground** ginger
- ½ teaspoon salt
- 2 tablespoons all-purpose flour
- 6 cups *dashi*, homemade (recipe follows), or *katsuo dashi* (bonito broth) instant concentrate (available in 6.7 ounce bottles at Asian food markets). Prepare according to directions on bottle. Each serving: 1 teaspoon dashi concentrate to 1 cup hot water
- 2 to 6 fresh parsley stems (each about 6 inches long), **blanched**
- 2 to 3 teaspoons **finely chopped** fresh parsley flakes, for **garnish** (optional)

Equipment: Food processor, rubber spatula, 2 plates, medium saucepan, slotted spoon, plastic wrap, cup, scissors, ladle

1. Put fish in food processor and process for about 10 seconds. Add egg, ginger, and salt and process for 5 seconds. Use rubber spatula to scrape down sides of container. Sprinkle flour over fish mixture and process for about 10 seconds into a smooth paste. Transfer to a plate. With wet hands, divide fish mixture into 6 portions and form each into an oval dumpling. Repeat making dumplings, and place side by side on plate.

2. Fill medium saucepan two-thirds full of water and bring to boil over high heat. Add dumplings, cook for about 2 minutes until they float to the surface. Remove with slotted spoon, and place on plate. Cool to room temperature and cover with plastic wrap. Refrigerate until serving time.

3. Prepare garnish: You will need either 2 or 6 stems of blanched fresh parsley, long enough to wrap around your finger and tie. Remove the tied ring from your finger and trim the ends with scissors so it will fit nicely in the soup cup. Place in cup of cold water until ready to serve. Repeat making rings.

4. Prepare to serve: Heat broth over medium-high heat until small bubbles appear around edge of pan (do not boil). Place a dumpling in each bowl and ladle over the hot soup. Garnish 2 bowls for the bride and groom with knotted sprigs of parsley and in the remaining bowl either garnish with a knotted sprig and/or sprinkle with the chopped fresh parsley flakes.

Serve the bride and groom first, then the parents of the bride and groom. It is customary to first, pick out and eat the dumpling using chopsticks, then pick up the cup with both hands, to drink the broth.

Dashi

Basic Broth

Yield: serves 6

6 cups water

1 piece (3-inch square) dried kelp (**kombu**) (available at Asian food stores)

½ cup (loosely packed) dried bonito flakes (katsuo bushi) (available at Asian food stores)

Equipment: Medium saucepan, metal tongs, mixing spoon, medium strainer, 1 or 2 coffee filters, medium bowl

1. In medium saucepan bring the water and kelp almost to a boil (it should not actually boil) over medium-high heat. Remove pan from heat. Immediately remove kelp from water with metal tongs, discard kelp.

2. Sprinkle bonito flakes over the hot water, stir, and let stand undisturbed for 2 or 3 minutes, until bonito flakes sink to the bottom.

3. Line medium strainer with 1 or 2 coffee filters and set over bowl. Strain liquid through filters and discard filter contents.

Use for tai no tsumire wan *(recipe precedes). Leftover broth can be cooled to room temperature, covered, and refrigerated for 2 to 3 days.*

Sushi means vinegar-flavored rice. The vinegar-flavored rice is molded into small shapes and combined with a range of meat, fish, shrimp, or vegetable pieces either left raw, cooked, or smoked and garnished with condiments for dipping. This recipe is made with cooked fish.

There are many different ways to assemble the *sushi* and each is a work of art. Plating and garnishing is an important part of the total *sushi* experience. The color and shape of *sushi* must be appealing to the eye and each piece is cut into bite-size pieces, that are easy to pop into the mouth. *Sushi* made without fish or meat is often included in the vegetarian meals after Buddhist wakes and funerals. When this recipe is made without fish, it is called *hana-zushi* (flowered rice). At banquets *sushi* is eaten as an appetizer.

Nori-maki Sushi

Vinegar Rice and Fish in Seaweed

Yield: serves 8 to 10

3 cups water

1 tablespoon vinegar

½ teaspoon salt

3 **coriander** seeds
6 strips (1 inch x 6 inches each) fresh, skin-on salmon **fillets**, about ½ inch thick (The skin will keep the fillets from falling apart.)
6 (7½ x 8½ inch) sheets yaki-sushi nori (toasted seaweed, available at Asian food stores)
3 cups *maki-zushi* (*sushi rice*) (recipe follows)
12 spinach leaves, **trimmed** and **blanched**, pat dry with paper towels
shredded omelet (recipe page 335)
1 carrot , for **garnish**
1 cucumber, for garnish
4 to 6 tablespoons Japanese soy sauce, for serving (available at all Asian food stores and some supermarkets)
1 or 2 tablespoons **wasabi** paste or powder, for serving (available at Asian food stores—use according to directions on package)

Equipment: Medium saucepan, slotted spatula, plate, baking sheet, oven mitts, plastic food wrap, work surface, kitchen string, **serrated knife**

1. Pour water into medium saucepan, add vinegar, salt, and coriander seeds. Bring to boil over high heat for 5 minutes. Reduce heat to **simmer**, add salmon strips, and **poach** gently for 4 minutes, or until fish is cooked through. (Fully cooked fish is opaque and it is no longer translucent in the center.) Remove from liquid with a slotted spatula and place on plate.

2. Spread sheets of seaweed, slightly overlapping, on baking sheet and slightly warm in 250° F oven for 5 to 8 minutes to enhance the flavor.

3. To assemble: Place a 10- to 12-inch square of plastic wrap on work surface and place 1 sheet seaweed on top. Spread one-sixth of the rice evenly on the seaweed leaving a 1 inch border on all sides. Pull or cut the skin off a salmon strip and place it on the rice. Cover the fish with 2 blanched spinach leaves. Sprinkle one-sixth of the omelet over the spinach. Using the plastic wrap as a guide, carefully roll ingredients in the sheet of seaweed, keeping the filling centered and making the roll as tight as possible. Wrap string around the plastic wrap and tie it in 3 places to hold it closed. Twist the ends of the plastic wrap closed. Repeat making the rolls and refrigerate for at least 4 hours before serving.

4. Prepare for serving: Remove string and plastic wrap. Using a serrated knife, cut rolls crosswise into slices about 1 inch thick. Arrange the slices, cut side-up, on individual plates. Turn the carrot and cucumber slices into flowers by cutting V-shaped notches around the edge of each vegetable and place on the plate as garnish.

Serve with 2 dipping sauces: (1) A small dish of equal parts water and Japanese soy sauce. (2) A small dish of prepared wasabi paste.

If using long grain rice instead of **short grain** rice for this recipe, use 2 cups of water instead of 1¾ cups.

Maki-Zushi (also Sushi Rice)

Japanese Vinegar-flavored Rice

Yield: 3 cups
1½ cups **short grain** rice (available at some supermarkets and Asian food stores)
1¾ cups water
2 tablespoons white vinegar
2 tablespoons sugar

Equipment: Medium saucepan with cover, kitchen towel, cup, Japanese wooden tub (handai or sushi-oké) or large bowl, Japanese wooden paddle (shamoji) or wooden mixing spoon, hand-held fan (Japanese lacquered flat fan, uchiwa) or a piece of stiff cardboard or folded newspaper

1. Combine rice and water in medium saucepan, and bring to a boil over high heat. Reduce heat to low, cover, and cook for 10 to 12 minutes, or until all the water is absorbed and the rice is tender. Remove from heat and remove pan cover. Place a folded towel over the pan of rice, set the pan cover on top of the towel, and let stand 15 minutes; The towel prevents moisture from dripping onto the rice.

2. Pour vinegar into a cup and stir in sugar until it is dissolved. Transfer the rice to the wooden tub or large bowl. Rinse shamoji or wooden spoon under cold water and use it to gently toss rice and at the same time fan the rice vigorously. (This combined tossing and fanning prevents the steam from condensing onto the rice.) While the rice is still warm, toss it and sprinkle with the vinegar, 2 tablespoons at a time until well mixed.

The rice can be made several hours ahead and covered with a damp towel and plastic wrap; keep at room temperature. (Do not refrigerate, it will turn hard and crusty.)

Shredded Omelet

2 eggs
1 teaspoon cold water
½ teaspoon sugar
1/2 teaspoon salt
1 teaspoon vegetable oil

Equipment: Small bowl, fork, medium skillet, metal pancake turner, work surface, **serrated knife**, large plate

1. Crack eggs into small bowl. Add water, sugar, and salt; using fork, beat well.

2. Heat oil in skillet over medium-high heat. Add egg mixture and swirl to cover bottom of pan evenly and thinly. Cook until set, about 1 minute, turn and cook briefly on other side until firm. Transfer omelet to work surface. When cool enough to handle, roll egg into a cylinder and cut crosswise into very thin strands. Separate strands on large plate to prevent them from sticking together.

Continue with nori-maki sushi *(recipe page 333).*

In Japan, *sekiban* is a festive dish served at weddings and birthdays. Red is the color of happiness, and in this dish, the rice has a reddish color.

Sekiban

Red Festive Rice

Yield: serves 6

1 cup red beans (*azuki*) (available at Asian food stores)
2 cups cold water
2 cups Japanese sweet rice (*mochi gome*), cook according to directions on package (available at Asian food stores)
1 teaspoon black **sesame seeds, toasted**, for **garnish** (available at Asian food stores)

Equipment: **Colander** or strainer, medium saucepan, mixing spoon

Place beans in a colander or strainer and wash them under cold running water. Transfer to saucepan, cover with cold water, and bring to a boil over high heat. Reduce heat to **simmer** and cook for 45 minutes, until they are firm and tender, not mushy. Add cooked beans to cooked rice and stir gently. Cover and set aside for 10 minutes.

Serve either hot or at room temperature. Transfer rice to individual rice bowls and sprinkle each serving with sesame seeds. Sekihan *can be served with* tai *(grilled red snapper) or as a sweet course with* kuri fukume-ni.

PHILIPPINES

The Philippines consists of a group of islands in the South China Sea, located south of Taiwan and east of mainland Asia.

For many centuries, the indigenous people of the Philippines have shared their islands with people who migrated from Europe, the Middle East, China, Malaysia, and the United States. The Spanish, however, have perhaps made the strongest cultural impact on the Filipino people. The Spanish not only brought Catholicism and Spanish customs, food, dress, and language to the Philippines, but in the nineteenth century, a Spanish decree required all natives, regardless of ancestry, to acquire a Spanish surname.

About 83 percent of Filipinos are Roman Catholic; the remaining percentage are Christian Protestant, Muslim, and Buddhist. For Filipino Catholic families, the church is the center of life and almost every *barangay* (village) has a church or chapel. Besides serving as a call to mass, church bells announce baptisms, weddings, and funerals. (See Protestant and Catholic Life-Cycle Rituals, page xlvi.)

Filipinos generally follow the custom that every relative, no matter how far removed, is recognized as a family member, forming a close kin group. The first important life-cycle event among the Catholic Filipino population is the infant's baptism, which often brings together this extended family. For such a festive occasion, the family might serve chicken dishes, such as *rellenong manok* (recipe page 337), or pork, such as *puerco horneado* (recipe page 404), and several rice and bean dishes. An important part of the happy celebration is a sweet table covered with cakes, cookies, puddings such as *dulce de leche* (recipe page 392), and candies such as *turrón* (recipe page 187). In Filipino Catholic tradition, godparents are selected who will oversee the rearing of the child if the parents are no longer able to do so, and to act as a source of guidance for the child, often extending into adulthood. This is called *compadrazco,* and it assures the child a secure future.

When Filipino boys reach puberty they are usually circumcised; village boys often try to prove their manhood by being circumcised without anesthesia.

The marriage ceremony for Filipino Catholics takes place in the church. The traditional Filipino wedding rituals of the veil, candle, and cord were introduced in the early eighteenth century by Spanish missionaries. The godparents of both the bride and groom, as primary sponsors, are usually looked upon as honored guests. Couples who are special relatives or friends of the bride and groom are selected to be the veil sponsors, candle sponsors, and cord sponsors for their wedding. The six sponsors and the godparents stand at the altar front as the bride and groom kneel during the Mass. The veil ceremony symbolizes the unity of the two families into one by placing a veil over the groom's shoulders and the bride's head. For the candle ceremony, which symbolizes enlightenment and God's presence in the ceremony, the candle sponsors light the candle at the altar and put it out before the end of the ceremony. The cord ceremony concludes the rituals when the *yugal* (nuptial tie—a cord made out of silk threads, flowers, coins or beads) is loosely entwined in a figure eight around the necks of both the bride and groom. The cord is a symbolic reminder of the bond of marriage. At the end of the ceremonies, sponsors sign the wedding papers as witnesses and they are expected to make small donations to the church.

The wedding reception usually includes great quantities of food and drink, music and dancing. A fun tradition is when relatives and friends pin money on the newlyweds, covering them from head to toe with money.

The centerpiece of many wedding feasts is the *lechón*, a grilled or spit roasted whole **suckling pig** (recipe page 348), and/or *rellenong manok* (recipe follows).

Food plays an important part in Filipino life, not only in times of joy, but also in times of sorrow. Wakes, which honor the life of the deceased person, often take on the air of a *fiesta* (celebration), with relatives and friends coming from far and near to attend. Great quantities of food and drink are served. The *novena* (Roman Catholic nine days of prayers) is held after the funeral, and death anniversaries are celebrated with a mass or a visit to the grave.

This recipe for *rellenong manok* is of Spanish origin. It has been adopted by the Filipinos who often serve it at weddings. Adding the hard-cooked eggs to the stuffing is symbolic of life and fertility.

Rellenong Manok

Roasted Stuffed Chicken

Note: Each time before and after handling raw chicken, wash work surface, utensils, and your hands with soapy water and rinse well.

Yield: serves 4 to 6

4½ to 6 pound whole chicken (Have butcher **bone** chicken, leaving wings and legs intact.)
¼ cup soy sauce
1 tablespoon vegetable oil
1½ cups onion, **finely chopped**
4 cloves garlic, finely chopped
1 pound lean Spanish or Italian pork sausage (not in casing)
½ pound **ground** lean pork
3 cups **cubed** white bread
½ cup grated cheddar cheese
3 **egg whites**
½ cup seedless raisins
salt and pepper to taste
4 hard-cooked eggs, peeled
6 tablespoons sweet pickle relish
½ cup melted butter

Equipment: Paper towels, work surface, large bowl, plastic food wrap, large skillet, mixing spoon, large mixing bowl, 12- x 9- x 2½-inch baking pan fitted with wire rack, 3 or 4 metal **truss** pins or skewers, kitchen string, **bulb baster**, aluminum foil, meat **thermometer** (optional), **pastry brush**, oven mitts

1. Since chicken is boned, the packet with liver and gizzard are already removed from cavity. Rinse chicken under cold running water, drain and pat dry with paper towels. Place chicken on work surface. Using your hands, rub soy sauce over skin and in cavity of chicken. Place chicken in large bowl, cover with plastic wrap, and refrigerate until ready to stuff.

2. Prepare stuffing: Heat oil in large skillet over medium-high heat. Add onions and garlic and stir and **sauté** until soft, 3 to 5 minutes. Reduce heat to medium, crumble in pork sausage and ground pork. Stirring constantly, sauté until meat is browned, 7 to 12 minutes. Transfer to large mixing bowl and cool to room temperature. Using your hands, combine cubed bread, cheese, egg whites, raisins, and salt and pepper to taste. Cover with plastic wrap and refrigerate for 2 to 3 hours. **Note:** The stuffing must be thoroughly chilled before filling cavity of chicken.

Preheat oven to 325° F.

3. Stuff chicken: Place chilled bird, breast-side up, on rack in baking pan. Fill neck cavity with about ½ cup of stuffing and close by fastening

neck skin to back with metal truss pin or skewer. Spread half remaining stuffing over bottom of cavity. Place peeled hard-cooked eggs, end to end, inside of cavity on top of stuffing, running length of bird. Sprinkle eggs with pickle relish, add remaining stuffing over and around eggs. Keep stuffing loosely packed, don't press it down.

4. Close opening: Insert truss pins or skewers into skin on either side of opening. Place them, one above the other, about ½-inch apart. Wrap string around pins or skewers and lace opening shut, like lacing a boot. Draw sides of opening tightly together and knot string. Use string to tie legs together so chicken holds its shape during baking. Using pastry brush, cover chicken with melted butter. Insert meat thermometer into meatiest part of chicken. Combine remaining melted butter and soy sauce; use it to **baste** chicken with bulb baster or spoon.

5. Bake in oven for 2 to 2½ hours, basting frequently with soy sauce mixture. If chicken browns too quickly, cover loosely with sheet of foil.

6. Test for **doneness**: Chicken is done when thermometer registers 185° F. You can also test for doneness by piercing chicken thigh with tip of knife; if juices trickle out clear, chicken is done. If juices are pinkish, roast another 15 to 20 minutes. Allow chicken to rest 10 to 15 minutes for easier carving.

To serve, since chicken is boned, slice it in half lengthwise and lay each half cut side down. Cut off drumsticks. Slice each half crosswise into thick pieces so everyone gets some egg.

Pancit bihon (also *bigon*, rice stick noodles) are Filipino longevity noodles. Most people in Asian countries eat long noodles that symbolize long life and prosperity at lifecycle celebrations. Rice stick noodles come in 8- or 16-ounce packages. They are available either in a white and fairly straight form or light tan and crinkly. Rice stick noodles are precooked when you buy them. They need only to be rehydrated, not boiled. Allow one to two ounces dried noodles per person.

Bigon (also Bihon)

Filipino Longevity Noodles

Yield: serves 4 to 6

8-ounces rice stick noodles, either white or tan (available at Asian food stores)
hot water, as needed
3 tablespoons vegetable oil, divided
2 onions, **finely chopped**
6 cloves garlic, finely chopped
3 carrots, **trimmed** and finely chopped
3 cups finely sliced **bok choy** (Chinese cabbage), including green tops (available at Asian food stores and most supermarkets)
4 or 5 cooked chicken thighs, cut into bite size pieces
2 cups oyster sauce (available at Asian food stores)
2 teaspoons curry powder, more or less to taste
1 teaspoon red chili paste, more or less to taste (available at Asian markets)
3 green onions, trimmed and finely sliced crosswise at an angle, for **garnish**
2 hard-cooked eggs, peeled and sliced, for garnish

Equipment: Large bowl, **colander**, **wok** or large skillet, mixing spoon, metal tongs

1. Put rice stick noodles in large bowl. To reconstitute: Soak white noodles in warm water for 10 to 20 minutes to soften or soak the light tan rice sticks in very hot water for 30 to 40 minutes to soften. Drain in colander and sprinkle with 1 tablespoon oil to keep from sticking together. Set aside.

2. Heat wok or large skillet over high heat, add remaining 2 tablespoons oil, and swirl to coat pan. Add finely chopped onions and garlic. Stir and **sauté** until onions are soft, 3 to 5 minutes. Add carrots, bok choy, and pieces of cooked chicken thighs and toss to mix. Reduce heat to medium, cover, and cook 7 to 12 minutes for flavor to develop. Remove from heat and keep covered.

3. In small bowl, combine oyster sauce, 2 teaspoons curry powder (more or less to taste), and 1 teaspoon red chili paste, more or less to taste. Stir into chicken mixture. Cook and stir chicken mixture over medium-high heat to heat through, 5 to 7 minutes. Remove from heat and add softened noodles. Using tongs, toss to mix and coat with sauce.

To serve, divide into individual soup bowls. Garnish each serving with a sprinkle of green onions and place 2 or 3 slices of hard-cooked eggs on top.

One of the many dishes on the celebration table is this salad recipe.

Habas con Chorizos

Sausage and Chickpea Salad

Yield: serves 4

- 1½ cups cooked chickpeas (also garbanzos), either dried, cooked (according to directions on package), and drained, or canned and drained
- ½ pound cooked chorizo or salami-type sausage, thinly sliced
- 2 red bell peppers, **trimmed**, **seeded**, and thinly sliced
- 1 green bell pepper, trimmed, seeded, and thinly sliced
- 3 tomatoes, trimmed and quartered
- 1 onion, **finely chopped**
- 2 cloves garlic, finely chopped
- 2 tablespoons vinegar
- 2 tablespoons olive oil
- salt and pepper to taste

Equipment: Medium salad bowl, small bowl, whisk, salad tools

1. Put chickpeas in salad bowl, add cooked sliced chorizo or salami-type sausage, red and green bell peppers, tomatoes, onions, and garlic.

2. In small bowl, whisk vinegar and oil, add salt and pepper to taste and pour over salad. Using salad tools, toss to mix well.

To serve, put bowl of salad with salad tools on the table and have guests help themselves to salad. Eat with rellenong manok *(recipe page 337).*

MALAYSIA & SINGAPORE

Malaysia consists of a narrow peninsula located south of Thailand in southeastern Asia, and the northern part of the island of Borneo.

Malaysia's population is among the most varied in East Asia, consisting of Malays, Chinese, Indians, and indigenous groups known as *bumiputra*, or "sons of the soil." Indigenous tribes have their own languages and religions, although many have become Muslim or Christian. Many Chinese and Indians in Malaysia are descendants of workers brought by the British to work on the rubber plantations or in tin factories. Malaysian life-cycle events vary according to the country of origin and religious preference.

Singapore is a small group of islands located between Malaysia and Indonesia, and Singapore City, its capital, is one of the world's busiest ports. Singapore is an ethnically diverse country where Buddhists, Hindus, Muslims, and some Christians live side-by-side. The largest portion of Singapore's population is Chinese, followed by Malay, then Indian. As in Malaysia, life-cycle events of the people of Singapore vary according to the country of origin and religious preference.

Some Malay women can be very superstitious and keep themselves and their newborn infant protected from bad weather and evil spirits at all times. According to this custom, the baby must not be exposed to wind and cold, nor must it be praised for fear of attracting jealous spirits. The baby's head is ceremonially shaved 40 days after birth, at the end of the mother's confinement. After this ceremony, family and friends gather to view the baby, which can be simple or elaborate affair depending upon family superstitions. If there is a feast, several rice dishes similar to Indonesian *nasi uduk/gurih* (recipe page 343) and/or the more elaborate Malaysian *nasi kuning lengkap* (recipe follows) might be served.

In both Malaysia and Singapore, wedding ceremonies are conducted according to religious preference. After the traditional ceremony, if the family can afford it, a big showy wedding reception with plenty of beautifully presented food is a current trend. It's not unusual for families to invite several hundred people to a hotel or restaurant to share the joy of their son's or daughter's marriage. Modern-day receptions are often a blending of the best of several cultures and include plenty of toasts, merrymaking, drinking and eating, picture-taking, and even the newlywed couple performing a karaoke duet.

Rice is fundamental to the existence of the Malays, and they believe it to possess an essential life force. For a Malay, rice is synonymous with food, and its presence is what distinguishes a meal. Therefore, ceremonials that mark every stage of life from birth through coming of age, marriage, and death, involve a symbolic meal of rice.

Rising like a golden mountain, yellow rice, made into a cone-shape, is the centerpiece of the banquet table. An Indonesian cone mold is available at some Asian food stores or a conical-shaped strainer, about 8½ -inches deep, available at most kitchenware stores, can also be used. Or make a mold using cardboard that can be cut and formed into a cone-shape about 8 inches tall and about 8 or 10 inches across at the base. Line the cardboard cone with foil, and spray the inside with vegetable cooking spray. Set the prepared mold, point end-down, in a container like a deep bowl or pitcher, so it can be filled easily without tipping over. ❂ ❂ ❂

Nasi Kuning Lengkap

Yellow Rice in Cone-shape

Yield: serves 8

- 3 tablespoons vegetable oil, divided
- 1 cup **finely chopped** onions
- 2 cloves garlic, finely chopped
- 6 cups fresh *coconut milk* (recipe page 346), or 6 cups canned coconut milk (available at some supermarkets and most Asian food stores)
- 2 pieces **lemon grass**, each **trimmed** to 4-inches long
- 4 teaspoons **ground** turmeric
- 1 tablespoon salt
- 3 cups long grain rice
- 3 hot, red chili peppers, for **garnish**
- 12 to 15 romaine lettuce leaves, trimmed, washed and separated, for garnish
- 2 cucumbers, cut crosswise into ¼-inch thick slices, for garnish
- 8 hard-cooked eggs, peeled, for garnish
- 2 eggs, lightly beaten
- ½ cup finely chopped celery leaves, for garnish

Equipment: Large saucepan, mixing spoon, prepare cone-shaped mold (see above), thread, small skillet, wide metal spatula

Note: Use care when handling peppers. Wrap your hands in plastic wrap or cover them with plastic sandwich bag. If you accidentally touch your eyes, rinse out at once under cold running water.

1. Heat 2 tablespoons oil in large saucepan over medium-high heat. Add onion and garlic, stir, and **sauté** 3 to 5 minutes until soft. Add coconut milk, lemon grass, turmeric, salt, and rice. Stir and cook until small bubbles appear around edge of pan. (Do not let milk boil.) Reduce heat to **simmer**, cover, and cook 20 to 25 minutes until rice is tender. Remove from heat and keep covered until all the liquid is absorbed. Remove and discard lemon grass.

2. Fill greased cone-shaped mold with cooked rice, packing it firmly. Cover opening with foil and refrigerate overnight to firm.

3. Unmold rice onto the center of a large round serving platter. Tie stems of 3 peppers together with thread. Place the tied ends at the very top and spread the peppers to cascade over the rice. Place lettuce leaves around base of rice. Arrange sliced cucumbers and quartered hard-cooked eggs on lettuce.

4. Heat remaining 1 tablespoon oil in small skillet over medium-high heat. Add lightly beaten eggs and cook undisturbed for 1 minute or until bottom is lightly browned. Using wide metal spatula, turn egg over and cook 1 minute more. Slide it onto a plate and cut into strips about ¼-inch wide. Decorate the rice cone by scattering strips of egg over the surface. Sprinkle with celery leaves.

To serve, place in the center of the banquet table for the centerpiece. Some side dishes served with the rice are rempah *(recipe follows) and others can be purchased at Asian food stores, such as* atjar kuning *(yellow pickles) and* rempejek *(peanut wafers).*

This is one of many side dishes served with *nasi kunig lengkap.*

Rempah

Coconut-Beef Patties

Yield: about 20 pieces

1 pound **ground** beef
4 cups **coconut,** finely grated (recipe page 346) or canned
1 egg
2 teaspoons ground **coriander**
1 clove **finely chopped** garlic
¼ teaspoon ground cumin
salt and pepper to taste
2 to 3 cups vegetable oil, for frying

Equipment: Baking sheet, paper towels, food processor, rubber spatula, large **heavy-based** skillet, wide metal spatula, oven mitts

Preheat oven to lowest setting. Line baking sheet with several layers of paper towels. Set aside.

1. Combine beef, grated coconut, egg, coriander, garlic, cumin, and salt and pepper to taste in food processor. Process until mixture is blended, smooth and fluffy, about 3 minutes.

Note: While processing, turn machine off once or twice and scrape down sides of container with a rubber spatula.

2. For each patty, scoop up about ¼-cup of mixture with your hands and pat into a round disk about 2 inches in diameter and ½-inch thick.

3. Heat oil in large heavy-based skillet over medium-high heat. Add patties a few at a time and fry for about 5 minutes on each side until browned and cooked through. Transfer cooked

patties to drain on paper towels covering baking sheet and place in oven to keep warm while cooking remaining patties.

To serve, arrange meat patties on platter and serve with nasi kuning lengkap *(recipe page 340).*

Another popular and easy to make side dish served on the buffet table with *nasi kuning lengkap* is *Begedil.*

Begedil

Potato Cutlets

Yield: serves 6

6 tablespoons vegetable oil, divided
1 onion, **finely chopped**
2 large potatoes, peeled, quartered, and boiled
½ cup celery, finely chopped
1 teaspoon nutmeg
salt to taste
1 cup dried **bread crumbs**

Equipment: Baking sheet, paper towels, food processor, rubber spatula, large **heavy-based** skillet, wide metal spatula, oven mitts

Preheat oven to lowest setting. Line baking sheet with several layers of paper towels. Set aside.

1. Heat 1 tablespoon oil in large heavy-based skillet over medium-high heat. Add onions and **sauté** until soft, 3 to 5 minutes.

2. Put cooked potatoes, sautéed onions, celery, nutmeg, and salt to taste in food processor and process until smooth and well mixed, about 1 minute.

Note: While processing, turn machine off once or twice and scrape down sides of container with a rubber spatula.

3. Put bread crumbs in shallow bowl. Divide dough-like mixture into 6 balls and shape each into ½-inch thick patty. Coat all sides of each cutlet with bread crumbs.

4. Heat remaining 5 tablespoons of oil in large heavy-based skillet over medium-high heat. Fry a few patties at a time until golden brown on all sides, about 5 minutes. Transfer cooked cutlets to drain on paper towels lining baking sheet and place in oven to keep warm until all are fried.

To serve, arrange cutlets on platter and place on the buffet table.

INDONESIA

Off the southeast Asian coast, Indonesia is a sprawling archipelago consisting of nearly 13,700 islands. Only about half of the islands are inhabited, with diversified cultures existing in diversified living conditions ranging from Stone Age to high-tech.

As the fourth most populous country in the world, Indonesia is home to Arabs, Chinese, Pakistanis, Indians, Dutch and other Europeans, Polynesians, Eurasians, and the indigenous Indonesian peoples. Most Indonesians are Muslim, making Indonesia the largest Islamic country in the world. Hinduism, once a major religion, now exists mostly on Bali. Less than 12 percent of the Indonesian population is Christian, with the majority Protestant. Most Indonesian Buddhists are of Chinese descent.

There can be a strong sense of nationalism among the different ethnic groups, and the population is encouraged to be Indonesian first and members of their *sukubangsa* (ethnic group) second. Generally, each ethnic group follows the life-cycle rituals of their particular religious traditions. (See Buddhism and Buddhist Life-Cycle Rituals, page liii; Protestant and Catholic Life-Cycle Rituals, page xlvi; Hinduism and Hindu Life-Cycle Rituals, page li; and Islam and

Islamic Life-Cycle Rituals, page xlix.) However, it is not unusual for Indonesians to mix traditions and religions, forming new rituals and celebrations.

Many Indonesians observe a bathing ceremony for mothers-to-be; after the baby is born there is another bathing ceremony. In Bali, the bathing ceremony is done at the third month; most other groups observe the *tujuh bulan* (seventh month) *selamatan*. A *selamatan* is a religious meal intended to assure harmony and good fortune. The seventh month is a time for other mothers with living children to give the mother-to-be emotional support. Infant mortality in Indonesia is very high, and so all the encouragement a soon-to-be mother can get is welcome. Elders always attend the *selamatan* to say the prayers. Everyone present partakes in a meal, which varies with each group. Usually several rice dishes are served, among them *nasi uduk/gurih* (recipe follows), as well as *ikan mas* (carp), fried whole and eaten to give strength and endurance, and the shrimp dish, *sambal goreng udang* (recipe page 344). The rituals include scented or blessed water, special fresh fruit and flowers, and ceremonial cloth (*kain batik*) worn by the mother.

In Bali, children are thought to be reincarnated from one of their ancestors, and they are treated as holy until they are 210 days old (the length of a Balinese calendar year). The infant's feet touch the ground for the first time when he or she is three months old (the crawling stage is bypassed, as being too "animalistic"). The family celebration, when the infant first walks, is called *nyambutan* and includes a feast with great quantities of rice and a large variety of sweets.

This is a popular way to cook rice, and it is served at most family celebrations.

Nasi Uduk/Gurih

Rice in Coconut Milk

Yield: serves 6 to 8

1 pound rice, such as **basmati** or jasmine (available at Asian food stores and most supermarkets)
3½ cups coconut milk, homemade (recipe page 346), or canned
4-inch length of **lemongrass**, washed and **trimmed**
½ teaspoon salt

Equipment: Large saucepan with cover, wooden mixing spoon, fork

Place rice in large saucepan, add coconut milk, lemongrass, and salt. Bring to a boil over medium-high heat. Stir rice and **reduce** heat to simmer. Cover and cook until all moisture is absorbed, 18 to 20 minutes. Remove and discard lemongrass. Cover and let rice sit 5 to 10 minutes before serving. Fluff with a fork before serving.

Serve rice with rendang *(recipe follows).*

This is an easy dish to prepare for a birthday celebration.

Rendang

Spiced Coconut Beef

Yield: serves 6

1 4-inch piece **lemongrass**, washed and trimmed to about 6 inches off the tender, whitish end
2 tablespoons peanut oil
6 cloves garlic, **finely chopped** or 1 tablespoon garlic granules
10 **shallots**, finely chopped
4 to 6 dried hot red chili peppers, more or less to taste (available at Asian food stores and most supermarkets)

1 tablespoon *galangal powder* (Thai or Laotian **ginger**, available at Asian food stores)
1 teaspoon **ground** turmeric
1 teaspoon ground **coriander**
1 teaspoon ground black pepper
1 tablespoon ground ginger
salt to taste
4 cups coconut milk, homemade (recipe page 346), or canned (available at Asian food stores and many supermarkets)
2 pounds beef chuck, cut into 1-inch cubes

Equipment: Work surface, paring knife, measuring cup, large skillet or **wok**, wooden mixing spoon

1. Cut lemon grass crosswise into ¼-inch pieces. You should have ¼ cup. Set aside.

2. Heat large skillet or wok over high heat. Add oil, garlic, shallots, and chili peppers. Stir and **sauté** for 1 to 2 minutes until shallots are soft. Reduce heat to medium-high and stir in galangal, turmeric, coriander, black pepper, ginger, lemongrass, and salt. Add beef cubes and toss constantly to lightly brown, 2 to 4 minutes.

3. Stir in coconut milk and cook for 3 to 5 minutes until bubbles appear around edge of pan. Reduce heat to low, stirring occasionally, and cook until coconut milk **reduces** and thickens to a gravy-like consistency, 1 to 1½ hours.

Serve over nasi uduk/gurih *(recipe precedes).*

Seafood is plentiful in Indonesia where this sweet and spicy dish is served with rice, peanuts, and fresh, thinly sliced vegetables.

Sambal Goreng Udang

Shrimp in Spicy Sauce

Yield: serves 4
¼ cup vegetable oil
2 onions, thinly sliced
1 clove garlic, **finely chopped**
1 pound medium shrimp, **peeled and deveined**
dried red pepper flakes, to taste
1 cup coconut milk, homemade (recipe page 346), or canned (available at Asian food stores and some supermarkets)
1 tomato, **trimmed** and **coarsely chopped**
1 green pepper, peeled and thinly sliced into rings
1 tablespoon packed brown sugar
salt and pepper to taste

Equipment: **Wok** or large skillet, mixing spoon

Heat oil in wok or large skillet over medium-high heat, add onion, garlic, and shrimp. Stir-fry ingredients until shrimp turn opaque pinkish-white and they are cooked through, 3 to 5 minutes. Add red pepper flakes, coconut milk, tomato, green pepper, brown sugar, and salt and pepper. Stir-fry for about 5 minutes for flavors to **blend**. Remove from heat.

To serve, transfer to serving bowl. To eat sambal goreng udang, *spoon it over rice.*

FIJI

Fiji is a group of more than 300 islands located in the Pacific Ocean northeast of Australia. The population is made up of Fijians who are descendants of Polynesians; Melanesians; and Indians, who are descendants of indentured laborers recruited over a century ago. The Indian population has increased more quickly than the native population, and there are now more Indians living on Fiji than indigenous peoples.

More than 85 percent of the indigenous Fijians are Christian. Christianity was brought to Fiji by Methodist missionaries, and superstitions, astrology beliefs, and nature events have been interwoven into their religion. Many native Fijians live in small villages centered around a Methodist church and mission schools.

Indians are not allowed to own land in Fiji (only native Fijians and the government can own land), which has added to the tension between Fijians and Indians. There is no social mixing and almost no intermarriage between the two groups. Fiji Indians have their own villages with their own places of worship and their own schools, and they prepare dishes from their Indian homeland. (See India and Subcontinent recipes pages 285–310.)

Indians introduced fire-walking to Fiji. The indigenous Fijians adopted the ritual, except that they walk on heated stones instead of hot embers. Wedding celebrations now often call for a display of fire-walkers.

Kava, a nonalcoholic drink made from the crushed root of a pepper plant, is a ceremonial drink among Fijians. It is served from a *bilo* (coconut cup). Onlookers perform ritual clapping, clapping once before the *kava* is drunk and three times after swallowing. *Kava* might be enjoyed at any auspicious occasion, such as child being born, a boat being completed, a roof being raised, a child returning home, etc.

The first important event in a Christian Fijian child's life is his or her christening. Feasts are prepared by Fijians for this celebratory occasion. Among native Fijians, a wedding or funeral is a community affair, and also involves feasting. A flotilla of boats often brings neighboring communities to the celebration. A *tambua*, a ceremonial object of respect made of the polished tooth of the sperm whale, is often given at births, presented to distinguished guests, given to show sympathy at funerals, or given when a contract or agreement is entered into. It is customary for a groom to presented a tooth to the father of the bride, prior to the wedding.

Feasts center around the **suckling pig** (recipe page 348), which is baked in a pit over heated stones covered with palm fronds and banana leaves. Baked with the suckling pig are chunks of plantains, sweet potato, peeled breadfruit, taro root, and fish and shrimp wrapped in large leaves. In Fiji, *shrimp palusami*, the following recipe, would be wrapped in leaves. For this recipe we're wrapping the shrimp in foil. ۞ ۞ ۞

Shrimp Palusami

Shrimp in Coconut Cream

Yield: serves 4

- 6 large cabbage leaves, washed and well drained, divided
- 2 to 3 pounds medium shrimp, chopped, shelled, **peeled**, and **deveined**
- 1 cup **finely chopped** onion
- salt and pepper to taste
- 1 cup *coconut cream*, homemade (recipe page 346), or canned (available at Asian food stores and some supermarkets)
- water, as needed

Equipment: Medium mixing bowl, mixing spoon, 4 (8 ½- x 10-inch) rectangles of aluminum foil, oven mitts, 9 to 10-inch square baking dish

Preheat oven to 350° F.

1. Finely chop 2 cabbage leaves and place in medium mixing bowl. Add chopped shrimp, onion, salt and pepper, and coconut cream, and stir well.

2. Place 4 sheets of foil side by side on work surface and set one of the 4 remaining whole cabbage leaves on top of each. Spoon equal amounts of shrimp mixture in the center of each leaf. Fold the leaves over the filling. Wrap and seal each stuffed leaf in foil. Arrange packages in baking dish, add about 1½ inches of water in bottom.

3. Bake in oven for 1 hour, until shrimp are fully cooked. Check shrimp doneness; they should be opaque pinkish-white when done.

To serve, each person gets one package as an appetizer during the wedding feast. The contents of the package are eaten by tearing open the foil.

Fresh Coconut for Grating

Yield: about 3 to 4 cups grated coconut

1 ripe coconut (at least 2 pounds) **Note:** When buying a fresh coconut, make sure that it has no cracks and that it contains liquid. Shake it, and if you do not hear swishing liquid, select another. When making coconut milk and cream it is not necessary to remove the brown inner skin before you grate coconut meat.

Equipment: Ice pick or metal skewer, kitchen towel, hard surface, oven mitts, hammer, food processor fitted with coarse grating attachment

1. ADULT HELP REQUIRED: Have an adult pierce the "eyes" of the coconut with an ice pick or metal skewer. Drain liquid, discard or save for another use.

2. Wrap coconut in towel and place on hard surface. Protect your hands with oven mitts and crack coconut open with hammer. Break into pieces small enough to fit in feed tube of food processor, for grating.

3. In food processor fitted with coarse **grater**, grate coconut pulp, about 4 minutes. (You should have about 4 cups loosely packed coconut pulp.)

Use grated coconut to make lolo *(coconut milk)* or coconut cream *(recipe follows) or pack in airtight container and freeze.*

Lolo

Coconut Milk

Yield: about 2 cups

2 cups grated fresh coconut, homemade (recipe precedes), or unsweetened, grated coconut (available canned or frozen at Asian food stores or most supermarkets)

2 cups boiling water, more if necessary

Equipment: Electric **blender** or food processor, strainer, double thickness cheesecloth or cotton napkin, small bowl, spoon

In blender or food processor, mix coconut and 2 cups boiling water for 2 minutes; let cool for 30 minutes. Line a strainer with double thickness dampened cheesecloth or napkin and set over small bowl. Pour coconut mixture into the cloth, a little at a time, making sure all liquid drains through cloth. Once all liquid has drained, pick up the four edges of cloth and twist it tightly to release as much coconut milk as possible into the small bowl. Discard coconut in cloth. This process makes thick coconut milk. For thinner coconut milk, add a little more water until you reach desired consistency.

Coconut Cream

Yield: about 1 cup

1 cup heavy cream

2 cups grated fresh coconut, homemade (recipe page 346), or unsweetened, grated coconut (available, canned or frozen at Asian food stores and most supermarkets)

Equipment: Small saucepan, electric **blender** or food processor, strainer, double thickness cheesecloth or cotton napkin, small bowl, spoon

1. In small saucepan, heat cream until small bubbles appear around edges of pan.

2. In blender or food processor, mix coconut and heated cream for about 2 minutes. Allow to cool for 30 minutes.

3. Line strainer with double thickness dampened cheesecloth or napkin and set over small bowl. Pour coconut mixture into cloth, a little at a time, making sure all liquid has drained through the cloth. Pick up four edges of cloth and twist tightly to release as much liquid as possible. Discard coconut in the cloth.

PAPUA NEW GUINEA

Papua New Guinea (PNG) lies about 90 miles northeast of Australia and includes the eastern half of the island of New Guinea and hundreds of neighboring islands. Plagued with frequent mud slides, earthquakes, volcanic eruptions, and drought, the islanders are no strangers to natural disasters. In recent years, a *tsunami* (a huge ocean wave produced by an underwater earthquake) did devastating damage and took many lives.

For over 100 years, PNG has been a destination for Christian missionaries, who have had a strong influence on the native people. Christian New Guineans combine Christianity with traditional beliefs; magic and sorcery remain powerful influences throughout their lives.

The indigenous population of PNG consists of several hundred groups or societies, each with their own language or dialect, customs, and traditions. Mainly due to the country's rugged, often impassable terrain, many clans live a near Stone-Age existence, isolated not only from the rest of the world, but from one another. Though modernization has begun in the country, for the vast majority of native peoples living in small villages, their way of life and social structure remains unchanged. The social structure is generally small, based on family, clan, or tribe. Loyalty and obligation to the extended family is an important part of life.

Contrasts abound in this land where the only form of communication between some villages are talking drums, while in other parts of PNG people converse via a high-tech microwave telephone system. Coastal villages consist of thatch-roofed houses, usually built on stilts, a school, and a *haus tambaran* ("spirit house"; also known as the men's ceremonial house). Most coastal villagers earn a living from the sea (fishers, coral divers, canoe builders, net makers, etc.) or farm. Highlanders live in similar villages, except their huts cling to the sides of mountains, and people forage from the forests or work on coconut and coffee plantations. Coffee, the nation's most profitable crop, grows well in the highland altitudes.

When young boys pass into adulthood, they are taken to the *haus tambaran*, which is the meeting place for the secret men's society and off-limits to women. Among some groups, the boys undergo a grueling initiation into manhood. Scarification is one of the acts performed on the boys. Mask and statue carvings, body painting with mud and ash, and the sacred flute are all used in the "boy-to-manhood" rituals. When the initiation is completed there is usually a great celebration (*sing-sing*).

Endless life-cycle customs and rituals can be found in PNG. Some groups have a food exchange ceremony honoring recently deceased elders. The clan comes together, each member bringing quantities of food to share at the festive occasion.

Like other life-cycle celebrations, weddings are communal, and the entire village might take part in the preparations and celebration. The husband-to-be customarily pays a bride's price to the family of his future wife. Since the pig is a prized possession and a form of wealth, the bride's price is often paid with a pig or two plus a little cash.

Funerals are usually momentous occasions and the rituals are very complex. Each clan has their own funerary traditions, which might include internment, cremation, or burial at sea. Some clans sink the body in the sea or set it adrift. Ancestral worship and spirit beliefs are usually part of death rituals. Among some groups the secret men's societies make *dukduks* (ritual costumes) or carve *malangans* (masks or totemic figures) to honor the dead. (*Malangan* refers to the carvings as well as a complex system of spiritual ideas, rites, and beliefs.)

Eating pork is reserved for important celebration feasts. For the people who can afford it, every important life-cycle celebration means the roasting of a whole suckling pig. The pig is roasted in a *mumu*, a traditional underground oven. A pit is dug, fire-heated stones are place in the bottom, and meat and vegetables are wrapped in herbs and leaves and placed on the stones. The pit is then sealed with palm fronds, banana leaves, and branches, and the contents roast and steam.

Celebrations are almost always communal, and it is not unusual for many weddings to take place on the same day. On such occasions the roasting pit can be several hundred yards long and filled with hundreds of whole pigs.

Baked in the pit with the pigs are chunks of plantains, sweet potato (*kaukau*), peeled **breadfruit**, **taro root**, and fish, each separately wrapped in banana leaves. Also wrapped in leaves and baked in the pit is *pota*, a mixture of chicken and salt pork. This recipe for roast suckling pig is adapted for the kitchen oven. ❁ ❁ ❁

Vuaka Vavi Ena Lovo

Roast Suckling Pig

Yield: serves 10 to 12

6 tablespoons dark brown sugar
1 cup Chinese soy sauce
6 cloves garlic, **finely chopped**
12-pound suckling pig (weighed when dressed), rinse and pat dry with paper towels
6 tablespoons vegetable oil
1cup butter or margarine, divided
6 ripe plantains, cut crosswise into 2-inch chunks, for **garnish**
2 pounds sweet potatoes, boiled to done, yet firm (not mushy), peeled and cut crosswise into 2-inch chunks, for garnish
1 lemon or large lime, for garnish

Equipment: Small saucepan, mixing spoon, paper towels, small bowl with cover, large plastic bag (about 24 x 30 inches), kitchen string, large roasting pan with rack, aluminum foil, **bulb baster**, oven mitts, large skillet with cover, large saucepan with cover

1. Prepare **marinade**: Put the brown sugar and soy sauce in a small saucepan, and over medium heat, stir to dissolve the sugar, 1 to 2 minutes. Remove from heat, stir in the garlic, and cool to room temperature. Using a crumpled wad of paper towel, dab the pig inside and out with half the soy sauce mixture. Slip the pig into a large plastic bag, seal, and refrigerate for 4 to 6 hours to absorb the marinade. Transfer remaining marinade to small bowl, cover, and refrigerate to use for basting the pig during roasting.

Preheat oven to 450° F.

2. Prepare pig to roast: Using string, tie the pig's legs. To do this, bend the back legs in a crouching position and tie them together, under the pig. Tie the front legs straight out in front. Place the pig upright on rack, in large roasting pan. Make a lemon-size wad of foil and place

it in the pig's mouth to keep it open. Cover the ears and tail with foil to prevent burning.

3. Mix remaining marinade with oil. Using a wad of paper towel, dab it all over the pig.

4. Roast pig: Roast at 450° F for 30 minutes and then reduce heat to 325° F for 4½ to 5 hours (allow 30 minutes for each pound), or until cooked through and registers 165° to 175° F on meat thermometer. Using a bulb baster, **baste** frequently with marinade. If necessary, make more marinade.

5. Prepare garnishes: 30 minutes before serving, melt ½ cup butter or margarine in large skillet over medium-high heat. Add plantain chunks and fry, tossing frequently, until golden, 15 to 20 minutes. Cover and keep on low heat. Melt remaining ½ cup butter or margarine in large saucepan over medium-high heat. Add sweet potatoes, reduce heat to medium and fry, carefully turning the pieces, until they are golden, 15 to 20 minutes. Cover and keep on low heat.

To serve, transfer the pig to large platter or tray. Remove the foil from ears and tail. Replace the foil in the mouth with whole lemon or lime. Arrange plantain and sweet potato chunks around the pig and serve as the centerpiece for the wedding feast.

Canned fish and bully beef, shipped from Australia, and mutton flaps, the belly portions of sheep, from New Zealand are very popular and often are included in the wedding feast or other life cycle *sing sing*.

Poe, not to be confused with *poi*, is made with assorted fruit and is usually one of the many dishes served along with *sucking pig*.

Poe

Baked Fruit Pudding

Yield: serves 6

1 large ripe **papaya**, **seeded**, peeled, and **coarsely chopped**
4 ripe bananas, peeled
3 ripe **mangoes**, peeled, seeded, and coarsely chopped
1 pineapple, peeled, cored, and **finely chopped**
1 cup brown sugar
1 teaspoon vanilla extract
½ cup **arrowroot** (available at supermarkets)
1 cup pineapple juice
1 cup *coconut cream*, homemade (recipe page 346), or canned (available at Asian food markets and some supermarkets)

Equipment: Food processor, rubber spatula, small mixing bowl, buttered shallow baking dish, oven mitts

Preheat oven to 350° F.

1. In food processor, **purée** the papaya, bananas, mangoes, and pineapple. Add brown sugar and vanilla, and continue processing. Put arrowroot in small mixing bowl, add pineapple juice, and stir until arrowroot is dissolved; pour into the fruit purée. Process to mix together. Pour the fruit mixture into the buttered baking dish and smooth top with the rubber spatula.

Note: While processing, turn machine off once or twice and scrape down sides of container with rubber spatula.

2. Bake in oven for 1 hour, or until the top is golden brown. Using oven mitts, remove from oven and let cool to room temperature. Refrigerate until ready to serve.

Serve poe *with a side dish of* coconut cream *to* ***drizzle*** *over each serving.*

AUSTRALIA

Australia, the sixth largest country (in land mass) and smallest continent in the world, is south of Papua New Guinea and Indonesia in the Indian Ocean. Most of the Australian population is clustered in towns and cities along the southeastern seaboard, between the cities of Adelaide and Brisbane. The vast inland regions of Australia, which are sparsely populated, are known as the *bush* and the *outback*. The outback encompasses nearly four-fifths of Australia's total area. Very few people live in this extremely flat and barren territory. The Australians who call the outback home live an isolated existence either in one-street towns or on the dusty plains. The bush, less desolate, has more wildlife and boasts a little rain.

Australia's original settlers, the Aborigines, arrived on the continent some 40,000 years ago. The next settlers, the British, came in the eighteenth and nineteenth centuries, many of whom were convicts sent to Australia when it was a penal colony. Australia was also settled by Germans, Chinese, Italians, and Greeks. Today, Australia is a multicultural country, with immigrants of many races, nationalities, and religions. The Eurasian population celebrates life-cycle events according to the religion, rituals, and festivities of their homeland. It is not unusual to have a combination of Italian, Greek, and Asian dishes served at the same banquet.

Many immigrants are forming new rituals, blending Australian customs with their traditional rites. For instance, some Asian couples have two wedding ceremonies; one Buddhist and one civil. The bride often makes several dress changes, wearing both traditional and Western wedding attire during the day-long celebration.

The Aborigines in Australia live between two worlds: one with their traditional customs and the other with modern Western culture. Many of the younger generations of Aborigines have moved from their tribal lands to join the Australian mainstream. Tribal Aborigines carry on the traditions of their ancestors, and social gatherings (*corroborees*) involve a great deal of singing and dancing and storytelling. Music is very important to Aboriginal culture and is used during sacred ceremonies to communicate with spirits.

Life-cycle rituals for Aborigine boys begin when they are about eight years old. At that time they go through very complex circumcision rituals followed by a celebration feast for the whole clan. When boys reach 12 or 13, they are sent to live in the bush for a few months and to fend for themselves. These "boy-to-manhood" rituals take more than a year to complete, and at the end of them, there is always a big ceremony and feast. Once into manhood, the young men take part in a *kunapipi* ceremony—fertility rites to prepare them for marriage.

The Aboriginal ceremonial feasts include what is called "bush tucker" (survival food). Crocodile, goanna (monitor lizard), kangaroo, possum, fatty muttonbird, and the witchetty grub (insect larvae that feed on the wood of the eucalyptus trees) are prized by Aborigines as good "tucker." Witchetty grubs (from the Aboriginal *Witjuti*, the name of roots in which the grubs are often found) are eaten either live and raw, or cooked, and are now considered a gourmet delicacy in Australia. Canned grub soup is available in some Australian supermarkets, and it can also be purchased over the Internet. Crocodile and kangaroo meat has become quite commonplace in most meat markets in Australia. Along with these meats, there are endless seeds, ferns, berries, and fruits that are part of the Aboriginal banquet fare.

Along Australian's eastern seaboard, about 80 percent of the population lives in middle-class suburban homes, many of which have a barbie (barbecue) and garden. During their summer (our winter), the barbecue pit is the center of many social events. (Barbie can also mean barbecue party.)

For Australians living in the outback, planning a life-cycle happening, such as a birthday, anniversary party, or wedding or funeral, can be no easy task. Guests often must travel great distances to attend, and usually plan to spend the night. Invitations are often issued over radio transceiver (a radio that receives and transmits), since many remote areas do not have telephones. Fruits, vegetables, and other foodstuffs must come by way of "mail lorry" (mail truck) over dirt roads or by "goods train" (freight train). In the most remote areas of the outback, such as along the barren Nullarbor Plain, a train referred to as the "Tea and Sugar" arrives in isolated communities once a week, and families of railroad workers and nearby cattle and sheep stations (ranches) come to do their weekly shopping for groceries and other sundries.

If there is a lake or river nearby, such things as wild ducks and yabbies (**crayfish**) will be on the menu. The standard way of cooking crayfish is in a pot of boiling water, and the crayfish are called "billy-boiled yabbies." The "billy," a carryover from early outback survival gear, is a large can-like metal container with a wire handle attached to the top. Anything cooked in a billy takes on the name, such as billy tea, which is simply tea made with water boiled in a billy can. ۞ ۞ ۞

Yabby Cocktail

Crayfish Cocktail

Yield: serves 6

- 4 dozen live **crayfish** (available at most fish markets) or 1 to 1½ pounds frozen crayfish meat (available in the freezer section of most fish markets and supermarkets)
- 1 gallon water and one teaspoon of salt (if using live crayfish)
- 1 cup ketchup
- 1 tablespoon Worcestershire sauce
- ¼ cup fresh lemon juice
- salt and **ground** red pepper to taste
- 2 tablespoons heavy cream
- 6 leaf lettuce leaves, separated, washed, and drained, for serving
- 1 lemon, cut into 6 wedges, for **garnish**

Equipment: Large saucepan, **colander**, 2 small bowls with covers, spoon, 6 salad plates

1. Prepare live crayfish: Pour water and 1 teaspoon of salt into large saucepan, and bring to a boil over high heat. When water boils, add live crayfish. (Discard any crayfish that appear dead and if their tails do not curl under them.)

2. When crayfish hit the boiling water, their shells turns bright red. When they float to the top, continue to boil 3 to 5 minutes; drain in a colander set in the sink. When cool enough to handle, **peel and devein** crayfish. Rinse crayfish meat under cold running water, drain well, and put in a small bowl. Cover and refrigerate until serving time.

3. Prepare fresh frozen crayfish: Thaw according to directions on package and put in small bowl. Cover and refrigerate until serving time.

4. Prepare sauce: Put ketchup in a small bowl and stir in Worcestershire sauce, lemon juice, salt and ground red pepper to taste, and heavy cream. Cover and refrigerate until serving time.

5. To assemble: Place 6 salad plates side by side on work surface. Set a crisp lettuce leaf on each plate. Using either the fresh or the thawed, frozen crayfish meat, place an equal portion on top of the lettuce and spoon a tablespoon of sauce over each serving. Garnish each serving with a lemon wedge.

To serve, place the yabby cocktail *at each place setting on the table. Serve as an appetizer with saltine crackers.*

Casseroles and large meat pies are favorites at large Australian family get-togethers and social gatherings. The old English classic, steak and kidney pie, which came with the early settlers, is being replaced by this more healthy recipe.

Puftaloons

Steak and Mushroom Pie

Yield: serves 6

1½ pounds lean top-round steak, cut into 1-inch cubes
¼ cup all-purpose flour
salt and pepper to taste
½ teaspoon **ground** nutmeg
2 tablespoons vegetable oil, divided, more as needed
4 tablespoons butter or margarine, divided, more as needed
2 onions, thinly sliced
2 cups sliced fresh white mushrooms (approximately 7 ounces)
2 tablespoons **finely chopped** fresh parsley
1 cup canned beef broth
¼ cup canned tomato paste
egg wash
½ box (1 sheet) frozen **puff pastry sheets**, thawed (available in most supermarkets)

Equipment: Medium mixing bowl, cup, large skillet, mixing spoon, large mixing bowl, buttered 9-inch deep-dish pie pan, lightly floured work surface, lightly floured rolling pin, knife, scissors, **pastry brush**, aluminum foil, oven mitts

1. Place meat cubes in medium mixing bowl. In cup, mix together flour, nutmeg, and salt and pepper to taste. Sprinkle nutmeg mixture over the meat and using clean hands, toss to coat. Set aside.

2. Heat 1 tablespoon oil and 2 tablespoons butter or margarine in large skillet over medium-high heat. Add onions and mushrooms. Stirring frequently, **sauté** until soft, 4 to 5 minutes. Using mixing spoon, transfer to large mixing bowl.

3. Place skillet back on the heat without cleaning and add 1 more tablespoon oil and 2 tablespoons butter or margarine. Heat over medium-high heat. Add meat cubes (a few at a time) and toss to lightly brown meat on all sides, 4 to 5 minutes. Add to onion and mushroom mixture. Continue sautéing until all the meat is browned. Add more oil and butter or margarine, as needed.

4. Add chopped parsley, beef broth, and tomato paste to meat mixture. Toss to mix and transfer to buttered deep-dish pie pan. Cool to room temperature and refrigerate for 1 hour.

Preheat oven to 400° F.

5. Place pastry sheet on lightly floured work surface and using lightly floured rolling pin, roll out pastry to about 10-inches square. Lay pastry over meat mixture and press down around the rim of the pie pan. Using a knife, trim off the overhang and save the pastry scraps. Using a knife, cut a 2-inch long crisscross, in the center of the pastry. Curl back the edges in the middle of the X to make a decorative vent for steam to escape. Cut the pastry scraps with the scissors into leaves, stars, or confetti-like shapes and scatter them over the top. Using a pastry brush, brush top of pastry well with egg wash. (If the pastry is rough looking, that's fine; it makes a more interesting looking pie.)

6. Place pie in oven and bake for 15 to 20 minutes, or until top is golden brown. Reduce the oven heat to 350° F and place a piece of foil over the pie to prevent the top from getting too brown. Continue baking for 15 to 20 minutes more. Using oven mitts, remove from oven.

Serve the pie while still warm, cutting the top into wedges and spooning out the meat filling.

No Australian meal is complete unless desserts, called "afters" (because they are eaten "after" the meal), are brought to the table and served with a "cuppa" (a cup of tea). An old favorite "after" served at life-cycle parties are *lamingtons*. These small cakes were named after Baron Lamington, who was the governor of Queensland from 1895 to 1901. They are a favorite and often baked for charity fund-raising events and school bake sales.

Recipe shortcut: Packaged white or pound cake mix can be used in this recipe. Make the cake (according to directions on package) and continue with steps 4 and 5. Use 16-ounce canned chocolate frosting to ice the cakes and continue with step 7.

Lamingtons

Small Coconut Cakes

Yield: 16 pieces

- 3/4 cup butter or margarine, at room temperature
- 3/4 cup sugar
- 3 eggs
- 1½ cups cake flour
- ¼ teaspoon salt
- 1 teaspoon baking powder
- 1 teaspoon vanilla extract
- 2 tablespoons milk
- ¼ cup raspberry jam, for filling
- 3½ cups confectioners' sugar, more as needed
- 3 tablespoons cocoa powder
- ¾ cup hot water, more or less as needed
- 1½ cups sweetened grated coconut, more if necessary

Equipment: Large mixing bowl, electric mixer or wooden mixing spoon, flour **sifter**, rubber spatula, scissors, wax paper, greased 8-inch square cake pan, toothpick, oven mitts, wire cake rack, **serrated knife**, baking sheet, plastic food wrap, medium bowl, fork, dinner knife or small spatula, small bowl

Preheat oven to 350° F.

1. Put butter or margarine and sugar in large mixing bowl. Using an electric mixer or wooden mixing spoon, beat until creamy, 2 to 4 minutes. Add eggs one at a time, beating well after each addition.

2. Combine flour, salt, and baking powder in sifter. **Sift** a small amount of the flour mixture over the egg mixture and fold in using rubber spatula or wooden spoon. Continue folding in small amounts of flour, alternating with milk, until mixture is smooth. Stir in vanilla. Using a scissors, cut a square of waxed paper to cover bottom of the greased cake pan. Set in pan and grease topside of waxed paper. Pour batter into prepared pan and smooth top with rubber spatula.

3. Bake in oven for 35 to 45 minutes, until toothpick inserted into center of cake comes out clean and cake is golden brown. Wearing oven mitts, remove from oven and set pan on cake rack to cool to room temperature.

4. Loosen the sides of the cake by running a small knife around the inside edge of pan. Place a piece of wax paper on a baking sheet and invert it over the cake. Holding the baking sheet and cake pan tightly together turn over; remove the cake pan with the wax paper. Wrap the cake in plastic wrap and refrigerate at least 8 hours or overnight.

5. Assemble cakes: Remove the plastic wrap. Using a serrated knife, cut the cake through the middle, separating the top from the bottom. Spread jam over the bottom piece and sandwich the top and bottom together. Cut cake into 2-inch squares (make 4 equal-size cuts the length and width of the cake) and place on wax-paper-covered sheet pan.

6. Prepare icing: Put 3½ cups confectioners' sugar in a medium bowl and add the cocoa. Using a mixing spoon, stir in ¾ cup of hot water, a little at a time, just until the mixture is a thick,

spreadable paste. Note: To thin the mixture, add a little more hot water; to thicken the mixture, add a little more confectioners' sugar.

7. Icing cakes: Poke a fork into the bottom of a cake square and holding the fork handle in one hand, spread the icing over the top and 4 sides of the cake using a dinner knife or small spatula held in the other hand. Put 1½ cups grated coconut into a small bowl and using your fingers, press the grated coconut onto the iced cake. Using your fingers or a spatula, carefully remove fork from bottom of pan and set cake back on wax-paper-covered baking sheet allowing space between cakes. Repeat icing each cake and allow to set for at least 4 hours before serving.

Serve the cakes on a platter for birthday parties, anniversaries, and other special life-cycle celebrations.

Another favorite treat are *bickies* (biscuits or cookies), especially when made with Macadamia nuts. Indigenous to Australia, Macadamia nuts were "bush tucker" food for the Aborigines long before the Europeans discovered them in the 1820s. They were originally called bush nuts, Queensland nuts, or bauple nuts.

Macadamia Bickies

Macadamia Nut Cookies

Note: This recipe takes 2 days.

Yield: about 90 pieces

3 eggs
¾ cup sugar
1 cup oil
1 teaspoon vanilla extract
1 cup **coarsely chopped** macadamia nuts
1 cup chocolate chips
2 cups all-purpose flour
1½ teaspoons baking powder
¼ teaspoon salt
1½ cups corn flakes

Equipment: Large mixing bowl, wooden mixing spoon, small bowl, rubber spatula, plastic wrap, greased baking sheet, aluminum foil, vegetable oil spray, lightly floured work surface, oven mitts, **serrated knife**

Note: Mix ingredients with a mixing spoon, do not use an electric mixer or food processor.

Preheat oven to 350° F.

1. Put eggs in large mixing bowl. Add sugar and oil and stir well using a wooden mixing spoon. Stir in vanilla extract, nuts, and chocolate chips until well mixed. Put flour, baking powder, and salt in small bowl and stir together. Add flour mixture a little at a time, stirring after each addition. Using rubber spatula, stir in corn flakes. Cover bowl with plastic wrap and refrigerate overnight.

2. Prepare to bake: Cover baking sheet with piece of foil and grease foil with vegetable oil spray. Divide dough into 3 balls. Using clean hands, roll one ball into the shape of a rope 1 inch wide and about 15 inches long on lightly floured work surface. Repeat making 2 more ropes and place them side by side, with space between them to allow for rising, on foil covered baking sheet. Bake in oven until golden, 25 to 30 minutes.

3. Using oven mitts, remove from oven and allow to rest 10 minutes. Using a serrated knife, slice each log diagonally across into ½-inch thick slices. Lay the slices side by side, with cut side on the baking sheet. Bake in the oven 3 to 5 minutes to lightly toast. Cool to room temperature.

Serve as a sweet treat at birthday parties or on the dessert buffet table for other life-cycle celebrations. These cookies freeze well; store in a resealable plastic freezer bag.

NEW ZEALAND

New Zealand, about 1200 miles southeast of Australia, consists of two islands, North Island and South Island, which are separated by the Cook Strait. The greatest concentration of people live on North Island. The descendants of Europeans, primarily from the British Isles, are generally city dwellers and belong to the Anglican church.

The indigenous people, the Maoris, live in settlements in remote regions of the country. Most Maoris combine traditional Maori beliefs with Christianity. The ancestors of the Maoris migrated centuries ago to New Zealand, which they called *Aoteuroa* ("the long white cloud"). They came by seagoing canoes from islands somewhere in the mid-Pacific and developed a unique culture, considered one of the most advanced in all of Polynesia.

According to Maori tradition, the land is sacred and it must be cared for and protected. The people get from the land not only their food, but also their identity; the cycle of birth and death springs from Mother Earth. At a Maori's birth, the father or a Maori priest recites a ritual prayer (*karakia*) to bestow supernatural powers on the child, especially if it is the first-born. After the ceremony a feast is held for everyone in the community.

New Zealand has some 40 different Maori groups. Many Maoris have fused the Western language and way of life (referred to as *pakena*) with their own. Traditional Maori social activities take place at the communal ceremonial gathering site (*marae*). The *marae* includes the meeting house, dining hall, utility buildings, and sometimes a church. There are about a thousand *marae* throughout New Zealand where only the Maori language is spoken and Maori food is eaten. This is where all meetings, ceremonial gatherings (*hui*), and such special events as weddings and funerals take place.

At the *marae* compound everything is communal, from gathering the food to sharing it in the dining hall. The men prepare the *hangi*, an earth oven, which is a pit filled with fire-heated stones that can cook hundreds of pounds of mutton, pork, beef, chicken, eel, cabbage, and *kumara* (sweet potatoes) at one time. Women do most of the food preparation, table setting, and cleanup work, with the help of the children. Men are called upon to bake bread leavened with homemade potato yeast. Potato yeast is very difficult to develop. A bread similar in flavor, but with a different, yet pleasant texture, is made with mashed potatoes and active dry yeast (recipe follows). Potato bread is prepared for all life-cycle celebrations.

Weddings are often planned for Easter or Christmas holidays, and many relatives gather to share in the celebration. Most brides wear the *pakeha* (Western-style) wedding attire. Vows are spoken in Maori, and the rite takes place either in the church or the meeting house, followed by speeches, singing, dancing, and feasting in the *marae* dining hall. Kinfolk bring their harvest of sweet potatoes, cabbages, seaweed, seafood, and assorted meats to be cooked in the *hangi*. A crew of women serve the food buffet-style to the throngs who attend the celebration.

The Maori rituals of death (*tangihanga*) are elaborate and long. The death rites take place in the meeting house where families spend three days and nights together, making speeches about the deceased, paying tribute to the ancestors, reciting ancient tales, expressing their grief and beliefs in chants, and singing Maori songs around the casket. Mourning is public; according to Maori traditions, the deceased belongs to the tribe, not to the individual family. Contributions of food, cash, and personal help are given by mourners for such ceremonial gatherings. On the third day of the funeral ritual, after a church service, the grave is dug by the men in the family, and the deceased is buried with cherished personal belongings. The rituals end with a cleansing rite followed by a celebration feast.

Potatoes are not native to New Zealand and were probably introduced to the Maoris by Christian missionaries in the early nineteenth century, who also probably showed the Maoris how to make the leavening agent for making bread. In the potato bread recipe following, freshly mashed potatoes and dry active yeast are used to speed up the procedure. ۞ ۞ ۞

Maori Potato Bread

Note: This recipe takes two days.

Yield: 1 round loaf (about 8 inches)

- 2 cups mashed potatoes, leftovers or prepared instant
- 2 cups **lukewarm** water
- 1 package active dry **yeast**
- 7 cups bread flour, divided, more or less as needed
- 2 teaspoons salt
- 2 teaspoons sugar
- ½ cup **cornmeal**
- 1 teaspoon cornstarch
- ½ cup cold water

Equipment: Large mixing bowl, wooden mixing spoon, plastic wrap, lightly floured work surface, kitchen towel, baking sheet, sharp knife, 8-inch square baking pan, small pan, heat-proof surface, **pastry brush**, oven mitts, wire cake rack

1. Prepare yeast sponge: Put mashed potatoes in large mixing bowl, add lukewarm water, yeast, and 4 cups flour, and stirring gently, mix ingredients. Cover with plastic wrap and allow to stand in warm place for 6 to 8 hours or overnight. The sponge is ready to use when it is very thick and bubbly.

2. Uncover the yeast sponge, and sprinkle in salt and sugar. Using wooden mixing spoon, carefully **fold in** 2½ cups flour. Do not stir, as stirring will toughen the dough. Using your hands, continue slowly folding in flour, ½ cup at a time, until dough is no longer sticky and can be formed into a ball. Transfer to lightly floured work surface and **knead** until smooth and **elastic**, 5 to 8 minutes. Grease large mixing bowl and place dough in bowl, turning to grease all sides. Cover with towel and let rise in a warm place until doubled in bulk, 1½ to 2 hours.

3. **Punch down** dough with your fist. Transfer to lightly floured work surface and shape into round loaf. Sprinkle loaf with cornmeal and place on baking sheet. Cover with towel and let rise for 1½ to 2 hours, until almost double in size. Using a sharp knife, make a crisscross slash, about ¼-inch deep on top center of loaf.

Preheat oven to 375° F.

4. Fill an 8-inch square baking pan with about ½-inch water and place on bottom of oven. (This helps the bread form a nice crust.)

5. In small saucepan, dissolve cornstarch in cold water and bring to a boil over high heat. Cool slightly and using pastry brush, coat top and sides of loaf with cornstarch mixture.

6. Bake bread in oven for 30 to 35 minutes, or until loaf is golden brown. Using oven mitts, remove from oven. Remove loaf from baking sheet and invert on wire rack to cool to warm.

Serve the bread fresh from the oven while still slightly warm for best flavor.

New Zealanders love sweet potatoes (*kumaras*). The Maoris cook them in the *hangi* (earth oven) while the *pakeha* bake them in a casserole.

Sweet Potato and Apple Casserole

Yield: serves 6 to 8

6 sweet potatoes, boiled and peeled
juice of 1 lemon
2 cups thinly sliced apples
½ cup brown sugar
1 teaspoon **cinnamon sugar**
¼ cup butter or margarine
½ cup thawed, frozen apple juice concentrate

Equipment: Work surface, knife, medium bowl, thickly buttered 8-inch square baking pan, oven mitts

Preheat oven to 350° F

1. Cut sweet potatoes crosswise into ½-inch thick slices. Put apple slices in medium bowl and sprinkle lemon juice over them to keep from discoloring.

2. In thickly buttered 8-inch baking pan, layer half of the sweet potato slices, slightly overlapping, over the bottom and sprinkle with cinnamon sugar. Cover with all the apple slices, and sprinkle with cinnamon sugar. Top with slightly overlapping layer of remaining sweet potato slices. Sprinkle with cinnamon sugar and dot top with small chunks of butter or margarine. Pour over apple juice.

3. Bake in oven for 35 to 45 minutes, until top is lightly browned and bubbly.

Serve from the pan as a side dish with pork, lamb, or beef.

Kiwi fruit is cultivated in New Zealand, and most New Zealanders seem to have a variety of fruit trees growing in their backyard. This salad made with easily available fruit would probably be included in the birthday or anniversary dinner menu.

Grapefruit, Kiwi, and Watercress Salad

Yield: serves 6

4 fresh grapefruit, peeled, **pith** removed, and **sectioned**, or two jars (26-ounces each) grapefruit sections (available in the refrigerated section of most supermarkets)
3 kiwis
2 tablespoons lemon juice
1 tablespoon cider vinegar
3 tablespoons vegetable oil
2 teaspoons honey
salt and pepper to taste
1 bunch fresh **watercress**, rinsed, patted dry, and **trimmed**
cinnamon sugar, to taste, for **garnish**

Equipment: Strainer, medium bowl, knife, work surface, small bowls with cover, pint jar with tight fitting lid, medium serving platter

1. Drain grapefruit sections in strainer placed over a medium bowl. Cover and refrigerate grapefruit juice for another use.

2. Peel kiwi on work surface, and slice crosswise into ¼-inch thick slices. Put slices in small bowl, cover, and refrigerate until ready to assemble.

3. Prepare dressing: In pint jar, combine lemon juice and vinegar. Add oil, honey, and salt and pepper to taste. Cover jar tightly and shake to mix. Refrigerate until ready to use.

4. Assemble: Arrange watercress in a ring around edge of medium serving platter. Fill in center with well drained grapefruit sections.

Place the kiwi slices on the top center of the grapefruit. Slightly overlap the kiwi slices in a decorative pattern. Do not completely cover the grapefruit. Cover with plastic wrap and refrigerate until ready to serve.

To serve, uncover salad. Shake dressing in jar and ***drizzle*** *over fruit. Sprinkle with cinnamon sugar to taste, for garnish.*

CARIBBEAN

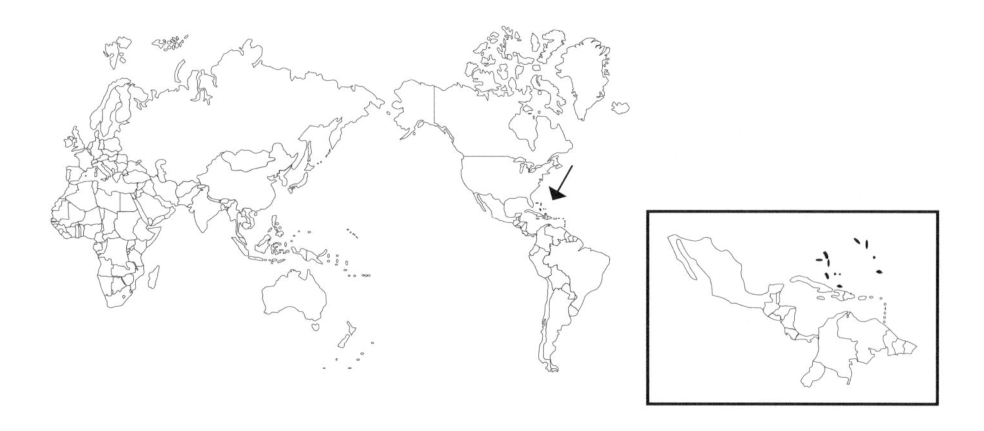

The Caribbean islands are located in the Caribbean Sea, which stretches from Venezuela in the south to the area between Florida and Mexico in the north. The popular image of the Caribbean is that it is a land of tropical breezes, palm trees, blue skies, gentle seas, and lush green vegetation and that all islands are alike. Behind this stereotyped image of island paradises are unique islands with marked differences in peoples and geography, ranging from tropical to arid semi-desert islands.

The original inhabitants, Arawak Indians and Caribs (they gave the region its name), disappeared after the arrival of Europeans, mostly through disease and war. Nearly everyone who calls the islands "home" is a transplant. Caribbean traditions, customs, and food arrived with the explorers, conquerors, settlers, slaves, and indentured workers from Europe, Africa, India, Asia, and Latin America.

Seventy-five percent of the Caribbean people are at least partially descended from African slaves. The remainder includes direct descendants of European colonists and the East Indians brought to the islands as indentured laborers when slavery was abolished in the nineteenth century. The Chinese also emigrated to the area in search of economic opportunities.

All of these ethnic groups have adapted the life-cycle traditions and foods of their homelands to conditions of the islands, creating new traditions and foods that spread throughout the Caribbean. A perfect example is the black wedding cake (recipe follows). It is a version of the English fruit cake, but it is made with ingredients native to the tropical islands.

This cake is called black cake because of its dark brown color. In the tropics, burnt sugar syrup is added to make the cake even darker. Burnt sugar syrup (available at Caribbean food stores and some supermarkets) is a thin, black, bitter liquid. It is also added to meat and fish stews to enrich the color. Burnt sugar syrup is not essential to the taste of this recipe but adds to the presentation. *Black wedding cake* is also known as bride's cake and Christmas cake. ۞ ۞ ۞

Black Wedding Cake

Caribbean Fruit Cake

Note: This recipe takes more than one day.

Yield: serves 35 to 45

- 5 cups chopped mixed candied fruit: **papaya**, pineapple, cherries, apricots, or **citron** (1¼ cups each or any combination)
- 1½ cups seedless raisins (9-ounce container equals 1½ cups)
- 1½ cups chopped dates (9-ounce container equals 1½ cups)
- 2 cups chopped nuts (walnuts or pecans)
- 7½ cups all-purpose flour, divided
- 1 teaspoon salt
- 6 teaspoons baking powder
- 1 teaspoon **ground** cinnamon
- 1½ teaspoons ground **allspice**
- ½ teaspoon ground cloves
- ½ teaspoon ground nutmeg
- 14 eggs, lightly beaten
- 2 cups unsalted butter, melted
- 1½ cups warm water
- 2 tablespoons burnt **sugar syrup** (optional)
- 3½ cups dark brown sugar
- ½ cup rum, for misting (optional)
- 4 to 5 (8 ounces each) tubes **almond paste**, for assembling (available at all supermarkets)
- 1 to 2 tablespoons water (optional)
- *butter cream icing* (recipe follows), for frosting

Equipment: 3 springform pans (each a different size: 6, 9, 12 inches), aluminum foil, 3 cake circle boards (each a different size: 6, 9, 12 inches), 2 large mixing bowls, flour **sifter**, electric mixer or mixing spoon, rubber spatula, oven mitts, toothpick, wire cake rack, small spray bottle (optional), medium bowl, 2 baking sheets, **icing spatula** or dinner knife, large round serving tray or platter, 10 (4- to 6-inch) skewers, small cutting pliers, pitcher of warm water, paper towels

1. Prepare springform pans: Cut a piece of foil large enough to cover one side of each cake circle board and fit smoothly over the edges. Open the side ring latch on each springform. Remove the metal pan bottom and replace it with a circle board of the same size. Place the cake board, foil-side up, in the side ring then close and tighten the side ring latch around it to secure the bottom in place. Repeat assembling all three pans. Butter the sides and the foil-covered bottom of each pan and sprinkle with flour, shake out excess, and set pans aside.

Preheat oven to 275° F.

2. Put candied fruit, raisins, dates, and nuts in a large mixing bowl. Add 1½ cups flour, and using your hands, toss to coat fruit mixture.

3. **Sift** remaining 6 cups flour, salt, baking powder, cinnamon, allspice, cloves, and nutmeg into the remaining large mixing bowl. Add lightly beaten eggs, melted butter, burnt sugar syrup (optional), and brown sugar into flour mixture. Using an electric mixer or mixing spoon, beat until batter is smooth, 3 to 5 minutes. Fill each springform pan about two-thirds full with batter.

4. Bake cakes in oven for 2½ to 3 hours or until toothpick inserted in center of each comes out clean and cakes pull away from sides of pans. Using oven mitts, remove from oven and place on wire rack. Let cakes cool for 1 hour before removing sides of pans.

5. Remove sides of springform pans but keep cakes on the cake boards. (The boards support the cakes.) Set the cakes on the wire rack to cool for at least 2 hours before continuing. When cakes are cool to the touch, carefully turn topside-down on work surface. Remove the cake boards, and if the foil sticks to the cake, carefully peel it off, and recover the circle boards

with a new piece of foil. Place the cake board, foil-side-up on the work surface then slide the topside-down cake onto it. The bottom of the cake, which has a smooth flat surface and sharp corners, is now the top; repeat with all 3 cakes.

6. Wrap each cake in foil and refrigerate overnight or up to a week for flavor to develop. Lightly mist the top and sides of cakes with rum from a spray bottle two or three times during the week to enhance the flavor (optional).

Preheat oven to 250° F.

7. Prepare to coat cakes with almond paste: Remove almond paste from packages and put in medium bowl. Allow paste to sit at room temperature for at least 2 hours and mix well. If almond paste seems too stiff to spread, beat in 1 to 2 tablespoons water.

8. Set cakes on baking sheets. Using icing spatula or dinner knife, spread a thin layer of almond paste over the top and sides of each cake. Place in oven for 20 to 30 minutes to dry almond paste. Cool cakes to room temperature before icing them.

9. Assemble 3-tier cake: Set largest (12-inch) cake on large round serving tray or platter. Poke one skewer in the center and space the other four skewers equally apart, in a 4-inch radius from the center skewer. Using small cutting pliers cut the exposed tops off of the 5 skewers so they are an even with the top of the cake. (The skewers give added support when the other cakes are placed on top.) Center the 9-inch cake on top of the trimmed skewers. Poke 1 skewer in the center of the 9-inch cake and space the other four skewers equally apart in a 2-inch radius from the center. Cut the skewers even with the top of the cake as before and center the 6-inch cake on top.

10. Prepare 2 batches *butter cream icing* (recipe follows).

11. Frost cakes with icing: Prepare a pitcher of warm water and paper towels to keep icing tool clean as you work. Keep surface around cake clean by covering with paper towels. Start icing from the top (6-inch) cake layer and work down the other two tiers. Smooth icing and place completed 3-tier cake in cool dry place until ready to serve.

To serve, decorate the cake with flowers of your choice and place cake in the center of the buffet or cake table. Set cake plates, dessert forks, napkins, and a silver cake knife and serving spatula next to the cake. Arrange to have a family member or dear friend cut the cake after the bride and groom take the first slice.

Two batches of this *butter cream icing* are needed to cover the wedding cake.

Butter Cream Icing

Yield: 9 cups

- ½ cup butter
- ½ cup solid vegetable shortening
- 8 cups confectioners' sugar, sifted, more if necessary
- ½ cup heavy cream, more if necessary
- 1 tablespoon vanilla extract

Equipment: Large mixing bowl, electric mixer or mixing spoon, rubber spatula

Put butter and shortening into large mixing bowl, and using an electric mixer or mixing spoon, beat until creamy. Beating constantly, add confectioners' sugar, a little at a time, alternately with ½ cup cream. If mixture seems too stiff, add a little more cream, ½ tablespoon at a time, to make icing a spreadable consistency. If too runny, add confectioners' sugar, 1 tablespoon at a time, to thicken. Beat in vanilla extract.

Use for black wedding cake *(recipe precedes: Step 10. Frost cakes with icing:), or cover and refrigerate for another use. Use within 1 week.*

TRINIDAD & TOBAGO

Trinidad and its tiny neighbor Tobago, just 20 miles to the northeast, sit just off the coast of Venezuela. Both islands have warm and humid climates typical of the tropics. The islands were united as a single British colony in 1888 and gained full independence in 1962.

Most citizens are descendants of African slaves and East Indian indentured servants. The East Indians were originally brought in to resolve the labor shortage created by the emancipation of the African slaves in 1833.

The blacks and East Indians retain distinct social patterns, with different diets, religions, cultural traditions, and lifestyles. Most blacks are Roman Catholics (about 33 percent), a remnant of the Spanish conquest of the region, and follow the life-cycle traditions of their Church. (See Protestant and Catholic Life-Cycle Rituals, page xlvi.) The East Indians are Hindu or Muslim. (See Hinduism and Hindu Life-Cycle Rituals, page li, and Islam and Islamic Life-Cycle Rituals, page xlix.)

Most Hindu East Indians living in the Caribbean follow, as much as possible, the religious traditions of their homeland, often adding their own touches of drama and color. For example, altars are covered with hibiscus and other native flowers, prayer beads and lamps are decorated with seashells, and Hindu priests often call worshipers to prayer by blowing on a conch shell.

The Roman Catholic blacks have also added local flavor to their life-cycle celebrations. Guests at celebrations, from a christening party, birthday, wedding, or funeral feast, expect meat and certain special occasion dishes, such as *pudding and souse*. *Pudding* refers to the blood or "black" sausage, and *souse* is lime-marinated meat, usually made with a whole pig's head and feet or similar parts of goats, sheep, or beef. *Souse* is also known as "headcheese," although it is not a cheese. Both blood sausage and headcheese are available in the deli section of most supermarkets and butcher shops. For serving, allow one or two slices for each per person. See step 4. in the following recipe for instructions on cooking the blood sausage before serving it. Headcheese requires no cooking. Arrange the slices, slightly overlapping, on a serving platter. It is best to buy the blood sausage but you can make the *souse*, (recipe follows).

One or two salads, several breads, such as fried yeast bread (recipe page 363) and banana bread (recipe page 420), and iced drinks are served along with *pudding and souse*.

PUDDING AND SOUSE

BLOOD SAUSAGE WITH LIME-MARINATED PORK

Yield: serves 4 to 6

4 pounds fresh pork jowls, tails, feet, or ears, in any combination
1 onion, peeled and quartered
3 teaspoons salt, divided
1½ cups fresh lime juice
1 tablespoon oil
1 cucumber, **trimmed** and sliced crosswise, for **garnish**
1 bunch **watercress** or Italian flat-leaf parsley, for garnish
½ teaspoon liquid hot sauce, more or less to taste, for serving
1 to 1½ pounds commercially made blood sausage (*pudding*), cut crosswise into ¼-inch thick circles, for serving

Equipment: Large **heavy-based** saucepan with cover or **Dutch oven**, mixing spoon, knife, metal tongs, large bowl, metal strainer, medium bowl, plastic food wrap, heavy-based skillet, large serving bowl, large serving platter

1. Wash pork thoroughly under cold running water and place in large heavy-based saucepan or Dutch oven. Add enough water to cover the pork by at least 2 inches. Add onion and 2 teaspoons salt, and bring to boil over high heat. Skim off and discard the particles and foam that form on the surface. Reduce heat to **simmer**, cover, and cook 30 minutes. Remove cover and cook 1½ hours longer. The pork pieces are done when they can be easily pierced with a knife. Using metal tongs, transfer pork pieces to a large bowl until cool enough to handle. Continue simmering the liquid until it is **reduced** to about 2 cups, 45 minutes to 1 hour.

2. Remove and discard bones, fat, gristle, and skin from meat. Cut or pull the meat apart into bite-size pieces. Sprinkle with remaining 1 teaspoon salt and lime juice. Toss to coat.

3. Place a metal strainer over a medium bowl, strain the cooking liquid, and discard residue left in strainer. Pour the strained liquid over the meat, stir, and set aside to cool. Transfer the meat mixture to a serving bowl, cover with plastic wrap, and refrigerate overnight to set.

4. At serving time: Heat 1 tablespoon vegetable oil in heavy-based skillet or on griddle over medium-high heat. **Sauté** blood sausage slices, a few at a time, until lightly browned, 3 to 5 minutes on each side.

5. To serve, spoon chunks of *souse* onto a serving platter and garnish with cucumber slices and watercress or parsley. **Drizzle** the *souse* with liquid hot sauce or serve it on the side. Arrange the blood sausage slices attractively around the *souse.*

Serve at room temperature. The pudding and souse *are eaten as finger food at a life-cycle celebration.*

Floats are a spin-off of the flat breads brought to the Caribbean by the East Indians. The fried bread "floats" to the surface of the oil when fully cooked. Many Caribbeans lack modern conveniences so deep-fat frying is done in large iron kettles, set out in the yard. The traditional frying oil is a combination of lard and coconut oil.

Floats

Fried Yeast Bread

CAUTION: HOT OIL USED

Yield: about 18 pieces

¾ cup **lukewarm** water, divided, more if necessary
1 package active **yeast**
3½ cups all-purpose flour
1 teaspoon salt
½ cup solid vegetable shortening
2 cups vegetable oil

Equipment: Small bowl, mixing spoon, flour **sifter**, large mixing bowl, lightly floured work surface, kitchen towel, lightly floured rolling pin, paper towels, 2 baking sheets, large **heavy-based** skillet, wooden mixing spoon, metal tongs or slotted metal spatula, bread basket or serving plate

1. Pour ¼ cup lukewarm water into small bowl, and sprinkle in the yeast. Let rest for about 3 minutes, and stir to dissolve yeast completely. Set yeast mixture in warm place for 5 minutes, or until it begins to bubble and almost doubles in volume.

2. **Sift** flour and salt into large mixing bowl, and add solid vegetable shortening. Using your fingers, rub the flour and shortening together until mixture resembles coarse meal. Pour in the yeast and remaining ½ cup lukewarm water, and using your hands, toss together to mix well. Form dough into a ball. If dough doesn't hold together,

add a little more lukewarm water, 1 tablespoon at a time, up to ½ cup. Transfer dough ball to lightly floured work surface and **knead** until smooth and elastic, 8 to 10 minutes. Lightly grease large mixing bowl, place dough in the bowl, and turn to grease all sides. Cover with towel and set in warm place to rise to double in bulk, about 1 hour.

3. Form into small loaves: **Punch down** dough and divide into 18 equal pieces. Using your hands, roll each piece into a ball. Place the balls about 2 inches apart on a baking sheet. Cover with towel and let rise in warm place for about 45 minutes, or until double in bulk.

4. On lightly floured work surface, using lightly floured rolling pin, roll each ball into a disk about 1/8-inch thick. Stack, slightly overlapping on work surface. Cover with a towel.

5. Prepare to fry: ADULT SUPERVISION REQUIRED. Place several layers of paper towels on baking sheet. Heat oil in large heavy-based skillet over medium-high heat. Oil is hot enough when small bubbles appear around a wooden spoon handle when it is dipped into the oil. Fry dough disks, one or two at a time, for 2 or 3 minutes on each side, or until golden brown. Carefully turn with metal tongs or slotted metal spatula. Transfer to paper towels to drain and keep warm until ready to serve. Continue frying in batches.

Serve floats *in a basket or plate to eat with* pudding and souse *or* codfish cakes *(recipe page 370).*

This pudding is a delicious combination of tropic flavors.

Papaya, Coconut, and Sweet Yam Pudding

Yield: serves 4

1 cup half & half
3 tablespoons butter or margarine
1 cup raw yam or sweet potato, peeled and grated
½ cup ripe **papaya**, mashed
3 eggs
4 tablespoons light brown sugar
¼ teaspoon salt
¼ teaspoon **ground** nutmeg
¼ teaspoon ground cinnamon
1 teaspoon vanilla extract
1 teaspoon grated lemon **zest**
½ teaspoon coconut extract
4 tablespoons canned grated coconut in heavy syrup (available at Asian food stores)
whipped cream or whipped evaporated milk (recipe page 366), for **garnish**

Equipment: Medium saucepan, wooden mixing spoon, fork or **whisk**, small bowl, buttered 6-inch soufflé dish or buttered oven-proof casserole, oven mitts, wire cake rack, knife, individual dessert dishes

Preheat oven to 300° F.

1. Put cream and butter or margarine in medium saucepan and cook over medium-high heat, until small bubbles appear around the edge of the pan. Reduce heat to low, add grated yam or sweet potato, and stir. Cook until potato is soft, 3 to 5 minutes. Stir in mashed papaya and remove from heat. Set aside.

2. Using fork or whisk, beat eggs in a small bowl. Beat in the brown sugar, salt, nutmeg, cinnamon, vanilla, lemon zest, and coconut extract. **Fold in** egg mixture and grated coconut (including the coconut syrup) with cream mixture. Pour into buttered soufflé dish or buttered oven-proof casserole.

3. Bake in oven for 1 hour and 45 minutes to 2 hours or until knife inserted in the center of pudding comes out clean. Remove from oven and set on wire rack to cool.

To serve, spoon pudding while still warm into individual dishes, and add dollop of whipped cream or whipped evaporated cream to each serving.

GRENADA

Grenada, part of the Windward Islands, is about 100 miles north of Venezuela. The overwhelming majority of Grenada's population is of African descent with small communities of East Indians brought to the island as indentured workers and a few descendants of early European settlers.

Grenada was originally colonized by France, which is reflected in the fact that more than 60 percent of the population are Roman Catholic. British forces invaded the island in 1762, and today English is the official language and the Church of England has the largest Protestant following on the island (more than 20 percent). Members of both religions celebrate the life-cycle events prescribed by their churches. (See Protestant and Catholic Life-Cycle Rituals, page xlvi.)

Religion is at the heart of all celebrations. Christenings, adult baptisms, weddings, and funerals are all celebrated with a Caribbean flare, using the foods native to the island, especially spices.

In fact, Grenada, known as the "isle of spice," grows about 40 percent of the worlds supply of nutmeg and mace. Nutmeg is the seed of the nutmeg tree, and mace is the bright red membrane that covers the nutmeg seed. A wonderful fruit dish using nutmeg is *matrimony* (recipe page 379).

In the hot, humid Caribbean, a cold soup is a welcome addition to the wedding buffet. Put the soup in a tureen or punch bowl, and provide a ladle and small cups. The guests can serve themselves and drink the soup from the cup. ۞ ۞ ۞

Cold Cream of Breadfruit Soup

Yield: serves 6

4 tablespoons butter or margarine
1 cup onions, **finely chopped**
2 cloves garlic, finely chopped, or 1 teaspoon garlic granules
2 cups fresh **breadfruit**, peeled, cored, **coarsely chopped**, **blanched** for 2 minutes, and drained, or 4 slices canned breadfruit, drained and coarsely chopped (available at most supermarkets and all Latin American food stores)
4 cups chicken broth, homemade (recipe page 106), or canned
1 cup half & half
salt and pepper to taste
1 tablespoon finely chopped fresh parsley, for **garnish**

Equipment: Medium **heavy-based** saucepan, mixing spoon, medium mixing bowl, food processor, ladle, tureen or punch bowl, individual soup bowls

1. Melt butter or margarine in medium heavy-based saucepan over medium-high heat. Add onions and garlic, and stirring constantly, **sauté** for 3 to 5 minutes, or until soft and transparent. Stir in chopped breadfruit, pour in chicken broth, and bring to a boil. Stir, reduce heat to **simmer**, cover, and cook for 20 to 25 minutes, or until breadfruit can easily be mashed against the side of the pan using the back of the spoon. Remove from heat, remove cover, and allow to cool to warm.

2. Ladle half of the breadfruit mixture into the food processor, and pour in ½ cup of half & half. Process for about 1 minute, or until smooth. Pour into medium mixing bowl. Ladle remaining breadfruit mixture into processor, and add the remaining half & half. Process 1 minute or until smooth, pour into bowl with first batch,

and add salt and pepper to taste. Cover and refrigerate until ready to serve.

Note: While processing, turn machine off once or twice and scrape down sides of container with rubber spatula.

To serve, pour into either a tureen or individual soup bowls. Sprinkle with parsley flakes, for garnish.

The fruit guava comes in many varieties, ranging in smell and flavor from sweet to offensive. Canned guava is recommended for this recipe.

Guava Pie

Yield: serves 8 to 10

16 ounces canned **guavas**, drained (available at Latin American food stores and most supermarkets)
2 to 3 tablespoons sugar
½ teaspoon **ground** nutmeg
juice of ½ lime
2 **egg whites**
2 (9-inch) unbaked pie crusts, homemade (recipe page 446), or frozen (thawed)
heavy cream or whipped evaporated milk (recipe follows), for serving

Equipment: Food processor, rubber spatula, medium mixing bowl, small mixing bowl, electric mixer or **whisk**, 9-inch pie pan, lightly floured work surface, ruler, paring knife, fork, oven mitts

Preheat oven to 400° F.

1. **Purée** canned, drained guava and 2 tablespoons sugar in food processor, about 1 minute. Taste for desired sweetness, if necessary add remaining 1 tablespoon sugar and process 6 seconds to make sweeter. Transfer to medium mixing bowl, and using rubber spatula, stir in nutmeg and lime.

Note: While processing, turn machine off once or twice and scrape down sides of container with rubber spatula.

2. Put egg whites in small mixing bowl, and using an electric mixer or whisk, beat until stiff peaks form. Using rubber spatula, **fold in** egg whites with guava mixture. Pour into unbaked pie crust, and smooth top with rubber spatula.

3. Place second crust on lightly floured work surface. Using a ruler and paring knife, cut ½-inch wide strips out of the crust, and lay them across the pie in a lattice (criss-cross) pattern. Press the ends of fork into the edge of pie crust to make a ridged, sealed border around the outer edge of the pie pan.

4. Bake in oven for 20 to 25 minutes, or until pie is lightly browned and filling is bubbly. Using oven mitts, remove pie from oven, and cool to warm.

Serve guava pie *at room temperature with a dollop of whipped cream or* whipped evaporated milk *(recipe follows) on each serving. Serve guava pie with coffee or tea after a baptism, christening, or funeral.*

Whipped cream and refrigeration have not always been available to the island cooks so they found a way of whipping canned evaporated milk. A can of evaporated milk triples in volume when whipped, whereas regular heavy cream only doubles in volume.

Whipped Evaporated Milk

Yield: about 3 cups

12 ounces canned evaporated milk
4 tablespoons confectioners' sugar, (optional, for soft icing)
1 teaspoon flavored extract of your choice: coconut, vanilla, almond, or rum (optional)
sweetened shredded coconut, for garnish (optional)

Equipment: Large saucepan, metal tongs, oven mitts, can opener, chilled medium metal bowl, chilled electric mixer or whisk, spoon

1. Fill large saucepan halfway with water, and bring to boil over high heat. Carefully place the unopened can of evaporated milk in the water; when the water comes back to boiling, boil can for 15 minutes. Wearing oven mitts and using metal tongs, remove the can from the water. Cool to room temperature and refrigerate for about 24 hours.

2. To whip: Pour contents of can into chilled bowl and whip with chilled electric mixer or whisk until soft peaks form. (The whipped evaporated milk makes softer peaks than whipped heavy cream.) The cream can be used at this time or continue to make soft icing.

3. Make soft icing: **Fold in** 4 tablespoons sifted confectioners' sugar with each 1 cup of whipped evaporated milk. Fold in 1 teaspoon of flavoring extract of your choice.

When the topping is sprinkled with sweetened shredded coconut it is called mont blanc, *an island specialty.*

PUERTO RICO

Puerto Rico is an island in the Caribbean Sea, located east of the Dominican Republic. It is a semi-autonomous commonwealth that has been under the protection of the United States since the Spanish-American War of 1898. Most Puerto Ricans are of Spanish decent, but after decades of intermarriage, racial lines are practically nonexistent. Puerto Rico is officially a bilingual country (English and Spanish), but island-born Puerto Ricans prefer to speak Spanish to one another as a matter of cultural pride.

Puerto Rico is an island of contrasts; the people living outside of the major cities are poor and live a very simple life with few modern comforts. Their diet is mostly rice, beans, and **salt cod**; for special occasions, roast pork or chicken might be prepared for the feast if the budget allows. Most city dwellers live with modern conveniences, high-rise apartments, department stores, and American television. Many urbanites are two-car families and eat food not unlike that eaten in American cities with large Hispanic communities.

More than 85 percent of the Puerto Ricans are Roman Catholics. Most life-cycle events, from christening the newborn infant to the burial of an elder, are celebrated according to the Catholic Church. (See Protestant and Catholic Life-Cycle Rituals, page xlvi.) The rituals are similar to other Latin American countries except among descendants of slaves who were brought from West Africa to Puerto Rico in the 1500s. People of African descent often combine African rituals and voodoo with Catholic traditions; the worship of African gods with Catholic saints is not uncommon. Spiritualism (*espiritismo*) and witchcraft (*brujeria*) are very much alive in Puerto Rico. It is common practice among all islanders, not only those of African descent, to consult *curanderos* (healers) and *espiritistas* (spiritualists) about love and marriage, health, childbirth, revenge, wealth, and death.

Life-cycle celebration feasts in the Puerto Rican cities call for **appetizers**, something to nibble on after the long church service and before the main meal is served. *Plantanos* (plantains) are popular throughout the Caribbean, but this easy-to-make Puerto Rican specialty, *mofongo*, is an unusual combination of ingredients. Use either green or yellow plantains (depending upon variety) that are partly ripe; they should have large black spots on the skin and be slightly soft when pressed between your fingers. The skin should peel away from the flesh fairly easy. If the plantains are firm to the touch and the skin cannot be peeled off, they are too green and the *mofongo* will be sticky. If the plantains are all black and soft to the touch, they are too ripe, making the *mofongo* too sweet. The plantains are combined with crisp pork rind, called pork cracklings, available at supermarkets. At Latin American food stores, they are called *chicharrón*.

Mofongo

Plantain Spread

Yield: 6 to 8

4 ounces pork cracklings (pork rind), break or cut into small pieces
3 partly ripe plantains
1 cup vegetable oil, more as needed
4 cloves garlic, **finely chopped**
3/4 to 1 1/4 cups water
salt and pepper to taste

Equipment: Knife, large, work surface, blender, rubber spatula, medium mixing bowl, baking sheet, paper towels, **heavy-based** skillet, wooden spoon, slotted metal spatula, fork, mixing spoon

1. Put small pieces of cracklings in blender, and in batches, pulse the blender on and off until the cracklings reach the consistency of fine breadcrumbs. Turn blender off once or twice and scrape down sides of container with rubber spatula. Transfer to medium mixing bowl and set aside. You should have about 2 to 2 1/2 cups of crumbs.

2. Peel plantains and cut crosswise into 1-inch pieces.

3. Prepare to pan-fry: ADULT SUPERVISION REQUIRED. Cover a baking sheet with several layers of paper towels. Heat 1 cup oil in large heavy-based skillet over medium-high heat. When tiny bubbles form around a wooden spoon handle dipped in the oil, it is hot enough. Add 10 to 14 plantain slices at a time and fry on all sides until golden brown and the centers are soft when poked with a fork, 3 to 5 minutes. Drain plantains on paper towels. Repeat frying in batches.

4. When cool enough to handle, put plantains in blender and add chopped garlic and 1/2 cup water. With blender running, add more water through the feed tube, 1/4 cup at a time, until mixture is smooth. While blending, turn machine off once or twice and scrape down sides of container with rubber spatula. Add blended plantains to crackling crumbs and stir to mix well. *Mofongo* should be spreadable and smooth; if too dry, add a little more water (1 to 4 tablespoons). Add salt and pepper to taste.

Serve mofongo *as an appetizer. Put in a small serving bowl and surround with savory chips or crackers. To eat, scoop a little* mofongo *on a chip or spread on a cracker.*

Weddings and other happy occasions call for meat on the table. The ultimate lifecycle celebration food is *lechoncito asado* (whole suckling pig recipe page 383); this can be expensive. Instead most Puerto Ricans would prepare *asopao de pollo*. Preparing an *asopao* usually makes a little meat feed a lot of people for little money. There is no one way to make *asopao*; it can be either soupy or thick, with shellfish and/or chicken and/or meat. *Asopao* means souplike in Spanish, but this Puerto Rican version is thicker, more of a casserole.

Asopao de Pollo

Chicken Casserole

Yield: 6 to 8

2 1/2 to 3 pound chicken, cut into serving-size pieces
1 teaspoon dried oregano leaves
1/2 teaspoon **ground coriander**
salt to taste

2 cups water
1 (16-ounce) can stewed tomatoes
1 onion, chopped
3 cloves garlic, chopped
1 cup raw white rice
1 (10-ounce) package frozen green peas, thawed
1 green pepper, **trimmed** and chopped
½ cup (about 2 ounces) fully cooked smoked ham, **cubed**
½ cup pitted small green olives
1 tablespoon capers (available at supermarkets)
grated Parmesan cheese

Equipment: Large **heavy-based** skillet with cover or **Dutch oven**, mixing spoon

1. Rinse chicken pieces thoroughly under cold running water and place on several layers of paper towels to drain well. Sprinkle chicken with oregano, coriander, and salt to taste.

2. Pour water, stewed tomatoes, chopped onion, and garlic in large skillet or Dutch oven, and stir. Add chicken pieces and bring to boil over medium-high heat. Reduce heat to simmer, cover, and cook 30 minutes.

3. Sprinkle in rice, cover, and cook 20 minutes longer. Test **chicken doneness**.

4. Add peas, ham, olives, and capers to chicken mixture. Cover and simmer 5 minutes to heat through.

To serve, transfer to large deep serving platter and sprinkle generously with cheese.

One of the many side dishes besides beans and rice would probably be this unusual Puerto Rican recipe of cucumbers and orange juice.

Pepinos en Salsa de Naranja

Stewed Cucumbers in Orange Sauce

Yield: serves 4
3 cucumbers, each about 8 inches long
½ teaspoon salt, more as needed
1 tablespoon cornstarch
1¼ cups fresh orange juice, strained
3 tablespoons butter or margarine
½ teaspoon white pepper
1 teaspoon grated orange rind

Equipment: Vegetable peeler, knife, work surface, teaspoon, medium saucepan, **colander**, cup, medium skillet, medium deep serving dish

1. Peel cucumbers and cut in half lengthwise. Using a teaspoon, scrape out and discard seeds. Cut cucumbers halves crosswise into ½-inch slices.

2. Fill medium saucepan halfway with water, add ½ teaspoon salt, and bring to boil over medium-high heat. Drop cucumber pieces into boiling water, reduce heat to **simmer**, and cook for 5 minutes. Drain in colander placed in sink.

3. Put cornstarch in cup and stir in ¼ cup orange juice to make **slurry**. Melt butter or margarine in medium skillet over medium-low heat. Add remaining 1 cup orange juice and when small bubbles appear around edge of pan, stir in slurry. Stirring constantly, increase heat to medium and cook until mixture thickens, 2 to 3 minutes. Add white pepper and grated orange rind. Add cucumber and toss to coat and heat through, 3 to 5 minutes.

To serve, transfer to bowl and serve as a side vegetable with asopao de pollo. Pepinos en salsa de naranja *is also a great side dish with pork.*

DOMINICAN REPUBLIC

The Dominican Republic shares the eastern two-thirds of the island of Hispaniola with Haiti. The subtropical Hispaniola sits to the south and east of Cuba.

Hispaniola was one of the first islands visited by Columbus, and the Dominican Republic has been heavily influenced by Spain. Roman Catholicism is the official religion, and all life-cycle events are celebrated according to the Church. (See Protestant and Catholic Life-Cycle Rituals, page xlvi.) The Dominican people, who are mostly mulatto, of mixed black and white ancestry, also speak Spanish, which is the official language

The Catholic Church plays such an important role in Dominican life that even the secular life-cycle event of high school graduation involves several visits to the church. . The day begins when students, each accompanied by his or her godfather (*compadrazgo*), meet on the school grounds. Together they march proudly to the church where mass is held honoring the godfathers and blessing the students. Afterwards the students and godfathers march back to the school for the graduation ceremony. Godfathers are included in the day-long activities, even attending the many parties for classmates. The following Sunday, after church, each family has a celebration dinner for friends and relatives.

The Catholic Church takes on an even greater role in weddings, which must take place in a church to be recognized officially. In Cibao, the most Spanish part of the country, traditions reflect the strict Spanish rules of courting, betrothal, and marriage. Young girls are chaperoned during the courting and the boys are expected to ask permission to marry from the girl's parents.

It is hard to imagine why people surrounded by an ocean full of seafood would even bother with **salt cod** for a life-cycle celebration. But ever since the Spanish and Portuguese brought salt cod to the Caribbean, it has remained a favorite food. Salt cod has a very distinct and delicious flavor; it stores much better than fresh fish and is easy to prepare. It can be prepared hundreds of ways, but this recipe is a party favorite.

BACALAITOS

FRIED COD FRITTERS

CAUTION: HOT OIL USED

Note: This recipe requires two days.

Yield: about 30 pieces

½ pound **salt cod** (boneless and skinless fillets) (available at most supermarkets and all Latin American food stores)
1½ cups all-purpose flour
1 teaspoon baking powder
1½ cups water
1 clove garlic, **finely chopped**, or 1 teaspoon garlic granules
¼ teaspoon black pepper
vegetable oil for deep frying

Equipment: Large glass or plastic bowl with cover, **colander**, medium saucepan, fork, **slotted spoon**, plate, large mixing bowl, mixing spoon, wax paper, 2 baking sheets, **deep fryer**, cooking **thermometer** or wooden spoon, paper towels

1. Prepare salt cod: Start this recipe a day before you plan on serving it to allow the cod to soak. Place salt cod in a large glass or plastic bowl, and cover generously with water. Cover the bowl and refrigerate to soak for at least 12 hours. It is

important to change the soaking water 3 or 4 times during the 12 hours.

2. Discard soaking water, transfer the cod to a colander, and rinse under cold running water. Drain well and place in medium saucepan. Add enough fresh water to the saucepan to cover the fish by 1 inch. Bring to a boil over high heat. Carefully taste the water; if it seems very salty, drain it, cover the cod with fresh water, and bring to a boil again. Reduce heat to **simmer** and cook for 20 minutes, or until fish flakes easily when poked with a fork. Using a slotted spoon, transfer cod to a plate and discard hot fish water. When cod is cool enough to handle, use your hands to gently flake the fish into small pieces, taking care to remove and discard any little fine bones or tendon particles.

3. In large mixing bowl, combine flour and baking powder. Make a well (hole) in the center and pour in the water, garlic, and pepper. With a mixing spoon or your fingers, gradually incorporate the flour mixture into the water mixture, stir until smooth, and **fold in** cod.

4. Using your hands, shape cod mixture into golf ball-size balls and place side by side on wax-paper-covered baking sheet. Moisten your hands from time to time, if necessary.

5. Prepare to deep-fry: ADULT SUPERVISION REQUIRED. Place several layers of paper towels on baking sheet. Heat oil to 375° F on thermometer or when small bubbles appear around a wooden spoon handle when it is dipped into the oil.

6. Fry cod balls in small batches, 3 to 5 minutes per batch. Turn frequently and when golden brown remove with slotted spoon. Drain on paper towels and keep warm while frying remaining balls.

Serve cod fritters while warm as an appetizer for the wedding banquet or as a birthday party snack.

Traditionally *frituras de ñame* are made with **yams**, not sweet potatoes. Since genuine yams are not readily available, sweet potatoes are a good substitute. Fried yam cakes are often served with the *bacalaitos* for a wedding buffet.

Frituras de Ñame

Fried Yam Cakes

Yield: about 20 pieces

1 pound fresh yams or sweet potatoes, peeled
1 onion, quartered
1 tablespoon melted butter
2 **egg yolks**
1 tablespoon **finely chopped** fresh parsley, or 2 teaspoons dried parsley flakes
salt and pepper to taste
¼ cup vegetable oil, divided

Equipment: Food processor with grating attachment, rubber spatula, medium mixing bowl, paper towels, baking sheet, large **heavy-based** skillet, tablespoon, slotted metal spatula

1. Using food processor fitted with grating attachment, grate yams or sweet potatoes and onion into container. Add melted butter, egg yolks, parsley, and salt and pepper to taste. Process until smooth and mixture comes away from sides of container. Transfer mixture to medium mixing bowl.

Note: While processing, turn machine off once or twice and scrape down sides of container with rubber spatula.

2. Prepare to fry: ADULT SUPERVISION REQUIRED. Place several layers of paper towels on baking sheet. Heat half the oil in large heavy-based skillet over medium-high heat. Use about 1 tablespoon yam mixture to make each cake and place cakes in heavy-based skillet. Using back of spoon, flatten cakes slightly. Fry in small batches, leaving space between each cake.

Fry for 2 to 3 minutes each side, or until golden and crisp around the edges. Using slotted metal spatula, remove cakes and drain on paper towels. Keep in warm place while frying remaining cakes.

Serve cakes, while they are still warm, as a side dish with bacalaitos *(recipe page 370) or with* pudding and souse *(recipe page 362).*

All celebrations, depending upon the budget, will have either pork, beef, goat, chicken, or pigeons as a main dish, with a large assortment of candies and cakes. The centerpiece of a Dominican wedding is the Caribbean *black wedding cake* (recipe page 360).

Pan dulce de harina de maíz is often included in the sweet assortment.

Pan Dulce de Harina de Maíz

Sweet Corn Bread

Yield: 2 loaves

- 1½ cups(8-ounces) mixed candied fruit, **finely chopped**
- 4¼ cups all-purpose flour, divided
- 3 cups yellow cornmeal
- 1 tablespoon baking powder
- ½ teaspoon **ground** cinnamon
- ½ teaspoon nutmeg
- ½ teaspoon cloves
- ½ cup coconut milk, homemade (recipe page 346), or canned (available at most supermarkets and all Latin American food stores)
- ½ cup milk
- 6 tablespoons solid vegetable shortening, at room temperature
- 6 tablespoons butter or margarine, at room temperature
- ¼ cup sugar
- 4 eggs
- 2 cups finely grated unsweetened **coconut**, fresh, canned, or frozen
- 1 teaspoon finely grated fresh lime rind

Equipment: Small bowl, flour **sifter**, medium mixing bowl, 12-ounce cup, large mixing bowl, electric mixer or whisk, rubber spatula, 2 buttered and floured 7- x 4- x 3-inch loaf pans, toothpick, oven mitts, knife, wire cake rack, serving platter

Preheat oven to 400° F.

1. Place candied fruit in small bowl, sprinkle with ¼ cup flour, and toss to coat evenly.

2. **Sift** remaining 4 cups flour, cornmeal, baking powder, cinnamon, nutmeg, and cloves into medium mixing bowl. Combine coconut milk and regular milk in cup, and set aside.

3. In large mixing bowl, combine solid vegetable shortening and butter or margarine. Using electric mixer or whisk, beat until light and fluffy, 1 to 2 minutes. Beat in sugar and eggs, one at a time, beating well after each addition. Beating constantly, alternate adding flour mixture, 1 cup at a time and ¼ cup milk mixture, beating well after each addition. Continue to beat until batter is smooth, 1 to 2 minutes. Using rubber spatula, **fold in** mixed candied fruit mixture, grated coconut, and fresh lime rind. Pour batter equally into the 2 prepared loaf pans.

4. Bake in oven for 35 to 45 minutes, or until toothpick inserted in the center comes out clean and the tops are golden brown. Using oven mitts, remove from oven and let cool in pans for about 5 minutes. To remove loaves from pan, run a knife around the inside edges and flip onto wire cake rack to cool completely.

To serve, slice the loaves crosswise and arrange the pieces decoratively on a serving platter.

On hot days in the Dominican Republic, and that's most of the time, this easy-to-make juice cooler can satisfy most kids having a name day or birthday party. *Frio-frio* (*frio* means cold in Spanish) are also called snow cones or snowballs. They are made by pouring a dollop of fruit syrup over a paper cupful of crushed ice. The fastest way of making fruit syrups is by mixing thawed, but not diluted, frozen fruit juice concentrates with **simple syrup**. Stick a straw into the crushed ice and sip the cool liquid through the straw.

HAITI

Haiti occupies the western third of the island Hispanolia, which is also home to the Dominican Republic. Hispanolia is a subtropical island that lies to the south and east of Cuba.

The majority of Haiti's population are peasant farmers, descendants of African slaves, brought to the island to work on the French-owned plantations. After an uprising and bitter struggle, the former slaves defeated Napoleon's forces and drove all the whites off the island. The former slaves gave the new nation the old Indian name "Haiti" (high hills) and on January 1, 1804, the republic of Haiti declared its independence. French, the official language of Haiti, is spoken by only 10 percent of the people; most Haitians speak Créole, a pidgin language.

While under French control, the African *vodun* (voodoo) was widely practiced by the slaves even though it was outlawed by the French. After the defeat of the French, voodoo resurfaced, and it is now accepted as a vital part of Haitian culture.

Most Haitians profess Catholicism and celebrate the traditional life-cycle events prescribed by the Church (see Protestant and Catholic Life-Cycle Rituals, page xlvi), but they also retain their voodoo practices. For almost three hundred years, the Haitians have blended the two together. For example, the use of candles, bells, crosses, and prayers and making the sign of the cross, elements of the Catholic Church, are used along with African dances, drumming, and the worship of ancestral spirits.

The birth of the firstborn son is a joyous addition to the family because he will carry on the family name and inherit the family farm. Most Haitians turn to the Catholic Church for the infant's christening, which is generally a colorful and noisy affair. The christening garments are traditionally handed down from past generations. After the ceremony, a celebration feast is held, usually in the church social hall. The christening feast will include *griots de porc* (recipe page 375), *extra-rich hominy grits* (recipe page 374), *riz Créole* (recipe follows), *pain Haïtien* (recipe page 374), *matrimony* (recipe page 379), and *planter's cake* (recipe page 378). Cookies, coffee, and cold beverages complete the menu. ۞ ۞ ۞

Riz Créole

Creole Rice

Yield: serves 4

2 tablespoons butter or margarine
1/4 cup green onions, **finely chopped**
1/2 red bell pepper, **trimmed**, seeded, and finely chopped
1 tomato, finely chopped
1/2 teaspoon **ground** turmeric
1/2 teaspoon paprika
salt and pepper to taste
2 cups water
1 cup long grain rice

Equipment: Medium saucepan with cover, mixing spoon, serving bowl

Melt butter or margarine in medium saucepan over medium-high heat. Add finely chopped green onions, red bell pepper, tomato, turmeric, paprika, and salt and pepper to taste. Stirring constantly, **sauté** for 2 to 3 minutes for flavors to develop. Add water and rice and bring to a boil. Stir, reduce heat to **simmer**, cover, and cook for 15 to 20 minutes, until rice is tender. Remove from heat. Let stand covered for 5 minutes.

To serve, transfer to serving bowl and serve warm as a side dish with griots de porc *(recipe page 375).*

Extra-Rich Hominy Grits

Yield: serves 8

- 4 cups water
- ½ teaspoon salt
- 1½ cups coarsely ground quick-to-cook **hominy grits** (also called grits) (available at all supermarkets)
- ½ cup whole milk or half & half
- 4 tablespoons butter or margarine
- ¾ cup shredded cheddar cheese

Equpment: Medium saucepan with cover, mixing spoon, serving bowl

1. Pour water in medium saucepan, add salt, and bring to boil over high heat. Add grits, and cook for 2 minutes, stirring constantly to prevent lumping. Reduce heat to medium-low, cover, and cook for 10 to 12 minutes, stirring occasionally.

2. Stir in milk or half & half and butter or margarine, and continue stirring until mixture is smooth and creamy. Add cheese and stir until completely melted.

To serve, pour into a serving bowl and serve as a side dish with one of the many Caribbean meat dishes in this section.

One of France's more positive legacies in Haiti is bread, which Haitians love and eat in great quantities. Most Haitians, especially farmers, don't have ovens in their kitchens but have outside clay-dome ovens in their yard where they bake their beloved *pain* with and without yeast. When made with yeast, as in this recipe, the bread has a lighter and more tender texture.

Pain Haïtien

Haitian Bread

Yield: 24 pieces

- 2 packages dry yeast
- 1½ cups **lukewarm** water
- ¼ cup honey
- 2 tablespoons vegetable oil
- 1 teaspoon salt
- 1 teaspoon **ground** nutmeg
- 4½ cups bread flour or all-purpose flour, divided
- ½ teaspoon freeze-dried instant coffee granules, for **glaze**
- 2 tablespoons milk, for glaze

Equipment: Large mixing bowl, mixing spoon, lightly floured work surface, lightly greased medium mixing bowl, clean kitchen towel, greased baking sheet, long knife, 4-ounce cup, **pastry brush**, oven mitts, bread basket, cloth napkin

1. Add yeast to lukewarm water in large mixing bowl, and stir to dissolve. Stir in honey, oil, salt, nutmeg, and 2 cups flour. Beat until very smooth, about 1 minute. Gradually add just enough of remaining 2½ cups flour to make a stiff dough that is no longer sticky. Transfer to lightly floured work surface. **Knead** until smooth, 5 to 8 minutes.

2. Put dough in lightly greased medium mixing bowl and turn to grease all sides. Cover with towel and set in warm place to rise to double in

bulk, 45 minutes to 1 hour. Dough is ready if indentation remains in it when gently poked with your finger.

3. **Punch down** dough with fist. Transfer to greased baking sheet, spread dough out evenly to cover bottom of pan, and smooth top of dough. Using the back side of a long knife, mark off 24 pieces in the dough by making 4 equally spaced marks in the dough, the length of the pan, and 6 across. Cut down into dough only halfway, not through to the bottom. Cover with towel and let rise in warm place until double in bulk, about 30 minutes.

Preheat oven to 350° F.

4. In cup, dissolve instant coffee granules in milk. Using pastry brush, brush top of dough with coffee mixture to give it a glaze. Bake in oven until golden brown, 30 to 35 minutes.

Serve fresh from the oven, break bread apart, and place in bread basket. Cover with napkin to keep warm.

Pork is reserved for special occasions, such as baptisms and wedding feasts. It is quite expensive, especially since the Haitian pig population was wiped out by swine fever a number of years ago. This recipe can be made with beef or goat instead of pork.

Griots De Porc

Marinated Spicy Pork

Note: Use care when handling peppers. Wrap your hands in plastic wrap or cover them with plastic sandwich bags. If you accidentally touch your eyes while handling peppers, rinse them out under cold running water at once.

Yield: serves 6

1 onion, **finely chopped**
1 teaspoon dried thyme
3/4 cup orange juice
1/4 cup lemon juice
1 hot chile pepper (**jalapeño**), seeded and finely chopped, or 1/2 teaspoon **ground** red pepper
2 cloves garlic, finely chopped
3 pounds lean pork shoulder, cut into 2-inch cubes
water as needed
1 tablespoon cornstarch
6 cups cooked white rice, for serving

Equipment: Large resealable plastic bag, large saucepan with cover, slotted mixing spoon, medium bowl, **bulb baster** or large spoon, **whisk**

1. Prepare **marinade**: Put onion, thyme, orange juice, lemon juice, finely chopped pepper or ground red pepper, and garlic in large plastic resealable bag. Seal bag tightly and shake to mix. Open bag, add meat, seal tightly, and shake to coat. Refrigerate overnight.

2. Put meat and marinade into large saucepan, and add water to cover. Bring to boil over high heat, reduce heat to **simmer**, cover, and cook until tender, about 1 hour.

3. Using slotted mixing spoon, transfer meat to medium bowl. Using bulb baster or large spoon, skim off and discard fat from marinade. Reheat marinade in saucepan over high heat, and bring to boil, stirring occasionally. Reduce heat to simmer and stirring frequently, cook, uncovered until **reduced** by half, 15 to 20 minutes.

4. Stir cornstarch into 1/2 cup water until smooth. Whisk cornstarch mixture into reduced marinade, and continue whisking until thickened, 2 to 3 minutes. Reduce heat to low.

5. Return meat to thickened sauce, and toss to coat. Increase heat to simmer, cover, and cook to heat through, 5 to 7 minutes.

Serve over rice with plenty of pain Haïtien *(recipe page 374)*. Stuffed plantains *(recipe page 384) are traditionally served with this dish.*

JAMAICA

An island in the West Indies, Jamaica is 90 miles south of Cuba and 100 miles east of Haiti. Originally colonized by Spain, Jamaica fell under British control in 1655 and did not become independent until 1962. Today, Jamaica is a multiracial society of Africans, East Indians, Scots, Chinese, and English.

About 60 percent of the population is Christian (about 55 percent Protestant and 5 percent Catholic) and celebrate life-cycle events in accordance with the Christian traditions. (See Protestant and Catholic Life-Cycle Rituals, page xlvi.) In addition to these Western religious traditions, Jamaica is also the birthplace of the *Rastafarian* religion, which has attracted many followers among Jamaicans of African descent. The aim of the "*Rastas*," as they are called, is to restore dignity and pride to the black race and to recreate the African way of life without the technology of the West, which in Rasta terminology is called Babylon.

Rasta men are easily noticed because of their "dreadlocks," braided strands of hair allowed to grow, often below the waist. The role of *Rasta* women is controversial, and although men enhance the status of women by giving them the title "queen," the belief is women are subordinate to men. Most *Rasta* men are known to be good fathers and take pride in caring for their children.

Rasta weddings are happy occasions, and everyone is free to do their own thing. There is no special person officiating, nor is there a special ceremony. *Rasta* marriages are common-law; however to be legal in Jamaica, couples must register at the office of records.

A dish known as *pudding and souse* (recipe page 362) is prepared for special occasions throughout the Caribbean. Jamaicans eat *souse* without the *pudding* for life-cycle celebrations. *Souse* is the same as head cheese which is available in the deli section of supermarkets or butcher shops. Hot **Scotch bonnet** peppers, native to Jamaica, **garnish** the platter and are eaten with the *souse*.

In Jamaica, *cho-cho*, a tropical squash, is often served with *souse*. Elsewhere *cho-cho* is known as **chayote,** mirliton, or its French name christophene.

Stuffed Cho-cho

Stuffed Chayote

Yield: serves 4

2 chayotes, (about 1 pound each) (available at all Latin American food stores and most supermarkets)
8 tablespoons butter or margarine, divided
1 large onion, **finely chopped**
½ cup grated Parmesan cheese, divided
salt and pepper, to taste

Equipment: Large saucepan, paring knife, tablespoon, medium bowl, paper towels, large **heavy-based** skillet, mixing spoon, greased baking sheet, oven mitts, serving platter

1. Put whole chayotes into large saucepan, and cover generously with water. Bring to boil over high heat, and reduce heat to **simmer** for 30 minutes, until tender. To test doneness, poke chayotes with a paring knife. If knife goes in easily they are done. Drain and rinse chayotes under cold water to cool. When cool enough to handle, slice in half, lengthwise, and remove and discard seeds.

2. Using a tablespoon and paring knife, carefully scoop out the pulp, leaving about ¼-inch thick boat-like shells. Put pulp into medium bowl. Set the chayote shells upside down on several layers of paper towels to drain. **Coarsely chop** the scooped-out pulp.

3. In large heavy-based skillet, melt 4 tablespoons butter or margarine over medium-high heat. Add onion and **sauté**, stirring frequently, until soft but not brown, 2 to 3 minutes. Add the chopped chayote, ¼ cup grated cheese, and salt and pepper to taste. Stirring frequently, reduce heat to medium-low, and cook until most of the liquid has cooked off and the mixture is the consistency of mashed potatoes, 5 to 10 minutes.

Preheat oven to 350° F.

4. Fill the 4 chayote shells equally with onion mixture. Place the filled shells side by side on greased baking sheet. Dot the top of each with remaining 4 tablespoons butter or margarine, and sprinkle with remaining ¼ cup grated cheese.

5. Bake in oven for 25 to 30 minutes, or until tops are lightly browned.

To serve, transfer to a serving platter. Eat chocho *while still warm.*

Some meat dishes, such as *roast pork calypso*, are always prepared for celebrations. In Jamaica, depending upon the budget, less expensive kid goat (*cabrito*) replaces the pork. *Calalou* (recipe page 381) is served with most pork dishes.

Roast Pork Calypso

Yield: serves 6

- 3 pounds lean pork roast
- 1 cup light brown sugar
- 2 cloves garlic, **finely chopped**
- 2 teaspoons **ground** ginger
- ½ teaspoon ground cloves
- salt and pepper to taste
- 3 tablespoons cold water, divided
- 2 cups chicken broth, homemade (recipe page 106), or canned
- 2 teaspoons **arrowroot**
- 3 tablespoons fresh lime juice
- lime slices, for **garnish**

Equipment: Large meat knife, shallow roasting pan with rack, oven mitts, heat-proof surface, plate, small saucepan, **bulb baster** (optional), spoon, small bowl, meat **thermometer** (optional), cutting board, small cup, serving platter, small bowl for serving (optional)

Preheat oven to 325° F.

1. With a large meat knife, make crisscross diagonal cuts ¼ inch deep about 1 inch apart in the fat side of the pork roast. Place roast, fat side up, on rack in roasting pan.

2. Bake in the oven for 1½ hours, or until golden brown.

3. Using oven mitts, remove roast from oven, and place pan on heatproof surface. Transfer meat to plate. Pour pan drippings into small saucepan, and using bulb baster or spoon, skim and discard fat from pan drippings. Set aside to use later for gravy.

4. In a small bowl, combine brown sugar, garlic, ginger, cloves, and salt and pepper to taste. Add 2 tablespoons cold water and stir into paste. Using back of spoon, spread the paste over surface of pork roast. Return meat to rack in roasting pan. Return to oven to continue baking 35 to 45 minutes, until the juices run clear when the roast is poked with a knife and the surface is crusty and brown. (A meat thermometer inserted into the middle of the roast should register 185° F when done.)

5. Transfer roast to cutting board and let rest for at least 10 minutes before slicing.

6. Prepare gravy: Stir chicken broth into fat-free pan drippings, bring to boil over medium-high heat, and reduce heat to low. Put arrowroot into cup and stir in remaining 1 tablespoon water to make smooth paste. Stirring constantly, add arrowroot mixture to broth mixture, and cook until thickened to gravy consistency. Re-

move from heat and stir in lime juice. Add salt and pepper to taste.

To serve, arrange pork slices on platter, and garnish with lime slices. Either pour gravy over the meat or serve separately in small bowl.

Jamaicans enjoy sweets, and any life-cycle celebration is a reason to stock up on plenty of candy and cakes. A birthday is really special when the cook makes *planter's cake* for the occasion. The average Jamaicans don't have kitchen ovens so the only home cake baking is done by the well-to-do urbanites.

Planter's Cake

Layer Cake with Mocha Icing

Yield: serves 8 to 10

- 5 **eggs, separated**
- 1 cup sugar
- 1 cup cake flour, **sifted**
- 1 tablespoon fresh lime juice, strained
- 1 teaspoon grated lime rind
- *mocha cream icing* (recipe follows)

Equipment: Large mixing bowl, electric mixer or **whisk**, medium mixing bowl, rubber spatula, 2 buttered and floured (9-inch) round cake pans, oven mitts, toothpick, wire cake rack, metal **icing spatula** or dinner knife, serving plate

Preheat oven to 350° F.

1. Put egg whites in large mixing bowl, and using an electric mixer or whisk, beat the egg whites to stiff peaks.

2. Put egg yolks in medium mixing bowl, and using the same electric mixer or whisk, beat yolks until light and fluffy, about 1 minute. Sprinkle in sugar, a little at a time, and continue beating until mixture is thick and falls off beater or whisk in ribbons when it is lifted above the bowl, 2 to 3 minutes. Using a rubber spatula, **fold in** about ¼ of the whipped egg whites to the full portion of egg yolks. Then using the rubber spatula, gently fold the egg yolk mixture back into the remaining whites. Sprinkle sifted cake flour, lime juice, and lime rind over egg mixture. Fold in until there is no trace of flour, about 2 minutes (don't over fold). Divide the batter equally between the 2 prepared cake pans. Using rubber spatula, spread batter to the edges of the pans, and smooth out top of batter.

3. Bake in oven for 20 to 30 minutes, or until a toothpick inserted in the center of the cakes comes out clean. Let the cakes cool in their pans for about 5 minutes, then turn over onto wire cake racks to cool completely.

4. Prepare *mocha cream icing* (recipe follows).

5. To assemble: Place one cake layer on a serving plate, and using a metal icing spatula or dinner knife, cover with a ¼ cup icing. Place the second layer on top. Spread remaining icing over the top and sides of cake, and refrigerate until ready to serve.

To serve, cut into wedges and serve with cup of coffee or tea.

Mocha Cream Icing

Yield: about 3 cups

- 2 tablespoons instant powdered coffee, preferably *espresso*
- 3 tablespoons dry cocoa powder
- ¼ cup hot water
- 1½ cups confectioners' sugar, more as needed
- 2 teaspoons rum flavored extract

Equipment: 8-ounce cup, medium mixing bowl, mixing spoon

1. Stir instant coffee and cocoa into ¼ cup hot water until dissolved.

2. Put 1½ cups confectioners' sugar in medium mixing bowl. Add coffee mixture and rum extract, and using mixing spoon, stir until smooth.

If icing seems too thin, add more confectioners' sugar, one tablespoon at a time, stirring after each addition until it becomes a spreadable consistency. Refrigerate for 1 hour to firm up before using.

Continue with planter's cake *(recipe precedes: Step 5. To assemble).*

Fresh fruit is very abundant on the Caribbean islands, and *matrimony* is a nice dessert at the end of a heavy birthday or wedding feast. How the dish got its name is a mystery, but it's perfect to serve at a wedding reception.

Matrimony

Fresh Fruit Medley

Yield: serves 6

- 8 **carambolas**, **trim** ends and slice ¼ inch thick crosswise
- 3 large oranges, peeled and **segmented**
- 1 (14-ounce) can sweetened condensed milk, or 1½ cups whipped evaporated milk (recipe page 366)
- 1 teaspoon **ground** nutmeg

Equipment: Medium glass or ceramic serving bowl, mixing spoon, plastic food wrap, serving spoon, small dessert bowls

1. Put carambolas and oranges in a medium glass or ceramic serving bowl, and toss to mix. Cover bowl with plastic wrap and refrigerate.

2. At serving time: Add sweetened condensed milk or whipped evaporated milk, sprinkle with nutmeg, and toss to mix.

To serve, place bowl of matrimony *on the dessert table with a serving spoon. Provide small dessert bowls and spoons for guests so they can help themselves. Eat with a slice of* pan dulce de harina de maíz *(recipe page* 372*).*

BAHAMAS

The Commonwealth of the Bahamas is made up of more than 750 islands and cays in the North Atlantic Ocean about 50 miles off the east coast of Florida. Only about 30 of the islands and cays are inhabited. While not geographically part of the Caribbean, the Bahamas does border the Caribbean Sea and the Bahamians have many social and historical ties to the rest of the region.

The original inhabitants of the Bahamas were the Arawak Indians, who were wiped out by disease when Europeans arrived. The Bahamas became a British colony and large numbers of African slaves were brought to the islands. Today about 85 percent of the population are of African descent.

The islands became an independent country in 1973, but legacy of British colonialism remains. The official language of the Bahamas is English, and the majority of the people are Christians, split fairly evenly among Baptists, Anglicans, and Roman Catholics. Bahamians generally celebrate the life-cycle events prescribed by their branch of Christianity. (See Protestant and Catholic Life-Cycle Rituals, page xlvi.)

Weddings are community celebrations, and the bride, if the budget allows, wears a long white wedding dress with veil. Most ceremonies are held in a church, followed by a reception of small sandwiches, cake, and punch in the church social hall or the home of the bride's parents. Or guests are invited to the reception at a restaurant or hotel.

Traditionally two cakes are prepared, one for the bride and one for the groom. The bride's cake is called silver wedding cake. It is a three-tier fruit cake (see recipe for *black wedding cake* page 360) covered with edible **silver leaf**, symbolizing prosperity. The groom's cake (recipe follows) is pound cake often covered with edible gold leaf, symbolizing his authority as head of the family. The cakes are covered with *butter cream icing* (recipe page 361) and allowed to dry for a day or two before decorating with gold or silver leaf.

Fresh English ivy and tiny pink rose buds are usually added as decorations on the wedding cake. A cedar seedling is placed on top of the cake, and according to tradition, the newlyweds plant the seedling together at their future homestead. The decorative cakes are not cut at the reception, but later when the bride's parents give a party in their home honoring the newlyweds. Many families save the top layer of the wedding cake and serve it at the christening of their first child.

The groom's cake is either the basic pound cake calling for all significant ingredients, flour, sugar, butter, and eggs be of the same weight. A similar cake called *sand torte* is also popular. ❂ ❂ ❂

Groom's Gold Wedding Cake

Sand Torte

Yield: serves 10 to 12

1 cup flour
1 cup cornstarch
2 teaspoons baking powder
1 cup unsalted butter, at room temperature
1 cup sugar
6 **eggs, separated**
2 tablespoons vanilla or rum extract
butter cream icing (recipe page 361), for **garnish**
gold leaf (available at some Middle East and Indian food stores), for garnish

Equipment: Flour **sifter**, medium mixing bowl, large mixing bowl, mixing spoon or electric mixer, rubber spatula, buttered 9-inch tube pan, oven mitts, toothpick, knife, wire cake rack, serving platter, **icing spatula** or dinner knife, small artist's paintbrush or feather (optional), serving platter

Preheat oven to 350° F.

1. **Sift** flour, cornstarch, and baking powder in medium mixing bowl.

2. Put butter and sugar in large mixing bowl, and using mixing spoon or electric mixer, beat until light and fluffy, 2 to 4 minutes. Add egg yolks, 2 at a time, beating well after each addition. Add sifted flour mixture, a little at a time, beating well after each addition. Beat in vanilla or rum extract.

3. Put egg whites into clean, dry, medium mixing bowl and using clean, dry electric mixer or mixing spoon, beat until soft peaks form. **Fold in** whites with batter, using rubber spatula. Transfer batter to buttered 9-inch tube pan.

4. Bake in oven for 45 to 50 minutes, or until toothpick inserted in centers comes out clean. Cool cake in pan for 10 minutes. Run knife around side of pan and flip onto wire cake rack.

5. Prepare *butter cream icing.*

6. Assemble cake: Place cake on serving platter. Beginning at the top, cover cake with icing, using icing spatula or dinner knife. Decorate cake with greenery, such as English ivy, placed around the base and in the center hole of the cake.

Continue to decorate with gold leaf, simply lay the small pieces on the icing with your fingers, they should stick by themselves. A small artist's paint brush or feather can be helpful to spread each piece.

At most wedding receptions only beverages and cakes are served. When more food is required, such dishes as *pudding and souse* (recipe page 362), local seafood such as fried conch (*lambi*), turtle soup (*calalou*, recipe follows), and boiled spiny lobsters might be prepared.

The comfort food of the Caribbean is *calalou* (also *callaloo* or *callilu*). Dasheen leaves, a variety of taro root grown in the southern United States, or spinach can be used for this recipe if calalou leaves are not available.

Calalou

Crab Stew with Okra and Greens

Yield: serves 6

2-ounce slice salt pork, diced, or 4 tablespoons butter or margarine
2 onions, sliced
2 cloves garlic, **finely chopped**
½ pound **dasheen** leaves or spinach, washed and chopped
salt and pepper to taste
1 potato, peeled and **diced**
½ pound okra, **trimmed** and sliced crosswise into 3 pieces
6 cups chicken broth, homemade (recipe page 106), or canned
½ pound cooked crab meat, fresh, canned, or frozen (available at most fish markets and supermarkets)
ground red pepper to taste
6 cups cooked white rice, for serving

Equipment: Large saucepan with cover, mixing spoon

1. In large saucepan over medium heat, **render** chopped salt pork until fat is released, about 5 minutes, or if not using salt pork, melt butter or margarine.

2. Increase heat to medium-high, and add onions and garlic. Stir and **sauté** until onions are soft, 3 to 5 minutes. Add dasheen or spinach and ½ teaspoon salt. Cover and cook until greens are limp, 1 to 2 minutes. Add potato, okra, and chicken broth and stir. Reduce heat to **simmer**, cover, and cook 20 to 25 minutes, or until potato and okra are tender. Add crab meat, salt and pepper to taste, and ground red pepper to taste. Stir, cover, and cook until crabmeat is heated through, 5 to 7 minutes.

Serve as a main dish over cooked rice with a basket of floats *(recipe page 363).*

Island dumplings, called *fungi* are an essential part of any Bahamian meal. City folks and farmers alike use them to soak up gravy left in the bowl or on the plate. Serve *fungi* with *calalou* (recipe precedes). In the Caribbean, a **Scotch bonnet pepper**, seeded and minced, would be added to this recipe. Substitute ground red pepper, to taste. *Fungi* is basically the same as cornmeal mush in the southern United States. The Italians call their version of cornmeal mush *polenta*, and the Romanians know it as *mamaliga*.

Fungi

Cornmeal Dumplings

Yield: serves 6

2½ cups water
2 tablespoons margarine
4 okra, **trimmed** and sliced crosswise
ground red pepper, to taste
1¼ cups plain yellow **cornmeal**

Equipment: Medium **heavy-based** saucepan with cover, mixing spoon, buttered 8-inch square baking pan, serving plate

1. Heat water in medium **heavy-based** saucepan over high heat, and bring to boil. Stir in butter or margarine, okra, and ground red pepper to taste. When butter or margarine is melted, stir in cornmeal, a little at a time, and continue stirring until mixture thickens, 2 to 4 minutes.

Reduce heat to **simmer**, cover, and cook 5 to 7 minutes.

2. Pour mixture into buttered 8-inch square baking pan, and cool to room temperature. When cool, use moistened knife to cut mixture into 1-inch squares.

To serve, arrange fungi *squares on a serving plate and each person can add a few to their soup or stew or eat them in place of bread to soak up gravy or sauce.*

Peas or beans with rice is one of the comfort foods of the Caribbean and each island has its own way of preparing it and naming it, e.g., *pois et ris* in Haiti (peas and rice); in Cuba it's *Morros y Chistianos*, which is Spanish for Moors and Christians (black beans and rice); or in the Bahamas, *gunga*. A christening, first communion, wedding, or funeral feast in the Bahamas would be incomplete if a big pot of *gunga* were not on the table. Pigeon peas (also called *Congo peas* or *no-eyed* peas) are native to Africa. They are available fresh, frozen, and canned, as well as dried and split in Latin American and Indian food stores and most supermarkets.

Gunga

Pigeon Peas and Rice

Yield: serves 6

- 2 tablespoons vegetable oil
- 1 onion, **finely chopped**
- 1 green bell pepper, **trimmed**, seeded, and finely chopped
- 2 tablespoons tomato paste
- 16 ounces canned stewed tomatoes, chopped
- 1 teaspoon dried thyme flakes
- 2 cups water
- 1 cup white rice
- 1 cup dried pigeon peas, (cooked according to directions on package), or 3 cups canned (see above)
- salt and pepper to taste
- 1 lemon, cut into 6 wedges, for serving

Equipment: Medium saucepan with cover, mixing spoon, strainer

1. Heat oil in medium saucepan over medium-high heat. Add finely chopped onion and bell pepper, stir, and **sauté** until onion is soft, 3 to 5 minutes. Add tomato paste, stewed tomatoes with juice, thyme, and water. Bring to boil, add rice, and stir. Reduce heat to **simmer**, cover, and cook 15 minutes.

2. Drain cooked or canned pigeon peas in strainer and discard juice. Add peas to tomato mixture, stir, cover, and continue cooking 7 to 12 minutes more, until rice is tender and peas are heated through. Add salt and pepper to taste.

Serve gunga *hot, with lemon wedges to squeeze over each serving.*

CUBA

Cuba is the largest island in the West Indies and sits just 90 miles south of Florida. It was one of the first islands visited by Columbus, and as with other Caribbean islands, the indigenous population of Arawak Indians was wiped out by disease soon after European contact. Cuba became a Spanish colony, and the Arawak Indians were replaced by African slaves brought by the Spaniards to work on the sugar and tobacco plantations. With the help of the United States, Cuba broke from Spain in 1899, though the Spanish influence remained in language and religion, which was predominantly Roman Catholic.

Although Cuba was nominally independent, it was greatly influenced by the United

States until a revolution led by Fidel Castro established a new regime in 1959. Intially, relations between the United States and Cuba remained friendly after Castro's takeover, but by 1961, the United States broke off relations with Cuba, and Castro formed an alliance with the Soviet Union. Castro embraced the Communist philosophy of his new partner, and even with the fall of Communism in Europe, Cuba remains a Communist society.

Today, Cuba is a multiracial society with a population of mainly Spanish and African origins. The largest organized religion is the Roman Catholic Church, although Cuba's Communist regime is officially atheist. After Pope John Paul's visit in 1997, there has been a resurgence of Catholic rituals and observances by people. (See Protestant and Catholic Life-Cycle Rituals, page xlvi.) Most Catholic life-cycle celebrations are once again being observed but not on the same grand scale of pre-Fidel Castro days.

One of these observances is baptism. Shortly after birth, babies are baptized so if they die they can become *angelitos* (little angels) and go to heaven. Children are usually named after a saint on whose day they are born, along with the name of either parent and/or a favorite relative, living or dead.

Among the rural Catholic families, when the baby is 40 days old, the mother and *compadres* (godparents) take it to church to hear *Missa* (Mass). This is called *sacamisa*, and commemorates the presentation of the Infant Jesus in the Temple by the Virgin Mary. It is customary, following the *sacamisa*, for the parents to invite the godparents for a feast meal, which, depending upon the budget, can be a grand *fiesta* (celebration) with music, singing, and dancing. The poor, who cannot afford the cost of a special *Missa*, can bring their baby to any scheduled *Missa* and join in the celebration.

In the rural areas of Cuba, marriages take place at an early age, depending upon regional customs. The girls are usually about 15 and the boys are 17 or 18. Civil weddings have been more common under Communism, but since the Pope's visit, more Cuban couples are being married in the Catholic Church. Most young people like the pageantry of the church wedding, but it is expensive and only a select group can afford it.

For the most elegant Cuban wedding, the *lechôncito asado* (recipe follows) is the centerpiece of the wedding feast table, and *bolo de frutas* (fruit cake) is the traditional Cuban wedding cake, which is the same or similar to Caribbean *black wedding cake* (recipe page 360).

Cubans love roast suckling pig: See directions to buy, prepare, roast, and carve (page 348). When budget allows, it is the centerpiece of the *sacamisa*, baptism, confirmation, or wedding celebration banquet. The expert who prepares the pig holds the distinguished title of *la lechónera* (suckling pig master).

Lechôncito Asado

Cuban Suckling Pig

Yield: serves 8 to 12

- 10- to 15-pound **oven-ready** suckling pig, (available at butcher shops and most supermarkets by special order)
- ¼ cup vegetable oil
- 2 tablespoons salt and pepper
- 1 whole lemon or lime, for **garnish**
- 4 large onions, **trimmed**, sliced across, and separated into rings, for garnish
- *mojo criollo* (recipe follows), for serving

Equipment: Paper towels, **pastry brush**, aluminum foil, large shallow roasting pan with wire rack, **meat thermometer** or paring knife, oven mitts, serving platter

Preheat oven to 350°

1. Follow directions in Papua New Guinea section (page 348) for more details on how to prepare and roast suckling pig.

2. Oil and season pig: Using pastry brush, cover pig all over with oil. Sprinkle salt and pepper in the inside cavity and over skin.

3. Roast the pig undisturbed in oven for 2½ to 4 hours (depending upon weight—allow 30 to 35 minutes per pound roasting time), remove foil from ears and tail and continue roasting for 30 minutes more. Test for doneness: Meat is done when meat thermometer registers 175° to 180° F and thigh joints move easily in their sockets.

4. Transfer to serving platter and replace the foil in the mouth with a lemon or lime. Arrange raw onion rings around the pig. Let the pig rest for at least 20 minutes for easier carving.

Serve pig with side dish of mojo criollo *to spoon over the slices. The onions are eaten with the pig. Roasted potatoes,* riz créole *(recipe page 373),* piononos, *and* calalou *(recipe page 381) would also be on the wedding menu.*

Mojo criollo is the classic Cuban sauce for roasted *lechôn* (pig). It is made with sour seville oranges (*naranjas agrias*) mixed with fatty pork. This recipe uses easily available ingredients and is an excellent sauce for most pork dishes.

Mojo Criollo

Cuban Pork Sauce

Yield: about 3 cups

- 3 cloves garlic, **finely chopped**
- ½ cup frozen lime juice concentrate, thawed
- 1 cup frozen orange juice concentrate, thawed
- 2 cups water
- 2 tablespoons vegetable oil
- 1 tablespoon **ground** cumin
- 1 tablespoon ground oregano
- salt and pepper to taste

Equipment: 1-quart glass jar with lid, small saucepan, spoon, small serving bowl

1. Put garlic, lime and orange juice concentrates, water, oil, cumin, oregano, and salt and pepper to taste in quart jar. Tightly cover jar with lid and shake well. Refrigerate at least 4 hours for flavor to develop, shaking occasionally.

2. Pour juice mixture into small saucepan and over medium-high heat, cook until heated through, 2 to 3 minutes.

To serve put into small bowl and spoon over each serving of lechôncito asado.

A wonderful side dish with the pork is *piononos*, which uses plantains. Plantains can be prepared dozens of ways, but this recipe is more elegant than most. It is a popular party dish throughout the Caribbean and Latin America.

Piononos

Stuffed Plantains

Yield: serves 4 to 6

- 2 or 3 large ripe **plantains**
- 2¼ cups vegetable oil, divided
- ¼ pound hot spicy bulk sausage meat, such as *chorizo*
- 1 pound lean **ground** meat (pork or beef or combination)
- 1 cup **finely chopped** onion
- 2 cloves garlic, finely chopped
- 1 green bell pepper, seeded and finely chopped
- 3 tomatoes, **peeled** and finely chopped
- 2 tablespoons cornstarch

½ cup water
salt and pepper to taste
1 cup grated cheddar cheese

Equipment: Baking sheet, paper towels, knife, large skillet, slotted metal spatula, work surface, greased standard muffin pan (12 cups *each* 2¾ inch wide), oven mitts, large oven-proof serving platter, toothpicks

1. Prepare plantains: Have ready paper-towel-covered baking sheet. Using a knife, **trim** ends off of each plantain and slice lengthwise into 3 or 4 strips, depending upon their size. Remove and discard peelings.

2. Heat ¼ cup oil in large skillet over medium-high heat, and fry plantains, a few at a time, 2 to 3 minutes on each side, until golden. Remove with slotted metal spatula and drain on paper towels. Remove and discard oil left in skillet.

3. Prepare stuffing: Crumble sausage and ground meat into skillet. Over medium-high heat, fry until cooked through, 3 to 5 minutes. Reduce heat to medium and add onions, garlic, green pepper, and tomatoes. Tossing frequently, cook until onions and pepper are soft, 5 to 7 minutes. Stir cornstarch into ½ cup water until smooth, and stir into meat mixture. Add salt and pepper to taste and cook until sauce thickens and meat mixture holds together, 3 to 5 minutes.

Preheat oven to 350° F.

4. Assemble: Place greased muffin pan on work surface. Line the sides of each muffin cup with a plantain slice, overlapping the ends to cover the whole side of the cup. Fill the center of each muffin cup with meat mixture. Pack down meat mixture and smooth the top even with the plantain. Repeat filling muffin cups using all the meat mixture.

5. Bake in oven 30 to 35 minutes, or until meat is browned. Remove from oven, sprinkle each patty generously with grated cheese, and return to oven to melt, 3 to 5 minutes. Allow to rest in pan for 10 minutes before removing from muffin cups. Transfer to serving platter, and if necessary to prevent plantains from unwrapping, poke a toothpick through overlapping ends.

Serve as a side dish with lechôncito asado *(recipe page 383) or* pastel de maíz *(recipe follows), and cooked black beans with sour cream and chopped onions.*

When pork is too expensive, the next best thing for a life-cycle celebration is chicken. This lovely casserole dish can be prepared ahead and heated through at serving time. When it's necessary to bring a covered dish for any occasion, this one is perfect.

Pastel de Maíz

Chicken Pie with Corn Topping

Yield: serves 6
2 ½ to 3 pound chicken, cut into serving-size pieces
2½ cups water
salt and pepper to taste
2 tablespoons vegetable oil
1 cup onions, **finely chopped**
3 tomatoes, **peeled** and chopped
12 prunes, soaked in warm water for 10 minutes and drained
½ cup seedless raisins, soaked in warm water for 10 minutes and drained
½ teaspoon ground cinnamon
4 cups corn kernels, fresh (cut from about 16 ears), or frozen (thawed)
1 tablespoon sugar
3 tablespoons butter or margarine
4 eggs
12 pimiento-stuffed olives, rinsed and halved
4 hard-cooked eggs, **coarsely chopped**

Equipment: Large saucepan with cover or **Dutch oven**, metal tongs, plate, 2 medium bowls, small bowl with cover, large **heavy-based** skillet, mixing spoon, food processor, rubber spatula, buttered large oven-proof casserole, oven mitts

1. Prepare filling: Put chicken pieces and water into large saucepan or Dutch oven, add salt and pepper to taste, and bring to boil over high heat. Reduce heat to **simmer**, cover, and cook for 40 to 50 minutes, or until tender. Let the chicken cool in broth until cool enough to handle. Using metal tongs, transfer chicken to plate. Cut or pull meat off bones, cut into bite-size pieces, and put into medium bowl. Discard bones and skin. Transfer broth to small bowl, cover, and refrigerate for another use.

2. Melt 2 tablespoons oil in large heavy-based skillet over medium-high heat. Add onions, stir, and **sauté** for 3 to 5 minutes, until soft. Add tomatoes, stir, reduce heat to simmer, and cook 5 to 7 minutes for flavors to develop. Remove from heat, add prunes, raisins, cinnamon, and chicken, and toss to mix. Transfer to medium bowl.

3. Prepare crust: Put corn kernels, 1 teaspoon salt, and sugar into food processor, and process until mixture is reduced to **purée**, 2 to 3 minutes.

Note: While processing, turn machine off once or twice and scrape down sides of container with rubber spatula.

4. Using the same heavy-based skillet, melt 3 tablespoons butter or margarine over medium-high heat. Add corn mixture, stir, and reduce heat to simmer. Add eggs, one at a time, stirring well after each addition. Reduce heat to low, stirring occasionally, and cook for 20 to 25 minutes, or until mixture has thickened to consistency of mashed potatoes. Cool for 10 minutes.

Preheat oven to 350° F.

5. Assemble: Spread about one-third of corn mixture evenly over bottom and sides of buttered oven-proof casserole. Spoon in chicken mixture, and cover with olives and chopped hard-cooked eggs. Spread remaining corn mixture over top olives and eggs, and using back of spoon, spread smooth.

6. Bake in oven 45 minutes to 1 hour, until top is firm and golden brown.

Serve with frituras de ñame *(recipe page 371),* floats *(recipe page 363), and* matrimony *(recipe page 379).*

LATIN AMERICA

Latin America, which includes the countries of Central and South America, is an area of great geographic, climatic, and topographic diversity. It includes jungles, rainforests, high mountains and glaciers, deserts, and fertile plains. Despite these physical differences, there are many similarities in the ways of life in Latin America. Without question, the Roman Catholic Church is the dominating force in South and Central America. (See Protestant and Catholic Life-Cycle Rituals, page xlvi.)

Originally inhabited by Native American tribes, including some advanced empires like the Aztecs of Mexico and Incas of Peru, Latin America changed dramatically with the arrival of Europeans. The conquering Spanish and Portuguese soldiers (*conquistadores*) were accompanied by Catholic missionaries who arrived during the fifteenth and sixteenth centuries and began converting the indigenous Indians to the Catholic religion. The Indians often combined their native rituals and traditions with Catholicism. The area remained under European control until the nineteenth century when independence movements swept through Latin America.

Today, the family is the cornerstone of Latin American life. Besides the husband, wife, and children, a family usually includes the grandparents, aunts, uncles, and cousins—an extended family. Most of the family's social life takes place within this kinfolk group, and the social life centers around the Catholic Church. Baptisms, confirmations, weddings, birthdays, name days, graduations, and funerals are occasions for huge family gatherings. In addition to these events, girls have a special honor, *quinceañeara*, the traditional Hispanic celebration of a girl's 15th birthday.

CHILE

Chile is a long, narrow country in South America between the Andes Mountains and the Pacific Ocean. Originally under the control of the Inca tribe, thousands of Indians were converted to Catholicism during the Spanish conquest, around the sixteenth century. Chile remained under Spanish control until it won its independence in 1818.

Today, most of the population are either descendants of the Spanish invaders, or people of mixed lineage (*mestizo*), both Indian and Spanish. Chileans have a strong sense of national unity, and like other Roman Catholic countries, all life-cycle events are celebrated according to the Church. (See Protestant and Catholic Life-Cycle Rituals, page xlvi.)

Baptisms are a particularly important life-cycle event in Chile. Due to high infant mortality, especially among *mestizos*, babies are baptized shortly after birth for fear they may die before becoming a Christian. As in many other Latin American countries, the godparents (*compadres*) play an important role in the lives of their godchildren. For the baptismal church service, first communion, and wedding of a godchild, godparents are involved in the rituals and take responsibility in the expenses of the events. After the Mass, the parents and godparents invite family and friends to the feast meal, which can be in the home, a restaurant, or hall.

Marriage takes place at an early age, though the age varies by region. In most cases, the marriages are arranged by the parents, except in the larger cities where couples are free to date and marry whomever they like. For a wedding to be recognized by the Catholic Church, it must be performed by a priest. Because church weddings can be very expensive, more and more couples are having a small civil ceremony.

The waters off the coast of Chile are known for the plentiful fish and seafood , and often both are included in the wedding feast. *Congrio* are very large fish found in Chilean waters. They are considered the finest of all fish according to Chilean fish lovers. *Congrio* is the Spanish word for eel, but Chilean *congrio* are not really eel. Substitute any firm-fleshed fish for this recipe.

Congrio en Fuente de Barro

Fish with Tomatoes and Onions

Yield: serves 4 to 6

- 2 pounds **fillets** of cod or other firm-fleshed fish
- salt and pepper to taste
- juice of 1 lemon
- 1 teaspoon **ground** paprika
- 4 to 6 tablespoons butter or margarine
- 6 onions, **finely chopped**
- 6 tomatoes, chopped
- 4 slices firm white bread, pan fried in butter or margarine
- 1 cup milk
- 2 hard-cooked eggs, sliced
- 1 tablespoon parsley, chopped for garnish

Equipment: Large skillet, mixing spoon, buttered medium ovenproof casserole with cover, oven mitts

1. Sprinkle fish fillets with salt and pepper, lemon juice, and paprika. Set aside.

2. Melt 4 tablespoons butter or margarine in large skillet over medium-high heat. Add onions, stir, and **sauté** until soft, 3 to 5 minutes. Add remaining 2 tablespoons butter or margarine, and reduce heat to medium. Add tomatoes, stir, and sauté for 5 minutes longer.

Preheat oven to 350° F.

3. Layer half tomato mixture in buttered casserole, cover tomatoes with fish, and add layer

of fried bread. Spread remaining tomato mixture over top fried bread. Arrange sliced hard-cooked eggs over tomato mixture, and pour milk over the top.

4. Cover and bake in oven for 30 minutes, or until fish flakes easily when poked with a fork.

Serve from casserole dish for a lovely, satisfying, full-flavored dish.

Throughout Latin America avocados are a favorite food. For a special occasion avocados are stuffed and served as an appetizer.

Aquacates Rellenos

Stuffed Avocados

Yield: serves 6

3 large avocados
juice of 1 lemon
1 cup chopped, cooked ham
3 hard-cooked eggs, chopped
1 cup commercial mayonnaise
salt and pepper, to taste
Iceberg lettuce, shredded, for **garnish**

Equipment: Sharp knife, medium bowl, mixing spoon, six salad plates

1. Cut avocados in half, and remove and discard pit. Sprinkle the cut sides of the avocados with lemon juice, and set aside.

2. In medium bowl, combine ham and chopped hard-cooked eggs. **Fold in** mayonnaise and salt and pepper to taste.

3. Make a bed of shredded lettuce on each of six salad plates. Place an avocado half, cut side up, on each plate. Spoon equal amounts of ham mixture over each of the 6 avocados.

Serve as the first course for a wedding reception or family dinner.

ARGENTINA

Situated in the southern half of Latin America, Argentina is bordered by Chile on the west, Bolivia and Paraguay on the north, and Uruguay and Brazil on the east, although the Atlantic coastline forms most of the eastern border. Argentina is the second largest country in Latin America in both population and area. (Brazil is first.)

Argentina was colonized by Spain in the sixteenth century and remained under Spanish control until 1810 when Argentina declared its independence after Spain was defeated by Napoleon. Today, Argentina is different from other South and Central American countries in that its population is mostly of European origin, with few Indians and *mestizos* (people of mixed Indian and European origins). Besides the Spanish, the Italians have had a profound influence on the country, and people of Italian descent make up a fairly large portion of the population.

More than 90 percent of the population are Roman Catholic and by law, the president and vice president of the country must be Roman Catholic. All life-cycle rituals are celebrated according to the Roman Catholic Church. (See Protestant and Catholic Life-Cycle Rituals, page xlvi.) Babies are baptized at a few weeks old, and first communion is celebrated around the ages of seven or eight. Weddings are generally held in a church.

As is the custom in many Catholic nations, a funeral feast is held after the burial. Depending upon the region and wealth of the bereaved family, the funeral feast almost always includes meat, usually beef. Among the people living in the Pampas (the cattle-raising region of Argentina), several cattle are slaughtered for the occasion and cooked over an open fire, an *asado* (barbecue). Part of the ritual to honor the departed soul involves the beverage *maté.* (See Paraguay's *yerba mate*, page 399.) Before the feasting begins, mourners take a turn to sip *maté* through a *bombilla* (metal straw). Everyone uses the same *bombilla,* and it is an insult to the bereaved family if anyone refuses.

Empanadas are a favorite Latin American appetizer and might be served at weddings and other family celebrations. They are filled with meat, vegetables, or fruit. The Argentine *empanadas* are crescent shaped with a distinctive braided *gaucho* (South American cowboy) rope border. The rope border takes practice to duplicate. This recipe for *empanadas* offers an easier way to make the border. ۞ ۞ ۞

Empanadas de Horno

Baked Meat-filled Turnovers

Yield: makes 12 to 14

1 tablespoons olive oil
1 cup onions, **finely chopped**
½ pound boneless lean beef, **coarsely chopped**
¼ cup seedless raisins, soaked in 1 cup boiling water for 10 minutes and drained well
¼ teaspoon **ground** red pepper, more or less to taste
¼ teaspoon ground cumin
salt and pepper to taste
turnover pastry dough (recipe follows), or frozen pie crust or pie crust mix
2 hard-cooked eggs, each cut vertically into 8 wedges
14 stuffed green olives, coarsely chopped, more if needed

Equipment: Large skillet, mixing spoon, lightly floured rolling pin, lightly floured work surface, 4-inch cookie cutter or 4-inch plate, paring knife, small cup of water, fork, baking sheet, oven mitts, metal spatula, serving platter

1. Prepare filling: Heat oil in large skillet over medium-high heat, add onions, and **sauté** until soft, 3 to 5 minutes. Crumble meat into the pan, stirring constantly, and cook until browned, 5 to 7 minutes. Stir in raisins, ¼ teaspoon ground red pepper, more or less to taste, cumin, and salt and pepper to taste. Set aside.

2. Prepare *turnover pastry dough.*

3. Assemble turnovers: Using a lightly floured rolling pin, roll the dough out on a lightly floured work surface to about ⅛ inch thick. Cut the dough into circles using a 4-inch cookie cutter or cut circles with a knife, using a 4-inch plate as a template. Gather remaining dough into a ball and roll out. Cut the remaining dough into circles as well.

Preheat oven to 350° F.

4. Place 1 tablespoon meat filling in the center of each dough circle, staying at least ½ inch from the edges. Place one wedge of egg on top of meat filling and sprinkle with chopped olives. Dip your finger into cup of water, and moisten edge of pastry. Fold top half of dough over filling to form a half circle, and press edges of dough together with fork to seal. Place turnovers side by side on baking sheet. Make vent holes in the top of each turnover by poking once or twice with fork.

5. Bake in oven for 15 to 20 minutes, or until lightly browned. Using oven mitts, remove from oven. With a metal spatula, transfer turnovers to serving platter.

Serve empanadas *while they are still warm as an appetizer.*

Turnover Pastry Dough

Yield: about 12 to 14

2½ cups all-purpose flour, more as needed

1 teaspoon salt
1 teaspoon baking powder
2 tablespoons sugar
¾ cup cold butter or margarine, cut into small pieces
½ cup ice water, more if necessary

Equipment: Large mixing bowl, **pastry blender** (optional), plastic wrap

In large mixing bowl, combine 2½ cups flour, salt, and baking powder. Add butter or margarine pieces, and using pastry blender or fingers, **blend** until mixture resembles coarse crumbs. Add ½ cup ice water and using your fingers blend to form into ball. If dough is too dry, add more water, and, if too sticky, add a little more flour. Wrap dough in plastic wrap and refrigerate for at least 1 hour to chill.

Continue to make empanadas de horno *(recipe precedes: Assemble: Step 3).*

The *alfajores*, an Argentine tradition served at first communion parties, are cake-like cookies filled with *dulce de leche*, creamy caramel-flavored milk.

Alfajores Santafecinos

Frosted Caramel-filled Cookies

Yield: about 20 cookies
2 cups *dulce de leche* (recipe follows)
1 cup all-purpose flour
½ teaspoon salt
3 **egg yolks**
1 teaspoon melted butter
1 cup confectioners' sugar, more if necessary
½ cup heavy cream, more if necessary

Equipment: Large mixing bowl, mixing spoon, lightly floured work surface, lightly floured rolling pin, 2-inch cookie cutter or water glass, 1 or 2 lightly greased cookie sheets, oven mitts, metal spatula, wire cake rack, small bowl, **pastry brush**, serving tray

1. Prepare *dulce de leche*. Cover and refrigerate until ready to use.

2. Put flour and salt in large mixing bowl. Make well (hole) in the center, and drop in the egg yolks and melted butter. Using your fingers, mix the ingredients together to form into a ball of dough. Transfer dough to lightly floured work surface and **knead** vigorously for 10 minutes, or until smooth and elastic. Let dough rest for 10 minutes.

Preheat oven to 350° F.

3. On lightly floured work surface, roll dough to about ⅛ inch thick with lightly floured rolling pin. Using 2-inch cookie cutter or the rim of glass, cut out as many circles as you can from the dough. Gather the scraps together and form them into another ball. Roll dough out again and cut into circles as with other dough. Repeat until all the dough has been used. Place the circles 1 inch apart on 1 or 2 lightly greased cookie sheets.

4. Bake in oven for 10 minutes, or until the cookies are lightly browned. Using a metal spatula, transfer cookies to a wire rack to cool.

5. Prepare icing: Put 1 cup confectioners' sugar into small bowl, stir in ½ cup heavy cream, a little at a time, and **blend** well. The icing should coat the spoon lightly. If it seems thin, add a few spoonfuls of confectioners' sugar; if it is too thick, add a little more cream.

6. Using a pastry brush, coat the tops of half the cookies with a thin layer of icing and let dry for 10 minutes.

7. Spread a thick layer of *dulce de leche* on the remaining cookies. Place the cookies on top of each other like a sandwich, with *dulce de leche* in the center and icing on top.

To serve, stack alfajores santafecinos *on a tray and serve as sweet treats at baptism celebrations and first communion parties.*

Dulce de leche is popular not only in Argentina but throughout Latin America. It is eaten as a dessert and even used as a spread on bread. *Dulce de leche* is also called *natillas piuranas*, *manjar blanco*, and *leche quemada*.

Dulce de Leche

Caramel-flavored Milk Pudding

Yield: about 4 cups

15 ounces canned condensed milk
3 cups whole milk
½ teaspoon baking soda
1 cup dark brown sugar
¼ cup water

Equipment: Small saucepan, wooden mixing spoon, medium **heavy-based** saucepan

1. In small saucepan, stirring constantly, bring condensed milk, whole milk, and baking soda to a boil over high heat, and immediately remove pan from heat.

2. Put sugar and water into medium heavy-based saucepan, and cook over low heat, stirring constantly, until the sugar dissolves. Stir in hot milk mixture and cook over very low heat for 1 to 1½ hours, stirring occasionally. The mixture becomes a thick amber-colored pudding when done.

Continue with alfajores santafecinos *(recipe precedes: Step 7:) or serve as dessert.*

URUGUAY

South America's smallest country, Uruguay, is situated on the east coast of South America, south of Brazil and east of Argentina. Unlike other South American countries, it has no rainforests, swamps, jungles, or deserts. It is a pleasant country of grasslands and an attractive coastal region.

Uruguay was originally colonized by the Portuguese in 1680, but it was seized by Spain by 1778. By the time of the Spanish victory, the native Indians of the region disappeared, and today Uruguay is the only South American country without an indigenous Indian population. Uruguay broke from Spain in 1811 but was taken over by the Portuguese from Brazil. Finally, independence was won with the help of Argentina in 1825.

About 90 percent of the people are descendants of Spanish immigrants. The remaining population are of mixed races—*mestizos*, part Spanish and part Indian, and mulattos, part African and part Spanish. The majority of Uruguayans are Roman Catholics, although religion is not as important a part of daily life as it is in most Latin countries, and a sizeable Protestant population exists there. Most life-cycle events are connected to Christian traditions (see Protestant and Catholic Life-Cycle Rituals, page xlvi), but marriage can take place outside of a church, and in some remote parts of the country, there are no churches.

An unusual custom of Uruguay, also found in several other South American countries, is the drinking of *yerba maté*. (See Paraguay's *yerba mate*, page 399.) The herbal tea is mixed in a *maté*, or gourd, and sipped through a *bombilla* (metal or silver straw). The tea is believed to have magical powers, and the Indians used it in religious ceremonies. Today, at the end of a wedding, everyone sips *yerba maté* through the same *bombilla* to show respect and unity to the newlyweds. To refuse to take a sip is an insult to everyone present.

All through Latin America, *albóndigas* (meatballs) are popular and would be one of the many dishes served for a wedding, family gathering after a baptism, or birthday party. They are easy to make and everyone seems to love them. Each country has its own special way of making them. ۞ ۞ ۞

Albóndigas

Meatballs Uruguay-style

Yield: serves 4 to 6

8 tablespoons vegetable oil, divided
2 onions, **finely chopped,** divided
1 tomato, **peeled** and chopped
1 teaspoon **ground** red pepper, more or less to taste
1 teaspoon sugar
salt and pepper to taste
1 pound veal, finely ground
1 cup **fresh bread crumbs**
4 tablespoons grated Parmesan cheese
¼ cup seedless raisins
½ teaspoon grated nutmeg
2 eggs
2 cups canned beef broth
2 cups dry red wine
1 bay leaf

Equipment: Large skillet, mixing spoon, large mixing bowl, shallow bowl, slotted spoon, large saucepan, large serving bowl

1. Heat 4 tablespoons oil in large skillet over medium-high heat. Add 1 chopped onion, stir, and **sauté** 3 to 5 minutes, until soft. Add tomato, 1 teaspoon ground red pepper, more or less to taste, sugar, and salt and pepper to taste. Reduce heat to medium, and stirring frequently, cook until mixture thickens and is quite dry, 3 to 5 minutes. Set aside to cool to room temperature.

2. In large mixing bowl, combine veal, bread crumbs, Parmesan cheese, raisins, nutmeg, and cooled tomato mixture. Add eggs and mix thoroughly. Form mixture into 2-inch balls.

3. Put flour in shallow bowl. Roll meatballs in flour to coat all sides, and shake off excess.

4. Heat remaining 4 tablespoons oil in large skillet over medium-high heat. Fry meatballs in batches until lightly browned on all sides, about 12 to 15 minutes. When they are done, lift them out with slotted spoon and set aside.

5. In large saucepan, sauté remaining chopped onion for 3 to 5 minutes until soft. Add beef broth, wine, and bay leaf. Stir and reduce heat to **simmer,** 5 to 7 minutes for flavor to develop. Add meatballs, cover, and cook over low heat until fully cooked, 30 to 40 minutes.

To serve, spoon meatballs into large serving bowl and pour sauce over them. Serve with bread for sopping up the sauce.

Meat is always served on special occasions. This recipe is very unusual and a favorite in Uruguay.

Lomo de Cerdo a la Caucana

Pork Loin Baked in Milk

Yield: serves 4 to 6

4 tablespoons butter or margarine
2 pounds boneless pork loin, or **boned** pork shoulder
4 cups milk
¼ cup lemon juice
salt and pepper to taste

Equipment: Large skillet, metal tongs, medium roasting pan, medium bowl, meat **thermometer** (optional), **bulb baster** or mixing spoon, oven mitts, slotted spoon, small serving bowl

Preheat oven to 325° F.

1. Melt butter or margarine in large skillet over medium high heat, add pork, and lightly brown all sides, about 12 to 15 minutes. Using metal tongs, transfer to medium roasting pan.

2. In medium bowl, mix milk and lemon juice. (The milk will curdle from the lemon juice.) Pour curdled milk mixture over pork. Sprinkle with salt and pepper to taste. Insert meat thermometer, if using one, into middle of roast.

3. Bake in oven for 2 to 2½ hours, until tender, basting frequently with bulb baster or mixing spoon. Meat thermometer should register 170° F when done.

4. Using oven mitts, remove meat from oven and keep warm. Using slotted spoon, remove and discard fat from the milk sauce in roasting pan. Carefully transfer sauce to medium saucepan. Cook over medium-high heat until **reduced** to about half and thickened, 7 to 12 minutes.

To serve, pour sauce into small bowl and serve separately. Slice the meat and serve hot with rice or potatoes.

BOLIVIA

Mountainous, landlocked Bolivia is located in the heart of South America, surrounded by Brazil, Chile, Peru, Paraguay, and Argentina. When the Spanish arrived in the sixteenth century, most of Bolivia was controlled by the Inca empire. After the Spanish defeated the Incas, the native population was enslaved, mainly in pursuit of the mineral wealth that made Bolivia famous. By the time of Bolivian independence in 1825, the mineral wealth was largely exhausted. Much of the history since independence has been dominated by disastrous wars fought in an attempt to gain access to the sea.

Over half the population of Bolivia lives on a high plateau (average altitude over 12,000) between two chains of the Andes mountains. The remoteness of this high plain protected the native population from European diseases that wiped out other Indians in Latin America, and today Indians make up more than 50 percent of the population. The next largest group are *mestizos* (mixed Indian and Spanish). The Roman Catholic Church dominates Bolivian life. Most *mestizos* and Indians combine ancient Inca and other Indian beliefs with Christian practices in their life-cycle ceremonies. (See Protestant and Catholic Life-Cycle Rituals, page xlvi.)

Marriage is the most significant event in a person's life. Every stage of the courtship, betrothal, and the wedding ceremony include set rituals with music, chanting, or singing and folk dances. Godparents (*compadrazgo*), usually are selected at birth or just prior to the marriage, are important to marriages. They are held in high esteem and are selected with great care by both Indian and Hispanic cultures. The godparents participate in the marriage ceremony and are given gifts by the bride and groom.

This recipe for cooked cabbage is a hearty, filling dish that goes well with meat or *pastel de chocio con relleno de pollo* (recipe follows). It would be served at a birthday party or other life-cycle celebration.

Guiso de Repollo

Cabbage in Sauce

Yield: serves 4

3 tablespoons vegetable oil
1 onion, **finely chopped**
3 tomatoes, chopped
dried red pepper flakes, to taste
1 tablespoon tomato sauce
salt and pepper, to taste
1 pound green or white cabbage, finely shredded, **blanched,** and drained
4 potatoes, peeled, cooked, and quartered

Equipment: Large skillet, mixing spoon, serving bowl

1. Heat oil in large skillet over medium-high heat, add onion, and sauté 3 to 5 minutes, until soft. Reduce heat to medium, and add tomatoes and dried red pepper flakes to taste. Stir and cook for 5 minutes for flavors to develop.

2. Stir in tomato sauce and **blend** well. Add salt and pepper to taste.

3. **Fold in** blanched and drained cabbage, and cooked potatoes. Continue to cook until heated through, 10 to 15 minutes. Add more salt and pepper if desired.

To serve, transfer to serving bowl and serve hot or at room temperature as a side dish.

This easy-to-prepare party dish is often served for the family wedding feast.

Pastel de Chocio con Relleno de Pollo

Chicken Pie Bolivian-style

Yield: serves 6

3½ pound chicken, cut into serving pieces
4 cups water
3 tablespoons vegetable oil
2 onions, **finely chopped**
3 tomatoes, chopped
salt, to taste
¼ cup seedless raisins, soaked in cup of warm water for 10 minutes and drained
1 teaspoon **ground** cinnamon
2 hard-cooked eggs, chopped
12 pimiento-stuffed green olives
½ cup butter or margarine
1 cup canned corn kernels, drained and **puréed**
1 tablespoon sugar, more or less to taste
4 eggs

Equipment: Large saucepan with cover or **Dutch oven**, mixing spoon, metal tongs, baking sheet, knife, large bowl, large skillet, medium saucepan, 2 quart ovenproof casserole, oven mitts

1. Put chicken in large saucepan or Dutch oven, add water, and bring to boil over medium-high heat. Reduce heat to **simmer**, cover, and cook until tender, 45 to 50 minutes. Check for **chicken doneness**. Allow chicken to cool in the broth until cool enough to handle. Remove cooled chicken from broth using tongs, and place chicken on baking sheet. Remove and discard skin and bones. Cut chicken meat into 1-inch pieces and put in large bowl. Set chicken pieces aside. Save broth for another use.

2. Heat oil in large skillet over medium-high heat, add onions, and **sauté** for 3 to 5 minutes until soft. Reduce heat to medium, add tomatoes and salt to taste, stir, and cook 5 minutes for flavors to develop. Add raisins, cinnamon, chopped eggs, olives, and chicken pieces. Set aside.

3. Prepare topping: Melt butter or margarine in medium saucepan over medium heat. Add puréed corn and 1 tablespoon sugar, more or less to taste, and stir to mix well. Reduce heat to low, and add eggs, one at a time, beating well after each addition. Mixture will quickly thicken as it is being beaten. After mixture thickens, remove from heat and allow to cool slightly before assembling, 12 to 15 minutes.

Preheat oven to 350° F.

4. To assemble: Spoon about ¼ of the corn mixture over bottom of buttered 2-quart ovenproof casserole. Spoon in chicken mixture to cover the corn mixture. Cover the chicken mixture with remaining corn mixture.

5. Bake in oven for 30 to 40 minutes, or until topping is lightly browned.

To serve, put the casserole on the table and serve hot. This is an ideal buffet dish served with guiso de repollo *(recipe precedes) as a side dish.*

BRAZIL

Brazil, South America's largest country, takes up nearly half the continent and shares a border with every other South American country except Chile and Ecuador. One of its most important features is the Amazon river basin, which drains more than a third of the country.

Unlike other Latin American countries whose recent histories were dominated by Spain, Brazil was conquered and populated by the Portuguese, who began settling in Brazil in the sixteenth century. Although Brazil declared independence in the nineteenth century, the Portuguese influence is still strong. Portuguese is the official language, and most Brazilians are Roman Catholics and follow the life-cycle traditions prescribed by the Church. (See Protestant and Catholic Life-Cycle Rituals, page xlvi.)

Beyond language and religion, though, Brazil is a land of different regions and people. The extremely diversified population is a result of geographic diversity and over 400 years of Africans, Europeans, and Indians melding together creating a complicated racial melting pot.

Of the life-cycle events, children's birthdays are similar to those in the United States. Adults often have a small family gathering, followed by a larger party to celebrate the event. In Brazil, friendships are important and to fail to attend a close friend's birthday party is taken as an insult and often severs the relationship.

Weddings generally begin with the couple signing civil documents in a small home ceremony attended by the immediate family, and it is followed by the religious ceremony in a church. After the Mass, if the family can afford it, a large reception is held at a hotel or club, complete with music, singing, and dancing.

For funerals, families usually bury their dead within 24 hours. The body, dressed in black, lies in state in a coffin at the family home. During an all-night vigil, mourners drink and have a light repast while they hover around the casket speaking only pleasantries about the deceased. At a designated hour, the hearse carrying the coffin, leads a procession to the church, where a requiem is offered. In small towns, the body is buried in the church's private cemetery, in the large cities, the procession moves to a large public cemetery. Masses are held in memory of the deceased after seven days, thirty days, and again after one year.

Eating is one of the great pleasures in Brazil and all life-cycle celebrations call for plenty of food. Bread, rolls, and other pastries are prepared for almost every celebration.

Pãezinhos de Batata Doce

Brazilian Sweet Potato Rolls

Yield: 24 rolls

- 6 tablespoons yellow **cornmeal**
- 3 cups all-purpose flour, sifted
- 1 teaspoon salt
- ½ cup **lukewarm** milk
- 1 package active dry **yeast**
- 2 eggs, lightly beaten
- ½ teaspoon anise seeds
- 1 sweet potato, boiled, peeled, mashed, and kept warm
- ¼ cup melted butter or margarine
- **egg wash**

Equipment: **Blender**, rubber spatula, flour **sifter**, medium mixing bowl, large mixing bowl, clean kitchen towel, small bowl, mixing spoon, 2 to 4 greased muffin pans to bake 24 standard (2¾-

inch) rolls, **pastry brush**, oven mitts, wire cake rack, bread basket or serving platter

1. Pulverize cornmeal in blender until fine and powdery. **Sift** flour, pulverized cornmeal, and salt into medium mixing bowl.

2. Pour lukewarm milk into large mixing bowl, stir in yeast, sugar, lightly beaten eggs, and anise seeds, and stir to mix well. Stir in about 1 cup flour mixture to make a batter. Cover with towel and set in warm place to rise for 30 to 35 minutes, until spongy. Add warm potatoes and melted butter or margarine, and stir to mix well. Add more flour mixture, ¼ cup at a time, until dough is no longer sticky.

3. Transfer dough to lightly floured work surface and **knead** until smooth, adding remaining flour, if necessary. Transfer dough to lightly greased large mixing bowl, and turn to grease all sides. Cover with towel and set in warm place to rise again to double in bulk, 45 minutes to 1 hour.

4. **Punch down** dough and divide into 72 walnut-size pieces and shape each into a ball. Fit 3 balls into each greased muffin cup to make 24 rolls. Cover with towel and set in warm place to rise to double in bulk, 35 to 45 minutes.

Preheat oven to 375° F.

5. Brush risen rolls with egg wash. Bake in oven for 20 to 25 minutes, or until golden brown and done. Remove from oven and transfer rolls to wire cake rack to cool to warm.

To serve, transfer to bread basket or serving platter and serve while still warm.

This unusual dish might be served at a family first communion dinner. *Pãezinhos de batata doce* (recipe precedes) would be served to sop up the sauce.

Xinxim de Galinha

Chicken with Shrimp and Peanut Sauce

Yield: serves 6

3½ to 4 pounds chicken, cut into serving pieces
4 tablespoons lime or lemon juice
2 cloves garlic, **finely chopped**
salt and pepper, to taste
2 tablespoons olive oil
1 onion, grated
1 cup dried shrimp, finely **ground** (available at all Asian and Latin American food stores)
½ cup dry roasted peanuts, ground
dried red pepper flakes, to taste
1 cup chicken broth, homemade (recipe page 106), or canned
¼ cup palm oil (*dendê*) (available at all Latin American food stores)

Equipment: Large bowl, mixing spoon, large **heavy-based** skillet with cover

1. **Marinate** chicken: Put chicken pieces in large bowl and sprinkle with lime or lemon juice, garlic, and salt and pepper to taste. Refrigerate to marinate for about 1 hour, turning often to coat well.

2. Heat oil in large heavy-based skillet over medium-high heat. Add onion, shrimp, peanuts, and dried pepper flakes, to taste, stir, and **sauté** for 5 minutes for flavor to develop. Add chicken pieces with marinade juice and chicken broth to skillet, and reduce heat to **simmer**. Cover and cook until chicken is tender, 45 to 50 minutes. Test for **chicken doneness**.

3. Add palm oil. Adjust seasoning, adding more salt and pepper if desired. Cook for 3 to 5 minutes longer, turning chicken to coat both sides.

Serve with white rice and farofa de azeite de dendê *(recipe follows).*

A Brazilian meal would not be complete without some form of cassava or manioc meal. It is put into a *farinheira*, a sort of shaker, and sprinkled on meat, poultry, and vegetables at the table. Or it is made into a *farofa*, which is more elaborate. It is put in a bowl and spooned over the main course of almost every meal.

Farofa de Azeite de Dendê

Cassava Meal with Palm Oil

Yield: serves 6 to 8

2 cups **cassava** (manioc) meal (available at all Latin American food stores)
4 tablespoons palm oil (*dendê*) (available at all Latin American food stores)

Equipment: Large **heavy-based** skillet, wooden mixing spoon, serving bowl

1. In a large heavy-based skillet over low heat, toast cassava meal until it begins to turn very pale tan, 15 to 20 minutes. Stir frequently so the meal does not burn.

2. Stir in palm oil and cook until it is well blended, and the mixture is bright yellow.

To serve, transfer to serving bowl. To eat, spoon a desired amount over each serving of xinxim de galinha *or with any meat or other poultry dish.*

PARAGUAY

Paraguay is a small landlocked country centrally located in South America in between Bolivia, Brazil, and Argentina. Guarani-speaking Indians were the original inhabitants of the region, and Guarani is the most often-used language after Spanish. Spanish explorers penetrated the region in the sixteenth century, and Jesuits set up settlements in the next century. Paraguay revolted against Spanish rule in 1811 and declared itself a republic. Since independence, Paraguay has been troubled by wars and dictatorships, and internal strife has left Paraguay less developed than many of its South American neighbors.

The majority of the *mestizo* (part Spanish, part Indian) population are Roman Catholic, and life-cycle celebrations are celebrated according to the traditions of the Church. (See Protestant and Catholic Life-Cycle Rituals, page xlvi.) At birth, babies are baptized, but the first religious ceremony children actively participate in is the first communion. Around seven years old, children make their first confession to the priest to cleanse them in preparation for receiving their first communion.

When the child is baptized, the family observes the happy occasion with a meal for relatives and friends. The celebration begins when everyone relaxes and takes a sip of the *yerba maté* as it is passed around. The meal begins when large bowls or baskets of freshly baked *sopa Paraguaya* (recipe page 400) are set out for guests to munch on while eating their thick soup of either *so'o-yosopy* (recipe follows) or *caldo de zapallo tierno* (recipe page 400). Along with the filling soup, there are always beans and rice and perhaps a chicken dish, such as *arroz con pollo* (recipe page 414). For first communion, no pecial celebration is observed, other than a family dinner.

As in much of Latin America, when a girl reaches 15 years of age in Paraguay, she takes part in *quinceañera*, a party to introduce her into womanhood. The party can be quite expensive, and families often go heavily in debt to give their daughter a beautiful *quinceañera*.

Wedding ceremonies take place in a church, followed by a *fiesta* either in a local hall or the bride's home. Musicians are plentiful in Paraguay, and small ensembles of three or four are easily available for weddings and other life-cycle celebrations. Many people prefer traditional folk music played on the Paraguayan harp and guitars over the modern music of today.

Funerals are solemn affairs and accompanied by specific songs and chants. The family holds a wake, in which the body is laid out, either in the home or church. After 24 hours the body is carried to the cemetery by a hearse or on the shoulders of male family members and friends. A funeral feast is held at the home of the deceased after the burial.

Paraguayans speak two languages, Spanish and Guarani. *So'o-yosopy* is the Guarani name for *sopa de carne* (beef soup). A superstition in Paraguay holds that if anyone who doesn't enjoy cooking is in the kitchen while *so'o-yosopy* is cooking on the stove, the soup will separate and spoil. ۞ ۞ ۞

So'O-Yosopy

Beef Soup

Yield: serves 6

- 2 pounds lean **ground** beef
- 8 cups water, divided
- 2 tablespoons vegetable oil
- 2 onions, **finely chopped**
- 1 green bell pepper, **trimmed**, seeded, and finely chopped
- 4 tomatoes, **peeled** and chopped
- ½ cup white rice
- grated Parmesan cheese, for serving

Equipment: Food processor, rubber spatula, large skillet, mixing spoon, large saucepan with cover, ladle, individual soup bowls

1. Put ground meat in food processor, add 1 cup water, and process until mashed and smooth, 2 to 3 minutes. Set aside.

Note: While processing, turn machine off once or twice and scrape down sides of container with rubber spatula.

2. Heat oil in large skillet over medium-high heat. Add onions and peppers, stir, and **sauté** until soft, 3 to 5 minutes. Reduce heat to medium, add tomatoes, stir, and cook until mixture is thick and well blended, 5 to 7 minutes. Cool slightly.

3. Transfer mashed beef and its juices to large saucepan. Stir in sautéed onion mixture. Add remaining 7 cups water, stir, and bring to a boil over medium-high heat. Reduce heat to **simmer**, add rice, and stir. Cover and cook until rice is tender, 20 to 25 minutes.

To serve, ladle into individual soup bowls and sprinkle each serving with Parmesan cheese.

In Paraguay, *yerba mate* is known as Paraguayan tea, a popular ceremonial drink. It is made from *yerba* leaves that are dried in an outdoor oven and pounded into a powder that is mixed with water. It is traditionally drunk from a *maté*, a vessel made from a vegetable gourd or cow horn, and sipped through a *bombilla*, a sort of metal or wooden drinking straw with a filter. The drink can be either hot or cold. On social occasions, such as a wedding, the silver-trimmed *maté* is passed around and everyone has a sip from the same silver *bombilla*.

Soups are very popular in Paraguay and are served at most life-cycle parties. *Caldo de zapallo tierno* is easy to make and inexpensive. When a large crowd is expected at a first communion party, a large batch of *caldo de zapallo tierno* can feed them cheaply.

Caldo de Zapallo Tierno

Zucchini Soup

Yield: serves 6

2 tablespoons vegetable oil
1 onion, **finely chopped**
1 clove garlic, finely chopped
5 cups chicken broth, homemade (recipe page 106), or canned
3 tablespoons raw rice
1 pound zucchini, grated
salt and pepper to taste
1 egg
3 tablespoons grated Parmesan cheese, for **garnish**
1 tablespoon parsley, finely chopped

Equipment: Large saucepan with cover, mixing spoon, small bowl, whisk, ladle, individual soup bowls

1. Heat oil in large saucepan over medium-high heat, and add onions and garlic. Stir and **sauté** until onions are soft, 3 to 5 minutes. Add chicken broth and rice, and reduce heat to **simmer**. Stir, cover, and cook for 10 minutes. Add zucchini, stir, and continue to simmer until zucchini is very tender, about 10 to 15 minutes. Add salt and pepper to taste.

2. Just before serving, beat egg with cheese and parsley in small bowl, and whisk into soup.

To serve, ladle soup into individual soup bowls to eat as the first course at a family dinner.

The following recipe is called *sopa* (soup), but its really a wonderful, hearty corn bread made with two kinds of cheese. It is traditionally served with *so'o-yosopy* (recipe page 399).

Sopa Paraguaya

Paraguayan Corn Bread

Yield: serves 6 to 8

8 tablespoons butter or margarine, at room temperature, divided
2 onions, **finely chopped**
½ pound cottage cheese
½ pound Münster cheese, grated
2 cups cornmeal
16 ounces canned cream-style corn
1 teaspoon salt
1 cup milk
6 **eggs, separated**

Equipment: Large skillet, food processor, rubber spatula, large mixing bowl, medium mixing bowl, **whisk,** greased and floured 10- x 13- x 2½-inch baking pan, oven mitts, toothpick

1. Heat 4 tablespoons butter or margarine in large skillet over medium-high heat. Add onions and **sauté** until soft, 3 to 5 minutes. Remove from heat and set aside.

2. In food processor, combine remaining 4 tablespoons butter or margarine and cottage cheese, and process until thoroughly blended, about 1 minute. Add grated Münster cheese, onions, cornmeal, cream-style corn, salt, milk, and egg yolks. Process about 1 minute to mix thoroughly but still retaining some texture. Transfer to large mixing bowl.

Note: While processing, turn machine off once or twice and scrape down sides of container with rubber spatula.

Preheat 375° F.

3. In medium mixing bowl, using whisk, beat egg whites until soft peaks form. Using rubber spatula, **fold in** egg whites, a little at a time, to cornmeal mixture. Pour batter into prepared 10- x 13- x 2½-inch baking pan.

4. Bake in oven for 45 to 55 minutes, or until toothpick inserted into center comes out clean.

To serve, cut into squares while still warm and keep covered with a cloth napkin to maintain freshness and warmth. Serve at once.

PERU

Peru is on the west coast of South America, bordered on the north by Colombia and Ecuador, on the east by Brazil and Bolivia, and on the south by Chile. It is a land of cold and rugged mountain regions; vast deserts; hot, humid plains; and jungles.

Peru was once part of the Inca empire until the Incas were conquered by the Spaniard Francisco Pizarro in 1533. Spain remained in control until 1824, making Peru a vice royalty, the seat of government.

Although the majority of Peruvians are Roman Catholics and follow all life-cycle rituals according to traditions of the Church (see Protestant and Catholic Life-Cycle Rituals, page xlvi), the people are as varied as the land. They range from wealthy descendants of Spanish landowners to pure-blooded Indians following the same customs and rituals practiced by their Inca ancestors. Most Inca descendants live in isolated mountain regions. In the Amazon region of Peru, other Indians live the same traditional lifestyle their ancestors did thousands of years ago. Most Indians, though, except for the most isolated tribes, combine Catholic rituals with their traditional practices.

Traditional wedding customs are gradually changing, especially in urban areas. Couples are mostly free to select their own marriage partner. In the past, marrying without parental approval was unacceptable. For a marriage to be legal, the law requires a civil service at city hall. All Catholic weddings are held in a church a few days after the civil ceremony.

It is customary for the wedding reception to follow the religious church ceremony. Depending upon the family's wealth, the reception can be a grand affair in a hotel ballroom or a small family supper. Or it can be a gathering of friends and relatives for a *pachamanca*, which means "earth oven," referring to an ancient way of cooking food over heated stones, like a pit barbecue. The centerpiece of the feast is either *lechoncito asado* (suckling pig, see Cuban recipe page 383) or *cabrito* (kid goat). Baked in the pit along with the pig and/or goat are *cuy* (guinea pig), chickens, and other meats depending upon the number of guests and budget. Both sweet and white potatoes, ears of corn, and other vegetables as well as tamales are cooked along with the meat. After the pit is filled with the food, it is sealed with earth and the top is decorated with flowers and greenery. The cooking begins early in the morning, and by late afternoon when guests begin arriving, the food is almost ready to eat. The guests work up an appetite singing and dancing and entertaining the newlyweds. A good time is had by all.

Potatoes are one of Peru's most valued crops. This traditional potato dish would be delicious to serve at life-cycle celebrations.

Ocopa à l'Arequipeña

Potatoes and Shrimp with Peanut Sauce

Yield: serves 6

- 4 to 5 medium potatoes, peeled and thinly sliced
- water, as needed
- salt and pepper to taste
- 1 cup peanut butter (either smooth or chunky)
- 1 cup milk
- 1 cup **finely chopped** onions

2 cloves garlic, finely chopped
¼ teaspoon **ground** red pepper, more or less to taste
½ teaspoon ground oregano
1 pound (31-35 count) medium shrimp, cooked, **peeled, and deveined**
½ pound grated mild cheddar cheese, divided

Equipment: Medium saucepan, **colander**, food processor, rubber spatula, large mixing bowl, buttered ovenproof medium casserole, oven mitts

1. Put the sliced potatoes in medium saucepan, and cover generously with water. Add ½ teaspoon salt and bring water to boil. Reduce heat to **simmer** for 7 to 10 minutes, until almost tender. Drain in colander and set aside.

2. Put peanut butter, milk, onions, garlic, ¼ teaspoon ground red pepper, more or less to taste, and oregano in food processor, and process, about 1 minute.

Note: While processing, turn machine off once or twice and scrape down sides of container with rubber spatula.

Preheat oven to 350° F.

3. Put potato slices and shrimp in large mixing bowl. Add peanut butter sauce and ¼ pound of the grated cheese. Using your hands, gently toss to coat. Transfer to buttered ovenproof medium casserole, smooth top, and sprinkle with remaining grated cheese.

4. Bake in oven for 15 to 20 minutes, until potatoes are soft and top is golden brown.

Serve either hot or at room temperature, from casserole.

The nuns in Latin American countries are known for making delicious candies and pastries. The tradition was brought by the first nuns arriving around 1600. The nuns sell the cakes and *dulces* (sweets) to support charity schools for girls.

In Lima, the capital of Peru, it is considered good luck for a bride to have her wedding cake made by the nuns. The recipe that follows for a cake made with fillings of pineapple and caramelized, sweetened condensed milk is a typical Peruvian treat. The recipe can easily be doubled or tripled to serve more people.

Alfajor de Huaura

Peruvian Pineapple Layer Cake

Yield: serves 10
2 (15-ounces each) cans sweetened condensed milk, for filling
2 teaspoons vanilla extract, divided
3 eggs
1 cup granulated sugar
½ cup water
¾ cup all-purpose flour
1 teaspoon baking powder
½ teaspoon salt
confectioners' sugar, as needed
16 ounces canned crushed pineapple, well drained
1 sweet potato, baked, peeled, and mashed
½ cup sugar

Equipment: Deep saucepan, tongs, can opener, rubber spatula, small bowl with cover, small saucepan, aluminum foil, mixing spoon, 15½- x 10½- x 1-inch jelly-roll pan, medium mixing bowl, electric mixer (optional), small bowl, oven mitts, toothpick, paring knife, clean kitchen towel, work surface, serving platter, cake knife

1. Prepare caramelized milk filling: Place 2 unopened cans sweetened condensed milk in deep saucepan, cover generously with water, and bring water to boil. Reduce heat to **simmer** and cook for 3 hours. (The sweetened condensed milk thickens to a caramel-like substance when heated in the can.) Using tongs, remove cans from water and cool enough to handle. Open cans and transfer caramelized milk to small bowl.

Add 1 teaspoon vanilla extract and stir well. Cover and refrigerate until ready to use.

2. Prepare pineapple filling: Put mashed sweet potato, drained crushed pineapple, and ½ cup sugar, more or less to taste, in small saucepan. Stir and heat through over medium heat, for flavor to develop, 5 to 7 minutes. Cool to room temperature, cover with foil, and refrigerate until ready to use.

3. To prepare baking pan: Line jelly-roll pan with piece of foil and generously grease with butter or margarine. Set aside.

Preheat oven to 350° F.

4. Prepare cake: Put eggs in medium mixing bowl, and using electric mixer or mixing spoon, beat until thick and bright yellow, 3 to 5 minutes. Beating constantly, add granulated sugar, a little at a time. Beat in water and vanilla extract until well mixed.

5. In a small bowl, mix flour, baking powder, and salt. Add flour mixture to egg mixture, a little at a time, and beat just until smooth. Pour batter into prepared jelly-roll pan and smooth out, using rubber spatula.

6. Bake in oven until toothpick inserted in center comes out clean, 12 to 15 minutes. Immediately loosen cake from sides of pan by running a paring knife around edge of cake.

7. Place clean towel on work surface and sprinkle generously with confectioners' sugar. Carefully flip cake over onto towel and remove and discard foil. Using paring knife, **trim** edges of cake, if necessary, to make them even and smooth.

8. Assemble cake: Cut cake into 4 rectangles, 10½ x 3¾ inches each. Place one piece on serving platter. Alternate using the two fillings with the layers of cake, leaving top and sides of cake plain. Sprinkle confectioners' sugar over top and sides of cake.

To serve, cut cake crosswise into slices about 1 inch thick.

ECUADOR

The name Ecuador means equator in Spanish, which is appropriate since the equator runs through the center of this country in the northwestern part of South America. The Pacific coastline forms one border, and Colombia and Peru the others.

By the time the Spanish arrived in the sixteenth century, the Inca empire had absorbed and conquered the Kingdom of Quito, which had flourished around A.D. 1000. Spain ruled the area until 1824, when, after a 14-year struggle, Ecuador joined Venezuela, Colombia, and Panama in a confederacy known as Greater Colombia. This union fell apart in 1830, and Ecuador became independent.

Today, the population is made up of *mestizos* (mixed Spanish and Indian), Indians, and people of Spanish descent. Almost all Ecuadorians are Roman Catholics and celebrate life-cycle events prescribed by the Church, with certain local touches added. (See Protestant and Catholic Life-Cycle Rituals, page xlvi.)

When Ecudorian Indians marry, they combine old local customs with those of the Catholic Church. On the night prior to the wedding day, *las cosas de mediano* (wedding food) is carried by the groom to the home of his bride. The food usually includes cooked guinea pigs and *pollo en salsa de huevos* (recipe page 405), baskets of bread, ears of corn, peeled potatoes with sauce, hard-cooked eggs, and bottles of rum. The two fathers say a blessing over the bride and groom, and then they bless the food.

Catholic weddings must always be held in a church. However, because of the cost of a church ceremony, it is not uncommon for *mestizos* to have a less expensive civil ceremony with a *maytro* (master of ceremonies) officiating. Most couples will add a few Catholic rituals to their civil ceremony. A ritual popular among most Hispanic Catholics is draping the long rosary over the shoulders of the kneeling bride and groom. In a church, the godparents perform the ritual, but in some Indian communities the *maytro* places the rosary around the newlyweds. After the placement of the rosary, more blessing are bestowed upon the couple, they exchange rings, and they declare their undying devotion to one another.

Most Ecuadorians live on soups and thick stews of beans and corn with other vegetables. For special happy occasions, such as a baptism or wedding, the least expensive and most available meat is *cuy* (guinea pig); it would be used in this recipe. We suggest using regular pork instead. ۞ ۞ ۞

Puerco Horneado

Ecuador Pork Roast

Note: This recipe takes over 8 hours.

Yield: serves 4 to 6

- 2 ¾- to 3-pound **oven-ready** pork loin, boned, rolled, and tied (available at most butcher shops and supermarkets)
- ½ teaspoon salt, more as needed, divided
- 3 cloves garlic, **finely chopped,** or 1 teaspoon garlic granules
- 1 teaspoon **ground** marjoram, divided
- 3 fresh basil leaves, finely chopped, or 1 teaspoon crushed basil
- 1 teaspoon ground cumin, divided
- ½ teaspoon ground red pepper, more or less to taste
- 3 cups boiling water, more if needed
- 2 tablespoons all-purpose flour
- 1 tablespoon wine vinegar
- 3 tablespoons cold water
- 1 teaspoon dried parsley flakes

Equipment: Small bowl, mixing spoon, plastic food wrap, medium roasting pan with wire rack, oven mitts, meat **thermometer** (optional), **bulb baster** or mixing spoon, small serving bowl, spoon, meat knife

1. In small bowl, combine ½ teaspoon salt, garlic, ½ teaspoon marjoram, basil, ½ teaspoon cumin, and ½ teaspoon ground red pepper, more or less to taste. Rub mixture on meat. Wrap meat in plastic wrap and refrigerate for 8 hours or overnight.

Preheat oven to 450° F.

2. Remove plastic wrap and place meat on rack in roasting pan. Bake in oven until browned, 10 to 15 minutes. Using oven mitts, remove from oven.

Reduce oven to 350° F.

3. Insert meat thermometer into center of meat if using one. Pour 3 cups boiling water around meat, and return to oven to bake, basting frequently with bulb baster or mixing spoon. Add more water if needed, bake until thermometer registers 170° F or for about 1 to 1 ½ hours. Remove from oven and allow to rest for 10 minutes before slicing.

4. Prepare sauce: Measure 2 cups greaseless pan drippings into a small saucepan. Whisk in flour, vinegar, 3 tablespoons water, remaining ½ teaspoon marjoram, basil, and remaining ½ teaspoon cumin. Cook, whisking constantly over medium-high heat until sauce thickens, 3 to 5 minutes. Stir in parsley flakes.

To serve, cut roast into ½-inch thick slices. Put gravy in small serving bowl and spoon over meat. Serve with medley of vegetables, such as squash, corn, and tomatoes.

This is a typical chicken dish in Ecuador where eggs are used often because they are a sign of fertility, good for wedding celebrations.

Pollo en Salsa de Huevos

Chicken in Egg Sauce

Yield: serves 4 to 6

- 1/4 cup vegetable oil
- 3 1/2 to 4 pound chicken, cut into serving pieces
- 1 large onion, **finely chopped**
- 1 clove garlic, finely chopped
- 1 tablespoon dry mustard
- salt and pepper to taste
- 2 cups chicken broth
- 6 hard-cooked eggs, finely chopped

Equipment: **Dutch oven** or large **heavy-based** skillet, mixing spoon, metal tongs, baking sheet, oven mitts, serving platter

1. Heat oil in Dutch oven or large heavy-based skillet over medium-high heat. **Sauté** chicken pieces, in batches, until golden on both sides, 7 to 12 minutes. Using metal tongs, transfer to baking sheet until all chicken pieces are cooked.

2. Sauté onions and garlic in the oil left over in Dutch oven or large skillet until onions are soft, 3 to 5 minutes. Reduce heat to medium, and stir in dry mustard and salt and pepper to taste.

3. Return chicken pieces to skillet or Dutch oven. Pour chicken broth over chicken, and bring to boil over medium-high heat. Reduce heat to **simmer**, cover, and cook for 45 to 55 minutes, until chicken is done. Test **chicken doneness.**

4. Transfer chicken to serving platter and keep warm. Increase heat to medium-high under sauce in Dutch oven or large skillet. Stir in chopped eggs and cook just long enough to slightly thicken the sauce, 3 to 5 minutes.

To serve, pour sauce over chicken. This dish is usually served with a side dish of rice or potatoes.

Being on the equator, Ecuador has 12 hours of sunshine all year round so that fruits and vegetables grow well. Because of their abundance, fruits and vegetables are an important part of the Ecuadorian diet.

Ensalada Mixta

Mixed Salad

Yield: serves 4

- *vinaigrette* (recipe follows)
- 2 cups chopped lettuce
- 2 hard-cooked eggs, chopped
- 2 cups cubed potatoes, cooked
- 2 cups green beans, cooked and cut into 1/2-inch pieces

Equipment: Large salad bowl, salad tools

1. Prepare *vinaigrette* (recipe follows), cover, and refrigerate until ready to serve.

2. In large salad bowl, combine lettuce, hard-cooked eggs, potatoes, and green beans. Using salad tools, toss to mix well.

3. Just before serving, pour dressing over mixed salad, and toss to coat well.

Serve at once with puerco horneado *(recipe page 404)*.

Vinaigrette

Oil and Vinegar Dressing

Yield: about 1/2 cup

- 2 tablespoons apple cider vinegar
- 2 tablespoons Dijon mustard
- 8 tablespoons olive oil
- salt and pepper to taste

Equipment: Small bowl with cover, fork

In small bowl, combine vinegar, mustard, olive oil, and salt and pepper to taste. Using a fork, beat until well blended. Cover and refrigerate.

Continue to use on ensalada de garbanzos *(recipe precedes: Step 3:).*

COLOMBIA

Located on the northwest corner of South America, Colombia is the only country on the continent to have coastlines on both the Atlantic and Pacific Oceans. It is bordered by Panama on the northwest, on the east by Venezuela and Brazil, and on the southwest by Peru and Ecuador.

The Spanish conquered the area in the sixteenth century, but in contrast to countries such as Peru, little is known about the history of the indigenous population prior to the arrival of the Spanish. Colombia remained under Spanish control until 1824 when the country joined with Venezuela, Ecuador, and Panama to form the Republic of Greater Colombia. Venezuela and Ecuador formed their own countries soon after, and Panama declared its independence in 1903 when Colombia refused to ratify the lease granting the United States rights to dig the Panama Canal.

Currently, Colombia's population is a diverse group, including *mestizos* (mixed Spanish and Indian), people of Spanish descent, mulattos (mixed white and black), black, mixed black-Indian, and Indians. The unifying force is the Catholic Church. Religious holidays and life-cycle events are observed according to strict religious guidelines. (See Protestant and Catholic Life-Cycle Rituals, page xlvi.)

In small villages and remote areas of the country, babies are often baptized by the midwife shortly after being born. This is done in case the infant should die during the fragile first days of its life. The baptism means the baby dies a Christian.

After baptism and first communion, confirmation is usual for young people between 12 and 15 years old. Confirmation takes a long time since the young people must study the Bible and make a commitment to the Catholic faith. For the confirmation ritual, the children make a circle around the Bishop as he puts a cross of holy oil on the forehead of each person and taps his hand on the cheek. The oil is a symbol that Christ lives and will forever be with the young person from that moment on. Tapping the cheek is a signal to wake up to the light of a new life through Jesus Christ. After the church service, families and friends of the confirmed children often join together to celebrate the happy occasion. This can be a dinner party in a restaurant or in someone's home. Today more and more families are opting for the more relaxing, less expensive outdoor gathering. After eating a picnic feast, parents loll around while the children play.

As far as foods for life-cycle celebrations, if the family can afford it, the most important events call for meat on the table. In the cities, especially Bogota, *sobrebarriga Bogotana* is prepared for baptisms, first communions, confirmations, and wedding feasts.

SOBREBARRIGA BOGOTANA

FLANK STEAK, BOGOTÁ-STYLE

Yield: serves 4 to 6

2 pounds flank steak with fat left on
1 onion, **finely chopped**
2 cloves garlic, finely chopped
2 tomatoes, chopped
2 or 3 parsley sprigs
½ teaspoon **ground** thyme
1 bay leaf
salt and pepper, to taste

6 cups canned beef broth
2 tablespoons butter or margarine, at room temperature
1 cup **fresh white bread crumbs**

Equipment: Large saucepan with cover, mixing spoon, fork, metal tongs or meat fork, paper towels, broiler pan with rack, small skillet, mixing spoon, oven mitts, meat fork and knife, strainer, serving bowl, serving platter

1. Put meat in large saucepan, add beef broth, onion, garlic, tomatoes, parsley, thyme, bay leaf, and salt and pepper to taste. Bring to boil over medium-high heat. Reduce heat to **simmer**, cover, and cook for 2 to 2½ hours, until fork tender.

Preheat oven to 350° F.

2. Lift out meat with metal tongs or meat fork, and pat dry with paper towels. Place meat, fat-side up, on rack of broiler pan. Save cooking liquid.

3. Melt butter or margarine in small skillet, add bread crumbs, and stir to coat well. Spoon buttered crumbs thickly onto surface of meat. Place in oven for 15 to 20 minutes until crumb coating is golden brown. Allow to rest for 20 minutes before cutting into ¼-inch thick slices and arranging on platter.

4. Reheat cooking liquid over medium heat. Strain into serving bowl and serve as gravy to spoon over meat.

Serve with papas chorreadas *(recipe follows) and salad.*

This marvelously rich potato dish goes well with flank steak. For the less fortunate, this recipe is often the main dish for life-cycle celebrations.

Papas Chorreadas

Potatoes with Cheese and Onion Sauce

Yield: serves 6
6 potatoes, scrubbed
2 tablespoons butter or margarine
1 onion, **finely chopped**
2 tomatoes, **peeled** and chopped
salt and pepper to taste
½ cup heavy cream
1 cup shredded Swiss or Monterey Jack cheese

Equipment: Large saucepan, knife, large skillet, mixing spoon, serving bowl

1. Peel and quarter potatoes and put into large saucepan. Cover generously with water and bring to boil over medium-high heat. Reduce heat to **simmer**, cover, and cook until very tender, 25 to 30 minutes. Drain and keep warm in serving bowl.

2. Melt butter or margarine in large skillet over medium-high heat. Add onion, stir, and **sauté** until soft, 3 to 5 minutes. Add tomatoes and salt and pepper to taste, and cook, stirring frequently, 5 to 7 minutes. Stir in heavy cream and cheese, until cheese is melted.

To serve, pour cheese and onion sauce over potatoes and eat while warm.

To complete the meal add a simple salad, such as *pico de gallo* (rooster's beak). Jicama, used in this salad, is a popular and tasty Latin American root vegetable. Buy jicama with smooth skin. The flesh inside should be moist and crunchy. Cut in half or quarter before using a vegetable peeler to remove the coarse skin. Jicama has a taste somewhere between a potato and apple. It is eaten both raw and cooked.

Pico de Gallo

Jicama Salad

Yield: serves 6

2 pounds jicama, peeled and **coarsely chopped** (available at all Latin food stores and most supermarkets)
4 navel oranges, peeled, **sectioned**, and coarsely chopped
salt, to taste
ground red pepper, to taste

Equipment: Medium salad bowl, salad tools, plastic food wrap

Put jicama and oranges in medium salad bowl, add salt, and ground red pepper to taste. Using salad tools, toss to mix. Cover with plastic wrap and refrigerate until ready to serve.

Serve salad cold as a refreshing side dish with sobrebarriga bogotana *(recipe page 406).*

VENEZUELA

Occupying most of the northern coast of South America, Venezuela is bordered by Colombia on the west, Guyana on the east, and Brazil on the south. Originally inhabited by the Arawak and Carib Indians, Venezuela was one of the first sites of European contact on the continent, explored by Columbus on his third voyage in 1498. Venezuela remained under Spanish control until the nineteenth century when it joined with Colombia and Ecuador to form the Greater Republic of Colombia, which lasted until 1830.

Today, Venezuela is one of the most prosperous countries in South America. The population consists of several different ethnic groups, including *mestizos* (mixed Spanish and Indians), Europeans, Africans, and Indians, but they are unified by their language, Spanish, and their religion, Roman Catholicism. Venezuelans generally follow the life-cycle traditions of the Catholic Church. (See Protestant and Catholic Life-Cycle Rituals, page xlvi.)

One of the unique Latin American life-cycle events is also celebrated in Venezuela. When girls turn 15, they have a *quinceañera*, or a special 15th birthday party. The ritual, a form of debutante or "coming out" ball, announces that the birthday girl is now a woman and ready to join the social world. The expense of the party varies according to the family's wealth. Families are known to go into debt for years to pay off the expense of a *quinceañera* party.

Weddings in Venezuela are often grand affairs. When families can afford it, they invite thousands of people and spare no expense to give their daughter a beautiful send-off. It is considered good luck for the bride and groom to sneak away from the wedding reception shortly after it begins without anyone seeing them leave.

A Venezuelan wedding feast would probably begin with bowls of *caviar criollo* (recipe follows) that they spread on *arepas* (recipe page 410) and a soup such as *sopa de chayote* (recipe 416), several salads, including *ensalada mixta* (recipe page 405). Beef is popular throughout South America, and the tender, lean and economical flank steak (*sobrebarriga*) is a special favorite.The highlight of the wedding reception is the table laden with sweets—the wedding cake; puddings, such as *dulce de leche* (recipe page 392); and fresh fruits and assorted candies, such as *cejeta de leche* (recipe page 415).

Although *pabellón caraqueño* is well-liked throughout South America, some Venezuelans think of it as their national dish. The way the plantains, black beans, rice, and meat are placed on the platter is said to resemble a striped flag (*pabellón*), similar to the Venezuelan flag. A simpler dish made with black beans is this recipe for *caviar criollo*. The word *Criollo* means Creole, which is a person originally of Spanish ancestry born in the New World and looked upon as a native Venezuelan. ۞ ۞ ۞

CAVIAR CRIOLLO

CREOLE CAVIAR

Yield: serves 6

1 cup dried black beans
water, as needed
5 tablespoons olive oil
1 onion, **coarsely chopped**
dried red chili flakes, to taste
3 cloves garlic, **finely chopped**
2 teaspoons **ground** cumin
salt, to taste

Equipment: Medium saucepan with cover, mixing spoon, large skillet, strainer, small serving bowl

1. Put beans in medium saucepan and cover generously with water. Bring to boil over medium-high heat. Reduce heat to **simmer**, cover, and cook about 1 hour or until tender. Drain well in strainer.

2. Heat 2 tablespoons oil in large skillet over medium-high heat, and add onion. Stir and **sauté** until soft, 3 to 5 minutes. Add red pepper flakes to taste, garlic, and cumin. Stir and cook for 2 minutes. Add drained beans, remaining 3 tablespoons oil, and salt to taste. Stir and cook to heat through.

To serve, transfer to small serving bowl and serve as side dish with chicken or grilled beef.

Venezuelans love cocktail nibbles and when *cachapas de jojoto* are made small and wrapped around a piece of cheese they become an ideal appetizer. These pancakes are often eaten instead of bread at a dinner party.

CACHAPAS DE JOJOTO

CORN PANCAKES

Yield: makes about 12

1½ cups corn kernels, if frozen thaw thoroughly
½ cup heavy cream
1 egg
3 tablespoons all-purpose flour
¼ teaspoon sugar
½ teaspoon salt
2 tablespoons melted butter or margarine
vegetable oil, as needed for frying
½ pound *queso blanco*, Münster, or Monterey Jack cheese, cut into 12 pieces about ¼ x 1½ inches long, for serving

Equipment: Electric **blender**, rubber spatula, large **heavy-based** skillet, metal spatula, baking sheet, paring knife, cloth napkin or serving platter

1. Put corn kernels, cream, egg, flour, sugar, salt, and melted butter or margarine in blender. Cover and **blend** until smooth, 1 to 2 minutes. Turn off blender once or twice and use rubber spatula to scrape down side of container.

2. Heat 2 tablespoons oil in large heavy-based skillet over medium-high heat. For each pancake, spoon out 2 tablespoons batter to make them about 1½ inches in diameter. Don't crowd the pan. Cook in batches, until lightly browned, 3 to 5 minutes each side, turning once using metal spatula. Keep on baking sheet in warm oven.

To serve as bread substitute, wrap in a napkin and serve warm. To serve as an appetizer, wrap each pancake around a piece of cheese and arrange them on a platter. Serve at once while still warm.

The *arepas* are a type of corn bread made from specially processed flour made from pre-cooked corn. It is not the same as the Mexican flour called *mesa*. *Arepas* flour is available at Latin American food stores.

Arepas

Venezuelan Corn Bread

Yield: makes 8 to 10

2 cups *arepas* corn flour (see above)
1 teaspoon salt
2 cups water, more or less as needed
oil, for frying

Equipment: Large mixing bowl, mixing spoon, large **heavy-based** griddle or skillet, metal spatula, baking sheet, oven mitts

1. Put flour and salt in large mixing bowl, and stir in about 2 cups water, a little at a time, to make a stiff dough. Let the dough rest for 5 minutes, then form into 8 to 10 balls flattened slightly to 3 inches across and about ½ inch thick.

Preheat oven to 350° F.

2. Prepare to fry: Put baking sheet into the preheated oven. Spread about ½ tablespoon oil over large heavy-based griddle or skillet to lightly coat surface. Over medium heat, cook breads, in batches, 5 minutes per side. Transfer to baking sheet in oven and continue to bake for 20 to 30 minutes, turning them with spatula 2 or 3 times during baking to lightly brown all sides.

To serve, split the warm bread open and spread butter or margarine on both sides. Some people pull out and discard the inside dough with their fingers, and they butter the remaining crispy crust.

GUYANA

Guyana is located on the northeast coast of South America, just above the equator. It is east of Venezuela, west of Suriname, and north of Brazil.

Unlike most of Latin America, Guyana was not colonized by the Spanish or the Portuguese. France, Britain, and the Netherlands all established settlements in the area, but the majority of settlements were Dutch. The British took control of the region in 1831.

In 1834, slavery was outlawed, and to fill the labor shortage on sugarcane plantations, Hindu workers were brought from India as indentured workers. Today the population is pretty evenly split between people of African descent and people of East Indian descent. The East Indians live in close-knit communities and follow the traditional Hindu rituals and ceremonies of their homeland. (See India, page 296, and Hinduism and Hindu Life-Cycle Rituals, page li.)

When a Hindu dies, the body is cremated three days later. It is customary for the family to hold a memorial ceremony for the deceased, and relatives, friends, and villagers are expected to attend. The Hindu ceremony (*puja*) is held to help remember the soul of the deceased. An altar is made of a small banana tree and garlands of tropical flowers set on a mud base. The Hindu priest (*pundit*) lights fires in tiny clay bowls (*deyas*), and he also lights sandalwood incense sticks. The priest then puts a round, white finger marking, called *tikkas*, on everyone's forehead. He chants *mantras* (repeated prayers) and makes food offerings to the sacred fire on the altar.

A male relative of the deceased also sits on the altar with the priest. He makes offerings of milk, rice, and *ghee* (recipe page

285) to the sacred fire. Both men wear white ritual garments (*kurtas*).

After the priest finishes the *puja*, everyone present partakes of the feast. The meal consists of *rotis* with coconut (recipe follows), several rice dishes including *meeta pilau* (recipe page 298), a curry dish, and pumpkin. Mourners sit on floor mats, and the meal that has been placed on banana leaves is eaten with their fingers.

Rotis is one of several Indian flatbreads. Hindus in Guyana add coconut to *rotis* recipe, making it more exotic.

Rotis

Flatbread with Coconut

Yield: about 12 loaves

1 cup finely shredded coconut (available at East Indian food stores or Asian food stores and some supermarkets), or place shredded coconut in blender until finely ground
2¼ cups **self-rising flour**
1 to 1¼ cups cold water
vegetable oil, for pan frying

Equipment: Medium mixing bowl, mixing spoon, lightly floured work surface, clean kitchen towel, large **heavy-based** skillet or griddle, **pastry brush**, wide metal spatula, plate

1. In medium mixing bowl, combine coconut and flour. Add water, a little at a time, stirring constantly until dough is soft, smooth, and pulls away from sides of bowl. Transfer dough to lightly floured work surface. Cover with towel for 30 minutes.

2. Divide dough into 12 equal balls. Using your hands, flatten each ball into thin circles, about 5 inches across, on lightly floured work surface. Place finished *rotis* on work surface and keep covered with towel until ready to fry.

3. Heat large heavy-based skillet or griddle over medium-high heat. Using pastry brush, brush griddle or skillet with oil. Cook breads, in batches until both sides are golden, about 2 minutes on each side. Remove from griddle or skillet with wide metal spatula and transfer to plate to keep warm while cooking remaining loaves. Add more oil, when necessary to keep bread from sticking to skillet.

Serve rotis *while still warm for best flavor.* Rotis *are used to scoop food from the plate to one's mouth.*

Seafood is plentiful in Guyana, and a popular shrimp dish is *prawn bhaji*.

Prawn Bhaji

Curried Shrimp

Yield: serves 6

4 tablespoons vegetable oil
2 onions, **finely chopped**
1 clove garlic, finely chopped
½ teaspoon **ground** ginger
4 tomatoes, **peeled** and chopped
1 teaspoon salt
1 teaspoon curry powder
1 teaspoon vinegar
½ teaspoon ground red pepper, more or less to taste
½ teaspoon turmeric
1 cup water
2 pounds headless medium shrimp (31-35 pieces to a pound), **peeled and deveined**
6 cups white rice (cooked according to directions on package), kept warm for serving

Equipment: Large skillet, mixing spoon, **colander**, deep serving bowl

1. Heat oil in large skillet over medium-high heat. Add onions and garlic, and **sauté** until onions are soft, 3 to 5 minutes. Reduce heat to

medium, stir in ginger, tomatoes, vinegar, salt, ½ teaspoon ground red pepper, more or less to taste, curry powder, turmeric, and water. Stirring frequently, cook for 5 minutes for flavor to develop.

2. Put peeled and deveined shrimp in colander and rinse under cold running water. Drain well. Add drained shrimp to curry mixture. Stirring frequently, cook until shrimp become opaque, pinkish-white, and are fully cooked, 7 to 12 minutes.

To serve, put rice in deep serving bowl and spoon shrimp mixture over the top.

PANAMA

The southernmost country of Central America, Panama is the narrowest point between North and South America, which is why the isthmus was chosen for the Panama canal that links the Pacific and Atlantic Oceans. Costa Rica is to the north of Panama, and Colombia is to the South.

After European contact, Panama became a center for shipments to Central and South America. When Colombia revolted against Spain, Panama joined the Greater Republic of Colombia, which included Venezuela, Colombia, and Ecuador, but unlike Venezuela and Ecuador, Panama was unable to break away from Colombia. After Colombia refused to grant a lease to the United States for the building of the canal, Panama broke from Colombia with the support of the United States.

Because of Panama's position as an isthmus between two continents, Panama has a diverse population. Most people are *mestizos,* part Spanish and part Indian, but the population includes many blacks whose ancestors came from the West Indies to work on the Panama Canal, and people of European descent. Several different indigenous Indian groups live in Panama, including the two largest groups the Guaymí and Cuna.

The majority of Panamanians belong to the Roman Catholic Church and follow the life-cycle traditions of the Church (see Protestant and Catholic Life-Cycle Rituals, page xlvi), although many of the black inhabitants from the Caribbean are Protestant.

The Indian tribes have their own traditions that have survived the European conquest. The Cuna tribe, for example, are matrilineal, which means that the women own the land and the husband comes to live with the wife's family after a wedding. One of the many unique customs among the Cunas is the coming out party, *inna-nega.* Depending upon the wealth of the family, several hundred people may attend. The three-day celebration can cost the family years of savings. The occasion is one of great importance to the *Cuna* since the girl is now of child bearing age. During the ceremony she is given a permanent name and her hair is cut. Following the ceremony, a feast is held for family and friends which might include either a*rroz con pollo* (recipe page 414) or *pebellón caraqueño* (recipe follows) and side dishes of black beans (canned, cook according to directions on can, available at all supermarkets); hard-cooked eggs, a symbol of fruitfulness; and plantains, such as *piononos* (recipe page 384).

Regardless of ethnic or religious background, a wedding celebration is a grand affair in Panama. It calls for *pebellón caraqueño,* a dish made with flank steak, a meat Latin Americans hold in high esteem for its fine flavor. The dish is especially popular for weddings because hard-cooked eggs, as a symbol of fertility, are added to the dish.

Pebellón Caraqueño

Steak with Rice, Black Beans, and Plantains

Yield: serves 6

1½ pounds flank steak, cut into 2 or 3 pieces
5 cups canned beef broth
1 onion, **finely chopped**
1 clove garlic, finely chopped
2 tomatoes, **peeled** and chopped
salt to taste
2 tablespoons olive oil
6 cups cooked white rice (cook according to directions on package), kept warm for serving
6 hard-cooked eggs, peeled and quartered, for serving
4 cups canned black beans, drained, for serving
3 plantains or regular bananas, fried (recipe follows), for serving

Equipment: Large saucepan with cover, fork, mixing spoon, **colander**, food storage container with cover, large mixing bowl, large skillet, large platter

1. Put meat in large saucepan, add beef broth, and bring to boil over medium-high heat. Reduce heat to **simmer**, cover, and cook 1½ to 2 hours, until fork tender. Allow meat to cool in the broth. Drain broth in colander over food storage container, cover, and refrigerate for another use. Shred the meat with your fingers. In large mixing bowl, combine the meat with onion, garlic, and tomatoes. Add salt to taste.

2. Heat olive oil in skillet over medium-high heat. Add shredded meat mixture, stir, and **sauté** until onion is cooked and mixture is very dry, 7 to 12 minutes.

3. Fry plantains or bananas (recipe follows).

To serve, put rice in center of large platter and heap the meat mixture on top. Arrange quartered hard-cooked eggs on top of meat. Surround the rice with black beans and decorate the edge of the platter with fried plantains or bananas.

Fried Plantains or Bananas

Yield: serves 4 to 6

3 plantains or regular bananas
4 tablespoons vegetable oil

Equipment: Paring knife, large skillet, slotted spoon

1. Peel plantains and cut in half lengthwise, then cut crosswise into thirds. If using bananas, peel and cut into thirds.

2. Heat oil in large skillet over medium-high heat, and fry plantains or bananas until golden brown on both sides, 3 to 5 minutes.

Continue: Use for pebellón caraqueño *(recipe precedes).*

COSTA RICA

Costa Rica is a small country in Central America between Panama to the south and Nicaragua to the north. At the time of Columbus's arrival in 1502, over 25,000 Indians lived in the area, but they were wiped out by European diseases and conquests. Costa Rica remained under Spanish control until it gained its independence in 1821. Independence was shortlived as Mexico took the area over until 1848.

The population of Costa Rica is dominated by people of European descent and *mestizos* (mixed Spanish and Indian). The majority of Costa Ricans belong to the Roman Catholic Church and celebrate the life-cycle events prescribed by the Church. (See Protestant and Catholic Life-Cycle Rituals, page xlvi.)

The first important celebration is the *baptisma* (baptism), which takes place when the baby is six to eight weeks old. After the church service, everyone goes to the home of the parents to partake in a buffet. The buffet most often includes two salads, *arroz con pollo* (recipe follows), and a favorite cake from Nicaragua, *pastel de tres leches* (recipe page 418). A dessert made with corn, *tamal de elote* (recipe page 414), is another traditional dish served. In most Latin American countries, corn, a symbol of motherhood, is an important food at life-cycle celebrations.

First communion is another family event celebrated with a family feast. The celebration goes on all afternoon when friends gather for cake (called *queque* in Costa Rica) and ice cream and games, such as smashing the *piñata*.

For weddings, most couples marry in the church. The bride's parents are hosts for the occasion, which can include a party before and after the wedding day. For up to three days, guests have a good time eating, drinking, and dancing. When the newlyweds leave for their honeymoon, the guests finally go home.

Wedding cakes are either the same in Costa Rica as they are in the United States or they can be the *black wedding cake* (recipe page 360) of the Caribbean. They are very grand and elaborately decorated with the traditional wedding couple on top.

The traditional feast dish is *arroz con pollo*. It can be prepared many ways, but this favorite is easy and delicious.

Arroz con Pollo

Chicken and Rice

Yield: serves 6 to 8

- 3 cups white rice
- 1 onion, **finely chopped**
- 1 green bell pepper, **trimmed** and finely chopped
- 2½ to 3 pounds chicken, cut into serving-size pieces
- 4 cups water
- ½ cup carrots, finely chopped and **blanched**
- ½ cup string beans, sliced and blanched
- ½ cup raisins
- ½ cup frozen peas, thawed
- ½ cup pitted green olives, sliced
- 2 tablespoons vegetable oil
- salt and pepper to taste

Equipment: Large ovenproof saucepan with cover, oven mitts, serving bowl

Preheat oven to 350° F.

1. Sprinkle rice, onion, and bell pepper over bottom of large ovenproof saucepan. Set chicken pieces on top and add water. Cover saucepan.

2. Place in oven and bake for 45 minutes to 1 hour. Before the last 10 minutes of baking, using oven mitts, remove from oven, and uncover. Sprinkle in carrots, string beans, raisins, peas, and sliced green olives. Cover and return to oven to heat through and finish the remaining 10 minutes of baking. Test for **doneness** of chicken.

To serve, transfer mixture to serving bowl and serve as main meal for the family baptism party.

For people who are on a limited budget, as many Costa Ricans are, it is necessary to be creative when making food. Making a cake-like dessert with corn is unusual, delicious, and inexpensive.

Tamal de Elote

Corn Pudding

Yield: serves 8 to 10

- 12 ounces canned condensed milk
- 6 cups canned whole kernel corn, drained

3 eggs
1 cup melted butter or margarine
1 teaspoon **ground** cinnamon
whipped cream (optional)

Equipment: Electric **blender**, rubber spatula, greased 8-inch square cake pan, toothpick, oven mitts

Preheat oven to 350° F.

1. Combine condensed milk, corn, eggs, melted butter or margarine, and cinnamon in blender. **Blend** for 3 minutes, or until smooth. Using rubber spatula, transfer mixture to greased cake pan.

2. Bake in oven for 45 to 50 minutes, or until a toothpick inserted in center comes out clean.

Serve as a dessert at room temperature for best flavor. Some people add a dollop of whipped cream to each serving.

Candy is served at most life-cycle celebrations, and this easy-to-make fudge is a Costa Rican specialty.

Cejeta de Leche

Milk Fudge

Yield: about 15 balls
12 ounces canned condensed milk
1 cup powdered milk
1½ tablespoons butter or margarine
sliced almonds, macadamia nuts, or small pieces of candied fruit, for **garnish**

Equipment: Large mixing bowl, wooden mixing spoon, candy-size or mini paper cupcake cups, baking sheet, paring knife, small serving dish

1. In large mixing bowl, combine condensed milk, powdered milk, and butter or margarine. Stir until smooth.

2. Separate candy-size or mini paper cupcake cups onto baking sheet. Using your hands, form mixture into 1-inch balls and set each in a paper cup. With a knife, cut a cross on the top of each ball. In the center of the cross, place either a slice of almond, macadamia nut, or small piece of candied fruit.

To serve, arrange the candies, in paper cups, on a serving dish. Traditionally the balls were placed on lemon leaves to absorb the lemon flavor.

NICARAGUA

Nicaragua is the largest Central American country, but it is also the most sparsely populated. Costa Rica is to the south, and Honduras is to the north. The geography of the Pacific side of the country is dominated by two large lakes, Nicaragua and Manugua. First settled by the Spanish in 1522, Nicaragua won its independence in 1838.

The majority of people living in Nicaragua are *mestizos* (mixed Spanish and Indian). The remaining population are mostly pure Spaniards, blacks, and Indians whose ancestors lived in the area before the Spaniards arrived 400 years ago. Nicaraguans are predominantly Catholic, except for the people living along the Caribbean Sea region called the Mosquito Coast. There the inhabitants, who came from the British-settled islands of the Caribbean, speak English and most are Protestant.

Among the Catholics, religious holidays and life-cycle celebrations are observed according to Church doctrine. (See Protestant and Catholic Life-Cycle Rituals, page xlvi.) Birthdays or name days, baptisms, communions, weddings, and funerals are celebrated with a feast, complete with drinking, especially the popular celebration drink *pinollo*, made from cocoa beans.

Many celebration feasts include soup, such as *sopa de chayote*. When even a little meat or chicken is added to a dish it becomes a special festive treat. ۞ ۞ ۞

Sopa de Chayote

Chayote Soup

Yield: serves 6

2 large **chayotes**, peeled and sliced (available at all Latin-American food stores and many supermarkets)
water, as needed
salt and pepper to taste
2 tablespoons butter or margarine
1 onion, **finely chopped**
1 clove garlic, finely chopped
1 tablespoon all-purpose flour
4 cups chicken broth, homemade (recipe page 106), or canned
1 cup cooked and shredded chicken breast, for serving

Equipment: Large saucepan, slotted spoon, food processor, rubber spatula, mixing spoon, medium saucepan with cover, measuring cup, ladle, individual soup bowls

1. Put chayotes in large saucepan and cover generously with water. Add salt to taste and bring to boil over medium-high heat. Reduce heat to **simmer**, cover, and cook until tender, 15 to 20 minutes.

2. When tender, using slotted spoon, transfer chayotes to food processor. Measure 2 cups cooking liquid in measuring cup, add to chayote, and process until smooth. Discard any remaining cooking liquid.

Note: While processing, turn machine off once or twice and scrape down sides of container with rubber spatula.

3. Melt butter or margarine in medium saucepan over medium-high heat. Add onion and garlic, stir, and **sauté** until onion is soft, 3 to 5 minutes. Reduce heat to medium, stir in flour, and cook, stirring constantly, for 1 minute. Stir in chicken broth until mixture is smooth.

4. Stir processed chayote mixture into chicken broth. Add salt and pepper to taste. Add chicken, stir, cover, and cook until heated through, 5 to 7 minutes.

To serve, ladle into individual soup bowls. Eat as the first course for a confirmation party or wedding reception.

Most life-cycle meals include *nacatamales*, a plate-size tamale, that is considered the national dish of Nicaragua. In Nicaragua, *nacatamales* are wrapped in banana leaves that have been simmered in boiling water for about 10 minutes to soften. The banana leaves are placed on cooking parchment, wrapped tightly to make waterproof, and tied with string. This recipe uses foil for each package instead.

Nacatamales

Nicaraguan Tamales

Yield: serves 12

2 cups distilled white vinegar, divided
3 tablespoons paprika
1½ teaspoons dried oregano leaves
3 cloves garlic, **finely chopped**
1 teaspoon **ground** cumin
1 cup orange juice
½ cup lime juice
3 pounds **boned** pork shoulder or butt, cut into 1- x 2-inch chunks
2½ cups long grain rice
masa (recipe follows)
2½ pounds (about 6) potatoes, peeled and sliced crosswise into ¼-inch thick circles and each circle cut in half
12 canned hot yellow chili peppers, drained (available at all Latin American food stores and some supermarkets)
12 pitted prunes

72 (2 cups) small pimiento-stuffed, Spanish-style olives
¾ cup seedless raisins
salt and pepper to taste
3 cups fresh mint leaves, lightly packed, rinsed, and drained
2 large onions, **trimmed** and *each* sliced into 6 (¼-inch thick) circles
2 green bell peppers, trimmed, seeded, and *each* sliced into 6 (¼-inch thick) rings
2 large tomatoes, trimmed and *each* sliced into 6 (¼-inch thick) circles

Equipment: Small bowl, mixing spoon, large resealable plastic bag, medium bowl, strainer, 12 pieces (12 x 18 inches each) aluminum foil, work surface, large saucepan with cover, heatproof plate, slotted metal spoon or metal tongs, plate

1. Prepare **marinade**: In small bowl, combine ½ cup vinegar, paprika, oregano, garlic, and cumin. Stir to mix well. Transfer paprika mixture to large resealable plastic bag, and add remaining 1½ cups vinegar, orange juice, and lime juice. Close bag and shake to mix well. Add meat chunks, close bag, and shake to coat meat with marinade. Refrigerate overnight. Turn bag several times to coat meat well.

2. Soak rice: Put rice in medium bowl, cover with water by 1 inch, and set aside to soak at least 8 hours or overnight. Drain in strainer.

3. Prepare *masa* (recipe follows).

4. Prepare to assemble: Put 1 piece foil on work surface. Spoon ¾ cup *masa* onto center of foil. Pat to flatten slightly. Poke 1 chili pepper, 1 prune, and 6 olives into the *masa*, and cover with ¼ cup rice. Top with 1 tablespoon raisins. Place 5 or 6 potato slices around edge of *masa*. Sprinkle with salt and pepper to taste.

5. Using slotted spoon or tongs, divide marinated pork into 12 equal portions. Set portions on baking sheet. Place one portion of meat on top of rice, and spoon 1 tablespoon marinade onto meat. Discard remaining marinade. Place 3 or 4 mint leaves on meat. Stack 1 slice *each* of onion, bell pepper, and tomato on top of each mint leaf.

6. Carefully enclose filling and fold foil edges together to seal in the ingredients and make the tamale wrap waterproof. Repeat assembling remaining tamale wraps.

7. Stack tamale wraps in large saucepan. Put a heatproof plate on top to keep tamale wraps from floating. Fill pan with enough water to cover tamale wraps. Bring water to boil over medium-high heat, and cook for 45 minutes. Add more hot water, when necessary, to keep tamale wraps immersed. Reduce heat to **simmer**, cover pan, and cook for 1 hour more. Check water level frequently, adding more when necessary to keep the tamale wraps covered.

8. Remove tamale wraps with slotted metal spoon or metal tongs, and drain well.

To serve, place each nacatamal *on a plate, with the seam side up. Guests get a packaged tamale wrap, which they open and eat while the contents are still warm.*

Masa for Nacatamales

Yield: serves 12
1¾ pounds russet potatoes, peeled, quartered, and boiled until tender, 15 to 20 minutes
1 cup vegetable oil
2 onions, **trimmed** and finely chopped
6 cloves garlic, **finely chopped**
4 cups corn *tortilla* flour (also called dehydrated *masa* flour) (available at all Latin American food store and most supermarkets)
2 cups beef broth or water
salt and pepper to taste

Equipment: Potato masher, large skillet, mixing spoon, food processor, medium bowl, rubber spatula, large bowl

1. Drain potatoes and mash, using potato masher

2. Heat oil in large skillet over medium-high heat. Add onions and garlic, stir, and reduce heat to medium. Fry, stirring frequently, until onions are very brown, 20 to 30 minutes.

3. Put mashed potatoes in food processor, add fried onion mixture, pan drippings, *tortilla* flour, and beef broth or water. Add salt and pepper to taste. Process until well mixed, 1 to 2 minutes. Transfer to medium bowl.

Note: While processing, turn machine off once or twice and scrape down sides of container with rubber spatula.

Continue: Use for nacatamales *(recipe precedes: step 2. Prepare to assemble).*

A special-occasion cake popular throughout Latin America is *pastel de tres leches* (For short it is called *tres leches*) three milks cake. It seems the cake originated in Nicaragua, but it also has become a favorite children's birthday cake in Mexico.

Pastel de Tres Leches

Three Milks Cake

Yield: serves 18 to 20

1 ½ cups all-purpose flour
2 teaspoons baking powder
4 **eggs, separated**
½ cup milk
1 ½ cups sugar
12 ounces canned evaporated milk, for topping
14 ounces canned sweetened condensed milk, for topping
2 cups heavy cream, for topping
meringue frosting (recipe follows)

Equipment: Flour **sifter**, small mixing bowl, large mixing bowl, whisk, medium mixing bowl with electric mixer or whisk, rubber spatula, greased and floured 13- x 9- x 2½-inch baking pan, oven mitts, medium bowl, mixing spoon, wire cake rack, fork or skewer, metal icing spatula, **cake knife**

Preheat oven to 350° F.

1. **Sift** flour with baking powder into small mixing bowl.

2. Put egg yolks and milk in large mixing bowl, and using a whisk, **blend** well. Whisk in flour mixture, a little at a time, to form a smooth batter.

3. In medium mixing bowl with electric mixer with clean beaters or whisk, beat egg whites until **frothy**. Add sugar, a little at a time, beating to form stiff peaks.

4. Using rubber spatula, **fold in** egg whites. Pour batter into prepared baking pan.

Bake in oven until edges are golden brown, about 45 minutes. Remove from oven and let cool on wire cake rack.

5. Prepare topping: In medium bowl, stir together evaporated milk, sweetened condensed milk, and heavy cream. Using the fork or skewer, poke holes about 1-inch apart into cake. Pour milk mixture over cake and let sit until all the milk is absorbed into the cake holes, about 30 minutes.

6. Prepare meringue frosting. Using metal icing spatula, spread frosting over top of cake, and refrigerate until ready to serve.

To serve, cut cake into squares.

Meringue Frosting

½ cup water
1 cup sugar
3 **egg whites**

Equipment: Medium saucepan, wooden spoon, electric mixer or large mixing bowl and mixing spoon, whisk

1. In medium saucepan, bring water and sugar to a boil over low heat, stirring frequently with wooden spoon. When syrup forms a fine thread when the spoon is lifted from the mixture, remove from heat.

2. In electric mixer or mixing bowl and whisk, beat egg whites to stiff peaks. Continue beating whites, and slowly pour in sugar syrup. Beat until meringue holds stiff peaks. The meringue will stay fresh, if covered, for up to 2 days in the refrigerator.

Continue: Use as frosting on three milk cake (recipe precedes: Step 6.).

HONDURAS

The second largest country in Central America, Honduras has a relatively long Caribbean coastline (400 miles) and a short Pacific coastline (40 miles). It is bordered by Nicaragua on the southeast, El Salvador on the south, and Guatemala to the west.

At one time, the region was part of the Mayan empire, and descendants of this ancient civilization live in Honduras today. Explored by Columbus on his last voyage in 1502, Honduras remained under Spanish control until 1821, when it joined a federation of Central American states. In 1838, Honduras seceded from the federation and became independent.

The majority of Hondurans are of European descent or *mestizos* (mixed Spanish and Indian), although the descendants of the Mayans and some other Indian groups make up a small percentage of the population. A group of people living on the Honduras islands in the Caribbean and along the Caribbean coast of Honduras are referred to as black Caribs. Although most black Caribs are Catholic, they add many African customs and rituals to life-cycle celebrations. Most *mestizo* and white Hondurans are Catholic and celebrate life-cycle events according to the doctrines of the Church. (See Protestant and Catholic Life-Cycle Rituals, page xlvi.) Protestant groups are a fast-growing minority in the country, and missionaries have helped attract members with social service programs.

Two important childhood rites in the Catholic Church are baptism and communion. Catholic children are baptized at a few months of age and families attend services. The first communion is held when children are seven years old. The girls dress like little brides. Each wears a long white dress, usually made of satin, and a veil on her head. A family dinner is held after the service when the child receives presents from family and friends.

Funerals are sad occasions, especially if a child dies. The child is referred to as *angelito* (little angel). The funeral procession traditionally walks to the cemetery and is led by the priest and several small children carrying flowers to lay on the grave. After the burial, the mourners go to the home of the deceased for a meal of soup, beans, and tortillas. If the family can afford it, meat is added to whatever is being served.

The foods of Honduras are similar to that in other Central American countries. Maize (corn) and frijoles (beans) are the staples. *Nacatamles* (recipe page 416) are favorites.

Bananas are a major export of Honduras, and *pan de banano* is a favorite treat, often served as dessert for life-cycle celebrations.

Pan de Banano

Banana Bread

Yield: 1 loaf

½ cup butter or margarine, at room temperature
½ cup sugar
1 pound ripe bananas (about 2 or 3), peeled and mashed
½ teaspoon salt
1 teaspoon **ground** cinnamon
1 tablespoon lemon juice
1 egg, well beaten
1½ cups all-purpose flour
2 teaspoons baking powder

Equipment: Large mixing bowl, electric mixer or whisk, medium bowl, flour **sifter**, rubber spatula, greased 9- x 5-inch loaf pan, oven mitts, toothpick, knife, small dessert bowls, serving spoon

Preheat oven to 350° F.

1. Put butter or margarine and sugar in large mixing bowl, and using electric mixer or whisk, beat until light and fluffy. Add mashed bananas, salt, cinnamon, lemon juice, and egg, and beat well.

2.In medium bowl, **sift** flour with baking powder. Using rubber spatula, **fold in** flour, a little at a time, with banana mixture. Transfer batter to prepared loaf pan.

3. Bake in oven for 45 to 50 minutes, until toothpick inserted in center comes out clean.

To serve as bread, cut into slices and serve with honey. To serve as pudding, put the slices in small bowls with a ***drizzle*** *of cream over each serving.*

To satisfy the sweet tooth when money is scarce, desserts are made from unexpected ingredients, such as this simple dessert made with cheese.

Dulce de Queso

Sweet Cheese

Yield: serves 4 to 6

1 pound mozzarella cheese, at room temperature
2 cups dark brown sugar
1 cup water
2 teaspoons **ground** cinnamon

Equipment: Sharp knife, shallow 8-inch square or round baking pan, small saucepan, mixing spoon

1. Using the sharp knife, cut cheese into ¼-inch strips and lay them in a shallow 8-inch square or round baking pan.

2. In a small saucepan, combine brown sugar, water, and cinnamon. Bring to a boil over medium-high heat, stirring constantly to dissolve sugar. Reduce heat to **simmer** for 5 minutes without stirring. Pour brown sugar mixture over the cheese.

Serve immediately either by spooning a serving over pan de banano *(recipe precedes), or simply spooning a helping into a bowl to eat as dessert.*

EL SALVADOR

El Salvador is the smallest of the Central American countries, and the only one without an Atlantic coastline. It is bordered by Honduras on the north and east, and by Guatemala on the west.

The original inhabitants were the Pipil Indians, descendants of the Aztecs. Spain conquered the area in 1525 and remained in control until 1821, when El Salvador joined the federation of Central American states, which lasted until 1838.

Today, the majority of the people are *mestizos* (mixed Indian and Spanish), and most people belong to the Roman Catholic Church and follow life-cycle events according to Church doctrine. (See Protestant and Catholic Life-Cycle Rituals, page xlvi.)

Major family events—birth and baptism, marriage, and death—are usually celebrated in church. A religious marriage connotes social status. Most El Salvadoran couples planning to marry would love a large church wedding, but they are too poor.

Almost every El Salvadoran meal includes beans and rice, but for special occasions sweet potato dishes, especially when made extra sweet, are symbolic of a sweeter life.

Los Camotes

Candied Sweet Potatoes

Yield: serves 6

- 6 cups water
- 4 cups sugar
- 4 cups dark brown sugar
- 3 teaspoons **ground** cinnamon
- 6 whole cloves
- 6 sweet potatoes, peeled and quartered
- ½ cup melted butter or margarine

Equipment: Medium saucepan, mixing spoon, buttered 12- x 10- x 2½-inch baking pan, aluminum foil, oven mitts, serving bowl

1. Prepare thick sugar sauce: Combine water, granulated sugar, cinnamon, cloves, and brown sugar in medium saucepan. Stirring constantly, bring to rolling boil over medium-high heat until sugar dissolves. Reduce heat at once to low, and cook for 2 hours until sauce thickens. Set aside.

Preheat oven to 350° F.

2. Put quartered sweet potatoes in a single layer in buttered baking pan. Brush potatoes with melted butter or margarine, and cover with foil.

3. Bake in oven for 40 to 50 minutes, until tender. Keep warm.

To serve, transfer sweet potatoes to serving bowl and cover with thick sugar sauce.

Pupusas de chicharrón originated in El Salvador and are now found in other Latin American countries. Whenever a family gathering or party is held, expect to eat *pupusas*. They are filled with either cheese or refried beans.

Pupusas de Chicharrón

Salvadoran Pies

Yield: makes 4

- 2 cups hot water
- 1 teaspoon salt
- 4 cups *masa harina* (available in the Mexican food section of most supermarkets or all Latin American food stores)
- ½ cup shredded cheese or refried beans (available in the Mexican food section of most supermarkets or all Latin American food stores)
- 4 tablespoons vegetable oil, more if necessary

Equipment: Large mixing bowl, mixing spoon, wax paper, work surface, large skillet, metal spatula, paper towels, serving plate

1. Pour hot water into large mixing bowl, add salt and masa harina, and stir well. Divide mixture into 8 equal-size balls (a little larger than golf ball-size) and place on wax-paper-covered work surface.

2. Using your hands, pat each ball into a disk about ¼ inch thick and 2½ inches across. Place on wax paper, and pile about 1 heaping teaspoon shredded cheese or refried beans on top of 4 disks, staying well within the edges. Cover each with one of the remaining 4 disks, making it into

a sandwich, and press edges together to seal in the cheese or beans.

3. Heat 4 tablespoons oil in large skillet over medium-high heat. Fry *pupusas*, in batches, for 3 to 5 minutes on each side, until golden brown. Drain on paper towels.

To serve, stack pupusas *on a serving plate. Pick up and eat with your fingers.*

GUATEMALA

The northernmost Central American country, Guatemala is one of the most populated countries in Central America. It is bordered by Mexico on the north, and by Belize, Honduras, and El Salvador on the east.

Guatemala, once part of the Mayan empire, was conquered by Spaniards in the sixteenth century. It remained under Spanish control until the nineteenth century when Guatemala joined the shortlived federation of Central American states. A republic was established in 1839 after this federation collapsed.

The population of Guatemala is nearly equally divided by people of Spanish heritage—people of European descent and *mestizos* (mixed Spanish and Indian)—and Indians. Most people belong to the Roman Catholic Church and follow the life-cycle traditions of the Church. (See Protestant and Catholic Life-Cycle Rituals, page xlvi.) Many of the Indians combine indigenous traditions with Catholicism, while others continue to follow their ancient traditions.

One Guatemalan life-cycle celebration that occurs outside the confines of religion is the coming of age ceremony at age 10. The 10th birthday is celebrated with a community party, much like Christian confirmations or Jewish bar mitzvahs. The parents explain what adulthood means and the responsibilities all young adults have to their family and community. The villagers slaughter pigs (recipe page 383) for the party. Everyone has a good time eating, drinking, and dancing.

In Guatemala, turkey holds a place of high esteem on the banquet menu. It is prepared for special occasions such as fiestas, weddings, and other family life-cycle celebrations.

Mole Pablano de Guajolote

Turkey Roasted in Chocolate Chili Sauce

Yield: serves 8 to 10

1 cup *mole pablano* concentrate (available at all Latin American food stores and some supermarkets)
4 cups chicken broth, homemade (recipe page 106), or canned
3 teaspoons sugar, more or less to taste
8 to 10 pounds turkey, cut into serving-size pieces
arroz Guatemalteo, (recipe page 423), keep warm for serving

Equipment: Small saucepan, mixing spoon, roasting pan with cover, meat **thermometer** (optional), oven mitts, **bulb baster** or mixing spoon, metal tongs, serving platter

1. Put *mole poblano* concentrate in small saucepan. Add chicken broth, stir, and heat over medium heat until blended, about 3 minutes. Taste mixture, add 3 teaspoons sugar, more or less to taste, and stir well.

2. Arrange turkey pieces in roasting pan and coat well with *mole* sauce. Cover and refrigerate for at least 2 hours. Turn turkey once or twice to keep well coated with *mole* sauce.

Preheat oven to 325° F.

3. Bake in oven 1½ to 2½ hours or until meat thermometer inserted in thigh registers 180°-185° F. **Baste** frequently.

To serve, mound arroz Guatemalteo *on serving platter and arrange turkey parts on top. Using bulb baster or mixing spoon, remove and discard grease from sauce in roasting pan. Pour sauce over turkey.*

All banquets in Guatemala include a variety of side dishes, such as this popular rice dish.

Arroz Guatemalteo

Guatemala-style Rice

Yield: serves 4 to 6

2 tablespoons vegetable oil
1 cup rice
1 cup mixed vegetables (carrots, celery, and sweet red bell peppers), **finely chopped**
½ cup sweet peas
2 cups water
salt and pepper to taste

Equipment: Large **heavy-based** skillet with cover, mixing spoon

Heat oil in large heavy-based skillet over medium-high heat. Add rice and mixed vegetables, stir, and **sauté** for 3 to 5 minutes to coat rice with oil. Add water, stir, and bring to boil. Reduce to low, cover, and cook for 20 minutes, until rice is tender. Add peas and salt and pepper to taste. Stir to mix well.

Serve as a side dish with mole pablano de guajolote *(recipe precedes).*

NORTH AMERICA

The three countries that make up North America—Canada, Mexico, and the United States—were conquered and settled by people from many different parts of the world. Although Canada and the United States are similar in many ways and share some cultural traits, all three countries of North America have their unique histories and cultures.

At first glance, Canada is hard to distinguish from the United States, especially along the border and the two coasts where most Canadians live. The constant interchange between Canadians and Americans living in those areas has led to similar lifestyles. But on closer examination, one finds regional communities, such as French-speaking Quebec, with completely different cultures. In addition, many indigenous peoples living in isolated areas of Canada, especially the far north, have preserved their cultures into modern times.

In contrast, Mexico appears to be very different from the United States. The major European influence was not Britain or France, but Spain. In addition, the Spanish settlers intermarried with the indigenous population, creating a new race of people known as *mestizos*, whereas in Canada and the United States, native populations were either wiped out or isolated from the cultural mainstream. But that is not to say that the United States and Mexico share nothing except a border. In fact, much of the southwestern United States used to be part of Mexico, and in many areas Americans of Mexican heritage outnumber non-Mexicans, and the Mexican influence can be seen in everything from foods to street names.

The United States itself is far from unified in its culture. If one travels from coast to coast and border to border, the differences in each region's foods, culture, and even speech is readily apparent, yet all these people would refer to themselves as American.

In the pages that follow, foods and life-cycle traditions from different regions of each of these North American countries will be presented and described. The variety of cultures and foods is amazing.

MEXICO

About one-fifth the size of the United States, Mexico is bordered on the south by Belize and Guatemala and on the north by the United States. The wealthy Aztec empire, which was conquered by the Spanish in the sixteenth century, was just the latest in a series of empires that included the Mayans and Toltecs. Under Spanish control, Mexico expanded beyond its current boundaries and controlled most of the southwestern United States. Some of the oldest settlements in the United States were founded in the sixteenth century by Spaniards. Mexico won its independence in 1821 after a long struggle with Spain.

Mexico is a country of extreme contrasts, from deserts to jungles, and from modern skyscrapers in Mexico City to primitive Indian villages in the remote mountain regions. The vast majority of Mexicans are *mestizo*, a mixture of Spanish and Indian people. But whether they live in the guarded, walled mansions of the wealthy, the tin-can hovels of the city slums, or the one-room, thatched adobe shacks of the small subsistence farmers, Mexicans have one thing in common, their religion. The Roman Catholic Church dominates every facet of life and life-cycle events are celebrated in accordance with its teachings. (See Protestant and Catholic Life-Cycle Rituals, page xlvi.)

Besides the Church-prescribed life-cycle events, Mexicans celebrate the *Quinceañera*, an important celebration for girls when they reach 15 years old. When the family can afford it, a big party is held with dancing, cake, and ice cream or an elaborate dinner, and lots of presents are given to the birthday girl.

Catholic weddings must be in the church. If the couple can afford it they have a lengthy nuptial Mass. The bride wears a white gown with a veil and the groom dons a tuxedo. Catholic weddings in Mexico are full of special rituals, such as the *lazo*, a huge rosary that is placed around the shoulders of the bride and groom as they are kneeling at the altar while the priest prays over them. They are also presented symbolic gifts during the ceremony—coins (silver or gold), a Bible, and a rosary. These are handed to the couple by *padrinos* who are usually two special people (not godparents) the couple have chosen. The coins symbolize prosperity. The Bible and rosary signify keeping the Catholic faith in their home.

Food plays an important role in life-cycle celebrations, and this cake is served on all special occasions—engagement parties, weddings, baptisms, first communions, and birthdays.

TORTA DEL CIELO

HEAVENLY CAKE

8 ounces almonds, **blanched**
1¼ cups sugar, divided
½ cup cake flour
1 teaspoon baking powder
10 **eggs, separated**
¼ teaspoon salt
1 teaspoon vanilla extract
confectioners' sugar, for **garnish** (optional)

Equipment: Pencil, scissors, parchment paper, 10-inch springform pan, food processor or **blender**, rubber **spatula,** 2 medium bowls, flour **sifter**, mixing spoon, large mixing bowl, electric mixer or egg beater, oven mitts, toothpick, wire cake rack, serving platter

1. Prepare pan: Using pencil and scissors, cut piece of parchment paper to fit bottom of 10-inch springform pan. Oil pan bottom, not the sides, then set paper in place and lightly oil the top surface of the paper.

Preheat oven to 325° F.

2. Finely grind almonds with 1/4 cup sugar in food processor or blender. Transfer to medium bowl. **Sift** cake flour and baking powder into nut mixture and stir thoroughly with mixing spoon.

Note: While processing, turn machine off once or twice and scrape down sides of container with rubber spatula.

3. In large mixing bowl, using electric mixer or egg beater, beat egg whites with salt until the mixture forms stiff peaks.

4. Using electric mixer or egg beater, beat egg yolks in second medium bowl until **frothy**. Add vanilla extract and remaining 1 cup sugar a little at a time and beat for 2 to 3 minutes or until mixture becomes thickened and lemon-colored and forms a ribbon when beaters are lifted from the bowl. Using rubber spatula, **fold** nut mixture into egg yolk mixture, then fold in whites. Pour into prepared springform pan and smooth top.

5. Bake in oven for 50 to 60 minutes, or until toothpick inserted in center comes out clean. Place on wire rack to cool for 1 to 2 hours. Release sides of pan, flip cake onto wire rack, remove pan bottom, and peel off paper.

To serve, transfer cake to serving platter and dust top with confectioners' sugar. The cake can also be frosted with butter cream icing (recipe page 361) or whipped evaporated cream (recipe page 366).

Mexicans love sweets, and although these are called cakes, they are really cookies.

Tejas de Boda

Wedding Cakes

Yield: about 4 dozen

1 cup butter or margarine, at room temperature
1/4 cup sugar
1 teaspoon vanilla extract
2 or 3 drops green food coloring
2 cups all-purpose flour
1 cup finely **ground** pecans
2 cups confectioners' sugar, for **garnish**

Equipment: Medium mixing bowl, electric mixer or egg beater, rubber **spatula,** cookie sheet, oven mitts, shallow bowl, wire cake rack, serving platter

Preheat oven to 325° F.

1. In medium mixing bowl, using electric mixer, beat butter or margarine until creamy. Beat in sugar and vanilla until light and fluffy. Add 2 or 3 drops food coloring to make a light green tint. Beating constantly, add flour and pecans and **blend** well.

2. Using your hands, roll into 1-inch balls and place 1 inch apart on ungreased cookie sheet.

3. Bake in oven, in batches if necessary, for 18 to 20 minutes or until lightly browned.

4. Place a shallow bowl filled with 2 cups confectioners' sugar next to oven. While the cookies are still warm, remove them one at a time from cookie sheet and roll them in confectioners' sugar in shallow bowl. Place on cake rack until set and cooled.

To serve, arrange cookies on serving platter and set out on wedding buffet table for guests to munch on.

Happy occasions, such as baptisms and christenings, call for plenty of sweets. *Yemitas* are perfect for the sweet table because they are made with eggs, the Mexican symbol for life.

Yemitas

Egg Yolk Candies

Yield: 25 to 30 pieces

1 quart heavy cream

¼ teaspoon baking soda
2½ cups sugar
12 **egg yolks**
1½ teaspoons **ground** cinnamon
1 cup **cinnamon sugar**, for **garnish**

Equipment: Large **heavy-based** saucepan, wooden mixing spoon, medium mixing bowl, whisk, **candy thermometer** (optional), baking sheet, 25 to 30 candy-size or mini-cupcake paper cups

1. Pour heavy cream into large heavy-based saucepan and add baking soda. Stirring constantly, bring to boil over medium-high heat. Remove from heat to prevent boiling over. When foam subsides, return to heat, bring back to boil, and then quickly remove from heat. Cool to warm, add sugar, and stirring constantly, return to medium heat and cook until mixture thickens, 20 to 30 minutes. **Note:** Mixture is sufficiently thickened if you can see the bottom of pan when mixture is separated with a spoon. Cool to room temperature.

2. Put egg yolks in medium mixing bowl and use whisk to beat in ground cinnamon. Beat yolk mixture into cooled cream mixture. Return to medium heat and stir constantly until mixture reaches hard ball stage, or 250° to 266° on candy thermometer. Remove from heat and cool to warm.

3. Using a wooden mixing spoon, beat mixture until it reaches a very thick, fudge-like consistency, 10 to 15 minutes. Using your hands, shape into marble-size balls. Put cinnamon-sugar in small shallow bowl. Roll balls in cinnamon-sugar to coat well. Place side by side on baking sheet until set.

To serve, put each ball in a candy-size or mini-cupcake paper cup.

Little tacos are a favorite snack at family gatherings or as an **appetizer** at other celebrations.

Taquitos

Little Tacos

CAUTION: HOT OIL USED

Yield: serves 10 to 12

48 small (3-inch-diameter) tortillas (available at Latin American food stores and most supermarkets)
2 to 3 cups vegetable oil
2 cups lettuce, shredded, for serving
12 ounces canned refried beans, for serving
1 pound lean pork, beef brisket, or chicken, cooked and shredded, for serving
1 pound Mozzarella or Monterey Jack cheese, shredded, for serving

Equipment: Paper towels, baking sheet, large **heavy-based** skillet or **Dutch oven**, fryer **thermometer** or wooden spoon, metal tongs, large ovenproof serving platter, oven mitts

1. Prepare to skillet-fry: ADULT SUPERVISION REQUIRED. Place several layers of paper towels on baking sheet. In heavy-based skillet or Dutch oven heat oil to 375° F on fryer thermometer or until small bubbles appear around a wooden spoon handle when it is dipped in the oil. Fry tacos in small batches, 2 or 3 at a time, until golden and crisp, 1 to 2 minutes. Remove with metal tongs and drain on paper towel-covered baking sheet.

Preheat broiler

2. Prepare to assemble: Place tacos side by side on large ovenproof serving platter. Sprinkle each with a little shredded lettuce. Add about 1 teaspoon refried beans, cover with shredded meat or chicken, and top with 1 or 2 teaspoons shredded cheese. Place under broiler for about 1 minutes to melt cheese.

Serve directly from the broiler, so tacos are nice and hot.

CANADA

Canada is the northernmost and largest of North American countries, stretching from its southern border with the United States up into the Arctic Ocean. The original inhabitants of Canada were Indians, particularly the Inuit (Eskimos) of the far north. The first European settlers were French, and Canada was a French colony until the 1763 Treaty of Paris ceded the territory to Britain. At the time, most European inhabitants were French, and large regions of Canada, especially the province of Quebec, retain French culture, language, and religion.

Today, Canada is home to people from many different cultures. As people settled in Canada, they had to modify their traditional life-cycle customs, especially the celebration feasts, to fit what they could catch, hunt, raise, and store in the harsh Canadian environment. Most Canadians are Christians, so life-cycle celebrations correspond with their religious beliefs (see Protestant and Catholic Life-Cycle Rituals, page xlvi), but some big differences can be found between the English and French-speaking parts of Canada. The French Canadians are generally Roman Catholic and follow the traditions of their Church, while most of the English-speaking Canadians belong to various Protestant churches.

Baptism is an important ritual among French-Canadian Catholics. The child is usually dressed in a family christening gown that was worn and handed down by many other family members. The shawl blanket the child is wrapped in is usually a family heirloom. After the church service, the family celebrates with food and gifts for the infant. *Petits fours* (recipe page 433) and candies, usually Jordan Almonds, *sucre a la crème* (recipe page 432), and *bâtons de noisettes* (recipe page 435) are set out for guests along with soft drinks, tea, coffee, and alcoholic beverages.

Among French Canadians, the nuptial wedding mass is generally held in the morning at the church, and the families of the bride and groom go either to the bride's home or to a hotel for the wedding luncheon. The traditional wedding cake is the same as *English wedding cake* (recipe page 202).

At French-Canadian funerals, special prayers are often said over the casket at the funeral home. Then the casket is taken to a church for the service with a procession of male mourners, dressed in black, walking behind the hearse. Following the burial service, the funeral feast is either catered at the home of the bereaved family, or it is held in a restaurant.

The Canadian North, bordering the Arctic Ocean, is home to the circumpolar ethnic group, once called Eskimos, now known as Inuit (the people). In the last half century, the Inuit have had to adjust from a Stone Age existence to a modern consumer society. Although most Inuit live by fishing and hunting, they no longer live in igloos, but rather in prefabricated houses in government-built settlements. They travel by motor-powered boat instead of a kayak. Despite the availability of snowmobiles, many Inuit keep the nine-dog sled team. They consider four-pawed traction more reliable: dogs don't stall uphill, nor do they run out of gas.

Among the Inuit, life-cycle celebrations begin with the birth of a baby, usually performed at home by a midwife. The Inuit believe dead ancestors are reborn in children and according to tradition, the name of a dead ancestor is given to a newborn, thus keeping the spirit of the ancestor alive.

Marriage is an important part of Inuit culture, and they have a saying, "Every woman needs a hunter and man should not be alone." When a wedding is announced, everyone in the settlement is expected not only to attend but also to help with the work. The wedding ceremony generally is a big celebration with plenty of food.

To outsiders, the Inuit seem to have unusual food and eating habits. Traditionally, groups prepared and ate only one meal a day together. Inuit used no salt, pepper, or sugar, and they preferred their food raw, even eggs. Whale oil was used for cooking and seal oil was used for light. In recent years, eating habits are changing. The younger generations seem to prefer cooked food. Many have two or more meals a day, sweets are causing dental problems, especially among children, and many prefer their food cooked. Frozen TV dinners are popular and available in the local stores. Some old customs haven't change, though. The raw liver of the seal is considered sacred, and like candy, it is a treat for children.

Cod is caught by the Inuit and it is usually eaten raw, especially by elderly Inuit. Fish soups are popular with all Canadians, and often the wedding and funeral feast begins with soup. ۞ ۞ ۞

Soupe à la Morue

Cod Soup

Yield: serves 6

8 cups water
2 potatoes, peeled and **coarsely chopped**
1 onion, **finely chopped**
1 celery rib, **trimmed** and finely chopped
salt and pepper to taste
1 pound fresh or frozen skinless fish **fillets** (cod, trout, snapper, or whiting) rinsed, patted dry with paper towels, and cut into 2-inch slices
2 tablespoons butter or margarine
2 tablespoons all-purpose flour
2 cups half & half
3 tablespoons parsley or chives, finely chopped for **garnish**

Equipment: Large saucepan with cover, mixing spoon, medium skillet, whisk

1. Put water, chopped potatoes, onion, celery, and salt and pepper to taste into large saucepan. Bring to boil over high heat. Reduce heat to **simmer**, cover, and cook for 15 to 20 minutes or until potatoes are tender. Add fish, stir, cover again, and cook for 7 to 12 minutes, until fish is opaque white and done. Keep covered and reduce heat to low.

2. Melt butter or margarine in medium skillet over medium-high heat. Remove skillet from heat and whisk in flour until smooth and well-blended. Whisk continuously while slowly adding half & half until well mixed. Return to medium heat and whisk constantly until smooth and thickened, 5 to 7 minutes. Slowly add cream mixture to fish mixture while stirring gently and constantly. Reduce heat to low and cook, uncovered for 5 to 7 minutes for flavor to develop.

To serve, sprinkle each serving with chopped parsley or chives.

These small meatballs are a favorite **appetizer** for all life-cycle celebrations.

Ragout de Boulettes

Small Meatballs

Yield: serves 6 to 8

1 pound lean **ground** beef
½ pound lean ground pork

¾ cup dry **bread crumbs**
¼ cup milk
1 egg
1 onion, **finely chopped**
¼ teaspoon ground nutmeg
salt and pepper to taste
3 tablespoons all-purpose flour
1 teaspoon instant beef bouillon
¾ cup water, divided
1 cup half & half
2 tablespoons fresh parsley, finely chopped, or 2 teaspoons dried parsley flakes

Equipment: Large mixing bowl, mixing spoon, **baking sheet,** oven mitts, medium ovenproof bowl, large skillet

1. In large mixing bowl, combine ground beef, ground pork, bread crumbs, milk, egg, onion, nutmeg, and salt and pepper. Using mixing spoon or hands, combine ingredients.

Preheat oven to 350° F.

2. Moistening your hands with water frequently, shape meat mixture into Ping-Pong-sized balls. Place side by side on baking sheet. There should be about 48 meatballs.

3. Bake in oven until lightly browned, about 20 minutes. Using oven mitts, remove pan of meatballs from oven. Transfer meatballs to ovenproof bowl and keep warm. Save pan juices.

4. Prepare sauce: Spoon 3 tablespoons saved pan juices in large skillet. Add flour, ¼ cup water, and bouillon, and stir until smooth. Heat over low heat, stirring constantly until bubbly, or about 1 minute. Remove from heat. Stirring constantly, add remaining ½ cup water and half & half. Increase heat to medium-high and continue to stir until smooth and thickened, 3 to 5 minutes. Before serving, pour sauce over meatballs and sprinkle with parsley.

*Serve while warm as an **appetizer** or as a side dish on the celebration table.*

Tourtière de la gaspesie is a classic Canadian recipe that is often made with wild game and/or waterfowl.

Tourtière de la Gaspesie

Three Meats Pie

Yield: serves 6 to 8
2 (9 inches each) unbaked pie crusts, homemade (recipe page 446), or frozen prepared crust (available at most supermarkets)
2 to 3½ pound stewing chicken, cut into serving-size pieces
water, as needed
salt and pepper to taste
1 bay leaf
2 tablespoons vegetable oil
1 onion, **finely chopped**
2 cloves garlic, finely chopped
½ pound lean pork, chopped
½ pound lean beef, chopped
4 tablespoons all-purpose flour

Equipment: 9-inch pie pan, damp kitchen towel, large saucepan with cover, slotted spoon, medium mixing bowl, knife, large mixing bowl, large skillet, fork, strainer, small saucepan, small bowl, whisk, oven mitts

1. Prepare 2 pie crusts: If homemade, fit 1 crust into pie pan. Place second on work surface and cover both with damp towel. If buying frozen pie crusts in pie pans, thaw according to directions on package.

2. Place chicken in large saucepan and pour in enough water to cover by at least 1 inch. Add salt and pepper to taste and bay leaf and bring to boil over medium-high heat. Reduce heat to **simmer**, cover, and cook for 1 to 1½ hours, until very tender.

3. Using slotted spoon, transfer chicken to medium mixing bowl. Save broth and cool both broth and chicken to room temperature. When

chicken is cool enough to handle, remove meat from bones. Cut chicken into bite-size pieces and put them into large mixing bowl. Discard bones.

Preheat oven to 375° F.

4. Heat oil in large skillet over medium-high heat. Add finely chopped onion and garlic, and **sauté** for 3 to 5 minutes until onion is soft. Crumble in chopped pork and beef and, stirring constantly, sauté until lightly browned, 5 to 7 minutes. Remove from heat and add to chicken; toss to mix. Add salt and pepper to taste and 4 tablespoons saved chicken broth.

5. Put meat mixture into prepared pie shell and spread evenly. Dampen edge of crust and cover with second crust. Pinch top and bottom edges together using fork or your fingers. Using paring knife, make 3 or 4 slits on top crust for steam vents.

6. Bake in oven for 40 to 45 minutes, or until crust is lightly browned.

7. Prepare sauce while pie is baking: Strain chicken broth into medium bowl. Measure out 4 cups of broth into small saucepan. Any remaining broth can be covered and refrigerated for another use. If there is not enough broth, add water to make 4 cups. Bring broth to boil over medium-high heat. Reduce heat to simmer.

8. Put flour into small bowl. Stirring constantly, slowly add ½ cup cold water to flour to make **slurry**. Whisking constantly, slowly add slurry to hot broth until smooth and thickened. Reduce heat to low, and cook 5 to 7 minutes for flavor to develop. Add salt and pepper to taste.

To serve, allow pie to rest for 10 to 15 minutes before cutting it into wedges. Serve sauce in small bowl. Each person can ladle some sauce over their serving.

This candy is served at life-cycle events from baptisms to funerals.

Sucre a la Crème

Sugar-Cream Confection

Yield: 64 to 100 pieces

2 pounds brown sugar or maple sugar
½ cup heavy cream
½ cup butter or margarine
1 cup walnuts, **coarsely chopped**

Equipment: Medium saucepan, wooden mixing spoon, buttered 8- to 10-inch square cake pan, **icing spatula**, plastic food wrap

1. Put sugar and cream in medium saucepan and, stirring constantly, bring to boil over medium-high heat. Reduce heat to **simmer**, then add butter or margarine and continue stirring until butter melts. Remove from heat and stir in chopped walnuts.

2. Beat mixture with wooden spoon until thick and creamy, about 7 to 12 minutes. Transfer mixture to buttered baking pan and spread evenly, using back of spoon or icing spatula. Cover with plastic wrap and refrigerate until set, 2 to 4 hours.

To serve, cut into 1-inch squares and place in serving dish.

Petits fours are very labor intensive, but well worth the effort. Adding special decorations make *petits fours* ideal for life-cycle parties. Use multi-colored, chocolate, silver or gold sprinkles (available at most supermarkets), **silver leaf**, nuts, heart-shaped candies, or edible flowers. For example, at a baby girl's baptism party, use raspberry preserves for the filling, spread pink icing over the cakes, and cover the top with pink and white sprinkles or place a pink candied heart on each cake. Before you begin, coordinate fillings(homemade and canned preserves), icing colors, and decorations for the cakes.

Petits Fours

Small Individual Cakes

Yield: Five dozen 1½-inch square cakes

½ cup all-purpose flour
½ cup cornstarch
6 tablespoons unsalted butter
water, as needed
6 eggs, at room temperature
1 cup granulated sugar
1 teaspoon vanilla extract
chocolate filling (recipe follows)
3 flavors of preserves (variety of colors) to be used as a filling
sweet icing (recipe page 435)
dried or fresh fruits for decorating cakes (optional)
decorating icing (assorted colors are available in 4.25-ounce tubes at most supermarkets) for decorating cakes (optional)

Equipment: 17- x 11- x 1-inch jelly-roll pan, paring knife or scissors, waxed paper, flour **sifter**, medium bowl, small **heavy-based** saucepan, spoon, small bowl, large saucepan, heatproof surface, large heatproof mixing bowl, electric mixer or whisk, rubber **spatula,** oven mitts, toothpick, ruler, 9- x 15-inch rectangular cardboard pattern, long **serrated knife**, plastic food wrap, wire cake rack, metal spatula

1. Prepare jelly-roll pan: Grease bottom and sides of pan. Use paring knife or scissors, cut wax paper to fit bottom of pan and press smooth. Grease surface of waxed paper and sprinkle with flour to coat. Shake out and discard excess flour.

2. **Sift** flour and cornstarch together into medium bowl.

3. Melt butter in small heavy-based saucepan over low heat. When butter separates, remove from heat. Skim off and discard any foam that forms on the top. Tip the pan slightly, spoon the clear butter into a small bowl and set aside. Discard milky solids that settled in bottom of pan.

Preheat oven to 350° F.

4. Fill large saucepan halfway with water and bring to boil over high heat. Remove from heat and set on a heatproof surface. Put eggs and sugar in large mixing bowl and set over pan of hot water. **Note**: Bottom of large mixing bowl should not touch water; if necessary, pour some water off. Using electric mixer or whisk, beat egg mixture until thick and foamy. When mixture is **lukewarm**, place bowl on work surface and continue to beat until egg mixture has almost tripled in volume. The mixture should stand in peaks when the beaters or whisk is lifted from the bowl. This will take about 15 minutes with an electric mixer or if using a whisk, about 30 minutes.

5. Using rubber spatula, **fold in** flour mixture, ¼ cup at a time. Fold in the clear melted butter, a little at a time, and add vanilla extract. Spread batter evenly over prepared paper-lined pan and smooth top with rubber spatula.

6. Bake for 25 to 30 minutes, or until the cake begins to pull away from sides of pan and toothpick inserted in center comes out clean. Using oven mitts, remove cake from oven and flip onto sheet of wax paper placed on work surface. Carefully peel off the wax paper that is now on the top side of cake and cool cake to room temperature.

7. Prepare *chocolate filling* (recipe follows). Place preserves fillings next to prepared *chocolate filling*.

8. Prepare *sweet icing* (recipe follows).

9. Center 9- x 15-inch cardboard pattern on cake. Using long serrated knife, cut around pattern, cutting off all edges of cake. Discard or save edges for another use. Cut 15-inch length in half, making two 7½- x 9-inch pieces. Cut both 7½- x 9-inch pieces in half, making four —4½- x 7½ cakes.

10. Make each cake two layers by cutting through the middle horizontally, separating the

top from the bottom. Place top on bottom, exactly as they were before cutting, so they don't become mixed up.

11. Add fillings: Work with one cake at a time. Carefully remove top layer, then place bottom layer, cut side up, on work surface. Spread prepared *chocolate filling* thinly over cut side of bottom layer and replace top layer, cut side down. Using the preserves as a different filling for each cake, repeat filling and reassembling. Wrap each cake separately in plastic wrap and place in freezer for at least one hour.

12. Remove 1 cake at a time from freezer, unwrap, and cut into 1½-inch squares. Using serrated knife, cut longest side into five strips, each 1½-inch wide. Cut each strip into three 1½-inch pieces, making 15 squares.

13. Cover cakes with *sweet icing*: Select a color of icing that corresponds or complements the color of the filling for each cake. Working with 1 colored icing at a time, transfer icing to heavy-based saucepan. (Keep other icings covered.) Rinse and dry jelly-roll pan, set wire cake rack in pan, and place on work surface. Cut 3 pieces of waxed paper to fit bottom of jelly-roll pan and layer them over the bottom before setting the wire cake rack on top. Set cake squares about 1 inch apart on wire cake rack. Warm icing over low heat to make it pourable, stirring constantly. Pour or spoon icing generously over tops of cakes, letting it run down the sides. With metal spatula, scrape up excess icing that dripped onto the waxed paper and return it to saucepan. Stirring constantly, warm icing over low heat until it is pourable again. Pour or spoon it over any cakes that were not evenly coated. You can repeat, remove waxed paper, scrape, warm, and pour icing as many times as necessary until all the cakes are evenly coated. Let iced cakes dry on rack for about 10 minutes before transferring to wax-paper-covered work surface. Repeat cutting and icing remaining 4½- x 7½- inch cakes, one at a time.

14. Each *petits four* can be decorated with pieces of dried or fresh fruit and/or you can draw whatever designs you like using colored decorating icing. Allow icing to dry at least 1 hour before lightly covering with wax paper.

To serve, arrange different colored cakes decoratively on serving platter.

Any fruit preserves you like can be used as filling for *petits fours*. Thin each ¾ cup of preserves with 3 tablespoons apple juice. A few drops of mint extract added to *chocolate filling* also gives it a nice flavor.

Chocolate Filling

Yield: about 2 cups

12 ounces semisweet chocolate, **coarsely chopped**
16 tablespoons unsalted butter
2 cups confectioners' sugar

Equipment: Medium **heavy-based** saucepan, wooden mixing spoon

1. Melt chocolate and butter in medium heavy-based saucepan over medium-low heat, stirring constantly. When mixture is fully melted, remove from heat.

2. Using wooden spoon, beat in confectioners' sugar, ½ cup at a time, beating well after each addition.

Continue: Use for petits fours *(recipe precedes: Step 10. Add filling:).*

Once you've decided on four flavors of preserves to be used as fillings, select a food coloring to add to the *sweet icing* that will match or complement the filling color and flavor. For instance, red or purple fruit preserves go well with pink icing. *Chocolate filling* (recipe precedes), or peach or orange preserves go well with yellow icing, and green icing goes well when mint extract is added to *chocolate filling*. White icing goes with any color filling.

Sweet Icing

Yield: enough for 60 *petits fours*

5 cups granulated sugar
$2\frac{1}{2}$ cups water
$1\frac{1}{2}$ cups light corn syrup
12 cups (4 pounds) confectioners' sugar, **sifted**
Red, green, and yellow liquid food coloring
mint extract (optional)

Equipment: Large **heavy-based** saucepan with cover, wooden mixing spoon, hair-bristled (not nylon) **pastry brush**, electric mixer or whisk, rubber spatula, 4 medium bowls, plastic food wrap

1. In large heavy-based saucepan, combine granulated sugar, water, and corn syrup. Stir over medium-low heat until sugar dissolves. Using a pastry brush dipped in cold water, wipe sugar crystals from around sides of pan back down into the syrup. Cover pan and cook syrup over low heat for 5 minutes; the steam will dissolve any remaining crystals.

2. Remove cover, increase heat to medium-high, and boil syrup, without stirring, for 5 minutes. Remove from heat and cool to room temperature.

3. Using electric mixer or whisk, beat constantly, add confectioners' sugar, about 1 cupful at a time, beating well after each addition, and continue to beat until mixture is well mixed.

4. Place sugar mixture over low heat, stirring constantly. Cook until mixture is **lukewarm** and appears smooth and shiny, 7 to 12 minutes. Do not overcook or icing will lose its gloss.

5. Color icing: Divide icing equally between 4 medium bowls. Select a different color of food coloring for 3 of the bowls of icing and leave the fourth bowl white. Stir in a few drops of the selected color of food coloring to that individual bowl. Cool icings to room temperature and cover with plastic warp.

Continue: Use for petits fours *(Step 11. Cover cakes with icing).*

In the afternoon after a baptism, a tray of assorted cookies is always a welcome treat for the friends and relatives who come by to see the baptized child. Cookies are also a popular addition at children's birthday parties.

Bâtons de Noisettes

Nut Stick Cookies

Yield: 28 to 30 pieces

1 cup unsalted butter, at room temperature
$\frac{1}{4}$ cup granulated sugar
$\frac{1}{4}$ teaspoon salt
2 cups all-purpose flour
2 teaspoons vanilla extract
1 cup **finely chopped** walnuts or filberts
1 cup confectioners' sugar

Equipment: Large mixing bowl, electric mixer or mixing spoon, rubber **spatula,** wax paper, work surface, buttered cookie sheet pan, oven mitts, wide metal spatula, wire cake rack, small shallow bowl, serving platter

1. Put butter in large mixing bowl and, using electric mixer or spoon, beat until creamy. Beating constantly, add granulated sugar a little at a time and continue beating until light and fluffy. Sprinkle salt over flour and add to the butter mixture about $\frac{1}{2}$ cup at a time, beating well after each addition. Beat in vanilla. Using rubber spatula, **fold in** nuts.

Preheat oven to 350° F.

2. Shape cookies: Place wax paper on work surface. Divide dough into 28 to 30 equal balls and set on wax paper. Roll each ball between the palms of your hands into a cylinder about $2\frac{1}{2}$ inches long and about $\frac{1}{2}$ inch thick. Place them about 1 inch apart on buttered cookie sheet.

3. Bake in oven for 10 to 12 minutes, or until light golden brown. Using oven mitts, remove pan from oven and let cookies rest for 10 minutes. Using wide metal spatula, transfer cookies to wire cake rack to cool.

4. Put confectioners' sugar into small shallow bowl. When cookies are cool, roll each in confectioners' sugar to coat all sides.

To serve, decoratively arrange cookies on serving platter. Bâtons de noisettes *keep well for several weeks in a tightly covered container.*

UNITED STATES

The United States is the middle country of North America, sitting between Mexico to the south and Canada to the north. Most of the original inhabitants of the country, the Indians, were wiped out shortly after contact with Europeans, though some tribes survived the wars and diseases brought by Europeans. Although originally colonized and ruled by England, the United States has attracted immigrants from all over the world.

The various waves of immigration from around the world have changed the American cultural landscape, but at the same time, each wave of immigrants is assimilated into the cultural mainstream in an everchanging mix. Americans choose from the cultures their ancestors brought with them and the new culture that has developed here. At times this process has been viewed optimistically as seen in the popular belief in United States as a "Melting Pot," a term coined by Israel Zangwell in a 1908 play describing the assimilation of the new immigrants into the American way of life.

Another metaphor that has been used in place of the "melting pot" is the "bread basket," which seems appropriate for a cookbook. Although the meaning of this metaphor implies that America is a large culture (the breadbasket) filled with many separate, distinct cultures (the breads), the literal meaning applies as well. The new American "bread basket" includes breads from the many different cultures that make it up, from white bread to brioches, *challah* to dark pumpernickel, from flat breads such as pita, tortillas, and nan to hard rolls, soft rolls, sweet rolls, bagels, croissants, and breadsticks

The reality probably falls somewhere between the two metaphors. Successive waves of immigrants have assimilated into the mainstream culture while retaining important rituals of their home culture, including life-cycle rituals. The rest of this section will detail a few of the cultures and their life-cycle rituals that have become part of the U.S. landscape.

African American

Unlike most immigrants to the United States who came seeking freedom or economic opportunity or fleeing trouble or persecution, the ancestors of most African Americans were brought to this country by force, as slaves. Although the slave owners discouraged the importation of African culture, many slaves kept their own traditions and created new ones in their harsh conditions of slavery.

Today, many African Americans are revisiting these traditions, and some couples have added a ritual called "jumping the broom" to their wedding ceremony.

This tradition developed during slavery when slaves were considered chattel and they had no legal or religious rights, including marriage. To mark their passage into marriage, the slaves devised a ritual that was known as "jumping the broom." To legitimize their union as husband and wife, the husband and wife would join hands and step over a broom lying on the floor, signifying their passage into married life.

Today, reviving the ritual gives newlyweds a connection with their past and allows them to show pride and respect for their ancestors. The "jumping the broom" ritual is included in modern weddings either after vows are exchanged or later, during the wedding reception.

The wedding feast often includes foods that have special meaning for African Americans. Black-eyed peas, for example, are said to have come to America from Africa by way of the West Indies, sometime before 1700. Today, they hold an important place in African American culinary history. For many centuries, black-eyed peas have been eaten at New Year's celebrations for good luck and more recently they have been eaten for good luck at weddings. *Hoppin' John* is made with black-eyed peas, and it is the same as Senegal's *thiebou nop niébé* (recipe page 75). A big pot of *hoppin' John* is a necessary addition to the southern African American wedding feast.

Other African American food traditions, such as "soul food," developed as a result of slave cooks "making do" with the poorest-quality ingredients allotted to them by slave owners, such as chitlins (small intestines), hog maw (pig's stomach), and pig's feet and ears. Today, descendants of slaves are keeping traditions alive by preparing their beloved *chitlins* and other soul food dishes for major holiday and life-cycle celebration feasts. ❂ ❂ ❂

Chitlins (also Chitterlings)

Skillet-fried Hog Intestines

Note: This recipe takes 2 days.

Yield: serves 6

- 2 pounds chitlins (available by special order at most butcher shops)
- water, as needed
- 2 onions, quartered
- 2 cloves garlic, **coarsely chopped**
- ½ teaspoon salt
- salt and pepper to taste
- juice of 1 lemon
- ½ cup all-purpose flour
- ½ cup butter or margarine, more if necessary
- 1 tablespoon **finely chopped** fresh parsley or 2 teaspoons dried parsley flakes, for **garnish**
- 1 lemon, cut into 6 wedges, for garnish

Equipment: Medium bowl with cover, **colander**, knife, medium saucepan with cover, fork, large skillet, metal spatula, serving platter

1. Rinse chitlins under cold running water, put in medium bowl, and cover with fresh cold water. Cover bowl and allow chitlins to soak for 24 hours in the refrigerator. During that time, make several changes of water. Transfer to colander and drain well.

2. Cut chitlins into 2-inch lengths. Turn inside out and peel away and discard most of the fat, leaving a little for flavor. Rinse again under cold running water.

3. Pour 4 cups water in medium saucepan and bring to boil over high heat. Reduce heat to **simmer**, and add chitlins, onions, garlic, ½ teaspoon salt, and lemon juice. Stir, cover, and simmer for 2 to 2½ hours or until tender when pierced with a fork. **Note**: Do not boil chitlins or they become tough. Transfer chitlins to colander in sink and drain thoroughly. Then, transfer chit-

lins to medium bowl, sprinkle with salt and pepper to taste and toss with flour until well coated.

4. Prepare to skillet-fry: Melt ½ cup butter or margarine in large skillet over medium-high heat. Fry chitlins a few at a time, turning with metal spatula, until golden brown, 3 to 5 minutes. Transfer to serving platter and keep warm while frying remaining chitlins in batches. Add more butter or margarine, if necessary, to prevent sticking.

To serve, sprinkle with chopped parsley and garnish with lemon wedges for guests to squeeze on serving if desired.

Another "make do" dish came about because masters decided lemons were a luxury, therefore too good for the slaves. With no lemons to cook with, ingenious slave cooks created this pie made with vinegar, a surprisingly good substitute for lemon. *Mock lemon (vinegar) pie* should be on the wedding feast table.

Mock Lemon Pie

Vinegar Pie

Yield: serves 10 to 12

9-inch baked pie shell, homemade (see recipe page 446) or commercial, frozen (prepared according to directions on package)
1¼ cups sugar, divided
3 tablespoons all-purpose flour
¼ teaspoon salt
3 **eggs, separated**
1 cup water
2 tablespoons butter or margarine
¼ cup cider vinegar
2 or 3 drops yellow food coloring
1 tablespoon lemon extract

Equipment: Oven mitts, wire cake rack, medium **heavy-based** saucepan, whisk, rubber **spatula,** electric mixer, medium mixing bowl

1. Prepare pie shell according to directions on package.

2. Set baked pie shell on wire cake rack to cool to room temperature.

3. Combine 1 cup sugar, flour, and salt in medium heavy-based saucepan. Whisk in egg yolks and water. Set over low heat, add butter or margarine, and whisking constantly, cook until smooth and thickened, 7 to 12 minutes. Remove from heat and, whisking constantly, slowly pour in vinegar. While whisking, add 2 or 3 drops yellow food coloring. Using rubber spatula, transfer vinegar filling to cooled, baked pie shell.

Preheat oven to 350° F.

4. Prepare meringue: If using whisk to beat egg whites, wash and dry whisk thoroughly. Using electric mixer or whisk, beat egg whites in medium mixing bowl until **frothy**. Beating constantly, add remaining ¼ cup sugar, a little at a time. Add lemon extract and beat until stiff peaks form. Using rubber spatula, spread meringue to completely cover and seal in filling. To make a more attractive meringue, swirl it into peaks and valleys, using rubber spatula.

5. Bake in oven for 8 to 10 minutes, or until meringue peaks are golden brown.

To serve, cool to room temperature and cut into wedges.

Today, a refreshing punch is almost always served at the wedding receptions.

Strawberry Iced Tea Punch

Yield: serves 14 to 18

2 cups water
1 cup sugar
2 cups strong tea
6-ounces canned frozen lemon juice concentrate

8 cups apple juice
24 ice cubes
1 lemon, thinly sliced, for **garnish**
8 strawberries, washed, **trimmed,** and sliced, for garnish

Equipment: Small saucepan, mixing spoon, large punch bowl, ladle

1. Pour water into small saucepan, add sugar, and stir and cook over medium heat until liquid is clear and sugar is dissolved. Remove from heat and cool to room temperature.

2. At serving time: Combine tea, frozen lemon juice concentrate, and apple juice and stir well. Stir in sugar mixture, a little at a time, to sweeten punch. Add ice cubes.

To serve, place the filled punch bowl on the buffet table. Float lemon slices and strawberries in the punch, for garnish. Set the ladle in the punch bowl and arrange the punch cups around the bowl. Fresh greenery and/or flowers placed around the base of the punch bowl also adds a festive touch.

The Amish

Early in the 1700s, southeastern Pennsylvania became a sanctuary for thousands of German Protestants of many diverse sects, such as Mennonites, Amish, Moravians, and Seventh-day Adventists, who came to America seeking religious freedom.

The settlers, mostly from Germany, were called Dutch, a corruption of the German word *Deutsch*, which means German, and has nothing to do with Dutch people from the Netherlands. The Pennsylvania Dutch (Deutsch) were divided into two groups, the "Plain People," such as the Amish and Mennonites, who followed a strict religious path, and the "Fancy Dutch" or "Church People," more worldly liberal members of the Lutheran and Reform Churches.

Both Plain and Fancy Dutch have two things in common, their local dialect, a blending of English with old south German, and their love of food. They have a word for it "feinschmeckers," which roughly means "those who know how good food should taste and who eat plenty of it."

Today Amish communities are located all over North America,. The Amish have a simple lifestyle and are against the use of modern technology such as electricity and motorized vehicles. They are easily identified by their plain, non-ornate style of dress. Amish women wear a white cap or bonnet over hair parted in the middle and pulled back into a bun. Amish men wear black or dark blue clothing with suspenders and black felt or straw hats with a flat crown and wide, flat brim. Most clothing is sewn by hand by the females of the community.

Eating is one of the pleasures the Amish consider legitimate, and they indulge themselves whenever an occasion arises, be it a wedding, a barn raising, or a huge dinner after Sunday church services. Throughout the year, Sunday worship takes place in a different parishioner's farmhouse each week and is always followed by a feast.

When a boy and girl are of marrying age, they follow very rigid courting customs. The boy usually calls on the girl at her home where they get to know each other in the sitting room.

When a couple wants to "bond," as the Amish call marriage, it is announced at Sunday service. Traditionally the bonding ceremony takes place after the harvest season, in the fall. The ceremony is either on Tuesday or Thursday so everyone can attend. During the bonding service, the bride and groom sit facing each other. The bonding ritual ends with the couple standing together to accept the bonding vows.

After the late morning service, everyone enjoys the wedding feast. Usually 300 to 400 guests are fed in shifts, which can often run into more than six seatings. The newlyweds sit facing the guests and must remain seated until everyone has eaten. After the feast, the rest of the day is spent singing hymns and snacking on cold food and beverages. A huge supper is served before everyone heads for home.

Guests do not bring gifts to an Amish wedding. Instead, in the weeks following, the gifts are picked up by the newlyweds as they fulfill their obligation to visit the home of each family who attended their bonding.

Schwingfelder is considered the traditional Amish wedding cake, although it is more like bread. The saffron and turmeric give it a yellowish color.

Schwingfelder

Saffron Wedding Cake Bread

Note: This recipe takes over 8 hours.

Yield: 2 loaves or cakes

- 6 saffron threads (available in spice section of most supermarkets)
- ¾ cup hot water
- ¾ cup milk
- ½ cup cold water
- 1 package active dry **yeast**
- 13 teaspoons sugar, divided
- 6 cups all-purpose flour, **sifted**
- 1 teaspoon salt
- ½ teaspoon **ground** turmeric
- 6 tablespoons vegetable shortening
- ½ cup currants
- ½ cup seedless raisins
- ½ teaspoon ground nutmeg

Equipment: Plastic food wrap, mixing spoon, work surface, small saucepan, cooking **thermometer**, large mixing bowl, **pastry blender** (optional), kitchen towel, lightly floured work surface, 2 (6-inches each) well-buttered round cake pans, oven mitts, white napkin-lined plate

1. Put saffron threads in ¾ cup hot water, cover with plastic wrap, and set on work surface for at least 8 hours.

2. In small pan, combine milk and ½ cup cold water and heat to **lukewarm**. Remove from heat and let rest 5 minutes. Stir in yeast and 1 teaspoon sugar and let stand for 5 to 10 minutes or until **frothy**.

3. Put flour, salt, ground turmeric, and remaining 12 teaspoons sugar in large mixing bowl. Using pastry blender or your fingers, cut or rub shortening into flour mixture until mixture resembles bread crumbs. Add currants, raisins, and nutmeg. Pour saffron liquid and frothy yeast mixture over flour mixture. Stir well or use your hands to form soft dough. Cover with towel and set in warm place to rise to double in bulk, 2 to 2½ hours.

4. **Punch down** and transfer dough to lightly floured work surface. **Knead** until smooth and firm, about 5 to 7 minutes. If dough is sticky, sprinkle lightly with flour and knead in. Divide dough in half and shape each piece to fit into a well-greased 6-inch cake pan. Cover pans with towel and set in warm place until dough has risen to tops of pans, 40 to 50 minutes.

Preheat oven to 400° F.

5. Bake in oven for 35 to 45 minutes, or until golden brown. Test **bread doneness**.

To serve, wrap each loaf separately in a white-napkin-lined plate and set one in front of the bride and the other in front of the groom. After the food is blessed, the newlyweds break off chunks from their loaf to share with each other. This symbolizes togetherness and that from this day forward, they will share everything in their lives.

Amish serve a great variety and quantity of farm food for the wedding feast. The menu usually includes roast chicken with stuffing, pork and sauerkraut, chicken pot pie, *scrapple* (recipe follows), egg noodles, fried chicken and mashed potatoes, *pickled eggs* (recipe page 224), pepper cabbage, *schmierkäse* (cottage cheese salad), and a great assortment of cakes, cookies, and pies, such as *shoo-fly pie* (recipe page 442).

Scrapple (also called *ponhaws*) got its name because it was made from scraps of meat scraped from cooked hog bones (usually the head). This is a perfect way to use leftover pork.

Scrapple (also Ponhaws)

Fried Pork Cakes

Yield: serves 6

cold water, as needed for cooking
4 cups boiling water
1 cup **cornmeal** (available at all health food stores and most supermarkets)
1 teaspoon salt, more if necessary
1 cup cold water
1½ cups **ground**, cooked pork
1 onion, **finely chopped**
½ teaspoon ground sage
¼ teaspoon ground nutmeg
salt to taste
ground red pepper to taste
4 to 6 tablespoons butter or margarine, for frying

Equipment: **Double boiler** with cover, medium bowl, mixing spoon, heatproof surface, scissors, wax paper, large loaf pan, plastic food wrap, knife, cutting board, large skillet, wide metal **spatula**, serving platter

Prepare to cook in double boiler: Fill bottom pan of double boiler halfway with cold water and bring to boil over high heat. Reduce heat to **simmer**.

1. Pour 1 cup cold water into a small bowl and stir in 1 cup ground cornmeal and 1 teaspoon salt until smooth.

2. Place top pan of double boiler over the simmering water and fill with 4 cups boiling water. Stirring constantly, slowly add the cornmeal mixture until smooth. Cover and continue cooking until mixture is thickened and cooked through, 20 to 25 minutes, stirring frequently. Remove double boiler from heat, then remove top pan with cornmeal mixture and place on heatproof surface.

3. Crumble in cooked ground pork, finely chopped onion, ground sage, ground nutmeg, and salt and ground red pepper to taste. Using mixing spoon, stir until well mixed.

4. Cut piece of wax paper to fit in bottom of medium loaf pan. Rinse loaf pan with cold water (do not dry). Place piece of wax paper in bottom of pan and fill with pork mixture, then press down with your hand or back of spoon and pat smooth. Cover with plastic wrap and refrigerate until cold and firm, about 3 to 4 hours, or place in freezer for 1 to 2 hours.

5. At serving time, uncover and remove pork mixture from pan by running a knife around the sides of pan, flip onto cutting board. Remove and discard wax paper. Cut loaf crosswise into about ½-inch slices.

6. Melt 4 tablespoons butter or margarine in large skillet over medium-high heat. Reduce heat to medium, and fry slices a few at a time until golden brown on both sides, 5 to 10 minutes. Fry in batches, adding more butter or margarine when necessary.

To serve, transfer to serving platter. Scrapple *can be eaten cold as an* ***appetizer*** *or hot as one of the many side dishes at the wedding luncheon.* Scrapple *keeps well, wrapped and refrigerated up to one week.*

Shoo-fly pie is sometimes called wet-bottom pie because the crust stays moist from the filling. It's a classic Pennsylvania Dutch pie that is included on the dessert table of the wedding feast.

SHOO-FLY PIE (ALSO SHOOFLY OR WET-BOTTOM PIE)

MOLASSES PIE

Yield: serves 6 to 8

9-inch unbaked pie crust, homemade (recipe page 446), or frozen (available at most supermarkets)
¼ cup vegetable shortening
2 cups all-purpose flour
½ cup brown sugar
1 teaspoon baking soda
1 cup hot water
½ cup light corn syrup
½ cup dark molasses
½ teaspoon **ground** nutmeg
¼ teaspoon ground **ginger**
¼ teaspoon ground cinnamon
¼ teaspoon ground cloves
¼ teaspoon salt
3 eggs, lightly beaten

Equipment: 9-inch pie pan, medium bowl, **pastry blender** (optional), large mixing bowl, mixing spoon, aluminum foil, baking sheet pan, oven mitts

Prepare pie crust: If homemade, fit crust in 9-inch pie pan. If buying frozen pie crust in pie pan, thaw according to directions on package.

1. Prepare crumb topping: Combine shortening, flour, and brown sugar in medium bowl. Using pastry blender or your fingers, cut or rub shortening into dry ingredients until mixture resembles moist bread crumbs. Set aside.

Preheat oven to 450° F.

2. Prepare filling: In large mixing bowl, stir baking soda in hot water to dissolve. Stir in corn syrup, molasses, nutmeg, ginger, cinnamon, cloves, salt, and lightly beaten eggs. Stir well and pour into unbaked prepared pie shell and spread smooth.

3. Assemble pie: Spoon crumb mixture over top of filling in pie pan, leaving about 1-inch circle of filling exposed in the center. This opening is like a steam vent and prevents the filling from bubbling over as it bakes. To be safe, place filled pie pan on foil-lined baking sheet and place in oven.

4. Bake 10 minutes, then reduce heat to 350° F and continue to bake 40 to 50 minutes or until filling thickens into custard. Wear oven mitts to test doneness. Pie should not quiver when you gently shake it from side to side. **Note**: Do not overbake or filling will become too dry.

To serve, cut in wedges. The pie has the best flavor while still warm. Serve plain or with a whipped cream or vanilla ice cream.

Acadian (Cajun)

Around 1755, a group of French settlers living in Acadia, an English colony on the North Atlantic seaboard, now known as Nova Scotia, refused to swear allegiance to the English flag; they refused to stop speaking French or to give up Catholicism, as ordered by the British. The British were unhappy with the group, known as the French Acadians and drove them out of the region.

The Acadians found a home in the French colony of Louisiana. Their Louisianan neighbors had trouble saying "Acadian" which they mispronounced "Cajun" and the name stuck. Most Cajuns are devout Roman Catholics, and all life-cycle events are celebrated according to doctrines of the Church. (See Protestant and Catholic Life-Cycle Rituals, page xlvi.)

Weddings are big celebrations for Cajuns. Besides the bride and groom, the cakes are the most important part of a Cajun wedding. There can't be too many and too few would be unacceptable. The cakes are made by members of the bride's family who spend weeks before the wedding getting them baked and decorated.

If the reception is in the home of the bride's parents, they often have a room designated as the Cake Room. On the wedding day it is filled with cakes of every description, like the *gâteau à la montagne blanche* (recipe page 446). The cakes are round, flat, square, and layered, then iced and decorated in every color imaginable. Other sweets served include trays of beautifully decorated *petits fours* (recipe page 433), crunchy brittle, fudge, and cookies, like *bâtons de noisettes* (recipe page 435).

At Cajun religious and life-cycle celebrations, the feast includes any number of spit-roasted hogs or suckling pigs (*lechonito asado*, recipe page 383). Cajuns use every part of a pig except the squeal. They pickle the pig's ears and feet and make some very unusual sausages. *Boudin noir* (black sausage) is made with blood and fat of hogs. *Boudin blanc* literally means "white pork pudding" and is a very white sausage. When you purchase the natural casing for this recipe, it need not be in one length, allow for some waste.

Boudin Blanc

White Meat Sausage

Yield: makes 12 sausages

- 7 to 9 feet natural **sausage casing** (available at most butcher shops and some supermarkets) (see above)
- 3 tablespoons vegetable oil
- 3 onions, **finely chopped**
- 2 green bell peppers, **trimmed**, **seeded**, and finely chopped
- 2 cloves garlic, finely chopped
- 2 cups finely **ground** chicken or turkey meat (buy ready-ground, available at most supermarkets)
- 1½ pounds finely ground lean pork (buy ready-ground, available at most supermarkets)
- 2 cups water, more as needed
- 3 cups cooked rice
- salt and ground white pepper to taste
- ground red pepper to taste
- 2 teaspoons ground **allspice**
- 2 cups milk
- 4 tablespoons butter or margarine, more if necessary

Equipment: Large skillet with cover, mixing spoon, food processor, rubber spatula, large mixing bowl, sausage stuffer or large funnel, kitchen string, wooden spoon, large saucepan, ice pick, metal tongs, large platter, sharp knife or scissors

1. **Pre-soak** casing. (See directions in glossary).

2. Heat oil in large skillet over medium-high heat. Add finely chopped onions, green peppers, and garlic, stir and **sauté** for 3 to 5 minutes, until soft. Crumble in ground chicken or turkey and ground pork. Add 2 cups water, stir, and bring to boil. Reduce heat to **simmer**, cover, and cook, stirring occasionally, 12 to 18 minutes or until done. Transfer to large mixing bowl and cool to room temperature.

3. Add cooked rice and sprinkle in salt and white pepper to taste, ground red pepper to taste, and allspice. Using your hands, toss to mix well.

4. Prepare to fill pre-soaked natural casing: Rinse casing under cold running water before filling. Insert the tube end of stuffer or large funnel into casing. Ease as much casing as possible onto the tube so it wrinkles up. Seal opposite end with a knot or tie with string.

5. Fill casing: Work with a few cups of meat mixture at a time, push it through tube into casing, easing the filling toward the sealed end. Use wooden spoon handle or something similar to push filling into casing. Continue to fill casing until all the mixture is used and evenly distributed in casing. Do not overfill casing. Allow room for expansion or the casing will burst during cooking. Twist and tie filled casing into 6-inch lengths.

6. Fill large saucepan half way with water, add milk, and bring to boil over medium-high heat. Coil sausages into boiling liquid, reduce heat to simmer, and cook 25 to 35 minutes until well done and mixture has firmed up. As sausages rise to the surface, prick each section once or twice with an ice pick to keep casing from bursting. Remove sausages with metal tongs and transfer to large platter to cool. Do not separate links. Links can be covered and refrigerated for up to 2 days.

7. At serving time, cut sausages into individual links with sharp knife or scissors. Melt 4 tablespoons butter or margarine in large skillet over medium-high heat. Sauté 3 or 4 links at a time, on both sides, to heat through and lightly brown. Sauté in batches, adding more butter or margarine, if necessary.

To serve, cut each link crosswise in 2 or 3 pieces and serve as an ***appetizer*** *on the buffet table. For dinner, serve 1 or 2 links of* boudin blanc *per person with mashed potatoes.*

Crawfish (also crayfish, mudbugs, crawdad, creekcrab, or yabbie) are plentiful in Cajun country. For most celebrations, crawfish are served boiled and eaten out of the shell. The crawfish meat is made into pies, patties, stews, salads, cocktails, and gumbo. Another delicacy is stuffed crawfish heads. The following are instructions for boiling and eating crawfish Cajun style. THIS IS A TASK FOR ADULTS.

Des Écrevisses Bouillies

Boiled Crawfish

Allow at least 1 to 3 pounds live **crawfish** per person.

Crawfish are dumped live into large kettles of boiling water set over a fire in the yard. **Note**: If any crawfish are dead, discard them. Lots of salt and crushed red pepper are added. When the water comes back to boiling, the crawfish turn bright red and rise to the top; allow them to cook for 12 to 15 minutes more. Take crawfish out with a long-handled heavy-duty metal strainer. Boil crawfish in batches using the same water. Add more fresh water, salt, and red pepper flakes, when necessary.

The boiled crawfish are piled in the middle of picnic tables that have been covered with newspapers. Crawfish eaters dig in, pulling or biting off crawfish heads and either digging out the meat in the tails with their fingers or using a crawfish claw as a pick. **Note**: Discard any crawfish that do not curl up before or after boiling.

Serve crawfish with a favorite dipping sauce, sauce rémoulade *(recipe follows).*

Rémoulade is a famous Cajun sauce served with everything from seafood to meats and vegetables. Bowls of it are always on the celebration buffet table.

Sauce Rémoulade

Famous Cajun Sauce

Yield: 5½ to 6 cups

- 2 cups hot, spicy mustard (such as Creole mustard or horseradish mustard available at most supermarkets)
- 4 hard-cooked eggs, peeled and **coarsely chopped**
- 1 tablespoon paprika
- ½ teaspoon **ground** red pepper to taste

2 teaspoons Kosher salt
2 tablespoons vinegar
juice of 1 lemon
1 cup extra-virgin olive oil
1 cup green onions, **finely chopped** (including 3 inches of top greens)
¼ cup fresh Italian (flat-leaf) parsley, finely chopped
1 cup celery, **trimmed** and finely chopped

Equipment: Electric **blender**, rubber **spatula,** medium mixing bowl with cover, mixing spoon

1. In blender, combine mustard, chopped hard-cooked eggs, paprika, ground red pepper to taste, salt, vinegar, and lemon juice. **Blend** for about 30 seconds or until well mixed and smooth.

2. With blender running on low, slowly pour oil through the feed tube in a thin line until mixture is thickened, about 1 minute. Transfer to medium bowl. Add green onions, parsley, and celery, and stir to mix well. Cover and refrigerate for at least 1 hour before serving.

Serve as dip with boiled ***crawfish, crudités****, or as sauce for* crawfish cocktail *(recipe page 351).*

The favorite way of serving food is called Ambigu, a French-Créole buffet service with all the dishes placed on the table at the same time. One of the most popular Cajun dishes served Ambigu-style for the wedding feast and funeral meals is *etouffee*.

Écrevisse Etouffée

Crawfish Stew

Yield: serves 4
½ cup butter or margarine
1 onion, **finely chopped**
1 green pepper, **trimmed**, **seeded**, and finely chopped
1 rib celery, trimmed and finely chopped
¼ cup cream
½ teaspoon cornstarch
1 pound frozen **crawfish** meat, thawed according to directions on package (available in Asian food stores and most supermarkets)
salt and pepper to taste
ground red pepper to taste
2 green onion tops, finely sliced
¼ cup fresh parsley, chopped, or 2 tablespoons dried parsley flakes
4 cups cooked rice, kept warm, for serving

Equipment: Large **heavy-based** saucepan with cover or **Dutch oven**, mixing spoon, small bowl

1. Melt butter or margarine in large heavy-based saucepan or Dutch oven over medium-high heat. Add finely chopped onion, green pepper, and celery. Stir, and **sauté** for 5 to 7 minutes, or until onions are soft. Reduce heat to medium.

2. Put cornstarch in small bowl and stir in half & half a little at a time, until smooth. Slowly stir cornstarch mixture into onion mixture. Add thawed crawfish, salt and pepper to taste, and ground red pepper to taste, and stir well. Cover and cook 10 to 12 minutes for flavor to develop, stirring frequently. Just before serving, **fold in** sliced green onion tops and parsley.

To serve, mound cooked rice in large serving bowl and pour crawfish mixture over the top or serve in separate bowls.

On the cake table, one cake is more important than the others, the wedding cake. *Gâteau de noce créole à l'ancienne* (old-fashioned Creole wedding cake) is the same as the Caribbean *black wedding cake* (recipe page 360). The following cake *gâteauà la montagne blanche* might accompany the wedding cake on the cake table.

Gâteau à la Montagne Blanche

White Mountain Cake

Yield: serves 24

2 cups cake flour
2 teaspoons baking powder
3 **egg whites**
½ cup butter
1 cup sugar
¾ cup milk
½ teaspoon almond extract
grated rind of 1 lemon
butter cream icing (recipe page 361), or confectioners' sugar, for **garnish**

Equipment: Flour **sifter**, 2 medium bowls, electric mixer or whisk, large mixing bowl, mixing spoon, rubber **spatula,** buttered and floured 12- x 8-inch cake pan, oven mitts, wire cake rack

Preheat oven to 350° F.

1. **Sift** together flour and baking powder into medium bowl.

2. Put egg whites in medium bowl and using electric mixer or whisk, beat until stiff but not dry, 2 to 3 minutes.

3. Put butter into large mixing bowl and using electric mixer or mixing spoon, beat until creamy. Slowly add sugar, beating constantly until fluffy and light. Add flour mixture alternately with milk while continuing to beat constantly. Add almond extract and beat until mixture is smooth. Using rubber spatula, **fold in** whipped egg whites. Transfer mixture to prepared cake pan and spread smooth.

4. Bake for about 1 hour, or until toothpick inserted in cake comes out clean and cake has pulled away from sides of pan. Using oven mitts, remove from oven and place on wire cake rack to cool to room temperature.

To serve, cover top with butter cream icing *or sprinkle with confectioners' sugar and cut into 2-inch squares.*

Basic Pie Crust

Yield: 2 crusts

2¼ cups all-purpose flour, more if necessary
1 teaspoon salt
¾ cup solid shortening
4 tablespoons ice water, more or less as needed

Equipment: Large mixing bowl, **pastry blender**, lightly floured work surface, floured rolling pin, 9-inch pie pan, aluminum foil, oven mitts

1. Combine 2¼ cups flour and salt into large mixing bowl. Using pastry blender, work in shortening until mixture resembles coarse crumbs. Sprinkle in water, 1 tablespoon at a time, until mixture holds together, using your hands, form dough in a ball. If dough is too dry, add a little more water, and, if too sticky, add a little more flour.

2. Divide into halves and shape each half into flattened round on lightly floured work surface. Using floured rolling pin, roll dough large enough to cover bottom and sides of pie pan, allowing at least ½-inch overhang. Either roll out second half of dough for top crust or wrap in foil and refrigerate for another use.

3. Preheated oven to 415° F., if pie shell is to be baked unfilled. Prick the crust surface in several places with a fork after fitting into the pie pan. To keep the crust from baking unevenly, place a sheet of foil over the crust. Spread about 1 cup uncooked beans on top of the foil to weigh the crust down while it bakes. Bake 10 to 15 minutes until golden.

Use in recipe calling for filled homemade prepared crust, continue to fill and bake accordingly.

BIBLIOGRAPHY

Adams, Thatcher. *Traditional Cookery in Bermuda.* Island Press Ltd., 1991.

Adeleke, Tunde. *Songhay.* Heritage Library of African People Series. New York: Rosen Publishing Group, 1996.

Africa News Service, Inc.*The Africa News Cookbook.* New York: Penguin Books, 1985.

Ayer, Eleanor H. *Germany, The Heartland of Europe.* Tarrytown, NY: Benchmark Books, Marshall Cavendish Corp., 1996.

Ayo, Yvonne. *Africa.* New York: Alfred A. Knopf, 1995.

Ayodo, Awuor. *Luo.* Heritage Library of African People Series. New York: Rosen Publishing Group, 1996.

Beckwith, Carol. "Niger's Wodaabe: 'People of the Taboo.'" *National Geographic,* October 1983, CD-ROM.

Benchley, Peter. "New Zealand's Bountiful South Island." *National Geographic,* January 1972, CD-ROM.

Bennett, Margaret. *Scottish Customs from the Cradle to the Grave.* Edinburgh, UK: Polygon, 1992.

Biddlecombe, Peter. *French Lessons in Africa: Travels with My Briefcase Through French Africa.* London: Abacus a division of Little, Brown & Co., 1995.

Broek, Jan O. M., and John W. Webb. *A Geography of Mankind.* New York: McGraw-Hill Book Co., 1978.

Clayton, Bernard Jr. *The Complete Bread Book.* New York: Simon & Schuster, 1973.

De Mente, Boye Lafayette. *Japan Encyclopedia.* Lincolnwood, IL: Passport Books, a division of NTC Publishing Group, 1995.

Devine, Elizabeth, and Nancy L Bragant. *The Travelers' Guide to African Customs & Manners.* New York: St. Martin's Press, 1995.

Dossey, Donald E. *Holiday Folklore, Phobias and Fun.* Los Angeles, CA: Outcomes Unlimited Press, 1992.

Eerdmans' Handbook to The World's Religions. Grand Rapids, MI: William B. Eerdmans Publishing Co., 1982.

Esposito, Mary Ann. *Celebrations Italian Style.* New York: William Morrow & Co., 1995.

Farley, Marta Pisetska. *Festive Ukrainian Cooking.* Pittsburgh, PA: University of Pittsburgh Press, 1990.

Fisher, Angela. *Africa Adorned.* New York: Harry N. Abrams, Inc., 1984.

Gaertner, Ursula. *Elmolo.* Heritage Library of African People Series. New York: Rosen Publishing Group, 1995.

Gillison, Gillian. "Fertility Rites and Sorcery in a New Guinea Village." *National Geographic,* July 1997, CD-ROM.

Goldstein, Darra. *A La Russe.* New York: Random House, 1983.

Goodman, Jim. *Cultures of the World, Thailand.* North Bellmore, NY: Marshall Cavendish Corp., 1991.

Harris, Andy. *A Taste of the Aegean.* New York: Abbeville Press, 1992.

Harris, Jonathan. *France.* New York: J. L. Lippincott, 1989.

Hodgson, Bryan. "Namibia, Nearly a Nation?" *National Geographic,* June 1982, CD-ROM.

Holtzman, Jon. *Samburu.* Heritage Library of African People Series. New York: Rosen Publishing Group, 1995.

Huyler, Stephen P. *Painted Prayers.* New York: Rizzoli International Publications, Inc., 1994.

Jomier, Jacques. *How to Understand Islam.* New York: Crossroad, 1989.

Kornblum, William. *Sociology in a Changing World.* 3rd ed. Fort Worth, TX: Harcourt Brace College Publishers, 1988.

Kraus, Barbara. *The Cookbook of The United Nations.* London: The Cookery Book Club, 1964.

Lands & People: Africa. Danbury, CT: America Grolier Incorporated, 1995.

Lands & People: Europe. Danbury, CT: America Grolier Incorporated, 1997.

Lands & Peoples: Central & South America. Danbury, CT: America Grolier Incorporated, 1993.

"Letter from the Editor by Arun Narayan Toké" *Skipping Stones Magazine,* vol. 9, no.1, 1997.

Leydet, François. "Journey Through Time, Papua New Guinea." *National Geographic,* August 1982, CD-ROM.

Livingstone, Sheila. *Scottish Customs*. Edinburgh, UK: Birlinn Ltd, 1996.

Marks, Copeland. *The Korean Kitchen*. San Francisco, CA: Chronicle Books, 1993.

Marquis, Vivienne, and Patricia Haskell. *The Cheese Book*. New York: Simon & Schuster, Inc., 1985.

Mathabane, Mark. *African Women*. New York: Harper Collins, 1994.

McDowell, Bart, Albert Moldvay, and Joseph J. Schersche. "Hungary, Changing Homeland of a Tough, Romantic People." *National Geographic*, April 1971, CD-ROM.

Merchant, Ismail. *Passionate Meals*. New York: Hyperion, 1994.

Momatiuk, Yva, and John Eastcott. "Maoris: At Home in Two Worlds." *National Geographic*, October 1984, CD-ROM.

Moosewood Collective. *Sundays at Moosewood Restaurant*. New York: Simon & Schuster, 1990.

The National Council of Negro Women, Inc. *Mother Africa's Table*. New York: Main Street Books/ Doubleday Dell Publishing, 1998.

Newton, Alex, and David Else. *West Africa*. Oakland, CA: Lonely Planet Publications, 1995.

Njoku, Onwuka N. *Mbundu*. Heritage Library of African People Series. New York: Rosen Publishing Group, 1997.

Nwanunobi, C.O. *Malinke*. Heritage Library of African People Series. New York: Rosen Publishing Group, 1996.

Nwanunobi, C.O. *Soninke*. Heritage Library of African People Series. New York: Rosen Publishing Group, 1996.

Ojakangas, Beatrice A. *The Finnish Cookbook*. New York: Crown Publishers, Inc., 1964.

Oluikpe, Benson O. *Swazi*. Heritage Library of African People Series. New York: Rosen Publishing Group, 1997.

Ortiz, Elizabeth Lambert. *The Book of Latin American Cooking*. New York: Vintage Books by Random House, 1969.

Papashvily, Helen. *Russian Cooking*. New York: Time-Life Books, 1969

Parris, Ronald *Hausa*. Heritage Library of African People Series. New York: Rosen Publishing Group, 1996.

Patten, Marguerite, and Betty Dunleavy. *Cakes and Cake Decorating*. Feltham, England: Hamlyn House; Sydney, Australia: Dee Way West, 1965.

The Picayune Creole Cookbook. New York: Weathervane Books, 1989.

Post, Laurens van der. *African Cooking*. New York: Time-Life Books, 1970.

Quintana, Patricia. *Mexico's Feasts of Life*. Tulsa, OK: Publisher Council Oak Books, 1989.

Richards, Chris. *World Religions*. New York: Element Books Limited, 1997.

Scot, Barbara J. *The Violet Shyness of Their Eyes—Notes From Nepal*. Corvallis, OR: CALYX Books, 1993.

Seah, Audrey. *Cultures of the World*. North Bellmore, NY: Marshall Cavendish Corp., 1994.

Sturgis, Ingrid. *The Nubian Wedding Book*. New York: Publisher Crown Publishers, 1997.

Taik, Aung Aung. *The Best of Burmese Cooking*. San Francisco, CA: Chronicle Books, 1993.

Tope, Lily Rose R. *Cultures of the World, Philippines*. North Bellmore, NY: Marshall Cavendish Corp., 1991.

Tornquist, David. *Vietnam, Then & Now*. London: Flint River Press Ltd., 1991.

Twagilimana, A. *Hutu & Tutsi*. Heritage Library of African People Series. New York: Rosen Publishing Group, 1998;

Wanasundera, Nanda P. *Sri Lanka*. North Bellmore, NY: Marshall Cavendish Corp., 1991.

Wangu, Madhu Bazaz. *Hinduism World Religions*. New York: Facts On File, Inc., 1991.

Warren, Janet. *A Feast of Scotland*. London: Published for Lomond Books by Reed Consumer Books Ltd, 1990.

Weeks, Gertrude S. "In The Heart of Africa." *National Geographic*, August 1956, CD-ROM.

Weiser, Francis X. *Christian Feasts and Customs*. New York: Harcourt, Brace & World, Inc., 1952.

Wells, Troth. *The Global Kitchen*. Freedom, CA: Crossing Press, Inc., 1990.

———. *The World in Your Kitchen*. Freedom, CA: Crossing Press, Inc., 1993.

Wentzel, Volkmar. "Zulu King Weds a Swazi Princess." *National Geographic*, January 1998, CD-ROM.

Whedon, Peggy, and John Kidner. *Great Embassies Cookbook*. Seattle, WA: Peanut Butter Publishing, 1987.

Wolf, Burt. *Gatherings and Celebrations*. New York: Doubleday, 1996.

Wyk, Gary N. van. *Basotho*. Heritage Library of African People Series. New York: Rosen Publishing Group, 1996.

Yin, Saw Myat. *Cultures of the World, Burma*. North Bellmore, NY: Marshall Cavendish Corp., 1990.

INDEX

by Linda Webster

Lois Sinaiko Webb is a restaurant consultant and caterer for Villa Capri Restaurant, Seabrook, Texas, whose specialty is multicultural weddings. Webb is also a member of the Roundtable for Women in Food Service (RWF); Houston Culinary Historians; and Confrerie de la Chaine des Rotisseurs, Houston Barilliage. She was recently nominated in the entrepreneur category for one of the Pacesetter Awards 2000. She owned and operated a seafood restaurant for 15 years, which she closed so that she could write and travel. She also has written for numerous food service publications. While in the People's Republic of China, Ms. Webb taught American cooking to 54 chefs in the Jilin Province. She is the coauthor of Oryx's bestselling *Multicultural Cookbook for Students* and *Holidays of the World Cookbook for Students*.